CONFLICTS OF EMPIRES

1585–1713

CONFLICTS OF EMPIRES

SPAIN, THE LOW COUNTRIES AND

THE STRUGGLE FOR WORLD SUPREMACY

1585–1713

JONATHAN I. ISRAEL

THE HAMBLEDON PRESS

LONDON AND RIO GRANDE

Published by The Hambledon Press 1997

102 Gloucester Avenue, London NW1 8HX (UK)

PO Box 162, Rio Grande, Ohio 45674 (USA)

ISBN 1 85285 161 9

A description of this book is available from the
British Library and from the Library of Congress

Typeset by The Midlands Book Typesetting Company, Loughborough
Printed on acid-free paper and bound in
Great Britain by Cambridge University Press

120497-700088

Contents

Illustrations
Plates between pages 100 and 101

Maps

Text Illustrations

Acknowledgements

Those articles which are reprinted here first appeared in the following publications and are reprinted by the kind permission of the original publishers.

1   Appears here for the first time.

2   Appears here for the first time.

3   Appears here for the first time.

4   R.L. Kagan and Geoffrey Parker (ed.), *Spain, Europe and the Atlantic World: Essays in Honour of John H. Elliott* (Cambridge, 1995), pp. 267–95. By permission of the Cambridge University Press.

5   Appears here for the first time.

6   Appears here for the first time.

7   D.S. Katz and J.I. Israel (ed.), *Sceptics, Millenarians and Jews* (Leiden, 1990), pp. 76–97. By permission of E.J. Brill.

8   *Bijdragen en mededelingen betreffende de geschiedenis der Nederlanden*, 98 (1983), pp. 167–90. By permission of the editors.

9   *Studia Rosenthaliana*, 28 (1994), pp. 99–119. By permission of the editors.

10   *Mediterranean Historical Review*, 9 (1994), pp. 235–55. By permission of Frank Cass Publishers.

11   S. Groenveld and M. Wintle (ed.), *The Exchange of Ideas: Religion, Scholarship and Art in Anglo-Dutch Relations in the Seventeenth Century*, Britain and the Netherlands, 11 (Zutphen, 1994), pp. 13–30. By permission of the Walburg Press.

12   O.P. Grell, J.I. Israel and N. Tyacke (ed.) *From Persecution to Toleration: The Glorious Revolution and Religion in England* (Oxford, 1991), pp. 129–70. By permission of the Oxford University Press.

13   S. Groenveld and M. Wintle (ed.) *State and Trade: Government and the Economy in Britain and the Netherlands since the Middle Ages*, Britain and the Netherlands, 10 (Zutphen, 1992), pp. 50–61. By permission of the Walburg Press.

14   *Tijdschrift voor geschiedenis*, 103 (1990), pp. 412–40. By permission of the editors.

15   D. Hoak and M. Feingold (ed.), *The World of William and Mary: Anglo-Dutch Perspectives on the Revolution of 1688–89* (Stanford, California, 1996), pp. 75–86. By permission of the Stanford University Press.

16   S. Roach (ed.), *Across the Narrow Seas: Studies in the History and Bibliography of Britain and the Low Countries* (London, 1991), pp. 167–77. By permission of the British Library.

17   A. Rapoport-Albert and S.J. Zipperstein (ed.) *Jewish History: Essays in Honour of Chimen Abramsky* (London, 1988), pp. 267–84. By permission of Peter Halban Publishers.

18   J. Michman (ed.), *Dutch Jewish History*, 2 (Assen and Jerusalem, 1989), pp. 117–36. By permission of Van Gorcum Publishers, Assen, The Netherlands.

Foreword

In writing these essays and also in bringing them together in what I hope will be seen as a coherent, if wide-ranging, volume I have incurred quite a number of scholarly debts. It is with great pleasure that I here take the opportunity to express my gratitude and appreciation to those who have in one way or another materially assisted me with stimulating discussion and criticism no less than with useful bibliographical information, archival references and help with illustrations and maps. First and foremost, I would like once again to record my debt to Sir John Elliott, who first introduced me to the world of Spanish and Ibero-American history at Cambridge more than thirty years ago, and to the late K.W. Swart who, more than a quarter of a century ago, first introduced me to the fascinating world of the Low Countries in early modern times. It is certainly true that a series of discussions with one or two key teachers can change the course of one's entire life. Those whom I would additionally like to thank for help with specific points or aspects are Edgar Samuel, Marcel Curiel, Reginald de Schryver, Daniel Swetschinski, Yosef Kaplan, Ole Grell, Paul Janssens, Christopher Brown, Rafael Valladares, David Parrott, Robert Oresko, Geoffrey Parker, Richard Kagan, Fernando González de León and Dale Hoak. Last but by no means least I would like to record my gratitude to Martin Sheppard of the Hambledon Press for his expert help and advice in organizing this volume and in getting it ready for the press.

Abbreviations

AGI	Archivo General de Indias, Seville
AGS	Archivo General de Simancas, Valladolid
AHU	Arquivo Histórico Ultramarino, Lisbon
ANTT	Arquivo Nacional da Torre do Tombo, Lisbon
ARA, WIC	Algemeen Rijksarchief, The Hague, Archives of the West India Company
ARB, SEG	Archives Générales du Royaume, Brussels, Secrétairerie d'État et de Guerre
ARH, SG	Algemeen Rijksarchief, The Hague, Archives of the States General
BL, MS	British Library, London, Department of Manuscripts
BND	Biblioteca Nacional, Madrid, Sala de Manuscritos
BRB, MS	Bibliothèque Royale, Brussels, Section des Manuscrits
GAA, NA	Gemeentearchief Amsterdam, Notarial Archives
GAA, PJG	Gemeentearchief Amsterdam, Archives of the Portuguese Jewish Community
GA, Rotterdam	Gemeentearchief, Rotterdam
PRO, SP	Public Record Office, London, State Papers

Introduction

The period of modern history from the late sixteenth to the early eighteenth century was one of tremendous, and ultimately decisive, shifts in the balance of political, military and economic power in both Europe and the wider world. After achieving a general hegemony in the Mediterranean and western Europe during the third quarter of the sixteenth century, the union of the crowns of Spain and Portugal, in 1580–1, appeared to many contemporaries to confirm Spain's dominance not only of Europe and the New World, of the Atlantic and the Pacific, but of Africa and Asia as well.[1] The early and mid 1580s when Spanish forces conquered the Azores, recovered Flanders and Brabant, retook Antwerp (1585) and restored Catholic control in the electorate of Cologne (1585–8), the years immediately preceding the sending of the great Armada of 1588 against England, were a period of near euphoria at the Spanish court. There were moments when it seemed that the Escorial was to be the headquarters of the whole world. But the Armada failed; and in the Netherlands, the concentrated might of Spain under the brilliant military leader ship of Alexander Farnese, duke of Parma, failed to extinguish the Dutch Revolt. Nevertheless, at the end of the sixteenth century, Spain bestrode the world and far surpassed in power and wealth all other European powers. France, potentially a match for Spain, was still weak and only gradually recovered from the disruption of the Wars of Religion (1562–94). England at that time was still a relatively minor power. The Dutch in the years around 1590 were only just beginning their meteoric rise to primacy in world commerce, shipping and finance.

During the early seventeenth century Spain was still the leading world empire and preeminent military power in Europe. But owing to the overstretching of Spanish resources, and the rapid decline of the cities of Castile, from the 1590s, Spanish means soon ceased to be sufficient to maintain the imposing façade. At the outset of the Thirty Years' War (1618–48) and latter part of the Eighty Years' War (1621–48), Spain still appeared to dominate the European scene. Spanish intervention in Germany looked decisive (see Chapter 3) and the Dutch situation became difficult, morale in the Republic sinking to a low-point during the siege of Breda (1624–5) by the Spanish army of Flanders. This was now

---

[1] A point recently emphasized by Geoffrey Parker in his essay 'David or Goliath? Philip II and his World in the 1580s', in R.L. Kagan and Geoffrey Parker (ed.), *Spain, Europe and the Atlantic World: Essays in Honour of John H. Elliott* (Cambridge, 1995), pp. 245–66.

commanded by the Genoese Ambrogio Spínola (1569–1630) who, since Philip III's special secret instructions to him, issued at Aranjuez in central Castile in April 1606, had been one of the most trusted and powerful, as well as politically and militarily competent, figures at the helm of Spain's world empire.[2] Breda capitulated to Spínola in June 1625. The victory, later commemorated by Velázquez in one of his greatest paintings, was the last of the era in which Spain was incontestably preponderant. Only a few years later, Spain suffered a series of major defeats and humiliations: in the Mantuan war in northern Italy (1628–31), losing 's-Hertogenbosch, one of the most important strongholds of the Spanish Netherlands, in 1629, surrendering Maastricht in 1632, suffering reverses in Brazil, naval defeat at the battle of the Downs (1639) and, finally, the culminating setback, the twin rebellions of Catalonia and Portugal in 1640.

Meanwhile, the relatively harmonious relations between Spain and France established in the second decade of the seventeenth century progressively deteriorated during the 1620s until, by the end of the decade, there prevailed a cold war verging on open conflict.[3] Full-scale war between France and the Habsburgs erupted in 1635; but since Spain, rather than the emperor, bore the brunt of fighting France, it was really a case of France and Spain grappling for the leadership, and eventual mastery, of Europe. After 1635, France was undeniably Spain's chief opponent, though the war with the Dutch (who were now in alliance with the French crown) continued. The fact that France was now Spain's principal foe, combined with the dramatic impact of the invasion of France mounted from Flanders by the Cardinal-Infante in 1636, which caused panic in Paris, has led historians to suppose that Spain's military capability was now directed chiefly against France and that, from 1635 onwards, the Dutch front was reduced to secondary status.[4] But this notion has been shown to be wrong and one of the aims of this present volume is to suggest a rather different way of explaining Spanish strategic decision-making in relation to France in the culminating period of Franco-Spanish struggle (see especially Chapters 5 and 7). Far from concentrating her offensive capability against France, the count-duke of Olivares and Philip IV directed Spain's armies to fight only defensively against the French through most of the period 1635–40 while the main attacking thrust of Spanish power was directed against the Dutch. The thinking behind this was that it would be both easier and quicker to bring matters to a conclusion and settle with the Dutch, on a basis which would remove the Dutch West India Company from Brazil and maintain the prestige of the

[2] Joseph Lefèvre, *Spinola et la Belgique* (Brussels, 1947), p. 30.

[3] A process described in Jean-Pierre Amalric, 'L'oeil et la main de l'Espagne dans les affaires françaises (1621–1632)', *Wolfenbütteler Forschungen*, 39 (1988), pp. 23–35.

[4] R.A. Stradling has laid particular stress on what he calls 'Olivares' master-plan' for attacking France see, R.A. Stradling, *Spain's Struggle for Europe, 1598–1668* (London and Rio Grande, 1994), pp. 117–18, 280–1; the same perspective has been set out again recently by Miguel Ángel Echevarría Bacigalupe, 'Las relaciones económicas hispanoholandesas y los tratados de 1648–50', in J. Lechner and H. den Boer (ed.), *España y Holanda: quinto coloquio hispanoholandés de historiadores* (Amsterdam, 1995), pp. 45–6.

Spanish crown. Once the Dutch were out of the picture, the French, on their own, would be much more vulnerable to Spanish power. An additional reason for concentrating on the Dutch, at this stage, was Olivares' insistence that Spain had to recover one, or more, of her lost strongholds on the Rhine, in north-western Germany, or lose her standing, and capacity to intervene, in the German empire (Chapters 3 and 4).

In retrospect, it appears obvious, especially for the period after the outbreak of the Catalan and Portuguese rebellions in 1640, that the era of Spanish great-ness was over and that Spanish hegemony in Europe was about to be replaced by that of France and, outside Europe, by the English, French and Dutch. But in the 1640s, and for most of the 1650s, it seemed much less clear than it ap-peared later that Spanish ascendancy was giving way to that of France. Remark-ably enough, the Spanish court did not abandon its ambitious imperialism in Europe after the double disaster of 1640 and the downfall of Olivares in 1643. Although one might logically expect that, from 1644, Spanish attention and resources were chiefly concentrated on endeavouring to quell the rebellions of Catalonia and Portugal,[5] in fact the southern Netherlands continued to be the main Spanish military base, or *plaza de armas*, the Spanish court taking the view that attacking France from the Low Countries, in alliance with disaffected French nobles and the duchy of Lorraine (which Richelieu and Mazarin were striving to break as an independent power and incorporate within France) of-fered the best chance of bringing France to her knees and restoring Spanish dominance — and, precisely by defeating France, removing the conditions which enabled Catalonia and Portugal to resist the might and authority of the Span-ish crown. The Low Countries, in other words, right down to the Peace of the Pyrenees of 1659, were seen in Madrid as the key to the successful suppression of both the Catalan and Portuguese revolts (see Chapter 7). Furthermore, it seemed for some years, from 1648 down to 1656–7, an entire decade, that this Spanish strategy might well succeed. Helped by the outbreak of the Frondes (1648–53), a period of chaotic conflict within France which temporarily, but substantially, weakened the French crown, Spanish power and prestige staged a marked revival which was evident throughout Europe and, not least, within France itself.

If the greatness of both Spain and France was beyond dispute during the first six decades of the seventeenth century, down to the Peace of the Pyrenees, the precise balance between the two principal western powers was subject to sudden, dramatic and unpredictable swings, and was constantly shifting. Major internal disruption, such as the outbreak of the Catalan and Portuguese rebel-lions, or the onset of the Frondes, in France, could transform the picture with breathtaking speed. Such episodes showed that the sinews, even the very founda-tions of power, were fragile and at times highly precarious. Again and again, royal courts swung from euphoria to the depths of gloom, almost overnight, at

---

[5] See, for instance, R.A. Stradling, *Europe and the Decline of Spain* (London, 1981), pp. 118–19, 133.

the news of some unexpected, and often very distant, reverse. The exact significance, moreover, for the overall balance of power on land and sea of even the most spectacular developments was exceedingly difficult to gage correctly. When Portugal broke away from Spain in 1640, for example, foreign observers were less impressed with the prospects for Portuguese success (which most doubted) than the opportunities offered to other powers for exploiting the situation to the disadvantage of Spain and for carving up the Portuguese overseas empire.

But what precisely were the opportunities? The French crown, expecting to be the chief beneficiary, hastened to take the Portuguese rebels under its protections (see Chapter VII); the Dutch though initially divided as to whether they could best exploit the situation by befriending Portugal in Europe, or attacking her overseas, expected to make solid gains on both fronts, weakening Spain in Europe while simultaneously dismantling the Portuguese colonial empire, not least in Africa where the Portuguese colonies of Angola and São Thomé came under West India Company occupation in the years (1641–8) but, after a few years, found that they had misjudged.[6] Eventually, in the 1660s, it was the English who emerged as the chief protectors of Portuguese independence (at the cost of utterly antagonizing Spain), obtaining, among other advantages, the former Portuguese colonies of Tangiers and Bombay, gains which dismayed the Dutch and French, as well as infuriated Philip IV — who still claimed those places as possessions of the Spanish crown.[7] Meanwhile, the Spanish court had not abandoned its aim of recovering both Portugal and Brazil and persevered in its efforts to do so until finally being compelled, by defeats and adverse circumstances, to accept the fact of Portuguese independence in 1668.

A perceptive contemporary contemplating the European and world scene, at the time of the peace of the Pyrenees in 1659 might well have been able to predict the further decline of Spain (where both agriculture and the towns of the interior were in a state of chronic decay), the continued expansion of French power within Europe, and the spectacular advances achieved by the English and Dutch outside Europe — as well as the mounting difficulty experienced by the Dutch in protecting their burgeoning trade and shipping from the envious glances of the English and French. Underlying forces — social, economic and political — were at work, and long-term trends in progress, of which contemporaries were sometimes dimly aware and which the modern historian makes it his, or her, business to identify. Nevertheless, it is certain that a great deal of what actually transpired after, as before, 1659 was also determined by extremely short-term, incidental factors and the play of personalities: a great deal, in other words, which did not fit the main trends and was often entirely

---

[6] J.I. Israel, *The Dutch Republic and the Hispanic World, 1606–1661* (Oxford, 1982), pp. 329–32.

[7] Rafael Valladares Ramirez, 'Inglaterra, Tánger y el "estrecho compartido": los inicios del asentamiento inglés en el Mediterráneo occidental durante la guerra hispano-portuguesa (1641–1661)', *Hispania*, 51 (1991), pp. 985–9.

unexpected and unpredictable. Given that it was not at all in England's long-term interest that Louis XIV should break the power of the Dutch Republic — for that would have not only made him master of Europe but greatly strengthened the French position in Asia, Africa and the Americas — it was not only the Dutch but also the Italian and German princes who were amazed and deeply disturbed by the joint Anglo-French attack on the United Provinces in 1672.[8] Once the assault began it seemed impossible that Dutch power, prosperity and colonies could survive the combined forces of France and England; yet somehow Admiral Michiel de Ruyter repeatedly beat the superior Anglo-French fleet in a series of battles in the North Sea and Louis XIV's invading army, after conquering Gelderland, Overijssel and Utrecht, was stopped at the last line of Dutch defence: a mere few miles from Amsterdam. Having suffered such reverses, it seemed inconceivable, despite their survival in 1672, that the Dutch should emerge from the war of 1672–8 with their territory, colonies and shipping largely intact. Yet that is precisely what happened.

No less astounding and unexpected in its results was the Glorious Revolution of 1688–91. Here again, just as in 1640 and 1672, was a momentous happening which very significantly altered the course of world history. Like all great revolutions, it was an event firmly rooted in long-term trends, as well as long-standing international tensions. But the event itself, and especially the Dutch invasion of Britain in November 1688, which triggered it off — a vast undertaking planned by the Dutch Stadholder, William III, and his advisers swiftly and amid the utmost secrecy — caused stupefaction in the courts of Europe. Scarcely less amazing than a Dutch invasion armada of some 500 vessels (approximately four times as large as the Spanish Armada of 1588),[9] and the risks run in attempting such an operation as late in the year as November, was the speed with which James II's authority crumbled. London came under the control of the invading Dutch,[10] and a somewhat reluctant Parliament was induced to dethrone James and make his son-in-law, William III, king of England, albeit nominally jointly with his wife, the new queen, Mary Stuart. Within a matter of months the resources of Britain were turned round, against France, and an English army, sent by William, was fighting in Flanders alongside the Dutch while at the same time Dutch troops and commanders played a key role in enabling William to defeat the Jacobites in Scotland and Ireland. The European war which followed, precipitated partly by the Glorious Revolution and partly by the differences between Louis XIV and the coalition of powers ranged against

---

[8] The mood in Venice is well described in PRO, SP 90/51, fo. 230v, Doddington to Arlington, Venice, 1 July 1672; see also J.I. Israel, *Dutch Primacy in World Trade, 1585–1740* (Oxford, 1989), pp. 295, 298; on the reaction in Brandenburg, see W. Troost, 'William III, Brandenburg and the Anti-French Coalition', in J.I. Israel (ed.), *The Anglo-Dutch Moment: Essays on the Glorious Revolution and its World Impact* (Cambridge, 1991), pp. 302–4.

[9] J.I. Israel and Geoffrey Parker, 'Of Providence and Protestant Winds: The Spanish Armada of 1588 and the Dutch Armada of 1688', ibid., pp. 335–63.

[10] J.I. Israel, 'The Dutch Role in the Glorious Revolution', ibid., pp. 125–35.

him over the Rhineland, lasted nine years and ended in a stalemate formalized by the Peace of Rijswijk (1698).

By that time it had become clear that the Glorious Revolution had created what has aptly been termed a 'crowned republic' in England, a state in which it was not the monarch but parliament which controlled the purse and, by William's last years, most of the levers of power. Financially and militarily, the power of the British state expanded spectacularly in the years after 1688 so much so that by the time of the War of the Spanish Succession (1702–13), Britain had emerged as unquestionably the strongest of the powers ranged against the might of France and Bourbon Spain, with the Dutch Republic playing an increasingly subsidiary role, especially at sea and outside Europe. One might argue that England's success in outstripping the Dutch as a maritime and colonial power after 1688 was entirely predictable, given England's larger territory, population and resources. But this was by no means altogether how matters had appeared in 1688, a time when England had been relatively weak, owing to internal divisions. An awareness of the deep rifts which existed in society in England, as well as Scotland and Ireland, inclined many observers (both in Britain and on the continent) to suspect that the Glorious Revolution, far from unleashing Britain's potential, might merely be the recipe for years of internal strife, turmoil and, very likely, civil war (see Chapter 12).[11]

Given the enormous impact of the major power shifts of the seventeenth century, the world-wide ramifications, and the often narrow margins by which the outcome of these momentous contests were decided, it is not surprising that the main players resorted to the use of printed and visual propaganda on an unprecedented scale. In any hotly-contested situation, the ability of either side to sway sections of the nobility, the merchants and the clergy, or the public at large, could make a decisive difference. Holland during the 'disaster year' of 1672 was inundated with prints displaying French atrocities real or alleged and patriotic pamphlets inciting the people to bend every effort to fight the invaders and save the 'Fatherland'. One appealed to the religious, patriotic and social preferences and prejudices of the people as a matter of course or, as with the propaganda of the Catalan and Portuguese revolts, uninhibitedly exploited popular resentment of a dominant neighbouring people — in these cases the Castilians. Manipulation of confessional antagonisms and popular xenophobia was part of the stock-in-trade of statecraft.[12] The large-scale and cleverly planned propaganda campaign launched in Britain by the Dutch stadholder and States General, in October 1688, is a vivid illustration of this: for it played a not inconsiderable role in the success of the Glorious Revolution and engineering James II's dethronement (see Chapters 12 and 14).

---

[11] J.L. Price, 'William III, England and the Balance of Power in Europe', *Groniek: Gronings historisch tijdschrift*, 101 (1988), pp. 75–7.

[12] Ibid., pp. 74–5; for a recent study on propaganda in the Glorious Revolution, T. Claydon, *William III and the Godly Revolution* (Cambridge, 1996).

Outside, as well as within Europe, the great power shifts of the seventeenth century had momentous consequences but also created pivotal situations in which the outcome was unpredictable — decided in part by leading personalities and short-term contingencies. Much of what to us, in retrospect, appears to follow an obvious, or logical, course seemed at the time utterly uncertain and volatile. What we regard, for example, as the almost unshakeable grip of Spain over vast American possessions, which had been, and were to remain, under Spanish rule for generations, looked far from secure to contemporaries. Especially the Dutch, during the first half of the seventeenth century, and the English, in the second (but also, at some moments, the French) looked set to transform the pattern of European domination in the New World out of all recognition. During the early years after the foundation of the Dutch West India Company in 1621–2, it was by no means only the company's investors and directors whose heads were filled with visions of entire Spanish viceroyalties and governorships tumbling like ripe fruit into Dutch hands. A Dutch fleet under Joris van Spilbergen defeated a Spanish fleet off the Peruvian coast in 1615, sinking two galleons and killing 450 Spaniards, blockaded Acapulco, and landed 400 musketeers who fought a six-hour battle with a force of Spaniards at Zacatula, on the Pacific coast of Mexico in November. Following this, there was widespread anxiety throughout Spanish America as to what the Dutch might achieve. The marqués de Gelves, viceroy of New Spain (Mexico) in the years 1621–4, was a military man who had served under Alva in the conquest of Portugal (1580–1), led an infantry *tercio* on the Invincible Armada in 1588, spent three years in Holland as a prisoner, and served his king as commander of the citadel in Milan and later as viceroy of Aragon;[13] he knew the Spanish empire better than most and was not easily daunted. But he was deeply alarmed by the vulnerable state of New Spain in the early 1620s and dispatched a stream of urgent warnings to the king and the *Consejo de Indias* in Madrid. His anxiety stemmed partly from the lack of coastal fortifications and standing garrisons in Mexico.[14] There were only two major fortresses — one on either coast: at San Juan de Ulúa, near Veracruz, on the Gulf of Mexico; and at Acapulco, on the Pacific. Due to pressure to send as much cash as possible to Spain, for the needs of the empire in Europe, the standing garrisons were tiny. He was fearful also because in his view the Spaniards of New Spain, though reliable in sentiment, would be of little use in combat owing to their poor sense of discipline and lack of skill with arms. His fears were further heightened by reports relayed to him by the Flemish engineer Adriaen Booth, sent from Madrid to help with the drainage works around Mexico City, who had received intelligence from the Netherlands concerning the formation and resources of the West India Company and the strategic

[13] AGI, Audiencia de Mexico legajo 2, ramo 4, fo. 234v.

[14] Gelves to Philip IV, Mexico City, 10 June 1622. in *Descripción de la Nueva España en el siglo XVII por el padre Fray Antonio Vázquez de Espinosa y otros documentos* (Mexico city), 1944) pp. 218–19.

debates taking place in the Dutch Republic.[15] Additional danger, in Gelves' opinion lay in the large number of supposedly Catholic Netherlanders and other non-Spanish Europeans to be found even in the remotest parts of Mexico.

As it happened, the Dutch launched their main effort against Brazil rather than New Spain or the Caribbean. In retrospect, it may seem unsurprising, even predictable, that the Dutch should have failed in their massive, hugely expensive attempt to conquer and colonize tropical Brazil. The Portuguese had put down deep roots, as had their religion and culture, and were not to be easily displaced from a land which, at that time, provided the bulk of Europe's sugar supply. Besides the large military garrison, and a substantial number of Sephardic Jews, there were never more than a handful of Dutchmen in the zone under the West India Company's control even during its most successful years (see Chapter 8). Yet, to contemporaries, the question whether the Portuguese or Dutch who would, in the end, secure control of the Brazilian sugar plantations seemed very much an open one from the 1620s down to 1654, with the Dutch looking the likelier victors in the later 1630s and early 1640s. Even after the capitulation of the remnant of Dutch Brazil to the Portuguese in 1654, it was by no means clear that the contest was over (see Chapter 8). When the Dutch Republic went to war with Portugal in the years 1657–61, there was still, at that stage, vigorous support, not only in Zeeland but also other Dutch provinces, for pressing on with the war until the States General did obtain restitution of former Dutch Brazil.[16] The Spanish crown meanwhile, having encouraged the Dutch to go to war with Portugal (and opposing the subsequent efforts of De Witt and the Dutch peace party to settle without regaining territory in Brazil), reminded the States General on several occasions that under the terms of Münster by which Spain and the Republic had made peace in 1648, Spain recognized former Netherlands Brazil as Dutch territory, and would help restore it to them, should Portugal be reduced to submission to its rightful Habsburg ruler.[17] Thus, the Spanish court was prepared to help put northern Brazil into 'heretic' hands if by doing so, Portugal and southern Brazil could be brought back under Spain.

Several of the essays in this volume reflect the centrality of confessional strife, and allegiance, in the great imperial conflicts of the seventeenth century, as well as the complex, halting moves towards religious toleration perceptible in a few countries. In the late sixteenth- and early seventeenth-century, the fact that only Spain, among the main maritime, colonial and military powers of Europe, was free from internal confessional splits and (at least outwardly) had achieved a convincing religious uniformity, meant that only Spain among the powers could infuse its imperial policies and strategy with a strong sense of

[15] AGI, Audiencia de México legajo 29, ramo 5, fo. 2, Gelves to Philip IV, Mexico City, 30 July 1622.

[16] For a recent reassessment of the Dutch role in Brazil and the southern Atlantic, see E. van den Boogaert et al., *La expansión holandesa en el Atlántico, 1580–1800* (Madrid, 1992), pp. 67–88, 105–33, 145–54.

[17] Israel, *Dutch Republic and the Hispanic World*, pp. 377, 399, 408–9.

confessional allegiance and purpose. The Spanish court claimed to be the faithful right arm of the Catholic Church in Europe and the wider world, and not only condemned the Dutch rebels, and other Protestants, as 'heretics' but exploited the propaganda possibilities offered by Richelieu's and Mazarin's alliances with Protestant states to try to vilify France in the Catholic world as a hypocritical, disloyal and fundamentally unsound Catholic power which also tolerated Protestantism at home. France and the other powers were caught up in a more complex cross-play of confessional pressures. But even the empires which were most divided internally over religion — such as the Dutch Republic and England — showed precious little commitment to the principle of toleration, as such, down to the early seventeenth century.[18] Only very gradually, and initially thanks to the Arminian (Remonstrant) tradition in the United Provinces, and subsequently the defeat of the royalists and established church in the English Civil War (1642–6) did the idea of toleration as a positive principle begin to gain ground in European culture and society (see Chapter 12). A secret Spanish report written in 1617, on the clandestine efforts of the Catholic clergy to revive Catholic allegiance among the common people in the Dutch Republic, stresses that the pro-Arminian provincial regimes in Holland and Utrecht (where the position of the Catholics, thanks to the attitude of the Remonstrant city government and provincial States, was strongest) allowed much greater scope for Catholic clergy to operate and for loyal Catholics to practise their religion, than did Counter-Remonstrant towns and provinces. Most of the roughly 150 secular priests and twenty concealed Jesuits (who were of 'los mas excellentes') active in the republic were reportedly working in Holland and Utrecht — no less than eighteen priests and two Jesuits in the city of Utrecht alone. By contrast, in other provinces, and especially 'Zeeland, Friesland and Gelderland' . . . there are few priests because the laws proclaimed by the States against the Catholic religion are enforced there more rigorously then elsewhere'.[19] Only from the 1630s' in the Dutch Republic, and from the 1640s in England, did theories of religious toleration evolve into a major force in society.

By the 1660s, 1670s and 1680s, however, matters had progressed to the point, notably in the Dutch Republic and Britain, that books and tracts championing the cause of toleration began to become more frequent (though there was also still much intolerance) and political rivals began to vie with each other as to who was offering the greater measure of toleration as, in certain contexts, James II and William III did during the struggle of 1688–91. Toleration indeed was one of the central issues of the Glorious Revolution which had the effect of both reinforcing toleration and extending its use as a instrument of statecraft, especially in Britain, America and in the United Provinces (see Chapter 13).

A group which stood to benefit particularly from the gradual extension of toleration and came to play a not inconsiderable part, down to the early

---

[18] H.A. Enno van Gelder, *Getemperde vrijheid* (Groningen, 1972), pp. 64–84; J.I. Israel, *The Dutch Republic: Its Rise, Greatness and Fall, 1477–1806* (Oxford, 1995), pp. 372–89, 499–505.

[19] AGS, Estado 2302, Juan de Mancicidor to Philip III, Mariemont, 7 July 1617.

eighteenth century, in Europe's conflicts and colonial rivalries were the Jews and especially the *Sephardim*, or Jews of Spanish and Portuguese background. Some of the 'New Christians', descendants of the Jews forcibly baptized in Spain and Portugal in the 1490s or earlier, persisted in adhering to a simplified crypto-Judaism in the Iberian Peninsula whilst outwardly living as 'New Christians'. Many of these then migrated during the sixteenth and seventeenth centuries to the Spanish and Portuguese colonies in the New World while a handful settled in the Portuguese possessions in Asia.[20] Others reverted to open Judaism after settling in Italy or France while, from the 1590s, small groups of Sephardic Jews began to form also in Amsterdam and Hamburg. Later additional Sephardic communities arose in London, the Caribbean and, from the 1650s, in New Amsterdam (New York). From the late sixteenth century onwards the role of this group in the seaborne trade of the Atlantic world was a substantial one. Of course there were other merchant diasporas in seventeenth century richer and more powerful than the Sephardic Jews. Most notably there were the Genoese in the western Mediterranean and the Spanish empire; the Flemish whose merchant communities abroad were found, especially after 1585, in most of the main commercial centres of Catholic Europe; and, after 1685, the Huguenots in England, the United Provinces and Protestant Germany. But, as a merchant diaspora, the Sephardic Jews displayed certain features which were unique. They alone created a trading network which cut across the Catholic-Protestant dividing line and they alone had an important and enduring merchant network in most of the Americas (English, Spanish, Dutch, Portuguese and French America), as well as throughout western Europe, North Africa and the Near East. These exceptional features made the Sephardic diaspora exceptionally adept at the rapid transmission of commercial, and also political and military, news over vast distances which, in an era when communications were generally slow and difficult, gave the Sephardim an edge that others lacked in those sectors of finance, commerce and political intelligence, which depended on news-gathering from overseas. During the War of the Spanish Succession, Dutch and English statesmen several times found that the earliest news they received regarding the outcome of battles fought in the interior of Spain was from the Sephardic communities in Amsterdam and London (see Chapter 17). This same phenomenon is undoubtedly the reason for the presiding position which Sephardic Jews achieved, and retained during the second half of the seventeenth century, and early eighteenth, in the functioning of the world's first real stock exchange — that of Amsterdam (see Chapter 14). Major shifts in great power politics were bound to be reflected in the workings of the stock exchange but none had a more dramatic or astounding impact than the Glorious Revolution. Not surprisingly resentment generated by the sudden, and severe, stock exchange crash of late August and September, 1688 rubbed off on the Sephardim who handled the bulk of the dealings in shares, even though the basic cause of

[20] For a recent study of Sephardic Jews and crypto-Jews in the New World, see Günter Böhm, *Los sefardíes en los dominios holandeses de América del Sur y del Caribe, 1630–1750* (Frankfurt, 1992).

the crash was the crisis of confidence which hit the Dutch business scene once it was realized that William III and the States General were planning to invade Britain: for it was clear that this meant inevitable war not only with the king of England, James II, but also with James's ally, Louis XIV.

A final theme of the book is the important connection between the great-power conflicts of the seventeenth century and the world of art. European courts and leading nobles assembled great art collections in part in order to reflect and broadcast their aspirations and claims, as well as their political and religious allegiances. If pictures entered diplomacy, as gifts intended to win favour and proclaim the greatness of powers, art was also used to project the images of rulers and their courts, to each other, and the wider European public, as well as to heighten awareness of gains in prestige accruing from successful battles and sieges as well as court marriages alliances and peace treaties. The career of Gerard Ter Borch (1617–81) at Münster during the years of the European peace congress held there at the end of the Thirty Years' War, provides a vivid illustration of how intimately seventeenth-century art and court rivalries and politics became entwined (see Chapter 5).

The court of Albert and Isabella went further than most in its systematic use of art and architecture in support of its political and religious aims and aspirations. In an age in which cheap copies, prints and engravings were becoming more widespread, art also served as a means by which princely courts and republics could reach out to a wide public and project their concerns, aspirations and objectives more effectively than ever before. If, as Hugh Trevor-Roper has remarked, the opening decades of the seventeenth century were the 'years when the European art-market was first organized to supply a whole continent; and it was a continent at peace'.[21] It is also true that those were the years in which the European art world, and art market, first began to reflect the confessional and great-power rivalries of Europe as a whole. In the 1620s Antwerp art-exporters for the first time engaged in the systematic, regular export of Flemish art, chiefly paintings and prints to Spain. If this stream pouring into the Peninsula, via Seville, Valencia and Lisbon, included few works by the best artists such as Rubens, Jan Breughel and Sebastian Vrancx, and these were very highly priced, there were literally thousands of cheap, often very cheap items, by lesser artists.[22] And while it is true that these included great quantities of devotional scenes, landscapes, marines and flower-pieces, it is striking that the Spanish and American markets also generated an appreciable demand for scenes of historic battles and sieges, as well as portraits of royalty, courtiers, commanders and statesmen.

---

[21] Hugh Trevor-Roper, 'The Plunder of the Arts in the Seventeenth Century', in Hugh Trevor-Roper, *From Counter-Reformation to Glorious Revolution* (London, 1992), p. 117.

[22] See the correspondence of the Antwerp art merchant based in Seville Chrisostomus van Immerseel in J. Denucé (ed.), *Letters and Documents concerning Jan Breughel: Historical Sources for the Study of Flemish Art*, iii (Antwerp, 1934), pp. 8–9, 35, 45, 49, 57–60, 62–3.

Two of the greatest artists of this period — Rubens and Velázquez — were among those most directly affected by confessional and great-power politics. Both men knew the Spanish court intimately and often found themselves in private conversation with Philip IV. Rubens was also a trusted courtier of Albert and Isabella and knew the courts of Paris and London. From the early 1620s down to the mid 1630s he was extensively employed, first by the Archduchess, later by Philip IV, as a diplomatic agent able to act under cover of his artistic activity and who played a not insignificant part in diplomatic negotiations between the Spanish crown and the Dutch, and between Spain and England. Both artists glorified monarchical power. On one occasion, in 1626, they even collaborated at a distance, Rubens, in Antwerp, designing an elaborate emblematic border for an engraved portrait of the conde-duque de Olivares, building the design around a reproduction sent from Spain of a from-life portrait of the great minister, painted by Velázquez.[23] But the art of both these great painters also proclaimed to the world something of the horror and misery of the great conflicts of the age, even perhaps (as one historian expressed it) unmistakeable feelings of revulsion against heroic posturing and the futility of war.[24] Rubens, in his *The Horrors of War*, painted in 1638, and Velázquez who in the early 1640s painted his decidedly unheroic *Mars*, god of war, a tired, drooping figure whose weapons lay in spent disarray on the ground, may indeed have been commenting on the waste and futility of the great-power conflicts raging around them.

[23] Christopher White, *Peter Paul Rubens: Man and Artist* (New Haven, 1987), pp. 202–3.
[24] T.K. Rabb, *The Struggle for Stability in Early Modern Europe* (New York, 1975), pp. 129–39.

1

The Court of Albert and Isabella, 1598–1621

The court of Albert and Isabella at Brussels in the years 1598–1621 has long been, and will long remain, a subject of abiding fascination for students of imperial and international history, cultural history and history of art. The return of a measure of prosperity to both the cities and countryside of the southern Netherlands, beginning in the 1590s, combined with the progressive cessation of warfare, first with the Franco-Spanish Peace of Vervins (1598), then with the Anglo-Spanish peace of 1604, and finally with the Twelve Years' Truce (1609–21) between Spain and the Dutch, gave the Habsburg Netherlands a period of respite, stability and steady growth, such as the region had not known for over forty years. While it is true that neither the trade, nor industries, of the southern Netherlands provinces ever again attained the heights, with Antwerp the chief entrepot of Europe, achieved in the mid sixteenth century — primacy had now shifted irreversibly to the northern Netherlands — the south nevertheless regained part of its former economic vigour; and there was certainly no loss of refinement, or quality, in the specialized skills which since the fifteenth century had rendered the arts and industries of the Flemish and Brabantine towns the envy of all northern Europe.

Besides respite from strife and partial economic recovery, there were several additional factors which contributed to the huge cultural impact and stunning artistic creativity of the Spanish Netherlands during the age of the Archdukes. In the first place, the disruption of the 1570s and 1580s had not only damaged the urban and rural fabric of south Netherlands society, it had also left virtually all churches, cloisters, and chapels in the Habsburg Netherlands in a state of devastation and ruin. The increasing momentum of the recatholicization of the country after 1585, and determined reconstruction of the churches and refurbishment of devotional images and art under Albert and Isabella, set in motion what was arguably the most spectacular spate of ecclesiastical restoration and building, and commissions for altar-pieces and other religious art, witnessed under any reign in early modern Europe.[1] A further stimulus derived from the fact that, over the previous quarter of a century, many noble residences and country retreats had been pillaged, or left to decay. These too were now

---

[1] J.H. Plantenga, *L'architecture religieuse dans l'ancien duché de Brabant, 1598–1713* (The Hague, 1926), pp. 43–50; A.K.L. Thijs, *Van Geuzenstad tot katholiek bolwerk* (n.p., 1990), pp. 45, 65–9, 120.

often rebuilt and refurbished, as well as hung with new tapestries and paintings. Given what was lost and not regained, one can not perhaps call the age of
Albert and Isabella a 'Golden Age'. But there can be no doubt that it was an
era of glittering cultural achievement centred round a princely court which
itself stood at the centre of the European stage. It was the first, and perhaps
most impressive, phase of what has been termed the 'Silver Age' of the southern
Netherlands.[2]

Albert and Isabella were fortunate in the timing of their arrival in Brussels.
Circumstances local and international, mostly far beyond their control, came
to their aid. None the less, to all appearances it seemed as if theirs was a model
instance of a princely court restoring unity and harmony to a torn and divided
society. Much of the credit for the easing of friction and internal tensions within
Flanders, Brabant and lesser southern provinces accrued to them. This casts
an enduring lustre on their persons and their court. Spanish ministers during
the early seventeenth century certainly regarded this, together with the successful recatholicization of the country, as the Archdukes' great achievement.
When pondering the new situation which arose in the Low Countries with the
death of Albert in July 1621, one of the members of Philip IV's *Consejo de Estado*,
in Madrid, commented that the 'loss of the señor Archiduque has been a great
one, for his rule was such that having found the three estates [the nobles, church
and towns] of those provinces utterly corrupted he reduced them to proper
order and obedience'.[3]

Given the element of autonomy which attached to the southern Netherlands
under the Archdukes, and the impressive political, social and cultural successes of their reign, it is not surprising that one encounters in nineteenth-
and early twentieth-century Belgian historiography a tendency to insist on the
supposedly 'sovereign' status of the Archdukes and to imply that they pursued
what was, embryonically at least, a 'national' policy, conceived in the interests
of the southern Netherlands and pursued at times even in opposition to the
wishes and intentions of the Spanish court. Thus, one enthusiastic scholar wrote
that

> en realité la Belgique pendant cette periode fut donc bien un vrai état separé, reconnu,
> exerçant activement en droit international toutes les prérogatives de la souveraineté,
> malgré des liens superficiels avec l'Empire, auxquels personne n'avait grand égard,
> malgré, d'autre part, l'entente, la subordination de fait, et les restrictions contractuelles
> vis-à-vis de l'Espagne.[4]

More recent historians, by contrast, have maintained that the sovereignty of
Albert and Isabella was, in most respects, a 'sham' and that, 'although they

---

[2] On the post-1598 revival of the southern Netherlands and the notion of a 'Silver Age', see
J.I. Israel, *The Dutch Republic: Its Rise, Greatness and Fall, 1477–1806* (Oxford, 1995), pp. 410–20.
[3] AGS, Estado leg. 2035, consulta, Madrid, 30 July 1621, fo. 11, 'voto del commendador mayor
de Leon'.
[4] Victor Brants, *La Belgique au XVIIe siècle: Albert et Isabelle* (Louvain-Paris, 1910), p. 27.

took one or two decisions on their own, they were normally bound hand and foot by the "Spanish ministry" in Brussels, acting on the direct commands of the Spanish king and his entourage'.[5]

It has become clear that the state entrusted by Philip II of Spain to his daughter Isabel Clara Eugenia and his prospective son-in-law and (since December 1595) governor-general of the Habsburg Netherlands, in 1598, was never intended to be an autonomous or fully sovereign branch of the Habsburg family of empires. It is well known that Philip stipulated, on ceding sovereignty, that if either Albert or Isabella died without their having an heir, even should she choose to remarry, that the southern Netherlands were to revert immediately to direct Spanish sovereignty, as indeed eventually happened on Albert's death in 1621. But there were many additional limitations placed from the outset on the 'sovereignty' of Albert and Isabella in the Habsburg Netherlands — that is the southern Netherlands, the 'rebel' provinces, the areas of France to which the Habsburgs laid claim, and the districts of north-west Germany occupied for the interim by the army of Flanders. Among the public articles of the act of transfer was the stipulation that the Archdukes could not marry off any children born to them without the approval of the Spanish court; and that their subjects were to be excluded from all direct contact with the Americas, Africa and Asia but could only trade indirectly with the colonial empires of Spain and Portugal through Seville and Lisbon respectively.[6] Among the secret articles were stipulations requiring the total exclusion of non-Catholics, and those suspect in religion, from the court of the Archdukes and guaranteeing that five principal military garrisons were to remain under the direct command of the king of Spain.[7]

In fact, the Spanish grip on the southern Netherlands in the era of the Archdukes went considerably further even than restrictions such as these would suggest. In the first place there were many more than five garrisons which consisted, at least partly, of Spanish troops and which were under Spanish military governors. We learn, for instance, from a secret report on the court and government of Albert and Isabella, sent to Spain in 1600 or 1601 by Don Balthasar de Zúñiga, Philip III's envoy in Brussels in the years 1599–1604, of some of the details. There were major garrisons such as those of Antwerp, where Don Agustin Mexía was then governor; Cambrai, then under the governorship of Don Sancho de Leyva, Ghent, where there was now a considerable body of Castilian troops (which had not been the case in the early years after Parma's reconquest of the city), commanded by Agustin de Herrera, and Dunkirk where 'el capitan

[5] Geoffrey Parker, *Spain and the Netherlands, 1559–1659: Ten Studies* (London, 1979), p. 171; see also Joseph Lefèvre, 'Les ambassadeurs d'Espagne à Bruxelles sous le règne de l'Archiduc Albert', *Revue Belge de philologie et d'histoire*, 2 (1923), pp. 64–7; Hugo de Schepper, 'De katholieke Nederlanden van 1589 tot 1609', *Algemene geschiedenis der Nederlanden*, vi (Haarlem, 1979), pp. 290–2; J.I. Israel, *Empires and Entrepots: The Dutch, the Spanish Monarchy and the Jews, 1585–1713* (London, 1990), pp. 163–6; idem, *Dutch Republic*, pp. 412, 419.

[6] H. Schmolke, *Philipps II Abschied von den Niederlanden: Ein Beitrag zur Geschichte der Erzherzöge Albert und Isabella* (Berlin, 1878), pp. 28–32.

[7] Ibid., pp. 33–4.

Hortiz' was governor. There was in addition, a whole string of other strongholds also garrisoned by Spanish troops, and under Spanish military governors, including Nieuwpoort where the governor's name was 'Olivares'; Sas van Gent, under Don Juan Ramírez; Lier, under Don Alonso de Lima; Grave under 'el capitán Antonio González'; and the great Rhine bastion of Rheinberg, recaptured from the Dutch in 1598 and held by crack Castilian troops under Don Luis Bernardo de Avila who, according to Zúñiga, was too harsh a disciplinarian but a 'very honourable soldier'.[8]

While the army of Flanders was substantially reduced following the ceasefire with the Dutch in April 1607, and especially after 1609, the Spanish crown not only continued to control the army as before, appointing many (though not all) its senior officers, and ensuring that its key administrative officials, the *veedores generales* (inspectors-general), the *pagadores generales* (paymasters-general) and the *contadores del sueldo* (wage accountants) were all Spaniards,[9] but also took good care that a high proportion of the army's troop-strength should be of Spanish or Italian provenance. Until and after the signing of the Truce, the Spanish court strove to ensure that there were always over 6,000 Spanish infantry in the country besides some Spanish cavalry and several thousand Italians. This meant, with the greatly reduced total size of the army, that the era of the Archdukes was one in which the Spanish and Italian preponderance in the army of Flanders was not less, but actually much greater, than at other times. Thus, whereas in 1591 when there 9,579 Spanish troops in the Low Countries, amounting to less than one sixth of the total size of the army of Flanders which stood at 62,164, by March 1609, there were 6,528 Spanish soldiers in the Habsburg Netherlands, which was then not far short of half of the army's total strength of 15,259.[10] During the early and middle years of the Truce, the Spanish infantry in the southern Netherlands undoubtedly slipped somewhat below the 6,000 mark. In August 1611, the figure was 5,566.[11] But no sooner had the Thirty Years' War commenced, in 1618, and the *Consejo de Estado* in Madrid began planning for the likely resumption of the war with the Dutch, on the expiry of the Truce in 1621, than Brussels was informed that the number of Spanish troops was to be substantially increased and that there was to be a full *tercio* of 3,000 Neapolitan troops, to supplement them, under a Neapolitan commander.[12] By June 1620, there were 10,449 Spanish infantry in the army besides several thousand Spanish cavalry and over 4,000 Italians.[13]

---

[8] Balthasar de Zúñiga, 'Relacion de las cosas de Flandes y de las personas de importancia que sirven a su Magd', BL, MS Egerton 2079, fos 241–2.

[9] Geoffrey Parker, *The Army of Flanders and the Spanish Road, 1567–1659* (Cambridge, 1972), pp. 282–5.

[10] Ibid., p. 272.

[11] Ibid.

[12] AGS, Estado leg. 2034, consulta, Madrid, 21 March 1621, fo. lv. The *Consejo* advises the king to repeat the instructions he sent in April 1618 on levels of Spanish and Neapolitan troop strength.

[13] Parker, *Army of Flanders*, p. 272.

Nor was it only the army which was dominated by Spaniards. From 1618 onwards strenuous efforts were made to establish a royal naval squadron in Dunkirk and Nieuwpoort which would be capable of attacking Dutch merchant shipping and fishing fleets in the Channel and North Sea. But, whilst the great majority of the seamen, soldiers, shipping and weaponry involved were Flemish, the higher officers and the senior administrative staff, as the Archduke reported to the newly enthroned Philip IV in April 1621, were, and as far as possible it was intended that they would continue to be, Spaniards.[14]

Albert had spent much of his earlier life in Spain and Portugal and that is where his religious and cultural outlook, including a veneration for religious relics almost as obsessive as that of his mentor in statecraft, Philip II, had been largely formed. Isabella had grown up, and her outlook moulded, at the Escorial. All this was reflected at their court in Brussels, and palaces at Tervuren and Mariemont, where their chief advisers in matters spiritual were exclusively Spaniards. Especially prominent in the world of the court was the Archduke's confessor, the Dominican Fray Iñigo de Brizuela, described by Zúñiga as a learned and knowledgeable ecclesiastic of 'mucha discreción y prudencia'.[15] After Albert's death, Brizuela returned to Spain where he became bishop of Segovia and an important figure at court, rising to the presidency of the Council of Flanders on account of his wide knowledge of the affairs and personalities of the Spanish Netherlands.[16] In addition, there was Padre Fray Andrés de Soto, of the Order of Saint Francis, who was confessor to the Infanta, and the court chaplain, or *capellán mayor de sus Altezas*, Don Pedro de Toledo, a man, we are told, of great virtue and finesse who knew how to deal with every category of courtier.[17]

Handling the dispatches between Brussels and Madrid and other high-level correspondence and papers concerning matters of state (most of which was written in Spanish) was entirely reserved for the Spanish officials at Albert's side. Especially crucial here were the *secretarios de estado y guerra* (secretaries of state and war), pre-eminent among whom in the era of Albert and Isabella was Juan de Mancicidor who had earlier served as a royal secretary in Madrid and who was the key government secretary in Brussels from 1595 until his death in 1618.[18] As regards the main lines of foreign policy, the Archdukes were expected to adhere to the decisions of the Spanish court and to follow Madrid's lead. It was apt to cause irritation in the *Consejo de Estado* in Madrid if Albert took even a relatively small, and uncontroversial, step without first obtaining permission in Spain, as happened in 1620 when the Dutch seized and fortified the island of Pfaffenmütze, in the Rhine between Bonn and Cologne, to the dismay of

---

[14] AGR, SEG 185, fo. 184. Albert to Philip IV, Brussels, 30 April 1621.

[15] Zúñiga, 'Relacion de las cosas de Flandes', BL, MS Eg. 2079, fo. 246.

[16] J.H. Elliott, *The Count-Duke of Olivares: The Statesman in an Age of Decline* (New Haven and London, 1986), pp. 134, 354.

[17] Zúñiga, 'Relacion de las cosas de Flandes', BL, MS Egerton 2079, fo. 246.

[18] Parker, *Army of Flanders*, pp. 108, 286; idem, *Spain and the Netherlands* pp. 170–1.

elector of Cologne. Albert, in vague terms, but without clearing this with Madrid first, assured his fellow Catholic ruler of his support.[19]

When pondering the most vital issues of statecraft and strategy involving the Low Countries, the Spanish king inevitably needed much advice and information from Brussels. But it was decided in Spain who precisely in the Habsburg Netherlands was to be confided in and consulted, and who was to provide advice. When, for example, Philip III wished to know the views of the court at Brussels on whether, as its expiry approached, the Twelve Years' Truce with the Dutch should be renewed, or ended, a matter which vitally concerned every segment of society in the Low Countries, Philip III instructed Albert to set up a special *junta* to deliberate, and report to Madrid, stipulating who its members were to be. Apart from Spínola who was Genoese and just one Netherlander, Petrus Peckius, the chancellor of Brabant who was there, as it were, to represent the southern Netherlands, all members of this key junta were Spanish — the conde de Añover, Don Juan de Villela who later became president of the Council of the Indies in Madrid, and Fray Iñigo de Brizuela.[20] The guidance from Madrid even extended to what papers were to be discussed, special emphasis being given to the recommendations of Don Balthasar de Zúñiga who at this point was dominant in the *Consejo de Estado* in Madrid. He wished to renew the war with the Dutch, launching a land offensive using two armies, one to defend Flanders and Brabant, the other to attack the Dutch north of the Rhine, from Germany ('uno para la defensa de Flandes y Brabante y otro para hazer la guerra por la parte del Rhin').[21] Subsequently, the *junta* was joined by the newly arrived marqués de Bedmar, fresh from his imperialistic schemes in northern Italy. At a later stage in the deliberations, Philip III and his ministers decided, in view of the vital importance of the question, to broaden the *junta* in Brussels further. Albert was instructed to add several extra advisers all of whom, however, were again Spaniards: Don Luis de Velasco (marqués de Belveder), Don Iñigo de Borja (governor of Antwerp), Don Pedro de Coloma and the *veedor-general* of the army, Don Cristóbal de Benavente y Benavides.[22]

Regarding high matters of state at the court of Albert and Isabella, then, nothing could be clearer than that only the views of Spanish commanders, officials and diplomats plus Spínola really counted while the voice of the Archdukes' Netherlandish courtiers, whether nobles, churchmen or bureaucrats, was an entirely minimal one. Nevertheless, it remains true, precisely because so much of Spain's military, financial and diplomatic muscle was concentrated in the Habsburg Netherlands, that the court in Brussels in the era of Albert and Isabella was one of the chief diplomatic centres of Europe and that its personalities

[19] AGS, Estado leg. 2034, consulta, Madrid, 12 November 1620.

[20] AGS, Estado leg. 634, consulta, Madrid, 13 April 1619; AGR, SEG 182, p. 274, Philip III to Albert, Madrid, 23 April 1619.

[21] Balthasar de Zúñiga, 'Papel que had dado en materia de la tregua con olandeses', AGR SEG 183, fos 169–71v; AGR, SEG 184, fo. 33, Albert to Philip III, Brussels, 14 April 1620.

[22] AGR, SEG 184, fo. 81, Philip III to Albert, Madrid, 3 June 1620.

and preoccupations were avidly scrutinized by German courts, as well as in The Hague, Rome, Paris and London. Moreover, despite the many restraints on their freedom of action, the court of the Archdukes, at any rate down to Albert's death in 1621, always amounted to much more than simply the glorified household of Spanish regents or governors-general of the Netherlands. It had much of the prestige as well as the trappings of a sovereign court.

The diplomacy of Albert and Isabella may have been tightly controlled from Madrid, and key decisions taken in Brussels may have been made almost exclusively by Spaniards, plus after a certain point Spínola, but the outward façade of the Archdukes' diplomacy, and rule in general, as well as the image of their court, presented to the provinces under their 'sovereignty' and the courts of non-Habsburg Europe, was largely moulded in the south Netherlands and reliant on Netherlanders. Court ceremony, publicity, etiquette, formal announcements and presenting of gifts to fellow rulers, as well as judicial and administrative supervision, were the domain of the Archdukes' Netherlandish courtiers. Whilst the States General was in session, in Brussels in 1600, Albert and Isabella relied on the leading noble of Brabant, the duke of Aerschot, to preside and manage the sessions. When James VI of Scotland succeeded Elizabeth and became James I of England, it was the count of Aremberg whom Albert sent to London, loaded with gifts, to offer his congratulations as well as to prepare the ground for the Anglo-Spanish peace negotiations which followed. Jean Richardot (1540–1609), an official who had become president of the *Conseil privé* in Brussels in 1597 and, until his death, was the most prominent non-noble Netherlander at the Archdukes' court, handled a great deal of the detailed business both at Vervins, in 1598, and during the peace negotiations in London during 1604. Petrus Peckius (1562–1625), son of a professional jurist, and Richardot's chief protégé, whom the Archdukes named chancellor of Brabant, in 1614, and who was the preeminent non-noble Netherlander at their court during the latter years of their reign, served as Albert and Isabella's resident ambassador in Paris for four years between 1607 and 1611, where he earned the epithet 'le Sage Flamand' from Henri IV.

What above all lent a distinctive and impressive air to the court of the Archdukes, enabling it to exert a cultural and social impact far greater than could the modest courts of the Habsburg governors-general (including Isabella herself after her husband's death in 1621) who preceded and followed them, was the Archdukes' autonomous control over the substantial revenues which they received from their Netherlands provinces. It is revealing that the chief advantage which the *Consejo de Estado* in Madrid saw as accruing to Spain from the demise of Albert, and the reversion of 'sovereignty' in 1621, was that the Spanish crown would now control the subsidies voted each year by the States of Flanders, Brabant and other southern provinces. They could henceforth ensure that most of this money was spent on the army, fortifications and Dunkirk naval squadron, rather than, as during the era of the Archdukes, on maintaining the court in Brussels. One member of the *Consejo*, the duke del Infantado, commented that it would now be possible to ascertain how much the provinces contributed to their Highnesses 'y ver lo que bastara dar a la señora Infanta para su casa y lo demas aplicarlo al exercito' (and see what will be sufficient to give the señora Infanta for her house and use the rest for the army).[23] Another member, the conde de Benavente, even hoped that by employing most of the money raised in the southern Netherlands on the army of Flanders it would be possible to reduce the amount which had to be remitted each year from Spain.[24]

With its own autonomous and substantial financial base, the court of Albert and Isabella differed fundamentally from those of governors-general such as Alva, Don Juan de Austria or Parma, or, at a later date, those of Isabella herself in the years 1621–33 or that of the Cardinal-Infante (1635–41). It provided a far wider and more elaborate arena for the convergence and interaction of the Habsburg dynasty, and Castilian military and diplomatic elite, on the one hand, with the aristocratic, bureaucratic and, not least, artistic elites of the southern Netherlands, on the other. The court of Albert and Isabella may have been a focal point of Spanish imperial power in northern Europe but it was a also a show-case of the Counter-Reformation in courtly context: a meeting-place where those nobles and officials of the southern Netherlands who agreed with Justus Lipsius' view that the future best interests of their country lay in close cooperation with Spain could parade their credentials, make contacts and launch their careers. The key diplomats may have been Spaniards but, with so much diplomatic activity in hand, there was also ample room for south Netherlanders to conduct business on behalf of the Archdukes and the king of Spain, not least in distant regions such as Poland, Scandinavia and northern Germany where traditionally the Spanish had scant diplomatic experience. The army of Flanders may have been dominated by Spaniards, and to a lesser extent, Italians, but it was also the largest standing army in Europe and more than half its manpower, even in the age of the Archdukes, was neither Spanish nor Italian. There was ample room for a large number of south Netherlands nobles to build military careers as senior officers serving the king.

Of the utmost importance in projecting the imagery, splendour and pretensions of the court of the Archdukes, both to the people of the southern Netherlands and its nobility, and to the world beyond, was the elaborate ceremonial which broadcast and glorified the activities and projects of the court from its very inception. On 16 July 1598 the Archduke, supplied from Spain with a special procuration, summoned the States General to gather, for the first time in many years, at Brussels. When the States General met it was officially informed of the cession of sovereignty by Philip II to Isabella and her prospective husband, the Archduke. On 21 August the provincial delegations rendered homage to their own sovereign, the leading nobles and other

[23] AGS, Estado leg. 2035. consulta, Madrid, 30 July 1621, fo. 3, 'Voto del duque del Infantado.
[24] Ibid., fo. 9, 'Voto del Conde de Benavente'.

representatives, lay and ecclesiastical, taking turns to kneel and place their hands between those of Albert as Isabella's representative and future consort.[25]

The marriage itself was celebrated at Ferrara, on 15 November 1598, in the presence of Pope Clement VIII but with Isabella represented by a proxy, the main pageantry and ceremonial surrounding the marriage taking place during the spring of 1599 at the Spanish court, where quite a few leading south Netherlands nobles, including the counts of Egmont, Solre and Berlaymont were in attendance. Then, in June 1599, Albert, Isabella and a large entourage, including both their Spanish advisers and the south Netherlands nobles who had journeyed to Spain, all embarked at Barcelona for the return journey via Genoa, Milan, the Swiss passes and Nancy to the Netherlands. On 20 August 1599 the procession entered the Habsburg Netherlands at Thionville, at that time the most southerly town of the province of Luxemburg, where the party was met, and accompanied onwards, by more south Netherlands nobles. Several days were spent in the town of Luxemburg where, amid much pomp and circumstance, the Archdukes twice appeared in the principal church. The archducal party also paid a visit, outside the town, to the country villa 'La Fontaine' of the governor of Luxemburg, Peter Ernest, count of Mansfelt, famous for its magnificent setting and gardens, as well as for its sumptuous decor, numerous fountains and collection of antiquities.[26]

The next grand entry, as the procession wound its way northwards, took place over the three days 28–30 August in the fortress town of Namur.[27] Here again there were parades and visits to churches as well as the firing of salvoes of artillery from the fortress, with the comte to Berlaymont, governor of the province, acting as host and with numerous leading nobles in attendance, including Charles-Philippe de Croy, marquis d'Havré who was to be a key figure at the court in Brussels. On entering Brabant the procession was met by the preeminent nobleman of the province, Charles, duke of Aerschot. Then, more magnificent than anything seen thus far, was the ceremonial entry into Brussels, on 5 September, an occasion marked by the unveiling of some splendid décor on which various artists had worked, including a triumphal arch allegorizing the cession of the 'Seventeen Provinces' to the Archdukes.[28]

One of Albert's chief prerogatives as joint 'sovereign' of the Habsburg Netherlands, and an extremely useful one for enhancing the public image of the court in Brussels, was the right to distribute honours and titles, including

[25] Jules Mersch, 'L'Infante Isabelle (1566–1633), princesse souveraine des Pays-Bas, duchesse de Luxembourg', *Biographie nationale du pays de Luxembourg*, xiv (Luxembourg, 1966), p. 412.

[26] Giles du Faing, 'Voyage de l'Archiduc Albert en Espagne en 1598', in L.P. Gachard (ed.), *Collection des voyages des souverains des Pays-Bas* (Brussels, 1882), iv, p. 459. 'Postridie', relates Bochius, 'suburbanum Mansfeldii comitis praedium perlustrarunt, situ loci opportunum, structura sumptuosum, rura supellectile et ornatu magnificum, fontibus amoenissimum', see Joannes Bochius, *Historica narratio profectionis et inavgvrationis serenissimorvm Belgii principvm Alberti et Isabellae Avstriae archdvcvm* (Antwerp, 1602), p. 107.

[27] Du Faing, 'Voyage', pp. 520–1.

[28] Ibid., p. 522; Bochius, *Historica narratio*, pp. 110–15.

membership of the prestigious Order of the Golden Fleece. The Archdukes lost no time in exploiting the opportunity to create a forum in which the nobles of the Netherlands would compete for favour and position. Besides Philips Willem, prince of Orange, and Lamoral, comte (later prince) de Ligne, who had already been proclaimed members of the order during the festivities in Spain, Aerschot, d'Havré, Egmont, Solre and the comte de Champlite were all made knights of the Golden Fleece at this time.[29] The Archdukes also announced a reshuffle of the provincial governorships which were the most valuable rewards in their gift. Berlaymont was presented with the governorship of Artois while Namur, which he now vacated, was bestowed on Egmont.

Hardly had this first round of ceremonial entries been completed than Albert and Isabella embarked on their *Joyeuse Entrée*, as count and countess of Brabant, commencing, as tradition dictated, with Louvain (Leuven).[30] Here there was much splendour and pageantry and the court party paid a lengthy visit to the university where they witnessed the graduation of a number of bachelors and doctors in theology and listened to a Latin discourse delivered by the southern Netherlands' leading scholar, Lipsius, on the significance of the advent of the Archdukes and the qualities a prince needed to rule his subjects well. After three days in Louvain, the court rode out to visit the country retreat of the duke of Aerschot, at Hevre, where they heard mass and admired the duke's family monuments and collections.

The following month, on 13 December, it was the turn of Antwerp to receive the court, an occasion which the burgomasters made sure surpassed all the rest in splendour.[31] The décor, organized around a series of triumphal arches, through which the Archdukes and their entourage rode, and which was later perpetuated by the publication at Antwerp of a lavish volume of engravings,[32] was organized under the artistic direction of Joos de Momper (1564–1635),[33] known today chiefly as a painter of fine fantasy landscapes, with the collaboration of numerous other artists including Rubens' teacher, Otto van Veen (1558–1628). The Habsburg pair were shown much of what was impressive in the city and admired a great deal of art, as well as visited the printing-works of the house of Plantin and the headquarters of the tapestry industry. The city of Antwerp presented their highnesses with a silk tapestry woven with gold thread on which were represented, in various scenes, the military exploits of the Archduke at Calais, Ardres, Hulst and Amiens.[34]

After Antwerp, it was the turn of Ghent, which the court visited early in January 1600. Then, the following February, in rapid succession, the Archdukes

[29] Du Faing, 'Voyage', p. 524.

[30] [Aubert Le Mire], *De vita Alberti Pii, sapientis prudentis Belgarum principis commentarius* (Antwerp, 1622), p. 34.

[31] Bochius, *Historica narratio*, pp. 182–34; I. von Roeder-Baumbach, *Versieringen bij blije Inkomsten gebruikt in de Zuidelijke Nederlanden gedurende de 16e en 17e eeuw* (Antwerp, 1943), pp. 114–15, 133–41.

[32] In Bochius, *Historica narratio*.

[33] Roeder-Baumbach, *Versieringen*, pp. 114–15.

[34] Du Faing, 'Voyage', p. 536.

appeared at Lille (6 February), Tournai (9 February), Douai (11 February) Arras (15 February), Valenciennes (20 February) and Mons (24 February).[35] On all these occasions, artists were employed to devise elaborate allegories and representations, not infrequently showing the Seventeen Provinces being reunited, and brought to repose, by the Archdukes. There were processions, music and banquets, the proceedings at Valenciennes again being presided over by the duke of Aerschot, this time in his capacity as governor of Hainault.

When it came to decision-making at the court of the Archdukes, it may have been virtually only the Spaniards who mattered; but when it was a question of projecting the image and the requirements of the court and communicating with the provinces, there was never any doubt that it was the nobles of the south Netherlands who led. This remained the case throughout the era of the Archdukes. The sumptuous obsequies which followed the Archduke's death in 1621 were dominated not by Spaniards or other foreigners but by provincial delegations and the knights of the Golden Fleece, with Florent, comte de Berlaymont (who had been a member of the order longest), in front, followed by Ligne, Solre, Aerschot, d'Havré, Charles de Lalaing, comte de Hoochstraten, and only then a Spaniard, Don Luis de Velasco, followed by Guillaume, prince d'Espinoy.[36]

After 1600 a high proportion of the public ceremonies in which the Archdukes participated directly or by proxy were connected with religious festivals or the inauguration of major new churches. Albert had been tutored by the Jesuits as a youth in Spain and became in the Netherlands a fervent patron and ally of the Jesuit order. In many parts of the Habsburg Low Countries, Jesuit building activity was the most conspicuous part of the frenzy of ecclesiastical construction (and reconstruction) which reached its climax in the period of the Archdukes. During these years Jesuit churches and colleges arose throughout the length and breadth of the country. The two chief buildings erected in the town of Luxemburg under Albert and Isabella, for example, were the Jesuit church — today the cathedral of Luxemburg — and the Jesuit College.[37] In the case of the Jesuit church in Brussels designed by the court architect Jacob Francart (1583–1651), Albert and Isabella were present, with their court, both at the ceremonial laying of the foundations, in 1606, and at the inauguration which was celebrated amid great pomp, early in 1621, shortly before Albert's death.[38] Most magnificent of all was the new Jesuit church of Antwerp, for which Rubens painted two great altar-pieces for the high altar, the 'Miracle of Saint Ignatius Loyola' and the 'Miracle of Saint Francis Xavier', and for which, in March 1620, Rubens and, as his chief assistant, Van Dyck, were commissioned

---

[35] T. Louise, *La Joyeuse Entrée d'Albert et d'Isabelle à Valenciennes (20 Fevrier 1600)* (Valenciennes, 1877), p. viii.

[36] *Pompa funebris optimi potentissimi principis Alberti Pii archiducis Avstriae* (Brussels, 1623), p. 56.

[37] Mersch, 'L'Infante Isabelle', pp. 440, 490.

[38] Israel, *The Dutch Republic*, p. 416.

to paint the thirty-nine great ceiling paintings. The church was completed shortly after Albert's death and magnificently inaugurated, in September 1621.[39]

If the court of Albert and Isabella constituted an arena for the meeting and interaction of elites, it was also a place of close scrutiny of intentions and attitudes and, not infrequently, intense suspicion. This was an inherent characteristic of a court situated in a society traumatized by forty years of political and religious turmoil and war, but which now looked to the princely pair to soothe and heal the divisions and restore an outward façade of unity. Numerous past acts of temporizing, or betrayal, had to be overlooked or forgiven; numerous important personages had to be given the benefit of the doubt. The point of Zúñiga's secret report of 1600 to the Spanish court was to comment individually on the principal personages surrounding the Archdukes and to assess their trustworthiness as far as he was able to do so.

Don Balthasar had nothing but praise for the elderly governor of Luxemburg, the count of Mansfelt (1517–1604), who had loyally served as acting governor-general during the chaotic period from the death of Parma, in December 1592, until February 1594, when Albert's elder brother, the Archduke Ernest, had arrived in Brussels to take Parma's place. Although he was now aged 'over eighty years and has served in arms for sixty-seven, since taking part in [Charles V's] expedition to Tunis' in 1535, Zúñiga noted that he was still in reasonably good health and should not be ignored but rather 'mereze ser muy estimado y honrado de su Magestad' (deserves to be much esteemed and honoured by your Majesty).[40] He also unreservedly praised Charles de Ligne, comte d'Aremberg (1550–1616), son of Jean, comte d'Aremberg (1525–68), stadholder of Friesland, Groningen and Drenthe, who had been killed fighting the Dutch rebels in the battle of Heiligerlee in May 1568. He described him as 'gentleman of the Chamber of His Highness and member of his Council of State' and 'Admiral' — Albert had made him 'admiral et lieutenant général de la mer' in 1599 — as well as knight of the Golden Fleece, a 'buena persona' who had always served the king's interest in the Low Countries. 'Y no he oido', continued Don Balthasar, 'de tantas vezes como de otros que tenga malas yntenciones y sus Altezas entiendo que tienen particular satisfacion del' (And I have not heard so often in his case, as in others, that he has bad intentions and I understand that their Highnesses are particularly content with him).[41] Zúñiga added that Aremberg possessed little wealth and would be grateful for any royal grant made to him. He was married to the sister and heiress of the duke of Aerschot.

Florent, comte de Berlaymont et Lalaing, baron de Hierges, de Lens and de Montigny (d. 1626), governor of Artois, knight of the Golden Fleece, Zúñiga describes as colonel of a regiment of Germans in the royal army and again a 'buena persona' but one who, for a time, had been outside the royal service: a

---

[39] Frans Baudouin, *Pietro Paulo Rubens* (New York, 1989), p. 143.

[40] Zúñiga, 'Relacion de las cosas de Flandes', fo. 236v.

[41] Ibid., fo. 237.

reference to his joining the revolt of the States General in 1576 before revert-
ing to his former loyalty and becoming governor of Namur and Artois in 1579.
His record since that time, though, had been exemplary and his military services
considerable.[42] Berlaymont had an interesting marital history having first married Helène de Melun, widow of Floris de Montmorency, baron de Montigny,
whom Philip II had had secretly strangled at Simancas in 1570; after her death,
he had married Marguerite, comtesse de Lalaing, a lively and brilliant court
lady who made no secret of the fact that she preferred other men to him, and
with whom he got on increasingly badly. On 20 July 1604 Albert and Isabella
appointed Berlaymont successor to the recently deceased Mansfeld as governor
of Luxemburg and the comté de Chiny.

More guarded was Zúñiga's view of Charles-Philippe de Croy, the marquis
d'Havré (1549–1613), knight of the Golden Fleece, member of Albert's Council
of State, and president of the Council of Finance in Brussels. D'Havré knew
the Spanish court and had been employed as a high-level messenger between
the Escorial and Brussels by Philip II at a crucial stage in the Revolt in 1575.
Zúñiga described him as a son of Aerschot and of a 'legitimate daughter' of
the duke of Lorraine, a man of appreciable standing in the southern Netherlands
but one who was held to be 'muy ambicioso'.[43] In the late 1570s he had, for a
time, joined the noble opposition to royal policy in the Netherlands. Zúñiga
stressed that he had served the king well since returning to his service, but
warned that, while the marquis made great profession of his loyalty to the Spanish crown, there were some at court who suspected him.[44] Nevertheless, he added
it would be best to continue to show him favour.

As for Aerschot, knight of the Golden Fleece, member of the Council of State,
governor of Hainault and head of the illustrious house of Croy, 'es la persona',
Zúñiga assured the king, 'que agora ay en estos reynos, digo estados, mas estimado
por la grandeza de su casa y familia' (is the person in these realms, I mean
provinces, who is most esteemed for greatness of house and family).[45] Aerschot
too, he remarked, 'estubo algun tiempo fuera de la obediencia de su Magestad',
in the late 1570s, but, since returning to obedience to the crown, had served
the king loyally and well.[46] Aerschot had the reputation of being a friend 'of

---

[42] Ibid.

[43] D'Havré, according to the Belgian *Biographie nationale*, was the son of Philippe, the first duke
of Aerschot and Anne de Lorraine, widow of René de Châlons, prince of Orange.

[44] Zúñiga, 'Relacion de las cosas de Flandes', fo. 237.

[45] Ibid., fo. 237v.

[46] However, after 1606 he played no further part in public affairs. The fourth duke of Aerschot
since the death of his father in 1596, Charles de Croy (1560–1612), was the last of the senior line
of his house to hold the title. On his death, his vast possessions were divided between the children
of his sister, Anne de Croy, who had married Charles, comte d'Aremberg, — these included the
duchy of Aerschot and principality of Chimay; and the line of the marquis d'Havré whose eldest
son, Charles-Philippe de Croy (1549–1613), comte de Fontenoy, inherited the rest, including the
duchy of Croy and the principality of Chateau-Porcien, *Biographie nationale de Belgique*, iii, pp. 551–2.

our nation', Don Balthasar added, and 'towards myself has made great profession of friendship'. However, the duke's health was poor and he was prey to bouts of depression. Presumably he was also fluent in Spanish, as well as French and Dutch, since Zúñiga concluded by praising him as eloquent as well as widely read.

Philippe de Croy, comte de Solre-le-Château, knight of the Golden Fleece, member of the Brussels Council of State, governor of Tournai, *caballerizo mayor del Archiduque* (master of the horse to the Archduke) was highly rated by Don Balthasar: 'asi como tiene mas oficios que otros, asi es de los mas capazes' (just as he holds more offices than others, so is he one of the most able), adding 'y verdaderamente tiene arte y entendimiento' (and truly he possesses both finesse and understanding).[47] However, he noted 'ay quien le tenga por muy doblado' (there are those who consider him very duplicious), though he had always been outwardly loyal to the king and the Archdukes were entirely satisfied with him. He advised, by way of conclusion, that Solre should be cultivated: 'he is a man who spends a lot but has little income and thus he will esteem whatever he is given'.[48]

One of the most fascinating and closely watched personalities at the court of the Archdukes was Philips Willem (Philippe Guillaume), prince of Orange, knight of the Golden Fleece, member of the Council of State of their Highnesses, — and eldest son of William the Silent. Philips Willem had suffered severely from the effects of his father's long struggle against the Spanish crown and, at this juncture, with lands and titles in both parts of the Netherlands and as the elder half-brother of the Dutch Stadholder, Maurits of Nassau, his position was still uncommonly painful and difficult. After being kidnapped by Alva from the university of Louvain and sent to Spain, as a youth in 1568, Philips Willem had never seen his father again. Known at that time as the count of Buren, he had been sent to study at the university of Alcalá de Henares and allowed rather more freedom, for a time, than Alva considered advisable. But after the collapse of Spanish authority in most of the Low Countries in 1576–7, Philip II, on the insistent advice of Alva, had had the young, and now thoroughly hispanicized, count arrested, in September 1577, and shut up in the half-ruined castle of Arévalo.[49] There the young man, who inherited the title 'prince of Orange', on his father's assassination at Philip II's instigation in 1584, remained a prisoner of the king for eighteen years, until 1595. Denied pen, ink and all contact with the outside world, he meditated, prayed and read. On occasion, for exercise, he was taken out on hunting expeditions. In all probability he knew nothing of the post-1577 progress of the Dutch Revolt until his release.

After Philip II decided to send the Archduke Albert to the Netherlands as his governor-general, in succession to the Archduke's elder brother, the Archduke

---

[47] Zúñiga, 'Relacion de las cosas de Flandes', fo. 238.

[48] Ibid.

[49] J.P.S. Lemmink, 'Philips Willem graaf van Buren, prins van Oranje in Spanje, 1568–1595', *Jaarboek Oranje-Nassau Museum 1995*, pp. 19–21.

Ernest who had died in February 1595, Philips Willem was released and informed that the king wished him to join Albert's entourage. In September 1595 he was brought to the Escorial, where he stayed for three days, savouring the sober splendour of the Spanish court and, for the first time in nearly twenty years, encountering a group of noblemen from his homeland. He had an audience with the king and was introduced to the crown prince, the future Philip III. It was there that he first met the Infanta Isabella.[50] From the Escorial he set out for Barcelona to join the Archduke, who had left the court some weeks earlier. On arriving in Italy, the prince of Orange performed his first service for Albert, which was to travel to Rome to pay the Archduke's respects to the Pope, after which he hastened northwards to rejoin the Archduke's party *en route* to the Netherlands.

On arriving in Luxemburg, in January 1596, the party was lavishly entertained by the count of Mansfelt, which was no doubt a bitter-sweet experience for Philips Willem who can hardly have been unaware that the extensive revenues of the House of Orange in Luxemburg had been assigned by the king to Mansfelt during the latter's lifetime. Entering Brussels, for the first time in nearly twenty-eight years, the prince took up residence in the ancestral palace of the Nassaus, the largest, and most impressive, palace in the city second only to the ducal palace occupied by the governors-general. Not surprisingly, the prince's pain-fully conspicuous position at the Archduke's court, not to mention his long imprisonment in Spain, rendered him far more taciturn than his father had ever been. 'Es hombre de quien dificultosamente haria juicio', commented Zúñiga, 'por que es muy retirado y tiene poco trato conmigo' (He is a man of whom it is hard to make a judgment since he is very reserved and has little contact with me). Beyond this, Don Balthasar remarked only that he considered him to be a sincere Catholic 'que no es poco siendo hijo de su padre' (which is no small thing being the son of his father).[51]

Although Orange was not asked to shoulder any major political, diplomatic or military responsibilities, he remained a more conspicuous, if baffling, figure at the Archdukes' court than virtually anyone else. Next to the Archdukes, he was also probably the figure most affected by the negotiations which led to the signing of the Twelve Years' Truce in April 1609. For an important element in the agreement was that rightful owners of lands, titles and revenues on either side, who had been denied access to their possessions by the war, should now have what was rightfully theirs restored to them. Even before the Truce was concluded, Philips Willem was able to resume his rights as lord of Breda, Steenbergen, Buren and other lordships. He participated in a series of remark-able festivities, including a celebration at Buren in Gelderland on 23 October 1608, when, forty years after the Escorial had recognized him in the title, the prince was publicly proclaimed 'count of Buren'. Since he was childless, not the least intriguing question surrounding his presence at the Archduke's court

[50] Lemmink, 'Philips Willem', p. 27.
[51] Zúñiga, 'Relacion de las cosas de Flandes', fo. 238v.

was that of the fate of his lands and titles. It transpired, on his death, in 1618, that his last will and testament left everything to his half-brother Maurits, his only full sibling, Maria van Nassau, having died two years before.

Another phenomenon at the Archdukes' court was the highly enigmatic presence of four martial brothers, Herman, Frederik, Oswald and Hendrik, the counts van den Bergh. Their father, Count Willem, had been one of William the Silent's principal military commanders against Philip II until he had conspired with Parma and betrayed the Revolt in, and after, 1581.[52] His sons, having fought on the Dutch side all subsequently fought for Spain. The family had long been influential in Gelderland of which Herman van den Bergh (1558–1611), having been the king's, was now Albert's Stadholder. This meant in practice that he had responsibility for Upper Gelderland and, after Spínola's military gains in eastern Gelderland in 1606, Grol and Bredevoort. The ancestral seat, Huis Bergh, and most of the family's lands in Gelderland, however, were in the areas occupied by the Dutch rebels.[53] Count Frederik van den Bergh was captain of the Archduke's halberdiers and was regarded by Zúñiga as a 'valiant gentleman', as was Oswald, a cavalry officer. Hendrik (1573–1638), who was later also to be Habsburg Stadholder of Gelderland, was accounted a particularly able soldier and, in the 1620s, emerged as Spínola's second-in-command, and the most senior Netherlander, in the army of Flanders.[54] Don Balthasar was far from complacent about the presence of these men at the Archduke's court. Their mother had been a sister of William the Silent and a committed Protestant, which meant they were cousins of Maurits and Frederik Hendrik. Furthermore, Zúñiga reported to Madrid, even among the Flemish themselves there were those who spoke ill of them, cast suspicion on their loyalty and pointed out how influential they were among the sections of the army raised in the Low Countries. 'Although I know nothing for certain that can be alleged against them', he warned, 'were they to change allegiance it would be cause for considerable concern', as they were among the best soldiers among their countrymen and there were four of them holding positions of no small prominence.[55]

In a scarcely less curious position was Charles, count of Egmont (d. 1620), son of the count executed by Alva in 1568. He had been one of the nobles who had journeyed to Spain, in 1599, to attend the festivities surrounding the marriage of Albert and Isabella and had, subsequently, returned with them to the Netherlands. Made governor of Namur and a knight of the Golden Fleece by the Archdukes, Zúñiga was satisfied as to his loyalty and called him a polished courtier with a pleasing manner and good intentions who deserved the favour of the Archdukes, and of the king, both on account of his exalted lineage and

[52] K.W. Swart, *Willem van Oranje en de Nederlandse Opstand, 1572–1584* (The Hague, 1994), pp. 185, 243.

[53] Israel, *The Dutch Republic*, pp. 68–9, 386–7.

[54] J.I. Israel, *The Dutch Republic and the Hispanic World, 1606–1661* (Oxford, 1982), pp. 98–100, 170–1; idem, *Empires and Entrepots*, pp. 170–1, 180–1.

[55] Zúñiga, 'Relacion de las cosas de Flandes', fos 239v–40.

also because his brother was fighting with the rebels and in possession of the lands and revenues of the House of Egmont north of the rivers.[56]

Although he allocated far more space to the nobles, Zúñiga also had something to say about the leading non-noble Netherlanders at the archducal court. In particular, Jean Richardot was impossible to ignore. He had joined the Revolt of 1576 and subsequently been somewhat slow to abandon the rebels and submit to Don Juan, but he had been extensively employed by Parma and eventually regained Philip II's trust, and was later a principal member of the archducal and Spanish delegation which negotiated the Twelve Years' Truce with the Dutch, during the years 1607–9. Zúñiga describes him as a man of 'singular prudencia' and great skill in formal negotiations who was widely regarded, inside and outside the Netherlands, as one of the most accomplished statesmen of the age. Whilst he was denied all real power, and had little influence on decision-making at the highest level, in Brussels he was a central figure in the outward façade of archducal government. Don Balthasar reminded the king, however, that Richardot 'estubo algun tiempo fuera de la obediencia de su Magestad y aun agora ay quien no lo tenga por muy seguro' (was for a time outside obedience to your Majesty and even now there are those who question his loyalty).[57] Zúñiga then added that he himself had doubts about Richardot's underlying attitude but strongly advised the king to make full use of his political skills, and show him favour, to keep him loyal. Of the other prominent non-able Netherlander at court, Louis Verreycken, Zúñiga says only that he had never heard anyone, Spaniard or Netherlander, speak ill of him.[58]

Like the leading nobles and churchmen of the country of which they became 'sovereigns', the Archdukes were eager to restore, and refurbish, the palaces and other great buildings with which they were associated, and which reflected their status and prestige. They wished to use the opportunity, as the conflict with the Dutch temporarily wound down, to put the scintillating skills of the artists and architects of the southern Netherlands to work on a impressive scale. From the moment of their joint arrival in 1599, the Archdukes began to commission work to renovate the ducal palace in Brussels and restore it to its ancient lustre.[59] One wing was entirely reconstructed and filled with costly tapestries. Before long it was the turn also of the archducal château at Tervuren to be refurbished and that at Mariemont to be extensively rebuilt.[60] Hundreds of

[56] Ibid., fo. 238v.

[57] Ibid., fo. 239.

[58] Ibid., fo. 239v.

[59] Paul Saintenoy, *Les arts et les artistes à la cour de Bruxelles: le palais royal du Coudenberg du règne d'Albert et Isabelle à celui d'Albert Ier* (Brussels, 1935); A. Balis, 'Mécénat espagnol et art flamand au XVIIe siècle', in J.M. Duvosquel and I. Vandevivere (ed.), *Splendeurs d'Espagne et les villes belges, 1500–1700* (Brussels, 1985), i, p. 284.

[60] Ibid.; several splendid views of the Archdukes' palaces were painted during their reign, notably Jan Breugel's view of Tervuren (Museo del Prado, no. 1453), Sebastiaen Vrancx' view of the palace in Brussels (Museo del Prado, no. 1603) and Denis van Alsloot's view of Mariemont (Brussels, Musées Royaux des Beaux-Arts, no. 197).

paintings and other art works were installed in all three palaces, more than two hundred pictures being hung at Tervuren alone, the bulk of these by contemporary Flemish and Antwerp masters, though there were also older Netherlandish and Italian works.

If, as we have seen, it was chiefly the conjunction of social, economic and political circumstances which explains the astounding effluorescence of artistic activity in the southern Netherlands during the opening years of the seventeenth century, as well as the important role which art played in the courtly world of Albert and Isabella, indubitably Albert's personal connoisseurship and enthusiasm for art played its part too. In a semi-official Latin eulogy of the Archduke, published by the Plantin press, in Antwerp, shortly after Albert's death, the Archduke's love and patronage of the arts were paraded as one of his essential princely qualities. In one particularly crucial passage, the author states that the Archduke 'among painters living today, besides [Wenzel] Cobergher, esteemed and held dear Otto Veen, Peter Paul Rubens, and Jan Breugel whom, not infrequently, at times when he was free from state business, he summoned to his presence and to whose conversation he listened for innocent pleasure albeit privately. Also he was wonderfully delighted by their pictures and their art.'[61]

There is no doubt that Albert, brother of the Emperor Rudolf of Habsburg who has been described as the 'greatest of all collectors', had a genuine passion for art and greatly admired Rubens' magnificent talent. As the artist's nephew, Philip Rubens, later expressed it in his brief account of Rubens' life, 'Albert had a particular fondness for Rubens'.[62] In September 1609, a short time after his return from Italy, Rubens was appointed 'painter to the household of their royal Highnesses' and, in effect, became a courtier himself. He was provided with the status and privileges of a member of the archducal court, and an annual pension of 500 florins, but the terms of his appointment did not oblige him to live in Brussels or involve any specific artistic duties.[63] Any work which the Archduke desired of Rubens would be commissioned separately. Philip Rubens states that the 'rulers Albert and Isabella wished him to paint their portraits' and this he did, as we see from the pair of portraits today hanging in the Prado (see illustrations 2 and 4) and from the lively pair of portraits of Albert and Isabella which Rubens painted in or around 1609 and which hang today in the Kunsthistorisches Museum in Vienna.[64] Nevertheless, throughout the Truce period Rubens was not principally a court painter but spent most of

[61] [Le Mire], *De vita Alberti Pii*, pp. 92, 98; De Bie too several times styles the Archduke 'een sonderlingh Beminder van Pictura', see Cornelis de Bie, *Het gulden cabinet vande edele vry schilder const ontsloten door den lanck ghewenschten vrede tusschen de tween machtighe croonen van Spaignien en Vrancryck* (Antwerp, 1661), pp. 41, 168.

[62] Christopher White, *Peter Paul Rubens: Man and Artist* (New Haven and London, 1987), p. 55.

[63] Ibid.

[64] Ibid., pp. 55–7.

his time working on ecclesiastical commissions or paintings for Antwerp patricians and officials.[65] He appears to have painted relatively little either for the Archdukes or for leading courtiers. Only very exceptionally did Rubens produce a work linking him to the noble elite of the southern Netherlands, such as his elaborate memorial portrait (today in the Leningrad Hermitage) of Charles-Bonaventure de Longueval, comte de Bucquoy (1571–1621), an Artois nobleman who had served in the army of Flanders since 1596, risen to become general of artillery in 1602 and in the latter years of their rule had been the Archdukes' governor of Hainault.[66] He earned a European reputation as a general, seconded to Vienna, in the opening phase of the Thirty Years' War.

But if the great Rubens was not chiefly a court painter, before the 1620s, it is nevertheless with considerable justification that Cornelis de Bie, author of the most important account of Flemish art published in the seventeenth century, considered the age of Albert and Isabella a decisive turning-point in its creative history.[67] For it was undoubtedly the new political and economic climate prevailing from the late 1590s, and the strong stimulus given by the Archdukes' court, as well as the upsurge of church-building and ecclesiastical art over which they presided, which revived the art of the south Netherlands from the deep recession in which it had languished since the 1570s, bringing it within a comparatively short space of time to the very zenith of its brilliance — as De Bie fervently hoped that the Peace of the Pyrenees (1659), signed shortly before he began to write, would generate a second great revival.[68]

De Bie notes that Otto van Veen, who had earlier been court painter to both Parma and the Archduke Ernst, was the first of the artists to be extensively favoured and patronized by the Archdukes, the early emphasis being on court portraits, including the pair depicting Albert and Isabella which they sent to London as gifts for James I in 1604, and which became part of the collection at Hampton Court. Subsequently, the Archdukes spread their patronage of painters, architects, engravers, sculptors and tapestry-makers far and wide, particularly after 1609 when the Twelve Years' Truce enabled them to spend larger sums on art than had been the case previously.[69] Jan Breughel the Elder (1568–1625) was a particular favourite of Albert both for the exquisite beauty of his own work and his pleasing personality, as well as far his capacity for organizing and exacting the best from a wide range of collaborators and assistants.[70] Denis van

[65] Ibid., pp. 79–116; Baudouin, *Pietro Paulo Rubens*, pp. 65–117.

[66] White, *Peter Paul Rubens*, pp. 139–40; 'El Conde Bucoy', commented Zúñiga, in his secret report, 'gentil hombre de la voca de su Magd. y coronel de valones es de los cavalleros mozos de estos estados de quien se tienen esperanzas que aya de valer mucho por la guerra', 'prozede bien', he added, 'con nuestra nacion', Zúñiga, 'Relacion de las cosas de Flandes', fo. 240v.

[67] De Bie, *Het gulden cabinet*, pp. B2, 41, 43; C. Terlinden, 'Le Mécénat de l'Archiduchesse-Infante Isabelle-Claire-Eugénie dans les Pays-Bas', *Revue belge d'archeologie et d'histoire de l'art*, 4 (1934), p. 216.

[68] Terlinden, 'Le Mécénat', p. 216.

[69] Ibid.

[70] Ibid., p. 217; Duvosquel and Vandevivere *Splendeurs d'Espagne*, i, pp. 610–11.

Alsloot (1570–1626), a specialist in painting civic processions, was regularly patronized by the court from 1599 onwards, culminating in 1616 when Isabella commissioned him to paint a series of six large canvasses of the Brussels festivities known as the *Brusselschen Ommegang* for the dining hall at Tervuren, at a cost of 10,000 florins.[71] As De Bie remarked, in his later years the Archduke was much taken with the skills of Pieter Snayers (1592–1667) so that he too was declared a court painter and 'domesticq van 't Hof' (domestic of the court).[72] During his long career, down to the 1660s, Snayers was to paint a mighty series of great siege- and battle-scenes for the rulers and governors-general in Brussels. One of the earliest, commissioned by the Archdukes, was his painting of the surrender of Ostend to Spinola, under the eyes of Albert and Isabella, in 1604.

Besides Van Veen, Breugel, Rubens, Alsloot and Snayers, the Archdukes employed the services of numerous other painters, including Joos de Momper, Anthonie Sallaert, Frans Francken the Younger, Frans Pourbus the Younger, Sebastiaen Vrancx (Snayers' teacher and another accomplished painter of sieges) and an entire family of artists, Pieter, David and Salomon Noveliers.[73] Large numbers of paintings were required for the three palaces but also as donations to churches, gifts to foreign rulers and courtiers and, not infrequently, for sending to the Spanish king and court.[74] The range and variety of the court art they produced, often of a highly innovative kind, was astonishing. Besides portraits, ceremonial processions, visits to churches, sieges and battles, we are shown views of the Archdukes' palaces and gardens, carnival processions, ball scenes, Albert and Isabella attending peasant weddings; even, on one anonymous canvas, probably by one of the Noveliers, hanging today in the Brussels Musées Royeaux des Beaux-Arts, the Infanta's entire collection of more than thirty dogs in the care of Doña Juana de Lunar, her *femme de chambre*.[75]

A particularly notable ball-scene (see illustration no. 7) was that painted in, or around, 1611 by the gifted artist Frans Francken the Younger, in collaboration with Frans Pourbus, which hangs today in the Mauritshuis in The Hague.[76] The picture shows Albert and Isabella, side by side, seated on a dais looking on whilst the *seigneurs* and elegant ladies of their court, converse, listen to the music, or dance, around them. Besides the Archdukes, several other figures in the painting have been identified, including the male figure who dances in the centre of the picture who turns out to be the prince of Orange, Philips Willem, whose likeness is known from various other pictures. His partner is

---

[71] C. Terlinden, *Aartshertogin Isabella* (Antwerp, 1943), p. 140.

[72] De Bie, *Het gulden cabinet*, p. 223.

[73] Terlinden, *Aartshertogin Isabella*, pp. 135–40; Balis, 'Mécénat espagnol', p. 286; Saintenoy, *Arts et les artistes à la cour*, pp.–31–2.

[74] Terlinden, *Aartshertogin Isabella*, p. 135.

[75] Duvosquel and Vandevivere, *Splendeurs d'Espagne*, i, pp. 637–8.

[76] Ibid., pp. 640–1.

Charlotte de Montmorency, princesse de Condé, who had then recently arrived at the Brussels court in order to escape the pressing ardour of the French king, Henri IV.

Yet it was less in direct representation than in flights of artistic fancy, stimulated by the Archdukes' eager patronage, that the flow of art for the court attained its most refined and original as well as lavish effects. Breugel stood at the centre of a collaborative effort, to which his friend Rubens also occasionally contributed, which was at its height in the years 1615–20 and which produced a stunning series of garden fantasies and 'cabinet' allegories for Albert and Isabella.[77] These were mostly allegories of sight, sound, taste, touch and smell, which combined the skills of portrait, still life, genre, landscape and flower-painting all in one, setting ancient mythological figures amid a plethora of rarities, antiquities, exotic fruit, jewellery and sculpture in the midst of fantasy galleries covered with a profusion of pictures alluding to all the genres of Flemish painting, as well as cascades of exquisite flowers, portraits of Albert and Isabella, and handsome views glimpsed through windows, in one case of the palace of Mariemont. Although several of these astounding works were later lost in the great fire which ravaged the ducal palace in Brussels in 1731, others, including several second versions painted by Breughel, had long since been sent to Spain where the choicest hang today, in all their brilliance, in the Museo del Prado.

[77] Ibid., pp. 610–14; see also Justus Muller Hofstede, 'Zur Theorie und Gestalt des Antwerpener Kabinettbildes um 1600', in E. Mai, K. Schütz and H. Vlieghe (ed.), *Die Malerei Antwerpens: Gattungen, Meister, Wirkungen: Studien zur flämischen Kunst des 16. und 17. Jahrhunderts* (Cologne, 1994), pp. 38–43.

Graaf Hendrik van den Bergh.

2

Garrisons and Empire: Spain's Strongholds in North-West Germany, 1589–1659

A potent and enduring factor in shaping the political and religious history of the Lower Rhine region of Germany, and neighbouring Westphalia, in early modern times was the presence of an entire network of Spanish military garrisons from the end of the War of Cologne (1583–1589) to the Peace of the Pyrenees (1659), that is for around three-quarters of a century. This not unremarkable historical phenomenon has attracted scant comment from historians but it is arguably worth close attention and for several reasons. In the first place, Spain's posture in north-west Germany clearly had some impact on the course of both the Thirty Years' War in Germany, and on the latter stages of the Eighty Years' War in the Low Countries. But, beyond this, it seems highly likely that the entire course of the Counter-Reformation in north-west Germany, and subsequent political and religious development in the seventeenth century was fundamentally influenced by Spain's impressive and sustained investment of men, money, supplies and political capital over some seven decades.[1]

The Spanish garrisons in north-west Germany, a handful of them very large by the standards of the time, the majority rather modest in size, were also far more numerous, and spread over a rather larger area, than the standard accounts of the Thirty Years' War would lead even the most vigilant reader to suppose. Indeed, whilst Spanish influence in the area was at its height — in the years from 1614 to 1633 — a large part of north-west Germany was effectively under Spanish occupation and control. But first we must pose the question why the Spanish crown, which at this time faced multiple challenges in and outside of Europe and was increasingly feeling the strain of striving to sustain an overstretched military establishment strung out from the Netherlands to Italy, and from Europe to the Far East, encompassing Spain's immense American possessions in between, saw fit to intervene in this part of Germany at all. The strategic thinking behind Spain's massive commitment of resources to the Lower Rhine and Westphalia was complex and needs to be viewed under several different heads.

In the first place, three successive Spanish monarchs sought, by establishing and maintaining a network of formidable bastions, to secure sufficient leverage to tip the balance politically and strategically in a part of Europe which for

---

[1] J.I. Israel, *The Dutch Republic: Its Rise, Greatness and Fall, 1477–1806* (Oxford, 1995), pp. 386–7, 417–19, 407–8.

some time had been immersed in a bitter religious and political conflict which was bound to have far-reaching implications for the balance of power, and the position of the Habsburgs, throughout Europe. Since the 1560s, the whole of this region had been caught in a merciless triangular struggle between three great confessional-political blocs: Lutheran, Calvinist and Catholic. While it was obvious that the potential for instability and strife was virtually endless, it was very difficult to see who, or what, could possibly have resolved the terrifying divisions tearing the region apart. Furthermore, there was nothing in the early stages of this three-cornered contest for confessional dominance that suggested that, left to themselves and without Spanish intervention, the Catholic rulers and population of the region were likely to triumph or even hold their own.[2] On the contrary, even though a large part of the region consisted of (ostensibly) Catholic ecclesiastical states — the electorate of Cologne and the prince-bishoprics of Münster, Osnabrück and Paderborn — the extensive inroads made by Lutheranism and Calvinism especially among the urban population of all these states, and the undisguised Protestant sympathies of many of the lay rulers and minor lords of the region, placed the Catholic cause in a mostly weak and vulnerable position.[3] It was, in fact, Spanish intervention more than any other factor which first arrested the progressive disintegration of the Catholic position in north-west Germany; and then, from the later 1580s onwards, made it possible for the Counter-Reformation to take root, establish a strong presence; and then, finally (as in the southern Netherlands) triumph in the larger part of the region over its Lutheran and Calvinist enemies.

A second major reason for Spain's military and political commitment in north-west Germany was the obvious strategic significance of this area for the continuing, and relentless, conflict between the Spanish crown and its rebels in the Low Countries. This strategic factor came into play at a slightly later stage than the general political and religious factor. Down to the early 1590s, whenever they were able to take the offensive, the Spanish commanders had encountered no particular difficulties in crossing the great rivers which flowed from east to west across the Netherlands, dividing the northern from the southern provinces. Especially after Parma's victories of the mid 1580s the Spaniards, holding Nijmegen, Zutphen and Deventer, as well as Groningen, controlled much of the north-eastern side of the Netherlands from the rivers to the Ems estuary, which meant that they had a choice of relatively easy routes of access to the areas under rebel control. The strategic situation was transformed only after Philip II's momentous decision, in 1590, to halt the advance of his armies in the northern Netherlands and concentrate instead on intervening in the French

[2] Ibid., pp. 386–7; Heinz Schilling, 'Die politische Elite nordwestdeutscher Städte in den religiösen Auseinandersetzungen des 16. Jahrhunderts', in W.J. Mommsen (ed.), *Stadtbürgertum und Adel in der Reformation* (Stuttgart, 1979), pp. 235–308; R. Po-chia Hsia, *Society and Religion in Münster, 1535–1618* (New Haven, 1984), pp. 200–1.
[3] Hsia, *Society and Religion*, pp. 59, 123–4; Heinz Schilling, 'Bürgerkämpfe in Aachen zu Beginn des 17. Jahrhunderts', *Zeitschrift für historische Forschung*, 1 (1974), pp. 175–231.

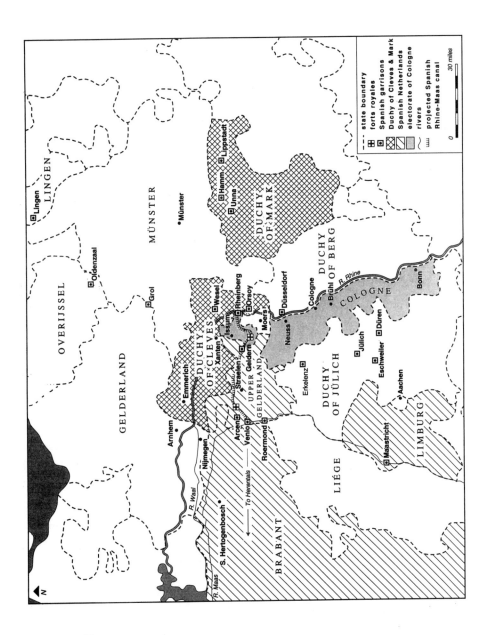

Map 1
The Spanish
garrisons in
north-west
Germany during
the 1620s.

Wars of Religion, in order to prevent Henry of Navarre and the Huguenots defeating the French Catholic League. The consequent weakening of the Spanish presence north of the rivers gave the Dutch Stadholder, Maurits of Nassau, the opportunity to launch two major offensives, in 1591 and 1597, in which he drove the Spaniards from the whole of the north-eastern Netherlands, including Nijmegen and their other main strongholds on the great rivers.[4] As a result of the Franco-Spanish war of 1590–1598, the Dutch States General were able to seal off every route of access from the south. They also made good use of the respite to extend and strengthen the fortifications of the strongholds they captured along the rivers in order to make the river barrier more formidable than it had ever been in the past. Thus, when the Spanish crown's intervention in France ended with the Peace of Vervins (1598) and planning began for a resumed offensive in the north, it rapidly became apparent that the only way that Spain could circumvent the daunting defensive line which the Dutch had now created was to attack the United Provinces indirectly, through north-west Germany, so as to tackle the Dutch defences north of the rivers, especially along the IJssel line between Zutphen and Coevorden, where lack of rivers and large towns conspired to render the Dutch defensive ring much more vulnerable than it was further south and west. This, in turn, meant that if Spain was going to mount a serious strategic threat to the United Provinces in the conditions prevailing after 1598 she had to establish a zone of political and military dominance on the Lower Rhine within Germany. And so it was, after 1598, for the rest of the Eighty Years' War, every single major Spanish thrust into Dutch territory — the most significant being Spínola's incursions in 1605–6; the invasion across the IJssel as far as Amersfoort in 1629; and the Cardinal-Infante's advance to Schenckenschanz in 1635 — was launched from north-west Germany rather than directly, from the southern Netherlands.

A third consideration which led the Spanish crown to strive to maintain hegemony in north-west Germany for some seven decades was the realization that the Spanish *plaza de armas* in the southern Netherlands, Spain's chief military base in Europe, could only be used to influence and intervene in the politics of the Holy Roman Empire as a whole, and in support of Habsburg initiatives in central Europe, if Spain possessed one or more secure, fortified crossing-points on the Rhine. Without a secure base on the Rhine it would simply be out of the question for Spain to attempt to intervene militarily in Austria, Bohemia or in the interior of Germany. Since the chief ministers of Philip III and Philip IV, especially from 1618 onwards, aspired to preside over Europe by interposing Spain as the chief protector and patron of the Catholic and Habsburg cause in the empire, and by consolidating the alliance between Spain and Habsburg Austria, it followed, as night follows day, that Spain needed secure bases on the Lower Rhine.

[4] Israel, *Dutch Republic*, pp. 244–53.

Lastly, there was also a consideration of a quite different kind. Possessing strongholds in north-west Germany proved in a number of ways useful to the Spanish crown as an instrument of economic and fiscal warfare and manipulation, useful against the Dutch and, on occasion, hostile or uncooperative neighbouring German states. This was especially evident during the great river blockade of 1625—9 when, over a four-year period, Spain endeavoured to paralyse the Dutch Republic's river trade by using her military garrisons on the Rhine, Ems, Weser and adjoining rivers, as well as on the Maas and Scheldt, to try to interrupt and suppress all Dutch river traffic with neighbouring lands as well as the Dutch overland trade to Brunswick, Hanover and other destinations in the interior of Germany.[5] But the garrisons were used to exert economic pressure also in other ways, and at other times, in particular by subjecting whole swathes of territory, with all their villages and undefended towns to 'contributions', payments exacted by cavalry patrols under threat of sack and devastation. It was not until the Dutch managed to capture the last of the major Spanish crossing-points on the Rhine, the fortress town of Rheinberg in 1633, that they could put an end to a situation whereby large areas of eastern Gelderland and Overijssel were paying regular 'contributions' to the king of Spain.[6] Although previous to the Twelve Years' Truce the districts of Borculo and Lichtenvoorde, which the Spanish crown recognized as belonging to the prince-bishopric of Münster, had been exempt from these exactions, they too had to pay 'contributions' after the resumption of the war in 1621, down to 1633, having been forcibly seized and annexed by the States General in 1616.[7]

Our story begins with the rise of Calvinism as a major force in north-west Germany, as well as the Low Countries, in the 1550s and 1560s; and the arrival of the duke of Alva and a strong Spanish army in the Netherlands, to restore the authority of the Spanish crown and the flagging fortunes of the Catholic Church, in 1567. If Alva was to succeed in his mission of repression, and reassertion of Spanish power, then it was impossible for him to ignore the situation in north-west Germany, which was intimately connected with that in the Low Countries in a host of ways, and where tens of thousands of Dutch rebels and Protestants now fled precisely to evade his stringent crack-down. One consequence of this exodus from the Netherlands was that it greatly strengthened the position of the Calvinists in the Lower Rhine duchies and Cologne, and intensified the triangular conflict between the three main confessions. This, in turn, rendered it all the more urgent, in the eyes of Philip II and Alva, that Spain should try to

[5] See J.I. Israel, *The Dutch Republic and the Hispanic World, 1606–1661* (Oxford, 1982), pp. 217–23.
[6] N.J. Tops, 'De heffing der Spaanse contributiën tot 1635 in het oosten der Republiek of de "landbederfelijke" rol van Grol, Oldenzaal en Lingen', in N.J. Tops, *Grol in de zeventiende en achttiende eeuw* (Groenlo, 1992), pp. 54, 59–60.
[7] Ibid., p. 58; T.A.M. Thielen, *Geschiedenis van de enclave Groenlo Lichtenvoorde* (Zutphen, 1966), pp. 89, 95, 103.

curb the advance of Protestantism and anti-Habsburg sentiment in the German territories bordering the Spanish Low Countries, and lend all possible help to those princely and civic regimes which continued to resist the Protestant tide.

At this juncture the preeminent princes of this part of Germany were the archbishop-elector of Cologne and Duke Wilhelm, ruler for more than half a century (1539–92) of the four duchies of Jülich, Cleves, Berg and Mark and the counties of Ravensberg and Ravenstein. Duke Wilhelm had been Lutheran and anti-Habsburg in the early part of his reign but subsequently modified his stance and, by the 1560s, professed to be a Catholic. Nevertheless, he was suspected by Alva of secretly sympathizing with, and abetting, William of Orange and the Dutch rebels. While, after 1567, he was cautious in the extreme it did not escape Alva's notice that there were clandestine supporters of Protestantism and the Dutch Revolt amongst his entourage.[8] During the crucial War of Cologne (1583–9), a struggle which was to have profound consequences for the whole of Germany, and into which both Spain and the Dutch rebels were soon drawn, Duke Wilhelm maintained a strict neutrality, striving to find a *Mittelweg* between the increasingly strident pro-Protestant and pro-Catholic factions competing to dominate the towns and localities of his own state.[9] Thus, while the duke's son and heir, the unbalanced Johann Wilhelm, had been raised as a Catholic and made no secret of his pro-Spanish sentiments, the duke offset this by marrying his three eldest daughters to Lutheran princes. In effect, the most powerful lay ruler in north-western Germany had by the 1580s been reduced to a helpless and passive role in which he was unable to influence the course of the struggle in Cologne, incapable of resisting Spanish pressure, and at the same time impotent to prevent the rapid advance of an aggressively anti-Spanish Calvinism in many, or most, of his towns.[10]

By the early 1580s it appeared that the Catholic cause in the German lands bordering the Low Countries was doomed to defeat. In May 1581 local Protestants seized control of the city of Aachen. Soon after this the War of Cologne erupted when the then archbishop-elector, Gebhard Truchsess von Waldburg, announced his conversion to Protestantism and attempted, with the assistance of the Dutch, to force through the Reformation in his electorate. This dramatic coup was answered, in April 1583, by a papal bull depriving the elector of his title and, in May, by the election, on the part of those members of the chapter who remained loyal to the Catholic Church of a new archbishop, in the shape of Ernest of Bavaria. With considerable support among the local population,

---

[8] 'El dicho duque', commented Alva, 'muestra vivir catolicamente, aunque la mayor parte de sus consejeros son de contraria opinion, si bien hay entre ellos algunos buenos católicos', quoted in Günter Bers, 'Wilhelm Herzog von Kleve-Jülich-Berg (1516–1592)', *Beiträge zur Jülicher Geschichte*, 31 (1970), p. 16.

[9] Ibid., p. 7.

[10] Ibid., pp. 6–7; F.L. Carsten, *Princes and Parliaments in Germany from the Fifteenth to the Eighteenth Century* (Oxford, 1959), pp. 280–3.

Archbishop Gebhard Truchsess had the upper hand, militarily, to begin with, but the tide turned and, in January 1584, Catholic nobles backed by Spanish troops seized the electoral capital, Bonn. In the following months, Ernst overran most of the electorate and then followed this up in 1585 by securing his election also as prince-bishop of Münster, the largest of the Westphalian ecclesiastical states. Ernst of Bavaria's double victory in Cologne and Münster marked the effective commencement of the Counter-Reformation in northwestern Germany and was to prove of great significance for every aspect of life and politics in the region. It should not go unnoticed that this crucial shift on the Lower Rhine occurred at the same time as Parma's reconquest of Flanders and Brabant and the effective start of the Counter-Reformation in the chief provinces of the southern Netherlands.

If Ernst and his adherents now had the upper hand they were not yet in control of the entire electorate. The conflict dragged on for several more years with both Spain and the Dutch becoming progressively more involved. Spanish troops recaptured Neuss for the elector, in July 1587, perpetrating a massacre of local Protestants. A force of 600 Protestants, descending from the north, stormed Bonn on 23 December 1587. In March 1588, as the Invincible Armada was being prepared in Lisbon and Corunna, a Spanish army, sent by Parma from Brabant, encircled Bonn.[11] The city surrendered to the Spaniards, after a six-month siege, in September. Finally, a year later in September 1589, Parma sent a substantial force, under the count of Mansfeld, to besiege Rheinberg, an outlying northerly enclave of the electorate which was one of the principal crossing-points over the Rhine on the stretch between Cologne and the Dutch border, and from which the Spaniards had already unsuccessfully tried to eject the Dutch in 1586. The starving garrison capitulated to the Spaniards in February 1590. It was the occupation of Rheinberg by Spanish troops in that month which marked the inauguration of the fixed network of Spanish garrisons in northwest Germany.

First, Rheinberg, then, and during the struggle for Groningen and Drenthe during the early 1590s also Lingen, a town and county entirely enclaved within Westphalia but which Charles V had annexed and attached to the Habsburg Netherlands,[12] became major Spanish bases with fixed garrisons. During Maurits' triumphant offensive of 1597, however, both of these bastions fell to the Dutch.[13] At the very start of his campaign, on 10 August, Maurits appeared before Rheinberg with 8,200 men and an impressive artillery train which had been

---

[11] Max Lossen, *Der kölnische Krieg* (2 vols, Gotha, 1882–97), ii, pp. 633–34; Carsten, *Princes and Parliaments*, p. 278; the defeat of the Invincible Armada in the Channel and North Sea took place in August.

[12] G.J. ter Kuile, 'Het graafschap Lingen onder de Oranjes', *Verslagen . . . van de Vereeniging tot beoefening van Overijsselsch regt en geschiedenis*, 68 (1953), pp. 13–31.

[13] Ter Kuile, 'Graafschap Lingen', p. 17.

shipped up the river. Ten days of bombardment by this river-borne siege artillery was enough to induce the Spanish garrison to surrender.[14] Opening his offensive by tackling the strongest Spanish bastion north of the rivers, and the one furthest away from the Dutch border, proved a shrewd strategy. In this way the two stadholders — Maurits was accompanied by the Frisian stadholder, Willem Lodweijk — cut the artery by which Spanish troops and supplies reached all the places still loyal to Philip II north of the great rivers. Cut off from all prospect of help, Grol, Bredevoort, Enschedé, Oldenzaal and, last of all, Lingen, fell to the army of the States General in rapid succession.[15]

The stunning success of Maurits' campaign of 1597, however, also served to underline the crucial strategic significance of the Lower Rhine crossing-points. Whether the Dutch were able to consolidate their grip north of the rivers, or Spain was able to restore her position in north-western Germany, was clearly going to depend in no small measure on who controlled the major crossing-points. When the Franco-Spanish war ended with the peace of Vervins (May 1598), and the semi-sovereign court of Albert and Isabella was established at Brussels, the attention of Spanish ministers in both Madrid and Brussels once again focused on how to reverse the tide of Dutch success. As early as the summer of 1598, while the Archduke Albert himself was away in Italy and Spain, formalizing his marriage to Isabella and the assumption of Habsburg sovereignty in the Low Countries, a Spanish army, commanded by Don Francisco de Mendoza, Admiral of Aragón, appeared in the Lower Rhine duchies and, after a short siege, recaptured Rheinberg for Spain and the Archdukes. The 'whore or war' (la puta de la guerra) as Rheinberg became known was to remain in Spanish hands for three years. Once the main part of the army of Flanders was tied down at the siege of Ostend, Maurits, on the direction of the States General, set siege to Rheinberg, for the second time, in June 1601. Although the town had a sizeable garrison including crack Castilian troops and Rheinberg's military governor, Don Luis Bernardo de Avila, was a capable and experienced officer, with adequate supplies at his disposal, the effect of Maurits siege works and artillery forced the Spaniards to surrender at the end of July.[16] To celebrate the victory a triumphal medal was issued in Holland showing a plan of Rheinberg's fortifications and Maurits' impressive siege works, adorned with the inscription 'Hostes dira minitans a Berga pellitur MDCI' (The enemy threatening fearful things is driven from Berg 1601).

For the next four years Spain had no military bases in north-west Germany. It was Spínola's two offensives north of the rivers of 1605 and 1606 which restored and stabilized the ascendancy of Spain and the Archdukes on the Lower Rhine

[14] R.H. Lemperts, 'Rheinbergs Belagerungen', *Mittheilungen des Vereins von Geschichtsfreunden zu Rheinberg,* 1 (1980), pp. 25–6.

[15] R. Fruin, *Tien Jaren uit den Tachtigjarigen Oorlog, 1588–1598* (The Hague, 1924), pp. 363–4.

[16] Lemperts, 'Rheinberg's Belagerungen', p. 26; Jean le Clerc, *Explication historique des principales medailles frapées pour servir à l'histoire des Provinces-Unies des Pays Bas* (Amsterdam, 1723), pp. 62–3.

and in Westphalia.[17] After being held by the Dutch since November 1597, the county and fortress of Lingen was reconquered by Spínola in August 1605. The town was placed under the command of Philippe de Croy, comte de Solre. Previously, in the same campaign, Spínola had taken Oldenzaal, the capital of the easternmost quarter of Overijssel. The following year, after capturing Grol and Breedevoort, Spínola besieged Rheinberg, the town being once again subjected to a heavy bombardment. The progress of the siege was followed with avid interest throughout the Low Countries and north-western Germany. An elaborate engraving depicting the scene was published whilst the outcome was still undecided, proclaiming to all Germany that 'Rhein Berck eine dess Stifts Colln Statt . . . von den Staten seher munijrt, von Spinola belegert wihrtt' (Rheinberg a city of the archbishopric of Cologne . . . amply supplied by the States is being besieged by Spínola).[18] The bombardment was reported to be continuous, fierce, and, despite the States General's efforts to extend and strengthen the town's fortifications, highly effective. The generalissimo's success in retaking the town for Spain and the Archdukes was generally regarded as one of his most resounding feats.

It was the onset of the Jülich-Cleves succession dispute, which began with the death of the pro-Spanish Duke Johann Wilhelm (the last of his line) in 1609, which provided both spur and opportunity for the acquisition by Spain of a more extensive network of bases in north-west Germany than had at any point been acquired, or even envisaged, hitherto. Since both rival claimants to the succession in Jülich-Cleves professed to be Lutherans, it was clear to the Spaniards and the Archdukes that great effort and vigilance would be needed to prevent a massive setback to Habsburg and Catholic interests on the Lower Rhine, as well as the possible collapse of the Twelve Years' Truce recently concluded with the Dutch and a resumption of war with France. Initially, Spain's policy was to resist the pretensions of both Lutheran claimants and support the emperor, who insisted on interposing an imperial administrator, the Archduke Leopold, to rule the duchies provisionally until all aspects of the succession had been resolved to the satisfaction of both the Protestant and Catholic sides. Leopold, however, found very little support in the predominantly Protestant towns and, in Cleves and Mark, also had a majority of the nobles against him.[19] Only in the duchy of Jülich could he claim to have most of the nobility on his side. His position (and the Emperor's policy) disintegrated, however, when the French and Dutch combined to invade the duchy and besiege the city, the most heavily fortified of the towns on the left bank of the Rhine ever since, in the years 1547–9, Duke Wilhelm had furnished Jülich with one of the earliest Italian designed, 'Renaissance' style, sets of fortifications in northern Europe.[20]

[17] Israel, *Dutch Republic and the Hispanic World*, p. 18; idem, *Dutch Republic*, pp. 260–62.

[18] Lemperts, 'Rheinbergs Belagerungen', p. 27.

[19] Carsten, *Princes and Parliaments*, pp. 288–92.

[20] Bers, 'Wilhelm Herzog von Kleve-Jülich-Berg', p. 5.

The events of 1609–10 in the Lower Rhine duchies, which ended with the Archduke Leopold's surrender of the city of Jülich to the besieging army in September 1610, constituted a serious reverse for the Spanish, Habsburg and Catholic cause albeit one mitigated by the assassination of Henri IV, in May 1610, an event which greatly weakened France and also put an end to Franco-Dutch collaboration in north-west Germany. Spain therefore had a much freer hand to intervene in 1614 when the fragile status quo, established in 1610, broke down and the rival 'princes pretendent' fell to blows. Furthermore, the lines of contest were now more clear cut. In 1613, the elector of Brandenburg had become a Calvinist and thrown in his lot with the Dutch and Calvinist towns of Cleves and Berg; while the Palatine Duke Wolfgang Wilhelm of Neuburg had recently married the sister of Maximilian, duke of Bavaria, and become a Catholic, which placed him firmly in the Habsburg camp. It was in the name of the emperor and Duke Wolfgang Wilhelm, and on the grounds of protect-ing their respective interests, that Spain was now able to expand dramatically her network of garrisons in the region. As a later Protestant German account expressed it, the Spaniards 'unter dem Praetext der Protection des Pfalzgrafens von Neuburg ihre Herrschafft in Teutschland fundiren wollten' (under the pretext of protecting the Palatine Count of Neuburg sought to establish their mastery of Germany).[21]

With the help of some Spanish officers, Neuburg seized Düsseldorf, the capital of Berg, expelling the troops and officials of the elector. Next, in August, Spinola appeared with a powerful army, reputedly of 22,500 men and toppled the Calvin-ist city government in Aachen, replacing it with a Catholic regime. Then Spínola reduced the Protestant town of Dueren which was obliged to write to the Elec-tor Georg Wilhelm, to whom it had wished to remain loyal, explaining that (under duress) it had been forced to hand over the keys of the town to Spínola and admit two companies of German soldiers in the pay of Spain but serving in the name of the 'Emperor, the King of Spain and Wolfgang Wilhelm'.[22] Spínola also occupied Berchem, Caster, Grevenbroich and several other nearby places before advancing into Cleves, where he seized Duisburg and Orsoy and then appeared before the heavily fortified Calvinist city of Wesel. Wesel, a town of some 6,000 inhabitants, had been predominantly Protestant for some seventy years and had become one of the most committed Calvinist centres in Germany: so much that, according to a Spanish newssheet published in Seville to an-nounce the fall of 'Bessel' to the Spanish public, it was designated 'mucho peor que Ginebra' (much worse than Geneva).[23] But, despite being as an English

---

[21] *Historischer Schau-Platz aller Rechts-Ansprüche auf Jülich, Cleve, Berg, Mark, Ravensberg . . . bis auf heutigen Tag* (Bremen, 1740), p. 173.

[22] *Resolutiën der Staten-General,* new series, ii, *1613–1616,* ed. by A.T. van Deursen (The Hague, 1984), p. 310; the missive from Dueren to Georg Wilhelm was dated 27 August 1614.

[23] *Relacion de la iornada qve hizo el Marqves Espinola con don Iñigo de Borja y don Luys de Velasco con veynte mil infantes y dos mil y quinientos cavallos, en Flandes, contra los Luteranos y . . . en particular de la toma de la fortissima villa de Bessel* (Seville, 1614), p. 3.

newssheet put it, 'wholie inhabited by Protestants', the town had no stomach to hold out against Spínola. After two days the city government came to terms, offering to admit a Spanish garrison in return for protection and the right to practise the Reformed faith without restriction and to keep most of the city's churches and schools in the hands of the Reformed.[24] After this 'kindly and friendly composition', Spínola quartered 1,200 troops in the city, about 1,000 of whom were Spaniards, and appointed the Castilian governor of Rheinberg, Don Juan González, provisional governor also of Wesel.[25] With this success Spínola placed Spain in a dominant position on the Lower Rhine, controlling the greater part of Cleves, where the Spaniards were now occupying ten different places; the greater part of Jülich, where Spanish troops were now quartered in twenty-eight different towns and villages; and much of Berg and Mark, where they were deployed in twenty-four locations.[26] Not only did Spain now garrison three major fortified crossing-points over the Rhine, Wesel and Orsoy, as well as Rheinberg, but, as the newssheet published in Seville noted, the links between the Spanish Netherlands and Cologne had been greatly tightened.

The granting of liberty not just of conscience but of exercise of the Reformed and Lutheran faiths, and the leaving of numerous churches and schools in Protestant hands, was a notable feature of the network of Spanish garrisons in north-western Germany as it developed after 1614. Not only were the Reformed and Lutherans permitted to exercise their respective faiths but, in Wesel at least, after the expulsion of the Remonstrants from the Dutch Reformed Church by the Synod of Dordt, in 1619, and the banning of the public exercise of Remonstrantism in the United Provinces by the States General, the Spanish governor gave permission, on instructions from Brussels, for the public practice of Remonstrantism also.[27] Rheinberg was also a predominantly Calvinist town and there too the Reformed community and tradition remained intact under Spanish rule. When the Dutch recovered the city in 1633, ending twenty-seven years of uninterrupted Spanish possession more than half the town's population adhered to the Reformed confession.[28] By contrast, Lingen had come under

---

[24] An English newssheet, translated from Dutch, which reports that Spínola's army was 20,000 strong, asserts that Wesel capitulated 'condicioning libertie of religion, and reserving their old privileges, but the towne should be kept with the Garrison of the marquesse Spinola', see *Newes from Gulick and Cleve: A True and Faithfull Relation of the Late Affaires in the Countries of Gulicke, Cleve and Bergh* (London, 1615), p. 7.

[25] *Relacion de la iornada*, p. 3; 'he metido dentro mil espanoles', Spínola reported to the king, 'y porque esta es poca gentè para tan gran plaza, y habia prometido no poner mas arrimados a ella, hago dos puestos para meter mas otros mil valones y alemanes y que la sujeten', Antonio Rodríguez Villa, *Ambrosio Spínola, primer marqués de los Balbases* (Madrid, 1905), p. 306.

[26] In Cleves these included, besides Wesel and Orsoy, the towns of Büderich and also Xanten where 200 Castilians were quartered; in Berg, Spanish troops penetrated at least as far south as Mülheim; large numbers of troops were quartered in the small towns of the duchy of Jülich, see Rodríguez Villa, *Ambrosio Spínola*, pp. 305–7, 311.

[27] Israel, *Dutch Republic*, p. 463.

[28] J. Kühlmann, 'Die "kleinere Kirche" zu Rheinberg', *Mittheilungen des Vereins von Geschichtsfreunden zu Rheinberg*, 1 (1880), pp. 81–8.

the influence of the Counter-Reformation at an earlier stage, in the 1580s. There, resumed Spanish rule, from 1605 onwards, served to eliminate the Protestant presence and render the town more or less solidly Catholic.[29]

When the Spaniards occupied yet more towns in Jülich, Cleves, Berg and Mark, as well as Ravensberg, in the 1620s, the same apparently tolerant policy was continued, at any rate in places where there was a strong Protestant presence. But it was taken for granted by Spain's enemies that this flexible policy was merely tactical and would end as soon as the Spanish crown felt strong enough in Germany to suppress Protestantism in the places under its military control. Commenting on the situation in the Palatinate town of Frankenthal, which its English garrison surrendered to the Spaniards in March 1623 under conditions which included the continued possession by the Reformed of their churches and schools, the younger Dudley Carleton, English envoy in The Hague, reported in July 1627 that the rights of the Reformed community of Frankenthal were being sorely infringed by the Spanish governor and that the 'Spaniards howsoever they temporise more than formerly with those of our religion in such places where they gett possession, yet theyre end and scope is to establish theyr conquests by their utter extirpation'.[30] But the Reformed congregations in the Spanish-occupied towns did have ways of bringing pressure to bear, even in periods when Spain and the United Provinces were openly at war. When, for example, in July 1628 the Reformed community of Wesel complained to The Hague that the Spanish governor of Wesel was behaving tyrannically towards them, the States General, through the *Raad van State*, wrote to the governor of Wesel threatening to expel the Catholic priests the Dutch tolerated in Rees and Emmerich unless the infringements ceased.[31]

Taken aback by the extent of the Spanish gains in 1614, Oldenbarnevelt and the States General took the risk of sending an army to the Lower Rhine to occupy such fortified towns and locations as the Spaniards had not yet seized. For the States General could not afford to see Spain exercising an unchallenged hegemony on the Lower Rhine and in Westphalia, or to give the impression they were ready to abandon the numerous Protestant communities of the region and see the Counter-Reformation triumph along the length of the Republic's eastern border. For the same reasons, it seemed in The Hague quite impossible either to evacuate the large Dutch garrison in the town of Jülich, which was now dangerously isolated from Dutch territory, or fail to make some gesture to bolster Dutch prestige and Protestant morale in the area. At length

[29] Ter Kuile, 'Graafschap Lingen', pp. 20–1.

[30] C. Ruelens (ed.), *Correspondence de Rubens et documents épistolaires concernant sa vie et ses oeuvres* (6 vols, Antwerp, 1887–1909), iv, p. 90; *Dudley Carleton to John Chamberlain, 1603–1624: Jacobean Letters*, ed. M. Lee (New Brunswick, New Jersey, 1972), Carleton to Lord Conway, The Hague, 2/12 July 1627.

[31] E. Hubert, *Les Pays-Bas espagnols et la République des Provinces-Unies depuis la paix de Munster jusqu'au traité d'Utrecht, 1648–1713* (Brussels, 1907), p. 76.

Maurits appeared on the scene with a considerable army and not only occupied Emmerich and reinforced the positions the Dutch already held in Cleves
but sent a substantial force, under his younger half-brother, Frederik Hendrik,
into the duchy of Mark to occupy Hamm, Lünen, Unna, Camen, Soest and
Lippstadt.[32] Maurits also sent orders to lieutenant-colonel Frederik Pithan, the
Dutch military governor of Jülich, to broaden the Dutch-occupied enclave in
the duchy by seizing the neighbouring towns of Linnich, Aldenhoven and Tetz,
once again all in the name of the elector of Brandenburg.

The crisis of 1614 subsided, remarkably enough, without a single clash between
the Spanish and Dutch forces. Nevertheless, the entire Lower Rhine region of
Germany remained gripped by tension, the periodic heightening of which rapidly
communicated itself to both Brussels and The Hague. In April 1616 the English
ambassador in The Hague, reported to London that there was a state of alarm
in Holland, owing to the 'marching of Spínola's troops to Wesel and making a
bridge over the Rhine at Berg [Rheinberg] which makes them believe they
shall have some stirring this summer'.[33] This was no exaggeration. At a plenary
secret session of the States General, together with the stadholder and the *Raad
van State*, on 5 April 1616, it was reported that Count Hendrik van den Bergh
and Don Luis de Velasco, had concentrated some 7,000 infantry and a strong
force of cavalry in the area between Rheinberg and Wesel and that Spínola was
expected. Some of those present suggested the Spaniards were preparing to
invade the county of Ravensberg, some that the Spaniards intended to seize
Essen or Bocholt, others that the plan was to attack Borculo.[34] The Dutch garrisons in Cleves, at Emmerich and Rees, were reinforced.

When the Spanish-Dutch war resumed, in 1621, the Spaniards launched their
opening offensive in the Lower Rhine region of Germany. While Spínola
positioned himself with one army at Wesel to block Maurits' path, a second
army, under Van den Bergh, of some 12,000 men, was sent to clear the Dutch
garrisons from the duchy of Jülich. After capturing the castle at Rheydt, near
Mönchengladbach, and other places in their path, the Spaniards set siege to
Jülich in September 1621. Aware that the garrison's supplies were low, Van den
Bergh simply blockaded the town without engaging in much fighting. After

---

[32] See *Resolutiën der Staten-Generaal*, new series, ii, *1613–1616*, p. 332; 'De gecommitterden in
het leger schrijven', we learn, 'dat Maurits op 28 September 24 compagnien ruiters onder Frederik
Hendrik naar het landschap Mark heeft gezonden, boven de drie compagnien die daar reeds onder
Brochem heen zijn getrokken, en zes compagnieen voetvolk, met twee halve kanonnen. De zes
compagnieen zullen in garnizoen gaan te Hamm, Lünen, Camen, Soest en Lippstadt, en andere
plaatse. Het voetvolk reist op wagens om de tocht te bespoedigen en de vijand voor te zijn. Maurits
heeft Roquelaure naar Pithan gezonden met last om zich meester te maken van enige bij Gulik
gelegen plaatsen, namelijk Linnich, Aldenhoven, Tetz en het Huis Hambach.'

[33] *Dudley Carleton to John Chamberlain*, p. 194, Carleton to Chamberlain, The Hague, 8 April 1616.

[34] *Resolutiën der Staten-Generaal*, new series, ii, *1613–1616*, p. 597; curiously there is no mention
here of Jülich, even though this was obviously a strong possibility. Carleton later wrote on 24 May,
whilst tension was still running high, that the Spaniards' 'first enterprise (it is thought) will be the
siege of Juleirs [ie. Jülich or, in Dutch, Gulik] which they think they may undertake under the
emperor's banners without breach of the truce', see *Dudley Carleton to John Chamberlain*, p. 202.

five months of siege the defenders, some 3,000 men, surrendered on 22 January. The Cardinal de la Cueva in Brussels reported to the king that 'han sentido mucho olandeses la perdida de Juliers' (The Dutch greatly regret the loss of Jülich).[35] In line with her instructions to appoint Spaniards rather than Netherlanders as military governors of towns conquered from the Dutch, the Archduchess Isabella named Don Diego de Salcedo, reportedly a 'persona de muy buenas partes' as governor of Jülich.[36]

During the summer of 1622 Spínola tried to advance on two fronts. Whilst he himself set siege to Bergen-op-Zoom, a second Spanish army, under Van den Bergh, advanced into Cleves so as to force Maurits to divide his forces and prevent any attempt to break the siege of Bergen. After bombarding and capturing the town of Goch, Van den Bergh, on Spínola's orders, dispatched a force southwards, into the electorate of Cologne, to lay siege to the fortress of Pfaffenmütze (or in Dutch Papenmutz). This was located on a strategically placed island in the Rhine between the city of Cologne and the electoral Residenz, Bonn, which the Dutch had seized and fortified in the summer of 1620 in order to overawe the elector of Cologne.[37] Though largely cut off from all sources of help and supply since the States General's forces had been ejected from the duchy of Jülich, the garrison obstinately withstood the Spanish bombardment for five months. Though the siege was conducted nominally on behalf of the elector, he refused to lend public support to the Spanish enterprise, insisting on remaining neutral so as to avoid Dutch hostility and retaliation.[38]

Despite the spirited resistance of Pfaffenmütze, Isabella assured her nephew Philip IV in August 1622 that the Dutch were now all but eliminated from the Lower Rhine. They had been ejected from all their posts in Jülich and Berg, and most of their positions in Mark 'y assi fuera de Rees y Emerick que poseen olandeses [in Cleves] no queda cosa de mucha substancia para ocupar' (and besides Rees and Emmerich, which the Dutch hold [in Cleves] there is not much left to occupy).[39] The surviving 500 defenders of Pfaffenmütze — around 200 of them wounded — surrendered the fortifications on 27 December 1622.[40]

---

[35] AGS, Estado leg. 2036, consulta, Madrid, 12 March 1622.

[36] In a letter to the king, of December 1621, Isabella acknowledges Philip's instruction 'que todos los governadores de plazas destos estados que estan agora en españoles se han de conservar en ellos quando vacarían y en las que de nuevo se gañaren se han de yntroduzir españoles en las que pareciere conviniente', see AGS, Estado leg. 2310, Infanta to Philip IV, Brussels, 17 December 1621.

[37] The Dutch justified their action on the grounds that the island — which the Archduke Albert, in his report to Madrid, calls 'Mondorp' — belonged to the lands recognized by the States General as territory of the elector of Brandenburg, see AGS, Estado leg. 2034, consulta, Madrid, 12 November 1620.

[38] Jürgen Kessel, *Spanien und die geistlichen Kurstaaten am Rhein während der Regierungszeit der Infantin Isabella, 1621–1633* (Frankfurt am Main, 1979), pp. 139–44.

[39] AGR, SEG 188, fo. 84, Infanta to Philip IV, Brussels, 16 August 1622.

[40] Heinrich Neu, 'Zur Geschichte der Insel Pfaffenmütze', *Bonner Geschichtsblätter*, 21 (1967), pp. 122–3. Dudley Carleton reported to London that 'Papenmutz the States' new fort betwixt Bon and Collen having sustayned the siege till from 700 they were brought to 100 able men there in

Thereupon, the Spanish crown garrisoned the fortress with German troops in its pay. This did not meet with the approval of the elector who dreaded becoming a pawn of the Spaniards more than he feared the Dutch, and who would have preferred to see the fortress demolished and the Spanish troops depart. He began pressing the court in Brussels for precisely this but Spínola advised the Infanta not to agree.[41] The populace of the surrounding area, however, did benefit from the replacement of a Dutch by a Spanish garrison for the latter did not, unlike the Dutch, hold the surrounding area under 'contribution'. The *Consejo de Estado* in Madrid approved the decision to garrison Pfaffenmütze indefinitely on 17 February 1623. Spain now possessed two major fortresses on the territory of the electorate of Cologne.

The Spanish, Habsburg and Catholic ascendancy in the Lower Rhine duchies and Westphalia was further reinforced by the crushing victory of the army of the Catholic League, under Tilly, over the Protestant army of Christian of Brunswick, virtually within sight of the Gelderland frontier, at Stadtlohn on 6 August 1623.[42] There was now no Protestant army in the field anywhere in the north Rhine-Westphalian region. Once again claiming to be protecting the interests of the House of Neuburg, Spanish troops expelled the Dutch and Brandenburgers from Hamm, Unna, Camen and Lippstadt in December 1623, overran the county of Ravensberg, occupying Herford and advancing as far as the River Weser.[43] The Dutch-held fortress of Schloss Sparemberg was captured and then garrisoned by the Spanish crown albeit in the name of Neuburg. Schloss Sparemberg provided a Spanish presence near an important river linking central Germany with the North Sea, at Bremen, on which the Dutch plied a busy trade. Possession of the fortress became an an element in the calculations which led Olivares and his colleagues to believe in the feasibility of the general blockade of the United Provinces which the Spaniards imposed on all the waterways around, and leading to, Dutch territory, in 1625.

Spanish power in north-western Germany was at its height during the five years from the battle of Stadtlohn, in August 1623, until late in 1628. Then the draining off of Spanish resources to Italy, as a result of the outbreak of the War of Mantua, led to a marked weakening in the Spanish position in both Germany

---

continued

garrison (the most part consumed by sickness) had surrendered' . . . 'now they repent themselves here, when it is too late, of 300,000 florins bestowed upon that fortificacion which will be held by the Spaniards as a place of the like use to Juliers now it is in theyr hands, as it was intended by the States when they were in possession of that towne', see PRO, SP 84/110, fo. 198, Carleton to Calvert, The Hague, 27 December 1622. According to the Infanta's report to Madrid 500 Dutch troops survived of whom 200 were wounded and 300 were 'buenos' (able), AGS, Estado leg. 2037, consulta, Madrid, 17 February 1623; the Spaniards renamed the fortress 'Fort Isabella' but, presumably at her request, the name was changed to 'Fuerte de San Estevan'.

[41] Kessel, *Spanien und die geistlichen Kurstaaten*, p. 142.

[42] Geoffrey Parker, *The Thirty Years' War* (London, 1984), p. 68.

[43] AGS, Estado leg. 2038, consulta, Madrid, 14 January 1624. The Dutch concentrated on trying to hold Lippstadt which was besieged for some weeks by a joint Spanish and Catholic League army, see PRO, SP 84/114, fo. 87, Carleton to Calvert, The Hague, 16 Sept. 1623.

and the Low Countries. During this period Spain was the unchallenged arbiter of the entire north Rhine-Westphalian region. Despite a growing lack of cooperation with Spanish plans and intentions on the part of the elector of Cologne and other Catholic princes in the area, on occasion even on the part of Neuburg, the Spaniards were able to initiate such ambitious and large-scale projects as their river blockade of the United Provinces in the years 1625–9 and the construction of the Fossa Eugeniana — the Spanish Rhine-Maas canal. It was also during these years when the network of Spanish garrisons in north-western Germany reached its maximum extent, amounting, if the smaller outlying posts are included together with those in and around Geldern and along the Fossa Eugeniana, to around fifty fortresses and forts.[44] The most important of these in the Lower Rhine duchies, Ravensberg, and the electorate of Cologne are as shown on Table 1.[45] The sizes of the garrisons shown in the third column are the figures 'adjusted' and agreed, in April 1628, by the special *junta* set up by Philip IV to resolve the continuing deadlock between Olivares and Spínola. The latter had left Flanders and travelled overland (via La Rochelle, where he visited the famous siege which was then in progress) to Madrid only to become embroiled, on arriving at the Spanish court, in deep disagreement with the Conde-duque over Spain's strategy and stance in the Low Countries. This special *junta*, besides Olivares and Spínola, included Don Agustín Mexía, Juan Manuel, third marqués de Montesclaros, Don Ferando Girón, an elderly and pessimistic veteran of the Low Countries Wars, the conde de Monterrey, Don Juan de Villela, Diego Mexía (marqués de Leganés), the duke of Feria and Pedro de Zúñiga, first marqués de Flores Dávila. Yet, despite the deep rift betwee Olivares and Spínola which was essentially about the size and cost of the minimum forces required to fight an effective defensive land war, shielding the Spanish Netherlands and north-west Germany from the Dutch and their allies indefinitely (Spínola insisting that Olivares' estimates of the men and money required were too low), there is no indication of any fundamental disagreement between them over the need to maintain large Spanish garrisons in the major Spanish bases on the Lower Rhine and in Westphalia. Actual Spanish troop strength in north-western Germany (excluding Geldern and the forts along the Fossa Eugeniana) in 1627–8, including the many minor garrisons of around fifty men, was probably in the region of around 11,000 men which could then be supported by

[44] AGS, Estado leg. 2040, consulta, Madrid, 30 March 1626.

[45] Table 1 is based on the following sources: AGS, Estado leg. 2041, consulta, Madrid, 10 March 1627; AGS, Estado leg. 2321, 'Relacion de los officiales y soldados . . . que ay en la infanteria y caballeria de todas naziones en los exercitos de Flandes y el Palatinado' (March 1628); AGS, Estado leg. 2320, 'Relacion de la gente de guerra de guarnicion que se ha ajustado que es conviniente y necessario que aya en los presidios y castillos de los estados de Flandes' (April ? 1628); Israel, *Dutch Republic and the Hispanic World*, p. 164.

Table 1. The Spanish Garrisons in North-Western Germany (1627–8)

Garrison	Territory	Troop Strength		Planned
		March 1627	March 1628	April 1628
Lingen	County of Lingen	2,000	1,353	2,200
Wesel	Duchy of Cleves	2,500	3,077	3,000
Büderich Orsoy	Duchy of Cleves	250	434	150
Rheinberg	Electorate of Cologne	800	1,695	800
Pfaffenmütze	Electorate of Cologne	*c.* 300	270	150
Jülich	Duchy of Jülich	500	397	400
Dueren	Duchy of Jülich	*c.* 200	186	0
Eschweiler (near Aachen)	Duchy of Jülich	*c.* 200	151	0
Grevenbroich	Duchy of Jülich	*c.* 100	61	0
Wassenberg	Duchy of Jülich	*c.* 100	78	0
Euskirchen	Duchy of Jülich	*c.* 100	91	0
Aldenhoven	Duchy of Jülich	*c.* 200	158	0
Linnich	Duchy of Jülich	*c.* 120	107	0
Tetz	Duchy of Jülich	*c.* 150	128	0
Erkelenz	Duchy of Jülich	*c.* 75	*c.* 75	0
Nideggen	Duchy of Jülich	*c.* 100	86	0
Düsseldorf	Duchy of Berg	600	581	200
Lippstadt	Duchy of Mark	1,000	696	700
Hamm	Duchy of Mark	800	*c.* 600	700
Unna	Duchy of Mark	?	?	0
Schloss Sparemberg	County of Ravensberg	150	134	200
Schloss Ringelberg	County of Ravensberg			200
Total		10,245	10,458	8,700

mobile forces sent from the Spanish Netherlands in times of danger. The reductions agreed in April 1628 would have significantly reduced the number of garrisons in north-west Germany being maintained by Spain but would only have reduced the total commitment of troops by between one fifth and a quarter.

It was not, therefore, Spain's decision in the late 1620s to abandon her offensive land war against the Dutch indefinitely, or the strategic review of 1628, which led to the collapse of most of the network of Spanish garrisons only a few years later. Rather it was the unexpectedly and disastrously heavy cost of the war of Mantua, leading to the excessive weakening of the Spanish army of Flanders, followed by the Dutch breakthrough of 1629 at 's-Hertogenbosch and Wesel and, finally, the impact of the Swedish invasion of Germany in 1630, which transformed the picture radically and forced the Spanish court to give up its hegemony over the Lower Rhine and Westphalia.

Frederik Hendrik's successful siege of 's-Hertogenbosch, which apart from Antwerp was the largest and most important Spanish stronghold in Brabant, was not only a deep humiliation for Philip IV but effectively broke the ring of Spanish bases surrounding the United Provinces by land. The simultaneous loss of Wesel was likewise regarded at the Spanish court as a deep humiliation, one which the king ascribed to the anger of the Almighty at his own sins and those of his people, leading him to order a general crack-down on vice and

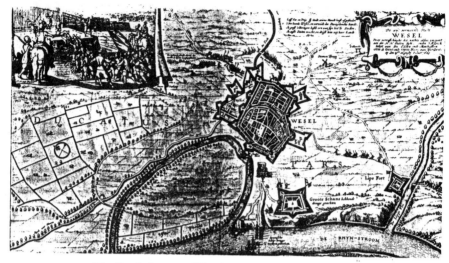

The Dutch Capture of Wesel from the Spaniards in 1629

profligacy in Madrid.[46] Wesel, its garrison temporarily depleted while many of
the troops based there participated in Van den Bergh's thrust across the IJssel
in an attempt to divert Frederik Hendrik from 's-Hertogenbosch, had been
surprised and stormed by some 2000 Dutch troops advancing from Rees and
Emmerich. The few Spaniards, including three captains, and 'some Walloons'
in the town had done their duty and fought, sixty of them being killed; but
most of the garrison, consisting of Germans had refused to fight and simply
called out for their (long delayed) pay instead.[47] The Dutch captured the town's
governor, Don Francisco Lozano and 890 defenders. In ensuing weeks the Dutch
also occupied Duisburg and ejected the Spaniards from Schloss Ringelberg.

Yet disastrous though the loss of Wesel was, the Conde-Duque insisted that
the fiasco was basically due to indiscipline, mismanagement and the lack of a
competent overall commander (with Spínola absent from Flanders) rather than
to an fundamental error in Spain's strategy and general stance. No change was
proposed in the overall posture of Spain on the Lower Rhine and in Westphalia.
On the contrary, the situation remained much as before except that, with Wesel
lost, Rheinberg and Orsoy, now heavily reinforced, became the principal Spanish crossing-points on the Lower Rhine. In December 1630, the marqués de
Aytona reported to the king from Brussels that Rheinberg was now garrisoned
by 3,000 men and that the garrison at Orsoy had risen to 600. 'Esta plaza, señor',
he added, referring to Rheinberg, 'es la mas bien pagada de Flandes porque
nos parecio que era la de mayor peligro' (This place, señor, is the best paid in

---

[46] BND, MS 2361, fo. 501, 'Copia de un decreto de su Magestad escrito de su real mano para el
consejo'.

[47] AGS, Estado leg. 2322, La Cueva to Philip IV, Brussels, 6 September 1629, and Infanta to
Philip IV, Brussels, 9 September 1629.

Flanders because we considered that it was the one in most danger),[48] an indication of the high priority given at this juncture to maintaining the Spanish posture on the Lower Rhine in Brussels and Madrid alike.

It was during the spring of 1630, whilst Aytona and the Spanish commanders in Flanders were planning their defensive campaign of that year, that it was decided in Brussels to urge the king to abandon his grip on Mark and Ravensberg and hand over his strongholds there (Lippstadt, Hamm, Unna, Camen, and Schloss Sparemberg — and also the fortress of Pfaffenmütze) to the army of the Catholic League and to the elector of Cologne. 'Ham, Lipstat, Sparemberg y Una que son los lugares del Duque de Neuburg en que Vuestra Magestad tiene presidio', Aytona advised the king, in March 1630, 'a mi parecer se hayan todos de dejar y valerse Vuestra Magestad de la gente . . .' (Ham, Lipstat, Sparemberg and Unna which are the places belonging to the duke of Neuburg [east of the Rhine] in which Your Majesty has garrisons should all be evacuated so that Your Majesty can use the troops elsewhere).[49] At the same time, Lingen came under scrutiny. It lay a considerable distance north of the Rhine and was relatively isolated. Although it was of great value strategically and served to keep Drenthe, Overijssel and the entire north of the Dutch Republic insecure, its walls were reportedly not in a good state of repair. Holding the base tied down over 2,000 troops and involved a considerable strain on Spanish logistics. The proposal that Lingen also should be handed over to the troops of the Catholic League provoked dismay and much soul-searching in Madrid. 'No es negable', remarked Olivares, 'la reputacion grande que se pierde en entregar plaza tan importante confesando en esta entrega la imposibilidad de defenderla' (It is undeniable that great *reputacion* is lost in handing over such an important place and confessing our inability to defend it.)[50] Nevertheless, very soon after Olivares uttered these words, the Spanish garrison — to the amazement of the Dutch — marched out of Lingen, leaving the fortress in the hands of imperialist troops. By late 1630, as Aytona reported to the king, the only Spanish garrison which remained on the right bank of the Rhine was that at Düsseldorf, capital of Berg and Residenz of the dukes of Jülich-Cleves.[51] Pfaffenmütze was dismantled and abandoned by its Spanish garrison, in September 1630, not under pressure from the elector of Cologne but out of sheer strategic necessity.[52]

Further retrenchment was soon forced on the Spaniards, who came under increasing pressure in their remaining Lower Rhine strongholds in the early

---

[48] BRB, MS 16149, fo. 46, Aytona to Philip IV, Brussels, 25 December 1630; only Breda, which then was defended by nearly 4,000 troops, had a larger garrison than Rheinberg.

[49] Ibid., fo. 10v, Aytona to Philip IV, Brussels, 8 March 1630; AGR, SEG leg. 203, fo. 28, Infanta to Philip IV, Brussels, 19 June 1630, where the Infanta claims that Lingen was tying down 3,000 men and costing 150,000 escudos per year.

[50] AGS, Estado leg. 2148, consulta, Madrid, 5 July 1630, 'voto del Conde-Duque'.

[51] See again BRB, MS 16149, fo. 46.

[52] Kessel, *Spanien und die geistlichen Kurstaaten*, p. 144; Israel, *Dutch Republic and the Hispanic World*, p. 181.

1630s. Frederik Hendrik's triumphant push up the Maas valley during the summer of 1632, in which he captured Venlo, Roermond, Straelen and finally, after
a bitter siege, Maastricht, the most important fortress town in the eastern part
of the Spanish Netherlands, drove a deep wedge between the remaining rump
of the Spanish Netherlands and the Spanish bases at Geldern, Rheinberg and
Orsoy. Not only were the surviving Spanish strongholds on the Lower Rhine
now effectively cut off from Spanish Brabant but, as a consequence, Spain's
whole posture in north-western Germany was now decisively weakened,[53] a
development noted by the electors of Cologne, Mainz and Trier with more than
faint misgivings — for they were now in great fear of the Swedes and anxious
for Spanish help and protection. A Dutch attempt to storm Orsoy by surprise,
in November 1632, almost succeeded but was finally beaten off after a fierce
battle inside the town which left 250 Dutch troops dead in the streets.[54] But, as
Aytona reported to Madrid, all the remaining Spanish bases on the Lower Rhine
were now in acute and constant danger.[55]

The marqués de Aytona, the king's right-hand man in the Spanish Netherlands
at this juncture, was a competent commander and statesman but, with the army
of Flanders still substantially weaker than that of the States General (since 1629)
and with the Dutch holding the length of the Maas valley between Venlo and
Maastricht, there was relatively littled that he could do to save Spain's position
on the Lower Rhine. On 11 June 1633 Frederik Hendrik appeared with a large
army before Rheinberg and began to dig his siege lines.[56] Aytona, with a smaller
army of 14,000 men, advanced rapidly from Brabant. While he was unable to
penetrate to the Rhine, or prevent Frederik Hendrik digging in, he was able to
capture Maaseik, Weert and the strategic crossing-point at Stevensweert, which
not only had the effect of isolating the large Dutch garrison at Maastricht but
provided the only means by which the Spanish grip on Geldern and Jülich could
be maintained.[57] After a furious three-week bombardment, the Spanish garrison at Rheinberg surrendered to the Dutch stadholder, on 2 June, and marched
away in defeat, with their women and priests, two days later. Within days of the
fall of Rheinberg the entire Spanish system of 'contributions' levied on the
Dutch undefended towns and villages east of the IJssel, in Gelderland and
Overijssel, came to an end.[58] The loss of Rheinberg also marked the definitive
abortion of the Spanish project to divert the Rhine trade away from the northern
Netherlands to Spanish Brabant by means of a heavily fortified Rhine-Maas canal
(see Chapter 4).

[53] Apart from anything else, it was now extremely difficult to supply Rheinberg, Orsoy, Geldern
and Jülich: see AGR, SEG 205, fo 263, Infanta to Philip IV, Brussels, 8 November 1632; Kessel,
Spanien und die geistlichen Kurstaaten, pp. 366–7.
[54] BRB, MS 16149, fo. 87v, Aytona to Philip IV, Brussels, 7 November 1632.
[55] Ibid., fo. 94. Aytona to Philip IV, Brussels, 7 February 1633.
[56] Lemperts, 'Rheinbergs Belagerungen', p. 29.
[57] BRB, MS 16149, fo. 110v, Aytona to Philip IV, Brussels, 16 June 1633.
[58] Tops, 'De heffing der Spaanse contributiën', pp. 59–61, 78; P. Holthuis, *Frontierstad bij het
scheiden van de markt: Deventer, militair, demografisch, economisch (1578–1648)* (Deventer, 1993), pp. 60–1.

With the Dutch capture of Rheinberg and Orsoy, in the summer of 1633, the Spanish hegemony in north-west Germany was a thing of the past. But, at the same time, Spain had not yet been finally eliminated from the Lower Rhine, nor was it the intention of the Spanish court, or the courts of the ecclesiastical princes of the Rhine and Westphalia, that Spain should be entirely removed from the picture. Olivares, in particular, continually stressed the need, if Spain was to maintain her role as a leading power in European politics, to recover Rheinberg and Orsoy at least. The Spanish counter-offensive of 1635, when the Cardinal-Infante swept into Cleves and his troops captured the key Rhine fortress of Schenckenschanz, on the Dutch-German border (see Chapter 6), briefly revived the Conde-Duque's hopes of a imminent restoration of Spanish power in the Rhineland; but the Spaniards were again dislodged from the Rhine in April 1636. At a meeting of the *Consejo de Estado*, in Madrid on 24 May 1637, Olivares saw little immediate prospect of peace with the United Provinces. Besides the thorny questions of Brazil and the East Indies, it was in his opinion impossible for Spain to accept her present position in, and around, the Low Countries since the loss of 'Esquenque' (Schenckenschanz): 'porque realmente nos hallamos estrechos en la Mosa y totalmente hechados del Rhin' (for really we are now boxed in on the Maas and totally eliminated from the Rhine)'.[59] He believed it was essential for Spain to recover a secure crossing-point over the Rhine and refused to share the opinion of some of his colleagues at the meeting that, in return for peace with the Dutch, Spain should simply acquiesce in her removal from north-west Germany. One member of the *Consejo*, the marqués de Santa Cruz, proposed that if restitution proved unobtainable, Spain should offer, in return for Dutch evacuation, that 'Rheinberg desmantelado se entregase al elector de Colonia cuya es y Orsoy a su dueño y Mastrique se entregase al arzobispo [sic] de Lieja' (that Rheinberg dismantled should be handed over to the elector of Cologne to whom it belongs and Orsoy to its owner [Neuburg] and Maastricht to the prince-bishop of Liège).[60] But it was Olivares' view which prevailed and in both Madrid and Brussels restoring Spain's position on the Lower Rhine remained a high priority objective. On 26 October 1637, at dawn, a Spanish force sent from Geldern launched a surprise attack on Rheinberg which almost succeeded, briefly capturing a section of the walls before finally being beaten off.[61] In his instructions to the Cardinal-Infante, of 17 March 1638, Philip IV reiterated to his brother that any peace or truce which the latter managed to negotiate with the Dutch must include restitution of Rheinberg and Orsoy to Spanish control.[62]

[59] AGS, Estado leg. 2052, consulta, Madrid, 24 May 1637, fo. 4. Olivares regarded the recovery of Rheinberg and Orsoy as indispensable: less, in the context of a new truce with the Dutch, with respect to the Netherlands than 'porque no tenemos otra puerta para Alemania . . .'

[60] Ibid., 'voto del marqués de Santa Cruz'.

[61] AGR, SEG 217, fo. 456, Cardinal-Infante to Philip IV, Brussels, 3 December 1637.

[62] AGR, SEG 218, fo. 455, Philip IV to Cardinal-Infante, Madrid, 17 March 1638.

After 1640, and the revolts of Catalonia and Portugal which did so much to weaken the Spanish monarchy, there was no longer any realistic likelihood that Spain would recover her lost footholds on the Rhine. Yet despite her greatly diminished weight in the international arena, Spain was still a significant power in western Germany, maintaining substantial garrisons at Jülich and Geldern, as well as (until 1652) further south at Frankenthal, in the Palatinate. She continued to have a number of important strategic and political interests in the Holy Roman Empire. The end of the war with the Dutch in 1647–8 and disintegration of the Austro-Spanish Habsburg family alliance, owing to the emperor's willingness to sign a separate peace with France, fundamentally transformed, but did not terminate, Spain's strategic involvement in Germany. With the temporary revival of Spanish power, and weakening of France, during the years 1648–52, the Spanish crown took the opportunity to restore its influence in the Rhenish ecclesiastical states and did so with some success (see Chapter 6). Between 1648 and 1659 Spain checked and largely neutralized French leverage and endeavours in the ecclesiastical electorates and dependent bishoprics, as part of her wider strategy of containing, and defeating France's quest for hegemony, in a way which led some German princes, including the emperor, to view Spain as a still useful buffer blocking French expansionist ambitions in the empire. After the final defeat of Spain by the French crown in alliance with England, in the years 1658–9, and the Peace of the Pyrenees which marked the end of the great Franco-Spanish contest for pre-eminence in Europe, Spanish power and Spanish garrisons were definitively removed from the Rhineland and Germany as a whole and were never to return. The inevitable result was a power vacuum which enabled Louis XIV to turn most of the Rhine valley into a French preserve and sphere of influence. It was not until the Glorious Revolution and the ensuing Nine Years' War (1688–97) that there emerged a European coalition strong enough to put an end to this French dominance of the region.

3

A Spanish Project to Defeat the Dutch without Fighting: The Rhine-Maas Canal, 1624–9

'Tiénese por obra fácil, y breve, y de no mucho gasto' (it is considered an easy project which can be speedily done without any great cost).[1]

The most ambitious engineering project ever undertaken by the Spanish Habsburg regime in the Low Countries, or the adjoining areas of Germany, was without doubt the grandiose scheme, vast in its scope and implications, for a Rhine-Maas canal which was attempted tenaciously in the years 1626–9 at heavy cost both financial and strategic. During its initial stages, the project aroused great excitement and enthusiasm in the southern Netherlands, not least in the mind of the great artist Rubens who (as we see from his letters) followed the progress of the undertaking with avid interest and upon whose imagination it evidently exerted a strong appeal. For a time the scheme came to supersede, in the minds of many influential persons in Antwerp and Brussels, all other forms of warfare waged by the Spanish crown on the 'rebel' Protestant provinces to the north. At the same time, the scheme aroused alarm in the United Provinces against which the project was chiefly directed. There was also widespread concern in the electorate of Cologne and the Lower Rhine duchies — Cleves, Jülich and Berg — all of which stood to see their Rhine traffic with the northern Netherlands diverted for good, via the new canal complex, to Antwerp., and their relationship with both parts of the Low Countries fundamentally transformed.

While the resources, political direction and indispensable military shield for the project were provided by the Spanish authorities in Brussels, the original inspiration for the scheme came from one of the most influential and energetic Flemish officials at the court of the Archduchess Isabella — Jan van den Wouvere, or Woverius, as he was called by his humanist friends; or, as he was known in Madrid, and to Spaniards in the Netherlands, Juan Voverio (Boberio). Van den Wouvere had played a leading part in projects to improve the harbours and fortifications of Dunkirk and Mardijk, in 1621–2, and was a leading figure in the financial administration of the Spanish Netherlands.[2] He was often seen at court and in the presence of the Archduchess. He also appears in Rubens' famous

---

[1] AGS, Estado leg. 2317, Cardenal de la Cueva to Philip IV, Brussels, 17 September 1626.

[2] José Alcalá-Zamora y Queipo de Llano, *España, Flandes y el Mar del Norte, 1618–1639* (Barcelona, 1975), pp. 101, 197–9.

painting 'The Four Philosophers' (1610) (Florence, Palazzo Pitti), seated to the left of the great humanist philosopher Justus Lipsius and under the bust of the Roman Stoic philosopher Seneca.[3] Many years later, Van Dyck included Van den Wouvere's portrait amongst twelve portraits of prominent contemporary statesmen and philosophers. These constituted the middle, or intervening, group among the three batches of portraits of famous contemporaries totalling eighty altogether — which made up his famous *Iconography* executed in the years 1628–36. In the middle section, Van den Wouvere appears alongside Rubens' friend and correspondent Claude Fabri de Peiresc, the Abbe Scaglia, the bishop of Ghent, Antonius Triest, and the Antwerp humanist Caspar Gaevartius.[4]

A humanist, the friend of the great Lipsius and an associate of Rubens, Van den Wouvere was a man of learning and refined taste, an able official endowed with real strategic and political vision. Like Rubens, he shared the unserving conviction of Lipsius that the best course for the southern Netherlands was to collaborate closely with the mighty world-empire of Spain, the Spanish crown alone being capable of providing the stability, order and security which the Low Countries so desperately needed. It is also clear from various reports he submitted in Brussels and Madrid that he was ardent mercantilist who believed that the global reach, and vast power, of the Spanish Habsburg monarchy could be mobilized to prise back to Antwerp, and the south, much of the commerce and prosperity which had shifted to the 'rebel' Netherlands since 1585. Whilst supervising operations at Dunkirk, in 1621–2, he assured his superiors that the new, improved harbour there would surpass in its facilities all the ports of 'Holland, Zeeland and Flanders'.[5] His greatest project, the Rhine-Maas canal, he saw as a means to divert the river trade of Germany from the United Provinces and to infuse a triumphant new economic vitality into Flanders and Brabant.

The plans for a vast canal project which emerged in 1626, and began to be implemented in September of that year, were the fruits of two years of deliberation and negotiation.[6] What was finally decided on, moreover, differed appreciably from earlier variants of the project. Originally, the plan had been to dig a comparatively modest canal to the west of the Maas, running from Maastricht to link up, in the prince-bishopric of Liège, with the River Demer, enabling river craft to continue westwards, via Hasselt, Diest and Aerschot, to Mechelen (Malines) from where traffic could continue down the River Scheldt to Antwerp and the Scheldt estuary.[7] The other wing of the original plan had been to

---

[3] Frans Baudouin, *Pietro Paulo Rubens* (New York, 1989), pp. 308–9.

[4] Christopher Brown, *Van Dyck* (Oxford, 1982), p. 136.

[5] Alcalá-Zamora, *España, Flandes y el Mar del Norte*, p. 198.

[6] [Jan van den Wouvere], *Relación tocante la obras de los canales propuestos a hacer entre los rios Rhin y Mosa y tambien desde la dicha Mosa entre Maestricht al rio Demer* (1626), appendix no. 5, in Alcalá-Zamora, *España, Flandes y el Mar del Norte*, p. 500; A.J. Veenendael, 'De Fossa Eugeniana', *Bijdragen voor de geschiedenis der Nederlanden*, 11 (1956), pp. 6, 8.

[7] [Van den Wouvere], *Relación tocante las obras*, pp. 500–1: accurately reflecting the state of the deliberations in Brussels and Antwerp at the time, Rubens reported to Pierre Dupuy, in July 1626, that the project west of the Maas envisaged 'un novo canale navigabile della Mosa vicino a Maestricht,

construct a second, and much more ambitious canal from the Rhine, at Rheinberg (see Map 1), in the electorate of Cologne, via Geldern, in the Spanish Netherlands province of Upper Gelderland, to the fort of Arcen (Aerssen) on the Maas, some miles to the north of Venlo.[8] The task of surveying the terrain for these linking canal systems was entrusted to the highest ranking engineer in the army of Flanders at the time — Giovanni de Medici, marchese di Sant' Angelo, a much-respected general on Spínola's staff, described by a fellow Italian officer in the Netherlands as an 'huomo nelle geometria, aritmetica e cosmografica dottissimo'.[9] Working under de Medici and De Wouwere, who were put in charge by the Infanta, was a team of the finest engineers and mathematicians in the Spanish Netherlands: Jacob Janssen, Jan Heimans Coeck, Sebastian Scroterrius, the architect Jan van Straatsburg and Michael Floris van Langeren, a young cosmographer and mathematician destined to have a long and distinguished career in the service of Spain, the scion of a family of mapmakers once resident in Amsterdam that had moved to Antwerp. Van Langeren had won his reputation as an engineer working, since 1624, on the new canal (Fossa Mariana) being built to connect Mardijk with Durkirk.[10] The Infanta, the chief Spanish minister in Brussels, the cardinal de la Cueva, and the commander-in-chief of the army of Flanders, Ambrogio Spínola, all appear to have been enthusiastic about the grandiose new undertaking from the outset, with Spínola evidently the most directly involved in supervising the planning and preparations for the project.[11]

By the early summer of 1626 the Infanta and her advisers had taken the decision in principle, to commit large resources — financial, material and military — to implementing the concept, though much detail remained to be worked out. In June 1626 Van den Wouwere, Van Langeren, Coeck and Janssen were sent to survey the River Demer and prepare charts for the work west of the Maas.[12] Meanwhile, Spínola and the Infanta, urged by Van den Wouwere, pondered an extension of the scheme which would mean undertaking something far more grandiose than previously envisaged. Van den Wouvere held, and the engineers seemed to agree, that it was possible, without prohibitive cost, to divert and reroute the River Rhine to flow into the Maas.[13] De Medici, Coeck, Janssen

continued
sino ad un altro fiume chiamato il Demer, circa Malines, per il spatio di quindici leghe', see Rubens to Dupuy, Antwerp, 24 July 1626, in *Correspondance de Rubens et documents épistolaires concernant sa vie et oeuvres*, ed. M. Rooses and C. Ruelens (6 vols, Antwerp, 1887–1909), iii, pp. 447–8.

[8] [Van den Wouvere], *Relación tocante las obras*, p. 501; Veenendaal, 'Fossa Eugeniana', pp. 11–12, 17.

[9] Veenendaal, 'Fossa Eugeniana', p. 10. Speaking of Sant' Angelo's fitness to supervise the construction work, Rubens described him to Dupuy, in January 1627 as 'cavagliere giudiciosissimo e di grandissima esperienza in simile cose', *Correspondance de Rubens*, iii, p. 36.

[10] Veenendaal, 'Fossa Eugeniana', p. 11.

[11] Antonio Rodríguez Villa, *Ambrosio Spínola, primer marqués de los Balbases* (Madrid, 1905), p. 457; [Van den Wouvere], *Relación tocante las obras*, pp. 501, 502.

[12] [Van den Wouvere], *Relación tocante las obras*, p. 501.

[13] Ibid., p. 502. The papal nuncio in Brussels reported to Rome, on 22 August 1626, that the

and 'el matematico' Van Langeren, having completed their survey of the Demer, were sent to study the terrain to the north west of Neuss, on the Rhine, to assess the feasibility of using the low area running north westwards to Gennep as the new main course of the Rhine, from where it was hoped to feed it into the Maas. It was envisaged that 'todo el Rhin se podría sacar de su cama y ser puesto en la Mosa, por donde Holanda quedaría desislada, de una parte, y ahogada, por otra' (it would be possible to divert the whole Rhine from its bed and feed it into the Maas, whereby Holland would be left high and dry on one side and drowned on the other).[14] This massive venture was to be attempted side by side with a new canal for river traffic, which would run to the south of the rerouted river, from Neuss, on the Rhine, to the Maas at Venlo (rather than Arcen). The engineers estimated that this canal 'se podría acabar en tiempo de siete u ocho meses, con moderado gasto de cuatrocientos o quinientos mil floreines' (it could be finished in seven or eight months, at the cost of 400 or 500,000 florins).[15]

In all versions, Van den Wouvere's canals scheme was a combined economic and strategic project. On the one hand, the result, fervently hoped for by de Wouvere and the Brussels court, would be the diversion of the river trade of Germany, especially the traffic in Rhine and Mosel wine, away from the Dutch Republic via the Maas, across Spanish Brabant to the Scheldt and Antwerp.[16] On the strategic side, the aim was to strip the Dutch of vital parts of their defensive ring — the curves of the Rhine in Cleves and Gelderland — while simultaneously interposing a massive strategic barrier between the Rhine and Maas which would prevent the Dutch penetrating down the left bank of the Rhine, threatening Jülich or raiding Upper Gelderland.[17] The papal nuncio in Brussels, Giovanni Guidi del Bagno, writing to Cardinal Barberini in Rome on 22 August 1626, reported the high hopes at the Infanta's court that diversion of the Rhine would engineer the drying up of the IJssel so that the east and north of the Dutch

---

continued

prime Spanish goal was to divert the Rhine from its normal course and make it run into the Maas, so that the north and east of the Dutch Republic would no longer be protected by the IJssel and other branches of the Rhine, see *Correspondance de Giovanni Guidi del Bagno (1621–1627)*, ed. B. de Meester, in *Analecta Vaticano-Belgica*, second series, 6 (2 vols, Brussels, 1936–8), ii, p. 766; [Carlos Scribani] *Den Oor-Sprongh Voort-gangh ende ghewenscht eynde van den Nederlantschen krygh* (Amsterdam, [1626]), pp. 94–5; Carlos Scribani, *Veridicvus Belgicvs* (n.p., 1626), p. 97.

[14] [Van den Wouvere], *Relación tocante las obras*, p. 502; [Scribani], *Oor-sprongh voort-gangh ende ghewenscht eynde*, p. 94.

[15] It 'could be completed in seven or eight months at a moderate cost of four or five hundred thousand florins', [Van den Wouvere], *Relación tocante las obras*, p. 502.

[16] Ibid. pp. 502–3. In the meeting of the *Consejo de Estado*, in Madrid, in 20 September 1626, the project was described as 'una obra que si llega a efecto sera muy dañosa para los olandeses y de beneficio para los payses de Vuestra Magestad que es la communicacion del Rin en la Mosa, abriendo un canal de una parte a la otra que aumentara mucho el trato con Alemania y menguara el de los olandeses', AGS, Estado leg. 2040, consulta, 20 September 1626, fo. 1; Scribani, *Veridicvus Belgicvs*, pp 98–9; Hugo Grotius, *Grollae obsidio cvm annexis anni 1627* (Amsterdam, 1629), p. 5.

[17] Veenendaal, 'Fossa Eugeniana', p. 6; J.D.M. Cornelissen, 'Het Maas- en Rijnkanaal van 1626', *Mededeelingen van het Nederlandsch Historisch Instituut te Rome*, 9 (1929), pp. 195–8.

Republic would be defenceless while, on the other side, the swollen Maas would inundate Dordrecht.[18]

Much impressed with what he had heard, Rubens wrote to his friend Pierre Dupuy in Paris, on 24 July 1626, describing the 'due imprese gloriosissime' (two most glorious undertakings), one for 'un novo canale navigabile' projected to run from Maastricht, via the Demer, to Mechelen, a plan for which he had seen 'il modello', and the other a scheme 'di divertir il Reno del suo corso ordinario', leaving most of the enemy's territory exposed and 'removing every obstacle posed by the tributary rivers of the Rhine' so that all Dutch territory, as far as Utrecht, would be vulnerable and could be brought under contribution.[19] But he added that he had not yet seen the plans for this latter project and did not believe that it had yet been firmly resolved on.

In fact, both concepts were destined to be radically altered during the course of the next weeks. A complex mix of political pressures, strategic considerations and technical difficulties obliged the Infanta and her advisers to adopt far-reaching modifications to almost every aspect of the plans. There was also some tough negotiating to be done. While the project, should it succeed, would confer immense benefits on Antwerp, Maastricht and the Spanish Netherlands as a whole, there were various neighbouring rulers, cities and localities who received the intimations emanating from Brussels with varying degrees of scepticism, anxiety and alarm. The nobles owning lands in Upper Gelderland the prince-bishopric of Liège, and parts of the electorate of Cologne which the authorities in Brussels planned to inundate or drive their canals through, saw only the risks and disruption such plans threatened for them.[20] Venlo was openly hostile, doubtless because the original scheme was to terminate the Rhine-Maas link to the north of the city, at Arcen, and the Demer-Maas canal to the south at Maastricht — leaving Venlo playing an unimportant part in between.[21]

In the lands where the Rhine-Maas canal was to be dug there was strong dislike and resentment of the fact that a large part of the Spanish army was to be billeted in what was a poor, thinly populated area.[22] For besides the tramping back and forth of the soldiery, and the fact that these troops frequently had to go for long periods without pay (and, when hungry, were none too particular how they obtained provisions), their deployment to hold a strategically and economically vital canal line was bound to turn the area into a fiercely contested war-zone, and provoke massive Dutch counter-action. But there was also robust support. The duke of Neuburg, ruler of the duchy of Jülich which lay to the

[18] *Correspondance de Giovanni Guidi del Bagno*, ii, p. 766.

[19] 'di divertir il Reno del suo corso ordinario, lasciando a scoperto gran paese del nemico, e levando ogni ostacolo d'altri fiumi derivati del Reno, per entrar nella Veluwe e rendere tributaria tutta la provincia sino a Utrecht, ma di questo non ho visto il dissegno ancora, ne credo esser risoluto ancora di tutto punto', *Correspondance de Rubens*, iii, p. 448.

[20] Cornelissen, 'Het Maas- en Rijnkanaal', p. 198; Veenendaal, 'Fossa Eugeniana', pp. 14, 16, 26.

[21] Veenendaal, 'Fossa Eugeniana', pp. 17–19.

[22] Cornelissen, 'Maas- en Rijnkanaal', p. 196.

south of the projected canal, was an enthusiastic backer of the project, since the Spanish plans would place a formidable obstacle between the Rhine and Maas which would shield Jülich and Upper Gelderland, as well as regions further south, as far as Luxemburg, from the raids of the States General's cavalry.[23]

The Infanta found herself besieged by representations from all these different interested parties. But the crucial negotiations, the ones on which the success or failure of the entire enterprise hinged, were those with the elector of Cologne who was also prince-bishop of Münster, Osnabrück and Liège. As ruler of both the electorate of Cologne, where Neuss, the original projected eastern terminus of both the new canal, and the new course of the Rhine, was situated, and as ruler of Liège, through which the Maas-Demer link would be dug, Ferdinand von Bayern was more than an interested party. If he saw, fit, he could block the entire project, while if it were to go ahead he would have to be a major partner in the undertaking.

The elector of Cologne, though an energetic champion of the Counter-Reformation and supporter of the German Catholic League was, as historians have often noted, not an automatic ally of Spain in its conflict with the Protestant Dutch.[24] On the contrary, the elector — like his colleagues the electors of Mainz and Trier — was anxious to avoid domination by Spain and to prevent the Catholic League becoming involved in any form of conflict with the Dutch. He was thus determined to remain neutral in the Low Countries conflict and evidently held that the best outcome of the Dutch war, for Cologne and all Catholic Germany, was an unbreakable deadlock in which the Spaniards and Dutch held each other firmly in check. In the very month in which the Infanta's engineers began their detailed surveying work, June 1626, Ferdinand wrote to his brother, the duke of Bavaria: 'Die Niederlanden muessen dividiert bleiben und einen so wenig als andern Meister lassen werden' (The Netherlands must remain divided with neither side letting the other be master).[25] Furthermore the elector keenly resented the stoppage in the Rhine trade with the Republic imposed, since 1625, by the Spanish garrisons at Rheinberg and Wesel; for the Spanish river blockade of the Dutch, for him, meant lost revenues, a deepening slump in the city of Cologne, and acute shortages of fish, salt and other items normally imported from the Netherlands.[26]

Nevertheless, he did not reject Spain's Rhine-Maas project out of hand and, after a period of intense negotiation, proved willing to participate in the final revised version which took account of his views. Very likely he was influenced initially, in adopting this comparatively amenable attitude, by the fresh anxiety

---

[23] Ibid.; [Scribani], *Oor-sprongh voort-gangh ende ghewenscht eynde*, p. 97, where Scribani states 'ende door dese rivieren sal het Landt van Over-maes, Limborch, Geldern Gulick ende Brabant uyt des vyandts contributie ontrocken worden . . .'

[24] Geoffrey Parker, *The Thirty Years' War* (London, 1984), pp. 255–6; Jürgen Kessel, *Spanien und die geistlichen Kurstaaten am Rhein während der Regierungszeit der Infantin Isabella (1621–1633)* (Frankfurt, 1979), pp. 65–69.

[25] Parker, *The Thirty Years' War*, p. 256; Kessel, *Spanien und die geistlichen Kurstaaten*, p. 190.

[26] Parker, *The Thirty Years' War*, p. 96; Kessel, *Spanien und die geistlichen Kurstaaten*, p. 209.

permeating the Westphalian ecclesiastical states which flowed from the Danish intervention in the Thirty Years' War and advance of the Danish forces, by July 1626, as far as Osnabrück,[27] one of Ferdinand's territories, as well as the unpalatable prospect of pending Dutch-Danish collaboration throughout northwest Germany. During the spring and early summer of 1626, with the power and prestige of Denmark in the ascendant, Bonn had no alternative but defer to Spain as the indispensable counter-weight to the threat of a Dutch-Danish condominium. But this soon ceased to be a major factor, for the Danish army in northern Germany was crushed by the army of the Catholic League, under Tilly, at Lutter, at the end of August, still several weeks before actual work on the canals began. In any case, whatever he decided about the canals, Spain would have been obliged to come to Ferdinand's assistance, had the Danes advanced further, to defend Cologne and their own bases at Lingen, Wesel, and Rheinberg.

No doubt Ferdinand also took note of the strategic advantages the Spanish project offered him. For the new canal system was intended to be not just a conduit for river traffic but a formidable defensive barrier which would put the lands behind them, to the south, securely out of reach of the Dutch.[28] This meant, for the elector, that the core of his state would henceforth be shielded from the kind of political and military pressure which Prince Maurits had brought to bear in the years 1619–23. Both Bonn and the city of Cologne were on the left bank of the Rhine and would therefore benefit from the new defensive line.

Yet this too can hardly have been decisive in swaying the elector. For the strategic gain was coupled with the disadvantage of bringing fresh Spanish garrisons onto Cologne territory to protect the new canal. What in all probability decided the elector was that the present (since 1625) Spanish river blockade which had brought Cologne's Rhine commerce to a virtual halt was set to continue indefinitely and that, even if it ended in the forseeable future, both the Spaniards and the Dutch would be able to interrupt, or manipulate it, at will without Cologne being able to influence the matter in any way. Were a new canal route to be opened, linking the Rhine to Antwerp, via the Maas, not only would Cologne's Rhine trade to the Low Countries resume but if the River Rhine itself was not diverted, but continued in its existing bed, then Cologne would, in future, have two routes to the Low Countries instead of one and would be in the enviable position of being able to play Antwerp off against the Dutch. No doubt the elector also realised, from the start, that it would be easy to obtain Spanish agreement to his levying a substantial toll on the barge traffic entering the new canal network from the Rhine, for without his consent Antwerp's projected link with the Rhine simply could not function.

---

[27] Kessel, *Spanien und die geistlichen Kurstaaten*, p. 189; in July 1626, Danish forces invaded Ferdinand's prince-bishopric of Osnabrück, see *Correspondance de Giovanni Guidi del Bagno*, ii, pp. 755–6.
[28] Veenendaal, 'Fossa Eugeniana', pp. 14–15.

Admittedly, several observers who reported on the negotiations surrounding the canal project, in the summer of 1626, including the papal nuncio in Brussels,[29] formed the impression that Ferdinand viewed the Spanish plans with a jaundiced eye and was trying to obstruct them. But it would be wrong to conclude from this, as have some historians, that Ferdinand really was basically opposed to the Rhine-Maas canal project as distinct from the scheme for diverting the Rhine from its normal course which the elector evidently rejected out of hand.[30] After initially sending a courtier, Ottavio Visconti, conte di Sforza, to lay the plans before Ferdinand, the Infanta subsequently sent, in June 1626, her chief engineer, the marquese di Sant' Angelo himself, to Bonn, a fact that strongly suggests that by that date it was no longer a question of if, but rather of how, and on what terms, the canal should be built.[31] Ferdinand was certainly anxious, as were most of his subjects, to prevent any attempt to divert the Rhine from its normal course. But beyond that his goal was seemingly to shape, not to block, the proceedings. He would have demanded a large say in the routes the two projected canals were to take and firm guarantees on the conduct and eventual withdrawal of the Spanish soldiery who would have to be stationed on the territory of his electorate to protect the canal during the duration of the Dutch war. He would doubtless also have held out for maximum compensation for unavoidable damage that construction of the canals would cause to land and property in the prince-bishopric of Liège as well as his electorate. But there is no evidence that Ferdinand tried to dissuade the Emperor from approving the Infanta's plans or that he refused to cooperate with the work of construction once it began.[32]

The most concrete evidence for this is that, once consultations between Brussels and Bonn were completed and construction work commenced, the Spaniards concentrated their main effort at the eastern end of the planned canal system, precisely on the territory of the elector of Cologne. However, it now emerged that the Rhine terminal was not, after all, to be Neuss, which lies opposite Düsseldorf, but, as originally intended, the fortress town of Rheinberg which was also situated in the electorate but much further north, near the border with the predominantly Calvinist duchy of Cleves.[33] By shifting the trajectory of the planned canal in this way to the north, the elector and the Infanta's

---

[29] *Correspondance de Giovanni Guidi del Bagno*, ii, pp. 766, 774.

[30] Both Veenendaal and Kessel, who speaks of 'die kölnische Verzögerungstaktik', suggest that Ferdinand was actively obstructing the construction of the canal, a view, I would argue, which is incorrect; see Veenendaal, 'Fossa Eugeniana', pp. 13–14; Kessel, *Spanien und die geistlichen Kurstaaten*, pp. 206–12.

[31] [Van den Wouvere], *Relación tocante a las obras*, pp. 501–2.

[32] AGS, Estado leg. 2318. Infanta Isabella to Philip IV, Brussels, 9 September 1626; Cornelissen, 'Maas- en Rijnkanaal', p. 199; Veenendaal, 'Fossa Eugeniana', pp. 13–14.

[33] AGS, Estado leg. 2317, cardenal de la Cueva to Philip IV, Brussels, 17 September 1626, specifies that Rheinberg is now the eastern terminal; see also Veenendaal, 'Fossa Eugeniana', p. 14, and J. Real, 'Die Fossa Eugeniana', *Gelre bijdragen en mededeelingen*, 8 (1905), pp. 233–4.

advisers were also shifting the protective umbrella of Spanish forts and garrisons, which were to protect the canal, from the core of the electorate to its northern tip, a locale roughly twice as far to the north of the city of Cologne as would have been the case with Neuss. The advantage for the elector was that, instead of dividing his lands, and leaving substantial areas to the north of the canal open to raiding and interference by the Dutch, virtually the whole of his electorate would now be safely tucked away to the south of the new fortified line. The duke of Neuburg too benefited from having more of his lands south of the barrier and therefore safe not only from the Dutch but also, from the Protestants of Cleves and the claims of the elector of Brandenburg to Jülich. Another alteration in the plans was that the planned trajectory was now to run from Rheinberg via Geldern but not as previously envisaged to Arcen. Despite the extra work, distance and cost involved, it was now to run to Venlo, a considerable distance further south. Presumably, this change was introduced to placate the latter city.

By mid September 1626 everything seems to have been agreed and the preparatory work of surveying, gathering workers and materials, and deploying troops commenced. Actual construction began near Rheinberg, on 21 September,[34] when the Spanish stadholder of Gelderland, Count Hendrik van den Bergh, after presiding over the celebration of mass in the open, took up a shovel in order to show that the work was not beneath the dignity of soldiers and dug out the first three spadefuls in full view of thousands of troops and labourers.[35] His example was then followed by several senior officers, after which the thousands of troops and hired peasants set to work in earnest. To protect the men working on the canal and its protective girdle of redoubts and forts, Van den Bergh encamped with the main Spanish field army close by, to the north, at the village of Issum, also on the territory of the elector.[36]

Protection of the eastern canal, once built, was to be the responsibility of the three main garrisons along its trajectory — at Rheinberg, Geldern and Venlo — and a guard force stationed along the length of the canal in twenty-four forts all but one of which were situated on the south side of the canal (which was planned to be seventy feet across), so as to make it more difficult to take them by surprise. These redoubts were spaced at regular intervals along the canal and were mostly rather small. Two, however, the so-called, 'forteresses royales' were considerably larger than the others and featured bridges across the canal, watch-towers and barracks for five hundred men.[37] One of these lay about the half the distance between Rheinberg and Geldern, on the soil of the electorate. The other, the only fort on the north side, lay at the strategic point, closest to Arcen, where the planned canal turned southwards towards Venlo and was called the Lintsfort.

---

[34] Friedrich Nettesheim, *Geschichte der Stadt und des Amtes Geldern* (Crefeld, 1863), pp. 386–8.
[35] Real, 'Fossa Eugeniana', p. 234; Nettesheim, *Geschichte*, p. 386.
[36] Nettesheim, *Geschichte*, pp. 387–8.
[37] Grotius, *Grollae obsidio*, p. 5 and map 2; Real, 'Fossa Eugeniana', p. 234.

Meanwhile the Dutch, while lacking the most up-to-date details of the Spanish plans, were in no doubt that their foes were engaged in a large-scale strategic
project which involved a major commitment of Spanish effort and resources,
and which posed an alarming threat, at least potentially, to themselves. On the
day before the ceremony in the open, near Rheinberg, the prince of Orange,
Frederik Hendrik, with the main Dutch field army, crossed the Rhine at Rees,
in the duchy of Cleves, only a few hours march to the north of Rheinberg. He
encamped near Xanten, still on the soil of Cleves but in striking distance of
the Spanish army encamped at Issum and no great distance either, albeit across
the River, from the Spanish base at Wesel.[38] The chief priority of the Stadholder
and his staff at that point was to try to check the progress of the construction
work. On 25 September 1626 the States General in The Hague passed a secret
resolution empowering Frederik Hendrik, at his own discretion, to undertake
whatever 'best shall serve to be done against the enemy's digging to divert the
Rhine'.[39]

Tension rose, not least among the men doing the digging, as the two armies
remained encamped in close proximity but without moving. The Spaniards
obstinately stayed where they were so as to cover the canal, as equally did the
Dutch in order to threaten it. After nearly two weeks of this motionless confrontation, it was Van den Bergh who delivered the first blow. He succeeded in leading a force, unnoticed, past the main Dutch encampment and in surprising a
Dutch cavalry camp further north, towards Kalkar, capturing several senior officers, including the camp commander, Count Herman Otto van Limburg Stirum,
a hundred or so men and some 250 horses.[40] But there was no change in the
overall situation until, a month later and with nothing gained, Frederik Hendrik
withdrew: 'The enemy', he reported to the States General, from near Emmerich,
on 31 October' 'busily continues to dig the new canal stretching from Rheinberg
to the city of Geldern and from there to the Maas below Venlo, using for that
purpose large numbers of peasants, as well as other diggers which they bring
from the Walloon country, Flanders and other areas.'[41]

That States General and stadholder committed their main military effort in
1626 to the area where the Spaniards were now concentrating their principal
effort on land demonstrates the seriousness with which the Spanish canal project
was taken in Holland. For by positioning his army, and keeping it immobile

---

[38] Spínola evidently planned to keep a regular garrison of 1,000 men in the canal forts, see
AGS, Estado leg. 2320, 'Relacion de la gente de guerra de guarnicion que se ha adjustado que es
conviniente y necessario que aya en los presidios y castillos de los estados de Flandes' (1627), where
1,000 men are allocated to 'los fuertes del canal que se haze de Rimberg a Mossa'.

[39] Veenendaal, 'Fossa Eugeniana', pp. 28–9; P.J. Blok, *Frederik Hendrik, Prins van Oranje* (Amsterdam,
1924), p. 100.

[40] AGS, Estado leg. 2040, consulta, *Consejo de Estado*, Madrid, 4 November 1626, fo. 2; Veenendaal,
'Fossa Eugeniana', p. 29.

[41] Ibid. Rubens reported the incident and the sale of some of the captured horses in Brussels
in a letter to Dupuy of 29 October 1626, *Correspondance de Rubens*, iv, pp. 2–3.

just to the north of the electorate of Cologne, the prince sacrificed the opportunity to strike at the enemy elsewhere where they had no field army in position to cover their defences.[42] But the Spaniards too paid a stiff price for immobilizing their main strike force on the left bank of the Rhine. When a comparatively small Dutch army of 7,000 men set siege to Oldenzaal, Spinola was unable to send a sufficient force north to Overijssel to try to break the Dutch siege, lest the main Dutch army should thereby gain the opportunity to ravage, or overrun, the area where the canal was being built.[43]

Initially, the Rhine-Maas canal made rapid progress. Writing to Madrid, on 10 November, the cardenal de la Cueva expressed satisfaction at the brisk rate of construction;[44] two days later, the Infanta, also reporting to the king, declared that 'en el dicho canal se va trabajando con todo diligencia posible' (work is taking place on the canal with all possible effort).[45] By mid November, though relatively little had thus far been done on the section from Geldern to the Maas, and only one redoubt had been constructed on that side, on the furthermost stretch, from Rheinberg to Geldern, the canal was almost complete; although for the moment it had only half the eventual planned width of seventy feet and one third of its eventual depth of water of fifteen feet.[46] Most of the twelve forts on this side stood ready to accommodate troops. During November, some 8,000 men were at work on the canal.[47]

Nor, contrary to what has been claimed, did the work cease over the winter of 1626–7. The weather that winter was very mixed but for most of the time sufficiently mild to enable the work on both the canal and the forts to continue. Reporting to the king, on 7 January, de la Cueva remarked that 'aunque ha elado dos vezes, no ha sido con tanta fuerza que aya facilitado el camino para dañar a los rebeldes, ni podido impedir la fabrica del canal del Rhin a la Mosa, que va muy adelante y habiendose entendido que el enemigo ha dexado muy gruessas guarniciones en Emmerich y Rees, y otras allí cerca, se esta a la mira para opponerse a qualquier insulto, que intentaren y particularmente sobre lo del canal'[48] (although it has frozen over twice, it has not been with such force as to facilitate access for cavalry to strike at the rebels, nor has it been able to prevent work on the canal between the Rhine and Maas which is now well advanced; and having heard that the enemy has stationed very large garrisons

---

[42] Veenendaal, 'Fossa Eugeniana', p. 29.

[43] Blok, *Frederik Hendrik*, pp. 100–1.

[44] AGS, Estado leg. 2317, De la Cueva to Philip IV, Brussels, 10 November 1626.

[45] Ibid., Isabella to Philip IV, Brussels, 12 November 1626; in part the Infanta was replying to the royal missive addressed to her, of 30 September, in which the king urged her to 'procurar venzer las difficultades que puede haver para el canal del Rhin a la Mosa'; it was in this same letter that Isabella explained that she and Spínola did not intend to try to 'recuperar y fortificar a Oldenzel para assegurar a Linghen', not only because winter was now close but also because the troops were occupied on building the canal.

[46] Real, 'Fossa Eugeniana', p. 234; Cornelissen, 'Maas- en Rijnkanaal', p. 201.

[47] *Correspondance de Giovanni Guildi del Bagno*, ii, p. 792.

[48] Veenendaal, 'Fossa Eugeniana', p. 23; Kessel, *Spanien und die geistlichen Kurstaaten*, p. 211.

at Emmerich and Rees, and others thereabouts, a good watch is being kept in order to oppose whatever affront they should attempt and especially against the work on the canal').[49] A month later, on 7 February, de la Cueva further reported that 'estos días ha elado fuertemente y assi fue forzoso suspender la fábrica del canal del Rhin a la Mosa' (in the last few days there has been a severe frost and therefore it has been necessary to suspend work on the Rhine-Maas canal).[50] But the interruption proved brief. 'Haviendo mejorado el tiempo', reported de la Cueva, on 28 February, 'se ha buelto a tratar de poner en perfección la fábrica del canal de la Mosa al Rhin' (The weather having improved, efforts have resumed to complete the work on the canal from the Maas to the Rhine).[51]

Rubens also mentioned the halting of the work due to the freezing weather in a letter to Dupoy, of 28 January. He added that the work had indeed now reached an advanced stage and there were high hopes, at Brussels and Antwerp, of its success. Nor, he, remarked, were the Infanta and Spínola content merely to complete the Rhine-Maas canal; for they were also still determined to construct a connecting link between the Maas and Antwerp: 'questo concetto e nobile e di gran consequenza, et al mio giudizio, como ho scritto a V.S. altre volte, questo canale sara il suggetto e palestra per molti anni della guerra di Fiandra' (this concept is a noble one and of great consequence and in my judgment, as I have written to you several times, this canal will be the subject and arena of the Low Countries wars for many years to come).[52]

In another letter to Dupuy, of 18 February 1627, Rubens confidently asserted that he has been assured by 'Don Giovanni de' Medici himself' that the successful completion of the canal project was 'certain' (infallibile), and that given the marchese's great expertise in such matters one could be confident that he was right. He added that the marchese had shown him the detailed plans which made it clear that that the aim was not now, 'as was thought', a cutting, or diversion, of the Rhine, or of the Maas, 'ma una fossa nova serrata de chiuse alle due estremita, da Rynbercq per Gueldres sino a Venloo, che sara navigabile . . .' (a new canal closed by locks at either end, from Rheinberg via Geldern to Venlo which will be navigable).[53] Once again Rubens assured his correspondent 'questa opera e molto avanzata'.

There was considerably less activity on and around the canal in the early spring of 1627 than there had been the previous autumn, but this did not prevent a good deal of excited speculation about the project both in the Low Countries and elsewhere. Grotius who, in a letter to his brother-in-law of March 1627 written from Paris, mentioned that he had seen one of Rubens' letters on the subject of the canal project circulating there, concluded that the Spaniards had given

[49] AGS, Estado leg. 2318, cardenal de la Cueva to Philip IV, Brussels, 7 January 1627.
[50] Ibid., De la Cueva to Philip IV, Brussels, 4 February 1627.
[51] Ibid., De la Cueva to Philip IV, Brussels, 28 February 1627.
[52] *Correspondance de Rubens*, iv, p. 30.
[53] Ibid., iv, pp. 34–6.

up trying to divert the course of the Rhine, being unable to overcome the difficulties posed by the higher ground lying between the valleys of the Rhine and Maas.[54] He agreed with Rubens that the main Spanish goal now was not to change the course of the Rhine but to suppress Dutch commerce with the southern Netherlands and Germany, by diverting the river traffic to Spanish Brabant with the secondary aim of preventing the Dutch from coming to the aid of the Protestants of the duchy of Jülich.

The papal authorities in Rome awaited further news of the canal project with keen anticipation and were by no means ill-informed on the subject, having been sent a copy of the master-plan together with notes on its progress by the nuncio in Brussels together with his letter to Cardinal Barberini of 14 November 1626. This elaborate chart, rediscovered in the twentieth century by J.D.M. Cornelissen in the *Biblioteca Barberiniana*, pin-points the locations of the new Spanish forts and sluices as well as indicating the precise trajectory of the canal from the Rhine to the Maas.[55] The acting nuncio, on 2 April 1627, reported to Rome that the project of the canals was at that moment the chief topic of conversation in Brussels.[56]

Meanwhile the suspension, initially due to the frost, seems to have partially continued for some weeks after the thaw owing to shortage of funds. This in turn, led to speculation in Paris that the Spaniards had despaired of the success of their canals project and that it had been all but abandoned.[57] Rubens wrote to Dupuy, from Antwerp on 22 April 1627, rejecting any such notion and beseeching his friend to believe that what was being said in Paris did not at all correspond to the reality of the situation. He admitted that the work had, since February, been going much more slowly, first owing to frost and subsequently to scarcity of funds. But he insisted that money was being found and that the work was about to resume with greater intensity. There were technical difficulties with regard to sluices which were to control the flow of water from the Rhine into the new canal at its eastern end but the marchese di Sant' Angelo, he claimed, was confident that he had found the solution to these. 'Solo posso dire a V.S. con verita', he concluded, 'che l'opera si va continuando con molto fervore sin adesso.'[58]

Rubens was undoubtedly right that it was shortage of cash from Spain, and not any loss of ardour for the canal scheme as such, which had caused the slackening of activity. One indication of the continuing confidence of the Spanish authorities in Brussels was the decision to prepare a map of the Rhine-Maas canal for publication as a publicity and propaganda coup. On 13 May 1627,

---

[54] *Briefwisseling van Hugo Grotius*, ed. P.C. Molhuysen and B.L. Meulenbroek, iii (The Hague, 1961), pp. 118–19, Grotius to Reigersberch, 6 March 1627.

[55] Veenendaal, 'Fossa Eugeniana', p. 22.

[56] *Correspondance de Giovanni Guidi del Bagno*, ii, p. 832.

[57] The impression in Paris was that 'l'opera del canale sia totalmente disperata et abbandonata', *Correspondance du Rubens*, iv, p. 245.

[58] Ibid., p. 246.

Rubens wrote to Dupuy that this official map of the new canal had been on the point of being published when the Infanta had expressed a desire 'che il titolo di Fossa Eugeniana si mutasse in Mariana, o di Nostra Signora che has causato ch'io non ho potuto havere sino adesso l'essemplare che mi era promesso, ma s'havera quanto prima' (that the name 'Fossa Eugeniana' be changed to 'Mariana', or 'of Our Lady', which is the reason that I have not yet been able to obtain the copy which I was promised but it will be available as soon as possible).[59]

Another indication, he noted in the same letter, was the speculation in Brussels that the Infanta and her closest advisers were planning an early summer tour of the new canal and forts 'che si deve tener per un indicio certo che quella impresa sia ridotta a buon porto e sia vicina alla sua perfettione non essendo verisimile che sua Altezza o il signore marchese Spínola e manco tutti duoi insieme con tutta la corte si vadino esporre temerariamente al pericolo d'esser irrisi di tutto il mondo (which should be taken as a certain indication that that enterprise is proceeding well, and is close to being perfected, as it is not likely that her Highness or the signor marchese, much less both of them together with the whole court, would rashly go and expose themselves to the risk of being mocked by the whole world).[60] He added that a team of engineers, covered by a force of cavalry, had been sent to survey the route proposed for the projected canal which was to link the Maas with Antwerp. The original concept of connecting the Maas at Maastricht with the River Demer had now been dropped, presumably for technical reasons but very likely also in order to make the route from Cologne to Antwerp shorter and more direct, in favour of a canal and river network far to the north extending from Venlo, via Herentals, across Brabant, to the Scheldt at Antwerp. Rubens did not hide his own scepticism about the feasibility of this new trajectory for the link to the west of the Maas: 'che mi par una impresa quasi sopra le forze del secolo nostro' (which seems to me an enterprise almost beyond the means of our century).[61]

Writing a week later, again to Dupuy in Paris, Rubens reiterated his opinion that the canals would be the pivot of military operations in 1627 and that 'non faremo altra impresa che de gli canali, vedendo che si fanno delle preparationi in questa città per cominciar un altra fossa da Herentals sino in Anversa' (we will not undertake any other enterprise other than the canals, seeing that preparations are being made in this city to begin another canal from Herentals to Antwerp).[62] It seemed, remarked Rubens, that the Spanish high command, not being able to 'conquer or subdue' the enemy 'with arms', was seeking to suffocate him in his entrenchments 'with all these canals.'

---

[59] Ibid., p. 255; see also *Lettres de Philippe et de Jean-Jacques Chifflet sur les affaires des Pays-Bas (1627–1639)*, ed. B. de Meester (Brussels, 1943), pp. 32–5.

[60] *Correspondance de Rubens*, iv, p. 255.

[61] Ibid.

[62] Ibid., iv, p. 259.

On the eve of the Infanta's tour of Upper Gelderland and the canals, the mood in Antwerp and Brussels regarding the great project was evidently still optimistic. 'Questi canali', wrote Rubens, in a letter to Dupuy from Antwerp on 4 June 1627, 'come ho detto sempre servono per essercitio della nostra militia e saranno utilissimi a noi per la commodita del commercio e rinfrancharanno gran paesi della scorrerie de' nemici et essattione di grossissime contributioni che forniscono buona somma quotannis al suo erario' (These canals, as I have always said, will serve to exercise our forces and will be extremely useful to us by facilitating commerce, and they will revive large areas by sealing them off from the raids of the enemy and by saving very large contributions since they furnish a great sum every year to their coffers).[63]

However, the acute shortage of funds experienced during the spring of 1627 was the worst the Brussels regime had yet had to contend with since the expiry of the truce, in 1621, and exerted a seriously debilitating effect on the army of Flanders and the royal administration alike.[64] 'Con tutto', reaffirmed Rubens, writing to Dupuy on 10 June 1627, 'cio l'opinione commune e che l'opera della Fossa Mariana si va avanzando felicissimamente sin adesso'.[65] Meanwhile, on 31 May, Isabella had set out from Brussels with her entourage to visit a sanctuary of Our Lady much favoured by her, close to Diest. She lingered there a fortnight. Then (despite reports in Brussels and Antwerp that she would not after all tour the new canal but would return directly to the capital) she set out, on 16 June, for Roermond, the regional capital of Upper Gelderland, accompanied by Spínola, De la Cueva, and her court ladies, and escorted by sixteen companies of cavalry and two regiments of infantry. From Roermond, she proceeded on 18 June to Venlo from where, the next day, she continued via Straelen to Waalbeek. From there, she and her escort followed the canal to Geldern. Then, the stretch from Geldern to Rheinberg being already open to barges, on 20 June she and her party sailed on a fleet of small boats along the canal to Rheinberg where she dined and then immediately set out again back to Geldern.[66] By 21 June she was back in Roermond where, the following day, she received a deputation from the nobles and towns of Upper Gelderland in the convent in which she was lodging. Pleading the extreme poverty of their region, they complained of the constant coming and going of the soldiery and disruptive impact of the canal works and construction of forts. The Infanta did her best to mollify them, promising that 'las tierras que se tomaran se pagarán'.[67]

To what extent the Infanta and her advisers were pleased with what they saw of the canals and forts, and the rate of progress, is not easy to judge. Rubens, in a letter of 25 June to Dupuy, in which he reported that the Archduchess had viewed the new canal from one end to the other, remarked 'ma sin adesso non

[63] Ibid., iv, p. 268.
[64] AGS, Estado leg. 2318, Isabella to Philip IV, Brussels, 22 April 1627.
[65] *Correspondance de Rubens*, iv, p. 274.
[66] *Kroniek der stad Roermond van 1562–1638*, ed. F. Nettesheim (Roermond, 1876), pp. 324–5.
[67] Veenendaal, 'Fossa Eugeniana', p. 26.

sappiamo come restera sodisfatta del opera' (But until now we don't know how far she is satisfied with the work).[68] But he added 'io non posso congetturar da questa andata di sua Altezza ch' ogni bene del successo del opera' (From this journey of Her Highness I cannot come to any other conjecture than the good success of the enterprise). De la Cueva wrote to the king, on 7 July 1627, reporting the Infanta's tour of Roermond, Venlo, Geldern and Rheinberg, confirming that she had viewed 'todo lo que está hecho del canal, que es mucho, por sí, y por los fuertes, que están acabados, mostrandose en ello la inteligencia y cuidado de Don Juan de Medicis, marqués de San Angelo, quien lo tiene a cargo' (having seen everything of the canal which is completed, which is a great deal both of the canal itself and the forts which have been finished, all showing the intelligence and care of Don Juan de Medicis, marqués de San Angelo, who is in charge of it).[69] But if this sounded reassuring there were also sceptical voices. The Franche-Comtois ecclesiastic Philippe Chifflet, who was one of the chaplains serving at Isabella's court, wrote to Bagno in Paris on 2 July, that work on the canals had come almost to a halt, in the first place owing to shortage of funds but also due to recent Dutch cavalry attacks.[70]

Here Chifflet was referring to the effect of a cavalry attack launched a few days before the Infanta's arrival on the scene. Undaunted by their lack of success the previous year, a large force of cavalry, under the 'lieutenant-general' of the Dutch cavalry, Thomas van Stakenbroeck, together with 800 infantry, succeeded in surprising the Spanish defenders of the new works and unfinished redoubts to the west of Geldern on 14 June. In the space of ten hours, Stakenbroecks' men overran and wrecked nine of the forts between Arcen and Geldern, killing some Spanish defenders and capturing 190. They drove off a large body 'peasants and labourers' and burnt numerous wagons and great quantities of tools as well as stores of timber and other materials.[71] They left the newly-dug westerly section of the 'Nieuwe Vaert', as the Dutch called the Fossa Mariana, a desolate and smoking ruin.[72]

During the summer campaign of 1627, the Spaniards deployed around the 'Nieuwe Vaert' as the pivot of their defensive strategy. Frederik Hendrik did likewise. During July he gathered his field army and spent several weeks encamped at Emmerich on the Rhine, in Cleves, a short distance to the north of Wesel

---

[68] *Correspondance de Rubens*, iv, p. 277.

[69] AGS, Estado leg. 2318, De la Cueva to Philip IV, Brussels, 7 July 1627.

[70] *Lettres de Philippe et Jean-Jacques Chifflet*, p. 43.

[71] Alexander van der Capellen, *Gedenkschriften* (2 vols, Utrecht, 1777–8), i, p. 425; N. Stellingwerff and S. Schot, *Particuliere notulen van de vergaderingen der Staten van Holland, 1620–1640*, ed. E.C.M. Huysman, iii, p. 301.

[72] Locally, in Upper Gelderland, the Fossa was likewise called the 'Nieuwe Vhaert', see *Kroniek der stad Roermond*, p. 324; Grotius, in his Latin account of the siege of Grol, calls it the Fossa Sanctae Mariae, see Grotius, *Grollae obsidio*, p. 5; in Germany it became known as the 'Mariengrift', see R. Verhuven-Hülferberg, 'Zur politischen und Verwaltungsgeschichte des Kreises Moers', in O. Constantin and E. Stein (ed.), *Der Landkreis Moers* (Berlin, 1926), p. 50; Nettesheim, *Geschichte*, p. 386.

from where, without moving, he could keep the enemy in a maximum state of uncertainty. It was impossible for his foes to know whether his intention was to cross the Rhine and advance southwards towards the nearby Nieuwe Vaert, embark on his fleet of river barges and sweep down river to Brabant or Flanders, or march northwards towards Grol or Lingen. The Spaniards already had large forces concentrated in the environs of the Rhine-Maas canal. Over the winter of 1626–7 2,500 men had been stationed in Wesel and its outforts, 800 in Rheinberg, 850 in Orsoy and Düsseldorf, 400 in Geldern and 400 in Venlo.[73] In July, the garrison of Rheinberg was reinforced to 2,500 men, some 4,000 were deployed along the canal and Venlo was strengthened while the garrison at Wesel was increased from 1,850 to 2,600 men.[74] When the prince finally broke camp, he marched north and set siege to Grol. Count Van den Bergh, who was in command of the Spanish forces on the Rhine and Maas, tried to gather a field army of sufficient strength to attempt to force the raising of the siege. But his efforts were greatly hampered by the unrelenting need to cover canals and by lack of money.[75] When finally he marched north he was too late to find any gap or weakness in the prince's entrenchments. Chronic lack of funds, and the emergency at Grol, meant that for the moment all work ceased on the canals themselves.

It was lack of funds, therefore, that led to the halting of work on the canals in the summer of 1627 and there was evidently no further progress over the whole of the following year. Inevitably, there was a great deal of talk and speculation as to the reasons for the suspension — and reports that it had been definitively abandoned owing to insuperable technical difficulties. There is no indication, however, in the dispatches from the Infanta's court, to Madrid, that this was in fact the case.[76] In July 1628, Rubens wrote to Dupuy admitting that nothing had been done on the Antwerp side of the planned Maas-Scheldt link but denying that the Rhine-Maas canal had been defeated by technical difficulties:

> questo canale vicino a questa città non si comincia ancora et poi che differiscono tanto, io non credo che si comminciara di questanno. Ma per conto di quel altro, io non so che sia cosi mal riuscito come V.S. scrive, rimamendo imperfetto solo per mancamento de dinari, che sono divertiti altrove, di sorte che per causa delle guerre d'Italia et Allemagna, noi restiamo qui a secco

[73] AGS, Estado 2320, 'Relacion de la gente de guerra de guarnicion que se ha ajustado que es conviniente y necessario que aya en los presidios y castillos de los estados de Flandes'.

[74] Stellingwerff and Schot, *Particuliere notulen*, pp. 372–3; according to a report from Wesel, of 29 July, there were then 2,500 men at Rheinberg and four to five thousand men 'in de Grifft', ibid., p. 372.

[75] ARB, SEG, 197, fo. 153, Infanta to Philip IV, Brussels, 28 July 1627; here she says that there was no money at all for the army, exclaiming 'Dios nos ayude'.

[76] Veenendaal, 'Fossa Eugeniana', p. 32.

(The canal adjoining this city has not yet been begun and since they put it off for so long, I do not believe that it will be begun this year. But as regards the other, I am not aware that it has turned out so badly as you maintain; it remains incomplete only because of lack of funds which have been diverted elsewhere, so that, owing to the wars of Italy and Germany, we find ourselves here without cash).[77]

The emergency in the Spanish Netherlands caused by the diversion of Spanish troops and money to the War of Mantua, in northern Italy, and exacerbated by the loss of the 1628 Mexican silver fleet, intercepted by a Dutch West India Company force under Piet Heyn off the Cuban coast, continued without respite down to the crisis of the summer of 1629 when the Dutch captured not only 's-Hertogenbosch, rendering the whole of north-eastern Brabant — insofar as this area remained in Spanish hands — insecure, but also Wesel, the principal Spanish garrison town on the Rhine, only a few miles north of Rheinberg.[78] The Dutch were now too close to several points of the projected canal system for it still to have been feasible to continue, even had the funds been available which was not the case. The concept was then definitively aborted by Frederik Hendrik's triumphant offensive up the Maas valley, in 1632, when Venlo, Roermond, Straelen and, after a bitter siege, Maastricht fell to the Dutch.[79] For Spain and the Spanish Netherlands the Fossa Sanctae Mariae was now just a painful reminder of what might have been: a costly but useless ditch in the earth. And thus it remained as the decades passed.

But it also served as a reminder of what a powerful ruler might one day achieve by way of rerouting the Rhine trade via the Maas and the southern Netherlands. In the eighteenth century the Spanish project was reviewed and intensively discussed by Frederick the Great and his ministers.[80] At the beginning of the nineteenth century Napoleon too was fascinated by the scheme. In September 1804, setting out from Venlo, Bonaparte inspected the entire length of what remained of the Fossa Eugeniana, riding as far as Rheinberg.[81] At first he toyed with the idea of completing it. But then, deciding that it hardly befitted a ruler of his stature to finish someone else's canal, ordered the construction of an entirely new but parallel canal system running further south, from the Rhine, at Neuss, to the Maas, again at Venlo. But the parallel turned out to be closer than the Emperor of the French would have wished. With three-quarters of this Napoleonic Rhine-Maas link completed, and expectations rising that the Rhine trade was about to be diverted from the Batavian Republic to a newly-enlarged France including the southern Netherlands, the work ceased never to be resumed owing to shortage of funds. Napoleon's emulation of the Spanish project of a Rhine-Maas canal served only to highlight both the overarching ambition and vast failure of its predecessor, and likewise survived only as a useless ditch in the ground.

[77] *Correspondance de Rubens*, iv, p. 442.

[78] J.I. Israel, *The Dutch Republic and the Hispanic World, 1606–1661* (Oxford, 1982), pp. 178–9.

[79] Ibid., pp. 185–9.

[80] Verhuven-Hülferberg, 'Zur politischen und Verwaltungsgeschichte', p. 50.

[81] Ibid., pp. 50–1.

4

Olivares, the Cardinal-Infante and Spain's Strategy in the Low Countries: The Road to Rocroi, 1635–43

In terms of territory and dependencies, the Spanish monarchy in early modern times was essentially a Mediterranean and trans-Atlantic empire. It extended across the southern flank of Europe and included an immense portion of the New World. Yet, paradoxically, during most of the age of Spanish greatness, the principal strategic pivot and main military base of the monarchy was located far from both the main territorial blocs of which the empire was composed – in northern Europe. In the opening decades of Spain's ascendancy down to the 1530s, its principal armies operated in Italy or the Iberian peninsula itself. But from the 1540s onwards, for well over a century, the Spanish crown chose to concentrate its military might, resources and expenditure, and thus its capacity to influence international affairs, in the Low Countries. This remarkable enduring strategic posture ceased only with the peace of the Pyrenees (1659) when Spain definitively lost its place at the head of the European powers, to France, and turned its efforts to attempting to recover Portugal.

There were several reasons for this, at first sight, rather illogical choice of main strategic base but the most compelling, during much of this long period, was the need to combat French power and influence, France being Spain's chief rival for hegemony in Europe. For France proved to be much more vulnerable to pressure from the Low Countries than to Spanish power

I would like to express my gratitude to both editors and also to Robert Oresko and Fernando González de León for their assistance with various matters discussed in this article. Translations are mine unless otherwise attributed.

exerted in the south. Of course, there were intervals when France was not the foremost danger facing the Spanish monarchy, such as the early 1560s when the spread of Ottoman power in the Mediterranean posed the chief threat, or the 1570s and 1580s when the rebellion in the northern Netherlands was the main preoccupation, or the opening years of the Thirty Years' War when the challenge to Habsburg ascendancy in the Holy Roman Empire seemed most urgent. But taking the period from 1540 to 1659 as a whole, France was, and was perceived to be, Spain's chief rival and the principal threat to Spain's preponderance in Europe.

For well over a century, then, the Netherlands was Spain's main strategic base or, as it was expressed then, *plaza de armas*. This is a point worth emphasizing for not a few historians, and generations of history students, have been convinced that (at least down to the fall of Breisach, in 1638) France was boxed in, all but encircled by Spanish and other Habsburg territories. A glance at a map of sixteenth- or early seventeenth-century Europe might indeed suggest precisely that; but such notions overlook the fact that the Franche-Comté (or Spanish Burgundy) was virtually indefensible and useless as a strategic base. Spanish Lombardy was a valuable possession and effective barrier, excluding French power from most of Italy, but was hardly suitable as a launching pad for Spanish offensives against, or any kind of intervention in, France, being separated from that monarchy by Piedmont and the Alpes Maritimes. Furthermore, the parts of Catalonia, Aragon and Navarre bordering on France, regions less densely populated and developed than southern France, were also for the most part weak links in what was, all considered, an exceedingly precarious chain. In fact, there was only one strong point among the Spanish territories adjoining France and that was the Spanish Netherlands. But so formidable and impenetrable was that bastion to sixteenth- and seventeenth-century armies, owing to the dense clustering of walled towns and new style fortifications, and the large number of rivers, dikes and canals to be found there, and so well-suited was that region to the maintenance of a large standing army, and the logistics of equipping and provisioning troops, that it served, on its own, to tip the strategic balance between Spain and France in such a way as to place France at a constant and appreciable disadvantage. Given that the Spanish Netherlands were difficult to invade from France, while on the French side the terrain lay invitingly open and Paris itself was only a short distance from the borders of Artois and Hainault – St Quentin, then just over the border in France being already over half way on the road from Brussels to Paris – Spain was, for as long as it possessed at least one large and well-equipped army, and stationed it in the Netherlands, capable of

Map 2   Spain's strategy in the Low Countries, 1635–1643

paralysing French offensives towards Italy or Spain, and pinning France helplessly to the defensive, whenever it chose. Whatever the position else-where, the Spanish army in the Netherlands could usually force the French to drop everything, and concentrate on defending the heart of the French monarchy merely by setting foot across the border. In this way, the Spanish Netherlands, though far from the two main territorial blocks of the empire, became what has been described as 'both the hammer and anvil of the Spanish Monarchy'.[1]

Consequently, during the war of 1635–59, the longest and most gruelling contest between Spain and France, there was never, at any stage, the slightest possibility that Spain's main army would be stationed anywhere other than in the south Netherlands. But there is a very real question as to when, precisely, the main Spanish effort came to be directed against France. It has been generally assumed that at the outset of this great struggle, Philip IV's chief minister, the count-duke of Olivares, was fully resolved on a large-scale offensive against France. However, it is open to doubt whether this was anything more than a momentary impulse if it was even that.[2] Since 1621, the Spanish army of Flanders had been locked in an arduous, slow moving war of sieges and counter-sieges with the Dutch. Did Spain now simply abandon, or give greatly reduced priority, to a struggle in to which such vast resources had been poured, over so many years, to turn its might against France which (at least on land) was undeniably its most powerful adversary? This is, indeed, a crucial question about Spanish strategy in 1635 and subsequent years, down to the battle of Rocroi (1643), the years in which Spain was still capable of mounting powerful offensives. When, and by what stages, did Spain scale down its war with the Dutch and unleash its principal effort against France?

By and large historians have simply taken it for granted that the Dutch front must have been relegated to secondary importance in Spanish strategic councils from 1635 onwards, and most general histories of the Thirty Years' War firmly give this impression. Even books which specifically deal with Spain's European strategy assert that this was the case. Thus, one historian claims that the Spanish–Dutch war 'faded into the background, ceasing to be a "hot war" (except in the maritime theatre) and by default, conditions approximating to those of armistice held sway until the Treaty of Mün-

---

[1] J. I. Israel, *The Dutch Republic and the Hispanic world, 1606–1661* (Oxford, 1982), pp. 251–2.
[2] John H. Elliott, *The count-duke of Olivares: the statesman in an age of decline* (New Haven and London, 1986), pp. 494–5.

ster'.[3] Admittedly, what I shall call the conventional view that Spain now gave priority to the French war, reversing its previous strategy in the Netherlands, appears to be vindicated by the fact that in 1636 the army of Flanders did enter France. In that year, the governor-general of the Spanish Netherlands, Philip IV's younger brother, the Cardinal-Infante, penetrated as far as Corbie, causing panic in Paris. Usually this episode is viewed as part of a massive, long-planned and major Spanish offensive. Moreover, this almost universally postulated 'great offensive' against France has been written about in rather dramatic terms. One scholar asserts that 'in 1636 the offensive directed by the Cardinal-Infante Ferdinand from the Low Countries had almost reached Paris', that Olivares at this juncture pressed the emperor 'to join in a decisive attack on France' and that the 'Cardinal-Infante together with Piccolomini and Gallas at the head of the Imperialist forces began a campaign directed at the very heart of France'.[4]

This interpretation remains predominant in recent publications. We are told of the 'offensive stage of the war against France' in the years 1635–7 and that the 'joint Spanish-Imperial invasion of France, at first promising much, petered out in 1637'.[5] Another scholar assures us that 'in 1635 the Cardinal-Infante took the offensive against France, striking hopefully from the Low Countries towards Paris; by August 1636 his army had reached Corbie'.[6] Yet another, in a widely read general work, claims that in 1635 Olivares 'planned the triple invasion of France in the following year' and that the 'conquest of an area as large as France was ... beyond the military capacities of the Habsburg forces' which, however, 'briefly approached Paris'.[7]

I have already made some attempt to challenge this prevailing interpretation and show that it has little or no basis in fact.[8] My purpose in this present essay is to restate my views of the matter in a more developed form and with more reference to the strategic relationship between Spain and France, arguing that there was no large-scale, concerted Spanish offensive against France in the years 1635–7, or subsequently (until the early 1640s),

[3] R. A. Stradling, *Europe and the decline of Spain: a study of the Spanish system, 1580–1720* (London, 1981), pp. 103–4.

[4] J. V. Polišenský, *The Thirty Years' War* (2nd edition, London, 1974), p. 219.

[5] R. A. Stradling, *Philip IV and the government of Spain (1621–1655)* (Cambridge, 1988), pp. 80, 130, 162.

[6] J. Lynch, *The Hispanic world in crisis and change, 1598–1700* (Oxford, 1992), p.140.

[7] Paul Kennedy, *The rise and fall of the great powers* (Lexington, Mass., 1987), p. 40; more guarded, but still to an extent giving the same impression, is R. J. Bonney's section 'France's war by diversion' in Geoffrey Parker, ed. *The Thirty Years' War* (London, 1984) pp. 144–53.

[8] Israel, *The Dutch Republic and the Hispanic world*, pp. 250–62.

ordered from Madrid or anywhere else. I hope to show that the 'French' front was not given priority over the 'Dutch' front, by Madrid or Brussels, in 1635–7 and that, furthermore, Olivares was as convinced as anyone of the need to concentrate Spain's main effort against the Dutch rather than the French and, over the winter of 1635–6, insisted on this in the most categorical terms. But, above all, my object is to explain the logic of Spanish strategic thinking in the later 1630s, the priorities which shaped Olivares' approach, the true reasons for the hastily improvised thrust to Corbie and, lastly, why, after 1640 Spanish ministers finally decided to drop the predominantly 'Dutch strategy' of the previous years and launch Spain's main effort against France.

It has been claimed, as recently as 1986, that Olivares' grand plan to attack France in 1635–7 was 'surely the most ambitious military conception of early modern Europe', that 'Olivares was relying to a significant extent on a rapid removal of France from the list of his enemies' and that the 'Cardinal-Infante was ordered to be prepared for all-out war with France'.[9] The same author admits that the reality was less grandiose than the concept but still insists on 'how close Olivares came to the outright defeat of France when a year later and considerably reduced in scale he actually launched his offensive'.[10] But in reality the Cardinal-Infante received no orders to attack France, following the French declaration of war and, during the early months of 1635, before the joint Franco-Dutch invasion of the Spanish Netherlands of that summer focused his mind instead on a plan to capture Philippine, one of the key Dutch strongholds around the Scheldt estuary.[11] Nor was Spain's principal ally, Philip IV's cousin, the Holy Roman Emperor Ferdinand II (1619–1637) either planning, or ready to contribute to, a major offensive against France at this stage.[12] Furthermore, it should not be forgotten that the original reason why the Cardinal-Infante was sent to the southern Netherlands with a powerful army in 1634 was not to fight France, or strike, from Flanders, into Germany, but for a different and very specific purpose: to restore Spanish power and authority in the Low Countries following the humiliating and disastrous setbacks at Dutch hands in 1629–33 and the severe weakening of the army in Flanders resulting from Spanish involvement in the

---

[9] R. A. Stradling, 'Olivares and the origins of the Franco-Spanish war, 1627–1635', *English Historical Review*, 101 (1986), 90–1; ironically Stradling criticizes John H. Elliott for not giving more emphasis to Olivares' plans to invade France.

[10] Stradling, 'Olivares and the origins', p. 91.   [11] Israel, *The Dutch Republic*, p. 252.

[12] E. Straub, *Pax et Imperium. Spaniens Kampf um seine Friedensordnung in Europa zwischen 1617 und 1635* (Paderborn, 1980), p. 471.

War of Mantua (1628–31).[13] By 1633 Spanish prestige in the Low Countries stood lower than at any time since the disastrous collapse of the late 1570s, during the governorship of don Juan de Austria, and its aftermath, so that for Olivares and Philip IV restoring Spain's might and *reputación* in the Netherlands was a priority of the utmost and overriding urgency. Given the extent of territory and large number of towns lost in the years 1629–33, it was inherent in this task of restoring Spain's position in the Netherlands that at least some of the strategically important lost towns and fortresses – which included Maastricht, Venlo, Roermond, Helmond, Eindhoven, Rheinberg, Wesel, Sittard, 's-Hertogenbosch and Limburg – should be recovered.

There were no orders, then, to concentrate against France. On the contrary, in a special meeting held in Madrid on 2 February 1635, before the French declaration of war (19 May 1635), but at a time when it was clearly pending, the count-duke and five other ministers, including the marquises of Leganés and Villahermosa, agreed on the necessity to launch an offensive against the Dutch and recapture Limburg and Maastricht as soon as possible, and then also Venlo, Roermond, Grave and crossing-points on the Lower Rhine, so as to restore Spain's strategic position in the chief river valleys of the Low Countries and revive its capacity to intervene in the German conflict.[14] On 18 March, the Cardinal-Infante wrote from Brussels confirming that he would follow his orders to concentrate against the Dutch and, if the expected quick successes were achieved, try to secure the now desperately needed truce with the Republic and thereby halt the escalating overseas conflict, above all in Brazil, and free Spain to confront France.[15]

In the event the Cardinal-Infante accomplished nothing in the interval before the Franco-Dutch invasion of June 1635. The advancing French and Dutch armies joined forces in the Maas valley in July, while the Cardinal-Infante fell back to cover Brussels. The invading army, some 60,000 strong, captured Diest, Tienen and several smaller places in Brabant before setting siege to Leuven (Louvain). But poor organization and logistics and the spread of sickness among the French, soon weakened the besieging army and this, together with their failure to make any impact on the walls of

---

[13] Israel, *The Dutch Republic*, pp. 238, 245, 250–1; Elliott, *The count-duke of Olivares*, pp. 453–4.

[14] AGS, Est. 2050. 'Junta particular sobre algunos propuestos de lo que se podría obrar este año con las armas en Flandes', Madrid, 22 February 1635; see especially Olivares' observations on fo. 5.

[15] AGR, Brussels, SEG, vol. 212, fo. 269. Cardinal-Infante to Philip, Brussels, 18 March 1635.

Leuven, rapidly transformed the strategic position.[16] Before long the
Spaniards had regained the initiative and both French and Dutch were
forced into a headlong retreat northwards towards the United Provinces.

The Cardinal-Infante could now counter-attack in whichever direction
he chose but opted (in accordance with his general instructions) to launch
his offensive towards the north.[17] After recapturing Diest and Tienen, he
advanced north-eastwards, towards the Rhine. Then, in late July, came the
sensational news that a small Spanish column, operating further north, had
succeeded in taking Schenckenschans (or Schenck or, in Spanish Esquenque), one of the most vital Dutch fortresses on the Lower Rhine, guarding
a major route of access into Gelderland from the east. Schenck had not the
slightest relevance to any conceivable attack on France but Olivares and
Philip IV were not just gratified on hearing the news: their spirits soared.
Over the next months Olivares was nothing less than euphoric. For he was
convinced that the capture of Schenck opened the way to much greater
strategic gains at Dutch expense than had been projected in the spring of
1635. Schenckenschans provided, or so it seemed, a heaven-sent opportunity to revive Spanish power on the Lower Rhine in dramatic fashion
and tip the balance in the Low Countries back in favour of Spain. Philip
and Olivares ordered the Cardinal-Infante to advance further north, pour
troops and resources into the Lower Rhine area and do everything possible
to secure his lines of communication with Schenck: 'so that from there we
can make war in the heart of Holland and, I hope, if we proceed thus and,
as you say, if we clear the enemy from the Maas, and with this fortress, you
will be able to make the peace or truce [with the Dutch] that we want'.[18]
Once confirmed, the Spanish public were told of the Cardinal-Infante's
glorious triumph against the 'Dutch' by means of a printed account
published in Seville.[19] The Dutch public, by contrast, was deeply disturbed by the unpalatable news. The Stadholder, Frederik Hendrik,
decided to keep his field army out in the open around Schenckenschans all

[16] AGR, SEG, vol. 213, fo. 1. Cardinal-Infante to Philip, Brussels, 11 July 1635.
[17] Diego de Luna y Mora, 'Relación de la campaña del año de 1635', in *Colección de documentos inéditos para la historia de España* (113 vols., Madrid, 1842–95), LXXV, p. 398; Henri Lonchay, *La rivalité de la France et de l'Espagne aux Pays-Bas (1635–1700)* (Brussels, 1896), pp. 76–7.
[18] BL, Add. 14007, fo. 53. 'Copia de carta de s.Magd. para el señor Infante Don Fernando', Madrid 25 October 1635: 'para que de allí se pueda poner la guerra en el coraçon de Holanda, y si se hace asi, espero, que con limpiar la Mosa, como decéis, y con este fuerte, avéis de hacer la paz o tregua que quisieremos ...'
[19] *Breve y verdadera relación de como por parte de su Magestad Católica ... se ganó el fuerte llamado de Eschenk* (Seville, 1635).

winter, to ensure recovery of the vital point of access at the earliest opportunity.[20]

During August and September 1635, a Spanish army of 20,000 men
occupied the duchy of Cleves (technically part of Brandenburg) and joined
forces with an imperialist contingent sent to assist. The plan was to create a
strategic wedge on the Lower Rhine, straddling the Dutch-German frontier
linking Schenck with the main body of the Spanish Netherlands.[21] The
Cardinal-Infante in person quartered, for over a month, at Goch, several
miles across the German border, supervising the activity of his commanders
in Cleves, northern Brabant and on the eastern side of Schenck. In a letter to
the king, he apologized for not spending the entire winter in Cleves,
explaining there was an acute shortage of provisions and forage in the area.[22]
During October, don Fernando fortified the town of Gennep on the Maas
(far to the north of Venlo) thereby creating a strategic cordon connecting the
Habsburg wedge in Cleves with Spanish Brabant, isolating Dutch-held
Venlo, Roermond, Limburg and Maastricht. At the same time, though, he
began preparing the king and Olivares for the possibility that Schenck
might not be secured. He assured Philip that Gennep was being fortified in
such a fashion that it would shortly be 'one of the best places which Your
Majesty possesses in these provinces … and it is of incomparably greater
significance than Schenck because it can be supplied and held whereas the
latter can not'.[23] Rounding off their success, in early November, Spanish
troops took the fortress town of Limburg and localities of Valkenburg and
's-Hertogenrade, thereby transforming the strategic situation in the Maas
valley.[24] For with these gains, the Spaniards liquidated most of the Dutch
wedge which had separated Spanish Brabant from the Rhine valley since
1632 and cut off the Dutch garrison in Maastricht.

On releasing his field army to winter quarters and returning to Brussels in
mid-November, don Fernando left 1,500 crack troops in Schenckenschans
with supplies for 'seven months', 2,000 men under don Francisco Toralto at
Cleves, and strong supporting garrisons in the positions between Cleves and

[20] J. J. Poelhekke, *Frederik Hendrik, Prins van Oranje: een biografisch drieluik* (Zutphen, 1978),
pp. 451–2.

[21] Ibid., p. 451; see also J. I. Israel, 'Olivares and the government of the Spanish Netherlands,
1621–1643', in J. I. Israel, *Empires and entrepots* (London, 1990) pp. 183–4.

[22] AGR, SEG, vol. 213, fo. 89. Cardinal-Infante to Philip, Goch, 20 August 1635.

[23] Ibid., fo. 166. Cardinal-Infante to Philip, Gennep, 11 October 1635: 'es incomparablemente
de mayor importancia que el Esquenque porque este se puede socorrer y mantener y aquel
no'.

[24] W. Jappe Alberts, *Geschiedenis van de beide Limburgen* (2 vols., Assen, 1972–4) II, p. 4; J. A.
K. Haas, *De verdeling van de landen van Overmaas, 1644–1662* (Assen, 1978), p. 5.

Schenck and at Gennep, Straelen and Geldern.[25] Additional forces were deployed around Limburg and Maastricht. Olivares and the king, however, were not convinced that don Fernando had done all he could to extend, and strengthen, Spain's newly won enclaves in the Maas valley and Cleves. In his instructions of 11 December 1635, the king instructed his brother to hold Schenckenschans 'at whatever cost', strengthen the Spanish positions between Schenck and Cleves and fortify Helmond so as to secure his line of communications across northern Brabant.[26]

The king's orders, and Olivares' strategy, could not have been clearer or more emphatic. Spain's effort was to be concentrated against the Dutch. There are no grounds for claiming 'that the government at Madrid was divided on whether it was preferable to concentrate the war effort on France or the Dutch Republic'.[27] It has been asserted that the French boundaries were more vulnerable to invasion and so the decision was taken to concentrate military action there. In 1636, the army of Flanders reached Corbie on the Somme, about eighty miles from Paris. The Spaniards also invaded from Franche-Comté in the east; and had their planned invasion of [sic] Catalonia not been deferred until 1637, this triple offensive might have knocked France out of the war...[28]

But the truth is that neither Olivares, nor the king, nor the Cardinal-Infante, nor any important minister – either over the winter of 1635–6, or at any point during the first five months of 1636 – proposed launching an offensive, major or minor, against France. Nor, as we shall see, did the Spaniards invade France from Spanish Burgundy – on the contrary the Spaniards almost lost the territory that year and there were no preparations of any kind for an invasion of France from Catalonia until the following year.[29]

Moreover, Olivares was the most categorical of all in insisting that Spain's efforts in 1636 should be concentrated against the Dutch. 'Your Majesty', he advised the king on 16 November 1635, 'may rest assured that neither your father, nor grandfather, had the opportunity which you now

[25] AGR, SEG, vol. 213, fo. 89. Cardinal-Infante to Philip, Brussels, 22 November 1635.

[26] Ibid., fos. 396–8. Philip to Cardinal-Infante, Madrid, 11 December 1635: 'aquello [Esquen-que] se ha de mantener a qualquier precio'; Israel, 'Olivares and the government of the Spanish Netherlands', p. 184.

[27] R. Bonney, *The European dynastic states, 1494–1660* (Oxford, 1991), p. 210.

[28] Ibid,. pp. 210–11.

[29] Paul Henrard, *Marie des Médicis dans les Pays-Bas (1631–1638)* (Brussels, 1876), p. 564; on the absence of preparations for an invasion of France from Catalonia in 1636, see John H. Elliott, *The revolt of the Catalans: a study in the decline of Spain (1598–1640)* (Cambridge, 1963), pp. 313–16.

have to settle the affairs of Holland with advantage and reputation, because God has been pleased to place the master-key in Your Majesty's hands.'[30] At the meeting of the council of State in Madrid, on 7 December, the count-duke again urged a maximum effort to secure and exploit Spain's gains on the Lower Rhine and in northern Brabant.[31] In one of his most insistent letters, in March 1636, Olivares assured the Cardinal-Infante that 'without Schenck we have nothing even if we were to capture Paris; and with it we have everything, even if we should lose Brussels and Madrid'.[32]

The Dutch, for their part, spared no effort to retake Schenckenschans. The fortress, on an island in the Rhine, was bombarded relentlessly from both shores, and by a flotilla of river gun-boats, a scene recorded subsequently on a large painting by Gerrit van Santen commissioned by the States-General. Finally, on 30 April 1636, the 600 survivors of the garrison, battered beyond endurance, surrendered to the Stadholder. The entire United Provinces erupted in jubilation and thanksgiving services. By contrast, the count-duke when he heard the news was beside himself with exasperation and grief. 'For I see', he wrote to the Cardinal-Infante, on 25 May 1636, 'that we have lost the best jewel which the king, our master, possessed in those states with which to settle his affairs successfully.' It was, he averred, a 'great blow for the king and all Spain'.[33]

The loss of Schenckenschans was a severe setback to Spanish hopes and to Olivares and the king. But it by no means nullified all the gains of the previous autumn or invalidated the logic of the offensive against the Dutch. If no offensive against France was planned during the winter of 1635–6, neither was there any talk of invading France, in Madrid or Brussels, in the aftermath of the fall of Schenck. There was, of course, a re-appraisal of Spain's strategy in the Low Countries in both capitals during May and June 1636. But in Spain, Olivares (and the king's other principal advisers) simply re-affirmed that the Dutch front was to have priority and that on the French side the army should fight purely defensively.[34] The count-duke continued to focus his attention on northern Brabant and the Lower Rhine, railing

---

[30] Quoted in Elliott, *The count-duke of Olivares*, p. 493.

[31] AGS, Est, 2050 consulta 7 December 1635, 'voto del Conde Duque'.

[32] Bayerische Staatsbibliothek, Munich, Cod. hisp. 22, fo. 12v. Olivares to Cardinal-Infante, Madrid, 14 March 1636: 'que sin el Squenque, no ay nada, aunque se tome a Paris, y con el, aunque se pierda Bruselas y Madrid, lo ay todo'.

[33] Ibid., fo. 17v. Olivares to Cardinal-Infante, Madrid, 25 May 1636: 'pues veo, señor, que se ha perdido la mayor joya que el rey nuestro señor tenia en esos estados para poder acomodar sus cosas con gloria ... grande golpe, señor, para el rey nuestro señor, grande para toda Espana'; see also Elliott, *The count-duke of Olivares*, p. 504 and Israel, 'Olivares and the government of the Spanish Netherlands', p. 184.

[34] AGS, Est. 2051, consulta of 17 June 1636.

about the vital importance of securing Helmond and Eindhoven and the failure to post enough Spaniards and Italians, the monarchy's best troops, in and around Schenck.

In the spring of 1636, the army of Flanders was a formidable engine of war, officially totalling 69,703 officers and men.[35] But, until late May, it was still the Dutch, and not France, that it was preparing to attack. In the event, however, the army of Flanders did not fight offensively against the Dutch Republic in the summer of 1636. Instead the decision was taken not in Madrid but at Brussels, late in May, to suspend this offensive and, instead, launch a secondary thrust, or 'diversion' as it was called, into France. Writing to the king, explaining this change of plan, on 26 May 1636, the Cardinal-Infante was at pains to stress that he and his commanders had been intending to launch a major attack against the Dutch, as the king and Olivares had instructed, but that the dramatic change in circumstances had persuaded him to switch to a French strategy.[36] For his, and the king's, plans had been based on the assumption that France would that year be pinned to the defensive by the projected imperialist invasion of eastern France with 40,000 men. Since the withdrawal of the Swedes to the northern fringes of Germany and the departure of the protestant electors from the war under the terms of the Peace of Prague (30 May 1635),[37] the emperor's position in Germany had indeed been greatly strengthened (albeit only temporarily) and a decision had been taken in Vienna, to strike at what now appeared to be the emperor's sole major enemy operating in the empire – France. But during May it emerged that logistical and financial difficulties had prevented the emperor's commanders amassing sufficient forces on the Rhine for them to invade France on their own; they informed Brussels they could only now do so in conjunction with the army of Flanders and to this don Fernando had agreed. In other words the Spanish invasion of France in the summer of 1636 was an entirely makeshift, secondary operation, improvised at exceedingly short notice, which had nothing what-soever to do with any grand Spanish design to invade France from several directions, in massive force, and which was decided on in Brussels purely in response to pressure from Vienna and the imperialist generals and because the Cardinal-Infante decided that he should not forgo the opportunity to combine his forces with those of the imperialists. . . .

Furthermore, even while announcing this change of plan, the Cardinal-

[35] Ibid., consulta 12 April 1636, citing figures sent the previous February by the *contador* Diego de Hernani.

[36] AGR, SEG, vol. 214, fos. 449–61v. Cardinal-Infante to Philip, Brussels, 26 May 1636.

[37] Polišenský, *Thirty Years' War*, pp. 216–17; Parker, *Thirty Years' War*, pp. 158–60.

Infante continued to reiterate that, as far as Spain was concerned, it was better to concentrate against the Dutch rather than France and that this was the view of his advisers in Brussels as well as of ministers at Madrid. Interestingly, one of the principal arguments advanced in Brussels for giving priority to the Dutch front, rather than the French, were the sentiments of the inhabitants of the Spanish Netherlands themselves. These, reportedly, had so great a preference for fighting the protestant Dutch, rather than the catholic French, that they would rather win a single mile of territory back from the United Provinces than entire provinces from France.[38]

Meanwhile, it is evident that Philip IV and Olivares were still expecting, as late as the second week of June 1636, that the main effort of the army of Flanders that year would be directed against the Dutch. Writing to the Cardinal-Infante, on 13 June 1636, Philip IV ordered him to advance into northern Brabant, fortify Helmond and Eindhoven and try to retake Schenck.[39] When they learnt of the change of plan, though, Philip and Olivares readily accepted that it was better to thrust into France together with the imperialists than invade Dutch territory without imperialist assistance, and without an imperialist attack on France, and all the more so since they now knew that a French army of 14,000 men, under Condé, had invaded Spanish Burgundy, during May, and set siege to its capital, Dôle.

Since no preparations of any kind were made for a thrust into France, from the Spanish Netherlands, before late May 1636, there was never any possibility of the invasion being coordinated with attacks by Spanish armies operating from Italy or Catalonia. The invasion turned into the sensational episode it did solely because of the unexpected weakness of the opposition and its extraordinary effect in France. The Cardinal-Infante, assured by his intelligence service that the Dutch were unprepared to assail him in his rear,[40] left Brussels at the end of June and gathered, at Mons, a lightly equipped invasion army of 18,000 men, a high proportion of which consisted of cavalry, including an imperialist contingent under Octavio Piccolomini.[41] He also published a manifesto in French blaming the war on France and accusing France of destabilizing the Holy Roman Empire and having brought in the Swedes which was cited as the cause of the devastation of

[38] AGR, SEG, vol. 214, fos. 254–60.
[39] AGR, SEG, vol. 214, fo. 565. Philip to Cardinal-Infante, Madrid, 13 June 1636.
[40] René Delplanche, *Pierre Roose, chef-président du Conseil-Privé des Pays-Bas (1586–1673)* (Brussels, 1945), p. 100.
[41] Henrard, *Marie des Médicis*, pp. 564–7; Lonchay, *La rivalité.* p. 83; see also David Parrott, 'Richelieu, the *Grands,* and the French army', in J. Bergin and L. Brockliss (eds.), *Richelieu and his age* (Oxford, 1992), p. 166.

Germany and sacking of innumerable catholic churches and monasteries as well as the destruction of the catholic faith in whole areas.[42] The French monarch was further accused of aiding and abetting the Dutch 'rebel vassals of His Majesty of Spain', usurping the lands of the duke of Lorraine, and persecuting his own mother, Marie des Médicis.

Advancing from Mons, via Avesnes, the Spaniards set siege to the key French frontier fortress of La Capelle. To their amazement, its large garrison, unnerved by the exploding shells fired by the Cardinal-Infante's siege mortars, a recent innovation as yet unfamiliar to the French, surrendered after only four days. The Cardinal-Infante was soon again astonished when Le Câtelet, one of the strongest fortresses in all France, capitulated – again after only three days.[43] His victorious troops then occupied Guise, Vervins and Bohain in rapid succession. As the Spaniards continued to advance westwards, towards the Somme, Louis XIII, in a state verging on panic, returned from Fontainebleau to Paris. On reaching the Somme, the imperialist contingent crossed over and captured Roye from where Piccolomini marched into a wide swathe of territory around Compiègne, causing utter consternation in Paris. On 7 August, the Cardinal-Infante set siege to Corbie – a vital fortress town on the Somme, certainly, but no great distance into France from the then Spanish Netherlands frontier – setting a large part of the town alight with his mortar bombs. Corbie surrendered a week later.

Meanwhile, on 8 August, the day after the commencement of the siege of Corbie, Louis XIII wrote to Condé, who was progressing with his siege of Dôle, ordering him (after making a final attempt) to abandon the siege and withdraw towards Paris to help preserve the heart of the French state.[44] But by the time Condé received these instructions, made his final unsuccessful attempt to take Dôle and withdrew from Spanish Burgundy, several more

---

[42] Juan Antonio Vincart, 'Relación y commentario de los sucessos de las Armas de S.M. ...d'esta Campaña de 1636', in *Colección de documentos inéditos*, LIX, p. 8; much of this propaganda had already appeared in the *Declaration de son Altèze touchant la guerre contre la covronne de France* (Brussels, 24 June 1635).

[43] Vincart, 'Relación y comentario', pp. 17–18.

[44] Louis XIII to Condé, Paris, 8 August 1636 in D. L. M. Avenel (ed.), *Lettres, instructions diplomatiques et papiers d'état du Cardinal de Richelieu* (Paris, 1853–77), V (1635–1637), pp. 534–5: 'Mon cousin, c'est avec beaucoup de deplaisir que je suis contraint de vous mander que le siège de Dôle tirant de longue, il est nécessaire de le lever pour retirer l'armée que vous commandez auprès de moy et conserver le coeur de l'estat, mais, comme j'estime que votre mine s'en va en estat de faire son effect, je désire qu'auparavant que vous leviez ce siège vous la faciez jouer, et faciez un dernier effort pour tascher à emporter cette place, qui porte tel coup à mes affaires qu'elle est capable de conserver ma réputation et mon royaume.'

weeks had elapsed and, by that time, the danger posed by the army of Flanders was already receding. At the French court, it was expected, after the fall of Corbie, that the Spaniards would penetrate further, though not necessarily towards Paris. On 17 August Richelieu confided to an underling: 'I do not know what the enemy will do but it is my view that they will advance on Abbeville or Amiens.'[45] Piccolomini was eager to advance further. He did his best, as he reported to Gallas, on 18 August, to persuade the Cardinal-Infante not to halt, urging that there would never be a better opportunity, such was the enemy's disarray, and that the Spanish army could cross the Somme with relatively little risk, but the Cardinal-Infante was firmly resolved to withdraw.[46] He had planned only a minor operation. He felt that he lacked the forces for anything more ambitious and should not risk the royal army. His army was also hampered by constant bickering among his generals.[47]

Consequently, by the time the Cardinal-Infante received definite word of the raising of the siege of Dôle, in early September, he was already back in Cambrai and the bulk of his invasion force had left France. Ironically (but typically in seventeenth-century conditions), the imperial army, under Gallas, despite the French evacuation of Spanish Burgundy (and having been handed the initiative on a plate) were, at that point, still not ready to launch their own thrust from the east. Condé raised the siege of Dôle on 15 August. Gallas' invasion force (which consisted of imperialists and Lorrainers but no Spanish troops) did indeed eventually cross Spanish Burgundy and penetrate into French Burgundy. But the main imperialist invasion of France from the east (such as it was) did not begin until mid-October – a whole month and a half after the Spanish withdrawal from the Somme.[48] This new invasion succeeded in taking Mirebeau after which the army's high command was riven by dispute. Charles, duke of Lorraine, whose duchy had been seized by the French king and who was striving to regain it through his alliance with Spain, urged an advance on nearby Dijon. But the slow and excessively cautious Gallas insisted on setting siege to the minor

[45] Ibid., v, p. 549. Richelieu to Chavigni, Paris, 17 August 1636: 'Je ne scay pas ce que feront les ennemis, mais ma pensée est qu'ils iront à Abbeville ou à Amiens.'
[46] Vincart, 'Relación y comentario', pp. 46, 50, 65; O. Elster, *Piccolomini-Studien* (Leipzig, 1911), pp. 70–1.
[47] See Fernando González de León, 'The road to Rocroi: the duke of Alba, the count duke of Olivares and the high command of the Spanish Army of Flanders in the Eighty Years' War, 1567–1659' (PhD thesis, The Johns Hopkins University, Baltimore, Md. 1991), pp. 166–8. (I am extremely grateful to Dr González de León for allowing me to see the relevant sections of his thesis.)
[48] Edmond de Vernisy, *L'invasion de Gallas. Tricentaire de l'invasion allemande en Bourgogne en 1636* (Paris, 1936), pp. 49,57.

fortress town of Saint Jean-de-Losne, west of Dôle, only a few miles across the French frontier. The invasion was destined to proceed no further. Saint Jean resisted tenaciously until, on 3 November, the imperialists were forced to raise the siege and retreat back to Spanish Burgundy by the approach of Condé's relief army.[49] In other words Gallas' invasion from the east was a fiasco which failed even to pose a serious threat to Dijon let alone to the 'heart of France'. Shortly after Gallas' undignified evacuation of the tiny morsel of France he had overrun, the Spanish garrison of Corbie capitulated to its French besiegers. On 17 November, Richelieu wrote triumphantly to the king, exclaiming that he hardly knew how to express his joy at the sudden and dramatic turnaround of the situation.[50] Olivares, for his part, was deeply distressed by the loss of Corbie, lamenting in a long missive to the Cardinal-Infante that the main Spanish force had been withdrawn from the Somme too soon and that not enough had been done to secure 'a place of such importance'.[51]

Yet the count-duke had also been greatly impressed by the general impact of the march to Corbie and the profound shock administered to the French court and all France. Consequently, it was at this point that Madrid and Vienna began planning a grand offensive against France. This time Olivares did indeed intend a large-scale invasion with the army of Flanders coordinating with the Spanish armies in Italy and Catalonia. Since the main attack could only be launched from the Spanish Netherlands, arrangements were made to send substantial reinforcements to the Cardinal-Infante from Naples as well as Spain, adding 8,000 Spaniards and Italians to the 65,000 men officially in the army of Flanders at the end of 1636.[52] The army of Lombardy was expanded to about 40,000 men. The plan was for the Cardinal-Infante to invade from the north, this time with some 30,000 men while the army of Lombardy crossed Savoy, entered Provence and thrust towards Marseilles, while the third and smallest of the three Spanish invasion armies, some 15,000 men based in Catalonia, penetrated the Languedoc.[53] For his part, the Emperor Ferdinand planned to send

[49] Ibid., pp. 116, 132–3.

[50] Richelieu to Louis XIII, Paris, 17 November 1636 in Avenel, *Lettres, instructions*, p. 681: 'Je ne scaurois assez témoigner à Vostre Majesté la joye que j'ay de voir qu'elles [ses affaires] changent de face. La prise de Corbie et le levement du siège de Saint-Jen-de-Losne, assiegé par toutes les forces de l'Empire, et ensuite la retraite de Galasse sont deux pièces de grande considération.'

[51] Bayerische Staatsbibliothek, Munich, Cod. hisp. 22, fo. 39v. Olivares to Cardinal-Infante, Madrid, 13 December 1636.

[52] AGS, Est. 2051, consulta 8 February 1637, fo. 5; Elliott, *The count-duke of Olivares*, p. 523; see also Elster, *Piccolomini-Studien*, pp. 72–4.

[53] Elliott, *The count-duke of Olivares*, pp. 522–4; Elliott, *Revolt of the Catalans*, pp. 324–5.

Piccolomini from the Spanish Netherlands into the Champagne, towards Rheims, while the imperialist army on the Rhine attacked the French in Alsace.

During the early months of 1637, there was unanimous agreement among the members of the council of state in Madrid that Spain should that year adopt an offensive strategy against France and fight defensively against the Dutch.[54] The duke of Albuquerque, at the meeting on 25 February, warmly seconded the count-duke's opinion that the army of Flanders should invade France that summer as swiftly and vigorously as possible, that this strategy best served Spain's interests both with regard to the war and 'the peace for which we hope', and that France should be invaded without any designs, or diversions, being attempted in the Netherlands, or any reserve forces being kept there beyond what was essential for defence against Holland.[55] He added that should Spain launch an offensive against the Dutch it would mean hazarding everything, including Spain's position in Italy, for little purpose.

And yet the strategic key, as always, lay in the Spanish Netherlands and, at Brussels, the Cardinal-Infante and his advisers continued to equivocate between the strategy of 1635–6 and what was now proposed. The Cardinal-Infante's trusted secretary, don Miguel de Salamanca, arrived in Madrid early in February 1637 and participated, expounding his master's views, in the crucial strategic debates of that month. He emphasized – and the relevance of this was to become plainer as the months passed – that the Cardinal-Infante's preference had all along been, and still was, for an offensive war against the Republic rather than France.[56] The Cardinal-Infante was inclined to a 'Dutch' strategy partly because this would be more popular with the inhabitants of the south Netherlands (by which was meant the Dutch speaking population of Flanders and Brabant rather than the inhabitants of Artois and Hainault), partly because towns and districts captured from the Dutch belonged to the king and would not be automatically returned (as would be anything taken from the French) and, finally, because the Dutch had been weighed down by war with Spain for many years and it was best not to give them any respite, especially as the king of France, with his present difficulties, was in no position to assist them. By concentrating Spain's might against the Republic, the Dutch could be brought to an 'acceptable' truce and Spain would then be far better placed to deal with France.

[54] AGS, Est. 2051, consultas of 25 and 26 February 1637.
[55] Ibid., consulta 25 February 1637. 'Voto del duque de Albuquerque', fos. 2v–3.
[56] Ibid., consulta of 8 February 1637. 'Voto' of Miguel de Salamanca, fo. 3.

Olivares insisted on a three-pronged assault on France in 1637 but not much, indeed practically nothing, came of it.[57] The small army operating from Catalonia crossed the French frontier on 29 August but, a month later, on 27 September, was routed by the French at Leucate. The army of Lombardy, embroiled in the fighting in Piedmont, was unable to cross into France at all. The council of State in Madrid approved the Cardinal-Infante's plan to strike deep into France, but no sooner did the army begin to mass on the French border than it had to be recalled owing to the descent of a Dutch field army of 18,000 men, under the Stadholder, on the northern borders of the Spanish Netherlands. After encamping for several weeks, poised to invade Flanders – he had hoped to be able to strike at Dunkirk – Frederik Hendrik marched into northern Brabant and set siege to Breda, taking advantage of the fact that much of the Cardinal-Infante's army was still in Artois and Hainault.[58]

Exploiting Frederik Hendrik's descent on Breda and the consequent transfer of Spanish forces northwards, the French then invaded from the south. In August, just a few days before the army of Catalonia entered the Languedoc, Olivares and the king received the unpalatable news that Breda was besieged, since 21 July, and that the French had captured Landrecies, a few miles to the east of Cambrai.[59] What made the siege of Breda so galling was that it was precisely Olivares' 'French' strategy which had given the Dutch their opportunity to dig in and complete their siege fortifications. For previously, while the main Spanish forces had been based in Brabant and Flanders, Frederik Hendrik's attempts to descend on Breda had each time been thwarted by a swift Spanish response.[60]

Thus, at the very moment that Olivares' grand three-pronged assault on France was supposed to begin, the bulk of the army of Flanders was recalled from the French frontier and concentrated against the Dutch.[61] Nor, from late August 1637 onwards, for the rest of that campaigning season, was there any question in the count-duke's mind that the Dutch front had to have priority. In the first place Breda with its garrison of over 3,000 men made up

[57] Elliott, *Revolt of the Catalans*, pp. 325–6; Elliott, *The count-duke of Olivares*, p. 523; see also José Alcalá-Zamora y Queipo de Llano, *España, Flandes y el mar del Norte (1618–1639)* (Barcelona, 1975), p. 365.

[58] A. Waddington, *La République des Provinces-Unies, la France et les Pays-Bas espagnols de 1630 à 1650* (Paris, 1895), I, pp. 295–6; Israel, *Dutch Republic and the Hispanic world*, p. 257.

[59] BL, Add. 14007, fo. 69. 'Copia de carta de S. Magestad para el Infante', Madrid, 25 August 1637.

[60] AGS, Est. 2052, consultas of 7 September and 7 October 1637 and the enclosed 'Discurso en que se pondere lo que se ha dejado de hazer y pudiera haver hecho en el socorro de Breda'.

[61] AGS, Est, 2052. Cardinal Infante to Philip, Antwerp, 28 July 1637.

of Spaniards, Italians and Walloons and Burgundians, was one of the most important strongholds of the Spanish Netherlands and a pillar of the king's *reputación*, representing as it did one of the most glorious successes of the early part of his reign. In the second place, the loss of slices of Brabant and Flanders to the protestant Dutch had a more disturbing impact on the States of Brabant and Flanders, the two principal contributing provinces of the Spanish Netherlands, than did loss of towns and districts to the French in Artois and Hainault.

Unable to relieve Breda, the Cardinal-Infante marched eastwards with 17,000 men, and opened an offensive against the Dutch in the Maas valley. After a few days' heavy bombardment, Venlo's garrison of 1,200 surrendered. Next, the Spaniards bombarded and forced the capitulation of Roermond.. After this, don Fernando considered besieging Grave, Nijmegen or perhaps Maastricht but then, on the advice of his military commanders – but against that of the principal civilian minister in his entourage, Olivares' special confidant, the president of the Secret Council at Brussels, Petrus Roose – he ceased his attack on the Dutch and turned back, alarmed by reports that the French were now making rapid progress in Artois, Hainault and Luxemburg.[62] Breda capitulated to the Dutch on 7 October. However, on 26 October, a Spanish column sent from Geldern scaled the walls of, and almost succeeded in capturing, the Dutch-arrisoned Rhine port of Rheinberg, in the electorate of Cologne.

The question of whether or not don Fernando judged correctly in turning back, in September 1637, was intensively debated both in Madrid and Brussels. At the gathering of the council of state on 7 October, Olivares strongly criticized the Cardinal-Infante's decision, insisting that he should have continued 'capturing places' from the Dutch and might, by this means, have forced Frederik Hendrik to raise the siege of Breda.[63] The king then wrote to his brother, instructing him to keep up the pressure on the Dutch, try to take Rheinberg so that Spain should again have a crossing-point on the Lower Rhine, and also tighten the blockade of Maastricht.[64] The Cardinal-Infante was also ordered, when campaigning ceased, to quarter his army for the winter over on the Dutch side, away from the French, so as to cover Antwerp which (since the loss of Breda) had now become more vulnerable. In addition, he was instructed to strengthen the garrisons of Gennep, Stevensweert, Geldern, Roermond and Venlo and improve the fortifications of Helmond, Eindhoven and Lier.

[62] AGR, SEG, vol. 217, fo. 382. Cardinal-Infante to Philip, Brussels, 1 November 1637.
[63] AGS, Est. 2052, consulta 7 October 1637. 'Voto del Conde Duque', fo. 1.
[64] AGR, SEG, vol. 217, fos. 353–v. Philip to Cardinal-Infante, The Escorial, 22 October 1637.

Olivares and the king aspired to make the army of Flanders stronger than ever in 1638. It was planned to send no less than 4,700,000 ducats to the Spanish Low Countries and expand the army there to over 80,000 men.[65] But how should Spain's main strike force be used? Scarcely surprisingly, after the fiasco of his grand, three-pronged, assault on France the previous year and the abrupt reversion to a 'Dutch' strategy since August 1637, the count-duke was now more convinced than ever that the Dutch front should have priority. At the meeting of the council of state on 8 January 1638, he declared that, ideally, it would be best to fight offensively against both France and the Republic but that since this was impossible 'and it is necessary to choose it is certain that concentrating against the Dutch is best'.[66] At the gathering of the council of state on 7 March, most ministers present openly disagreed, warning that if the king decided on 'offensive war' against the Dutch, and 'defensive' against France this would leave France with a free hand which could have disastrous consequences for Spain and Italy as well as the Spanish Netherlands.[67] But the count-duke, never one to be deterred by the objections of his colleagues, remained adamant. In his instructions to the Cardinal-Infante of 17 March 1638, the king stressed the urgency of settling with the Dutch while at the same time insisting that no settlement with the 'rebel' provinces would be acceptable unless they agreed to abandon their conquests in Brazil and restore Breda, Maastricht, Rheinberg and Orsoy.[68] The last two, crossing-points over the Lower Rhine, were deemed essential to Spain's standing in Germany. Obviously no such settlement would be attainable without subjecting the Dutch to massive new pressure. In the gathering of the council of state of 11 May 1638, Olivares again stressed that the most urgent priority now was to break the Franco-Dutch alliance by securing a favourable 'truce' with the Dutch and that the only way to accomplish this was to press them hard by both sea and land.[69] Already Olivares had his eye on the great armada he was amassing in Spain and which he was to send against the Dutch the following year, and how best to combine this pending maritime offensive with Spanish strategy on land.

Thus, for the campaign of 1638 Spanish strategy was again one of offensive war against the Dutch and a purely defensive effort against the French. In the event, however, neither Olivares' preference for a Dutch

[65] Ibid., fo. 462.
[66] AGS, Est. 2156, consulta, 8 January 1638. 'Voto del Conde-Duque': 'pero haviendo de escoger es cierto que es lo mejor (guerra offensiva) a Olanda, siendo flaquisima la razón de dezir que a olandeses siempre se les tiene allí...'
[67] AGS, Est. 2053, consulta of the *junta de estado*, 7 March 1638, fos. 6–11.
[68] AGR, SEG, vol. 218, fo. 455. Philip to Cardinal-Infante, Madrid, 17 March 1638.
[69] AGS, Est. 2053, consulta 11 May 1638, fos. 11v–12.

offensive, nor the disagreement among ministers at Madrid, made much difference since the Spaniards were pinned to the defensive by coordinated Dutch and French attacks. Nevertheless, it should be noted that the main military effort still had to be made against the Dutch rather than the French, because Antwerp was a great deal more important to the Spanish crown than St Omer. For many weeks the French border was left with only a skeleton defence. To the great joy of Olivares and the king, the Cardinal-Infante's defensive campaign of that year was exceptionally successful. The Dutch did indeed make a determined thrust towards Antwerp but their vanguard was caught in the open, at Kallo, by a crack force of Spanish troops, in what was the only pitched battle of the second part of the Eighty Years' War, and overwhelmed. The Spaniards captured 2,500 prisoners, eighty-one river barges and a good quantity of Dutch artillery. Writing to the king shortly afterwards, the Cardinal-Infante described his success rather grandly as the 'greatest victory which you Majesty's arms have achieved since the war in the Low Countries began'.[70] Soon after, the French army besieging St Omer was routed by a joint imperialist-Spanish force under Piccolomini.[71] During August, the focus of the war shifted north-eastwards to the Maas valley. Frederik Hendrik encircled Geldern with 16,000 men but was forced into a humiliating and costly retreat by the Cardinal-Infante's counter-thrust which was again backed by Piccolomini whose troops remained in Cleves, over the winter of 1638–9.[72]

During 1639, the army of Flanders was again pinned to the defensive. But it was still a uniquely well-entrenched and powerful force of some 70,000 men and the expectation was, in both Brussels and Madrid, that the Cardinal-Infante would be able to resume the offensive in 1640, given a measure of imperialist support, and assuming that the reinforcements which were sent on the huge armada (100 ships; 2,000 guns; 20,000 men), under Antonio de Oquendo, reached their destination safely. The Cardinal-Infante was told, in late July, to expect 9,000 'Spaniards with some Italians' for his army.[73] In the event, the armada which set sail from Corunna on 6 September met with disaster at the hands of the Dutch fleet in the Channel. But before Tromp ordered the final Dutch attack which destroyed the bulk

[70] AGR, SEG, vol. 219. fo. 255v. undated June 1638: 'la mayor victoria que han tenido las armas de Vuestra Magestad después que se començo la guerra en Flandes'.
[71] Lonchay, *La rivalité*, p. 91.
[72] F. Nettesheim, *Geschichte der Stadt und des Amtes Geldern* (2nd edition, 1963), pp. 214–15; O. Elster, *Die Piccolomini-Regimenter während des 30 jährigen Krieges* (Vienna, 1903), pp. 73–4.
[73] BL, Add. 14007, fo. 71. 'Copia de carta de S.Magestad para el Infante,' Madrid, 30 August 1639; Israel, *The Dutch Republic*, p. 317.

of the ships, at the Downs, some three-quarters of the Cardinal-Infante's reinforcements were successfully ferried across to Flanders from England.[74] By December 1639, the Cardinal-Infante had 77,000 men, of high quality, poised for action against either the French or Dutch.[75]

From August 1639, before the armada set sail, and in anticipation of striking a major blow at Dutch sea power, as well as reinforcing the army of Flanders, a new phase began in the strategic debate in progress since 1635 at Madrid and Brussels. Olivares and the king wanted an early offensive – to begin in March 1640 – launched before the French and Dutch were in a position to react. But how should the army of Flanders be used? One might readily suppose, with the mounting pressure of Spain's Catalan front, following the fall of the vital fortress of Salces to the French, on 19 July 1639, and the subsequent determined efforts on the Spanish side to regain the stronghold, that the obvious strategy would be to invade France from the Spanish Netherlands thereby relieving the pressure in the south. Yet, once again, this is not how Olivares and the king viewed the situation – they hoped to recover Salces before the onset of the main campaign season of 1640 in any case, and neither during 1639, nor over the winter of 1639–40, was any decision taken in Madrid to launch 'a general assault on France'.

What then was the strategy adopted by Spain for 1640? Setting out the available options in his instructions to the Cardinal-Infante of 30 August 1639, the king emphasized that the crucial thing was to achieve some notable success, either against the French or their Dutch allies, which would demonstrate the revived offensive capacity of the army of Flanders, and therefore of the Spanish monarchy as a whole, and enhance *reputación* sufficiently to facilitate the obtaining of the 'peace we desire so much [*la paz que tanto se desea*]'.[76] On balance, the king expressed a slight preference for a thrust into France, provided the Cardinal-Infante was reasonably sure he could capture one of the major strongholds along the Somme – Abbeville, Amiens, Péronne, Saint Quentin or Corbie – and this time hold it. If this seemed unattainable, the Cardinal-Infante was ordered to strike at the Dutch and specifically at one of five key strongholds which Olivares and Philip were anxious to regain – Sluis, on the Scheldt estuary, was their first choice but if this appeared too difficult, then Grave or Maastricht, on the Maas, or Rheinberg or Wesel, on the Rhine.[77] Madrid's preference, after

---

[74] Alcalá-Zamora, *España, Flandes y el mar del Norte*, pp. 444–5.
[75] Geoffrey Parker, *The military revolution: military innovation and the rise of the West, 1500–1800* (Cambridge, 1988), pp. 40,168.
[76] BL, Add. 14007, fos. 73–4v. Philip to Cardinal-Infante, Madrid, 30 August 1639.
[77] Ibid., fo. 74.

Sluis, was for Rheinberg. Should neither offensive seem feasible then the Cardinal-Infante was to try to recover the (only two) major strongholds the French had thus far managed to capture in the Spanish Netherlands – Landrecies and Hesdin (taken in 1639).

The Cardinal-Infante replied, from Dunkirk, on 7 October, in a less than optimistic tone. He was dismayed by the emperor's decision to recall Piccolomini and his troops, due to the revival of Swedish power and Swedish advances in Silesia and Saxony, remarking that 'if he goes, it will be a miracle if Your Majesty does not lose these states in the coming year'.[78] But should the emperor relent, and imperialist support be forthcoming, then there would be the possibility of an early offensive. He firmly ruled out, however, any attack on the Somme line, explaining that this year large French forces had gone into winter quarters near enough to the Somme to react quickly to any surprise thrust.[79] It would be too dangerous to attempt any of the French towns specified in Madrid. If he were to invade France, don Fernando suggested that Charleville-Mézières, far to the east, in the Meuse valley, a tiny independent sovereignty under the Nevers branch of the House of Gonzaga, would be both an easier, and safer, target and yet also one which would yield worthwhile strategic dividends. For, from there, Spanish troops would be able to bring the whole of the Champagne under threat of attack and render Rheims (a city which was not fortified) insecure. There was also the prospect, with the Spanish army operating in the area, that Louis, count of Soissons and other local malcontents might rise against their king.[80] Nevertheless, all considered, he and his advisers still thought it best to launch the offensive against the Dutch. For there were better, and more important, strategic gains to be made by thrusting to the north. Sluis, though, was definitely ruled out. 'What everyone here considers most suitable', he wrote, 'and I above all, is that we attempt Maastricht, because it is a place in the centre of these lands from where the Dutch range over Brabant, Luxemburg, Namur, Limburg and Geldern, raising contributions from the villages and unfortified places as much as they want, without our being able to stop it, something which causes much discontent in the land.'[81] Maastricht, he urged, would also be an excellent base from which to attack Grave and Rheinberg.

[78] Ibid., fo. 76. 'Copia de la respuesta que hico el señor Infante', Dunkirk, 7 October 1639.

[79] Ibid., fo. 77.

[80] On Soissons, see John H. Elliott, *Richelieu and Olivares* (Cambridge, 1984), pp. 89, 146.

[81] BL, Add. 14007, fo. 78: 'señor son tantas las razones que ay para librarse de una vez de este embarazo, que mi opinión es, deve precede el emprender esta plaza a todas las demas, y se podra yntentar con mucha facilidad en el tiempo que V.Magestad quiere, que se salga en campaña por la comodidad que havra en las prebenciones de todo...'

The basic pattern, and logic, of Spanish strategy in the Low Countries in the years 1635–9 was only finally broken by the (for Spain) catastrophic events of the year 1640. The Cardinal-Infante was unable to strike in March, partly owing to the late arrival of remittances from Spain but also because Piccolomini was withdrawn.[82] In May 1640, the Spanish Netherlands were invaded by both the French and the Dutch. The French set siege to Arras but, as in the previous year, the Cardinal-Infante had to give priority to the Dutch front, rather than the French,[83] so that no real effort was made to save Arras. Frederik Hendrik advanced cautiously from Flanders, probing the defences of Bruges. Finding no gap, he next tried to invest the Spanish forts facing Sluis and then attempted Hulst, each time being checked by Spanish counter-movements and a series of clashes. On 3 July 1640, the Frisian Stadholder, Hendrik Casimir, was killed in a fight on a redoubt near Hulst.

By this time, with the Cardinal-Infante boxed in between the French and the Dutch, Olivares and the king were confronted by a rapidly deteriorating situation both on the Italian front and in Catalonia. As disaster followed disaster, the year 1640 effectively removed all prospect of gaining the upper hand against the French or Dutch. Catalonia slid from sullen disobedience into open rebellion. On 7 June armed insurgents seized Barcelona and murdered the viceroy of Catalonia as he sought to escape, on the shore. Arras fell to the French on 9 August. On 24 September, the Catalan rebels officially requested a military alliance with the French king against the king of Spain.[84] Early in November, the victorious French entered Turin, re-establishing the authority of the pro-French claimant to the duchy, duchess Marie-Christine. Then, and most disastrous of all, on 1 December, a *coup d'état* toppled the Habsburg régime in Lisbon and all Portugal rose against the Spanish crown. To round off this catalogue of disaster, on 26 January 1641, a combined Catalan–French force decisively repulsed the Castilian army which Olivares and the king had sent to subdue Catalonia, at Montjuich, outside Barcelona.

Such massive setbacks as the rebellions of Catalonia and Portugal inevitably administered a severe shock to the entire Spanish monarchy and weakened it fundamentally. The strategic position of Spain was transformed and, in the following months, the standing and prestige of Spain were heftily marked down in all the capitals of Europe. Spain's enemies

---

[82] Elster, *Die Piccolomini-Regimenter*, pp. 70, 75.

[83] Waddington, *La République*, pp. 316–17.

[84] Elliott, *Revolt of the Catalans*, pp. 500–4

were encouraged by the spectacle to expect greater and more rapid gains at its expense, while many of Spain's friends and allies began to distance themselves from the court at Madrid which, in turn, further debilitated Philip IV's overall strategic position. Hitherto, one of Spain's most useful allies in the war with France had been duke Charles of Lorraine who, besides much else, had, as we have seen, played a major role in the campaigns in Burgundy in 1636. But Lorraine, from March 1641, entered into dealings with Richelieu and even though the duke subsequently played something of a double game he had, from this point on, to be largely discounted as an ally of Spain.[85]

But what strategy did Spain now adopt? Just as one would expect, Madrid's initial response was to raise armies in the peninsula and seek to crush the rebels as swiftly as possible. Owing to its proximity to France, priority had to be given to the Catalan front so that while repeated efforts to subdue Catalonia failed, no significant pressure was exerted on Portugal.[86] Hence, as the year 1641 unfolded, Olivares and the king had to decide whether now to divert most of Spain's military spending, and its best troops, from Flanders, giving priority to the new Iberian fronts, or continue with the old strategy of concentrating Spain's military muscle in the Netherlands. No one at the Spanish Habsburg court was in any doubt as to the extreme seriousness of the situation they now faced in the Iberian peninsula. Nothing was plainer than that the French would do their upmost to exploit the gaps which had opened up in Spain's defences, bolstering both rebellions and especially that of the Catalans.

Yet it was precisely because the Spanish monarchy was in such a dangerous conjuncture that Olivares and the king re-affirmed their strategy of keeping their principal army, their best troops and the bulk of their military spending in the south Netherlands.[87] The remittances sent from Madrid to the Spanish Netherlands in the years 1640–2 were indeed astonishingly high, among the largest ever seen.[88] It was not until the year 1643 that the adverse impact of the Catalan and Portuguese revolts on the monarchy's fortunes was reflected in a serious reduction in the flow of royal funds to

[85] Waddington, *La République*, I, p. 330.
[86] Elliott, *The count-duke of Olivares*, pp. 604, 612, 635–7.
[87] Israel, 'Olivares and the government of the Spanish Netherlands', pp. 186–7.
[88] Ibid.; according to official figures recorded in Brussels, the royal treasury in the Spanish Netherlands received 4,746,000 ducats from Spain in 1640, almost as much in 1641 and only somewhat less in 1642, with a large drop in 1643: see Rafael Valladares Ramirez, 'La peninsula y Europa. Los Habsburgos españoles y la alianza anglo-portuguesa (1640–1670)' (doctoral thesis, University of Madrid, 1992), p. 129.

Flanders. Even after the catastrophe at Rocroi, the official strength of the army of Flanders, as late as December 1643, was still 77,517 men.[89]

It was basic to Spain's European strategy in the years 1641–3 to use its principal military bastion to exert such pressure on France as to prevent Louis XIII and Richelieu sending the bulk of their forces to Catalonia and other southern fronts. What had changed fundamentally is that there was now no longer any question of giving priority, at least as regards offensive action, to the Dutch war. From the summer of 1640 onwards there was no more talk, in Madrid or Brussels, of besieging Maastricht, Sluis or Rheinberg, securing northern Brabant, or compelling the Dutch to relinquish their conquests in Brazil. Henceforth, the point of concentrating Spain's military might in the Low Countries was to pose a convincing strategic threat to France and, by this means to thwart the French offensive in southern Europe. The Spanish monarchy was now in a desperate plight. Yet the army of Flanders was still an impressive force. In a memorandum which he wrote at Douai, in October 1640, Miguel de Salamanca could still, with some justification, list the superior 'valour and military experience' of Spain's officers and soldiers in the Netherlands as a major strategic asset in the war against the French.[90]

In the years 1641–2 both the Catalan and Portuguese revolts prospered. French intervention was slowly stepped up. In the spring of 1642, a powerful French army reached Lérida from where it proceeded to invade Aragon, capturing Monzón in June. On 10 September 1642, the key Spanish border fortress town of Perpignan surrendered to its French besiegers. On 7 October, a combined Catalan–French army decisively defeated the Castilian counter-offensive at Lérida.

Logistical difficulties, inexperienced troops, lack of up-to-date fortifications and sheer incompetence all contributed to the repeated failures of Spanish arms in Catalonia, Aragon and against Portugal.[91] As defeat followed defeat and humiliation was heaped on humiliation, it became ever plainer that the only feasible way to redeem the honour and *reputación* of Spain and its king, raise morale in Castile and at court, and restore Spain's standing in Europe both strategically and diplomatically was to strike into France from Flanders. It is thus a mistake to view Olivares' refusal to concentrate Spain's military might within the peninsula as misplaced obstinacy. Given the overall situation, it made good strategic sense to preserve the army of Flanders and keep it where it was.

[89] Geoffrey Parker, *The Army of Flanders and the Spanish Road, 1567–1659* (Cambridge, 1972), p. 272.
[90] BL, Add. 14007, fo. 100.   [91] Elliott, *The count-duke of Olivares*, pp. 635–8.

The Cardinal-Infante having been carried off by smallpox in November 1641, at the age of 39, the destiny of the army, and of the Spanish Netherlands, lay in the hands of his successor as governor-general, don Francisco de Melo, soon to become marquis of Tordelaguna. He was in no doubt as to what was expected of him. Philip IV and Olivares instructed Melo to take the field early in 1642 and stay on campaign for as long as he could, making the 'greatest effort possible in the Netherlands to divert (the French king) from his design' of pouring his armies into Spain and Italy.[92] He was to be helped in his task by the imperialists, whose approach on the Lower Rhine sufficed to cover Geldern (which Frederik Hendrik was still endeavouring to take) and force the Dutch to spend the summer fruitlessly shielding Rheinberg and Orsoy. For much of the summer Melo thus had a fairly free hand. He was also given exceptionally wide powers to determine strategy and make decisions.[93]

His original plan was to invade France and try to penetrate to the Somme; but finding his path blocked, he advanced westwards from Douai to attack the French garrisons in Artois.[94] He recaptured Lens on 19 April and then besieged the important fortress of La Bassée. The 2,400 survivors of its original 3,000 man garrison surrendered on 11 May. Melo next marched, via Inchy, to tackle two French armies approaching from the south. He succeeded in surprising and inflicting a heavy defeat on the 'army of Champagne', under the maréchal de Guiche, on 26 May, at Honnecourt. The French reportedly lost over 4,000 casualties killed and wounded and another 3,000 men taken prisoner. Enthusiasts in the Spanish Netherlands ranked the battle the best Spanish victory since Nördlingen. Guiche himself escaped but Melo captured all his artillery and banners and twenty-two marquises, counts and barons. The army of Flanders next blockaded the French garrison at Landrecies but then had to march far to the east to meet another threat. By September, though, Melo was back at La Bassée with his full field army and from there he recovered and fortified Bouchain, Lillers and Aire.[95] In all, he was in the field for seven months, throwing his whole strength into harassing French garrisons and the French border, pursuing a strategy which had not, at any time, been pursued in the years 1635–40.

But the very success of the army of Flanders' campaign of 1642 lured it to disaster. For it lulled Melo into a false sense of his, and his army's,

92 Juan Antonio Vincart, 'Relación de la campaña de 1642', in *Colección de documentos inéditos*, LIX, pp. 118–19.
93 González de León, 'The road to Rocroi', p. 172.
94 Vincart, 'Relación de la campaña de 1642', pp. 120–6; Lonchay, *La rivalité*, pp. 101–2.
95 Vincart, 'Relación de la Campaña de 1642', pp. 195–6, 201.

capability and exerted an immense pressure on him to perform similar feats in 1643. Olivares ensured that he had even wider powers than before.[96] Within the Iberian peninsula the Spanish crown was now in desperate straits. The governor-general of the Spanish Netherlands had the money and troops and was now the only Spanish commander with the means to deliver the French a stinging blow. His strategy in 1643 was to invade France, in full force, via the valley of the Oise.[97] Advancing from Namur, with 17,000 men, he crossed into France and set siege to Rocroi. But expecting to capture the town in a few days and supposing Condé, with his relief army, to be further away than he was, he simply encamped around its walls without digging elaborate entrenchments, and erecting the siege fortifications used for a full-scale siege.[98] It was to prove a fatal error. Condé arrived on the scene, on 19 May, with some 23,000 men, and at once advanced to attack. The army of Flanders just had time to draw up in battle formation. The ensuing battle lasted six hours for much of which the outcome hung in the balance. Finally some of the non-Spanish contingents of the army of Flanders wavered and broke. The day ended with the core of the army, the proud Spanish veterans, being cut down where they stood.

Rocroi marked the end of an era, destroying the reputation of the army of Flanders for invincibility in the field. The bulk of Melo's high-grade troops were killed or captured. But the wider significance of the battle can only be properly grasped if it is viewed in the context of the new and peculiarly difficult strategic situation in which Spain found herself following the revolts of Catalonia and Portugal. The disaster resulted from attempting to strike hard into France at a time of overall military weakness, a strategy for which there was mounting pressure, from Madrid, on the governor-general of the Spanish Netherlands in the early 1640s. But this should be regarded as an entirely new phenomenon which arose only after, and as a consequence of, the catastrophic developments of 1640. Throughout the earlier phase of the Franco-Spanish conflict (1635–40) very different strategic priorities had prevailed leading, in the main, to a concentration of Spain's offensive power not against France but against the Dutch.

Finally, Rocroi marked the end not only of a legend but also of a strategic phase. For after 1643, it was no longer possible for Spain to launch an offensive from the Spanish Netherlands into France – not even, to any significant extent, when France in turn was gravely weakened, in the years

[96] González de León, 'The road to Rocroi', pp. 173, 208–9.
[97] Lonchay, *La rivalité*, p. 114.
[98] Henri d'Orléans, duc d'Aumâle, *Histoire des princes de Condé pendant les XVIe et XVIIe siècles* (Paris, 1889–96), IV, pp. 66, 79–80.

1648–53, by the Frondes. Yet Rocroi by no means ended the Spanish Netherlands' role as Spain's principal military bastion and base. This the region was to continue to be for another sixteen years, until the conclusion of the great war with France, in 1659.

5

Art and Diplomacy: Gerard Ter Borch and the Münster Peace Negotiations, 1646–8

Gerard Ter Borch (1617–81), one of the greatest artists of the Dutch Golden Age, was also, as a German exhibition catalogue expressed it, 'der einzige holländische Maler von Rang im 17. Jahrhundert, der längere Zeit in Westfalen gelebt und hier bedeutende Werke geschaffen hat (the only Dutch painter of standing who lived for any length of time in Westphalia and executed some significant works here).[1] He travelled to Münster at the end of 1645, or in January 1646, possibly as part of the entourage of Adriaen Pauw, Holland's plenipotentiary at the Münster peace talks, certainly in connection with Pauw's pending arrival.[2] Very likely Ter Borch had been commissioned beforehand to come to Münster in order to paint the large (98.5 × 158 cm.) and remarkable picture depicting Pauw's diplomatic entry, seated with his wife and child in a six-horse carriage, which was painted at Münster, early in 1646, and which hangs today in the Stadtmuseum in Münster.

The European peace congress in Münster and Osnabrück during the years 1645 to 1648 was beyond question an unprecedented, and unparalleled, episode in European history. Not only was this on account of the number of European powers, greater and lesser, represented at the twin gatherings, and the importance of the statecraft practised and agreements signed there, but also as a European cultural event. Münster in those years was nothing less than a vast theatre of statecraft in which Europe's princely courts and republics displayed their status, legitimacy, and pretensions to grandeur, and rivalled each other in splendour, and the quest for *reputación*, as well as diplomatic finesse.

Given this special context, Münster and Osnabrück were bound to be, for several years, the stage of Europe, the chief arena of prestige, statecraft, and ambassadorial splendour of every sort, including décor, fine cuisine and art from all over Europe. In particular, given Münster's location between the Low Countries and a Germany devastated by war, for the choicest manufactures and arts of the two Netherlands — north and south. Diplomats, their families and supporting staff converged in droves from all over Germany, France, Italy, Spain and the Netherlands. This mass of dignitaries together with their households,

---

[1] Exhibition catalogue, *Gerard Ter Borch*, published by the Landesmuseum für Kunst und Kulturgeschichte (Münster, 1974), p. 11.

[2] S.J. Gudlaugsson, *Geraert Ter Borch* (2 vols, The Hague, 1959–60), i, p. 51; idem, 'Gerard Ter Borch, 1617–1681', in the catalogue *Gerard Ter Borch*, p. 20.

servants, cooks, coachmen, lawyers, chaplains, medical staff, tailors, confection-
ers and guards had an immense impact on the city. The population of Münster
which, in the early 1640s, stood at around 11,000, increased during the period
of the European peace congress, between 1645 and late 1648, by between three
and four thousand.[3] Including every conceivable category of staff, the French
establishment alone was reported to exceed a thousand people.[4]

Of course France and Spain, as the two pre-eminent powers of Europe, felt
obliged to stage a more resplendent show than other powers. The chief Spanish plenipotentiary, Don Gaspar de Bracamonte y Guzmán, conde de Peñaranda,
was sick and in great discomfort when he arrived in Münster, from Brussels via
Antwerp, on 5 July 1645, and implored the city's burgomasters to keep the entry
ceremonies to an absolute minimum. But even this involved artillery salvoes,
the Münster civic militia being brought out on parade, and a considerable procession of coaches, guards and other riders attired in splendid costume. Once
established in Münster, Peñaranda resided in style in the Franciscan friary with
his twenty pages, a dozen halberdiers, two dozen footmen and lackeys, eighteen
gentlemen companions and *gentiles-hombres*, and a mere seven coaches, six of
them large, fitted to take the special ambassadorial six-horse teams.[5] Peñaranda's
household amounted to 150 persons. But, as he himself pointed out in a report
to Madrid, the Spanish establishment in Münster positively paled by comparison
with the French establishment, headed by Henri d'Orleans, duc de Longueville,
one of the most illustrious *seigneurs* of France, who had arrived in Münster a
few days before his Spanish counterpart, having shipped great quantities of
furniture and domestic staff down the Meuse and transported it all to Münster
via Venlo. Longueville had with him a dozen parade archers, as well as a dozen
halberdiers, and a guard of twenty-five cavalry, besides pages and lackeys too
numerous to mention. The splendour of the French presence in Münster reached
its height, however, during the months from July 1646 to March 1647 when the
duke's beautiful young wife, the prince of Condé's sister, the brilliant and politically ambitious Anne-Geneviève de Bourbon-Condé, madame de Longueville
(1619–79), was also resident in Münster.[6] Anne-Geneviève, who was later to
play a not inconsiderable role in the Frondes, and was to emerge as one of
Cardinal Mazarin's foremost enemies, was reputed to have had numerous lovers and to be one of the most impressive, as well as attractive, of the chief ladies
of the French court. Certainly she was the first lady of the Münster peace congress.
Her arrival was celebrated with a stream of receptions and banquets. During

---

[3] Hans Gelen (ed.), exhibition catalogue, *Münster, 800–1800: 1000 Jahre Geschichte der Stadt*
(Münster, 1984), p. 258. The names of 184 ambassadors and envoys who resided in Münster and
Osnabrück during the years of the peace congress are known, 111 of these being the representatives of German princes and Imperial Free Cities, see Fritz Dickmann, *Der Westfälische Frieden* (Münster,
1972), p. 193.

[4] Peñaranda to Pedro Coloma, Münster, 11 July 1645. *Colección de documentos inéditos para la
historia de España* (CODOIN), lxxxii, p. 89.

[5] Ibid.

[6] Dickmann, *Westfälische Frieden*, p. 196; Galen, *Münster*, pp. 272, 290.

these months, her portrait was painted by the Flemish artist Anselmus van Hulle, who had come to Münster specially to exploit the artistic opportunities offered by the occasion. The engraving made from Van Hulle's portrait was later published, accompanied by a caption proclaiming her 'beautés' and 'doux attrais' and suggesting that her gorgeous looks summoned up the very image of 'concord and peace' which the assembled diplomats were so assiduously in search of.[7]

All reports confirm that jewellery, tapestries, silverware, medals and gold chains were not only constantly on display but often passed from hand to hand as part of the diplomatic round. Very likely even most of this glitter was on the modest side compared with the handsome bribes which key plenipotentiaries offered to leading figures among those with whom they had to negotiate. In such a milieu there were also excellent opportunities for skilled artists to find work which was not only well paid but also socially rewarding, and which brought them to the margins of high society and the diplomatic whirl.

Since there were no resident artists of any importance there before 1645, it is surprising neither that a number of artists should have converged on Münster in, and around, that year, nor that all of these seem to have come from the Low Countries.[8] Among them was Van Hulle (1594–1673), who came from Ghent but had worked in the northern as well as southern Netherlands, who seems to have come to Münster, at least in part, on behalf of the Dutch Stadholder, Frederik Hendrik. Also present were the Haarlem artist Pieter Holsteijn (1614–87) and the industrious, if mediocre, Antwerp artist Jan Baptista Floris, who, having worked with Van Hulle, was commissioned by the Münster city government to supply thirty-four portraits of leading diplomats at the peace congress. In 1649 these pictures were mounted on the walls of the council chamber in the city hall. But by far the greatest artist to participate in the proceedings, a painter who was indeed one of the finest of the Dutch Golden Age, was Gerard Ter Borch (1677–1681). Besides being a great artist, Ter Borch, who while at Münster painted portraits and other pictures involving members of at least three of the principal diplomatic contingents, was undoubtedly also one of the best known, and most discussed, artists working in the city during the peace congress.

However, it was probably not Ter Borch but Van Hulle to whom accrued the the most prestige during the proceedings. While at Münster, Van Hulle painted many dozens, possibly more than a hundred, portraits of officials and diplomats which were afterwards copied as engravings by Paul Pontius, Pieter de Jode and Cornelis Galle, all well-known Antwerp engravers, and published together, as a magnificent set, at Antwerp in 1648, with expanded editions in later years.[9] The most complete series of Van Hulle's portraits was published half a century later, at Rotterdam in 1697, under the title *Pacificatores orbis Christiani sive icones*

[7] See the published engraving of Anselmus van Hulle, portrait of Anne de Bourbon, duchesse de Longueville; Galen, *Münster*, p. 271.

[8] Gudlaugsson, *Geraert Ter Borch*, i, p. 56; C.J.A. Genders, 'De bevestiging van de Vrede van Munster 1648 door Gerard Ter Borch', *Spiegel Historiael*, 8 (1973), p. 643.

[9] Galen, *Münster*, p. 259.

principium, ducum et legatorum, qui Monasterii atque Osnabrugae pacem Europae reconciliarunt. Among the most striking of Van Hulle's portraits, was his superb picture — there is a copy of the engraving in the Münster Stadtmuseum — of the papal representative Fabio Chigi (1599–1667), who had been one of the first important diplomats to arrive in Münster (March 1644) and who, with his entourage of fifteen, stayed longer than almost any other, until December 1649. Chigi was a famous art lover and connoisseur of classical literature and philosophy as well as one of the most polished conversationalists gathered in the city.[10] Another notable portrait of Van Hulle's was that of Count Maximilian von Trauttmansdorff (1584–1650), representative of the emperor, Ferdinand III, who stayed only a year and a half in Münster, from the end of 1645 until the summer of 1647, but who had a huge impact on the proceedings by making offers to the French which laid the basis for a separate Franco-Austrian peace, splitting asunder the traditional Habsburg family alliance between the emperor and Spain.[11]

Initially, Ter Borch's artistic activity in Münster was confined to the Dutch diplomatic delegation. His painting depicting Pauw's arrival and entry into Münster was one of the artist's largest, as well as most important, pictures and has a definite political significance.[12] A crucial feature of the diplomatic context, at this juncture, was that the Spanish crown as well as the emperor — and the international community generally — were now ready to recognize the free and sovereign status of the United Provinces unconditionally. This implied that the European powers, including Spain, recognized the Dutch plenipotentiaries as full ambassadors of a sovereign power with all the immunities and privileges which that status bestowed. The reception of the Dutch plenipotentiaries in Münster, on their arrival, was thus a key scene in the drama played out at Münster and presaged the momentous concession, signalled on the very first day of the Spanish-Dutch peace negotiations, the 16 January 1646, when Peñaranda delivered a stirring address, in Latin, calling on both sides, to lay aside the animosities of the past and labour together in the noble task of creating a sound and lasting peace.[13] He announced that Philip IV acknowledged the United Provinces as free and sovereign provinces.

If the arrival of the Dutch plenipotentiaries marked the commencement of a new era in the Dutch Republic's European standing, they made no attempt to stage a common entry. Ter Borch's picture, presumably privately commissioned by Pauw himself, is concerned only with the arrival of Holland's plenipotentiary seated in a six-horse carriage — the right to ride in such a carriage was one of the best-known prerogatives of ambassadorial status. Pauw belonged to an Amsterdam regent family and thus, unlike the other Dutch plenipotentiaries, was not a nobleman. Since all the other full ambassadors at

[10] Ibid., pp. 266–7.
[11] Dickmann, *Westfälische Frieden*, pp. 195–6.
[12] Exhibition catalogue, *Gerard Ter Borch*, pp. 68–9.
[13] J.I. Israel, *The Dutch Republic and the Hispanic World, 1606–1661* (Oxford, 1982), p. 360.

Münster were nobles, and Pauw alone was a non-noble representing a republic, his position was a visibly exceptional and delicate one. While Ter Borch's painting does not attempt to depict him as if he were a noble, it does imply that, as Holland's representative, Pauw possessed all the prestige and dignity of the most aristocratic of his colleagues at the peace congress. Ter Borch highlights the ambiguity of the 'entry' by contrasting Pauw's deliberately sober attire, the costume of a Dutch burgher, with the brilliance of the setting and splendid outfits of the accompanying coachmen and guards. Although, in reality, the event took place in the bleakness of January, when there would have been no leaves on the trees, Ter Borch made full use of the bright spring light and exuberance of foliage, prevailing at the time, in the spring of 1646, when he was actually working on the picture, to enhance its impact.

Yet while Ter Borch's arrival in Münster, and his initial activity there, was clearly linked to the appearance on the scene of the Dutch delegation, there is no indication that he was employed in any formal capacity by the Dutch plenipotentiaries.[14] Rather his artistic activity in Münster seems to have grown out of the contacts which he made there and from his own initiatives. Certainly, he painted no more pictures depicting the Dutch representatives in any kind of official capacity. Indeed, at no point does he appear to have received any official commission from the States General or the States of Holland or any other Dutch authority.

The milling concourse of members of diplomatic delegations found themselves pressed together, within the confines of what normally was a small provincial city with no princely court, university, local school of artists or literary society, not just for months but for several years. This meant that virtually all the high culture which was suddenly required — books, rareties, antiquities, pastimes, high-brow entertainment of every description — had to be imported from outside; also that familiarity with languages, and an ability to talk well about literature and the arts, was in constant, and heavy, demand. It meant as well that polished individuals with the travel experience, knowledge of culture, and the linguistic ability to serve as intermediaries of an informal kind, creating links between the delegations, were a valued asset. An obvious example of such a cultural intermediary was the young Caspar van Kinschot (1622–49), who though only twenty-three years of age was chosen to accompany the Dutch delegation in 1645, in part owing to his legal expertise, and the prominence of his family in administrative circles, in The Hague, but also because of his fluency in French, his skill in conversation, and renown as a neo-Latin poet. The treasurer of the French delegation described Van Kinschot in his diary as a 'jeune homme de la Haye qui promet beaucoup de soi par ses poesies latines et par la connaissance qu'il a des belles lettres'.[15] His Latin poems, under the title *Poemata* were later published, many years after his premature death, in 1685. One of those with whom Van Kinschot formed a close friendship, whilst he was at Münster, was

[14] Gudlaugsson, *Geraert Ter Borch*, i, p. 51.
[15] Ibid., i, p. 59.

the papal delegate, Chigi, who was later to become Pope Alexander VII (pope, 1655–67), and who was also to be one of the three greatest papal art patrons of the High Baroque era, along with Urban VIII Barberini (1623–44) and Innocent X Pamphili (1644–55).[16] Chigi indeed was a lover of art as well as literature who in the 1650s and 1660s was to transform the artistic and architectural face of Rome, not least by providing the crucial support which made possible the realization of Bernini's great project for the *piazza* of Saint Peter's.

Van Kinschot was one of the personalities of the Dutch delegation whose portrait Ter Borch painted during the months after his completion of the picture depicting Pauw's entry. This tiny miniature (11 × 8 cm.) survives today in the collection of his family's descendants. Van Kinschot died, probably from consumption, the year after the conclusion of the peace congress and it has been plausibly argued that the young man's portrait as it appears on the great painting of the ratification ceremony (see illustration no. 10), where he looks pale and thin, shows the impact of the disease.[17] He does indeed look more robust on the earlier picture which was probably painted in 1646 or 1647. On the great picture, Van Kinschot is standing between, and slightly behind, Holland's two plenipotentiaries — Pauw and the nobleman Johan van Mathenesse — both depicted with their right hands uplifted, to whom he had served as assistant.

Among the other miniature portraits painted by Ter Borch at Münster during 1646 and 1647 were his painting of Adriaen Pauw (see illustration no. 8), a picture subsequently used by Pieter Holsteijn to produce a portrait engraving of Pauw in two different versions,[18] and paintings of Anna van Ruytenburgh who was Pauw's wife, and who accompanied him to Münster; of the Groningen plenipotentiary, Adriaen Clant van Stedum (1599–1655) 15 × 11 cm.), which hangs today in the Groningen city museum; of the Utrecht plenipotentiary Godard van Reede, heer van Nederhorst (1588–1648) (15 × 11 cm.), a noble who opposed Pauw's efforts to settle all the disagreements with Spain, and to distance the Dutch delegation from the French, and became a tool of Mazarin's diplomacy,[19] a personality whose portrait was also painted by Holsteijn; and a portrait of the Reformed preacher, Eleazer Lootius, who acted as chaplain to the Dutch contingent at Münster.

By the beginning of 1647, Ter Borch had also made contacts within the French delegation and not least with its nominal leader, the duc de Longueville, who had little liking for Mazarin and who was attempting to negotiate in earnest with Spain.[20] The duke commissioned Ter Borch to paint an equestrian portrait

---

[16] Exhibition catalogue, *Gerard Ter Borch*, pp. 76–7.

[17] Ibid., pp. 76–7.

[18] Ibid., p. 64. Holsteyn also rendered a complimentary engraving of Pauw's wife; Pauw also had his portrait painted by Van Hulle and which in turn was rendered into an engraving by Paul Pontius, signed and dated 1648, Galen, *Münster*, p. 192.

[19] Israel, *Dutch Republic and the Hispanic World*, pp. 370–3.

[20] Dickmann, *Westfälische Frieden*, p. 478; O. Ranum, *The Fronde: A French Revolution, 1648–1652* (New York, 1993), p. 192.

of himself wearing a sumptuous gold-embroidered blouse and seated on a gold-embossed saddle, a picture which from 1867 to 1980 belonged to the New York Historical Society but which hangs today in the Stadtmuseum in Münster. The duke himself is splendidly rendered, complete with an aristocratic, rather supercilious, smile. He was not pleased, apparently, to find himself portrayed, in the original version, astride a somewhat stolid Dutch mount instead of an elegant Arabian thoroughbred. The duke, who was a connoisseur of horsemanship and had brought two dozen horses with him to Münster, obliged the artist to to correct his *faux pas*.[21] In altering the picture, Ter Borch ran into evident problems with his proportions, resulting in a certain ungainliness which occurred again, somewhat after the same fashion: two years later, in 1649, he undertook a second grand equestrian portrait of an illustrious personage, this time of the Elector Karl Ludwig (son of the 'Winter King and Queen', Frederick of Bohemia and Elizabeth Stuart, daughter of Charles I of England), who at that juncture had emerged as one of the major beneficiaries of the Münster peace treaties and, with the acquiescence of Spain and the Emperor, had recovered possession of the Rhenish Palatinate. The posture of Karl Ludwig in the later picture, which hangs today in the city museum at Mannheim, is indeed in every respect reminiscent of that of Longueville in the earlier painting.

Ter Borch was an artist who had travelled widely in his earlier years, mastering several languages besides his native Dutch, in particular Spanish, and who would seem to have been consciously using the exceptional context of the Münster peace congress to enhance his personal social status as well as to find commissions. During his years at Münster, he developed into a kind of court painter or, at any rate, a painter of greater and lesser aristocrats. An essential ingredient in his success in becoming a cultural intermediary, contributing to the interaction between the delegations, as well as in obtaining commissions, was precisely his earlier travels around Europe. Unfortunately, relatively little is known about these other than the fact that in 1635–6 he spent a period in England and that, during the late 1630s, he spent long periods in France and Italy as well as in Spain.[22]

In any case, it is certain that, during the latter part of his stay in Münster, Ter Borch had far fewer dealings than previously with the Dutch delegation. He joined the entourage of the conde de Peñaranda, spending a good deal of time with the Spaniards inhabiting the Franciscan friary, and came to be counted, for ceremonial purposes, as one of the conde's *gentileshombres*.[23] Besides the fact that Ter Borch's later artistic activity in Münster was chiefly concerned with

---

[21] Gudlaugsson, *Geraert Ter Borch*, i, p. 59; Galen, *Münster*, pp. 290–1; Longueville was also painted by Van Hulle, from which an engraving was prepared by Paulus Pontius and published at Antwerp in 1648.

[22] Gudlaugsson, *Geraert Ter Borch*, i, p. 38; Gudlaugsson, 'Gerard Ter Borch', pp. 19–20. McNeil Kettering considers that Ter Borch's journies to Italy and Spain took place over a roughly two-year period between late 1636 and 1639, see A. McNeil Kettering, *Drawings from the Ter Borch Studio Estate in the Rijksmuseum* (2 vols, The Hague, 1988), i, p. 86.

[23] Gudlaugsson, *Geraert Ter Borch*, i, pp. 60–2, 68–9.

members, or associates, of the Spanish delegation, and the remarkable circumstance that he portrayed himself on the extreme left-hand side of the gathering, in his great picture of the ratification of the Dutch-Spanish peace, dressed in Spanish court costume, there are also two references to this special episode in his life in the surviving documents preserved by Ter Borch's family. In one of her poems, the painter's gifted sister, Gesina Ter Borch, refers to him as an 'edelman int Spaansche hof van den graef van Penerande . . . int jaer 47' (nobleman in the Spanish court of the count of Peñaranda . . . in the year 1647).[24] In a poem written by his friend, the Zwolle schoolmaster, Joost Hermans Roldanus (c. 1595–1682), his stay in Spain is mentioned and he is again referred to as a Spanish courtier.[25] That Ter Borch became one of Peñaranda's *gentileshombres* points not only to a high level of sophistication, courtly manners and a knowledge of Spanish but also almost certainly to a high degree of sympathy for, if not outright allegiance to, the Catholic faith.[26]

Ter Borch executed a number of important pictures during this latter phase of his activity in Münster. In the first place, leaving aside for the moment his great picture of the ratification ceremony, there is his scintillating miniature portrait (10.5 × 9 cm.) of Peñaranda which hangs today in the Museum Boymans-Van Beuningen in Rotterdam (see illustration no. 9). This tiny masterpiece depicts the highly intelligent and aristocratic but delicate and constantly ailing count wearing a Spanish collar (*golilla*) and a silver-studded Spanish court costume powerfully conveying his sophistication, self-control, sensitivity, dignified bearing and suppressed irritability. It has been asserted with every justification that 'unter allen Miniaturen die Ter Borch je gemalt hat ist es gewiss die allerschönste' (Of all the miniatures that Ter Borch ever painted it is undoubtedly the most beautiful of all).[27] Another fine miniature portrait of this period is that of Hugo Eberhard Kratz, Graf von Scharfenstein (1610–63), envoy to the Münster peace congress of the archbishop-elector of Mainz, a diplomat who was regarded as anti-French and pro-Spanish and who played a significant role as an intermediary in the Dutch-Spanish negotiations at Münster.[28] In the picture of the ratification ceremony, Ter Borch includes him together with the Spanish party, standing in the front row, third from the right. In the Franco-Spanish struggle for influence in the electorate of Trier and bishopric of Speyer during the next few years, Scharfenstein as 'archdeacon' of the chapter of Trier played a large part in building the ascendancy of the 'Spanish' party. A report to Mazarin, of March

[24] Genders, 'Bevestiging van de Vrede van Munster', p. 645.

[25] Gudlaugsson, *Geraert Ter Borch*, i, p. 38; and ii, pp. 9, 23–4.

[26] One of the hints, in my view, is the prominent way Ter Borch has rendered the Madonna hanging from the ceiling in the city hall where the ratification ceremony took place.

[27] Gudlaugsson, *Geraert Ter Borch*, i, p. 61; F. Hannema, *Gerard Terborch* (Amsterdam, 1943), p. 71.

[28] Gudlaugsson, *Geraert Ter Borch*, i, p. 62; Genders, 'Bevestiging van de Vrede van Munster', p. 645.

1. The Marquis Ambrogio Spínola (1569–1630). Portrait by Peter Paul Rubens, painted after the successful conclusion of his siege of Breda in 1625. (*Herzog Anton-Ulrich Museum, Braunschweig*)

2. The Archduke Albert of Austria (1559–1621), with the palace of Tervuren in the background. Portrait by Peter Paul Rubens with background and flowers attributed to Jan Bruegel. (*Museo del Prado, Madrid*)

3. View of the palace of Tervuren by Jan Bruegel. (*Museo del Prado, Madrid*)

4. The Archduchess Isabel Clara Eugenia (1566–1633, with the palance of Mariemont in the background. Portrait by Peter Paul Rubens; background by Jan Bruegel. (*Museo del Prado, Madrid*)

5. The palace of Coudenberg (ducal palace) in Brussels.

6. Allegory of Sight and Smell by Jan Bruegel. Note the monkeys studying Hieronymous Bosch's *Temptation of Saint Antony*, in the foreground, the portrait of Charles the Bold in the lower centre and, on the table to the right, a small double portrait of Albert and Isabella in Spanish costume. (*Museo del Prado, Madrid*)

7. A ball at the court of Albert and Isabella in 1611. Painting by Frans Francken the Younger and François Pourbus the Younger. (*Mauritshius, The Hague*)

8. Adrien Pauw (1585–1653), pleni-potentiary of the province of Holland at the Münster Peace Congress in the years 1645–48. Portait by Gerard Ter Borch.

9. Don Gaspar de Bracamonte y Guzmán, conde de Peñaranda (1596–1676), Spanish plenipotentiary at the Münster Peace Congress. Portrait by Gerard Ter Borch. (*Museum Boymans-Van Beuningen, Rotterdam*)

10. The oath-taking ceremony of the Dutch–Spanish peace in the Münster Town Hall on 15 May 1648. Signed G. T. Borch, F. Monasterij A. 1648. The sickly-looking youth left-centre is Caspar van Kinschot; to his left, with the beard, is Adrian Pauw; next, on the left, also with his hand uplifted, is Adrian Clant van Stedum, plenipotentiary of Groningen;

behind him, with a beard and fingers uplifted, is Frans van Donia, the Frisian representative; next to him, hand uplifted, William Ripperda, representative of Overijssel; at the extreme left, fixing the onlooker with his stare, is Gerard Ter Borch. (The National Gallery, London)

11. The siege of Jülich by the Spanish army of Flanders (September 1621 to February 1622). A large painting (144 × 236 cm) by Pieter Snayers for the Spanish court.

12. The surrender of Jülich to the Spanish army of Flanders.

1650, on the canons of the chapter of Trier, mentions Scharfenstein first among the 'mal intentionnés' towards France.[29] In 1654, he became bishop of Worms.

One of Ter Borch's undated pictures which hangs today in the National Gallery of Ireland, in Dublin, is a sizeable canvas (72 × 97 cm.) depicting four Franciscan friars which at one time was supposed by art historians to have been a product of Ter Borch's stay in Spain — not a single one of Ter Borch's surviving paintings can with any real justification be assigned to his Spanish period.[30] It is now thought to have been painted in the Franciscan friary in Münster at some point in 1647 or 1648. The oldest of the four friars has a book in his hand on the spine of which the word *enfermeros* is legible. This term, corresponding to 'male nurses', strongly suggests that these are the persons who cared for Peñaranda during his frequent bouts of sickness and that it was at his prompting that the painting was commissioned.[31] The most senior of the four, thought to be the prior of the Franciscan friary, is the eminent friar that Ter Borch includes, standing at the extreme right of the front row, behind the rest of the Spanish party, in his painting of the ratification ceremony.

Ter Borch's crowning artistic achievement at Münster — though considerably smaller than the painting of the four friars — is of course the picture showing the oath-swearing which marked the culmination of the formal ratification of the Spanish-Dutch peace, an event which took place on 15 May 1648. This great painting, which hangs today in the National Gallery in London, is of remarkably small size (45.5 × 58.5 cm.) for such an exceptionally complex group portrait. No less than seventy-five different figures of whom more than twenty can be identified today with a reasonable degree of certainty, including Van Kinschot, Lootius, Clant van Stedum, Pauw, Mathenesse, Scharfenstein, Antoine Brun (the Franche-Comtois who acted as Spain's second plenipotentiary and who, the following year, became the first Spanish ambassador to be posted to The Hague), Peñaranda and his two chaplains (Don Miguel López de Barnuevo and Diego Bahac), and, of course, Ter Borch himself, at the extreme left-hand edge.

The moment which Ter Borch records with such artistic virtuosity was the climax of the proceedings which had begun at 8 a.m. that morning when Antoine Brun arrived at the Münster city hall, accompanied by the secretary of the Spanish delegation, Don Pedro Fernández del Campoy Angulo (who must be one of the figures standing close to Peñaranda in the painting but who has not been positively identified), to inspect the elaborate decorations erected in, and around, the city hall and meet two of the Dutch plenipotentiaries in order to

[29] Georges Livet (ed.), *Recueil des instructions données aux ambassadeurs et ministres de France depuis les traités de Westphalie jusqu'à la Revolution française: les états allemands,* iii *L'electorat de Trèves* (Paris, 1966), pp. 21–4.

[30] Hannema, *Gerard Terborch,* p. 71; B. Haak, *The Golden Age: Dutch Painters of the Seventeenth Century* (London, 1984), p. 396.

[31] Gudlaugsson, *Geraert Ter Borch,* i, p. 61.

'collect and prepare all the papers'. The task of arranging on tables the various copies in French and Dutch of the treaty, of the plenipotentiaries' powers and authorizations, and of the deeds of ratification, checking that the translations corresponded and that all was in order reportedly 'took two hours'.[32] Next, the rest of the Dutch plenipotentiaries present in Münster arrived, with their entourages, after which everyone awaited the arrival of the main Spanish party, headed by Peñaranda. The city militia were drawn up in the open space and adjoining streets, which were also packed with onlookers.

Peñaranda's procession was headed by the first of his six-horse coaches, containing eight splendidly-attired *gentileshombres*, one of whom quite possibly was Ter Borch; followed by a second in which rode the Spanish delegation's secretary 'for languages', Antoine Richard, who later became secretary of the Spanish embassy in The Hague; the delegation's treasurer, Peñaranda's mayordomo, Captain Juan Baptista Berenquel, who is certainly one of the personages on Ter Borch's painting; and the conde's two chaplains.[33] Next came two trumpeters followed by twenty-four civilian employees, followed by twelve cavalry guards followed by Peñaranda's twelve Spanish halberdiers. Next came the captain of Peñaranda's guard, Don Gabriel del Aquila y Bracamonte, who in the painting is very likely the figure overlooking the scene, standing above the main mass of participants and looking down, protectively, on the count. After him came a third six-horse carriage in which Peñaranda rode alone, dressed in 'finest cloth of Amsterdam' in a dark colour embroidered with silver in the Spanish court fashion and adorned with 'red plumes and very rich jewels'.[34] The carriage was surrounded by fourteen glittering pages adorned with 'many plumes of various colours', as well as gold and silver embroidery on their costumes. The rest of the count's coaches and entourage followed.

With Peñaranda and his entourage inside the city hall, another half an hour passed while final signatures to documents were appended in a side room. Only after this did the entire body of those present ascend to the main hall, the setting for Ter Borch's painting. There were chairs only for the most important participants. When these were seated, Brun delivered a stirring oration with much 'elegance' and 'discretion' to which the plenipotentiary of Gelderland, the province which enjoyed formal precedence among the United Provinces, replied. Next the text of the peace treaty and deeds of ratification were read out in French, a language which many of those present can have understood only very imperfectly, after which copies of the treaty, encased in velvet-covered boxes with corners and clasps of silver (clearly visible in the painting), were exchanged. To lend cohesion to the picture, Ter Borch, in composing his painting, decided to remove most of the chairs that were in the room and placed

---

[32] Peñaranda to Philip IV, Münster, 18 May 1648, *CODOIN*, lxxxiv, p. 202.

[33] *Relación de la forma con que se han hecho las entregas de las ratificaciones de la paz de España y los Estados Generales de las Provincias Unidas, y de su publicación, que se celebró en la ciudad de Munster de Westfalia a 15 y 16 de Mayo de este año de 1648, CODOIN*, lxxxiv, pp. 210–11.

[34] Ibid., p. 212.

the group differently from how they had stood in reality, turning their faces towards the imaginary onlooker. As Ter Borch records, only Peñaranda and Brun swore to uphold the treaty 'on the part of His Majesty . . . with their hands on a cross and on the Gospel', the Dutch plenipotentiaries swearing in their fashion with their right hands raised, holding up two fingers. In reality, according to Peñaranda's account of the proceedings, he and Brun swore first, reading out their text, while the Dutch did so only after they had finished.[35] This indeed would have been more logical than swearing together, since the two texts which Ter Borch shows being held up by Peñaranda and the Gelderland plenipotentiary, Barthold van Gent, are hardly likely to have been read out simultaneously. Clearly, Ter Borch opted for the appearance of simultaneity again to lend cohesion and heighten the drama of the scene.

When this procedure was completed, the ambassadors of the two sides embraced each other 'con grandísimas demostraciones de amor, gusto, alegría y contento' (with great display of love, delight, joy and contentment) after which their assistants, gentlemen, guards and servants did likewise.[36] All this had taken five hours and it was now one in the afternoon. The companies of civic militia, which had been standing to attention for hours outside, now had their chance to fire off several volleys into the air with their muskets, interspersed with salvoes of artillery and mortar fire. At the 'palacio' of the conde de Peñaranda a fountain spurting different wines was set in motion and masses of people, many of them women, rushed forward to cup wine in their hands. The general fiesta which now began continued *incesamente* until nine in the evening.[37] Peñaranda's Flemish tapestries, meanwhile, were publicly displayed near the town hall.

The work involved in executing such an intricate painting as Ter Borch's rendering of the ratification ceremony, in what has ever since been known as the *Friedenssaal*, was enormous. Presumably, Ter Borch made sketches of the assembly on the day and sketches also of the portraits of those whom he had not previously painted but wanted to include, with a fair degree of accuracy, in the picture. The overall authenticity and exactitude that he achieved make his picture one of the most impressive, and fascinating, paintings of the entire Dutch Golden Age. The principal remaining puzzle connected with the picture is that of why it was not acquired by Peñaranda, on behalf of the Spanish crown, or alternatively, by the States General or States of Holland. The story that the artist simply demanded too high a price, asking the sum of 6,000 guilders for it, and thus found no purchaser, may provide the right answer, or perhaps Ter Borch simply preferred to keep the picture as a momento of the great event which he had witnessed. Peñaranda, who left Münster for Brussels, never to return, at the

---

[35] Peñaranda to Philip IV, Münster, 18 May 1648, *CODOIN*, lxxxiv, p. 202; both Peñaranda and the *Relación de la forma* confirm that the text of peace treaty was read out to the assembled gathering in French.

[36] *Relación de la forma*, p. 213.

[37] Ibid.

end of June 1648,[38] some six weeks after the ceremony of ratification, probably saw the painting in a near completed state before he left — there is a note in the diary of the papal delegate, Chigi, that he saw the completed painting on 9 July 1648.[39] This would seem to imply that Ter Borch himself was then still in Münster and that he had completed the great picture in a mere seven or eight weeks. The picture remained in the possession of Ter Borch himself, and then of various relatives, for several generations.

This does not mean that the wider world had no knowledge or awareness of Ter Borch's great masterpiece. On the contrary, the picture became widely known since the artist who was evidently proud of his achievement and conscious of its significance, commissioned an engraver, Jonas Suijderhoef, to reproduce the picture as an engraving, faithfully rendering the detail of the original, an engraving executed to a high standard which was subsequently published. Thanks to Suijderhoef's work, Ter Borch's magnificent representation of the ratification ceremony at Münster could be hung on the walls of major public buildings in the United Provinces and elsewhere.[40] The only slight change introduced in the engraving, presumably by agreement with Ter Borch, was that instead of Ter Borch's signature on the board affixed high on the wall to the left, the engraver substituted the adage — more sincerely propagated in republics perhaps than by rulers of early modern monarchies — 'Pax optima rerum'.

[38] On the eve of his departure, Peñaranda wrote to Don Luis de Haro, enclosing a copy of the medal which he and Jean Friquet had had designed and struck, at Münster, to celebrate the conclusion of the peace; see Peñaranda to Luis de Haro, Münster, 26 June 1648, *CODOIN*, lxxxiv, p. 303. The medal must have had a lengthy Latin inscription, since Peñaranda remarks that 'por acá ha parecido muy bien a los eruditos'. It may thus be the medal designed by Engelbert Ketteler, mintmaster of Münster, and issued there during 1648, see H. Galen (ed.), *Der Westfälische Frieden: Die Friedensfreude auf Münzen und Medaillen* (Münster, 1987), pp. 45–8.

[39] Chigi wrote, 'vedo la pittura della ratificatione della pace di Spagna con gli olandesi . . .', see Genders, 'Besetiging van de Vrede van Munster', p. 649.

[40] Ibid., p. 650.

6

Spain and Europe from the Peace of Münster to the Peace of the Pyrenees, 1648–59

A crucial episode in European history which has been curiously neglected by historians, despite its far-reaching ramifications for large parts of the continent, was the late resurgence of Spanish power and influence which began in 1648, with the onset of the Frondes in France, and which slowly gathered momentum during the years 1649–52 whilst the disturbances in France continued. This unexpected reassertion of something approaching Spanish hegemony in Europe then gradually receded during the mid 1650s, being only finally overthrown by the combined Anglo-French onslaught on the Spanish forces in Flanders in 1657–9. Momentarily, it seemed that Spain's old ascendancy, which had prevailed in much of Europe from the early sixteenth century down to the 1620s, was reviving. Admittedly, the foundations on which this belated recovery in Spain's fortunes and prestige were based were more than a little precarious. Nevertheless, it appears that between 1648 and 1656 there was a real possibility that the Spanish crown might succeed in imposing a very different kind of political order, and distribution of power, on western and southern Europe, than that which actually emerged in the wake of Spain's final defeat, in 1659, after which Europe experienced several decades of domination by an overtly absolutist, mercantilist, and militarily ambitious, France under the rule of Louis XIV.

Between 1648 and 1656, then, Spain and her allies temporarily reversed what, ever since 1640, had looked like the rapid and inexorable rise of France to hegemony in Europe. The Frondes revealed with brutal clarity the deep rifts, and unresolved tensions, besetting French society and showed that it was entirely possible that France, staggering under the weight of her inner contradictions, and prodded by Spanish deep-penetration tactics, might lapse into a prolonged period of chronic instability and international weakness, leaving the Spanish court free to dictate the contours of the new European order. It may be true, as historians frequently assert, that Spain by the 1640s was financially and militarily exhausted and that the twin revolts of Catalonia and Portugal had left the monarchy in an exceedingly awkward and dangerous strategic position and that Castile, the hub of the empire, had for decades been in the grip of relentless demographic and economic decline. It may be that what Spain really needed, if she were to recover from her prostration of the 1640s and allow the cities of Castile to revive, was not a further round of warfare but a complete respite from the pressures and burdens of war. But it is also true that no other European power, aside from France, then possessed anything like the military and financial resources which remained at the disposal of the Spanish crown, or could rival its influence, and capacity to intervene, in Italy, Germany and the Low Countries and France was partially paralyzed by the Frondes for six years and continued to suffer from its disruptive effects for several years after.

In the existing accounts of Spanish policy in Europe during the 1640s and 1650s one encounters a number of accepted notions which are, arguably, in some need of revision. There is the idea that Spanish statecraft after Olivares' dismissal in January 1643 was weak and irresolute and at times even self-contradictory, revealing a 'lack of a controlling intelligence', as one scholar put it, 'having an uncertain cast caused by the king's vacillation and basic self-doubt and the inexperience of the new regime'.[1] As we shall see, what is really remarkable is, on the contrary, the tenacity and consistency of Spanish policy. Equally questionable is the view that 'Spain was unable to exploit the anti-Mazarin Fronde, as she did not have the resources for a major effort'.[2] In fact, Spain did mount a major effort and intervened extensively in northern and in southern France, as well as in Alsace and Lorraine. A third contention which seems more than a little dubious is the idea that the continuing revolts of Catalonia and Portugal forced the Spanish crown to drain resources away from the Spanish Netherlands:[3] in reality, as we shall see, the Spanish Netherlands continued, just as before 1640, to be both the hammer and anvil of the monarchy.

Yet another *idée fixe* likely to require radical revision is the notion that it was Cardinal Mazarin who took the initiative in exploring the possibilities for peace between France and Spain; and that it was the Spanish court which, through a combination of obstinacy, supineness and duplicity allowed the opportunities for a peace which Spain so desperately needed to slip away.[4] In fact there is very little truth in this idea, although it is true that Mazarin went to some lengths to contrive precisely this impression. Historians have been particularly prone to blame the failure of the peace negotiations of 1656 on Philip IV, a king, we are told, who 'against the advice of his ministers . . . refused to negotiate, insisting on conditions as unreasonable as those which Cromwell demanded of Spain'.[5] Far from this being the case, it was, in reality, none other than Mazarin who was chiefly responsible — time and time again — for blocking peace on conditions other than such as would reinforce his own position within France and

[1] R.A. Stradling, *Europe and the Decline of Spain: A Study of the Spanish System, 1580–1720* (London, 1981), p. 133; see also idem, 'A Spanish Statesman of Appeasement: Medina de las Torres and Spanish Policy, 1639–70', in R.A. Stradling, *Spain's Struggle for Europe, 1598–1668* (London and Rio Grande, 1994), pp. 159–60.

[2] Stradling, *Europe and the Decline of Spain*, pp. 122–9; see also Paul Kennedy, *The Rise and Fall of the Great Powers* (New York, 1989) pp. 58–9.

[3] 'Münster', argues Stradling, 'was in line with the important decision, taken in 1644, to allocate the new rebellions priority over the old', Stradling, *Europe and the Decline of Spain*, p. 133.

[4] This claim abounds in recent historical literature: see Richard Bonney, *The European Dynastic States, 1494–1660* (Oxford, 1991), pp. 212, 239; Stradling, *Europe and the Decline of Spain*, p. 123; John Lynch, *The Hispanic World in Crisis and Change, 1598–1700* (Oxford, 1992), pp. 169, 171.

[5] Lynch, *The Hispanic World*, p. 169.

establish French hegemony, and further opportunities for French expansion, within Europe. Furthermore, Philip IV did not act against the advice of his ministers in 1656, except only for the duke of Medina de las Torres whose influence has been somewhat exaggerated by historians and whose views were (with considerable justification) normally disregarded by the real architects of Spanish policy at this time — Don Luis de Haro and the conde de Peñaranda — and by the king.

A final doubtful contention about Spain's strategy is the idea that Philip IV's central objective, adhered to with the utmost rigidity, regardless of the consequences for the population of Spain, was to preserve intact the lands and possessions of the Habsburg dynasty. While it is correct that Philip had 'no conception of a national monarchy transcending dynastic interests', it is not the case that he 'saw himself primarily as the representative of the Habsburg dynasty, charged with the preservation of its possessions' or that his 'only criterion was his legal rights' and the need to safeguard 'his sacred inheritance'.[6] Like all seventeenth-century monarchs Philip IV's outlook was basically courtly and dynastic but this implied much more than simply a tenacious desire to retain territories which he had inherited wherever they were situated. In essence, what Philip IV and his advisers were striving for was to preserve the Spanish monarchy in its 'greatness', by which they meant its status as one of the two preponderant Catholic monarchies, with the leverage and *reputación* to exercise a dominant influence in wide areas of Europe as well as the world outside Europe. From this concept of the 'greatness' of the king of Spain it followed, ineluctably, that Spain could not simply abandon her traditional claims to preside in the crucial patchwork of territories wedged between France and the larger German states — that is the southern Low Countries, Lorraine, Spanish Burgundy (Franche-Comté), and the Rhenish ecclesiastical states as well as Alsace — or her hegemony in Italy without losing both her strategic advantages in relation to France and her status as a predominant power. If Spain withdrew from the network of principalities between France and the large German states, and gave up her role in Italy, she would be creating a power vacuum which would inevitably be filled by France, thereby conceding French mastery of Europe. It may be that all this amounted to a struggle for primacy, a contest for power and status, but it also true that by striving for dominance around the eastern fringes of France, and in Italy, Philip and his ministers were endeavouring to create a new stability out of conflict, a particular kind of political and ecclesiastical order in Europe built on the fixing of limits to the power, and the reach, of the French crown inside, as well as outside, of France.

If obtainable, this was their goal. But, amid the dismal circumstances which confronted them in 1647 and at the beginning of 1648, Philip IV and his ministers concluded that they had no choice but to sign a peace with France on Mazarin's terms. It was a bitter pill to swallow but Philip and his ministers felt that they

---

[6] Ibid., pp. 170–1.

must swallow it if the vast crisis within the Spanish monarchy brought on by the revolts of Catalonia and Portugal, and now also in 1647 the rebellion in Naples, was to be surmounted. Accordingly, in January 1648, at the same time that he agreed on final terms for peace between Spain and the Dutch, the conde de Peñaranda, Spain's plenipotentiary at the Münster peace congress, signed the draft peace treaty negotiated with the French. 'In retrospect', it has been claimed, 'Spanish duplicity in the peace negotiations and their wish to make a separate peace with the Dutch is very evident.'[7] But in reality there was no duplicity. The Spanish evidence shows that Philip and his ministers, deeply shaken by their many setbacks in the 1640s and by the insurrection in Naples (as well as the loss in 1646 of Dunkirk, Spain's chief port on the Flemish coast), were perfectly sincere in wanting to settle and in their willingness to accept defeat. It was, on the contrary, Mazarin's persistent stalling and holding out for yet more concessions from Spain (of which there had already been many) which prevented finalization of the Franco-Spanish peace in 1648.[8]

Against all expectation, over the next few months Spain's general strategic position in Europe improved markedly — to the extent of altering fundamentally the balance of power between Spain and France. As Peñaranda noted, in a report to the king, there were three basic reasons for this crucial shift.[9] First, despite the Dutch States General's undertaking to the French crown to do no such thing, and French efforts to prevent it, a majority of the United Provinces, five against two, voted to conclude a separate peace with Spain. The Eighty Years' War was now over and the Spanish commanders no longer needed to worry about the possibility of a Dutch army attacking their rear and posing a threat to Antwerp and the Flemish cities. This in itself appreciably weakened Mazarin's hand. Secondly, French efforts to exploit and widen the crisis facing the Spanish crown in Italy failed. In the spring of 1648, a punitive force sent from Spain, under Philip IV's acknowledged, illegitimate son, Don Juan José, crushed the rebel Neapolitan republic and restored Spanish control in southern Italy. Thirdly, it became apparent that there was growing unrest within France. The turmoil of the Frondes was now beginning, a rebellion against the centralizing policies of the French crown, and their fiscal consequences, on the part not just of sections of the bureaucracy and nobility but also broad sections of the population, particularly in the towns. Among the demands of the *Frondeurs* was a strident call for peace with Spain and a virtually universal insistence that Mazarin (who was extremely unpopular with most of the nobility and general public alike) be removed.[10] The massive burdens and heavy taxes necessitated by the long

---

[7] Bonney, *European Dynastic States*, p. 212.

[8] Conde de Peñaranda to Don Luis de Haro, Münster, 18 April and 18 May 1648, in *CODOIN*, lxxxiv, pp. 165, 230–1.

[9] Peñaranda to Philip IV, Münster, 11 June 1648, *CODOIN*, lxxxiv, pp. 244–6.

[10] Peñaranda to Philip IV, Münster, 2 March 1649, *CODOIN*, lxxxiv, pp. 359–61; nearly 5,000 pamphlets or *mazarinades*, denouncing Mazarin and his policies, and not least his refusal to make peace with Spain, were written during the Frondes, see R. Bonney, 'The English and French Civil Wars', *History* 65 (1980), pp. 376–7.

war may have placed an excessive burden on Spain but, at this point, it appeared that the strain of the conflict was wreaking even greater havoc in France.

It was not Spanish duplicity or intransigence, then, but a combination of Mazarin's prevarication and a change in the general strategic situation during the early months of 1648 which undid the provisional Franco-Spanish peace of January 1648. In May 1648, only a few days before the ceremonies surrounding the ratification of the Spanish-Dutch peace in the Münster city hall, Peñaranda received instructions from Madrid that he should not, after all, accept the 'condiciones exorbitantes' which Spain had been willing to concede to France back in January, the king now having definitely changed his mind following the 'reduction' of Naples and decision of the Dutch States General.[11] Although Franco-Spanish peace negotiations dragged on at Münster until late June, with the Dutch acting as intermediaries and Peñaranda endeavouring to absolve the Spanish court of blame for the deadlock, these later rounds of talks were completely sterile, Mazarin being no more willing to moderate his demands than were the Spaniards willing to agree to the terms they had provisionally conceded in January.

Philip IV, using his principal army, the army of Flanders, lost no time in attempting to translate the more favourable situation, which had developed since the spring of 1648, into gains on the map. There was indeed much lost ground to recover, in the Spanish Low Countries as well as in Italy and the peninsula itself. In the southern Netherlands, during the course of the 1640s, the French had overrun much of of western Flanders, including Gravelines, Mardijk, Dunkirk, Kortrijk (captured in 1643), Sint Winoxbergen (Bergues-Saint Winox) and Furnes (Veurne), and occupied most of Artois, establishing strong garrisons in Arras, Hesdin, Lens and Bethune, as well as La Bassée, in the district of Lille, while in Luxemburg they had taken Thionville and Damvillers.[12] The Spaniards marched into west Flanders and Artois, recapturing Kortrijk and Lens. But almost at once the Spanish offensive met with a crushing reverse. On 20 August 1648, the advancing Spanish army of 18,000 men was cut to pieces, with great loss of life, cannon, banners and prestige, by a slightly smaller French army commanded by the prince de Condé, almost under the walls of Lens.

In Madrid there was little zest to prolong a conflict which had already dragged on for over eighteen years. Philip IV certainly insisted on some softening of the terms of January 1648 which were highly unfavourable, even humiliating, for Spain. But if the French would go some way to meet him, the Spanish king professed his readiness to sign a peace with France even on terms which were, on balance, favourable towards France. Nevertheless, there was practically no prospect of peace being concluded at this stage, essentially because of Mazarin's attitude and the still very weak position of Spanish arms in Catalonia, on the

---

[11] Peñaranda to Philip IV, Münster, 11 June 1648, *CODOIN*, lxxxiv, pp. 244–5.

[12] H. Lonchay, *La rivalité de la France et de l'Espagne aux Pays-Bas, 1635–1700* (Brussels, 1896), p. 127.

Portuguese front and in Italy. It is true that it was Mazarin who took the initiative which led to the resumption of secret peace negotiations between the French and Spanish courts, in January 1649, but his motive at this juncture may simply have been to demonstrate to the *Frondeur* opposition, in Paris and in the rest of France, that he *was* engaged in efforts to end the Spanish war. In any case when Peñaranda, now in Brussels, sent one of his best diplomats, the Franche-Comtois Jean-Claude Friquet (1593–1667) to negotiate with Mazarin and the French court — which had had to leave Paris and was now residing at Saint-Germain-en-Laye — he found the cardinal not a whit more flexible than he had been the previous year. Friquet assured Mazarin that the Spanish king was ready to 'conclude peace on honourable terms and even on conditions favourable to France' and would do so 'without waiting to see what would result from those disturbances in Paris'.[13] There were, however, three major stumbling-blocks which would have to be resolved first. The most important — Catalonia — Friquet avoided in his opening remarks, hoping to lay a favourable basis by making early progress on the other two. The second main Spanish objection to the terms of January 1648 was to a clause stipulating the French court's right to continue to 'assist the Portuguese', after France had made peace with Spain, Philip insisted that, if there was to be peace, then France must agree *not* to assist the Portuguese in their rebellion against the Spanish crown.[14] The third Spanish objection was to the clause in which the French court had agreed to restitute the confiscated lands of Spain's ally, Duke Charles IV of Lorraine, but only in part. Philip and his client now required full restitution.[15]

Mazarin showed little willingness to shift his ground on any of these points. He clearly regarded the French occupation of Catalonia as a trump card which would eventually secure big gains for France. He warned Friquet that Peñaranda and the king should not place their hopes in the present turmoil in Paris. The agitation directed against himself and the court would immediately cease, he predicted, were the Spaniards to try to exploit the situation by invading France.[16] He also intimated that he was close to an agreement with the Portuguese whereby they would provide France with some of their warships, contribute to the cost of the war in Catalonia and hand Tangiers over to the French crown. He was adamant that France would not cease her support for the Portuguese secession, claiming that the French crown's obligations to Portugal, set out in written treaties, were of a different order from Philip IV's unpublished commitments

---

[13] BL., MS Add. 14000, fos 173–173v, 'Relacion de la jornada que Don Juan Friquet ha echo a la corte de Francia en San German por horden del señor conde de Peñaranda a principios de 1649'.

[14] Ibid., fo. 173v.

[15] Ibid., fos 175v–176; in his letter to the king, of 28 November 1648, from Brussels, Peñaranda explained that Lorraine in effect consisted of three entities: the duchy proper, the duchy of Bar and some lands within the bishoprics of Metz, Verdun and Thoul. Under the terms of January 1648 the French crown had been prepared to restitute the duchy proper but nothing else, CODOIN, lxxxiv, p. 329.

[16] Ibid., fo. 174v.

to the duke of Lorraine.[17] He added that if Philip persisted in demanding full restoration of the lands and independence of Lorraine, the French Queen Regent, on his advice, would negotiate a separate peace with Duke Charles whose troops would then be detached from Spain and fight as allies of France. Friquet replied that he saw little likelihood that the duke would desert Spain to settle separately with France for besides his solemn promises and the 'word of a prince of such blood' — a remark which must have drawn a smile from Mazarin, the duke being notoriously unreliable — prudence scarcely allowed that he should hand over his army to, and rely for his future security on, those who had despoiled him of his lands and revenues in the first place.

After a first round of talks, Friquet found himself dining not just with Mazarin but also with various other courtiers, which meant that it was not Mazarins intention that his visit should remain secret. This fact persuaded Friquet that the real motive for the talks was Mazarin's desire to convince the parlement of Paris, and *Frondeur* nobility, that he and Anne of Austria were actively seeking peace with Spain.[18] On the second day, after consulting with the queen and the royal council, Mazarin moderated his tone, implying that the French crown would give 'satisfaction to the duke of Lorraine', and consider abandoning Portugal, but nothing concrete was offered. These talks, like those before them, came to nothing. At this juncture, Mazarin's confidence appeared justified. From February, with the French royal army under Condé (who was then still loyal to the queen regent and the government) blockading the *Frondeurs* in Paris, Mazarin's position substantially (albeit only temporarily) strengthened.[19] On the orders of the governor-general in Brussels, the Archduke Leopold Wilhem, the Spanish army of Flanders did now invade France, penetrating from Mons, beyond Vervins, as far as Laon from where they were in striking distance of Reims and Soissons. But this attempt to rekindle *Frondeur* opposition to Mazarin failed and, in April, Mazarin succeeded in negotiating an end to the first, the so-called 'Parliamentary Fronde'.

The war, then, was set to continue. For Spain, this was a war in the first place for the recovery of Catalonia and Portugal, as well as the Portuguese colonial empire (despite the remarkable, but in the circumstances unavoidable, strategic reality that Spain was unable to launch any offensive against Portugal whilst the Franco-Spanish war lasted),[20] as well as for the effective reconstitution of Lorraine, together with the neighbouring duchy of Bar, as a substantial state adjoining the Spanish Low Countries and dependent on Spain, wedged between France and the German Empire. But, besides these fundamental aims, Spain also had several other far-reaching concerns. Mazarin had made and despite the failure of the Neoplitan revolution — was still making a determined effort

[17] Ibid., fo. 175.

[18] Ibid., fos 178v–179.

[19] O. Ranum, *The Fronde: A French Revolution, 1648–1652* (New York, 1993) pp. 206–14.

[20] Though an initial offensive foray was made in 1657, see Rafael Valladares, *Felipe IV y la Restauración de Portugal* (Málaga, 1994), pp. 39, 313–15.

to overthrow Spain's more than a century old hegemony in Italy by undermining her grip over Milan, Naples and Sicily, and by detaching her allies and inducing them to sign alliances with France. Then there was the question of the German empire. If France had succeeded in driving a wedge between Spain and the emperor, at Münster, and the Emperor had conceded French control of Alsace and the Rhine fortresses of Breisach and Philippsburg, Spain was not yet ready to accept either French possession of Alsace, in particular, or French domination of the Rhine corridor, in general. Owing to their military weakness, the Catholic ecclesiastical states of the Rhine were almost inevitably going to be dominated either by France or by Spain, and Spain appeared to be the only power available which might be capable of checking France's Rhenish ambitions. Spain still garrisoned Jülich and, further south, on the left bank of the Rhine, occupied the town of Frankenthal (until 1652), which meant that Spain was still firmly ensconced in the heart of the Palatinate and close to the key bishopric of Speyer.[21] Meanwhile, in the electorate of Trier, strategically situated between Lorraine, the Rhine and the Spanish territory of Luxemburg, the archbishop-elector, Philipp Christoph von Sötern (who ruled 1623–52), had in the past followed a consistently pro-French policy; but he was now old and frail, while troops of the duke of Lorraine had — with Spanish connivance — occupied several fortresses and towns in the southern part of the electorate, adjoining Lorraine.[22] The voting canons of Trier who would elect the new ruler were deeply split into French and Spanish factions but with the Metternichs and their allies, the pro-Spanish faction, hopeful of winning the next election[23]

Peñaranda, commenting on the overall balance of power in western Europe, in a report to the king of 2 March 1649, observed that Spain could now rebuild her influence in Germany, as well as recover lost territory in Flanders and Artois and reconstitute the duchy of Lorraine as a substantial Spanish client state. Furthermore, he urged, Philip now had an 'extraordinaria oportunidad' to retrieve Breisach for the Habsburgs and expel the French from Alsace which would then depend on Spain for its future security as part of the empire.[24] Nor was Peñaranda less sanguine about prospects for defeating the French attempts to overthrow Spain's ascendancy in Italy. He agreed with Don Luis de Haro that the next step was to recover the two Tuscan *presidios* of Piombino and Porto Longone (on the isle of Elba),[25] which the French had captured in

---

[21] Georges Livet, *L'intendance d'Alsace sous Louis XIV (1648–1715)* (Strasbourg 1956), pp. 143, 147; on Spain's continued questioning of the validity of the Emperor's renunciation of Alsace to France, see BL, MS 14004, fo. 32v, 'Notizias de la . . . division de la casa de Austria'.

[22] Joseph Baur, *Philipp von Sötern, geistlicher Kurfürst zu Trier, und seine Politik während des Dreissigjährigen Krieges* (2 vols, Speyer, 1897), i, pp. 241–7.

[23] *Recueil des instructions données aux ambassadeurs et ministres de France depuis les traités de Westphalie jusqu'à la Revolution Française: états Allemands*, iii, *L'electorat de Trèves*, ed. Georges Livet (Paris, 1966), pp. 20–4.

[24] Peñaranda to Philip IV, Brussels, 2 March 1649, *CODOIN*, lxxxiv, pp. 359–61.

[25] Thus *not* in the republic of Genoa, as stated in Bonney, *European Dynastic States*, p. 239.

1646, after which Spain should proceed to expel the remaining French garrisons from Savoy and the Montferrat and 'punish' the duke of Modena for his disloyalty to Spain.[26]

In the Rhineland, Spain did indeed make substantial gains at French expense in the years 1648–52, especially in Trier and Speyer. Since the 1630s, Von Sötern, in close alliance with France, had amassed lands and titles in both of these ecclesiastical territories, for his own family, and pursued his vendetta against the opposing sections of the Trier nobility and ecclesiastical hierarchy, headed by the Metternich family. In 1635 the Metternichs and their allies, backed by the Cardinal-Infante (who sent supporting troops from Luxemburg), had seized the electorate, arrested Philipp-Christoph and delivered him into the custody of the emperor whose troops had then occupied the most important fortress in Trier — Ehrenbreitstein, opposite Coblenz, commanding the confluence of the Moselle and Rhine. In 1645, however, Mazarin had secured the elector's release, as part of the Münster negotiations, and reinstalled him in Trier bringing the electorate back under French control; French troops were admitted to the great Rhine fortress of Philippsburg, on the territory of Speyer, while the Meternichs had to go back into exile.[27]

It was the revival of Spanish fortunes in 1648–9, and the outbreak of the Frondes, which enabled the Metternichs and their allies to regain the upper hand. Backed by Spain, and the elector of Mainz (who had now shifted to a pro-Habsburg stance), one of the younger canons of the electoral chapter, Karl-Kaspar von der Leyen, led a small army of local malcontents into the electorate and captured the town of Trier on 31 May 1649, imprisoning Philipp-Christoph in his own palace. In June 1650, the fifteen canons of the chapter, a majority of whom now adhered to the 'Spanish Party', elected Von der Leyen — whose heavy drinking, according to one of Mazarin's informants, was the 'seule et unique chose en quoi il excelloit' coadjutor of Trier and effective wielder of power in the electorate. For the time being Trier was secure as a Spanish client state and served as the new 'Spanish Road' for troops and supplies sent from the south to the Spanish Netherlands.[28] Duke Charles also continued to use the southern part of the electorate as a base for operations against the French troops in neighbouring Lorraine, the Trier towns and fortresses of Homburg, Landstuhl, Saarweden and Hammerstein remaining in the hands of his Lorrainers. After Philipp-Christoph's death on 4 February 1652, Karl-Kaspar was appointed his successor as archbishop-elector of Trier, whilst his ally, Lothar-Friedrich von Metternich, was elected bishop of Speyer. So both states remained

[26] Francesco I d'Este, duke of Modena, having pursued a pro-Habsburg policy in the 1630s, had become an ally of France during the 1640s and was to remain Mazarin's most consistent ally in Italy during the 1650s: see Robert Oresko, 'The Marriages of the Nieces of Cardinal Mazarin', in Rainer Babel (ed.), *Frankreich im europäischen Staatensystem der frühen Neuzeit, Beihefte der Francia*, 35 (Sigmaringen, 1995), p. 128.

[27] Fritz Dickmann, *Der Westfälische Frieden* (Münster, 1972; new edn, 1992), pp. 286–7.

[28] Baur, *Philipp von Sötern*, ii, pp. 309–15.

firmly within the Spanish orbit, except only for Philippsburg which remained in French hands but which served also as an excuse for the Spaniards to retain their garrison at Frankenthal.[29]

Despite the signing of the Peace of Rueil (11 March 1649), which ended the first phase of the Frondes and temporarily restored the ascendancy of the French court inside France, the Spaniards retained the upper hand on the Franco-Netherlands border. On 8 May, after a short siege, the Flemish city of Ieper (Ypres), which had recently fallen to Condé and was held by French troops, surrendered to the army of Flanders.[30] Mazarin's attempt to reply by laying siege to Cambrai, in June, failed owing to lack of money and troops and the robustness of anti-French sentiment in the Walloon border areas; Pieter Snayers was subsequently commissioned to paint a magnificent picture of the Archduke's siege of Ieper which eventually found its way to Madrid. Meanwhile, the French army of Catalonia which had received little pay since the summer of 1648, and was increasingly afflicted by poor discipline, had been definitely thrown on the defensive by the summer of 1649.[31]

Spain and the Princely Fronde, 1650–1

The year 1650 was a dramatic one on all fronts and, while amply showing the precariousness of the shifting balance between France and Spain, was overall one of substantial success for Spanish arms and the advancement of Spanish influence throughout western Europe. Especially helpful to the Spanish cause was the recrudescence of armed resistance to the royal government within France. After months of complex intrigue and mounting tension, Mazarin tried to resolve matters by an audacious coup, on 18 January 1650, when he had the prince de Condé arrested together with his brother, the prince de Conti, and the governor of Normandy, Henri, duc de Longueville. The three princely captives were incarcerated, at Le Havre, but their seizure merely provoked an escalation of opposition in many parts of France.[32]

There was also a rather disturbing development from the Spanish point of view and one capable of offsetting their advantages elsewhere — the simultaneous political crisis unfolding in the Dutch Republic. The new stadholder, William II of Orange, was a bitter critic of the Dutch peace with Spain and a firm ally of Mazarin. Locked in conflict with the States of Holland over issues of army size and military expenditure, it was clear by the end of 1649 that the ambitious young prince was striving for nothing less than mastery of the Dutch

[29] Livet, *L'intendance*, p. 147.

[30] CODOIN, lxxxiv, pp. 375–6.

[31] José Sanabre, *La acción de Francia en Cataluña en la pugna por la hegemonía de Europa, 1640–1659* (Barcelona, 1956), pp. 421–2, 432, 437.

[32] Richard Bonney, 'Cardinal Mazarin and the Great Nobility during the Fronde', *English Historical Review*, 96 (1981), p. 820.

state: if he succeeded, the probable result would be a new military alliance between France and the United Provinces and, very likely, the resumption of war between Spain and the Dutch.[33] The French court was greatly encouraged, in January 1650, when the duke of Lorraine's marauding, undisciplined troops ravaged part of the Dutch Generality Lands, causing a fierce public outcry in the republic, and backlash against Spain, which proved useful ammunition for William II in his political contest with the States of Holland.

While keeping a nervous eye on the United Provinces, the Archduke Leopold Wilhelm, closely advised by his army commander, the conde de Fuensaldaña, launched a summer offensive in 1650 south of Valenciennes, along the valley of the Oise, assisted by a *Frondeur* force led by the maréchal de Turenne who, at this point was in rebellion against the French court. The Spaniards, penetrating into France beyond Landrecies (which they had retaken in 1647), captured the strategic stronghold of Châtelet, failed to take Guise, but did take the key frontier fortress of La Capelle (see Map 2), which surrendered after thirteen days of siege, on 3 August. Amid the uncertainty over whether the invading army would continue to advance towards Paris, or swivel north west to invade Artois, Mazarin found himself 'en grande inquiétude' especially with regard to Arras. In fact, the Spaniards concentrated on widening their enclave towards the south east, into Champagne, capturing Vervins and later Château Porcien and Rethel, a short distance north of Reims.[34]

The contest in the United Provinces, meanwhile, intensified. On 30 July William II, using troops drawn from the garrisons in Gelderland, mounted his partially successful *coup d'état*, arresting six leading regents of the States of Holland and intimidating Amsterdam with a show of force. Pondering the seeming likelihood of civil war erupting in the United Provinces, Philip IV's advisers, after discussing the point at their meeting of 16 August 1650, instructed the Archduke in Brussels (and the Spanish ambassador in The Hague, Antoine Brun) to remain neutral as long as possible but to come to the assistance of Holland, against the stadholder, and lesser provinces, if Holland seemed about to be overwhelmed).[35] In the meantime, the Spanish diplomatic machine concentrated on removing every possible pretext that might be used by William II for provoking a confrontation with Spain. On Peñaranda's advice, additional trade concessions were offered to the States General and efforts were made to inflame the quarrel between the Dutch and Portuguese, who, since 1645, had reconquered most of Netherlands Brazil. When William II and the States General, now largely under his thumb, announced they were interceding between France and Spain to mediate an end to the war, an offer accompanied by a none too

[33] J.I. Israel, *The Dutch Republic and the Hispanic World, 1606–1661* (Oxford, 1982), pp. 385–92.

[34] Lonchay, *La rivalité*, 154.

[35] AGS, Estado 2072, consulta, Madrid, 16 August 1650; Spanish ministers were deliberating after William II's coup in Holland had taken place.

subtle threat to join France against Spain if Dutch mediation was rejected,[36] the Spanish governor-general in Brussels and ambassador in The Hague were instructed to proceed with the utmost circumspection, treating the Dutch proposals as a ploy devised in collusion with Mazarin, and to delay their reply for as long as possible. When they did finally respond, they were to assure the Dutch that the Spanish court was ready to negotiate peace with France but in vague terms, without expressly either accepting or rebuffing, the Dutch offer of mediation.[37] Such prevarication was unlikely to extract the Spanish court from their new predicament for long but, fortunately for Spain, the crisis ended with the sudden and unexpected death of the young prince (from smallpox) on 6 November 1650.

In the meantime, Spanish arms had been registering further gains in Italy and Catalonia. Don Juan José de Austria, having assembled a considerable armada in Naples and Sicily, set sail from Naples on 11 May with thirty warships, transports and gallies, and some 9,000 troops, with which he appeared off Piombino and Porto Longone, a fortnight later.[38] Additional troops were sent from Milan by the governor there, the marqués de Caracena. After a month's siege, Piombino fell to a Spanish assault on 21 June. After weeks of continuous bombardment, the 1,000 strong French garrison of Porto Longone, on the isle of Elba, surrendered ten days later. Mazarin, who had expended an immense amount of time and ingenuity, as well as men and money, on his efforts to advance French (and his own) ambitions in Italy, was in the highest degree alarmed, especially with regard to Casale, which he regarded as the strategic key to Italy and which, owing to the disarray ensuing from the Frondes, was now 'en très mauvais estat'. 'Nous sçavons', he remarked, in a letter to Le Tellier, 'que leur dessein est de venir fondre avec toute cette armée-là qu'ils joindront à celles qu'ils ont dans l'estat de Milan pour attaquer Casal, dont ils viendront à bout avec facilité, si on n'y remedie promptement, et ainsy nous perdrions aussytôt toute la maison de Savoye et aurions la guerre l'année prochaine dans le Dauphiné'.[39] Predictably, the weakening of the French, and corresponding revival of the Spanish presence, in Italy, was causing a general drift among the Italian princes back towards an attitude of deference towards Spain. Mazarin's chief fear, as far as Italy was concerned, was that Savoy would settle with Philip IV, which would virtually eliminate French influence from Italy and expose the Dauphiné to invasion.

---

[36] J.J. Poelhekke, *Geen blijder maer in tachtigh jaer: verspreide studien over de Crisisperiode, 1648–1651* (Zutphen, 1973), pp. 163–79.

[37] AGS, Archivo de la antigua embajada española en La Haya, leg. 32, fo. 170, Philip IV to Antoine Brun, Madrid, 30 November 1650; Israel, *Dutch Republic and the Hispanic World*, p. 392.

[38] 'Diario de lo sucedido al señor Don Juan de Austria en la navegacion y conquista de las plazas de Pumblin y Puerto Longon' (Palermo, 1 September 1650), BL, MS Add. 14009, fos 785, 822.

[39] *Lettres du Cardinal Mazarin pendant son ministère*, ed. P.A. Chéruel and G. d'Avenel (9 vols, Paris, 1872–1906), iii, p. 697.

Equally unpalatable to Mazarin were developments in Catalonia, where a Castilian army of 6,000 troops, advancing from Lérida, captured Flix, overran the lower Ebro valley and, in October, set siege to Tortosa. All along Mazarin had insisted, in strategic debates at the French court, that the Catalan front should be given the highest priority. But the efforts of the French forces in Catalonia, commanded by Louis de Vendôme, duc de Mercoeur, to break the siege remained unavailing. A French galley fleet which attempted to relieve Tortosa was repulsed by the Castilian blocking fleet, under the same duke of Albuquerque who subsequently became viceroy of Mexico, within sight of Tarragona on 24 November.[40] Tortosa capitulated three days later. Scarcely less alarming for Mazarin than these military and naval setbacks was a rash of attacks by gangs of Catalan peasants on the increasingly ill-disciplined French soldiery who had been driven by lack of pay to pilfer food and livestock from the peasantry: 'le roy d'Espagne' observed the cardinal, 'n'a perdu cette province-là que par les mauvais traitements que ses armées firent aux peuples. Je crains fort que cette mesme raison ne la fasse encore reperdre au Roy [de France].[41]

On the north-eastern French border, Spain also kept the upper hand, though the Archduke Leopold Wilhelm felt frustrated that he could not do more owing to shortage of Spaniards and Italians who formed the backbone of the army of Flanders. By the spring of 1651, the Spanish infantry *tercios* in Flanders were down to only 3,000 men and the Italians to scarcely 700.[42] Nevertheless, there were substantial gains as well as some reverses. A notable development in Lorraine was the capture of the key fortress of Stenay by a *Frondeur* force under Madame de Longueville. Though originally belonging to the duke of Lorraine, the court had assigned the town to Condé as a reward for his services. The duchess lost no time in summoning a Spanish garrison from nearby Luxemburg, though Philip subsequently decided that Stenay should be handed over to *Frondeur* troops lest, by keeping Spanish troops in Lorraine, he should create the impression in France that he was endeavouring to annex parts of the country. The chief French success was their recapture of Rethel, in December 1650, and subsequent defeat of the mixed *Frondeur*-Spanish force which had been sent to relieve the town.

With Spain in the ascendant but not decisively so, the courts of both France and Spain were alive with rumours over the winter of 1650–1 that the war was about to end, and peace talks about to begin in earnest. But if others thought that peace was around the corner, Mazarin, who was always apt to insist on 'l'opiniâtreté que les Espagnols ont pour la continuation de la guerre', could see no reason to expect any progress. On the contrary, he took the view that,

[40] C. de la Roncière, *Histoire de la marine française*, v, *La Guerre de Trente Ans: Colbert* (3rd edn, Paris, 1934), pp. 164–7.

[41] *Lettres du Cardinal Mazarin*, iii, p. 846.

[42] AGR, SEG 249, fo. 233v, Philip IV to Leopold Wilhelm, 26 February 1651; ibid., fos 292v–3, Leopold Wilhelm to Philip IV, Brussels, 13 March 1651.

for the moment, his hand was just too weak to obtain a settlement on terms
anything like what he would regard as acceptable. 'Il est à craindre', he remarked,

> que le bruit qu'on fait à Paris, faisant espérer, et à Bruxelles et à Madrid, qu'il arrivera
> tousjours de plus grands desordres dans le royaume, ne les oblige aussy à n'escouter
> aucunes propositions de paix, et que l'archiduc et comte de Fuensaldaña, conseillez
> et pressez par Madame de Longueville et [Turenne] ne fassent quelque declaration
> à mon prejudice, comme de ne vouloir pas traicter la paix avec moi, sachant que j'y
> suis tout-à-fait contraire et choses semblables . . .[43]

The position of the French court weakened further during the opening weeks
of 1651. Anne d'Autriche, under pressure from all sides, was obliged to agree
in February to the release of Condé and his companions imprisoned at Le
Havre.[44] This sensational event compelled Mazarin to leave court, and go into
exile in the electorate of Cologne, and appeared to have definitively broken
his grip on power. It seemed also to have cleared the obstacles which had previously prevented the negotiation of peace between France and Spain. Yet Condé's
release did nothing to modify Mazarin's reluctance to contemplate an early
peace with Spain. When the papal nuncio at Cologne, Fabio Chigi, alerted by
his colleague in Madrid, informed Mazarin that the Spanish court remained
adamant on the three points, relating to Portugal, Catalonia and Lorraine which
had blocked the peace in 1648 and 1649,[45] Mazarin was as obdurate as ever in
refusing to countenance withdrawal of the French armies from Catalonia and
Lorraine or to agree that France should cease supporting the Portuguese Revolt.

Unaware at first that Mazarin remained in secret contact with the French
queen regent, or that his influence at the French court remained intact, Spanish ministers and diplomats began to treat Mazarin as a potentially useful pawn.
On his way to Cologne, the cardinal passed through the city of Jülich which
had been occupied by the Spaniards in 1622 (see Chapter 2) and was still in
Spanish hands. Mazarin penned a description of his reception:

> toute la cavallerie qui estoit dans la dicte place me vint au-devant à une journée de
> là. Je trouvay la garnison sous les armes, à mon entrée. On me salua trois fois de tout
> le canon de la ville et de la citadelle chargé à balle, et on mit en garde devant mon
> logis une compagnie d'Espagnols avec un capitaine de la mesme nation . . . Enfin si
> l'Empereur y avoit esté, on n'auroit pas pu le traiter avec plus de respect. On fit le
> mesme salut royal à ma sortie, et comme je tesmoignois au dict seigneur Antonio de
> Pimentel qui m'accompagnoit, que j'estois confus de tous les honneurs que je recevois,
> il me repartit de fort bonne grace qu'ils m'estoient deubs en tout temps et en tous
> lieux, mais que les Espagnols particulièrement ne pouvaient assez m'en rendre dans
> le temps que je quittois la France.[46]

[43] *Lettres du Cardial Mazarin*, iii, p. 944, Mazarin to le Tellier, 24 December 1650.
[44] Bonney, 'Cardinal Mazarin and the Great Nobility', p. 280.
[45] *Lettres de Cardinal Mazarin*, iv, p. 115.
[46] Ibid., iv, p. 122.

A reply which Mazarin found gratifying though he can hardly have been entirely oblivious to the sarcasm lurking behind the Spaniard's words.

From his place of exile, the Residenzschloss of the elector of Cologne at Brühl, Mazarin urged the ministers in Paris to make every effort to strengthen the French defences in Italy, Alsace and the Low Countries. 'Pour la Flandre, j'ay dict et escrit beaucoup de fois qu'il falloit donner ordre à Arras; c'est une place dont la conquête donneroit plus d'avantage et de reputation aux ennemys que nulle autre'.[47] Saint Quentin and Dunkirk, too, he urged must be strongly defended. But the highest priority in Mazarin's eyes was still, as before, to retain control of Catalonia, which the Cardinal considered the key to obtaining the kind of peace with Spain he wished to achieve. When Spanish fortunes had been at their lowest, in 1646, he had confided to the French plenipotentiaries at Münster his hopes that a Catalonia securely held by France could eventually be exchanged for the Spanish Netherlands.[48] Such an acquisition would render the Paris basin invulnerable; it would also make France supreme in Europe. Writing to Le Tellier, from Brühl on 2 May, Mazarin judged the importance of the Catalan question 'incomparablement plus que tous les autres qui sont à present sur le tapis, puisque c'est par là que le Roy aura une paix honorable, et quelque advantage que l'on puisse avoir ailleurs, s'il réussit aux Espagnols de remettre cette province-là dans leur obeissance, on ne peut pas espérer, à mon avis, d'obtenir la paix qu'à des conditions tres préjudiciables, pour ne pas dire honteuses'.[49]

Clearly, the gap between the two courts was, as it had been since May 1648, simply too wide to be bridged. For, by May 1651, large parts of Catalonia (including the towns of Lérida, Tortosa, Tarragona, and Vich) were all securely back in the king of Spain's hands. Only Barcelona — which had hitherto refused to admit a French garrison but which now, as the Castilian armies advanced, finally did so — and Montblanch, Cadaqués, Rosas, Balaguer and Cervera remained under French occupation, together with some mountanous areas in the interior. In instructions sent to the Archduke in Brussels, at this time, Philip IV directed him to enter into peace negotiations but stipulated that the French would have to withdraw from the principality of Catalonia in its entirety, though the king was prepared, owing to the 'deseo que tengo de la paz y de castigar debidamente al revelde de Portugal' (the desire I have for peace and to punish as he deserves the rebel [the new king] of Portugal), to abandon and cede to France the counties of Roussillon and Cerdanya (Cerdagne), a small but strategically located territory astride the Pyrenees.[50]

---

[47] Ibid., iv, p. 158.
[48] Ibid., iv, p. 156n.
[49] Ibid.
[50] 'Copia de carta de su Magestad para el señor Archiduque Leopoldo Guillermo sobre el tratado de la paz (1 May 1651), BL, MS Add. 14000, fos 190v–191v; José Sanabre, *El tractat dels Pirineus: els seus antecedents* (Barcelona, 1961), pp. 26–7.

In the same instructions, it was also required that the the French should withdraw all their troops from Portugal and generally cease assisting the Portuguese Revolt.[51] In Italy, the main objective, now that Piombino and Porto Longone had been recovered, was to remove the French from the lands of the duke of Mantua, including Monferrat and especially Casale. In return, the Spanish king was willing to evacuate various towns and fortresses captured from the French and Savoyards the previous year, the most important of which was the Savoyard frontier fortress of Vercelli. The king stressed, though, that he would only return Vercelli to Savoy if the French *did* evacuate Casale.[52] In the Low Countries, the chief Spanish aim, as Mazarin had surmised, was the recovery of Arras rather than Dunkirk — an indication that Philip planned to keep the strategic upper hand, station large forces in heavily fortified towns on the road to Paris and maximize Spain's leverage within France.[53] Finally, on top of his requirements for Catalonia, Italy and the southern Netherlands, the Spanish king continued to insist on full restitution of the lands of the duke of Lorraine.[54] As to where the negotiations should be held, Philip agreed that it would be both easier and quicker to negotiate between Paris and Brussels, rather than between Paris and Madrid, nominating the conde de Fuensaldaña as his chief plenipotentiary.

Mazarin found the Spanish attitude insufferable. He complained to Lionne that, even though Spain's resources were exhausted and her empire on the point of collapse . . . les Espagnols . . . se conduisent avec un insolence non pareille dans la négociation de la paix, faisant des propositions avec un tel mespris, qu'ils auroient honte de les faire au dernier prince de l'Europe'.[55] From his refuge at Brühl, the cardinal not only remained in close contact with the queen regent and her advisers but cleverly played on the tensions and jealousies between different sections of the *Frondeur* opposition, especially the prevailing suspicion about the motives and intentions of Condé. Weaving a skilful web of bribery and intrigue, the cardinal detached various powerful figures from the ranks of the *Frondeur* opposition, notably Turenne and his older brother, the duc de Bouillon. The latter had long intrigued against the power of the French king and, in 1642, had been compelled to surrender his sovereign principality of Sedan to the crown, but now he too was won back (albeit at a steep price) to his allegiance to the king — and animosity towards Condé.[56] At the same time, Mazarin succeeded in his efforts to prevent Condé, who was striving to dominate the court, removing his own key clients and allies from positions of power and

[51] BL, MS Add. 14000, fo. 192.

[52] Ibid., fo. 192v; Sanabre, *El Tractat*, p. 27.

[53] 'La villa de Arras', the king says he has asserted several times in dispatches to Brussels 'es la que mas he deseado recuperar', ibid., fo. 194.

[54] Ibid., fo. 194v.

[55] *Lettres du Cardinal Mazarin*, iv, p. 254.

[56] Bonney, 'Cardinal Mazarin and the Great Nobility', pp. 827–8.

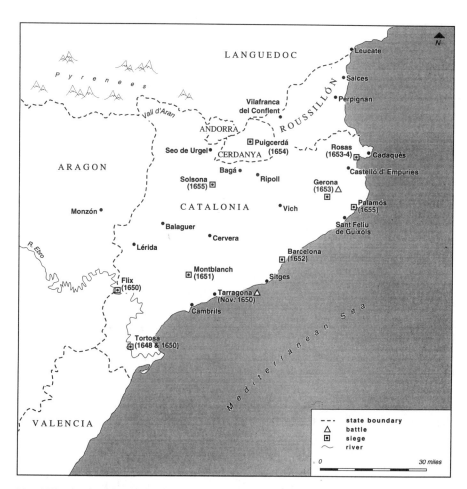

Map 3 The Catalan War, 1648–59

influence. As early as June, Mazarin suspected that Condé was in collusion with Spain and that this was a prime reason for the 'insolence' of the Spanish authorities at Brussels.[57]

By early June the Spaniards were beginning to suspect that at Brühl, Mazarin was engaged in activity 'très prejudiciable aux interests du roy d'Espagne et à l'*Augustissima Casa*'. In turn, the cardinal began to worry about his safety, despite the protection of the elector. He knew that if Spanish ministers in Brussels decided to try to arrest him, they could easily send two or three hundred cavalry and might well succeed in snatching him from under the elector's nose. 'Il ne faut pas douter', he noted, a fortnight later, after an exchange of messages, via the Spanish commander at Jülich, with Peñaranda, 'que ledict comte ne soit informé que la reine continue d'avoir toute confiance en moy.'[58]

Meanwhile, the Spanish offensive continued on all fronts. In Catalonia, the Castilians took Montblanch, encircled Barcelona and, in August 1651, began the close siege of the city by land, whilst a fleet of sixteen warships and twenty-three gallies blockaded the port from the sea.[59] The besieging army included some 3,300 Germans and Italians sent from Milan. In the Low Countries, the army of Flanders enveloped the French salient in west Flanders, early in September, retaking Furnes (Veurne) followed by Bergues-Saint-Vinox (Sint-Winoxbergen). 'Je crains fort', wrote Mazarin to the governor of Dunkirk, on 8 October, 'que la perte de Bergues, qui vous empeschera de vous ayder des contributions, comme vous avez faict par le passé, n'entraîne aussy celle de Dunquerque.'[60] In a letter to Mercoeur, written a few weeks later, after his flight from Brühl, Mazarin railed against the princely opposition and especially Condé, whom he accused of exposing 'la Catalogne à une perte evidente, dont la conservation estoit le fondement le plus solide qu'on pouvoit avoir pour contraindre les ennemis à la paix', and of being the cause 'de toutes les pertes qu'on a faictes du costé de la mer, qui seront bientost suivies de celles de Mardik et de Dunkerque, les ennemis n'oubliant rien pour profiter de l'occasion présente'.[61]

Condé, meanwhile, giving up his attempts to overawe the court, abandoned Paris in September and threw in his lot with the widening *Frondeur* rebellion at Bordeaux, and in Guyenne (of which province he had been nominated governor), while at the same time intensifying his contacts, through his agent Pierre Lenet, with the Spanish court.[62] These led to a formal alliance between Condé and the Spanish crown, signed on 6 November 1651, under the terms

[57] *Lettres du Cardinal Mazarin*, iv, p. 254.

[58] Ibid., iv, pp. 288, 311.

[59] De la Roncière, *Histoire*, v, pp.195–200.

[60] *Lettres du Cardinal Mazarin*, iv, pp. 458, 472; A. Chéruel, *Histoire de France sous le ministère de Mazarin, 1651–1661* (3 vols, Paris, 1882), i, p. 29.

[61] *Lettres du Cardinal Mazarin*, iv, p. 472.

[62] Chéruel, *Histoire de France*, i, pp. 31–2.

of which Condé agreed to collaborate with Spain by land and sea, not to negoti-ate with the French crown except jointly with Spain, and to provide the Spaniards with military and naval bases in Guyenne. Not long after this a Spanish armada, under the command of the baron de Batteville, sent from San Sebastian, ar-rived in the Gironde estuary. The Spaniards captured Talmont and the fortress of Bourg-sur-Gironde which was garrisoned with Irish troops in Spanish pay, under the command of Don Joseph Osorio.[63] Condé and his little army, meanwhile, captured Libourne and Périgueux.

Mazarin, as fertile in expedients as ever, was quick to exploit the failure of Spanish ministers to reconcile the duke of Lorraine with his old foe, Condé, and to persuade him to join the new league. Lorraine, for the moment, preferred to keep his options open and entered into negotiations with Mazarin. Duke Charles offered to bring his 10,000 troops across to the French side, against Spain and the *Frondeurs*, in return for restitution of his lands. To induce Lor-raine to enter his league with Spain, Condé had offered to transfer to the duke the three *places fortes* in Lorraine — Stenay, Clermont and Jametz — held by *Frondeur* troops loyal to himself. In a confident letter, from Dinant in the bishopric of Liège, of 29 November 1651, Mazarin reported that Lorraine's secretary (with whom he was negotiating) had seen the treaty between Condé and the Spaniards and that 'Fuensaldaña avoit faict ses derniers efforts pour obliger M. de Lor-raine de le signer aussy' but without success; he, for his part, advised the court to close the deal with Duke Charles, offering to restitute most of his lost terri-tory but with the French crown continuing to garrison Nancy, Stenay and Marsal to ensure that Lorraine would no longer represent a strategic check to France[64] These negotiations continued intensively over the next weeks. On 20 December 1651, Mazarin reported from Bouillon 'que j'ay fort avancé l'accommodement de M. de Lorraine et empesché jusqu'à present qu'il ne s'engageast pour de nouveaux traitez, avec les Espagnols', or entering into the league between Condé and Spain whereby 'on ne feroit point de paix avec le Roy que conjoinctement'.[65]

The Culmination of the Spanish Offensive (1652)

The Spanish resurgence achieved its most impressive successes during 1652 — though Spanish arms also suffered some notable reverses during that crucial year. Ministers in Madrid and Brussels were eager to make the most of the op-portunity to restore Spain's hegemony in Europe, presented by the turmoil in France, but at the same time the Spanish court was clearly anxious to settle and end the struggle whilst the overall strategic situation favoured Spain. Philip was satisfied with the victories and conquests achieved but was also determined to extract terms which would accord with his 'greatness', maintain *reputación*

---

[63] Ibid.
[64] *Lettres du Cardinal Mazarin*, iv, pp. 523–4.
[65] Ibid., iv, p. 552.

and reflect the shift which had taken place in the balance of power. But it was precisely this which made a settlement impossible as long as Mazarin remained at the helm in France. For the cardinal was incorrigibly opposed to anything less than Spanish acknowledgement of the French crown's general supremacy.

Most of Catalonia was now back under Castilian control. The horrendous siege of Barcelona dragged on month after month, the tenacious resistance of its inhabitants stiffened by a garrison of 3,000 French and Swiss troops.[66] Mazarin did all he could to mobilize resources for a counter-offensive to save Barcelona but with much of France in a state of chronic disorder there was not a great deal he could do. Meanwhile, the strife in Guyenne continued whilst the Spaniards resumed their offensive in Flanders. Having obtained from the States of Flanders a substantial grant for the purpose of recovering the parts of the province still in French hands,[67] the Archduke set siege to Gravelines on 11 April. After a five-week siege, the coastal fortress town surrendered late in May. With Gravelines in their possession, the Spaniards could tighten their blockade of Mardijk and Dunkirk, though the Archduke decided not to set siege to Dunkirk itself at this point, owing to the situation in France and Condé's repeated requests for the army of Flanders to come to his aid.[68]

The struggle in progress in France had indeed reached a crucial juncture. Mazarin, having returned in January 1652 at the head of 6,000 German mercenary troops, had skirted Paris where *Frondeur* sentiment remained strong, and set about pacifying the Loire valley. Condé, after the defeat of his forces in Guyenne, at Agen in March, but confident that Bordeaux was under no immediate threat, had hastened from the south-west to Paris, aware that the outcome of the contest for power would be decided there.[69] Meanwhile, the duke of Lorraine simultaneously invaded from the east and also encamped near Paris, though it was far from clear which side he was on — or would join.[70] Still refusing to cooperate with Condé, he resumed his negotiations with Mazarin. Next, a royal army, under Turenne, trapped and almost destroyed Condé's *Frondeur* force in a battle near the Bastille, in the Paris suburb of Faubourg Saint-Antoine, a setback which set alarm bells ringing in both Madrid and Brussels. But despite this near disaster, on 2 July 1652, for the moment Condé succeeded in barricading himself in Paris, aided by the continuing strength of *Frondeur* feeling in the city, and in keeping the royal army outside. The royal court, meanwhile, perambulated during the summer months around the city, from Saint-Denis to Pontoise to Compiègne. The Archduke, having been instructed from Madrid to give priority to assisting Condé over everything else, including the chance to regain Durkirk, launched the army of Flanders, under

[66] Chéruel, *Histoire de France*, i, 30.

[67] AGR, SEG 253, fo. 37, Philip IV to Leopold Wilhelm, Madrid, 11 July 1652.

[68] Ibid., fo. 58, Philip IV to Leopold Wilhelm, Madrid, 16 July 1652.

[69] Ranum, *The Fronde*, p. 323.

[70] Ibid., pp. 324–6.

Fuensaldaña, into France, towards Paris.[71] The Spaniards advanced as far as Chauny, a short distance from Compiègne and more than two-thirds of the distance between Brussels and Paris. Writing to Don Luis de Haro from his camp at Chauny on 20 July, Fuensaldaña reported that the duke of Lorraine was now again collaborating with him and had joined his forces with those of Spain.[72] With the Lorrainers, the Spanish army at Chauny was 25,000 strong.

Meanwhile the conflict in the south west had reached a decisive but unpredictable stage. In Bordeaux, the ruling group had been overthrown by a radical movement of shop-keepers and artisans, known as the Ormée, which soon envinced not just anti-Mazarin but strong anti-royalist and republican sentiments. The Ormée tightened the city's alliance with Condé and with Spain. During July, with the contest in Paris at its height, a Bordelais-*Frondeur* naval force under the comte du Daugnon succeeded in capturing Brouage and repulsing a counter-attack by a royalist marine force. The Bordelais then joined their ships with the armada from San Sebastian which included Spanish and Flemish vessels but the largest contingent of which was made up of ten Neapolitan ships under the command of Marino di Masibradi. This combined Spanish-Neopolitan-Flemish-Bordelais fleet then sailed northwards up the French coast and attempted to capture La Rochelle but was defeated, on 9 August, by a royalist fleet of twenty-six vessels and 5,300 men, under the duc de Vendôme, in a battle off the Île-de-Ré.[73]

Spain was not trying to dismember France and not endeavouring to conquer more territory. It is abundantly clear from the Spanish dispatches that the two-pronged Spanish invasion of France in 1652, penetrating to Chauny, in the north, and to the Île-de-Re, in the south west, was envisaged in Madrid as preparing the ground for a pending, negotiated peace. Nor was there anything unreasonable, inconsistent or vague about the Spanish objectives. Following the thrusts of his armada and army into France, the king sent fresh instructions to Brussels, dated 21 August, authorizing the Archduke, through Fuensaldaña, to enter into immediate talks, at the highest level, to end the war.[74] As a preliminary step, Philip asked that the French court order the garrison at Barcelona to capitulate to his armies and certainly hardened his terms also in some other respects. For example, he now reversed his stance on Roussillon, requiring restitution of the county and, in the Low Countries, demanded the return of Arras, Dunkirk and La Bassée. Moreover, while the Spanish court continued to insist on complete evacuation of Catalonia, repudiation of the Portuguese Revolt and restitution of all of Lorraine to Duke Charles, Philip IV's ministers were now also demanding restoration of all their lands and offices to Condé and the other rebel princes.[75] As a sop to French pride, Spain would cede to France a number

---

[71] AGR, SEG 253, fo. 99v, Leopold Wilhelm to Philip IV, undated (12 June ?) 1652.
[72] BL, MS Add. 14000, fo. 199v; Chéruel, *Histoire de France*, i, pp. 249–52; ii, p. 91.
[73] De la Roncière, *Histoire*, v, pp. 183–8.
[74] BL, MS Add. 14000, fos 199v–201, Philip IV to Leopold Wilhelm, Madrid, 21 August 1652.
[75] Ibid., fo. 200.

of towns in Artois and Luxembourg captured in the 1640s which were still in French hands, namely Hesdin, Thionville and Damvillers.

Whilst Mazarin remained in the ascendant in France there was not the slightest prospect that Louis XIV's ministers would agree to anything resembling these terms. On the contrary, Mazarin obdurately persisted in maintaining that it was vital for France to retain hold of Barcelona 'qui seule est capable de nous donner la paix générale'. If Catalonia did not receive prompt and large-scale assistance, he wrote to Le Tellier from Sedan on 7 September, 'elle se perdra; et avec cette province-là, les esperances de la paix'.[76] Without Catalonia, Mazarin could not see how the French crown could exercise a general supremacy over Spain, remove the Spanish strategic strategic threat to Paris and 'le coeur de la France', or enforce its hegemony in Europe. For the same reasons, Mazarin had not the slightest intention of abandoning Portugal to be reconquered by the Castilians and was absolutely opposed to the reincorporation of Arras and Dunkirk into the Spanish Low Countries. Nor was he in any way willing to yield ground in Italy or Lorraine, give up Roussillon or compensate the princes.

The gulf was unbridgeable. Mazarin may have been self-seeking, rapacious and intransigent in the extreme but he also accurately grasped that the monarchy he served had now reached a crucial juncture. If the princely rebellion, nurtured and bolstered by Spain, were permitted to succeed in bringing the French king to his knees, the inevitable result would be an enduring, perhaps even irreversible, subordination of royal power and authority to a combination of internal and external forces which would lock France into a position of structural inferiority in Europe for as long as the alliance between the princes and the Spanish crown lasted. It was in precisely these terms that Mazarin understood the situation: 'Comme les princes', he wrote, in September 1652

> ont interest à l'affoiblissement de l'authorité et de la puissance du Roy, lequel ne pourrait recevoir un plus rude coup que s'il estoit obligé de faire la paix aux conditions qu'on propose, et d'ailleurs M. de Lorraine ayant le mesme interest, et en outre celuy de se voir hautement restably dans ses estats par la paix générale, il est à craindre que tous conjoinctement n'employassent l'artifice et la force pour nous contraindre à consentir à ce que ledict sieur duc auroit ... proposé aux Espagnols, qui ne consiste pas seulement à abandonner le Portugal et la Catalogne, rendre le Roussillon, Arras, Béthune, et la Bassée, à restituter ses Estats à M. de Lorraine, et de restablir les princes et tous leurs adhérens (ce qui veut dire perdre généralement de tous costez); mais le Roy et l'estat souffriroient encore un préjudice plus notable qui seroit de souffrir, avec une honte et un dommage irréparable, que les Espagnols fussent les arbitres, tant dedans que dehors le royaume; que M. de Lorraine, restably par leur moyen, leur en eust toute obligation et demeurast à jamais lié avec eux, et que les princes en fissent de mesme, conservant, par ce moyen, un party formé en France, à la devotion de l'Espagne, pour empescher l'authorité royale de se relever et pour remuer toutes fois et quantes qu'ils le croiroient nécessaire pour leurs interests, avec asseurance d'estre assistez des Espagnols.

[76] *Lettres du Cardinal Mazarin*, v, pp. 171, 219.

The inevitable consequence in Mazarin's view, would be that the French king would be 'tousjours foible et languissant, son pouvoir soumis à celuy des princes, et enfin les affaires du royaume en un estat mille fois pire que lorsque les grands et ceux de la religion le partageoient, et qu'on n'avoit encore faict aucun progrez sur les Espagnols', worse, that is, than during the sixteenth-century Wars of Religion.[77]

Mazarin's prescription for rescuing the French crown from its predicament was, on the one hand, to bend every effort to restoring the king's authority within France, bribing but making only minimal political concessions to Condé, Lorraine and the other princes, whilst simultaneously straining every nerve to retain Catalonia and the conquered *places fortes* in the Low Countries and Italy, until eventually the military tide should turn. Working to detach either Condé or Lorraine from Spain was crucial but what mattered most of all, in Mazarin's opinion, was to send reinforcements to Flanders, Italy and, especially Catalonia: 'si Dieu nous faisoit la grace que nous puissions sauver Barcelonne', he held, 'j'oserois respondre de la paix à d'autres conditions qu'à celles que les Espagnols esperent de la faire; c'est pourquoy', he urged Le Tellier, 'au nom de Dieu, pressez toutes choses pour cela.'[78] 'Nonobstant toutes les peines que j'ay prises', he added gloomily, three days later, 'la Catalogue se perd, et le Roy [de France] en souffre un prejudice qu'on ne scauroit réparer en des siècles entiers.'[79]

By this time, however, it was becoming obvious that it was not only in Catalonia, but also in Flanders and Italy, that the French were facing major defeat. Some weeks earlier, in part under pressure from the States of Flanders, the Archduke had withdrawn the army of Flanders from France, leaving only the duke of Lorraine to check the French royal force under Turenne (as well as ravage the Champagne).[80] Soon after, the Spanish offensive in west Flanders resumed, the Spaniards steadily advancing their siege lines around Dunkirk. After repeated assaults, and a heavy bombardment, the French garrison at Dunkirk surrendered in mid September. Meanwhile, in Italy, where Duke Carlo II of Mantua-Monferrat had been in collusion with the Spanish authorities in Milan for some time, Mantua had formally broken its neutrality and signed an alliance with Spain. Under a supplementary treaty, signed in September 1651, the governor of Milan, the marqués de Caracena, promised, in return for the duke's help in ejecting the French from Casale, to hand the fortress over, once it had been captured, to be garrisoned by the duke's own troops.[81] In July 1652 the Spanish army of Milan laid siege to Casale for the fourth time in its history. After three months of siege, the city's inhabitants revolted against the French and

[77] Ibid., v, p. 267.
[78] Ibid., v, p. 269.
[79] Ibid., v, p. 291.
[80] AGR, SEG 253, fos 150, 192, Leopold Wilhelm to Philip IV, Brussels, 23 August and 18 September 1652.
[81] Robert Oresko and David Parrott, 'The Sovereignty of Monferrato and the Citadel of Casale as European Problems in the Early Modern Period', in D. Ferrari and A. Quondam (ed.) *Stefano Guazzo e Casale tra cinque e seicento* (Milan, 1997), pp. 59–61.

forced the garrison to withdraw into the citadel, letting the Spaniards enter the city. Finally, on 20 October, the Spaniards sprang a siege mine, severely damaging the citadel and leading, two days later, to the surrender of the French. A week later, under the terms of their agreement with Mantua, the Spanish troops marched off, leaving the long-contested fortress in the hands of ducal troops where it remained for the rest of the Franco-Spanish war and beyond.[82]

Meanwhile, Mazarin's final attempt to save Barcelona failed. A relief squadron of transports carrying troops and supplies, and escorted by eight warships, sailed from Marseille and reached San Feliu de Guíxols at the end of July. The French were sighted from Barcelona on 3 August. There then ensued four days of vigorous manoeuvring in which the French endeavoured to slip past Don Juan's blocking fleet. Unable to do so, and unwilling to risk a full-scale battle with the stronger Spanish fleet, the French withdrew on 7 August and sailed back to France. Barcelona held out for another two months before finally surrendering on 11 October. In the following weeks, the Castilian army also made swift progress in the northernmost parts of Catalonia, capturing Cadaqués, blockading Rosas — the last major French garrison inside the principality and, before long, recovering control of large parts of Roussillon and Cerdanya. The Catalan war seemed all but over. Amid the rising euphoria at the Spanish court over the string of victories at Gravelines, Dunkirk, Chauny, Casale, Barcelona and Cadaqués, Philip IV wrote to the Archduke Leopold Wilhelm in Brussels, on 31 October, expressing his eager desire to reach a final accord with the French court very shortly.[83] The Archduke was instructed to initiate talks and to collaborate closely with Condé so as to ensure that in the final peace terms the interests of the rebellious princes were safeguarded in every respect. With virtually the whole of Catalonia back under the Spanish crown, all that was required for peace, in the view of Philip and his ministers, was that the French court should agree to restore the entire territory and independence of Lorraine, satisfy Condé, promise not to assist Portugal, cede Arras and most of Artois, and hand over the rest of Roussillon in exchange for Hesdin, Thionville and Damvillers (which the French already held).

Needless to say, there was no more chance after the fall of Dunkirk, Barcelona and Casale to the Spaniards, than there had been before, that the French court would agree to anything resembling these terms. Mazarin was adamant that it would have catastrophic consequences for the French crown were he to yield to the pressure for peace at this juncture: 'je vous laisse à penser', he wrote to Le Tellier, on 14 October,

> si le Roy, aprez la perte de plusieurs batailles, pourroit estre conseillé à faire une
> paix par laquelle le Roy d'Espagne, non seulement eust son compte, mais aussy devinst

---

[82] Ibid., p. 62. Stradling's assertion that 'when Caracena captured Casale in 1652, it had to be abandoned immediately, since he had not the men to spare for a garrison' is, of course, absurd, see Stradling, *Europe and the Decline of Spain*, p. 126.

[83] BL, MS Add. 14000, fo. 203, Philip IV to Leopold Wilhelm, Madrid, 31 October 1652.

l'arbitre de toutes choses en France, en forçant sa Majesté à restablir M. de Lorraine et M. le Prince, et a leur departir des graces, lesquels, par gratitude et par interest, seroient tousjours attachez aux interests d'Espagne et à sa devotion; joint que cette paix ne dureroit qu'autant de temps que sa dite Majesté seroit resolue de faire aveuglement tout ce que le Roy d'Espagne et lesdicts princes voudroient.[84]

Spain and the Suppression of the Frondes (1653–4)

Adamant or not, it is clear that Mazarin was deeply shaken by the French defeats of the autumn of 1652, which did indeed seem to presage a new Spanish hegemony in Europe. He had been reluctant to believe the early reports of the loss of both Barcelona and Casale and, as late as 12 November, intimated to Le Tellier that if 'ces deux malheurs-là sont veritables, j'ay trop de passion pour le service du Roy pour avoir aucune joye de ma vie, voyant qu'il est presque impossible de remedier à ceux qui arriveront ensuite à l'estat, et je vous diray, en outre, du meilleur de mon coeur, que Dieu m'auroit faict une grande grace d'abreger mes jours pour ne me laisser voir tant de funestes effects de la rage des mauvais François'.[85] Amongst the most disastrous consequences, in Mazarin's judgment, was the blow to French prestige in Italy. The most serious immediate risk to France's position was the possible defection of Savoy: it was of the utmost urgency, he admonished his colleagues, to take all 'precautions necessaires avec la maison de Savoye, afin que, par l'apprehension des Espagnols, ou par leurs cajoleries, elle ne se laisse pas aller a faire quelque union avec eux au prejudice du Roy'.[86]

Yet, impressive though the triple triumph of Spanish arms in Italy, Catalonia and Flanders of the autumn of 1652 was, by that stage the pendulum had already began to swing back in favour of the French crown, and against the allies of Spain, at least within France itself. In the very month of October 1652 in which Barcelona and Casale had capitulated to the armies of Spain, Condé, accompanied by some 3,000 men who remained loyal to him was forced to abandon Paris where support for the Frondes was now receding, and withdraw eastwards, across Champagne, towards the Spanish Netherlands, besieging and capturing Rethel as he went.[87] In November, Condé's little army also captured Sainte Menehould and Bar-le-Duc. But, as the Archduke Leopold Wilhelm reported to Madrid on 2 November, the prince's support within France had now been eroded to the point that it was only possible for him to continue the struggle as an adjunct of the Spanish forces in the Netherlands.[88] Even so, Condé now

---

[84] *Lettres du Cardinal Mazarin*, v, p. 390.

[85] Ibid., v, p. 458.

[86] Ibid.

[87] Ranum, *The Fronde*, p. 340; J.J. Inglis-Jones, 'The Grand Condé in Exile: Power Politics in France, Spain and the Spanish Netherlands' (unpublished Oxford D.Phil. thesis, 1994), pp. 47–8.

[88] AGR, SEG 253, fo. 296v, Leopold Wilhelm to Philip IV, Brussels, 2 November 1652.

held a formidable cordon of *places fortes* in Champagne and Lorraine bordering the Spanish Netherlands. Over the winter of 1652–3, Condé quartered his
troops partly in Champagne-Lorraine and partly in Spanish Luxemburg.

Secure at the centre, to all appearances, Mazarin and the boy-king Louis XIV
(who had reached the age of fifteen) were now in a position to mount a more
determined effort than had been possible hitherto to suppress the Frondes in
the outlying regions of France while, at the same time, attempting to counter
the recent Spanish gains in Italy, Catalonia and Flanders. During the opening
months of 1653, French royal armies took the offensive both in the south west
and in Alsace and restored large areas to the king's control. At the same time,
fresh forces were dispatched to Italy where Mazarin launched a carefully
orchestrated diplomatic offensive to convince the princes and republics of the
French monarch's 'bonnes intentions pour la liberté de l'Italie pourvu qu'elle
soit secondée par les princes qui ont plus d'interest que jamais de s'y appliquer,
vu la puissance dont sont accrus les Espagnols, et le dessein qu'ils font paroître
plus que jamais, par l'oppression de cette noble province, de parvenir à la
monarchie universelle'.[89] This was a message which did not go unheeded. There
was, in various Italian states at this time, a flurry of anxiety arising from the
recent Spanish successes and something of an anti-Spanish back-lash, not least
in Genoa where the traditional alliance with Spain came under considerable
strain during the years 1652–5 owing to the strengthening of the local pro-
French faction and deepening of the internal divisions within the republic.[90]

Especially crucial at this juncture was the progress of the French royal armies
in south-western France, where Mazarin had prepared the way by winning over
the admiral du Daugnon with a magnificent bribe of 500,000 livres, a full amnesty,
the rank of 'marshal of France' and admission to the august order of Saint
Esprit. With this he engineered the recovery of Brouage and secured La
Rochelle.[91] Royalist troops fanned out across the south west and, by March 1653,
controlled much of the region. More royal victories followed. 'Bazas has
capitulated', Conti reported to Condé on 17 April, observing that besides
Bordeaux only Libourne, Bourg, Bergerac, Sainte Foix, Tartas and Périgueux
were still in open rebellion to the crown and that, over the last few days, the
Frondeurs had lost all their posts on the Garonne.[92]

Even so, the Ormistes for the moment retained their grip on Bordeaux and
seemed as resolute as ever in resisting Mazarin in alliance with Condé and Spain,
their hopes buoyed by repeated assurances from Spain, promising the imminent return of the armada from San Sebastian. The Spanish king, having

---

[89] *Recueil des instructions données aux ambassadeurs et ministres de France depuis les traités de Westphalie
jusqu'à la Revolution Française: Savoie Sardaigne et Mantoue*, i, ed. H. de Beaucaire (Paris, 1898), pp. 26–9.
[90] Felipe Ruiz Martín, *Las finanzas de la monarquía hispánica en tiempos de Felipe IV (1621–1665)*
(Madrid, 1990), pp. 148–9.
[91] De la Roncière, *Histoire*, v, p. 201.
[92] Quoted in S.A.Westrich, *The Ormée of Bordeaux: A Revolution during the Fronde* (Baltimore,
Maryland, 1972), p. 117.

withdrawn his fleet over the winter to refit and resupply, was indeed endeavouring to send a sizeable force back to the Garonne.[93] Meanwhile, in April 1653, categorical orders were sent from Madrid to Brussels that the archduke must give priority to intervening in France, to support Condé and fan the embers of the Frondes, over all other objectives and considerations.[94] But soon most remaining towns in rebel and Spanish hands in south-west France fell to the royal armies. Lormont-sur-Gironde, garrisoned by 575 Irish in Spanish pay, surrendered on 26 May. On 15 June, the archduke reported gloomily to Madrid that, despite the urgent need to revive the Frondes, he had been forced to delay putting his army into the field owing to lack of funds and the obstreperous attitude of the States of Flanders and Brabant which evidently disagreed with the royal opinion that invading France was more important than recovering the French-occupied towns of Artois.[95] On 4 July Bourg-sur-Gironde, garrisoned by 800 Irish, surrendered, followed by Libourne a fortnight later.[96]

The armada from San Sebastian eventually reappeared at the mouth of Gironde but too late to save Bordeaux where the Ormée was overthrown by a royalist coup from within at the end of July.[97] Conti and the *Frondeur* leadership in the south west abandoned the struggle and made their peace with Mazarin and the king in August.[98] All this, needless to say, was exceedingly frustrating for the Spanish court, the archduke in Brussels, and for Condé. In addition, there was a rising tension between Condé and his hosts in the Spanish Netherlands. Whilst the Archduke and Fuensaldaña complained to Madrid about Condé's haughty airs and desire to lay down the law to them,[99] Condé furiously complained about the attitude of both men, especially Fuensaldaña whom he accused of being obstructive and unhelpful in every respect. He blamed the Spaniards for being so slow to pay him the subsidy stipulated in his treaty of alliance with Philip IV that he had been unable to take the field until July, by which time a royal army, under Turenne, was besieging Rethel. Since the Spaniards had preferred to penetrate France further west, towards Saint-Quentin, rather than march towards Rethel, Condé had had no choice but to agree. The army of Flanders had then invaded as far as Roye and Montdidier, but far too slowly and hesitantly for Condé, who believed that a swift, bold thrust towards Paris (where both his own, and Spanish, intelligence indicated that *Frondeur* discontent with Mazarin and the crown was still simmering) was the best strategy.[100] The

[93] AGR, SEG 254, fo. 13, Philip IV to Leopold Wilhelm, Madrid, 9 January 1653.

[94] Ibid., fo. 221, Philip IV to Leopold Wilhelm, Madrid, 26 April 1653.

[95] AGR, SEG 255, fo. 80, Leopold Wilhelm to Philip IV, Brussels, 15 June 1653.

[96] [Pierre Coste], *Histoire de Louis de Bourbon II du nom Prince de Condé, premier prince du sang* (Cologne, 1693), p. 435.

[97] Westrich, *Ormée of Bordeaux*, pp. 123–4.

[98] He married one of Mazarin's nieces, Anna-Maria Martinozzi, and was subsequently loaded with favours, see Oresko, 'Marriages of the Nieces', pp. 122–3.

[99] AGR, SEG 255, fo. 126, Philip IV to Leopold Wilhelm, Madrid, 12 July 1653.

[100] BL, MS Add. 14007, fos 136–7, Condé to comte de Fiesque, 28 August 1653.

situation was all the more frustrating in that the joint Spanish-Condéan-Lorraine army, of nearly 30,000 men, was substantially stronger than the opposing French army, but hampered by poor cooperation between its constituent elements was unable to exploit its advantage.[101] When Condé surprised Turenne's army (encamped on the Somme, near Péronne, on 13 August), Fuensaldaña had been so slow to come up that he had lost the opportunity to launch a full-scale attack. This was the fourth major Spanish invasion of northern France since 1648 but the only tangible result, after a three-week siege, was the capture of Rocroy, in September.

With the king's approval, Rocroy was garrisoned with 1,500 troops under Condé's sole command. A disagreeable encounter between the archduke and Condé, to review the whole question of their strategic collaboration, held at Châtelet at the beginning of September, brought relations between the two men to a new low. Finding Condé insufferably arrogant and difficult to work with, the archduke assured the king that the prince had now lost virtually all his backing in France and having been abandoned by his 'brother, wife, sister, the duke de Rochefoucauld and the inhabitants of Bordeaux . . . was hated by all and without hope of ever being reconciled'.[102] Leopold Wilhelm pleaded with Philip to end, or at least scale down, his support, and especially his subsidies, for Condé. He warned that the king must either make peace or substantially strengthen the army of Flanders. If neither of these things was done 'whole provinces and realms will be lost'.

Condé, for his part, was infuriated by what he regarded as the excessively cautious attitude, and obstinacy, of the Spanish commanders, the consequence of which, in his opinion, was a veritable catalogue of missed opportunities. Nearly all of France was now back under royal control at any rate superficially. Yet it would be wrong to maintain that, for all practical purposes, the Frondes were now at an end. After August 1653 there was still a widespread mood of sullen opposition to royal authority, and by no means only in Bordeaux where disgruntlement was strongest. It was with some justification — if also a cynical disregard of anyone's interests but his own — that Condé persisted in his hopes that further Spanish intervention in France, especially the return of the Spanish armada from San Sebastian to disrupt the wine exports of the Bordeaux region, might yet provoke fresh outbreaks of rebellion against the crown.[103] If Rethel was lost, a whole cordon of strategically vital fortresses — La Capelle, Châtelet, Rocroy, Stenay, Landrecies — remained in *Frondeur* and Spanish hands, posing a direct threat to the Paris basin and the authority of the French crown. If most of Alsace

---

[101] AGR, SEG 255, fo. 190, Leopold Wilhelm to Philip IV, Brussels, 1 August 1653. The total size of the army of Flanders, in March 1653, was officially estimated at 53,500 men in total, infantry and cavalry, of whom 3,545 were Spanish and 2,414 Italian infantry, see AGS, Estado, leg. 2081, 'Relacion de los oficiales y soldados que ay en la infanteria y cavaleria del exercito de su Magestad en los estados de Flandes'.

[102] AGR, SEG 256, fos 35v–36v. Leopold Wilhelm to Philip IV, 6 and 7 September 1653.

[103] BL, MS Add. 14007, fo. 138; Westrich, *Ormée of Bordeaux*, pp. 132–3.

was back under the sway of Mazarin and the crown, the province's rebel governor, the comte d'Harcourt, remained defiant and, in September 1653, signed a fresh alliance with Spain and the duke of Lorraine, a treaty which provided for the transfer of Philippsburg to the Lorrainers and the marriage of Harcourt's eldest son to the duke of Lorraine's daughter, Anne.

Meanwhile, the French launched their counter-offensive in Catalonia. A large army of French troops and Catalan exiles, in all some 17,000 men, under the mareschal Hocquincourt, thrust southwards from Roussillon, capturing Figueres and San Feliu de Guíxols, and on 12 July set siege to Gerona. The siege of Gerona lasted for seventy days until finally, after experiencing considerable difficulty in scraping together a sufficient force, Don Juan advanced and, after some bitter fighting, forced the raising of the siege and the flight of the French back to Roussillon.

Reviewing the strategic situation at the close of 1653, the Spanish court and Condé agreed that it was essential to avoid spreading Spain's resources too thinly. In contrast to the prevous several years, the commitment of large forces to southwest France would now have to cease. While the fighting in Catalonia had not ended, it was obvious that Catalonia was both too poor and too devastated by the war to serve as a base for a large-scale invasion of southern France. In any case, the French continued to hold Rosas and, in December 1653, defeated a Spanish force near Gerona. It was thus considered 'yndubitable' that the only effective way to pin France to the defensive and keep the initiative in Spanish hands was to concentrate Spain's military resources in Flanders.[104] Only from that direction did it seem possible to exert the kind of pressure which would prevent the French from sending fresh armies into Catalonia and Italy, and renewing their attempts to stir up 'revolution' in Naples, pressure sufficient to pose a serious threat to the core of France and induce the French court to agree to a 'reasonable' peace.

The revival of French power continued during 1654. The maréchal de la Ferté completed the subjugation of Alsace, the comte d'Harcourt finally submitting to Mazarin and the king in May 1654 and handing Breisach over to royal troops. La Ferté's army then marched into Lorraine to reduce the strongholds of Stenay and Clermont which were held by the Condéans. Despite Don Luis de Haro's efforts to intercede, the quarrel between Condé and Fuensaldaña continued unabated.[105] Condé did everything he could to secure the recall of

---

[104] BL, MS Add. 14007, fos 140–44, 'Memoria . . . refiriendo lo que contienen dos despachos del señor Principe de Conde de 9 y 25 de Diciembre del ano de 1653'. Needless to say neither the pro-Spanish Catalans nor the pro-Habsburg Portuguese exiles in Spain agreed with this general strategy and there were also dissenting voices among courtiers in Madrid. The marqués de Velada, for example, advised at the time of the start of the siege of Barcelona, in 1651, that the Spanish crown would do best to scale down its effort in Flanders, Italy and Catalonia, and concentrate on recovering Portugal and its extensive overseas empire: see Rafael Valladares, 'Portugal y el fin de la hegemonía hispánica', *Hispania: revista española de historia*, 56 (1996), p. 529.

[105] BL, MS Add. 14007, fo. 152, Condé to Fiesque, Brussels, 9 May 1654.

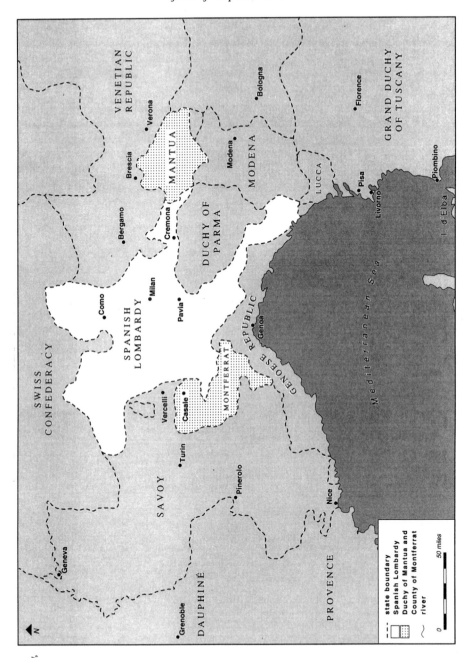

Map 4
Spanish Lombardy,
Mantua-
Montferrat,
and their
neighbours
during the
mid seventeenth
century

VENETIAN
REPUBLIC

GRAND DUCHY
OF TUSCANY

Verona

Bologna

Florence

Brescia

MANTUA

Modena

MODENA

Piombino

LUCCA

Pisa

Bergamo

Cremona

Livorno

DUCHY OF
PARMA

I. d'Elba

Como

Milan

SPANISH
LOMBARDY

Pavia

Genoa

GENOESE REPUBLIC

Mediterranean Sea

SWISS
CONFEDERACY

Vercelli

Casale

MONTFERRAT

Turin

SAVOY

Pinerolo

Nice

Geneva

PROVENCE

Grenoble

DAUPHINÉ

N

state boundary
Spanish Lombardy
Duchy of Mantua and
County of Montferrat
river

0   50 miles

Fuensaldaña and to undermine the position of the archduke, repeatedly warning the Spanish court that unless the quality of the military leadership in Flanders was improved Spain was likely to lose all her enclaves in north-eastern France that very year.

Condé was undoubtedly the most talented and energetic of the commanders in the Spanish Netherlands. Nevertheless, while the king was prepared to back Condé to the extent of confirming that he had absolute command over his own men (notwithstanding the fact that for the most part these were now being paid for by Spain), he was equally firm in laying down that the archduke alone had the authority to determine the overall strategy of the allies in and around the Low Countries.[106] Thus, when the French royal army laid siege to Stenay late in June, Condé was obliged to go along with Leopold Wilhelm's decision that the army of Flanders should launch its counter-offensive not into Lorraine, to save Stenay, but rather into Artois to threaten Arras. Seeing that the Spanish troops in Luxemburg were marching north westwards, and not towards the Lorraine, Mazarin alerted Turenne who was just in time to reinforce Arras before the town was sealed off by a joint Spanish-Condéan-Lorrainer army of 22,000 men. Despite shortage of provisions and the evident risks of pressing on with the siege with a substantial French royal army, under Turenne, not far away, Fuensaldaña and Condé persisted in fortifying their siege lines. Stenay, meanwhile, its walls breached by mines, surrendered to Louis XIV on 6 August. For several weeks the outcome of the drama in Artois hung in the balance. Finally, on 25 August, in a violent dénouement, Turenne successfully stormed a section of the Spanish lines outside Arras, forcing the immediate abandonment of the siege and the headlong flight of the Spanish army. Only the energy and dexterity of Condé saved the Spaniards, Lorrainers and his own men alike from a catastrophic defeat. As it was, Turenne captured 3,000 men and over sixty siege guns, as well as great quantities of other equipment and supplies. The defeat damaged Spain's revived prestige in Europe, and Condé's sagging prestige in France, but enhanced Condé's standing in the Spanish Netherlands and at the Spanish court, where he credited with having prevented a still worse disaster.[107]

Meanwhile France also recouped prestige on the Spanish border. Condé's younger brother, Conti, now an ally of Mazarin, having been named 'viceroy of Catalonia' in May, had gathered an army together at Perpignan and, in July, captured Vilafranca del Conflent and overran the rest of Roussillon still in Spanish hands. In September, Conti invaded Cerdanya and set siege to Puigcerdá. The town, held by a mixed garrison of 1,000 Italians, Germans, Irish and pro-Spanish Catalans, held out only briefly, capitulating on 21 September. In the ensuing weeks, the French and their Catalan allies reconquered the rest of Cerdanya.

Amid the bad news from Flanders and Catalonia, the Spanish monarch could

---

[106] Ibid., fos 154–6, 'Memoria' of comte de Fiesque for Don Luis de Haro, 18 June 1654.
[107] Lonchay, *Rivalité*, p. 167; Inglis-Jones, 'The Grand Condé', pp. 75–116.

at least take some comfort from the fiasco of Mazarin's latest attempt to overthrow Spanish rule in Naples. On 14 November a French naval force, which had sailed from Toulon, entered the Bay of Naples and seized the port of Castellammare, near Sorrento. But the French received little support and when they tried to adance were rapidly defeated by the Spanish garrison of Naples. They withdrew to their ships and sailed back to France.

Over the winter of 1654–5 Mazarin instigated a fresh round of peace talks with the Spanish court. Moreover, this time the terms which Mazarin offered appeared to represent a genuine softening of his previous position. For the first time since the outbreak of the Catalan revolt, in 1640, the French court signalled its willingness to evacuate the whole of the principality, retaining only Roussillon, and to cease all assistance for Portugal.[108] Besides this, France would restore Béthune, La Bassée, Quesnoy, Thionville and Damvillers to Spain in exchange for the key strongholds held by the Spaniards in north-eastern France: La Capelle, Châtelet and Rocroy, as well as Arras, Hesdin and Bapaume.[109] But this new moderation of Mazarin on territorial issues, at least regarding Catalonia and Flanders, was arguably motivated by his desire to drive a deep wedge between the Spanish court and its allies. Concerning Lorraine, Mazarin offered neither to restore the duke's lands nor his independence but only to compensate him for his losses in cash. Regarding Condé, Mazarin offered nothing at all except fulsome assurances that in Louis' royal clemency the prince would find 'every satisfaction'.[110]

Leopold Wilhelm tried to persuade Philip to respond favourably. He urged that the southern Netherlands were exhausted, that the military outlook was highly uncertain, and that the concession which the French were offering with respect to Portugal was 'un grandissimo punto' (a very big point).[111] He acknowledged that the king was bound by oath to negotiate with France only jointly with Condé, and to safeguard the latter's interests, but implored Don Luis and Philip's other chief advisers to consider whether it was reasonable that the Spanish monarchy 'should continue in a ceaseless and such a costly war' solely to buttress the pretensions of a prince which were not altogether justified and some of which might be termed 'extravagant'. Neither did he think that the question of Lorraine should be allowed to prevent the making of peace between France and Spain. But his views were not shared by Philip and Don Luis. The king and his chief advisers believed that they could not abandon Condé,

[108] BL, MS Add. 1400, fos 211–13, 'Copia de los apuntamientos que hizo Don Gaspar Bonifaz de las condiciones para la paz entre ambas coronas, que le propuso el Cardenal Mazarino al pasar por Paris'.

[109] Ibid.

[110] Ibid., fo. 212v, 'Respuesta que llevo de parte del señor Don Luis de Haro el sergento general . . . Don Gaspar Bonifaz'.

[111] Ibid., fos 209–209v, Leopold Wilhelm to Philip IV, Brussels, 29 January 1655.

or the duke of Lorraine, either honourably or without sacrificing Spain's leverage and influence around the borders of France; and that to do so was fundamentally against Spain's interest.[112]

Deadlock, 1655–6

The continuing revival of French power placed Spain in a rapidly deepening quandary and predicament. This was exacerbated by the worsening financial crisis at Madrid, which resulted in part from the increasingly strained relations between the Spanish court and the republic of Genoa.[113] Chronic shortage of cash meant that Spain's armies in all theatres were smaller and weaker than in previous years and this, in turn, lent added momentum to the French counter-offensive. In Catalonia a French army under Conti, invading from Roussillon, restored the French grip over the area around Rosas and laid siege to Cadaqués which was also bombarded from the sea. After two and a half years back under Spanish control, Cadaqués capitulated to the French on 27 May 1655.[114] Soon after this, Turenne and La Ferté led a powerful French army into the border zone of the Spanish Netherlands, setting siege to Landrecies. The French could calmly fortify their siege lines under the noses of the Spaniards and Condé who were too weak to interfere. Still more menacing was the advance of a joint Franco-Savoyard army right across Spanish Lombardy, threatening Milan itself at one point and laying siege to Pavia. The French and Savoyards were joined in ravaging large tracts of the Milanese by contingents of Modenese soldiery. Nevertheless, the Spanish army of Lombardy, under Caracena, eventually succeeded in winning a major victory over the French, breaking the siege of Pavia and putting their enemies to flight.

Meanwhile, fresh peace talks had begun. A Spanish envoy, Don Pedro de Vaus, conferred secretly with Mazarin at Soissons on 3 July 1655.[115] According to Mazarin, Condé was the fundamental obstacle to peace. The cardinal urged the Spanish monarch to desist from his unreasoning support for the pretensions of the prince. Louis XIV, he argued, was ready to abandon the 'duke of Braganza', as the Spaniards called the king of Portugal, and give the Portuguese no more assistance, even though he was a formal ally of France against Spain; reciprocity, he urged, required Philip to proceed likewise with Condé. Mazarin insisted that, once peace was signed, Condé would be given 'satisfaction' by the French king. He also reminded the Spanish court that Landrecies was besieged; that the French were regaining ground in Catalonia; and that Cromwell, now that England was released from her maritime war with the Dutch, was planning to attack Spain in the West Indies. Finally, he urged that Condé no longer

---

[112] Ibid., fo. 212v, 'Respuesta'.

[113] Ruiz Martín, *Finanzas de la monarquía hispánica*, pp. 148–51.

[114] De la Roncière, *Histoire*, v, p. 213; Sanabre, *La acción de Francia*, pp. 562–3.

[115] BL, MS Add. 14000, fos 213–21, 'Copia de lo que paso a Pedro de Baos en las conferencias que tubo con el Cardenal Mazarini (Soissons, 3 July, 1655).

represented a significant accretion to Spanish strength since his army of 10,000 men was largely paid for by Spain and the few French troops still with him were unreliable rebels whom the French king could easily induce to return to France.[116]

Spain's situation was indeed a difficult one. There was now a serious risk of major and general defeat. All the Spanish armies were in a poor state, the financial predicament was acute, and it was undoubtedly true that the English were planning to attack Spain in the Caribbean. Landrecies would fall — the town surrendered, after an eighteen day siege, on 14 July — after which Turenne would doubtless attempt La Capelle, the town of Condé, or another nearby *place forte*. Yet Philip and his ministers persisted in their view that what Mazarin was offering did not provide the basis for a secure and honourable peace. The royal objections were set out in a missive dispatched to the Archduke from Madrid on 14 August.[117] First, Philip had no intention of underwriting those of Condé's pretensions which were excessive but was determined to negotiate with the French king, as he had promised in his treaty with Condé, only jointly with the prince and safeguard those of the prince's interests which seemed just in Madrid. This much was pronounced 'ynescusable para mantener el honor, y las conbeniencias y consequencias futuras', indispensable, that is, both for the king's honour and for maintaining Spain's position as a great power in relation to France. Secondly, Philip (like Condé and the Archduke) had long lost patience with the duke of Lorraine, whose unreliability and secret dealings with Mazarin were not only notorious but positively dangerous. This led, in February 1654, to the duke being arrested in Flanders, imprisoned in Antwerp castle and soon sent into custody in Spain.[118] The king remained resolved, however, to secure the restoration of Lorraine as a large and independent client state of Spain wedged between France and the Empire. Mazarin's insistence on treating Lorraine and Bar as parts of France, and the duke as a rebellious *Frondeur*, was deemed totally unacceptable in Madrid. Nor were Mazarin's proposals on Italy considered very constructive; quite the contrary, they were judged so obscure that it was impossible to make out 'what is being offered and what is being demanded'. Finally, the king had not failed to notice that Mazarin's offer of peace lacked any undertaking to evacuate all of Catalonia, including Rosas and Cadaqués, or to discuss restitution of Artois. If for the moment the French had the upper hand in all theatres, the king pointed out that the fortunes of war can turn quickly, urging the archduke to remind the French of all the strongholds and territory which they had lost to Spain since 1648 in Flanders, Catalonia and Italy. He was also to emphasise that while, for the moment, the Spanish finances were in dire straits, the inhabitants of France were also feeling the strain and there was

---

[116] Ibid., fo. 216v.

[117] Ibid., fos 223–4, Philip IV to Leopold Wilhelm, Madrid, 14 August 1655.

[118] He was arrested on 25 February in the archducal palace in Brussels, from where he was transferred to the Spanish citadel in Antwerp and then by sea to Spain, where he was kept under house arrest in Toledo, [Coste], *Histoire*, pp. 449–50.

still a formidable malcontent faction within France sympathetic to Condé and the aims of the Frondes and which, at the first favourable opportunity, was likely to rise again.

With the gap between the two courts still very wide, there was no alternative but for the war to drag on. The French advance in Catalonia was halted in September when the arrival of a Spanish fleet forced the French to abandon their siege of Palamós. But in the southern Netherlands the French push continued. By this stage Leopold Wilhelm was in a state of acute anxiety owing to the poor state of Flanders' defences and the chronic lack of 'Spaniards and Italians, the principal nerve of war here'.[119] The strategic town of Condé, situated to the north of Valenciennes, capitulated on 18 August. With a large and powerful French army seizing and fortifying positions all around Condé, Arleux, Saint-Amand and nearby localities, it looked as if the Spaniards were about to lose a sizeable slice of territory containing several important towns. With no small satisfaction, Mazarin wrote to Turenne and La Ferté on 3 September concerning 'la consternation des ennemis et de toute la Flandre, qui est plus grande que vous ne scauriez imaginer. Ils sont tousjours dans la crainte qu'on ne fortifie Arleux et l'Escluse pour incommoder Douay et couper plus qu'ils ne le sont Bouchain, Valenciennes et Cambray'.[120] Tournai too was under threat.

An urgent political priority of the Spanish court at this juncture was to try to preserve Spain's leverage over the house of Lorraine. By arresting Duke Charles, Philip had shown that he was no longer willing to tolerate the political and military independence of the duke from Spain, though — as had been pointed out in reply to Leopold Wilhelm's declaration of 25 February 1654, announcing the reasons for the arrest of the duke in Brussels — Charles had never signed any commitment obliging him to negotiate with France only jointly with Spain.[121] In the negotiations of the autumn of 1655 between the Spanish court and Duke Charles (who was held in captivity in Toledo) there were two main issues. The first was the king's demand that the army of Lorraine — which, since the duke's arrest had been under the command of his brother, Duke Francis — should now be fully integrated into the army of Flanders and be part of the same structure of command, discipline and pay as the king's own troops. The second was the king's requirement that the duke must bind himself 'not to make any peace or alliance with another king or prince at my expense'.[122] In return for his assent, the duke was promised compensation in land and effects and also his personal freedom from the moment the transfer of his regiments to Spanish command was completed. However, the duke refused to submit to these demands and his detention in Toledo continued. In fact, by arresting

[119] AGR, SEG 261, fo. 99v, Leopold Wilhelm to Philip IV, Brussels, 20 February 1655.

[120] *Lettres du Cardinal Mazarin*, vii, p. 72.

[121] *Risposta al manifesto dell' Arciduca Leopoldo, il quale pretende di giustificar la prigionia del duca di Lorena* (n.p., March ? 1654), fo. 2; Inglis-Jones, 'The Grand Condé', p. 101.

[122] BL, MS Add. 14004, fos 697–701, 'Instrución' to Don Miguel de Salamanca, who was being sent to Toledo to negotiate with Duke Charles.

the duke Philip had so alienated him that he had little alternative but to keep him as his prisoner for the duration of the war. He also faced the tricky problem of how to ensure the continued loyalty to Spain of the duke's brother and commanding officers. For even had the duke signed a treaty under duress the likelihood that he would repudiate it as soon as he was released was too great for his release to be contemplated. In any case, Philip's bid to consolidate his grip over the house, troops and interest of Lorraine rapidly unravelled.[123] Duke Francis, choosing his moment, defected to the French in November 1655, fleeing via Landrecies and taking the bulk of his soldiery with him. There was no hiding the blow to Spanish prestige or the damage done to Spanish interests in Lorraine, Trier and on the middle Rhine. The Lorrainers fought with the French against the Spanish during the 1656 campaign.

The new governor-general in Brussels (who was also to be the last to command a powerful army in the southern Netherlands under the Spanish flag), Don Juan José de Austria, arrived early in 1656. Though he established a better working relationship with Condé than had his predecessor, he found few reasons for optimism. In his letter to the king of 15 April 1656, he insisted that a comprehensive peace with France was now a matter of the utmost urgency for the Spanish monarchy in general and the southern Netherlands in particular.[124] The expected French offensive in the north materialized in the early summer. The main French army, under Turenne and La Ferté, penetrated deep into Spanish territory, beyond Douai and Cambrai, seeking to exploit the inroads made the previous year. On 15 June 1656 the French army laid siege to Valenciennes. The siege and bombardment lasted for a month during which, Don Juan José was heartened to hear, the inhabitants displayed a solid loyalty to Spain. Finally, on the night of 15 July, Don Juan and Condé exacted their revenge for the defeat at Arras two years before. After repeated assaults, their troops broke through the besiegers' lines, throwing the French army into a headlong, panicky retreat in which the Spaniards and Condéans captured some 4,000 men, including Maréchal La Ferté himself, besides great quantities of guns and stores. This was in fact Spain's (and Condé's) last great victory; but no one knew that at the time and it was loudly trumpeted around Europe. It was also later commemorated, albeit stressing the role of the Spaniards rather than Condé, in a large painting 'very beautiful and well set out' by the celebrated Flemish battle artist Pieter Snayers.[125] Spain's prestige in Europe revived appreciably.

More than a little shaken by the 'malheur qui nous est arrivé', Mazarin urged Turenne to do everything possible to limit the damage and contain the Spaniards

---

[123] Ibid., fo. 717, consulta, 21 March 1658; Augustin Calmet, *Histoire ecclésiastique et civile de Lorraine* (3 vols, Nancy, 1728), iii, p. 532.

[124] AGR, SEG 261, fo. 203, Don Juan José to Philip IV, Brussels, 15 April 1656.

[125] De Bie devotes more space to Snayers' painting of the Spanish victory at Valenciennes, in July 1656, than virtually any other picture discussed in his book, see Cornelis de Bie, *Het gulden cabinet vande edele vry schilder-const* (Antwerp, 1661), pp. 223–4.

and, in particular, not to lose the nearby strategic towns of Condé and Saint-Guillan, 'car, outre que ces postes sont d'importance, ce sera un coup de haute reputation de les conserver'.[126] But Turenne could not prevent Don Juan entering Condé in triumph, an event which produced a fresh shower of congratulations from Madrid and more celebrations throughout the Spanish Low Countries.

Meanwhile, both before and after these Spanish successes of the summer of 1656, the French and Spanish courts were once again absorbed in peace negotiations. It has been claimed that it was 'Mazarin who made the strongest attempt to break the vicious circle' and that through his efforts and those of his closest aide, Hugues de Lionne, the two courts 'crawled painfully towards agreement'.[127] Were this view correct then Mazarin must indeed have shifted his ground substantially since the early 1650s, despite the fact that France's military position was, on the whole, now much stronger than it had been then. But while it is true that the talks were arduous and intensive, that the Spanish king participated personally during many hours in the deliberations, and also that, on territorial matters, the French were now more moderate than they had been earlier, it is plain that Mazarin and Louis XIV were as determined as ever not to settle with Spain without extracting the kind of political gains and advantages which would unambiguously proclaim the supremacy of France.[128]

The French crown agreed to abandon Portugal, the Spanish court to recognize the emperor's ceding of Alsace to France under the terms of the peace of 1648.[129] On Catalonia, it was agreed the French would evacuate the entire principality, including Rosas and Cadaqués, and restitute Cerdanya, but retain Roussillon so that the line of the Pyrenees would mark the final border between France and Spain. More difficult was the question of what territory the Spanish crown would cede to France in the Low Countries. After much wrangling, and with 'great repugnance', Philip agreed to sign away all of Artois to France, as well as to return the captured *places fortes* of Rocroy, La Capelle and Châtelet, while the French would restitute slices of Luxemburg they had conquered (Thionville and Damvillers) and Béthune, besides Quesnoy and La Bassée.[130] In addition,

---

[126] *Lettres du Cardinal Mazarin*, vii, p. 281.

[127] Stradling, *Europe and the Decline of Spain*, p. 134; more recently this author has written of what he calls the 'extremely reasonable overture of 1656, rejected by Philip IV purely on grounds of prestige', see Stradling, *Spain's Struggle for Europe*, pp. 26–7. Bonney writes, 'Philip IV was not interested in a just peace, only one that was favourable to Spanish interests, and his confidence in ultimate victory led him to spurn the French offer of a reasonable compromise during the mission of the French secretary of state, Lionne, to Madrid in 1656', see Bonney, *European Dynastic States*, p. 239. Lynch writes, 'in 1656 there was a distinct opportunity of peace with France; Catalonia had now been recovered and the French promised not to assist the Portuguese. Against the advice of his ministers Philip IV refused to negotiate, insisting on conditions as unreasonable as those which Cromwell demanded of Spain', Lynch, *The Hispanic World*, p. 169.

[128] BL, MS Add. 14000, fos 235–7, 'Copia de Carta de su Magestad para el serenissimo señor Don Juan de Austria avissando la rotura del tratado de paz para que vino Monsieur de Leoni', Madrid, 26 September 1656.

[129] Ibid., fo. 235v.

[130] Ibid.

the French would evacuate Charolais and other parts of Spanish Burgundy which they had occupied. More difficult still was the problem of Italy. Philip was ready to return Vercelli to Savoy and, after much argument, it was settled that Casale would have to be demilitarized and its walls demolished. Each side agreed to return captured enclaves in the Milanese and Monferrat but stubborn differences concerning Mantua and Modena remained unresolved.[131] Regarding Lorraine, Mazarin offered only to restitute the duchy proper without the duchy of Bar and with the walls of Nancy dismantled and France retaining a strategic corridor to Alsace,[132] stipulations which would have irretrievably converted Lorraine into a defenceless pawn of France.

Nevertheless, had the difficulties been confined to territorial and political disputes such as these, the peace negotiations of 1656 would perhaps have eventually ended in a comprehensive settlement. But the remaining obstacles were still more fundamental and it is by no means surprising that, in the end, the entire process collapsed. To claim, as one historian put it, that 'only one or two matters of form, even of protocol, were left to be finalised' is to fail totally to grasp what was at stake. For, as in 1655, Mazarin's relative moderation on territorial matters was designed to reinforce his bid to extract political advantages of a different kind and order. In fact, Mazarin never expected the talks to succeed but was anxious to contrive matters so that the Spanish crown should be saddled with the blame in the eyes of foreign courts, the papacy and the French public. 'Quoyque nous fussions bien asseurez', he explained, on 28 August 1656,

> que les Espagnols n'estoient nullement disposez à la paix, on jugea pour chose absolument necessaire de faire cette mission [de Lionne] afin que leur intention fust cognue de tout le monde, d'autant plus qu'ils publioient hautement que, si le Roy eust seulement consenty à envoyer une personne en Espagne, la paix auroit esté conclue en deux jours, le Roy Catholique estant tout-à-fait disposé à y apporter les dernières facilitez; et ç'a esté un grand bonheur pour nous d'avoir pu faire paroistre à tous, nonobstant ces artifices des Espagnols et les autres, dont ils se sont servis pour persuader au Pape et à tous les princes de la Chrestienté qu'ils souhaitoient avec passion de contribuer à son repos et que la France seule en empeschoit l'establissement, qu'ils en sont, en effect, plus esloignez que jamais, prétendant des conditions si injustes, que le Roy fera la guerre toute sa vie, avec une approbation générale, plustost que les accorder. Nous attendons le retour de M. de Lionne avec l'esclaircissement en bonne forme pour faire advouer aux plus critiques et à ceux qui sont les plus mal intentionnez pour la France, que, si la paix ne se faict pas, la seule injustice des Espagnols en est cause.[133]

Two obstacles were especially formidable, the chief of which, as before, was Condé. Since the recall of Leopold Wilhelm and Fuensaldaña, in which Condé

---

[131] Ibid., fo. 236.

[132] Ibid., fo. 237–237v; see also fo. 240, 'Resumen de la negociación de paz entre España y Francia' (1656).

[133] *Lettres du Cardinal Mazarin*, vii, p. 328.

had had a hand, and the arrival of Don Juan José, Mazarin had been struck by the growth of Condé's influence in Spanish deliberations and strategic decisions in the Low Countries. He judged that it was now the 'prince de Condé qui est maistre de toutes les resolutions', and that Condé was converting his Spanish hosts to his own preference for a bold offensive strategy of deep thrusts into the interior of France designed to provoke 'de grands desordres dans le royaume et quelque soulèvement dans la ville capitale'.[134] Mazarin knew that Condé had a network of secret contacts in France, and not least in Paris, and was by no means inclined to underestimate the threat to French royal authority and power posed by the armed collaboration of Condé with Spain.

Condé for his part had realized beforehand that Mazarin would try to persuade the world that it was only his own interests which obstructed the repose of Christendom and had begged Luis de Haro not to allow his own concerns to be left to last on the agenda.[135] Don Luis had indeed made strenuous efforts to discuss Condé's affairs before anything else. But this Mazarin had absolutely refused to accept, threatening to break off the negotiations altogether unless that issue was put off until last. When finally the negotiators had got around to the question of Condé, it emerged that Mazarin was willing to restore the prince's confiscated lands and revenues but not his governorships, offices, courtly functions and influence. This Philip refused to accept.[136] For, by abandoning Condé, Spain would be sacrificing all her leverage within France. It was over this that the talks broke down.

There may also have been some serious talk of Louis XIV asking for the hand of the Infanta, the Spanish king's daughter, Maria Theresa. Mazarin and his young master aspired to conclude the marriage because she was still, at this point, heir to the Spanish throne (the sickly Carlos II was not born until November 1661); and because, by this means, the French crown would acquire an immense leverage and influence throughout the Spanish empire and not least in the Spanish Netherlands and Italy. Lionne later recollected that Mazarin would have conceded numerous points in the 1656 negotiations in return for such a huge concession.[137] But Philip IV was not yet so worn down as to contemplate such a humiliating outcome. Thus while the Franco-Spanish peace talks of 1656 expressly collapsed over the issue of Condé and his political status and offices in France, it is clear that there were also numerous other reasons why Philip and his advisers decided that it was fundamentally against the Spanish interest to settle on any basis that Mazarin was prepared to agree to. In spite of the chronic lack of troops, weapons and money, and the general exhaustion of the monarchy, and in spite of the king's impatient desire to turn his arms

[134] Ibid. vii, p. 316.
[135] BL, MS Add. 14000, fos 231–231v, Spanish trans. of Condé to Luis de Haro, 5 February 1656.
[136] Ibid., fos 235v, 237v.
[137] J. Valfrey, *La diplomatie française au XVII siècle: Hugues de Lionne, ses ambassades en Espagne et en Allemagne* (Paris, 1881), pp. 56–7.

against what he regarded as the treason and rebellion in Portugal, it seemed that their best and only advisable course was to fight on.

In retrospect, it may appear obvious that the decision to reject Mazarin's terms in august 1656, and prolong the war, was a grievous mistake. The gathering collusion between France and England led to a combined offensive against the Spanish Netherlands, in 1658, which was simply too powerful for the Spaniards to counter. The army of Flanders was decisively defeated at the battle of the Dunes, on 14 June 1658, as a result of which the defences of the southern Netherlands were torn wide open. In the ensuing weeks Spanish morale in Flanders disintegrated. While the English occupied Dunkirk with French agreement, the French in rapid succession overran Gravelines, Veurne, Diksmuide and Ieper. In Spanish Lombardy too the French made rapid progress. The Spanish court was forced to settle.

Yet Philip IV's decision of August 1656 was perhaps not so wrong-headed as historians generally assert. In Catalonia, French efforts to break back in during the years 1657–8 were effectively rebuffed. In 1656, it had not been clear that Cromwell would opt for full-scale strategic collaboration with France (which arguably was not at all in England's interest) or that Spain's overall position was as disadvantageous as it rapidly became in 1657–8.[138] Furthermore, contrary to what is often claimed, the terms Spain finally accepted under the Peace of the Pyrenees, in 1659, were *not* practically the same as those which the Spanish court rejected in 1656. For, in 1659, Louis and Mazarin secured both the favourable marriage with Maria Theresa *and* extensive territorial gains, a combination of concessions which had at no point been considered in 1656. Given this difference, and in view of the disastrous slump in Spain's power and prestige in Europe during the 1660s, it seems to me entirely justifiable to characterize the Peace of the Pyrenees as a comprehensive defeat for the Spanish crown of a kind which Philip had striven to avoid since 1648: a defeat which brought in its wake the very consequences which the Spanish court had chiefly feared; the loss of all Spanish influence within and around the fringes of France; the consolidation of French power in Alsace, Lorraine and the Rhine corridor; and the isolation and emasculation of Spanish power in the Low Countries.

[138] As well as aligning with the United Provinces and Denmark and undoing the Anglo-French alliance, the Spanish court hoped to draw closer once again to the emperor and by this means defeat the French efforts — which by 1658 had succeeded — to oust Spanish influence from the Rhine corridor: see Paul Janssens, 'De spaanse ambassade in Den Haag onder Esteban de Gamarra van 1654 tot aan de vrede van de Pyrenees' (unpublished University of Leuven Ph.D. thesis, 1966), pp. 128–9, 197.

7

Dutch Sephardi Jewry, Millenarian Politics and the Struggle for Brazil, 1650–54

The notion that Jews were a marginal, isolated group which took no significant part in the great political struggles and rivalries of early modern times is so ingrained in the historiography of the period that any contention to the contrary is bound to seem startling and be looked on with scepticism. But the evidence that western Sephardi Jewry (and the Portuguese New Christians in Portugal) played a central role in the vast triangular, trans-Atlantic struggle between Portugal, Spain and the Dutch in the 1640s is extensive and deserves to be analyzed more systematically than has been the case hitherto.

The secession of Portugal from the Spanish crown in December 1640, the outcome of a conspiracy among the Portuguese nobility against Philip IV of Spain, and in favor of the Duke of Braganza, who was now proclaimed King John IV of Portugal, was one of the most dramatic events of the mid-seventeenth century – and one of the most far-reaching in its implications. Its effects, especially after Portuguese Brazil and the Portuguese East Indies followed Portugal itself in throwing off allegiance to the Spanish crown, during 1641, were indeed world-wide in scope. Portugal, a key market and hub of a global empire severed its links with the Spanish Monarchy, at that time still the largest and most powerful world *imperium*, starting a war in the Iberian Peninsula which was to last for over a quarter of a century[1]. But if the Lisbon *coup d'état* of December 1640 represented a new beginning for the kingdom of Portugal after sixty years under the hegemony of Spain in Europe and the Indies, the secession also marked the onset of major new dilemmas for the Dutch. For in the period from 1580 to 1640 the Portuguese, under Spain, and the Dutch had been enemies locked in a bitter conflict for supremacy in Brazil, West Africa and the Far East. For the Portuguese, independence presented a desperately needed opportunity to halt the war with the Dutch outside Europe, consolidate what remained of their empire in Brazil,

---

[1] C.R. Boxer, *The Dutch in Brazil, 1624-1654* (Hamden, Connecticut, 1973), pp. 100-104; J.H. Elliott, *The Count-Duke of Olivares. The Statesman in an Age of Decline* (New Haven and London, 1986), pp. 597-615; it was not until the Spanish-Portuguese peace of 1668 that the Spanish crown was finally forced to recognize the independence of Portugal.

Africa and Asia, and deploy all their resources against Spain. For the Dutch, the secession presented an opportunity to weaken Spain permanently. By helping the Portuguese against Spain, the Dutch could also expect to conquer more territory in the Spanish Netherlands – the Stadholder Frederick Henry in effect captured Hulst, Sas van Gent, and other enclaves in Flanders during the early 1640s – and make fresh gains at Spanish expense in the Caribbean. On the other hand, halting the struggle with the Portuguese and helping them against Philip IV also held serious disadvantages for the Dutch colonial companies[2]. A volteface in Dutch policy towards Portugal would mean giving up plans to extend the Dutch-occupied zone in Brazil and for further expansion at Portuguese expense in Africa, Ceylon, and southern India.

Initially, though, the secession of Portugal posed less of a dilemma for Dutch Sephardi Jewry than it did for the Dutch regent class which dominated the politics of the Republic. In 1640, Amsterdam Jews were not yet major share-holders in the colonial companies and as their principal traffic, that with Portugal had been seriously eroded by the resumption of war with Spain, since 1621, they were bound to look with enthusiasm on any circumstances likely to restore it[3]. Thus the Portuguese secession offered the prospect of Dutch ships and goods being allowed back legally into the ports of Portugal which, in turn, could be expected to revive Sephardi business activity in Holland and reverse the decline of the Amsterdam community which had been in progress for two decades, since Philip IV had imposed his total embargo on Dutch ships and merchandise in the ports of Spain and Portugal in April 1621[4].

The break-away of Portugal from Spain was also bound to find favor among most of the Portuguese New Christian diaspora in western Europe. The Portuguese New Christians resident at Rouen, Bordeaux, and Bayonne, who enjoyed the protection of Cardinal Richelieu as long as they were discreet about their private Judaism, could now re-establish their links with Portugal, broken since France had entered the Thirty Years' War against Spain in 1635 and at the same time support Richelieu's policy of helping the Portuguese achieve their independence so as to weaken Spain, a policy in which the Cardinal's New Christian favor-

---

[2] Lieuwe van Aitzema, *Historie of verhael van saken van staet en oorlogh in, ende ontrent de Vereenigde Nederlanden* (The Hague, 1667-1671), iv. 197-199; Boxer, *The Dutch in Brazil*, pp. 103-104.

[3] Jonathan I. Israel, "Spain and the Dutch Sephardim, 1609-1660", *Studia Rosenthaliana*, iii (1978), 29-31.

[4] *Ibid.*; John IV readmitted Dutch ships and cargoes to the ports of Portugal by edict of 21 January 1641: see Edgar Prestage, *A embaixada de Tristão de Mendonça Furtado a Holanda em 1641* (Coimbra, 1920), p. 14.

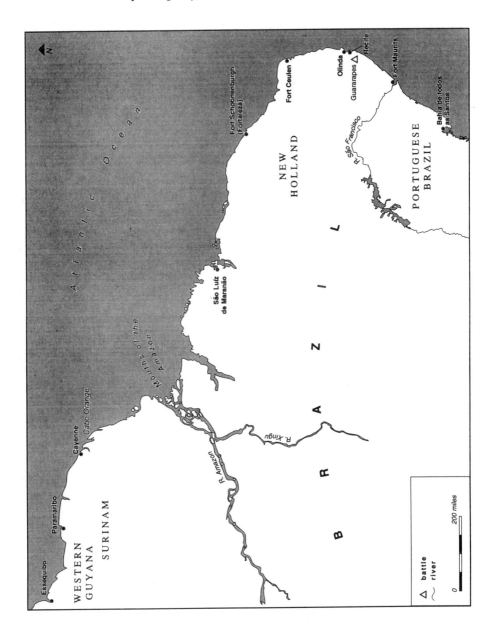

Map 5 The
Dutch–Portuguese
struggle for
Brazil, 1630–54.

ite, Alphonse López, was associated[5]. It is true that in Spain, the Portuguese New Christians, who had greatly benefited from the policies of the Count-Duke of Olivares since he had begun to rely heavily on their financial resources in 1627[6], were bound to remain loyal to the Spanish crown. And at Lisbon several factors of the great Portuguese bankers at Madrid joined in the conspiracy of 1641 to overthrow the new king of Portugal, John IV, and bring about the resubmission of the country to Spain[7]. But Olivares's policy of drawing the New Christians and their capital from Portugal into Spain[8], and granting special concessions to their nominees and factors at Lisbon, had also meant alienating the majority who were excluded from these opportunities[9]. Most of the Portuguese New Christians remaining in Portugal had no links with the *asentistas* in Madrid and Seville and no interest in opposing the Portuguese secession. On the contrary, the political restoration of Portugal could not succeed without forging a whole new financial apparatus centered on Lisbon and it was natural enough that leading Lisbon *conversos* who were free of links with Madrid, such as the merchant-bankers Manoel Garcia Franco, Balthasar Rodrigues da Mattos and Duarte da Silva, should wholeheartedly have backed a revolt which simultaneously enabled them to demonstrate their loyalty to the "patria", Portugal and gain a dominant position in Portuguese finance and trade.

Thus, in 1641 the interests of Dutch Sephardi Jewry converged with those of their New Christian relatives, associates and correspondents in Portugal and in France. All three groups had a material stake in backing the Portuguese restoration against Spain and in supporting the peace moves between Portugal and the United Provinces which were already in alliance with France. During the first three or four years of its struggle for independence, Portugal was in fact in an extremely precarious position militarily and financially and had Olivares and his fellow ministers not concentrated their efforts on trying to suppress the revolt of Catalonia (which had broken out earlier in 1640) before that of Portugal, the secession would, in all probability, have collapsed[10]. In the years 1641-1643,

---

[5] I.S. Revah, *Le Cardinal Richelieu et la restauration du Portugal* (Lisbon, 1950), pp. 10-16.

[6] James C. Boyajian, *Portuguese Bankers at the Madrid Court, 1626-1650* (New Brunswick, 1982), ch. 2; Elliott, *Olivares*, pp. 300-304.

[7] In particular Pedro de Baeça da Silveira, brother of Jorge de Paz, one of the leading bankers in Madrid: Boyajian, *Portuguese Bankers*, pp. 125-126.

[8] António Vieira was alluding to this in his 1643 *proposta* when he wrote: "se o Castelhano, para reduzir Portugal a província e lhe quebrantar as forças, tomou por arbitrio retirar-lhe os mercadores e chamar para as praças de Castela os homens de negócio, chame-os Vossa Majestade e restitua-os a Portugal": A. Vieira, *Obras Escolhidas*, ed. A. Sergio and H. Cidade (Lisbon, 1951-1954), iv. 15.

[9] Boyajian, *Portuguese Bankers*, pp. 125-126.

[10] Elliott, *Olivares*, pp. 608-610, 612.

John IV lacked the resources to sustain more than an wholly inadequate army and a token fleet. Portugal's seaborne communications with her empire in Brazil, Africa, and Asia, on which her future prospects largely depended, were at the mercy of the Dutch. Not surprisingly therefore, one of John IV's first priorities in the desperate struggle on which he now embarked was to end the conflict with the Dutch as quickly as possible and secure Dutch aid not only in the form of political support, but also arms, munitions and naval stores. The first Portuguese ambassador to the Dutch Republic, Dom Tristão de Mendonça Furtado, was sent off in January 1641, a mere few weeks after the Lisbon coup, with instructions to procure a ten-year truce in Brazil, Africa, and Asia, and carrying credit notes, including a credit for 100,000 *cruzados* issued by the Lisbon New Christian banker Manoel Garcia Franco, for the purchase of arms and munitions at Amsterdam[11].

The negotiations between the States General's delegates for Portuguese affairs and Dom Tristão were the principal talking-point of the early months of 1641 not only among the diplomatic community at The Hague but among the merchant élite and the Sephardi community at Amsterdam. The directors of East and West India Companies looked on with growing displeasure as the value of their shares began to slide[12]. The shares of both companies lost over ten per cent of their value on the Amsterdam Exchange during these months as it became clear that those elements in the States of Holland and States General in favor of a Dutch-Portuguese truce had the upper hand. The Jews, the evidence shows, were in the thick of the deliberations surrounding the truce talks as well as the discussions over arms purchases. Although the Jewish subjects of the Republic are nowhere mentioned by name in the text of the truce terms finalized in June 1641, they are referred to three times in the text by means of an obvious circumlocution which, as was later made clear, was mutually intended to refer specifically to the Jews[13]. Those Amster-

---

[11] Virginia Rau, "A embaixada de Tristão de Mendonça Furtado e os arquivos notariais holandeses", *Anais da Academia Portuguesa da História*, 2nd ser., viii (1958), 102.

[12] Aitzema, *Historie*, iv. 198-1988.

[13] Cornelis Musch in interview with the next Portuguese ambassador to the United Provinces, Sousa Coutinho, asserted in reference to clause 25 of the Truce "que esta clauzula metêrão expreçamente sò pelos judeus, porque os não quizerão nomear": see the *Correspondência diplomática de Francisco de Sousa Coutinho durante a sua embaixada em Holanda* (Coimbra, 1920-1955), ii. 146-147. Sousa Coutinho to Marquês de Niza, The Hague, 8 July 1647. Some months later, again referring to clause 25, Sousa Coutinho reported to King John IV 'que claramente querem que falle dos judeus, e que sem os nomear se faça delles expreça menção naquella particula que diz os subditos destas Provincias nascidos nellas ou em qualquer outra parte: e não ha duvida Senhor que por isso o fizerão naquella forma e que pois o primeiro embaxador de Vostra Magestade o acordou assym": *ibid.*, ii. 313-314: Sousa Coutinho to John IV, The Hague, 24 February 1648.

dam Sephardim consulted by the States General's deputies in the drawing up of the truce terms would certainly have included members of the
Mahamad and the leading Sephardi merchants then trading with Portugal and its empire. Garcia Franco's credit note for 100,000 *cruzados* was
drawn on the wealthy Amsterdam Sephardi merchant Francisco Ramires
Pina (Isaac Naar), who had long been trading with Lisbon, was a specialist in jewellery, especially pearls from Portuguese India, and was well-
known to the Portuguese New Christian financial elite in Portugal[14].
Francisco Ramires Pina was also a member of the *Mahamad* at this time
though he died during these months, and the servicing of the contract for
100,000 *cruzados* worth of guns, gunpowder, siege equipment and naval
stores was taken over by his brother-in-law, Lopo Ramires (David Curiel), another merchant-banker who had long been trading with Lisbon,
and his relative (and Lopo's business associate) Duarte Ramires Pina
(also Isaac Naar)[15]. Bento (David) Osorio who had been *parnas* the previous year, and who also had major financial connections with Lisbon,
would, we can be sure, also have been involved.

There is no doubt that Dutch Sephardi Jewry as a group had a major
stake in the Dutch-Portuguese truce terms of June 1641. The most vital
point for them was that they should be permitted to trade legally from
Holland and Dutch Brazil with Portugal and, through Portugal, with the
Portuguese empire and that their goods and cash in the hands of their
factors in Portuguese ports should be expressly exempt from the atten-
tions of the Inquisition even where such property was found in the possession of New Christians arrested in Portugal on suspicion of judaizing.
In theory, the truce terms gave them more than this for a key clause,
Clause XXV, also gave them protection for their persons on Portuguese
territory, something which the States General had previously attempted
to obtain for its Jewish subjects during the abortive 1632-1633 peace talks
with Spain[16]. On that occasion Spanish ministers had rejected Dutch de-

---

[14] Rau, "A embaixada de Tristão de Mendonça Furtado", pp. 102, 107, 111.

[15] *Ibid.*; Gemeente Archief Amsterdam PA 334/1323, "Registro dos parnasim" for
the year 5400. For more on the relations of the Ramires Pina and Lopo Ramires, see L.
Fuks, "Een rechtsstrijd onder Amsterdamse Sefardim in de 17e eeuw", *'t Exempel
dwinght, Opstellen aangeboden aan Prof.Mr. I. Kisch* (Zwolle, 1977), pp. 178-179.

[16] After demanding freedom of movement for all subjects of the Dutch state in the
European territories of the Spanish crown, the Dutch delegates during these talks demanded (Article IX): "Dat die van de Portugeesche natie, inwoonders ende ingesetenen
van de Vereenichde Provintien die zijn ofte naemals sullen komen, van wat religie of
geloof die souden mogen wesen, so wel als andere ingesetenen van de voors. Provintien
het effect van 't jegenwoordigen Tractaet soo in Nederlandt, als in Spaegnien ende
alomme in 't Spaensche gebiet, volkomentlick sullen geniten": Aitzema, *Historie*, iii. 78;
M.G. de Boer, *Die Friedensunterhandlungen zwischen Spanien und den Niederlanden in den Jahren
1632 und 1633* (Groningen, 1898), pp. 67, 89-90: on that occasion, one of the Spanish

mands regarding the Jews domiciled in the Republic out of hand. But in June 1641 the Portuguese gave way on this point[17]. Clause XXV reads:

> Et liberum esto utriusque partis subditis, cujuscunque nationis, conditionis, qualitatis et religionis, nullis exceptis (sive illi in alterius Ditione nati sunt, sive inibi habitasse dicantur) frequentare, navigare et commercari qualibet mercium et mercaturae forte in regnis, provinciis, territoriis ac insulis respective in Europa atque aliorsum ab hac Lineae parte sitis; nec fas esto neutrius subditos mercandi gratia, confluentes in alterius terris, sitis ut supra, in mercibus asportandis aut vero exportandis magis aggravare gabellis, impositionibus aliisve jurisbus, quam ipsissimos incolas et subditos carundum Terrerum; sed gaudeant pariter respective hujusmodi indultis et privilegiis quibus antehac illi usi sunt, priusquam Lusitania a Castilianis fuerit subacta.[18] [For translation, see p. 168 below]

On the other hand, Dom Tristão and his staff were careful to minimize the concessions that had to be made on the religious front. The Dutch had begun by demanding full liberty of conscience for their subjects in Portugal[19]. The final text conceded the right of private practice to subjects of the United Provinces on Portuguese territory but expressly excluded non-Christians, i.e., Jews, from this provision (Clause XXVI): "subditi ac incolae harum Provinciarum qui Christiani sunt . . . utentur et fruentur libertate conscientiae in domibus suis privatis ac intra naves libero religionis exercitio"[20]. In theory, then, the persons as well as property of Dutch Jews on Portuguese territory were protected but Jewish practice was forbidden to Dutch subjects even in private.

The truce agreement did incorporate, however, one other significant concession to the Jews. It was of concern to the Amsterdam Sephardi community that Jews resident in Netherlands Brazil should be expressly guaranteed the same protection and rights under the Truce as were

---

ministers of state, using the same circumlocution, but again directly (and only) referring to the Jews, commented 'que no se debe por ningun casso dar las ventajas a Portugueses que piden, pero bien se ajustaria a que en los nabios donde van sus haciendas, no fuese confiscado mas de lo que les pertenece, punto que seria de gran satisfacion para los rebeldes'': see Israel, ''Spain and the Dutch Sephardim'', p. 27.

[17] Antonio de Sousa de Tavares, *Relação do tratado de 1641 entre Portugal e Holanda (August, 1641)* (Lisbon, 1917), p. 10; Prestage, *A embaixada de Tristão de Mendonça*, p. 80.

[18] J. du Mont, *Corps universel diplomatique du droit des gens*, vi, part 1 (Amsterdam, 1728), p. 217. For the Dutch text, see Aitzema, *Historie*, p. 208; the first part of Clause XXV was rendered in Portuguese: ''E será livre aos subditos de huma e outra parte de qualquer nação, condição, qualidade e religião, sem excepção de algum, ou elles sejão nacidos em a jurisdição de cada huma das partes, ou nellas tenhão seu domicilio, assistir, navegar e comerciar com qualquer sorte de mercadorias e empregos em os Reynos, Provincias, termos e Ilhas em Europa, e em qualquer outra parte situadas daquem da linha''; see Prestage, *A embaixada de Tristão de Mendonça*, p. 80.

[19] Sousa de Tavares, *Relação do tratado de 1641*, p. 16.

[20] Du Mont, *Corps universel diplomatique*, vi, part 1, p. 217.

granted to subjects of the States General in Europe. This they obtained in Clause IX which stipulates that the same protection and recognition was to be enjoyed by residents in the territories and conquests of the Dutch West India Company "cujuscunque nationis, conditionis aut religionis sint"[21].

Dutch trade with Portugal underwent a marked revival in the early 1640s and the recognized, protected participation of the Dutch Sephardim in this traffic was clearly of immense benefit to the community as a whole, as well as to élite merchants such as Lopo Ramires, David Osorio, Diogo Martines, Francisco Lopes de Azevedo, Duarte Ramires Pina and Jeronimo Nunes da Costa (Moseh Curiel). In the three years 1643-1645, Dutch ships accounted for over half the total of non-Portuguese vessels entering the port of Lisbon[22]. As a result of their participation, the economic decline of the Dutch Sephardim, so evident in the 1620s and 1630s, was decisively halted.[23] In 1641, the number of Jewish accounts with the Amsterdam Exchange Bank stood at only 89 as compared with 106 twenty years earlier, in 1620, the Jewish share of the total number of accounts having fallen back from nine to six per cent[24]. By 1646, by contrast, the number of Jewish deposits had risen sharply to 126, or eight per cent of the total[25]. The economic position of Dutch Sephardi Jewry had been transformed. Decline had given way to steady expansion.

But the gains accruing to Dutch Sephardi Jewry and their New Christian relatives in France and Portugal were by no means limited to the economic sphere. A Portugal free of Spanish control initially appeared to open up a whole range of new possibilities. Since John IV needed all the financial assistance he could get, and the merchant community of Amsterdam during 1641 put, as we know, great emphasis on his financial weakness[26], there was seemingly every prospect of extracting, in return for financial help, sweeping improvements in the lot of Portugal's New Christians despite the vociferous opposition displayed by the Portuguese Cortes and clergy at this time to any suggestion of relaxing the systematic

[21] *Ibid.*

[22] Virginia Rau, 'Subsidios para o estudo do movimento dos portos de Faro e Lisboa durante o século XVII'', *Anais da Academia Portuguesa de História*, 2nd ser., v (1954), 241.

[23] Jonathan I. Israel, "The Economic Contribution of Dutch Sephardi Jewry to Holland's Golden Age, 1595-1713'', *Tijdschrift voor Geschiedenis*, xcvi (1983), 510, 516, 519-520.

[24] J.G. van Dillen, "Vreemdelingen te Amsterdam in de eerste helft der zeventiende eeuw. 1. De Portugeesche Joden", *Tijdschrift voor Geschiedenis*, i (1935), 14.

[25] *Ibid.*

[26] *Brieven van Nicolaes van Reigersberch aan Hugo de Groot*, Werken van het Historisch Genootschap, ser. III, no. 15 (Amsterdam, 1901).

discrimination to which they were subject[27]. Amid their initial euphoria, it seems, Jewish leaders even suggested that in return for their help, the king should consider permitting the establishment of two public synagogues in Portugal (one in Lisbon and one in Oporto?). Antonio de Sousa de Macedo, one of the propagandists of the Portuguese secession, records that "regem (habemus) ita catholicum, ut in necessitatibus principii Regni sui non admiserit propositiones Hebraeorum petentes duas synagogas in Lusitania pro quibus offerebant ingentes pecunias"[28]. Amid the atmosphere of rabid judeophobia prevailing in Portugal at that time this was not practical politics. But what definitely was on the agenda, as we see from Antonio Vieira's *propostas* of 1643 and 1646 to the Portuguese king on the subject of the New Christians[29], was the proposal to obtain a general amnesty from the Pope for past religious offences against the Catholic Church and to curb the powers of the Inquisition, it was hoped, to an even greater extent than the Count-Duke of Olivares had achieved in Spain[30]. Also demanded was the exemption of New Christian capital invested in commerce from confiscation by the Inquisition and abolition of the ban on New Christians holding public offices in Portugal or being admitted to the military orders. These proposals were put to John IV by the great Jesuit, Vieira, a committed opponent of the Inquisition, but there is little doubt that they were drawn up in consultation with the New Christian leadership in Lisbon or that they mirrored the immediate aspirations of the New Christians in Portugal. A key section of Vieira's 1646 *proposta* is actually entitled "O que querem os homens de nação"[31].

But there were, or so it seemed, still further possibilities beyond increased security for, and improvements in the status of Portugal's New Christians. Dutch Sephardim saw in the Portuguese restoration a chance to tighten their links with Portugal and her overseas empire at every level and erase from their minds all feelings of divided loyalties. They could participate fully in creating the sense of a new beginning, in the mystical, Sebastianist speculations which surrounded the political restoration of Portugal and which were to culminate in Vieira's dream of a Portugal which would lead and redeem mankind. Remarking on this general enthusiasm among the Dutch Sephardim for the Portuguese cause, in May 1644, the then Portuguese ambassador at The Hague, Francisco de

---

[27] J. Lúcio de Azevedo, *História dos cristãos novos portugueses* (2nd edn., Lisbon, 1975), pp. 238-239.

[28] Lúcio de Azevedo, *História dos cristãos novos portugueses*, p. 238.

[29] Vieira, *Obras Escolhidas*, iv. 1-62.

[30] *Ibid.*, iv. 48-49.

[31] *Ibid.*, iv. 42-44.

Sousa Coutinho, advised the king to entrust the funds for diplomatic expenses in central and northern Europe to the Sephardi bankers in Amsterdam:

> ... e advirto a V. Magestade que por mais judeos que sejão os portuguezes que ali há, emfim lá tem huma afeição a Portugal que fas desejarem mais servir a V. Magestade do que os flamengos, e não o digo sem cauza ... [32]

The zeal for the Portuguese cause shown by Duarte Nunes da Costa (Jacob Curiel) of Hamburg who, though a Jew, was made a knight (*cavaleiro fidalgo*) of the Portuguese royal household, in June 1641, and "Agent" of the crown of Portugal at Hamburg in 1644, his son, Jeronimo, who moved to Amsterdam in 1642, was also knighted and made "Agent" of the Portuguese crown in that city in 1645 and, initially at least, of Duarte's brother, Lopo Ramires who though a Jew and residing at Amsterdam was made a *cavaleiro fidalgo da casa real* in June 1642, was, therefore, merely the most overt and public example of an enthusiasm which, for a time, infused almost the entire western Sephardi diaspora outside of Spain[33]. In 1643, Antonio Vieira took the "love" of the Sephardim of north-west Europe for their former *patria* to be so intense that he assured John IV that

> Todos estes, pelo amor que tem a Portugal, como patria sua, e a Vossa Majestade, como seu rei natural, estão desejosos de poderem tornar para o Reino e servirem a Vossa Majestade com suas fazendas, como fazem aos reis estranhos[34].

Indeed, Vieira clearly believed that this "love" for Portugal could be used by the king to weaken and eventually destroy these Portuguese exiles' Judaism[35]. Duarte Nunes da Costa, whose allegiance to Judaism was strong, presumably did not envisage a mass return to Portugal. We can probably assume that he was hoping, rather, to strengthen the private practice of Judaism in Portugal by bridling the Inquisition and, at the same time, reinforce the Sephardi diaspora by strengthening the links between the New Christians in Portugal and the exiles in north-west Europe. In one of his letters to the Portuguese ambassador at Paris, Duarte deplores the failure to make it safe in Portugal for the exiles to

---

[32] *Correspondência diplomática de Francisco de Sousa Coutinho*, i. 149: Sousa Coutinho to John IV, The Hague, 3 May 1644.

[33] Jonathan I. Israel, "The Diplomatic Career of Jeronimo Nunes da Costa: an Episode in Dutch-Portuguese Relations of the Seventeenth Century", *Bijdragen en Mededelingen betreffende de Geschiedenis der Nederlanden*, xcviii (1983), 168-169; below, 172-3.

[34] Vieira, *Obras Escolhidas*, iv. 11.

[35] *Ibid.*, pp. 52-54.

return there for temporary visits. Referring to the loyalty to Portugal of the Jews of north-west Europe, he wrote:

> mas bem sabe V. excelencia que os que estamos desterados da nossa patria, somos imposibilitados de ir a ella, e isso he o que me inpide não mandar meu filho [Jeronimo Nunes da Costa], que se não for esse inconveniente não reparata em elle los mays irem a China por terra . . .[36]

The idea that in 1643 most Sephardi Jews of north-west Europe would have been willing to travel overland to China to demonstrate their zeal for a king and country which still championed the most virulent persecution of Jews and Judaism then to be found in the world may strike us today as far-fetched or comical, but there can be no doubting the intensity of the feeling to which Duarte alludes. Even a rabbi such as Menasseh ben Israel was swept up in the tide of enthusiasm for the Portuguese restoration during the early 1640s. Thus Menasseh remarked in the dedication of the second part of his *Conciliador*, in 1641, that it was now especially appropriate to dedicate such a work to the directors of the West India Company, as he did, as Portugal was now free of Spain, the struggle between Portuguese and Dutch over, the truce between Portugal and the Dutch about to be signed and the "ancient hatred" between the two nations at an end:

> Mayormente a tiempo que el benigno rey João IV, buelto a su natural y hereditario regno injustamente hasta agora de otro poseido, cessando el antigo odio, seguira la desseada paz: la qual siendo yo Lusitano con animo Batavo, me sera gratissima[37].

The great Jesuit António Vieira was intent on forging closer links between Portugal and the western Sephardi diaspora in order to strengthen the Portuguese state and increase its chances of surviving its struggle for independence and to retain its empire. As part of this policy he wished to curb the Inquisition and ease the pressure on the New Christians. But his ultimate purpose was to undermine Judaism and bring both Sephardim and New Christians back to Christ[38]. Conversely, Jewish leaders such as Duarte Nunes da Costa who was one of the leading figures in the Sephardi community at Hamburg, and Menasseh ben Israel, were eager to use the power of the Portuguese state, at a moment when it seemed

---

[36] Arquivo Nacional da Torro do Tombo (Lisbon), Miscellanea da Graça, Cela O, Caixa 17, tomo 4B.fo.549v: Duarte Nunes da Costa to Vidigueira, Hamburg, 7/27 June 1643.

[37] Menasseh ben Israel, *Segunda Parte del Conciliador o de la conviniencia de los lugares de la S. Escriptura, que repugnantes entre si parecen* (Amsterdam, 1641), epistola dedicatoria.

[38] A.J. Saraiva, "António Vieira, Menasseh ben Israel et le cinquième empire" *Studia Rosenthaliana*, vi (1972), 35.

possible to exert real influence, not just to ease the pressure on the New Christians and strengthen communications between them and the Sephardi diaspora in the material interests of both but, surely, because it seemed to them that Judaism – and rejection of Christ – both in Portugal and northern Europe would gain by this. To many in the Sephardi diaspora bridling the Inquisition and improving communications with Portugal and Portuguese Brazil spelt above all an opportunity to proselytize among the New Christians and draw them decisively away from Christianity – and nowhere were the chances of this more promising than in Brazil[39]. A figure such as Isaac de Castro Tartas who migrated from Holland to Netherlands Brazil in 1641, at the age of sixteen, and then crossed, in October 1644, to Bahia in the Portuguese zone, in order to proselytize among the New Christians there[40], was, in a way, giving expression to a general impulse then permeating the western Sephardi world, and which very likely inspired Menasseh's own stated intention at that time to emigrate to Brazil.

In Netherlands Brazil itself, the Dutch-Portuguese Truce greatly strengthened the position of the Jews, or rather appeared to do so. It was in the short period of peace in Brazil (1641-1644) that the Jewish population of Netherlands Brazil reached its peak, approximately 1,450 in 1644[41]. The peaceful conditions of those years encouraged the expansion of sugar output and induced more Jews to acquire plantations and settle well away from the main community in Recife. There are indications that during these years small Sephardi congregations formed at such places as Paraíba and at Itamaracá.

But the dream of Dutch-Portuguese reconciliation and the peaceful co-existence of the two Brazils was soon to be rudely shattered. Already in 1644 there was trouble in Maranhão, in the north, and a further slump in West India Company shares demonstrated a strong underlying anxiety about the future of Netherlands Brazil[42]. But this was as nothing compared to the shock of the insurrection of the Portuguese Catholic planters in the Dutch zone of Brazil, in June 1645[43]. The Dutch garrisons in Brazil (pared down to a minimum since the 1641 as the Company had switched its attention to the Caribbean) were too weak to react. The

[39] Anita Novinsky, *Cristaos Novos na Baha* (São Paulo, 1972), pp. 135-136.
[40] Arnold Wiznitzer, "Isaac de Castro, Brazilian Jewish Martyr", *Publications of the American Jeiwsh Historical Society*, xlviii (1957), 65-67.
[41] Arnold Wiznitzer, *The Jews of Colonial Brazil* (New York, 1960), pp. 120-138; I.S. Emmanuel, "Seventeenth-Century Brazilian Jewry: A Critical Review", *American Jewish Archives*, xiv (1962), 32-68.
[42] *Correspondência diplomática de Francisco de Sousa Coutinho*, i. 128, 139, 162, 181.
[43] Evaldo Cabral de Mello, *Olinda Restaurada. Guerra e açúcar no Nordeste, 1630-1654* (Rio de Janeiro, 1975), pp. 76-79.

insurgents swept across the whole expanse of the Dutch zone beyond the fortifications of Recife, Mauricia, Paraíba, Itamaracá, and one or two other forts, sacking the property of Dutchmen and Jews as they went. Within three months practically the whole of Netherlands Brazil outside five or six fortified bases was either conquered or devastated[44]. Morale throughout Netherlands Brazil collapsed. The outlying Sephardi communities disappeared, the Jews being from now on effectively shut up in Recife and Mauricia. The previously flourishing sugar trade between Dutch Brazil and Holland was suddenly totally paralyzed. All confidence in the future of the colony was gone. Jewish refugees began to stream back to Holland and soon also to Zealand.

The revolt of the Portuguese planters in Dutch Brazil in the summer of 1645 was a stunning blow to Dutch Sephardi Jewry. It was a blow not just to its trade and colonizing activities but to its entire political and emotional world. For the rebels, fired with Catholic zeal, acted in the name of John IV and received arms, supplies and encouragement from Portugal via Bahia. It is true that for the rest of the 1640s John IV and his ministers in Europe constantly reiterated that the revolt in Dutch Brazil had nothing to do with them, hoping by thus disowning the rebellion to avoid war with the Dutch in the Atlantic, Africa and the Far East. But in the Republic no-one was fooled by the subterfuge or failed to realize that the king was surreptitiously supporting the war against his ostensible Dutch allies.

The change in the previously euphoric mood of Dutch Sephardi Jewry was immediate and palpable. As realization of the magnitude of the disaster sank in, the community at Amsterdam quickly turned against the Portuguese diplomatic mission at The Hague. Later in the summer of 1645, Sousa Coutinho wrote to his superior, the Conde de Vidigueira, at Paris, in a mood of evident anxiety:

> Deos nos acuda e do hum expedente a estes negocios em forma que acabemos por huma vez. O povo de Amsterdam fes bravuras, os judeos me condenarão a pedradas e aqui he muito facil a execução, e o que peor he que
> · os que cuidamos são amigos são os peores, e o certo e que todos são huns[45].

The image of a Jewish public so menacing that its threats to stone an ambassador in the streets were taken seriously may not fit in with our usual perceptions of Jewish life in the seventeenth century, but there can be no doubt that this was the reality in Amsterdam in the summer of 1645. The

---

[44] *Ibid.*, p. 46: the losses suffered by the Dutch in Brazil in 1645, according to Vieira, "verdadeiramente foram grandíssimas, porque os levantados queimaram capitanias inteiras, e nelas muito engenhos": Vieira, *Obras Escolhidas*, i. 128.

[45] *Correspondência diplomática de Francisco de Sousa Coutinho* 1, i. 308.

tide of emotion reached such proportions that there were warnings from the burgomasters and on 22 Elul 5405 the Amsterdam *Mahamad* passed a resolution forbidding members of the community to utter public insults, "palavras descompostas contra o senhor embaixador de Portugal", or cause "scandal" when discussing Brazilian affairs[46].

The fury is understandable when we consider how basic was Netherlands Brazil in the life of Dutch Sephardi Jewry at that time. One of the pillars of its existence had collapsed. Menasseh ben Israel was among those who lost heavily financially, the collapse of Dutch Brazil being partly responsible for the subsequent failure of his printing business[47]. Manuel Martínez (David Abrabanel) Dormido, who was to become one of the founders of the Sephardi community in London in the mid-1650s, later recalled in 1654 how in 1641 he had sent his two sons to Brazil "with great cargazons of goods of which proseedes I did looke for above 500 chests of suggars which they had to send me in the yeare 1646 . . . it happened (though) foure months before that the Portugalls and dwellers in the country of Pernambuco (Recife) did rize, amongst whom were my debtors and possessors of my estate"[48]. Dormido claimed to have lost 150,000 guilders in Brazil in 1645, mostly owed to him by Portuguese planters who joined the insurrection.

The angry menaces uttered by Amsterdam Jews in the late summer and autumn of 1645 included much talk of the launching of a powerful Dutch counter-offensive in Brazil which would teach the Portuguese their lesson[49]. In fact, the revolt of the planters in Netherlands Brazil marked the parting of the ways politically between the Dutch Sephardim and the New Christian merchant élite of Lisbon. The many New Christians who had backed the Portuguese restoration in the early 1640s continued to lend strong support to the new régime, and its initiatives in Brazil and West Africa, during the later 1640s. The finance for the major Portuguese expedition sent to Brazil in 1647 which eventually gave Portugal the upper hand in its long struggle with the Dutch in the South Atlantic was arranged by Duarte da Silva, the best-known Lisbon New Christian merchant of the period, and a consortium of other New Christians, through the mediation of António Vieira[50]. Duarte da Silva was also instrumental in organizing the finance for the subsequent expedition of Sal-

---

[46] Gemeentearchief Amsterdam, Archives of the Portuguese Jewish Community vol. XIX (Hascamoth), p. 281: resolution of the Mahamad, 22 Elul 2405.

[47] Cecil Roth, *The Life of Menasseh ben Israel* (Philadelphia, 1934), p. 69.

[48] Lucien Wolf, "American Elements in the Re-Settlement", *Transactions of the Jewish Historical Society of England*, iii (1899), 91.

[49] *Correspondência diplomática de Francisco de Sousa Coutinho*, iii. 314.

[50] Boxer, *The Dutch in Brazil*, p. 189.

vador de Sá which culminated, in 1648, in the recapture of Angola from the Dutch[51]. Among the most active of the Lisbon New Christians supplying arms and munitions to Portuguese Brazil and therefore also to the insurgents in Netherlands Brazil in the late 1640s was Jerónimo Gomes Pessoa who subsequently fled from the Portuguese Inquisition first to Italy and then to Amsterdam where he took the Jewish name Abraham Israel Pessoa[52]. The Sephardim in Holland, by contrast, stirred up by relatives streaming back from Brazil, threw their support behind those elements in the Republic pressing for decisive action against the Portuguese in Brazil. This placed the Jews in a curious position within the labyrinth of Dutch politics. The Amsterdam city council and most of the other towns of the States of Holland, absorbed in intricate negotiations with Spain and anxious to safeguard their commerce with Portugal, were unwilling to be drawn into a major conflict in Brazil[53]. Apart from the West India Company whose financial position now looked hopeless, the party committed to a powerful counter-offensive in Brazil looked distinctly meager. The Jews thus became the adherents of a restricted pressure group headed by the States of Zealand, the province with the largest stake in the West India Company and Brazil, and a minority of Holland towns, led by Leiden[54]. Nevertheless even Amsterdam agreed that something had to be done to rescue Dutch Brazil and in 1647, after the main Portuguese battle fleet was sent across to Brazil, the States General belatedly prepared a major expedition. The strategy in the minds of the planners of this Dutch expedition of 1647 was to save Netherlands Brazil by taking the offensive in Portuguese Brazil and capturing Bahia; for without Bahia, it was believed, Dutch Brazil could not be safe.

During 1647 the Dutch Sephardim, determined to increase the pressure on Portugal, did all they could to undermine John IV's standing in the Republic, convey a sense of Portuguese weakness, and whip up a general outcry against Portugal. In July Sousa Coutinho reported to his superior at Paris that:

> Tem lançado fama que ha revoltas no reyno e que S. Magestade esta arrestado pela nobreza, e que a fortaleza de S. Evão estava por Castella, e antes destas novas, que os judeos são os que mais publicão e solemnizão, dizião que S. Magestade tinha arrestado todos os navios que se achevão nos ports do reino todo, por mandar armada ao Brasil[55].

---

[51] David Grant Smith, "The Mercantile Class of Portugal and Brazil in the Seventeenth Century: A Socio-Economic Study of the Merchants of Lisbon and Bahia, 1620-1690" (unpublished Ph.D. thesis), pp. 78-80.

[52] *Ibid.*, pp. 201-202; Cabral de Mello, *Olinda Restaurada*, p. 103.

[53] Boxer, *The Dutch in Brazil, pp. 186-188.*

[54] *Correspondência diplomática de Francisco de Sousa Coutinho*, ii. 237.

[55] *Ibid.*, ii. 154: Sousa de Coutinho to Niza, The Hague, 22 July 1647.

In fact John IV and his ministers did feel highly vulnerable. They knew that Portugal could not fight Spain and the Dutch Republic at the same time and that if the Dutch did launch a full-scale war against Portugal there was every possibility that the empire would collapse and be shared out between Spain and the Dutch. Officially the Portuguese crown was only too willing to allocate the whole of Dutch Brazil as it had been at its fullest extent in 1645 to the Dutch and might have been so in practice had the king been able to control the Catholic zeal of the Portuguese planters on the spot. As the preparations for the Dutch expedition went ahead, Sousa Coutinho made frantic efforts to win over Dutch opinion outside Zeeland and to achieve a compromise solution.

After long delays a Dutch war-fleet commanded by Withe de With finallyt sailed for Brazil in December 1647. There is no doubt that the entire Dutch Sephardi community, even Jeronimo Nunes da Costa, "Agent" of the Portuguese Crown in the United Provinces, pinned great hopes on this expedition. Jeronimo's uncle, Lopo Ramires had by this time already switched his allegiance from Portugal to Spain[56]. Jeronimo continued to promote Portugal's interests at Amsterdam – only his notion of "Portuguese interests" was one which centered on their compatibility with those of Dutch Sephardi Jewry. It is quite clear that in late 1647, a crucial juncture in the great drama, he used his influence to exaggerate Dutch strength in the eyes of John IV and his ministers and in trying to ensure the full restoration of Dutch Brazil[57]. Advising the Marquês de Niza, early in December 1647, that the Dutch were still having difficulties in getting their "armada" and troops for Brazil ready, he added

> e ainda que Jeronimo Nunes (da Costa) avise a V. Excelencia outra cosa, he porque não sabe se não dar roins novas contra nos, e per que conste a V. Excelencia quão velhaco he o seu tio Lopo Ramires, e como estes cães não andão mais que a dar-nos pezar, mando essas cartas suas pera que V. Excelencia as lea, porque tambem determino manda-las a S. Magestade per a que acabem de conhecer em Portugal que não ha nestos nem fe nem lealdade[58].

A week later Sousa Coutinho again accuses Jeronimo of deliberately exaggerating Dutch strength and advises Niza that whilst it was a good idea that the Portuguese garrisons in Brazil should be warned, Jeronimo's version of the situation would not be transmitted as it woud serve only

---

[56] From 1646 he was in secret correspondence with the Conde de Peñaranda, the Spanish minister in charge of negotiations with the Dutch, see my forthcoming history of the Curiel family.

[57] *Correspondência diplomática de Francisco de Sousa Coutinho*, ii. 270-271, 276-277.

[58] *Correspondência diplomática de Francisco de Sousa Coutinho*, ii. 265-266: Sousa Coutinho to Niza, The Hague, 9 December 1647.

to demoralize the troops and make them believe 'que vae contra elles o poder do mundo'' [59]. Shortly after, the ambassador reported to Niza that the Dutch were facing mounting difficulties and that Jeronimo was deliberately concealing the truth from him:

> A sua armada ainda esta destas partes, porque o vento não da lugar a fazer viagem; dizem que lhes morrem muitos nella de bexigas, mas esta nova não chegara a V. Excelencia por via de Jeronimo Nunes, assim como não chegou a da perda dos navios, no que me affirmo he que se fora em nosso odio e dano que elle a avizara por vias duplicadas [60].

Outraged and appalled by the immensity of the disaster in Brazil, Dutch Jewish opinion was particularly incensed by the treatment meted out by the Portuguese to Jews captured in Brazil. This issue attained great importance in the years 1646-1648 for not only did it arouse very strong emotions among Dutch Sephardi Jewry as a whole, it offered the *Mahamad* in Amsterdam a basis for political intervention with the city council of Amsterdam, States of Holland and States General to a greater extent than any other aspect of the Brazilian debâcle. It enabled Dutch Sephardi Jews to confirm their status as Dutch subjects, tighten the links between the community and the Dutch state, and present the Portuguese crown as the party which had broken faith. The question of the treatment of the Jewish prisoners captured in Brazil in 1645 thus became a major political controversy out of all proportion to the relatively small number of captives actually involved. Apart from the proselytizer Isaac de Castro Tartas who had been arrested at Bahia in December 1644 and shipped back to Lisbon where he was handed over to the Inquisition early in 1645, two Jews, one called Moseh Mendes, were caught by rebel forces north of Recife in the summer of 1645 and hanged on the spot, while a group of Jews, including several Ashkenazim, were captured at or near Fort Maurits, at the estuary of the São Francisco river, between Recife and Bahia and sent, via Bahia, to Portugal [61]. Of this group, four Ashkenazim and three Sephardi Jews born in Holland and never baptized were soon released [62]. However, several others who had been born and baptized in Portugal were held and tried by the Lisbon Inquisition.

The Amsterdam *Mahamad* lost no time in taking up the case of these captives, appealing to the Amsterdam city countil, States of Holland and States General that Dutch subjects had been seized by the Portuguese

[59] *Ibid.*, ii. 271: Sousa Coutinho to Niza, The Hague, 16 December 1647.
[60] *Ibid.*, ii. 276-277: Sousa Coutinho to Niza, The Hague, 30 December 1647.
[61] Wiznitzer, *Jews in Colonial Brazil*, p. 108.
[62] *Ibid.*; the Ashkenazim are listed as Samuel Israel, David Michael de Alemagna, Jacob Polaco and Salaman bar Jacob.

authorities and handed over to the Inquisition in violation of article twenty-five of the Dutch-Portuguese Truce. Petitions signed by the *parnasim* were lodged with the States General in October 1646, May and June 1647 and in January 1648[63]. Each time the States General wrote to John IV demanding the immediate release of the captives. But more importantly, the *Mahamad* was able to use the episode to mobilize the full weight of Jewish opinion against Portugal and exert intense pressure on the Portuguese ambassador.

This build-up of the issue into a major political *cause célèbre* served to greatly heighten the impact of the news of the *Auto-da-fé* staged in Lisbon in December 1647. Isaac de Castro's death at the age of twenty-two at the hands of the Inquisition in full view of the Lisbon populace was, in any case, one of the most sensational instances of Jewish martyrdom of the entire seventeenth century. In the words of a French onlooker so unsympathetic to the victim's Jewish beliefs that he refers to "cette peste du Judaisme", this remarkable young man who had lived in Portugal, France, Holland and Netherlands Brazil was

> . . . bruslé vif publiant et professant hautement la loy de Moyse qui possedait et parloit toutes sortes de langues . . . persista tousjours en sa malheureuse créance jusques au dermier soupir criant a haute voix Ely, Adonay, Sabatot; jamais l'On n'a veu une telle resolution et constance . . . [64].

But within the tense religio-political framework emanating from the Dutch-Portuguese confrontation over Brazil, and the mobilization of Dutch Sephardi opinion against Portugal – it is no accident that the *Mahamad* petitioned the States General from 1646 onwards in the name of the "gemeene Joodsche Natie" and not of the "Portuguese nation" of Amsterdam which in the past had been the customary terminology used by the Sephardi authorities when petitioning the States – the impact of Isaac de Castro's martyrdom, together with the penancing of three of the Jews captured on the São Francisco river, Abraham (Gabriel) Mendes, Samuel (João Nunes) Velho, and Abraham Bueno (Diogo Henriques)[65] at the same *Auto-da-fé*, was overwhelming.

Sousa Coutinho reported back to the king that unless one was in Holland, and witnessed it in person, one would not believe the strength of feeling and the general revulsion which the news aroused. He warned

---

[63] Algemeen Rijksarchief, The Hague SG 7011/i. petitions "representeert uyt den naem ende van wegen de gemeene Joodsche Natie residerende binnen Amsterdam gesecondeert met voorschryvens vande heeren burgemeesteren ende regeerders deselver stede", May and June 1647, and also the copy of the letter of the States General to John IV, The Hague, 10 October 1646.

[64] Wiznitzer, "Isaac de Castro, Brazilian Jewish Martyr", p. 74.

[65] Wiznitzer, *Jews in Colonial Brazil*, p. 108.

that a delegate of the Amsterdam *parnasim* had been sent to The Hague to foment the anger of the States of Holland and States General and that the episode was giving the Jews an undue influence on the moulding of Dutch-Portuguese relations:

> ... e não tem assoprado mal este fogo o que ahi so poz ao judeu prizioneiro da Bahia. He força, Senhor, dize-lo, porque não se pode crer a furia em que tem entrado os Estados, e a em que os mete hum procurador que nesta corte tem os judeus que a todas as horas lhe anda gritando nos ouvidos ...[66].

The ambassador explained to the king that the Jews constituted a "considerable" force in the United Provinces and that the present situation was enabling them to mobilize the States General against Portugal. He warned that in the aftermath of the agitation at Amsterdam and The Hague, a States General delegation had been sent to admonish him

> ... chegando-me a dizer que tinhão feito paz com Castella, e que lhes fica-vão as mãos livres para acodir por seos subditos aos quais se lhe faltara duas vezes com o direito das gentes; a primeira rendendo-se a partido na forta-leza de São Francisco, sem embargo de que forão levados a Portugal e ally metidos na Inquisição; e a segunda quebrando-se lhe o contrato da Tregoa no capitulo 25 que claramente querem que falle dos judeos, e que sem os nomear se faça delles expreça menção naquella particula que diz os subditos destas Provincias nascidos nellas ou em qualquer outra parte;[67].

Sousa Coutinho then went on to ask the king whether he was willing to risk war with the States General rather than free three Jews from the hands of the Inquisition.

The king instructed Sousa Coutinho to explain that the trials of the Jews were beyond his jurisdiction being an ecclesiastical matter. But just at this time a looming clash between the States General and the Spanish crown over four captured Dutch Jews in Spain who had been handed over to the Inquisition was settled by their being released. Reiterating his view that the episode was enabling the Jews to swing opinion in Holland against Portugal, Sousa Coutinho urged the king to follow the Spanish example. If reason of state had induced the Spanish king to compel his Inquisition to surrender four Jews to the Dutch why should not the king of Portugal act likewise[68]?

But in the years 1645-1649 Dutch Sephardi Jewry did more than wage

---

[66] *Correspondência diplomática de Francisco de Sousa Coutinho*, ii. 306: Sousa Coutinho to John IV, The Hague, 10 February 1648.

[67] *Ibid.*, pp. 313-314: Sousa Coutinho to John IV, The Hague, 24 February 1648; conference between Sousa Coutinho and the States General delegation took place on 30 January 1648.

[68] *Ibid.*, ii. 296.

a propaganda war against Portugal: it literally went to war against the Portuguese. The dispatch of the fleet of December 1647 was by no means the only armed action taken against the Portuguese, even though Portugal and the United Provinces were not officially at war. The States of Zeeland obtained agreement of the States General to restart the privateering war against Portuguese shipping in the South Atlantic. This war, a tradition among the Zeelanders, had ceased with the signing of the Truce, in 1641 but before that, in the 1620s and 1630s the campaign had had some success, at times capturing as many as forty to sixty Portuguese ships per year. But this time the plan was to hit the Portuguese much harder, fit out more privateers than ever before and bring the Portuguese traffic with Brazil to its knees. The question was, though, how was this to be organized? The West India Company was now so weakened financially, and by the revolt in Brazil, that it was no longer able to participate in raiding activity[69]. For this reason the States of Zeeland set up a special directorate in Middelburg to organize the massive privateering campaign that was now to be launched. Zeeland had no lack of hardened captains and seamen to man a large privateering fleet. The problem was to find enough financial backing for such a campaign; for this could not be done with local resources alone. On the whole, Christian merchants in Amsterdam and other Holland towns showed no interest in putting money into this venture. But the Sephardi Jews of Amsterdam did and thus they came forward as a group at this juncture to form a privateering alliance with the Zeelanders against Portugal[70].

According to Sousa Coutinho, Amsterdam Jews were already negotiating with the Zeelanders before permission for the campaign was secured from the States General and were in on its planning from the outset. Reporting the attempts of the Middelburg directorate to find backing in Amsterdam during the spring of 1647, he wrote

> a Amsterdam mandarão procura os que querião entrar, e não ouve framengo nenhum que quizesse; jueus, sim, muitos, ou seja pelo amor que nos tem, ou porque são os mois empenhados em Pernambuco (Recife) . . .[71].

When the furore over the burning of Isaac de Castro and the penancing of three other Brazilian Jewish captives at Lisbon was at its height, in

---

[69] J.W. van Hoboken, "De West-Indische Compagnie en de vrede van Munster", *Tijdschrift voor Geschiedenis*, lxx (1957), 361-362; the so-called "Brasilse directie tot Middelburg" was set up in December 1646, see Franz Binder, "Die Zeeländische Kaperfahrt, 1654-1662", *Archief uitgegeven door het Koninklijk zeeuwsch Genootschap der Wetenschappen*, (1976), 41, 77.

[70] *Correspondência diplomática de Francisco de Sousa Coutinho*, ii. 53, 314.

[71] *Ibid.*, ii. 53: Sousa Coutinho to John IV, The Hague, 6 March 1647.

February 1648, Sousa˙Coutinho further reported to the king:

> ... sey que os judeus tratão com os de Zellanda para que por conta de huns e outros se armen fragatas para irem infestar os mares e costas desse reino, para o que ja pedem licença aos Estados, e se ainda a não tem a virão a ter, se Vossa Magestade não for servido de lhes mandar responder a sua satisfação[72].

In the years 1647-1648, this privateering war organized by the *Brasilse directie* at Middelburg, and backed by Amsterdam Sephardi capital, had a devastating impact on the Portuguese traffic to Brazil. Nothing like it had been seen before. In the two years 1647-1648, the Zeelanders captured approximately 220 Portuguese ships sailing to and from Brazil, a majority of the vessels which attempted the voyage[73]. In fact, in 1648 unescorted Portuguese navigation to Bahia and Rio de Janeiro collapsed. What saved the Portuguese traffic to Brazil was the setting up of the so-called "Brazil Company" at Lisbon in 1649, a joint-stock company based on New Christian capital designed to operate a heavily armed convoy system[74]. As a result, from 1649 onwards, Portuguese shipping losses to the Zeeland privateers were cut to a mere handful[75]. In setting up the Brazil Company, John IV, as is well known, made his one really substantial concession to the New Christians in the face of bitter opposition from the Inquisition: capital invested in the Brazil Company was declared to be wholly exempt from confiscation by the Inquisition even when belonging to sentenced judaizers[76]. Thus the irony is that Dutch Sephardi hostility to Portugal in the years 1647-1648 had the unintended effect of gaining more for the New Christians than had Dutch Sephardi support for the Portuguese cause in the early 1640s. It was presumably on account of this major concession to the New Christians that Jeronimo da Costa's father, Duarte, at Hamburg decided to help procure large vessels suitable for conversion into warships, stores and supplies for the Company at a time when the Sephardi merchants in Amsterdam flatly refused to provide what was needed[77].

Dutch Sephardi Jewry's hopes that Netherlands Brazil could be saved and restored were finally dashed in the years 1649-1651. The troops that

---

[72] *Ibid.*, ii. 314: Sousa Coutinho to John IV, The Hague, 24 February 1648.

[73] Boxer, *The Dutch in Brazil*, pp. 280-290; Binder, "Die Zeeländische Kaperfahrt", pp. 41, 77.

[74] Boxer, *The Dutch in Brazil*, pp. 208-211; the "Companhia Geral do Comercio do Brasil" was financed largely by New Christians, see C.A. Hanson, *Economy and Society in Baroque Portugal, 1668-1703* (Ann Arbor, 1981), pp. 178, 217.

[75] Cabral de Mello, *Olinda Restaurada*, pp. 83-84, 88, 92.

[76] Boxer, *The Dutch in Brazil*, p. 212.

[77] Vieira, *Obras Escolhidas*, i. 100-105.

arrived with Withe de With, in 1648, proved insufficient to make the attempt on Bahia. The authorities in Recife then decided to throw what offensive power they had into an attempt to break the siege of Recife which culminated in the debacle of the first battle of Guararapes (April 1648) when the Dutch army of Brazil, some 4,500 men, was defeated by an inferior Portuguese force and driven back, with over 1,000 casualties, into Recife. This left the Portuguese free to surround Recife again and reoccupy Olinda. The last attempt to break out and gain the upper hand was launched in February 1649 and culminated in the second battle of Guararapes. Again the Dutch were beaten, this time more ignominiously and with heavier losses than before. With this hopes faded. Nevertheless, it was still expected in the Republic that Dutch Brazil could be saved, by means of either an all-out or a partial war against Portugal. But plans for an all-out war, or a blockade of Lisbon, met with stiff opposition in Amsterdam and at Hoorn which was the center for the importing of Portuguese salt, and no agreed strategy had yet emerged by 1651 when the Republic was dragged into its dangerous confrontation with England which led directly on to the first Anglo-Dutch War (1652-1654). With this the fate of Recife was sealed and early in 1654, the garrison capitulated along with the other remaining Dutch forts in Brazil to the Portuguese.

The collapse of Dutch Brazil was a crushing blow to Dutch Sephardi Jewry, indeed to all western Sephardi Jewry, and by no means only in an economic sense. Brazil had appeared to be the land of promise, the land on which western Sephardi Jewry's future prospects rested. Only in Brazil, or so it seemed, was there room for Jewish settlement on an unlimited scale and a guarantee of terms more favorable than existed, or were likely to be obtained, anywhere else in the world. And if the privileges and rights conceded by the West India Company to the Jews in Brazil were already the most liberal available anywhere before 1645, in the aftermath of the planters' revolt, in 1645, the States General, at the prompting of the Amsterdam *Mahamad*, directed the West India Company to reward the loyalty the Jews were showing by proferring to them every favor and protection and not discriminating against them in favor of Christians in any sphere of administration, taxation or commerce[78]. In fact in Netherlands Brazil, albeit as a result of a great crisis, the Jews were effectively granted equality of status and opportunity with Christians, a unique phenomenon, needless to say, in that age.

The Dutch-Portuguese truce of 1641 which had raised so many hopes, and which seemed to guarantee a secure and flourishing future for western Sephardi Jewry had, in the end, undermined and shattered all such

[78] Wiznitzer, *Jews in Colonial Brazil*, p. 100.

expectations. The inevitable result was a major shift in the political outlook of Dutch Sephardi Jewry. To proclaim an enthusiastic loyalty to
Portugal as well as to the United Provinces as Menasseh ben Israel had
done in 1641 was now inconceivable. The community at Amsterdam no
longer wanted to be known as the ''Portuguese nation'' but as the ''Jewish nation'' of Amsterdam. The planters' revolt of 1645 had meant a
parting of the ways politically between the Jews of the Republic and the
New Christians of Portugal and Brazil. But the shift in Dutch Sephardi
allegiance was not just a matter of political realism and a tightening of
links with the Dutch state. The idea of a political restoration of the Jews
so vividly lodged in Sephardi minds as a result of the stirring events of
the 1640s could not, once aroused, be simply packed away and discarded
on the shattering of prospects for Brazil. The likelihood was that so intoxicating a notion would continue to permeate the western Sephardi
world. Can it be mere coincidence, for example, that the year of the second battle of Guarapares which effectively aborted the Dutch counter-
offensive in Brazil was also the year of Menasseh ben Israel's *Esperança
de Israel*? The message of Menasseh's *Esperança* surely was that the political restoration of Israel was, after all, close at hand. The book is a retreat
from active hopes based on current political actuality to no less urgent
political expectations of a mystical character based on signs and symbols
which, he believed, pointed to the fulfillment of a spiritual process. One
of the key signs to which Menasseh points are the several recent Jewish
martyrdoms including that of Isaac de Castro, the Jew from Dutch Brazil
burnt alive in Lisbon[79]. The burning of Isaac de Castro aroused more
emotion among western Sephardim than any comparable event of the
age. It became a symbol of the destruction of Jewish hopes in Portugal's
restoration. But Menasseh urged his contemporaries to find also in this
terrible event consolation and a token of divine promise. Isaac de Castro's inspiring heroicism, according to Menasseh, was a God-given sign
that ''our redemption'' is now very near.

---

[79] Menasseh ben Israel, *Mikveh Israel. Esto es, Esperança de Israel* (Amsterdam, 1650),
pp. 99-100.

Appendix

Translations of the Passages in Latin and Portuguese Cited in the Text

Note 18
And it will be freely allowed to the subjects of either side, of whatever nation, condition, quality or religion without any exception, whether they are born under the jurisdiction of either side, or have their residence in either, to visit, come in ships, and trade in whatever kind of goods or employment in the kingdoms, provinces, territories and islands of the other in Europe and in whatever other parts situated on this side of the Line. Nor will it be lawful for either party to burden the subjects of either side carrying on trade in the lands of the other situated as stated above, whether importing or exporting goods, with higher taxes, duties, tariffs or other impositions than they impose on their own inhabitants and subjects, rather they shall enjoy equally the concessions and privileges which were in use hitherto until Portugal was subjected to the Castilians.

Note 20
'subjects and inhabitants of their provinces who are Christians may use and enjoy liberty of conscience in their private dwellings and free exercise of their religion inside their ships.'

Note 28
We had such a Catholic king that during the difficult times at the commencement of his reign he did not listen to the propositions of the Jews petitioning for two synagogues in Portugal for which they were offering huge sums of money.

Note 32
I call your Majesty's attention to the fact that although most of the Portuguese that are there are Jews, nonetheless they have an affection for Portugal that makes them wish to serve your Majesty more than do the Dutch and I do not say this without reason.

Note 34
All these men, owing to their love of Portugal as their homeland and of your Majesty as their natural monarch, are desirous to return to the kingdom and to serve your Majesty with their resources, as they do foreign kings.

Note 36
. . . but your Excellency well knows that we who are exiled from our homeland are prevented from going there and this is what prevents me from sending my son, Jeronimo

Nunes da Costa [Moseh Curiel] and if it were not for that hindrance most of us would not mind going to China overland [to serve the king].

Note 37
. . . especially at a time when the benign King João IV has been restored to his natural and hereditary kingdom, until now unjustly possessed by another, and when the old hatred [between the Dutch and Portuguese] is coming to an end and the much desired peace will follow — which, being a Portuguese with a Dutch soul, will be most pleasing to myself.

Note 45
. . . God help us and provide an expedient enabling us to settle these matters once and for all. The people of Amsterdam is growing hostile, the Jews would condemn me to be stoned and here that could easily happen, and what is worse still is that those who we imagine are our friends are the worst . . .

Note 55
They have spread the rumour that rebellion is rife in the kingdom and that his Majesty has been arrested by the nobles and that the fortress of São Evão is in Castilian hands; and preceding those reports, which are chiefly put about and published by the Jews, they were alleging that his Majesty had seized all the ships which were arriving in all the ports of the kingdom in order to be able to send an armada to Brazil.

Note 58
. . . and if Jeronimo Nunes da Costa advises your Excellency otherwise it is because he only knows how to spread damaging reports against us and, in order that it should be apparent to your Excellency what an old scoundrel his uncle Lope Ramires [David Curiel] is, and how these dogs do nothing other than cause us grief, I am sending these latters of his so that your Excellency may read them and may decide to send them to his Majesty in order that they may know in Portugal that there is in these men neither good faith nor loyalty.

Note 60
Their fleet is still in these parts held back by a contrary wind. It is said that many of their men are dyeing on board from small-pox but this report will not have reached your Excellency via Jeronimo Nunes da Costa, just as that of the loss of two [Dutch] ships did not arrive, which confirms me in thinking that if it were something to our disadvantage or detriment he would pass on the report by two different routes.

Note 67
. . . coming to me to say that they have concluded peace with Castile and that they will now have their hands free to assist their subjects with regard to whom the law of the peoples has been infringed in two respects: firstly, having surrendered with others in the fortress of São Francisco, nevertheless they were taken to Portugal and there handed over to the Inquisition; and secondly, that we are breaking article 25 of the Truce [of 1641] which they say clearly refers to the Jews, and which, without naming them, expressly mentions them in that particular which speaks of the subjects of these provinces whether

born in them or in whatever other place [ie. including New Christians born in Portugal who had reverted to Judaism in the United Provinces].

Note 71

... at Amsterdam they sought out those who wished to participate but there was not one Dutchman who wished to, only Jews of whom there were many whether through the love [ie hatred] that they have for us or because most of them have investments in Pernambuco.

Note 72

I know that the Jews are negotiating with the Zeelanders in order that together they will fit out and arm privateering frigates with which to infest the seas and coasts of that kingdom [ie Portugal] for which they are already petitioning permission from the States General and if they do not have it yet they will obtain it if your Majesty sends no order that they should be responded to and given satisfaction.

8

The Diplomatic Career of Jeronimo Nunes da Costa: An Episode in Dutch-Portuguese Relations of the Seventeenth Century*

The merchant and diplomatic agent Jeronimo Nunes da Costa, one of the most prominent figures of the Amsterdam Portuguese Jewish community of the later seventeenth century, has been referred to in passing in a good many books[1]. Renowned for his wealth, the prestige he enjoyed among non-Jews (the Stadholder William III is said to have stayed in his house for three days during one of his later visits to Amsterdam[2]), and his handsome donations to the Amsterdam Portuguese Synagogue, his name figured constantly in Dutch Jewish community life and synagogue politics for over half a century. His opulent residence on the Nieuwe Herengracht, then called the Joden Herengracht, in Amsterdam, testified both to the seigneurial grandeur of his life-style and his pretensions to leadership among the Portuguese Jewish 'nation' as the community was known in Holland. Over a period of decades, he was one, if not the most important, of all Dutch traders with Portugal and its colonies. He also traded quite extensively with Curaçao and, via Curaçao, with the neighbouring Spanish American mainland. His innumerable dealings in salt from Setúbal, sugar from Brazil and São Thomé, Algarve figs, Brazil tobacco, diamonds, grain, timber, silver, slaves, arms and munitions were unrivalled in scale or diversity among Dutch Jews of his day. But besides his prominence in commerce

*   I would like to express my deep gratitude for their help with this article to Dr. Marcel Curiel, of Caracas, a descendant of the former Nunes da Costa family much devoted to research into its history, to António de Vasconcelos Simão who greatly assisted me with obtaining copies of Jeronimo's dispatches from Lisbon, and to Edgar Samuel of London. I also gladly acknowledge my debt to Daniel Swetschinski who devoted a section of his as yet unpublished Ph.d. thesis to Jeronimo which I have had occasion to cite repeatedly in the following footnotes.
1.   In particular, see Isaac da Costa, *Noble Families among the Sephardic Jews,* B. Brewster and C. Roth, ed. (London, 1936) 151 f; J.S. da Silva Rosa, *Geschiedenis der Portugeesche joden te Amsterdam, 1593-1925* (Amsterdam, 1925) 100-101; H. Kellenbenz, *Sephardim an der unteren Elbe* (Wiesbaden, 1958) 167-169, 352-363; W.Chr. Pieterse, *Daniel Levi de Barrios als geschiedschrijver van de Portugees-Israelietische gemeente te Amsterdam* (Amsterdam, 1968) 75, 76, 89; Daniel M. Swetschinski, 'The Portuguese Jewish Merchants of Seventeenth-Century Amsterdam: a Social Profile' (Unpublished Ph.d. thesis Brandeis University, 1979) chapter iii, section v.
2.   David Franco Mendes, 'Memorias', *Studia Rosenthaliana,* IX, ii (July 1975) 95.

and Jewish community life, Jeronimo also spent considerable periods at The Hague immersed in diplomacy, acting as an important intermediary in Dutch-Portuguese relations. It is this latter aspect of his remarkable career which provides the subject matter of this present article.

Jeronimo Nunes da Costa, or Moseh Curiel, as he was known in the synagogue, was born at Florence, in the Grand Duchy of Tuscany, in May 1620 and was the eldest son of Duarte Nunes da Costa (Jacob Curiel), a Lisbon New Christian merchant who fled from the Inquisition in Portugal in or around 1609. After some years first in Madrid and then at Florence, Jeronimo's father moved to Amsterdam where his brother, Jeronimo's uncle, Lopo Ramires (David Curiel) had for some years been a leading figure in the Jewish community. But he stayed only five or six years before moving on, in 1626, to Hamburg. From then until 1640, Duarte imported to Hamburg a good deal of Brazil sugar and other goods from Lisbon and also became involved in the international munitions trade. Among other things, he shipped Danish gunpowder, via Dover, to the Spanish Netherlands. Following the secession of Portugal from the Spanish Monarchy, in December 1640, Duarte emerged as the most active and vocal champion of the Portuguese cause among the Portuguese Jewish diaspora in northern Europe. He shipped munitions and naval stores to Lisbon and played a notable part in the attempts to secure the release of Dom Duarte, younger brother of João IV, the new king of Portugal, who had been seized whilst serving in the wars in Germany by the Habsburg Emperor, at the instigation of the latter's cousin, Philip IV of Spain[3]. For his contributions to Portugal's struggle for independence from Spain, Duarte Nunes da Costa was made a knight of the Portuguese royal household, in 1641[4], and named 'Agent of Portugal' at Hamburg in 1644.

While Duarte's other sons remained with him at Hamburg, he sent his eldest, Jeronimo, at the age of twenty-two, early in 1642, to Amsterdam where he was to remain for the rest of his long life. This he did at the request of João IV's ministers who were keen to reinforce the small group of Portuguese representatives who were then in Holland[5]. This is why, many years later, in 1664, the English king, Charles II, was apprised by the Portuguese ambassador in London that

---

3. For further details about Duarte and Lopo Ramires, see my forthcoming book on the history of the Curiel family, 'The Curiels. An Ibero-Dutch Patrician Family in the Old World and New, 1492-1980'.

4. According to Jeronimo's letter of appointment as Portuguese Agent in the Dutch Provinces, Duarte was ennobled by João IV as a *cavaleiro fidalgo* on 14 June 1641, British Library (hereafter BL) MS Add. 46912, fos. 11r-v.

5. Biblioteca Nacional. Lisbon (BNL) MS 661, caixa 14, fos. 89v-90: J. Nunes da Costa to Vidigueira, Amsterdam, 19 september 1644.

Jeronimo Nunes da Costa who is, and has been these twenty yeares Agent for the king my master, in Amsterdam, for providing him with munition for war and all necessaryes for shipping, as well for his royall navy, as allsoe for that belonging to the Brasill Company; is the only person that acts these and such like businesses, for which end the king my master sent for him from Hamburgh to reside at Amsterdam[6].

The ambassador's object in stressing that Jeronimo had been asked to settle in Holland by the Portuguese was to secure immunity for his cargoes from seizure by the English in the event of a second Anglo-Dutch war. But the point is indeed crucial to understanding Jeronimo's pattern of loyalties. His Jewish loyalties were clear. Like his father, who was an important figure in synagogue affairs in Hamburg and beyond, Jeronimo always devoted a good deal of time and energy to Jewish community matters and, on occasion, took initiatives on behalf of his people at diplomatic level as in 1682 when he wrote to Louis XIV, pleading on behalf of the Jews of Martinique who were then under threat of expulsion by the French crown[7]. But, at least in the early part of his career, he showed little or no sense of obligation to the Dutch Republic and steadfastly refused to consider himself a Dutch subject. He insisted in his communications with the States General and States of Holland that he was an accredited representative of the Portuguese crown and that he owed allegiance to Portugal alone. Only in later years, as the hopes that he and his father had placed in the willingness and ability of the restored Portuguese monarchy to ameliorate the lot of the Portuguese New Christians faded, did he develop an increasing rapport with Dutch leaders and perform significant services on behalf of the Republic.

Initially, in the years 1642-1645, Jeronimo operated in Amsterdam on behalf of Portuguese diplomats and of his father, and trading on his own account, without holding any official title or position[8]. But he made himself increasingly useful not only to the Portuguese ambassador to The Hague, Francisco de Sousa Coutinho, but to Portuguese diplomats at Paris, London and at the Westphalian peace congresses, at Münster and Osnabrück. A service particularly valued by Sousa Coutinho in the early and mid-1640s was his procuring of news and information from Portugal's arch-enemy, Spain, by means of his fellow Jews at Amsterdam, several of whom specialized in clandestine trade, often via Bayonne, with a country from which Dutch ships and merchants were still officially

---

6. Public Record Office, London (PRO) SP 89/6, fo. 200: petition dated 28 December 1664.
7. Abraham Cahen, 'Les juifs de la Martinique au XVIIe siècle', *Revue des études juives,* II (1981) !06.
8. BNL, MS 661, caixa 14. no. 64: J. Nunes da Costa to Vidigueira, Amsterdam, 22 August 1644; Swetschinski, 'Portuguese Jewish Merchants', I, 228.

excluded[9]. He was appointed Agent of the Portuguese crown, not only in Amsterdam but in Holland and all the Dutch provinces, in May 1645. The implication, in much of the existing secondary literature which refers to Jeronimo's career, that his official activities were limited to Amsterdam is indeed entirely misleading.

By 1645, Jeronimo was in regular contact with the Portuguese ambassador in Paris, the conde de Vidigueira (later the marquês de Niza) who was serving as Portugal's senior diplomat in northern Europe, co-ordinating his country's efforts in France, England, the Netherlands and Germany. Jeronimo provided much information about the Dutch West India Company (in which he and his father were substantial investors) and its forces and operations in Brazil and West Africa[10], about the Dutch-Spanish negotiations then in progress, and about numerous other matters of interest to the Portuguese. He acted as the main clearing-house for Portuguese diplomatic correspondance passing from Lisbon, Paris, and London to and from the Portuguese delegations at the Westphalian congresses. He did also provide some financial services for Portuguese diplomats but his role in this sphere was very limited during the 1640s when his uncle, Lopo Ramires, acted as Portugal's main Amsterdam banker. One of Jeronimo's principal tasks was to obtain maximum publicity in Dutch news-sheets and pamphlets for Portuguese successes against Spain and he was regularly sent the details of Portuguese land and sea victories from Lisbon for this purpose[11].

After his appointment as Agent, Jeronimo also regularly sent dispatches direct to João IV's ministers in Lisbon. In 1646, for instance, the number of his reports to the Portuguese government, crammed with diplomatic and Dutch political and colonial news, was easily comparable with the quantities dispatched by his full-time professional colleagues[12]. To fully grasp the significance of Jeronimo's early role, one must bear in mind that not only was Holland then the diplomatic

---

9.   Pleased with some news procured by Jeronimo from Madrid, Sousa Coutinho reported to Lisbon in July 1643 that 'with him and his father it matters much to His Majesty that there should be the good correspondance which their services merit and, were it not for the fact that they are Jews, I do not know how His Majesty could repay what he owes them', *Correspondência diplomática de Francisco de Sousa Coutinho durante a sua embaixada em Holanda,* E. Prestage, e.a., ed. (3 vols.; Coimbra-Lisbon, 1920-1955} I, 14, 179.

10.   See, for instance, B(iblioteca da) Ajuda 49-x-24, fo. 339: J. Nunes da Costa, to L. Pereira de Castro, Amsterdam, 20 October 1645; Biblioteca Publica de Evora (BPE) CVI-2II: Niza to J. Nunes da Costa, Paris, 4 September 1648, thanking him for papers concerning the Portuguese reconquest of São Thomé; *Correspondência Sousa Coutinho,* II, 265-266.

11.   BPE CVI-2-1, fos. 150-151: Vidigueira to J. Nunes da Costa, Paris, 27 August 1644; and Affonso VI, 'Carta de padrão', *Anais da Academia Portuguesa,* 2nd ser. VIII (1958) 120-121.

12.   *Cartas de el-rei D. João IV ao conde de Vidigueira (Marquês de Niza) embaixador em Franca,* P.M. Laranjo Coelho, ed. (2 vols.; Lisbon, 1940-1942) II, 5-40.

nerve-centre of Europe and the principal source of news from Asia, Africa and Brazil but that what was happening in Holland was of crucial importance to a newly reborn Portuguese state fighting for its survival not only against Spain but against the colonial ambitions of the Dutch East and West India Companies. News supplied by Jeronimo about Dutch activity in Brazil was especially vital, for it was in 1645 that began the revolt of the Portuguese planters in the Dutch zone of Brazil which ended the fragile cease-fire which had held since July 1642 and initiated the last phase of the Dutch-Portuguese struggle for possession of the area. While both sides were anxious to avoid a full-scale war, relations between the Republic and Portugal were increasingly embittered from 1645 onwards. Having appointed him his Agent in the United Provinces, João IV further expressed his appreciation of Jeronimo's role as a supplier of Dutch news, by elevating him to the rank of 'knight and nobleman *(cavaleiro fidalgo)* of my house'[13], the same honour which he had previously conferred upon his father. In general, there is little to distinguish Jeronimo's dispatches from the usual type of diplomatic reports of the day, though Sousa Coutinho did note that in one letter he named the Island of St. Helena simply as Helena, remarking that he is such a religious Jew that if he called it 'Saint' he would be failing in his obligations[14].

As Dutch-Portuguese relations progressively deteriorated under the strain of the bitter contest for Brazil and West Africa, Jeronimo became more deeply involved in activity inimical to Dutch interests. King João IV himself expressed his pleasure at information supplied by Jeronimo through Niza concerning the weakness of the Dutch garrison of the West African island of São Thomé[15], information which was possibly of material assistance to the Portuguese in recovering the island from the Dutch, following their reconquest of Angola, in August 1648. In May 1649, Sousa Coutinho received from Lisbon the terms of the Dutch surrender in Angola. When the States General angrily refused to acknowledge the humiliating capitulation, the ambassador sent the document to Jeronimo who circulated copies in Amsterdam and arranged for their publication[16]. Jeronimo's standing in the Portuguese diplomatic service in the later 1640s clearly rested on his growing prestige among royal officials in Lisbon and with the marquês de Niza, ambassador at Paris, rather than on his

13. BL MS 46912, fos. llr-v.
14. *Correspondência Sousa Coutinho,* I, 318.
15. João IV to Niza, Lisbon, 8 July 1647 in *Cartas de el-rei D. João IV,* II, 119.
16. *Correspondência Sousa Coutinho,* III, 244-245.

relationship with Sousa Coutinho, Portuguese ambassador at The Hague, with whom, in fact, he was on increasingly bad terms[17].

A notable feature of Jeronimo's activity on behalf of Portugal in the late 1640s was his collaboration with the great Portuguese Jesuit preacher, missionary and diplomat, António Vieira. Vieira was a man close to the ear of João IV and of considerable importance in the events of his reign. Although little is known about Vieira's first visit to Holland (April-July 1646), it is clear that he was handling secret business on behalf of the king which involved close contact with Jeronimo, and other Amsterdam Jews, and with the Portuguese crypto-Jews of Rouen. In a letter written to these Portuguese New Christians of Rouen from The Hague, of 20 April 1646, Vieira states that the schemes which he had been endeavouring to persuade the king to adopt would undoubtedly be strengthened now that he had been in direct contact with the Rouen community[18]. Vieira was referring to his famous project for the restraining of the Inquisition in Portugal and its colonies on the part of João IV as part of a new relationship between the crown and the Portuguese Jewish diaspora, intended to enable the king to harness Jewish capital and resources behind the struggle for Brazil and Africa, and behind Portugal's fight for survival as an independent state. In particular, Vieira's plan for a joint-stock Brazil Company to take over commerce with Brazil in which Jewish and New Christian capital would be immune from confiscation by the Inquisition, though conceived of some years before, was only far enough advanced to be adopted by João IV after Vieira's return from Holland, in 1646[19]. This was just the sort of measure that Jeronimo and his father had longed to see from João IV who had, in fact, already taken some initial hesitant steps towards curbing the virulence of the Portuguese Inquisition[20] and Jeronimo and Duarte would certainly have promised Vieira their enthusiastic support. When the Brazil Company, which was to play a not inconsiderable part in clinching Portuguese success in the fight for Brazil, was finally set up, in 1649, both Jeronimo and Duarte Nunes da Costa were extremely active in procuring the necessary ships, naval stores, munitions and additional support. In return

17.   Late in 1647, Jeronimo and Sousa Coutinho were sharply at variance in their assessments of the chances of an early dispatch of Dutch reinforcements to Brazil and the ambassador accused Jeronimo of deliberately trying to mislead the kings' ministers, *Correspondência Sousa Coutinho,* II, 265-266; he also grumbled over what he considered Jeronimo's shortcomings in the sphere of financial services.
18.   António Vieira S.J., *Obras Escolhidas,* António Sérgio and Hernâni Cidade, ed. (12. vols.; Lisbon, 1951) I, 87-89.
19.   See C.R. Boxer, 'Padre Antonio Vieira S.J. and the Institution of the Brazil Company in 1649', *Hispanic American Historical Review,* XXIX (1949) 474-497.
20.   *Instruções inéditas de D. Luis da Cunha a Marco António de Azevedo Coutinho,* Pedro de Azevedo, ed. (Coimbra, 1929) 75-76.

Jeronimo and his father were respectively appointed the Company's Amsterdam and Hamburg representatives[21].

During his second stay in Holland, in 1647-1648, António Vieira was again in close contact with Jeronimo Nunes da Costa[22]. On this occasion, the Jesuit's mission was to purchase on behalf of the king newly-built fregates, fast, light, and constructed to the latest design. Although in the end most of the ships and munitions that Vieira was seeking were purchased in Hamburg and Lübeck by Duarte Nunes da Costa and Jeronimo's younger brothers, Manoel and Jorge Nunes da Costa (Selomoh and David Curiel), Jeronimo worked closely with Vieira constantly advising and assisting him. Jeronimo and his uncle, Lopo Ramires, did also purchase at least one fregate on behalf of Vieira, the *Fortuna,* which they bought from the Amsterdam merchant and ship-dealer, Jeremiah van Collen[23].

An amusing anecdote pertains to this period of Jeronimo's life. Throughout his career there were occasions when he found himself introducing Christian notables to the Synagogue and to Judaism. Indeed, Jewish leaders of the age of mercantilism regularly sought not only to convince influential non-Jews of the usefulness of Jewish skills and resources but consciously strove to improve the image of the Jewish faith among Christians. For the first time since the rise of Christianity to supremacy, a stream of rulers, noblemen, and ecclesiastics visited the synagogues and witnessed Jewish services and rituals, especially in Venice and Amsterdam. Vieira was one of numerous notables escorted to the Amsterdam Portuguese synagogue by Jeronimo Nunes da Costa. During the sermon, however, Vieira was so angered by certain words of the rabbi that he loudly interrupted the proceedings. The situation demanded all of Jeronimo's famed tact. He dragged the Jesuit out 'not without some violence' and reportedly calmed him with the following observation:

a man as eminent as yourself will either persuade or be persuaded; if you persuade us, it will be a bad day for the synagogue and should you be convinced, for the King of Portugal, so I judge it best that we avoid the issue[24].

Until 1651, Jeronimo continued to act for Portugal in an auxiliary capacity, essentially as an assistant of Sousa Coutinho. He supplied valuable reports. He

21. H. Kellenbenz, 'Phasen des hanseatischen-nordeuropäischen Südamerikahandels', *Hansische Geschichtsblätter,* LXXVIII (1966) 98-99; Swetschinski, 'Portuguese Jewish Merchants', i, 234.
22. *Cartas do Padre António Vieira,* J. Lúcio d'Azevedo, ed. (3 vols.; Coimbra, 1925-1928) I, 162-164.
23. Virginia Rau, 'O Padre António Vieira e a Fragata Fortuna', *Studia,* II (1958) 98-102.
24. *Memorias inéditas de Fr. João de S. Joseph* (s.a.) 160-161.

advanced sums for the repatriation of a considerable number of Portuguese soldiers and seamen brought back by the Dutch from the Indies east and west, feeding them until shipping space was available and then paying their passage back to Portugal[25]. In 1650, advancing a substantial sum to the king, he shipped a sizeable consignment of urgently needed arms and munitions back to Portugal[26]. Sousa Coutinho's transfer to Paris was followed, later in 1651, by the short extraordinary embassy of Antonio de Sousa de Macedo who was likewise assisted in various ways by Jeronimo, though on one occasion, Sousa de Macedo was much angered by Jeronimo's refusal to advance him 500 *cruzados* which he required to bribe an unnamed Gelderland delegate to the States General[27]. On Sousa de Macedo's departure, Dutch-Portuguese relations were near to a total break, the Dutch refusing to admit another ambassador from João IV until they were offered some satisfaction for their complaints over Brazil and West Africa. Several times during 1651, the States General discussed going to war with Portugal and blockading Lisbon.

In principle, João IV was anxious to mollify the Dutch, for he did not consider himself strong enough to fight Spain and the Republic simultaneously. At this stage he was still willing to partition Brazil and to repeat his assurances that no official help was being given to the rebels in the Dutch zone. However, the outbreak of the first Anglo-Dutch War in 1652 prevented the Republic from taking action against Portugal for the time being and emboldened the Portuguese monarch to take advantage of the opportunity and risk a full-scale offensive to finally dislodge the Dutch from the north-east of Brazil. The main Dutch stronghold, Recife, fell to the Portuguese forces in January 1654. But the collapse of the Dutch colony was closely followed by the treaty of Westminster which freed the Dutch from their English entanglement, enabling the States General once again to consider action against Portugal. At this critical juncture, Jeronimo Nunes da Costa was effectively Portuguese *chargé d'affaires* in the Republic and it fell to him to negotiate vital matters of state at the highest level not only in The Hague, with members of the States General's special committee for Portuguese affairs, and in Amsterdam, but in other Dutch towns. Some months after the fall of Recife, in the summer of 1654, when Antonio da Silva de Sousa, Portuguese envoy at Stockholm, visited Hamburg, he received instructions from the king to

---

25. There are a number of references to this in Sousa Coutinho's letters, see also the 'Carta de padrão', *Anais*, 2nd ser. VIII, 121.
26. *Ibidem*, 121; BPE CVL 2-1/123: J. Nunes da Costa to C. Soares de Abreu, Amsterdam, 3 November 1649.
27. Algemeen Rijksarchief, The Hague (ARH) SG 7011-1: De Chapelle to States General, The Hague, 28 August 1653.

proceed directly to Amsterdam and speak with Jeronimo Nunes about the prospects of an accommodation with the Dutch and whether or not they will forget what has happened in Brazil, and about obtaining the peace and understanding between this realm and that nation which I desire, and, in particular, you will discover whether they will now receive an ambassador from me[28].

The initial response from The Hague was negative, but Jeronimo continued with his soundings and sending secret reports to Lisbon. On 20 April 1655, the Council of State in Lisbon discussed a dispatch from Jeronimo of 30 March in which he advised that in the aftermath of the Dutch defeats by England, despite disagreement among the provinces, 'that the States General was inclined to negotiate peace and that it seemed unlikely that they would make war this year'[29]. Jeronimo appraised João IV's ministers that he was about to travel to Utrecht and the Overijssel towns to work at persuading more city magistrates to reconcile themselves to the permanent loss of Brazil. Three days later, the Council debated further reports from Jeronimo. He recounted that he had again talked with the 'Count of Nassau' who 'promised him to work vigorously on our behalf and find out for certain whether the States General will now receive an ambassador from Portugal'[30]. Jeronimo reiterated his previous assessment that the Dutch could be swayed to abandon Brazil without further conflict, assuring the king that negotiation was now possible. He even ventured to advise the king that Antonio de Sousa de Macedo was the man to send. Additionally, he suggested that the king write to the 'Conde de Nassau' thanking him for his assistance. On this occasion, as on numerous others, the Council expressed warm appreciation of Jeronimo's services. And several times subsequently, as on 16 December 1655, the Council returned to considering Jeronimo's assessments of the balance of views among the Dutch towns and provinces[31].

At the same time, Jeronimo's dispatches during the 1650s were the sole regular source of information available to Portuguese ministers as to the intentions and

28. João IV to Silva de Sousa, 17 July 1654 in *Um diplomata português da Restauração – António da Silva de Sousa* (Lisbon, 1940) 24; in the early eighteenth century, the Portuguese Protestant writer, Oliveira, a friend of Jeronimo's youngest son, Alvaro Nunes da Costa, wrote that 'lorsque les ambassadeurs de Portugal se retirerent de la Haya à cause des différens qui survinrent entres les deux puissances ...ce juif y resta seul chargé des plus grandes negociations de cette couronne. Il s'en acquitta avec honneur...'.
29. Bibliotheca dos Duques de Cadaval (Muge) (BDC) k-VIII-6b, 'Memórias do Conselho de Estado' fo. 86v.
30. BDC k-VIII-6b, fo. 91v.; the 'Count of Nassau' referred to here is presumably Willem Frederik, Stadholder of Friesland, a province which was traditionally cool towards the interests of the West India Company and firmly opposed going to war with Portugal over Brazil; Jeronimo would have talked with him at his town-house in The Hague.
31. BDC k-VIII-6b, fo. 260v: session of Conselho de Estado, 16 December 1655.

activities of the Dutch colonial companies. Besides being a major investor, Jeronimo clearly followed colonial affairs, including the movements in commodity prices, very closely. Thus his advices were essential subject matter for the *Conselho Ultramarino,* responsible for colonial affairs, as well as for the Council of State and the Brazil Company. In June 1655, for example, Jeronimo remitted details of Dutch and English reinforcements being sent out to the Far East which caused the *Conselho Ultramarino* to urge João IV to dispatch additional Portuguese forces to India and Ceylon[32], the latter having been a focus of bitter Dutch-Portuguese rivalry since the 1630s. Apparently, Jeronimo regularly sent to Lisbon details as to the number, tonnage, and cargoes both of outgoing and incoming Dutch East India fleets[33].

As the Republic was in so many ways central to their concerns in this period, the king's ministers were anxious that Portuguese diplomats in other parts of northern Europe should also receive regular reports from Jeronimo. In effect, Dutch ambassadors needed the most recent news from The Hague and Amsterdam. Thus when a new Portuguese ambassador, Francisco Mello Torres, was sent to London, in 1657, there were five other Portuguese representatives in northern Europe with whom he was instructed to maintain regular correspondance. Of these, two were Jeronimo and Duarte Nunes da Costa, royal Agents at Amsterdam and Hamburg[34]. Mello Torres, who frequently asked Jeronimo and his relatives to obtain books and other items for him in Holland, was generally highly appreciative of both father and son and several times praised them in his reports to Lisbon as also Jeronimo's cousin, Duarte Rodrigues Lamego, a prosperous Rouen crypto-Jew who forwarded Portuguese diplomats, as well as his Dutch and Hamburg relatives, information from the French court.

The indecision over Portuguese affairs that prevailed at The Hague during 1655-1656 could not last. The heavy setbacks suffered at Portuguese hands were indeed the greatest humiliation and most costly failure that the Republic ever endured during the Golden Age. In fact, there was rather greater support both in Amsterdam, where opinion was split, and in Holland generally, for a war against Portugal than is usually recognized. Only Friesland (and, we may take it, Willem Frederik, its Stadholder) was solidly against. Zeeland, Gelderland,

---

32. Arquivo Histórico Ultramarino, Lisbon (AHU) India ex. 23. doc. 63: proceedings of the *Conselho,* 9 June 1655.
33. Filmoteca Ultramarina Portuguesa, Lisbon (FUP), 'Livro das Monções 22B, fo. 354: dispatches of J. Nunes da Costa, 10 August and 22 September 1651.
34. T. Schedel de Castello Branco, *Vida de Francisco Mello Torres, conde da Ponte, marquês de Sande, soldado e diplomata da Restauração* (1620-1667) (Lisbon, 1971) 289-290, 302; Duarte Rodrigues Lamego was a son of Sarah, younger sister of Duarte Nunes da Costa.

and Groningen were ardent for war. In September 1657, ten months after the death of João IV a powerful fleet under the Baron van Obdam was sent to Lisbon, over the objections of Friesland alone, bearing diplomatic envoys and an ultimatum for the Portuguese Queen-Regent, Dona Luisa. The Dutch demanded outright the restitution of the lost territories in Brazil. The Portuguese rejected the ultimatum and war was declared. There ensued the sporadic maritime conflict of 1657-1661, a war which had seriously disruptive effects on Dutch trade, though it enabled the East India Company to complete its conquest of Ceylon. On the outbreak of war, the Pensionary of Holland, Johan de Witt, the dominant figure in Dutch politics, had 'Hijeronijmo Nunes da Costa' whom he described as being 'in charge of the affairs of the Queen of Portugal here' placed under surveillance and had at least part of his correspondance intercepted[35].

The adverse impact of the war on trade, notably the loss of high-grade Setúbal salt vital to the Dutch herring fleets, inevitably widened the division of opinion over the struggle in Holland. Consequently, in the summer of 1658, the States General deliberated whether to retreat from its previous uncompromising stand and agree to admit a Portuguese envoy. Four provinces – Zeeland, Gelderland, Utrecht, and Groningen – still refused to contemplate peace without the restitution of territory in Brazil, but Friesland, Overijssel, and all-important Holland were now eager to negotiate. This was also Johan de Witt's position. The split generated a furious political battle into which Jeronimo hurled himself with his customary zeal and persuasiveness. He travelled many times to The Hague and, on occasion, to see city magistrates outside Holland, striving to influence as many regents as possible in favour of receiving an envoy from Lisbon[36]. He also developed a harmonious relationship with the French ambassador, Jacques Auguste de Thou, who was under instructions from Mazarin to sustain Portugal as a means of weakening Spain[37]. Active on the other side was the Spanish ambassador to The Hague, Don Esteban de Gamarra, who strove to drum up support for the Dutch war-party being determined to prolong the Dutch-Portuguese conflict as long as possible in the interests of Spain.

Finally, much to the indignation of Gamarra[38] and the assemblies of at least

35.   ARH SH 2648: J. de Witt to Obdam, 16 November 1657; H.H. Rowen, *John de Witt, Grand Pensionary of Holland, 1625-1672* (Princeton, N.J., 1978) 292.

36.   'Carta de Padrão, *Anais*, 2nd ser. VIII, 121; Oliveira, *Discours pathétique*, 67-68.

37.   According to Oliveira, 'Monsieur de Thou... n'avoit jamais connu, disoit-il, un homme comparable à ce juif, soit par sa bonne foi, soit par le nombre des grandes qualités qui'il réunissoit dans sa personne', *Discours pathétique*, 67.

38.   'Cet evènement', reports Oliveira, 'mortifia beaucoup Mr. Gamarra, et il dit publiquement qu'il ne comprénoit point comment les Etats pouvoient se resoudre à favoriser un juif jusqu' à ce point là.

three provinces, the States General did vote to admit a Portuguese envoy. The personage chosen for this crucial mission by the Queen-Regent's ministers was a high noble, Fernando Telles de Faro who, in the event, proved a lamentable choice. He was required to show his secret instructions to Jeronimo and work with him as well as with his embassy secretary, Luis Alvares Ribeiro, in negotiating with the Dutch. But Jeronimo was soon baffled by the ambassador's tardiness in getting down to essentials, despite his repeatedly reminding him of the urgency of this 'so necessary peace'[39]. In fact, Telles de Faro had entered into secret, treasonable, liaison with the Spanish ambassador, Gamarra, and was deliberately spinning out the proceedings in the interests of Spain. Apparently, De Thou, whose spies had some inkling of what was afoot, warned Alvares Ribeiro and Jeronimo who was back in Amsterdam. They were nevertheless stunned when, on 28 May 1659, on the excuse of travelling to Amsterdam for some 'amorous diversion', Telles de Faro fled with the embassy's papers and cash and placed himself under Gamarra's protection[40].

Telles de Faro's dramatic defection was a calamity for Portugal and the Dutch peace-party alike. It was also a personal affront to Jeronimo in whose debt the ambassador was to the tune of f4,000 for a diamond necklace and a comparable amount in loans[41]. The affair caused a sensation throughout the diplomatic circles of Europe. The culprit was subsequently tried in his absence, in Lisbon, and sentenced to be strangled as well as burned in effigy before the public. His residences were declared forfeit and demolished and the ground on which they stood sown with salt.

Amidst this crisis, Jeronimo was at once summoned back to The Hague where in effect he promptly took matters in hand. His greater knowledge of the foreign diplomats, Dutch politicians and the way things were done in The Hague, not to mention the Dutch language, meant that Alvares Ribeiro merely followed his lead. After a two-hour conference with De Thou, Jeronimo decided to submit a joint representation to the States General, together with Alvares Ribeiro, with behind-the-scenes support from the French embassy, requesting recognition and diplomatic protection for the secretary and himself as accredited negotiators on

39. Arquivo Nacional da Torre do Tombo, Lisbon (ANTT) Ms. da Graça, 2 L, 'Corresp. Luis Alvares Ribeiro', fo. 14: J. Nunes da Costa to Queen-Regent, 3 June 1659.
40. L. van Aitzema, *Historie of verhael van saken van staet en oorlogh, in ende ontrent de Vereenigde Nederlanden* (14 vols.; The Hague, 1667-1671) IX, 660, 662-663, 667; E.C. Molsbergen, *Frankrijk en de Republiek der Vereenigde Nederlanden, 1648-1662* (Rotterdam, 1902) 183-184; C. van de Haar, *De diplomatieke betrekkingen tussen de Republiek en Portugal, 1640-1661* (Groningen, 1961) 163; Castello Branco, *Vida de Francisco Mello Torres*, 314-316.
41. *Ibidem.*

behalf of Portugal in place of Telles de Faro[42]. This petition was duly submitted on 7 June 1659[43]. De Witt dealt with the inevitable objections from some of the provinces with his usual dexterity and, despite the fact that this was a highly unorthodox procedure, the States General voted ten days later, on 17 June, to acknowledge the 'Agent d'Acosta', as the Dutch called him, and Alvares Ribeiro, as joint negotiators even though they lacked any kind of authorisation from Lisbon for assuming this role[44]. Jeronimo also advanced the cash that was needed until more funds could arrive from Lisbon.

During the next months, Jeronimo was almost continuously in The Hague. He had numerous meetings with De Thou and with the English resident, as well as with members of the States General's special committee for Portuguese affairs, especially Pieter de Groot who was one of De Witt's principal confidants and who collaborated closely with the two Portuguese representatives[45]. From these discussions emerged the outline of a draft treaty between the Republic and Portugal, the twenty-five agreed provisional articles of which De Witt outlined to the States of Holland on 19 October[46]. Holland's Pensionary, like De Thou and Jeronimo, was probably anxious for rapid progress owing to recent developments in the Franco-Spanish peace talks which led to the successful conclusion of the treaty of the Pyrenees in November 1659. The ending of the long war between France and Spain was likely to mean some diminution in French pressure on the Dutch to settle with Portugal. Under the provisional terms agreed in The Hague, in October, Portugal would restore former Dutch territory neither in Brazil nor Africa, but would compensate the Dutch government and the West India Company with an indemnity of 4 million *cruzados*. Equally, if not more important, the Dutch were also to receive the same advantageous commercial privileges in Portugal which the English had enjoyed since 1654.

The Portuguese ambassador chosen to replace Telles de Faro, the Conde de Miranda, arrived in the Republic late in November and had his first audience with the States General on 12 December 1659. There was still a lot of hard bargaining to be done, not to mention the opposition of four Dutch provinces to be overcome. At this time, there was much excited discussion among the merchants of Amsterdam over the Brazil and West Africa trades[47]. While the States of Holland accepted trade concessions with Portugal itself on the same

---

42. ANTT Ms. da Graça, 2L, 'Coresp. Luis Alvares Ribeiro', fo. 14.
43. *Ibidem*, fo. 16v.
44. ANTT Ms. da Graça, 2L, 'Coresp. Luis Alvares Ribeiro', fos. 8-11.
45. *Ibidem*, fo. 55: Alvares Ribeiro to Mello Torres, 22 August 1659.
46. *Resolutien Staten van Holland*, 19, 20 October 1659; De Haar, *Diplomatieke betrekkingen*, 165.
47. ANTT Ms. da Graça, 3L, fo. 43: Miranda to Mello Torres, 27 February 1660.

basis as that previously conceded to England, there was strong pressure for special privileges over and above anything possessed by the English as regarded the Brazil and Guinea trades. The Dutch negotiators demanded the right to sail direct to and from Brazil, Angola, and São Thomé by-passing the royal customs house in Lisbon. Miranda and Jeronimo, who acted as his interpreter and principal aid, countered with the argument that direct navigation would totally subvert the traditional rights of supervision of colonial trade by the Portuguese crown and breach the Brazil Company's monopoly of wine, flour, cod, and olive oil exports to Brazil[48]. There were a series of meetings between Jeronimo and Pieter de Groot in which they hammered at these and related points and argued over the form of the Portuguese indemnity as well as over the price to be agreed for Setúbal salt[49].

If the early months of 1660 were devoted to hard bargaining between the Dutch and Portuguese negotiators, the Dutch were eventually forced to settle for privileges similar to those possessed by the English and the substantial 4 million *cruzado* (*f* 8 million) indemnity. From the summer of 1660, the focus of attention increasingly shifted to the major political battle that De Witt now had on hand to force the terms through the provincial assemblies and the States General. Once again, Jeronimo took to visiting provincial centres, seeking to persuade city magistrates of the merits of the proposed treaty. He also strove his hardest to sway opinion among the by no means uninfluential Portuguese Jewish community of Amsterdam which accounted for a considerable slice of Dutch trade with the Portuguese-speaking lands. As Miranda noted in March 1660, many of the Jews, especially those expelled from Recife, in 1654, were actively supporting the West India Company in opposing the draft treaty[50]. The collapse of Dutch Brazil had undoubtedly been a calamity for Amsterdam Jewry and the issue must have caused Jeronimo endless heart-searching and agonizing discussion. It is unlikely that he was ever keen on the prospect of Portuguese conquest of Dutch Brazil. We may be sure that he much preferred João IV's stated policy in the 1640s of keeping peace with the Republic, recognizing the Dutch zone of Brazil, and disclaiming any links with the planter rebels in that zone. It may also be that there was some truth in Sousa Coutinho's charge, back in 1647, that Jeronimo had deliberately sought to mislead João IV over the strength of Dutch reinforcements for Brazil[51]. In any case, in 1660-1661,

48. *Ibidem,* fos. 38-46: Miranda to Mello Torres, 13 and 27 February and 4 March 1660.
49. *Ibidem,* fos. 18, 20.
50. *Ibidem,* fo. 46: Miranda to Mello Torres, 4 March 1660.
51. *Correspondência Sousa Coutinho,* II, 265-266; On João IV's policy of not helping the rebels in Dutch Brazil, see Joaquin Veríssimo Serrão, *História de Portugal V. A Restauração e a monarquia absoluta (1640-1750)* (Lisbon, 1980) 112-113, 122.

Jeronimo concentrated on trying to convince his co-religionists that there was no hope of retrieving what was lost in Brazil and that what mattered now was to buttress Amsterdam's role in Portuguese commerce and forestall English ambitions to dominate trade with Portugal and its colonies.

Gamarra who was still seeking to prevent a lasting Dutch-Portuguese agreement reported to Madrid, in January 1661, on both aspects of Jeronimo's publicity campaign. Noting that Miranda had sent his secretary to Zeeland to bribe the burgomasters of Flushing, he continued

Geronimo Nunez da Costa, Agent of the Tyrant, has been negotiating hard in the city of Utrecht and here [in Holland] has won over two Jews, one called Abraham de Azevedo who came here as a deputy from Brazil before it was lost, to seek aid, a man much interested in the Company, and the other Abraham Balverde who was also a delegate and, though both men did all they could in past years to persuade government leaders here and the directors of the Company to refuse any settlement without restitution of the territories, now they go urging one and all that they should accept the offers of the Tyrant, for otherwise they will lose everything[52].

But even as De Witt and his allies made headway on the home front, at least in Holland, and in Utrecht and Groningen, the two provinces most prone to be dislodged from opposition to the treaty[53], a new factor arose which appreciably complicated the situation. Once securely restored to the throne of England, Charles II took to instilling new vigour into what had already been the English policy on Dutch-Portuguese relations, though somewhat muted since the death of Oliver Cromwell, in 1658, namely to encourage the Dutch to acquiesce in the loss of Brazil while simultaneously seeking to prevent the States General obtaining commercial concessions as generous as those possessed by the English[54]. 'I can say no more of the business of Portugal', declared the English minister, Clarendon, at this time, 'than that the king our master must never endure that the Hollanders should enjoy equal privileges with him in point of trade'[55]. And while there was some disagreement at the Portuguese court as between the faction which leaned heavily towards England and another more inclined to appease the Dutch, on balance Affonso VI's government gave priority to cultivating close relations with Charles II. The Anglo-Portuguese alliance of

52. Archivo General de Simancas, libros de la Haya XLIII, fo. 4: Gamarra to Philip IV, The Hague, 10 January 1661.
53. BL MS Egerton 2537, fo. 349: Sir George Downing to Nicholas, 24 June 1661.
54. *Brieven aan Johan de Witt*, R. Fruin and N. Japikse, ed. (2 vols.; Amsterdam, 1919-1922) II, 42; Van de Haar, *Diplomatieke betrekkingen,* 177; C.R. Boxer, *The Dutch in Brazil, 1624-1654* (2nd ed.; Hamden, Conn., 1973) 252-253.
55. *Ibidem,* 252.

1654 was, indeed, renewed and updated in 1661 and it was at this time that the preparations were on hand for the marriage of Affonso's sister, Catherine of Braganza, to the English monarch.

Accordingly, whilst Miranda came under heavy pressure in The Hague from Charles II's somewhat aggressive and vociferously anti-Dutch ambassador extraordinary to the Republic, Sir George Downing, not to concede advantageous commercial privileges to the Dutch, he also received instructions from Lisbon to prevaricate for as long as he could. The undeniable fact was that the pro-English party were in the ascendant at Lisbon. At this crucial point, it is evident that Jeronimo Nunes da Costa began to follow his own policy which diverged significantly from that of Miranda. For an Amsterdam merchant trading primarily with the Portuguese lands, a Dutch-Portuguese treaty which failed to provide a commercial framework at least as beneficial as that already possessed by the English would have been as disasterous as a failure to sign a treaty at all. Thus, Jeronimo took to interpreting Portugal's interests in his own way assigning priority to restoring Dutch-Portuguese relations. During the spring and summer of 1661, Jeronimo had a series of talks with Pieter de Groot and other members of the States General's special committee, detailing the contradictory pressures on King Affonso, on Miranda, and on other Portuguese ministers and, in effect, advised the Dutch leadership as to how to deal with his own superior, Miranda, and with the English pressure. Assuring De Groot that De Witt would achieve nothing at this juncture by attempting further persuasion in Lisbon or London, he argued that heavy counter-pressure alone would achieve what was desired and that the States General should now confront Miranda with an ultimatum[56]. Jeronimo was thus an accomplice of the Dutch leadership in the issuing of the States General's ultimatum of 31 July 1661, demanding that the ambassador either sign the draft treaty, assuring the Dutch commercial privileges equal to those of the English, within ten days, or else leave the country pending a resumption of full hostilities[57]. The gamble paid off. Miranda promptly ceased his prevarication and signed the treaty, to the fury of Downing, on 6 August.

The next step was to secure ratification on both sides while at the same time clearing the air on a number of still outstanding points. In one of their last audiences before Miranda departed for Lisbon to present the draft treaty to the

---

56.   De Groot to De Witt, 9 July 1661 in *Brieven aan Johan de Witt*, 42-44.

57.   *Brieven geschreven ende gewisselt tusschen den ¡‌eer Johan de Witt... ende de Gevolmaghtigden van den Staedt der Vereenighde Nederlanden* (7 vols.; The Hague, 1723-1727) I, 410, 413-414; Abraham de Wicquefort, *Histoire des Provinces-Unies des Pais-Bas, depuis le parfait établissement de cet état par la paix de Munster* (4 vols.; Amsterdam, 1861-1874) III, 70-71; Van de Haar, *Diplomatieke betrekkingen*, 178; Boxer, *The Dutch in Brazil*, 253.

king, the States General presented the ambassador with a golden chain worth *f* 6,000 and the 'Agent d'Acosta' who, as usual, was at his side, acting as his aid and interpreter, with another worth *f* 800[58]. The two provinces which had refused to sign the treaty, Zeeland and Gelderland, angrily protested at this presentation of chains. Miranda's confidence in Jeromino appears to have been unimpaired by the episode of the ultimatum. Before leaving for Portugal, the ambassador presented two petitions to the States General concerning Jeronimo, testifying to his 'dilligence et zèlle ...specialement en tout ce qui dependoit à la conclusion de la paix entre sa Magesté et Mrs. les Estats' and asserting that during his absence Jeronimo Nunes da Costa alone was authorised to represent the Portuguese crown in dealings with the Dutch leadership and to discuss matters pertaining to the peace treaty[59].

During Miranda's absence in Portugal, Jeronimo did indeed continue to spend most of his time in The Hague and remained active diplomatically. In particular, he continued seeing De Groot and discoursing to the Dutch leadership on the split at the Portuguese court between the pro-English and pro-Dutch factions, headed respectively by Mello Torres 'who had been in England' and the Conde de Soure, as well as other intricacies of Portuguese relations with England and the Republic[60]. Again it emerges that Jeronimo was in some degree pursuing his own policy, or one particular Portuguese policy, which did not accord with the preponderant mood in Lisbon at the time. Whether or not this policy was in the best interests of Portugal, his conduct was certainly advantageous to Amsterdam, Dutch Jewry and to himself personally.

Miranda returned to Holland in December 1661 but without yet having had the treaty ratified by Affonso who was determined not to offend the English monarch. Portuguese ratification followed only in May 1662 when Charles, in one of the steps that he took to defuse the mounting tension between England and the Republic over a whole range of commercial, colonial, and fishery issues, withdrew his opposition to Affonso's signing the treaty. In part, this English move was intended to prevent the Dutch seizing more Portuguese territory in Asia. However, there now followed months of further delay before the treaty was in turn ratified by the States General. Besides the continued opposition of Zeeland and Gelderland, Groningen now withdrew its previous approval while a furious new Dutch-Portuguese dispute broke out over Cochin, on the Malabar coast of south-west India, seized by East India Company forces from the Portuguese in January 1663. Once again, Jeronimo assiduously aided Miranda

58. Aitzema, *Historie,* X, 109-110.
59. ARH SG 7011-11: Miranda to States General, 23 and 26 August 1661.
60. *Brieven aan Johan de Witt,* 46.

both in petitioning the States General and in interceding with numerous Dutch regents.

Publication of the Dutch-Portuguese peace treaty of 1661 took place at Lisbon and The Hague in March and April 1663. The Portuguese monarch formally thanked Jeronimo for his very considerable part in the making of this treaty and, in recognition of his services, granted him a royal pension of 700 *cruzados* yearly[61]. Certainly, it was one of the most important treaties for both the Dutch and the Portuguese of the seventeenth century, for the agreement put an end to more than sixty years of bitter colonial conflict and established the specific framework of peaceful relations which was to prevail well into the next century. The new Dutch-Portuguese relationship that arose was assuredly weighted, at least in the economic sphere, heavily in favour of the Dutch, and, on this ground, has been sharply criticized by some modern Portuguese historians[62]. The treaty recognized and confirmed an economic dominance over the Portuguese empire which Holland now shared with the English. Payment of the *f* 8 million indemnity took far longer in practice than the sixteen years envisaged in the treaty and continued far into the eighteenth century. Meanwhile, Dutch merchants and ships resumed a key role both in the trade of Portugal itself and that of West Africa and Brazil.

But the treaty was not yet quite firmly rooted. Dutch complaints over excessive tardiness in indemnity payments, and Portuguese insistence on the restitution of Cochin, led to a fresh deterioration in relations in 1665-1667. The diversion of Dutch attention during the second Anglo-Dutch war encouraged the Portuguese to go further than they would have otherwise have dared. But when the States General ended its second conflict with England with the signing of the treaty of Breda, in July 1667, there was talk of a new war with Portugal. To defuse this crisis, Francisco de Mello Manuel da Camara was sent from Portugal to The Hague as ambassador extraordinary[63]. During 1667-1669, Jeronimo acted as his chief aid and interpreter much as he had previously done for Miranda. In July 1669, a supplementary agreement was signed by which the Portuguese reconciled themselves to the loss of Cochin and fixed a precise schedule of tax-exempt salt consignments to be shipped from Setúbal to Holland. Jeronimo had long been a major importer of Setúbal salt and, being an expert on the subject, it is natural that he was the person who handled the details of the salt talks on behalf of

---

61. 'Carta de padrão', *Anais,* 2nd ser. VIII, 121.
62. See, for instance, Virginia Rau, *Os holandeses e a exportação do sal de Setúbal nos fins do século XVII* (Coimbra, 1950) 12.
63. Rau, *Os holandeses,* 10; E. Prestage, *The Diplomatic Relations of Portugal with France, England and Holland from 1640 to 1668* (Watford, 1925) 235-237.

The house of Jeronimo Nunes da Costa at Amsterdam. Engraving by Romeyn de Hooghe.

Portugal as he did in the subsequent periodic Dutch-Portuguese conferences at The Hague over salt. It was agreed in July 1669 that tax-exempt salt should be shipped from Portugal to Holland at the rate of 85.000 *moyos* yearly for twenty years, a rate that presupposed the use of approximately 130 ships each year. Problems arose later because the actual rate of shipments during the 1670s and 1680s fell far short of this. In 1678, for instance, only 43.283 *moyos* and, in 1680, 45.476 *moyos* were shipped[64]. Jeronimo had the continuing task of collating the figures and reviewing the position periodically with Dutch officials as, for instance, in the autumn of 1675 and in July 1679[65].

From 1669, Dutch-Portuguese relations can be said to have remained on a stable footing, without any major points of dissension. In the years 1663-1667, between the missions of Miranda and Manuel da Camara, the Portuguese crown retained a resident at The Hague, Diogo Lopes de Ulhoa, in addition to Jeronimo, as Agent in the United Provinces, at Amsterdam. But peace between Portugal and the Republic and the end of the Portugal's long struggle for independence from Spain, in 1668, removed the need for a full-time professional envoy at The Hague. From 1669, as far as Portugal was concerned, Holland ceased to be a major focus of diplomatic activity. Accordingly, except for one or two temporary envoys, Jeronimo Nunes da Costa served during the later half of his diplomatic career as sole representative of the Portuguese crown in the United Provinces and its permanent *chargé d'affaires,* though there was no change in his relatively lowly title of Agent. This, of course, immensely enhanced his personal and social prestige and meant that from now on he tended to appear before the States of Holland and States General on his own rather than at the side of a diplomatic superior.

Even so, there was still some question as to precise status. In 1667, there took place a significant shift in power in Lisbon whereby Affonso VI's brother, Dom Pedro, took over the reins of government. Among his other policies, Pedro encouraged, now that Portugal was secure, a much more harshly anti-New Christian and anti-Jewish attitude in official circles than had been feasible previously. The Inquisition, curbed by João IV, was restored to the full power and influence which it had enjoyed under the Spanish régime. These developments must in some measure have alienated Jeronimo's feelings from the Portuguese cause and given rise to some reconsideration in Lisbon as to whether

---

64.   ARH SG 7015-1: J. Wolfson to States General, Lisbon 31 July 1685; Jeronimo was also entrusted with authorising and issuing the passes to Dutch skippers sailing to Setúbal for salt, ARH SG 7013-11: C. Barlaeus to States General, Lisbon, 28 March 1673.
65.   ARH SG 7014-1: J. Nunes da Costa to States General, The Hague, 7 October and 7 December 1675; ARH SG 7014-11: J. Nunes da Costa to States General, The Hague, 10 July 1679.

he was still suitable to represent the crown in the United Provinces. We may surmise that it was his unrivalled knowledge of Dutch affairs which led to his being retained. Dom Pedro, who had taken the title Prince-Regent, eventually confirmed Jeronimo's position as Agent, in August 1668, and wrote to the States General asking that he be acknowledged in that role as representative of the Portuguese crown within the seven provinces[66]. In December 1668, Jeronimo also submitted a request to the States of Holland on the basis of Dom Pedro's patent, asking to be confirmed in his position as Portuguese Agent in Holland[67]. The States of Holland did so but under the proviso that 'he shall not thereby be exempt from the obligations of citizenship and obedience with respect to payment of all ordinary and extraordinary taxes'.

This restriction on his diplomatic status clearly involved a good deal financially as Jeronimo was by this time one of the four or five wealthiest members of the Amsterdam Jewish community. He had always insisted that he was not a Dutch subject but a minister of the crown of Portugal and during the course of the next few years he repeatedly sought to persuade the States General to recognize this, claiming that 'hy soude mogen werden getracteert als andere ministers van uytheemsche princen die onder de gehoorsaemheyt van desen staet niet gebooren zijn'[68]. After the fall of De Witt and the change of régime in the Republic, Dom Pedro again confirmed Jeronimo's appointment as 'sijn Agent alhier' and, on 6 May 1673, the States General once again recognized him as such, still stipulating that he was a subject and liable to all taxes[69]. To this, Jeronimo replied a few days later repeating that he was not a native of the Republic,

qui'il ne se soit retiré en ce pais que depuis les dernières revolutions de Portugal, et que pendant le séjour qu'il y a fait, il n'y a point acquis de biens ny mesmes le droit de bourgeoisie de la ville d'Amsterdam[70].

The States General referred this appeal to the States of Holland which delegated a committee to peruse Jeronimo's position and status. Some months later, Holland and the States General rejected his suit, confirming their earlier pronouncement. At this, Jeronimo submitted yet another petition further

---

66. ARH SG 7013-I: J. Nunes da Costa to States General, The Hague, 5, 25 and 28 November 1668.
67. *Resolutien Staten van Holland,* 15 December 1668: 'Is ter vergaderinge gelesen seecker memoriael van Jeronimus Nunes da Costa, houdende dat hy by den Heere Prince van Portuguael ordre hadde bekomen omme in qualiteyt van Agent van dat koninghrijck in dese Provincie te continueren'.
68. ARH SG 7013-II: J. Nunes da Costa to States General, The Hague, 22 January 1671.
69. *Resolutien Staten van Holland,* 12 August 1673.
70. ARH SG 7013-II: J. Nunes da Costa to States General, The Hague, 15 May 1673.

amplifying his argument as why he should not be considered a Dutch subject[71]. Remarkably enough, on this occasion the same committee to which the States of Holland had delegated the matter before now reversed its previous finding and proposed that Jeronimo should be exempted from extraordinary taxes not, however, on the ground that he was not a Dutch subject, but specifically out of recognition for his exceptional services to the state. Following this advice, the States of Holland resolved

> dat den voorschreven Jeronimo Nunes da Costa, om de goede diensten die hy soo geduyrende de onderhandelinge met Portugael als andersints aen den staet heeft ghedaen, van alle extraordinaris lasten en impositien die by haer Ed. Groot Mog. albereyts zijn ofte noch in 't toekomende souden mogen werden geïntroduceert, vry ende exempt sal wesen[72].

It is this exemption of 1673 which explains why Jeronimo's name is omitted from the list of Amsterdam Portuguese Jews assessed for the 200th penny levy in 1674[73].

Although Jeronimo Nunes da Costa was no longer involved in what might be termed major matters of state after 1669, it would be wrong to suppose that his role as Agent of Portugal after that date was merely decorative or honorary. He still had a number of important functions. One of these was as the official supplier of arms and naval munitions from Holland to the Portuguese lands. A substantial part of the stores used to equip the Brazil fleets, the Portuguese royal navy, the dockyards of Lisbon, Porto, Madeira, and the Azores were furnished by Jeronimo. Whilst Portugal had remained at war with Spain, he was in the habit of covering these shipments with false papers using the Dutch alias 'Nicholas Joris' and usually specifying Cadiz as the destination. This was to minimize the risk of having his cargoes seized *en route* by Spanish privateers[74]. On the eve of the second Anglo-Dutch War, the Portuguese ambassador in London requested Charles II that 'all such goods as shall come under the name of Nicholas Joris shall goe free as belonging to Jeronimo Nunes da Costa', attaching a list of five ships chartered by Jeronimo which 'are going now out of

71. *Resolutien Staten van Holland,* 12 August, 26 September and 26 October 1673.
72. *Ibidem,* 22 December 1673.
73. A.M. Vaz Dias, 'Over den vermogentoestand der Amsterdamsche Joden in de 17e en 18e eeuw', *Tijdschrift voor Geschiedenis,* LI (1936) 170.
74. Gamarra refers in a letter of August 1663 to a Dutch ship, loaded with naval munitions and carrying papers for Cadiz, which was intercepted by a Basque privateer, on which were found letters showing that the consignment was really being shipped to Lisbon by 'Geronimo Nunes da Costa, Jewish merchant of Amsterdam and adherent of the Rebel', AGS Libros, de La Haya, XLVII, fo. 68: Gamarra to Philip IV, 31 August 1663.

Holland to Portugal uppon the account of His Majestie', loaded with anchors, masts, ropes and grain[75]. It is true that after 1668 there is likely to have been a considerable falling off in this type of traffic between Holland and Portugal, but right until the end of his long life Jeronimo periodically requested permission from the States General for large consignments of munitions. In 1674, he asked permission for a cargo of gunpowder, sail canvas and ropes for the Portuguese navy[76]. In August 1689, he requested permission to export 100,000lb of gunpowder for the Portuguese forces and, in August 1691, for 80,000lb of gun and musket fuses for the royal arsenals[77].

Although the era of confrontation in the Indies was over, the Portuguese crown still took some interest in the affairs of the Dutch colonial companies and there was, of course, in certain regions, notably Guinea, India, and the South China Sea, a good deal of continuing peaceful interaction between the Dutch and Portuguese. Accordingly, Jeronimo was intermittently involved in some extremely wide-ranging deliberations. During 1682, for instance, he had several discussions with East India Company directors in Amsterdam about the severely depressed state of trade at Macão which was affected by upheavals in neighbouring China[78]. The directors proposed a deal between the Company and the Portuguese with the latter handing over Macão to the Dutch in exchange for Cochin. In reporting to Lisbon, Jeronimo explained that the difficulties the Dutch were then experiencing in southern India were saddling the Company with mounting garrison costs in Cochin. In the same dispatch, Jeronimo also discussed the continuing dispute between Portugal and Denmark over a Danish base on the Guinea coast which the Portuguese had seized in 1679[79]. Jeronimo mentions that he was in touch with correspondents in Copenhagen and following the steps being taken by the Royal Danish Africa Company and the Danish crown to recover the fortress.

As was usual with the diplomatic dispatches of the time, much of what Jeronimo reported to Lisbon concerned movements of armies and fleets in different parts of Europe. At times, though, he also offered analysis. A good

75. PRO SP 89/6, fo. 200: petition dated 28 December 1664. Jeronimo had been using the cover 'Nicholas Joris' since well before 1650, see PRO HCA 30495, prize claim of 31 December 1650 submitted by Nicholas Joris alias J. Nunes da Costa.
76. ARH SG 7014-I: J. Nunes da Costa to States General, The Hague, 11 April and 19 June 1674.
77. ARH SG 7015-II: J. Nunes da Costa to States General, The Hague, 20 August 1689 and 29 August 1691.
78. FUP 'Livro das monções' no. 47 34/41: J. Nunes da Costa to Dr. Manoel Pereira, Amsterdam, 12 December 1682.
79. This was the fortress of Christiansborg betrayed by its governor to the Portuguese, see K. Larsen, *De Danske i Guinea* (Copenhagen, 1918) 25-26, 28.

example is the long dispatch that he sent to the Conde de Castelmelhor, in February 1689, during the opening stages of the Nine Years War (1689-1698)[80]. Having previously sent a copy of the Anglo-Dutch treaty of alliance against France to Lisbon, he discoursed at length on the overall strategic situation, detailing the disposition of forces in Flanders, pointing out that the French naval arsenals at Brest and Toulon were poorly stocked and would remain so as the Dutch were in a position to block off a large part of the supply and since it was probable that Sweden would co-operate with the Republic. He expressed confidence that the combined Dutch and English fleets would prevent any significant French assistance from reaching James, pretender to the English throne, in Ireland.

A crowning episode in Jeronimo's long career as Agent of Portugal in the United Provinces were the events surrounding Pedro II's second marriage in 1687. Having dispatched to Lisbon a magnificent silver dining service which he had had made in Holland for the royal wedding table, Jeronimo arranged for the passage, via Holland, of Pedro's envoy sent to Heidelberg to collect the bride, Maria Sophia of Neuburg, daughter of the Elector Palatine[81]. With the envoy, Jeronimo sent coaches, gifts, and 'forty handsome horses' which he had shipped to Amsterdam from Hamburg for the purpose. When the queen-to-be approached the Republic, Jeronimo sent his sons to Düsseldorf to escort her for the rest of her journey and accompanied her to The Hague where he arranged everything, including several receptions and a famous fire-work display, in grand style. Later when the wedding took place, in Lisbon, he organised further festivities in The Hague and subsequently published, in Catholic Brussels, a handsomely produced poetic celebration of the event, the *Triumpho Lusitano,* couched in the extravagant Baroque verses of the time[82].

Jeronimo's activities as Agent of Portugal in the Dutch Republic plainly involved him in a huge commitment of time and energy. At certain periods, notably in the years 1658-1663, he spent months on end at The Hague immersed in diplomatic activity away from his family and business. And yet, though it is equally clear that he gave a great deal of time, especially after 1666, to the synagogue and Jewish community affairs, he continued to be extremely active as a merchant. His agency work brought him the repeated thanks of three

80. BNL MS. caixa 208, no. 45: J. Nunes da Costa to Conde de Castelmelhor, Amsterdam, 26 February 1689.
81. ARH SG 7015-I: J. Nunes da Costa to States General, The Hague, 21 September 1686 and 11 April 1687.
82. Manuel de Leon, *Triumpho Lusitano, Applausos festivos* (Brussels, 1688), the work is dedicated to Jeronimo; see also M. Kayserling, *Biblioteca Española-Portugueza-Judaica* (Strasbourg, 1890) 57.

Portuguese monarchs, noble rank and both a modest salary and his pension of 700 *cruzados* yearly. But the real rewards for his diplomatic efforts were much greater. His own business was furthered and enhanced in all manner of ways by his official connection with the Portuguese crown. Not the least of these was that as Amsterdam factor of the Brazil Company he had a favoured position in the sugar trade and eventually virtually monopolized the sale of Brazil-wood in Holland. Certainly, his agency post also enhanced Jeronimo's standing in Dutch and Jewish society and was a prime factor in his election as one of the two permanent representatives of the Amsterdam Portuguese Jewish community delegated to negotiate with the city magistrates and other Dutch authorities[83]. In this way, and also internationally, as in the case of his intercession on behalf of the Jews of Martinique, he can be said to have placed his diplomatic status at the disposal of his own people.

On the death, in 1697, of this noteworthy personality of the Dutch Golden Age, a man who began by working for Portugal against Dutch interests but later came to be publicly honoured by the States of Holland and States General for his services to the Republic, his title as Agent of Portugal in the United Provinces passed to his eldest surviving son, Alexandre Nunes da Costa (Selomoh Curiel) and, on his death, in 1712, to Jeronimo's youngest son, Alvaro Nunes da Costa (Nathan Curiel). Oddly enough, on Alvaro's death, in 1738, his heir, a nephew, was refused the title by the Portuguese government of the day on the grounds that he was a 'Jew'[84].

83. Daniel Levi de Barrios, 'Govierno Politico Judayco', *Triumpho del Govierno Popular* (Amsterdam, 1684) 4; W.Ch. Pieterse, *Daniel Levi de Barrios als geschiedschrijver van de Portugees-Israelietische gemeente te Amsterdam in zijn* ʻ*Triumpho del Govierno Popular*' (Amsterdam, 1968) 89; I.S. and S.A. Emmanuel, *History of the Jews of the Netherlands Antilles* (2 vols.; Cincinnati, 1970) I, 76.
84. D. Luis da Cunha, *Obras Inéditas do grande exemplar da sciencia do estado,* I (Lisbon, 1821): 'mas S. Magestade não quiz confirmar este emprego a seu neto, por ser judeo, como se seu pai e avos fossem christãos'.

9

Lopo Ramirez (David Curiel) and the Attempt to Establish a Sephardi Community in Antwerp in 1653–1654

AMONG THE LEADING patrician figures of the golden age of Dutch Sephardi Jewry one of the most contentious, as well as one of the most remarkable, was Lopo Ramirez alias David Curiel (b. Lisbon 11 May 1594 – d. Rotterdam 4 Oct. 1666). In the existing literature he is best known for his role in the communal crisis at Amsterdam of 1618 when, as a young man of twenty-four, he participated as *gabay* (treasurer) of the Beth Jacob congregation in the bitter quarrel which led to the secession of part of the congregation and the setting up of the Beth Israel synagogue.[1] But in what follows I shall suggest that Lopo Ramirez deserves to be better known for his involvement in other, and later, episodes and especially as the main agent of the Spanish crown at Amsterdam in the late 1640s and the man behind the efforts to establish an organized Sephardi community at Antwerp in the years 1653 – 1654.

Lopo Ramirez was the younger brother, nearly nine years younger, of Duarte Nunes da Costa alias Jacob Curiel (1585 – 1664) who was appointed 'Agent' of the Portuguese Crown at Hamburg, in 1641, and was, for many years, a leading figure of the Sephardi community of Hamburg.[2] Lopo and Duarte were sons of a well-known New Christian physician of Lisbon, Dr Jeronimo Nunes Ramires (1545 -1609), author of a 360-page Latin treatise on blood-letting, inspired in a large part by Galen, the *De Ratione Curandi per Sanguinis Missionem* (1st edn. Lisbon 1608, 2nd edn. Antwerp 1610). Shortly after Dr Nunes Ramires' death, in 1609, the inquisition in Lisbon arrested, imprisoned, and began to investigate his brother-in-law, Thomas da Fonseca, as a judaizer. This development placed other members of the family in danger and, at this point, Lopo and Duarte together with their mother, and

---

[1] See A. M. Vaz Dias, 'Losse bijdragen tot de geschiedenis der joden in Amsterdam: de scheiding in de oudste Amsterdamsche Portugeesche gemeente Beth Jaäcob (1618)', *De Vrijdagavond* 7 (1930-1931) p. 387-388, 402-404, and 8 (1931-1932), p. 7-9, 22-24; J. d'Ancona, 'Komst der Marranen in Noord-Nederland; de Portugeesche gemeenten te Amsterdam tot de vereniging (1639)', in: H. Brugmans and A. Frank, eds., *Geschiedenis der Joden in Nederland* 1 (*tot circa 1795*) (Amsterdam 1940) p. 229-246.

[2] On Duarte Nunes da Costa, see J. I. Israel, 'Duarte Nunes da Costa (Jacob Curiel) of Hamburg, Sephardi Nobleman and Communal Leader, 1585-1664', *Studia Rosenthaliana* 21 (1987) p. 14-34 (reprinted in J. I. Israel, *Empires and Entrepots* (London 1990) p. 333-354).

other relatives, left Lisbon and fled Portugal, travelling overland, across Spain, to the safety of the port of Saint Jean de Luz, in the extreme south-west corner of France. From Inquisition proceedings against various members of the family, we know that regular crypto-Jewish gatherings had been held in the house of Dr Nunes Ramires[3]; and that the family's spiritual guide in Lisbon, during the years preceding the doctor's death, had been none other than the (later) famous Dr Felipe Rodrigues Montalto (Eliahu Montalto), the physician who was summoned to the French court from Italy in 1612, and given a unique personal privilege of being allowed to practice Judaism openly in France.[4] Although his anti-Christian writings (in Portuguese) could not be published, Montalto was known throughout the Portuguese New Christian diaspora as a leading anti-Christian polemicist. Early contact with Montalto might well have played an important part in Lopo's development. For however inconsistent and reprehensible he was to prove in other respects, Lopo evinced throughout his subsequent life, and amid dramatically changing circumstances, which eventually led to his residing for seven years in the Spanish Netherlands, in virtual exile from the Amsterdam Sephardi community, an unswerving and punctilious commitment to Jewish observance.

Lopo remained at Saint Jean with his mother until her death, in February 1614. He then sailed from there, with his youngest sister, to Amsterdam, where he was to remain, with only occasional brief absences, for almost forty years. He was married in Amsterdam in June 1617, one month after his twenty-third birthday, to Maria de Pina, daughter of his aunt, Guiomar da Costa, who had died the previous year in Antwerp.[5] Maria had then moved from Antwerp to Amsterdam, together with her elder brother Duarte Ramires Pina (Moseh Naar) and taken the Jewish name of Rachel Naar.

Collaborating with his elder brother, Duarte, who resided between 1611 and 1621 in Italy, at Livorno and Pisa, as well as his wealthy Ramires Pina cousins in Amsterdam, Lopo engaged in a wide-ranging commerce with Portugal and with Tuscany, which centered around the importing of rough diamonds from India, via Goa and Lisbon, and the jewellery business.[6] Duarte's trade with North Africa was an integral part of the brothers' shipments, via Lisbon, to Portuguese India and presumably was chiefly intended to obtain the North African red coral which was

[3]   My research into the Portuguese background of the Curiel family was greatly assisted by Marcel Curiel, of Caracas, a direct descendant of Duarte Nunes da Costa and by Edgar Samuel, director of the Jewish Museum in London.

[4]   Arquivo Nacional da Torre do Tombo, Lisbon (= ANTT), Inquisicão de Lisboa tom. 7192, 'Proceso de Duarte Nunes da Costa', fos. 9, 12v.; on Montalto's anti-Christian polemicizing, see C. Roth, 'Quatre lettres d'Elie de Montalto', *Revue des Études Juives* 87 (1929) p. 137-168.

[5]   See I. S. Revah, 'Pour l'histoire des Nouveaux-Chrétiens portugais. La relation généalogique d'Isaac de Mathatias Aboab', *Boletim internacional de bibliografia Luso-Brasileira* 2 (1961) p. 301, 309.

[6]   See 'Notarial Records Relating to the Portuguese Jews in Amsterdam up to 1639', in *Studia Rosenthaliana*, deeds nos. 767, 1027, 1449, 1470, 1867.

[7]   W. C. Pieterse, *Livro de Bet Haim do Kahal Kados de Bet Yahacob* (Assen 1970) p. 175.

so highly prized as jewellery in India and which played a crucial part in the Indian diamond traffic in early modern times. In 1617, goods which Lopo had shipped to Livorno and which had then been sent by Duarte, with other merchandise, on a vessel bound for Tunis, were lost when the ship was wrecked off the coast of Sardinia. Besides his soon celebrated stock of diamonds, Lopo apparently also stored musk and other costly essences for perfumes in his home. It is worth noting in this connection that Eliahu Montalto's son, Dr Moseh Montalto, husband of Lopo's youngest sister, Esther (Isabel), was a dealer in, and keeper of, African civet-cats, a creature from the anal glands of which a costly, musk-like substance was extracted for use in making perfumes, an occupation in which he may well have been placed by Lopo.

Lopo Ramirez was, even before 1618, clearly one of the more affluent members of the Amsterdam Sephardi community[7], as is indeed evident from the fact that he was chosen whilst still a young man, and only recently married, to be *gabay* of the Beth Jacob synagogue. After the communal split, in 1618, one of his main tasks in his capacity as treasurer of the parent congregation was to confer with the treasurer of the new secessionist synagogue over the division of the list of registered communal poor eligible to receive alms so as to preclude the possibility of anyone receiving a double distribution of charity.[8]

After the resumption of the Spanish-Dutch conflict, in April 1621, and the re-imposition of the Spanish embargoes on Dutch ships and goods in Portugal as well as Spain[9], Lopo contrived to continue his trade with Portugal and Portuguese India by means of various ploys and subterfuges. To evade the embargoes, he and his brother, Duarte (who moved from Italy to Amsterdam in 1621) made frequent use of North German ships and crews. Thus, for example, in October 1623, Lopo and Duarte together chartered a vessel and crew from East Friesland to fetch a cargo of salt from Setúbal – after 1621 the price of good quality salt in Holland rose very sharply – providing the skipper with false documents, stating that the ship was engaged to return to a North German (and therefore neutral) port but with verbal instructions to return instead to Amsterdam. Duarte's subsequent decision to move, first to Glückstadt, and then to Hamburg, in 1626, was doubtless chiefly intended to safeguard the brothers' now tenuous links with Portugal and likewise, via Lisbon, with India.[10] Thus, for instance, a Hamburg vessel, the *St Peter,* sailed from Lisbon to Hamburg in the autumn of 1630, carrying several packets of diamonds and pearls marked DNdC and officially consigned to Duarte in Hamburg, but in fact destined, via Hamburg, for Lopo Ramirez and his cousin Francisco Ramires Pina (a leading pearl dealer) at Amsterdam.[11] But the brothers also operated through their contacts in Antwerp and the Spanish Netherlands. In November 1631, Lopo authorized a

8   'Notarial Records' (n. 6), no. 1781.
9   Israel, *Empires and Entrepots* (n. 2), p. 18-26, 202-210.
10   *Ibid.,* p. 340-341.
11   GAA NA 257, fos. 703v-704v (23 Dec. 1630).

Dutch merchant in London to act on his behalf, and Duarte's, in recovering a consignment of Hondschoote new drapery ('says') which had been transported across the border between the Spanish Netherlands and France and loaded onto a French vessel at Calais, but had been seized by the English *en route* to Oporto and brought into Dartmouth.[12]

Meanwhile, through the 1620s and 1630s, Lopo remained a leading and respected member of the Beth Jacob congregation. When, in 1621-1622, the now three congregations in Amsterdam decided – in the face of the economic dislocation resulting from the resumption of the Dutch-Spanish conflict and disruption of trade with the Iberian peninsula – to set up a steering committtee to deal with the mounting problem of destitution and poor relief in the community, Lopo was one of the *parnasim* who signed the founding articles on behalf of Beth Jacob. The resulting 'Imposta Board' was an important development in the history of Amsterdam Sephardi Jewry and helped pave the way for the eventual unification of the three congregations into one community and synagogue in 1639.[13] Besides dealing with poor relief, the Imposta Board represented Amsterdam Sephardi Jewry as a whole in its dealings with the rest of the Sephardi world. Thus, in February 1627, the Imposta Board considered letters from Venice describing the emergency facing the Jews of Jerusalem caused by the despotic actions of the then Ottoman governor. The board, sensible to this injury to the 'whole people of Israel' resolved to aid 'our brothers, the inhabitants of the holy city of Jerusalem', voting a substantial subsidy of 2,400 guilders which was to be in addition to the regular annual remittance to the Holy Land.[14] Lopo was again treasurer of his congregation in 1630 and several meetings of the *parnasim*, and of the Imposta Board, were held at his house. When, in January 1630, the Beth Jacob congregation had the opportunity to purchase the house 'Antwerpen' which it had rented, and used as its synagogue, since 1614 (on a canal which has since disappeared under the Waterlooplein), it was Lopo who negotiated the transaction on behalf of his community.[15]

Commerce in jewels was probably less severely affected by the Spanish embargoes and resulting diversion of trade, and by the need to employ German ships, crews and ports, than trade in other, and bulkier, commodities where the cost and difficulties of transportation would have been greater. In any case, despite the obstacles, it is clear that Lopo and his cousin Francisco Ramires Pina prospered and that, as the data for the Imposta returns, the tax levied by the Imposta Board on the whole community, show, they were each among the half dozen or so wealthiest Sephardi merchants of Amsterdam at that time.[16]

[12] GAA NA 941, fo. 410 (25 Nov. 1631).
[13] O. Vlessing, 'New Light on the Earliest History of the Amsterdam Portuguese Jews' in: J. Michman, ed., *Dutch Jewish History* III (Assen 1993) p. 43-75: 54, 60-63.
[14] GAA Archives of the Portuguese Jewish Community, 13, 'Libro dos termos da ymposta da nação', fo. 19v.
[15] GAA NA 638, fo. 77; see also J. F. van Agt, *Synagogen in Amsterdam* (The Hague 1974) p. 9.
[16] Vlessing, 'New Light' (n. 13), p. 75.

The cabinet of diamonds in Lopo's large house, on the Sint Anthoniesbree-straat, was undoubtedly one of the choicest in the city. A highly traumatic incident in his life occurred on 12 February 1628 whilst he was showing his stock of jewels to a German visitor from Leipzig.[17] The man suddenly attacked him from behind, with a knife, and all but cut his throat. Lopo somehow broke free and, bleeding profuse-ly, yelled out 'murder!' several times. The culprit fled but was chased through the streets by Sephardi neighbours and caught. He was subsequently tried and executed by the city authorities, his corpse being sold to the university of Leiden for one hundred guilders to be used for anatomical demonstrations. The doctors who ten-ded Lopo deemed it a virtual miracle that he recovered. Lopo subsequently wrote an account of the episode in Portuguese which survives in the Ets Haim collection to this day, and then had the text rendered into Hebrew verse, as a Purim scroll, by Moseh Gideon Abudiente of Hamburg. This Purim scroll is said to have accompa-nied Lopo on his subsequent migrations from Amsterdam to Antwerp, Middelburg and Rotterdam, and to have been recited in his home every year at Purim together with the Book of Esther.[18]

Lopo may have shown exemplary loyalty to his religion but displayed little sense of loyalty, as events were to show, to his wider family, community and city, or to the Dutch state. His contacts in the Spanish Netherlands, and experience in evading war-time regulations and inspections, doubtless contributed to his being drawn, in the later 1630s, into a regular collaboration with ministers at the Spanish court in Brussels and especially with several of the Portuguese New Christian con-tractors at Antwerp, such as 'our good friend Garcia de Yllan', as Lopo called him in a letter later, who supplied the Spanish army of Flanders with grain and munitions. Garcia de Yllan, who had the most splendid house in Antwerp of any of the Portu-guese New Christians living there at this time, was reputed to be the most zealous Catholic among their number[19]; but he also cultivated contacts with Lopo in Am-sterdam, and Duarte Nunes da Costa and other Sephardi Jews in Hamburg, and was one of the most active of the Antwerp New Christians in obtaining vitally needed supplies for the Spanish forces, from all over northern Europe.[20] This applied not only to the army of Flanders but also to the royal fleets in Spain and Portugal which were dependent for vital naval stores such as masts, pitch and ropes on supplies obtained from the Baltic and North Germany.

Exactly when Lopo became a collaborator of Garcia de Yllan and the Spanish regime in Brussels is not clear but it must have been at least as early as 1636, for in September of that year he chartered a ship to sail to Lisbon carrying supplies, which

[17] See Luis Crespo Fabião, 'O Cazo de David Curiel com o alemão', *Biblos* 38 (1965) p. 1-53.
[18] *Ibid.*, p. 52.
[19] See H. P. Salomon, 'The "De Pinto" Manuscript', *Studia Rosenthaliana* 9 (1975) p. 1-62: 30.
[20] Israel, *Empires and Entrepots* (n. 2), p. 341.
[21] *Ibid.*
[22] GAA NA 675, fos. 69v-70.
[23] Israel, *Empires and Entrepots* (n. 2), p. 341-342.

was provided with an official Spanish pass.[21] In June 1637, Lopo was prominently involved in chartering two Dutch vessels for Spanish service, ferrying grain and other supplies between Sicily and Naples, which were also provided with official passes.[22] Probably Lopo was also the link between Garcia de Yllan and Duarte Nunes da Costa in Hamburg. During the years 1639-1640, Duarte's name came to the attention both of the Cardinal-Infante, governor-general in Brussels, and the Danish king, for his part in arranging several consignments of gunpowder which were transported via Glückstadt, and the Dover entrepot, to Dunkirk (then in the Spanish Netherlands) for use by the army of Flanders.[23] In any case, there is incontrovertible evidence that at this time Lopo was regularly sending secret information to Brussels (doubtless via de Yllan in Antwerp) for use by the Spanish regime. Some years later, in 1648, in a letter to the Spanish king Philip IV, his chief plenipotentiary to the Münster Peace Congress, the conde de Peñaranda, described Lopo as a man who, since the time of the Cardinal-Infante as governor-general (1635-1641) 'was esteemed [in Brussels] for his zeal and useful advices and that he had supplied some very important intelligence'.[24]

Following the secession of Portugal from Spain in December 1640, and the elevation of the duke of Braganza to the Portuguese throne as king João IV, Lopo, like Duarte, ceased his activity on behalf of Spain and assumed the role of a leading backer of the Portuguese cause among the Dutch Sephardim. The first Portuguese ambassador to the United Provinces, Tristão de Mendonça Furtado, arrived in The Hague, in April 1641, with instructions to negotiate an end to hostilities between the Dutch and Portuguese and a letter of credit for 10,000 *cruzados* with which to pay for his diplomatic mission.[25] The letter was issued by the Lisbon New Christian banker Manoel Garcia Franco and drawn on Lopo's cousin, Francisco Ramires Pina who, however, had died a few weeks before the ambassador's arrival. Lopo came to his rescue by agreeing to cash the draft and consequently found little difficulty in netting the resulting contracts. Especially important was the contract signed, in the presence of the Amsterdam notary Jan Volkaerts Oli, on 14 July 1641, whereby Lopo undertook to supply 100,000 *cruzados* of arms and munitions to Portugal.[26] The list of items to be furnished included 4,000 muskets, 30,000 pounds of gunpowder immediately with 50,000 pounds to follow, 20,000 pounds of shot, artillery, siege mortars, ship's rigging and 113 'large grenades' for demolishing besiegers' mine-shafts. Under the contract a commission of 12% was payable to Lopo, which, it has to be said, was by no means an exorbitant charge given the risks involved for

24   'el secretario desta embajada empezo a confiarme del con decir que desde el tiempo del Senor Infante, que haya gloria, era estimado por hombre de buen celo y de buenas noticias, y que habia dado avisos importantisimos', Peñaranda to Philip IV, Münster, 3 Feb. 1648, in *Colección de documentos inéditos para la historia de España* 84 (Madrid 1885) p. 114.

25   GAA NA 1555B, p. 1355 (14 July 1641); Antonio de Sousa de Tavares, *Relação do tratado de 1641 entre Portugal e Holanda* (Lisbon 1917) p. 7-8, 14.

26   GAA NA 1555B, p. 1103-1104; V. Rau, 'A embaixada de Tristão de Mendonça Furtado e os arquivos notariais holandeses', *Anais de Academia Portuguesa de História* 2nd ser. 8 (1958) p. 115-116.

the supplier and the likelihood that the Portuguese Revolt might collapse before long in the face of Spanish counter-pressure, an eventuality which would have left the supplier without any prospect of being repaid. To help finance the package, Lopo loaned the ambassador an exceptionally large and fine diamond set in gold which he valued at 24,000 *cruzados* and which was then pawned, on behalf of the Portuguese crown, with the Amsterdam firm of Jan Bicker, albeit for a much smaller amount.

During the next five years or so, most of the cash remitted on behalf of the Portuguese king to finance Portugal's diplomacy and purchases of munitions in northern Europe – especially The Netherlands, Germany and Scandinavia – was forwarded through the Lisbon bankers Manoel Garcia Franco and Balthasar Rodrigues de Mattos via their Amsterdam agent, Lopo Ramirez. During 1642-1643, even the Portuguese ambassador at Paris, the conde da Vidigueira, received his ambassadorial pay and expenses from Lopo at Amsterdam.[27] Nor were Lopo's services on behalf of the Portuguese crown by any means limited to handling cash remittances from Lisbon and furnishing munitions. Among other roles he performed, he arranged the shipping back to Portugal of several hundred Portuguese soldiers who had deserted from the Spanish army of Flanders on the news of the rebellion in their homeland, and fled to the Dutch side, hoping to find passage back to Portugal.[28] He also arranged the repatriation of the Portuguese soldiers and sailors taken by the Dutch West India Company when its forces seized Angola in 1642. Lopo paid the passage and board for these men on Dutch cargo vessels sailing to Portugal, remitting his bills for expenses to the royal treasury in Lisbon. In this way some of Portugal's most experienced fighting men found their way back from the Low Countries and were able to participate in the war against Spain in the Peninsula. These were all appreciable services but they were undertaken in an undeviatingly businesslike spirit.[29] It was noticed at an early stage that his sense of commitment to the Portuguese cause was less wholehearted than that of his brother Duarte in Hamburg. In July 1643, for instance, the new Portuguese ambassador at The Hague, Francisco de Sousa Coutinho, advised the king and his ministers in Lisbon to pay Lopo's bills promptly, if the intention was to retain him in Portuguese service, because he was not so disinterested as Duarte: 'o tal Lopo Ramirez não he tão dizenterecedo como seu irmão Duarte Nunes da Costa'.[30]

Lopo supported the Portuguese secession from Spain in the years 1641-1644 which, it is worth noting, also coincided with the last period in which he played a leading part in the general affairs of the Amsterdam Sephardi community. He served

[27]   *Cartas de el-rei D. João IV ao conde da Vidigueira (Marquês de Niza), embaixador em França* (Lisbon 1942), vol. 1, p. 20-21.
[28]   J. I. Israel, *The Dutch Republic and the Hispanic World, 1606-1661* (Oxford 1982) p. 315.
[29]   *Correspondência diplomática de Francisco de Sousa Coutinho durante a sua embaixada em Holanda* (3 vols., Coimbra 1920-1955), vol. 1, p. 12, 17, 46, 195.
[30]   *Ibid.*

as *parnas* on the *Mahamad* only once after the unification of the three synagogues into one combined community in 1639, and that was in the year 1644, at a time when it was still a matter of great importance for the community to have at its helm someone with such high-level links with the Portuguese kingdom and its overseas empire.[31] For until 1645 it looked as if Dutch Brazil would be secure, and with it the now flourishing Dutch Sephardi sugar traffic with Recife, and that the newly independent Portuguese kingdom would accept the partition of Brazil within the context of a general alliance with the United Provinces against Spain. That Lopo was the man with the connections not only with the Portuguese ambassador at The Hague, but also with ministers and the king's bankers in Lisbon, would have been generally known amongst the Amsterdam Portuguese Jewish community. Presumably, it was also widely known that Lopo – who by patent of 18 June 1642 had been declared a 'cavaleiro fidalgo da casa real' in Lisbon – had been ennobled by the Portuguese king as a reward for his services.[32]

Lopo at this point was in an unrivalled position amongst the Sephardi merchants of Amsterdam as regards connections with the Portuguese business world and the Portuguese court. Yet, after their initial dealings, relations between Lopo and Mendonça Furtado rapidly soured, probably owing to the latter's tardiness in repaying cash which Lopo had lent him. Lopo was still awaiting repayment of money he had advanced to the ambassador in 1641, in July 1646, when he empowered a Lisbon merchant, João Baptista da Fonseca (presumably a distant relative on his mother's side, she being the daughter of the Lisbon physician Dr Lopo da Fonseca), to act for him in legal proceedings against the Mendonça Furtado family.[33] Similarly, relations between Lopo and Mendonça Furtado's successor at The Hague, Sousa Coutinho, soon began to deteriorate.[34] Lopo was no longer willing to advance cash on the basis of promises. When, for example, in May 1644 Sousa Coutinho requested an advance in anticipation of bank remittances from Lisbon, Lopo firmly refused. Gradually, the references to Lopo in Sousa Coutinho's letters to the king became more negative in tone. The ambassador was also highly dissatisfied with Lopo's Lisbon correspondent, Rodrigues de Mattos, whom he virtually accused of embezzling royal funds. An incident which enfuriated the ambassador, in the summer of 1645, was a letter to Lopo, from a minister in Lisbon, relating that at court there was talk of recalling Sousa Coutinho. The latter regarded it as an affront to his honour that such information should be confided to a 'resident of Amsterdam and a Jew'.[35]

[31]   GAA 334/1323, 'Registro dos parnasim' anno 5404.
[32]   The text of the patent is quoted in GAA NA 1556, deed of 4 July 1644, and signed as authentic by Lopo and two witnesses before notary Jan Volkaertsz. Oli.
[33]   GAA NA 1556B, p. 891 (20 July 1646).
[34]   *Correspondência diplomática de Francisco de Sousa Coutinho* (n. 29), vol. 1, p. 12, 17, 46, 195.
[35]   *Ibid.*, p. 288.

Thus, even before the news of the revolt of the Catholic Portugugese planters against Dutch rule in northern Brazil in 1645, a rebellion which devastated the sugar plantations and caused huge losses to the Dutch Sephardi merchant community and their relatives in Recife, there were definite signs of a cooling off of relations between Lopo and the Portuguese court. It is therefore possible that Lopo's decision to change his allegiance which he did, apparently, in the autumn of 1645, owed as much to personal disgruntlement as to the wave of anti-Portuguese sentiment which swept the Dutch Sephardi community in the wake of the events in Brazil.[36] Be that as it may, in November 1645, at a moment when there was intense resentment and anger against Portugal among the Amsterdam Sephardi community, the head of the Spanish delegation to the Münster Peace Congress, the great convention of European diplomats which eventually negotiated an end to the Thirty and Eighty Years' Wars, sent a confidant to Amsterdam to sound out those deemed likely to be useful to the Spanish diplomatic machine at this crucial juncture in European history.[37] In this way, the Spanish authorities again made contact with Lopo. One of those who recommended him to the Spanish plenipotentiary at Münster, the conde de Peñaranda, was the secretary of his delegation at the peace congress, an official who knew about Lopo's previous activity, in the late 1630s, on behalf of the Spanish regime in Brussels. In this way Lopo became the Amsterdam agent of the figure who was the most important Spanish negotiator in northern Europe in the late 1640s.

After Peñaranda's arrival at Münster with his delegation in December 1645, the remitting of his pay and expenses, and those of his staff, from Antwerp passed via Amsterdam and was handled by Lopo. A large part of Peñaranda's secret correspondence apparently passed between Münster and Antwerp by the same route. This is highly ironic not only because Spain and Portugal were at war and Lopo's brother, at Hamburg, had been publicly proclaimed 'Agent' of the Portuguese crown there the previous year, but even more since his nephew, Duarte's eldest son, Jeronimo Nunes da Costa (Moseh Curiel) (1620-1697) had recently been appointed Agent of the Portuguese crown in the United Provinces, in May 1645[38], and Lopo himself, despite Sousa Countinho's dislike of him, continued to handle the official remittances for the Portuguese crown from Lisbon for the Portuguese embassy in Holland, until as late as 1648, when his nephew took over this role from him[39], presumably because until then the Lisbon bankers had more confidence in Lopo's financial status than that of his as yet relatively unknown nephew. Indeed, at the same time

---

[36] On this backlash, see J. I. Israel, 'Dutch Sephardi Jewry, Millenarian Politics, and the Struggle for Brazil (1640-1654)', in: D. S. Katz and J. I. Israel, eds., *Sceptics, Millenarians and Jews* (Leiden 1990) p. 87-97; above, pp. 156-67.

[37] *Colección de documentos inéditos* (n. 24), vol. 82, p. 238-240. Peñaranda to Philip IV, Münster, 19 Dec. 1645.

[38] D. Swetschinski, 'An Amsterdam Jewish Merchant-Diplomat: Jeronimo Nunes da Costa alias Moseh Curiel (1620-1697), Agent of the King of Portugal', in: L. Dasberg and J. N. Cohen, eds., *Neveh Ya'akov. Jubilee Volume presented to Dr. Jaap Meijer* (Assen 1982) p. 3-30: 14.

[39] *Correspondência diplomática de Francisco de Sousa Coutinho* (n. 29), vol. 2, p. 62, 216, and vol. 3, p. 6, 354.

that Lopo was becoming increasingly active as Peñaranda's agent in the United Provinces he was still supplying at least some information to the Portuguese court.[40]

When the Dutch-Spanish peace talks at Münster reached their critical point, early in 1647, and the political debate in the Dutch provincial assemblies and town councils about whether or not to make peace with Spain was at its height, Peñaranda sent his deputy (and later the first Spanish ambassador to the United Provinces), Antoine Brun, to Amsterdam, Utrecht, Leiden and other towns whose votes were likely to be crucial, to canvass support among the regents for the proposed treaty. This sort of political mission, which included placing bribes, was expensive and to cover the costs Peñaranda supplied Brun with letters of credit for 50,000 guilders drawn on Lopo. Evidently the money was drawn off from the funds assigned at Antwerp for the upkeep of Peñaranda and his deputation at Münster. In a letter to the then governor-general of the Spanish Netherlands the marqués de Castel-Rodrigo, Peñaranda wrote that, as a result, he and his party 'would have nothing to eat', but that the expenditure was vital for the king's service.[41]

During Brun's mission to Holland, his movements were closely followed by French informers since France remained at war with Spain (in alliance with Portugal) and was attempting to dissuade the Dutch regents from settling with the Spanish king.[42] The fact that when Brun was in Amsterdam he was visited by a certain 'Portuguese' called 'Ramirez' consequently soon came to the attention of the French envoy at The Hague who then, at once, became suspicious, especially when he learnt that this personage transacted business in the United Provinces on behalf of the Portuguese king. The French envoy demanded to know from Sousa Countinho who this 'Lopo Ramirez' was. Sousa Countinho was then placed in the highly embarrassing situation of having to explain to his French allies that a Jew whom he considered utterly untrustworthy – the following year when reporting to Lisbon that Lopo was paying the costs of the Spanish delegation at Münster, he described him as the 'worst dog in all Jewry' ('o mais mao perro que ha em toda a judearia')[43] – was not really acting on behalf of the Portuguese court but 'only pays the money which is remitted from Portugal', being the 'correspondent' of the Lisbon bankers and therefore the banker of the Portuguese ambassadors at The Hague.[44]

Lopo assisted Peñaranda and the Brussels regime from his house and the merchants' exchange in Amsterdam, mostly without leaving the city. Amsterdam with its unrivalled financial and commercial facilities, and opportunities for gathering information from all parts of Europe, was ultimately the basis of Lopo's activity on behalf of Spain, as it had been on behalf of Portugal. Apparently, the only journey

[40]   *Ibid.*, vol. 3, p. 11.
[41]   *Colección de documentos inéditos* (n. 24), vol. 83, p. 5. Peñaranda to Castel-Rodrigo, Münster, 7. Jan. 1647.
[42]   On Brun's mission to the Republic in January 1647, see Israel, *The Dutch Republic and the Hispanic World* (n. 28), p. 370.
[43]   *Correspondência diplomática de Francisco de Sousa Coutinho* (n. 29), vol. 3, p. 10.
[44]   *Ibid.*, vol. 2, p. 47-48.

of any significance which he made during the years prior to his move to Antwerp was in June 1647, after the formal Dutch-Spanish cease-fire, when he and his wife (who was then ailing) travelled down to Spa, south of Verviers, a place in the south Netherlands famous for its waters and a long way from Amsterdam, but convenient for meetings between Spanish officials converging from Brussels and Münster.[45] He seems to have spent most of that summer at Spa, leaving his business affairs in Amsterdam in the hands of a certain 'Jacome Curiel' who was very probably Jacob Curiel, the second son of Duarte Nunes Victoria who had long been a close associate of Lopo.

Lopo was useful to Spanish statecraft and diplomacy in these years as a financial agent through his unrivalled access to information emanating from Lisbon[46], (which was always of great interest to Spanish officials in the years between 1640 and 1668 while Spain was still striving to reconquer Portugal and Brazil), and as a representative at the Amsterdam Exchange at a time when the Dutch-Spanish relationship was undergoing fundamental change. For the end of the Eighty Years War, and lifting of the Spanish embargoes, opened up a whole array of new opportunities and forms of interaction. One of the most sensational pieces of news which Lopo conveyed to the Spanish authorities concerned the commencement, very suddenly, of a massive illegal flow of silver bullion from the Bay of Cadiz to Amsterdam which, for Spain, was one of the less desireable consequences of the peace. In a letter to Peñaranda of November 1649, Lopo related that four ships had arrived in Amsterdam from Cadiz, carrying unregistered silver ingots and other untaxed merchandise from Spain's American viceroyalties, which had been removed from the last returning Indies fleet in the Bay of Cadiz before inspection and registration.[47] According to Lopo, the illegal cargo was worth over three million ducats. Peñaranda sent Lopo's *aviso* to Madrid where it was discussed with formal mention of 'Lopo Ramirez' by the *Consejo de Estado* at its meeting of 26 December 1649.

No doubt Lopo was keenly aware, from the resumption of his dealings with Spanish officials and the Portuguese New Christian contractors in Antwerp in 1645-1646, that if Spain and the Republic did make peace, all kinds of transactions and dealings, linking Amsterdam and Spain, would ensue and that he would then be ideally placed to participate advantageously in the proceedings. When the peace treaty was finally ratified, in May 1648, Peñaranda returned to Brussels entrusted with overseeing the smooth implementation of the treaty's provisions. It was expected, initially, that Peñaranda would also become Spain's first ambassador to the United Provinces. But it turned out that the Dutch States General were in no hurry

---

[45]   See Stadsarchief Antwerpen (= SAA) IB 84, p. 114, Lopo Ramirez to Thomas de Sampayo, Spa, 11 July 1647, and IB 1933, Jacome Curiel to Sampayo, Amsterdam, 1 July and 22 Aug. 1647.

[46]   *Colección de documentos inéditos* (n. 24), vol. 84, p. 113-120. Peñaranda to Philip IV, Münster, 3 Feb. 1648.

[47]   Archivo General de Simancas, Valladolid, Estado 2070. *Consulta* of the *Consejo de Estado*, Madrid, 26 Dec. 1649.

to receive a Spanish envoy at The Hague and a lengthy delay ensued until, in June 1649, Brun was sent, in Peñaranda's place, to take up the post. Lopo, for his part, applied to ministers in Brussels to be granted an official appointment and title, as Spanish 'consul' in Amsterdam or else a comparable position in Hamburg. The question of whether to confer an official title on Lopo, as the Spanish crown did later, in the 1660s, on first Andrés, and then Manuel de Belmonte, who each became 'Agent' of the Spanish crown at Amsterdam, was discussed several times by ministers at Brussels, during 1648, but, in the end, it was decided not to do so, presumably because Lopo was a Jew.[48]

After May 1648, Lopo remained in regular contact both with Peñaranda at Brussels and the contractors acting for the Spanish crown at Antwerp. A number of letters from Lopo to the Antwerp Portuguese New Christian financier Thomas de Sampayo survive in the Antwerp city archives (the earliest dated September 1646)[49] which not only confirm that Lopo was sending political information, as well as remittances, to Peñaranda at Münster, down to May 1648, but provide an indication of his developing role as Spain's agent at Amsterdam subsequently. After the lifting of the ban on the transporting of grain from the United provinces to the Spanish Netherlands in the summer of 1647, one of Lopo's functions was to inform the Antwerp contractors on the state of the Amsterdam grain market. For grain for the Spanish army of Flanders, still locked in struggle with the French, could usually be obtained more cheaply and conveniently at Amsterdam than elsewhere but, at the same time, much depended on knowing what and when to buy. Thus, in December 1647, Sampayo asked Lopo about the current price and quality of wheat and rye at Amsterdam and Lopo supplied the required information, offering to buy and transport whatever was needed.[50] In May 1648, Lopo reported the arrival of several grain convoys from the Baltic, and resulting fall in grain prices at Amsterdam, recommending that the time was ripe for bulk purchases of grain for the army.[51]

On various occasions Lopo was asked to procure munitions. In July 1649, for example, Peñaranda asked 'el buen Lopo Ramires', as he called him in a letter to Brun, to purchase 100,000 pounds of gunpowder which was urgently needed in Spain. Lopo did so, we are told, despite having no assurance of being reimbursed by the Spanish crown other than Peñaranda's own word.[52] This particular request led to a bizarre political incident because Brun, who had only just arrived as Spanish ambassador at The Hague, and was as yet unfamiliar with how things worked, made the mistake of requesting an export license for the powder in a week when the

[48] H. Lonchay, J. Cuvelier and J. Fefèvre, eds., *Correspondance de la Cour d'Espagne sur les affaires des Pays-Bas au XVIIe siècle* (6 vols., Brussels 1923-1937), vol. 4, p. 88.
[49] Stadsarchief Antwerpen (=SAA) IB 1932, 1933 and 1934, covering the years 1646-1648.
[50] SAA IB 1933. Lopo Ramirez to Thomas de Sampayo, Amsterdam, 13 Jan. 1648.
[51] SAA IB 1934. Lopo Ramirez to Thomas de Sampayo, Amsterdam, 18 May 1648.
[52] Archives Générales du Royaume, Brussels (= AGR) SEG 604, fos. p. 213v-216v. Peñaranda to Brun, Brussels, 22 and 26 July 1649.

chairman of the States General belonged to the anti-Spanish, pro-French faction among the Dutch ruling elite. French diplomats were soon informed about what was happening and the Dutch public (which was still predominantly anti-Spanish in attitude) aroused. The result was a general furore from which Brun (and behind the scenes Ramirez) were only extricated by the intervention, in favour of granting the license, of the Amsterdam burgomasters.

Even more political acrimony surrounded Lopo's purchases of warships for Spain. Almost immediately after the signing of the Dutch-Spanish peace, construction began at Amsterdam of twelve fregates for the Spanish navy. Lopo and his cousin Duarte Ramires Pina were at the centre of this undertaking together with the firm Gaspar and Jeremiah van Collen with which Lopo had had business dealings reaching back over many years. As the ships neared completion, complaints were lodged in the States General by the representatives of Zeeland and Utrecht, the two provinces which had obstinately opposed the Spanish peace in 1647-1648 and which remained most strongly pro-French. Naturally, there were also emphatic protests from both the French and Portuguese ambassadors. After a tussle in the States General, it was eventually resolved that the warships should not be supplied to Spain. Nevertheless, as the Portuguese envoy reported to Lisbon, work continued surreptitiously on two of the vessels, including one which we are expressly told was made ready, and armed, by Lopo Ramirez 'who shows his affection for Spain at every turn.'[53] It was this, or possibly another, fregate fitted out by Lopo which, armed and filled with ropes for the Spanish navy, was intercepted and sunk by French warships *en route* to Spain, in December 1648.[54]

What was probably Lopo's last service for Peñaranda was to arrange, in March 1650, the transportation of his furniture and baggage, accompanied by ten or twelve servants, from Brussels back to Spain. Peñaranda was keen to see his belongings conveyed in a Dutch vessel so as to minimize the risk of their being intercepted by the French. The operation was entrusted to Brun who, in turn, delegated the practicalities to Lopo. When the requisite shipping space was booked, Brun had Peñaranda's servants and numerous boxes and trunks shipped from Antwerp, via the inland waterways, to Amsterdam where, the servants were told everything would be attended to by 'Lopo Ramires who will show them which ship and organize their departure'.[55]

It was precisely at this time that Lopo's relations with the *Mahamad* of the Sephardi community in Amsterdam rapidly deteriorated. Francisco Ramirez Pina, brother of Lopo's wife and a wealthy merchant with whom he had often collaborated, had died in 1641, leaving his huge fortune of around 250,000 guilders to his tiny four-month old daughter Rebecca Naar. The Amsterdam civic orphans' chamber

53 *Correspondência diplomática de Francisco de Sousa Coutinho* (n. 29), vol. 3, p. 39.
54 *Ibid.,* vol. 3, p. 243.
55 AGR SEG 605, fos. 186, 190v, 200v. Brun to Peñaranda, The Hague, 17 and 21 March 1650.

(Weeskamer) had then appointed Lopo and Manoel Diaz Henriques (alias Matatia Aboab) (b. Oporto 19 May 1594 – d. Amsterdam, 5 Oct. 1667) who was married to another sister of the deceased – Isabel de Pina (alias Esther Naar) – as the child's guardians. What precisely the two guardians did with the infant's money remains unclear, but they evidently felt that much of it ought to have been bequeathed to their respective wives and children. After considering the matter for nine years, they took the sensational step, early in 1650, of attempting to dispossess their niece of her inheritance by filing a suit with the city magistrates, alleging that Rebecca's parents had failed to register their marriage in accordance with the law and that Rebecca was therefore illegitimate with the consequence that Ramirez Pina's fortune should be inherited by his sisters – their own wives.[56] These proceedings caused a great commotion among the Sephardi community since it had always been the policy of the *Mahamad* and the rabbis that questions of marriage, legitimacy and inheritance lay solely within the domain and under the authority of the community itself. Furthermore, since many couples were married only in accordance with Jewish law, without their marriages being formally registered with the city, if the marriage of Rebecca's parents were to be ruled invalid numerous others would appear to be so also. Determined to assert their authoriy, the *parnasim* demanded that the two men withdraw their application to the city magistracy. Lopo and Matatia refused. The *Mahamad* then placed the two men under the so-called *niduy*, or minor ban, a measure short of full excommunication (the *herem*).[57] The minor ban allowed them to continue contact with the community to a certain extent, including business dealings, but still punished the offender by a degree of isolation and by placing him in a position of contempt. The offender could not appear in the synagogue or be counted as one of the ten adult males (*minyan*) required for communal prayers. Lopo and Matatia reacted by lodging a complaint with the burgomasters to the effect that the *parnasim* were obstructing them in the performance of their religious obligations without just cause. The burgomasters ruled that the two men must be allowed to pray in the synagogue and, on 28 April 1651, one of the *parnasim* announced, in the synagogue, that the two men were about to appear among the congregation, that they had the permission of the burgomasters to do so and that no member of the congregation must interfere with them.[58] Lopo and Matatia duly took part in the service but, on their leaving the building, were insulted and jostled outside.

A second quarrel between Lopo and the *Mahamad* ensued when Lopo – whose first wife had died in March 1650 – sought permission to remarry. The chosen bride of the now fifty-six year old Lopo was the twenty-two year old daughter of his ally

[56] L. Fuks, 'Een rechtsstrijd onder Amsterdamse Sefardim in de 17e eeuw' in: *'T Exempel dwinght'. Opstellen aangeboden aan I. Kisch ter gelegenheid van zijn zeventigste verjaardag* (Zwolle 1975) p. 175-189: 178-179.
[57] *Ibid.*, p. 179.
[58] *Ibid.*, p. 179-180.

Matatia, Rachel Aboab. However, the marriage was objected to by a niece of Lopo's, Sara Curiel, daughter of Duarte Nunes Victoria (Abraham Curiel) who, with the support of a large part of the Curiel family, claimed that Lopo had previously promised to marry her and that her illegitimate, son, Abraham, was the child of Lopo[59]. The *parnasim* decided to back her plea that Lopo should marry her and forbade the marriage with Rachel Aboab. The *Mahamad*'s ruling was more than a little dubious under Jewish law, though, and Lopo had little difficulty, by appealing to respected rabbis in Italy, in obtaining rabbinic authorization for his marriage to Rachel. Armed with a favourable judgment from, among others, Simcha ben Isaac Luzzatto of Venice, Lopo married Rachel on 19 June 1651.[60] He also eventually obtained a favourable ruling from the city magistracy in March 1653 regarding his dispute with Sara Curiel.[61] The proceedings concerning the inheritance of Rebecca Naar, however, for the time being remained unresolved by the courts.

Lopo was now on the worst possible terms with the Amsterdam *Mahamad*, the congregation and part of the Curiel family. Probably he was already contemplating leaving Amsterdam and establishing himself and his family elsewhere, at least as early as 1651. For the moment, though, he remained in Amsterdam and his first child (his first marriage had been childless), Sara, was born there in July 1652.[62] Previously, it has been assumed by scholars that Lopo only moved to Antwerp 'around 1655' or in any case after June 1654, since the Aboab geneaology states that his first son, Imanuel, was 'born in Amsterdam' on 4 June 1654.[63] But a key notarial deed preserved in the Amsterdam city archives to which I shall refer several times in concluding this article, states that Lopo Ramirez 'lived in Antwerp from the year 1653 until the year 1660'[64], that is for approximately seven years, and in my view the conclusion that Lopo transferred to Antwerp in 1653, even if he subsequently made visits to Amsterdam, fits better with the other evidence that we have.

In the year 1653, a group of Amsterdam Sephardi Jews applied to the then governor-general of the Spanish Netherlands, the Archduke Leopold Wilhelm, asking permission, and offering a cash sum, to be allowed to live openly as Jews (which was forbidden in the Spanish Netherlands) at Antwerp.[65] We lack direct

[59] *Ibid.*, p. 180.
[60] Revah, 'Relation généalogique' (n. 5), p. 309.
[61] Fuks, 'Een Rechtsstrijd' (n. 56), p. 183.
[62] Revah, *ibid.*
[63] *Ibid.*; Fuks, 'Een Rechtsstrijd' (n. 56), p. 184; Swetschinski, 'An Amsterdam Jewish Merchant-Diplomat' (n. 38), p. 14.
[64] In July 1673, Isaac Aboab attested before the Amsterdam notary Adriaen Lock that 'hij met de voornoemde Lopo Ramires sijn oom van den jaere 1653 af tot den jaere 1660 toe tot Antwerpen gewoont heeft', GAA NA 242A, fo. 14. (4 July 1673); see also Swetschinski, *ibid.*
[65] See E. Ouverleaux, *Notes et documents sur les juifs de Belgique sous l'ancien régime* (Paris 1885) p. 29-41; S. Ullmann, *Studien zur Geschichte der Juden in Belgien bis zum XVIII. Jahrhundert* (Antwerp 1909) p. 38-41; E. Schmidt, *L'Histoire des juifs à Anvers* (2nd edn. Antwerp 1969) p. 41-45; J. I. Israel, *European Jewry in the Age of Mercantilism, 1550-1750* (Oxford 1985) p. 156; L. Dequeker, 'Heropleving van het Jodendom te Antwerpen in de zeventiende eeuw?', *De Zeventiende Eeuw* 5 (1989) p. 154-156, 160.

proof that the principal author of this proposal was Lopo Ramirez but, in my view, the circumstantial evidence that it was is so compelling that we can safely conclude that the scheme was Lopo's. We know that the project began through meetings with the Spanish Ambassador, Brun[66], at The Hague, and that it was not done on the initiative of the *Mahamad* in Amsterdam[67], and clearly only a leading member of the Amsterdam Sephardi community with exceptional contacts and standing, with the authorities in the Spanish Netherlands, making his approach without liaising with the *parnasim* in Amsterdam, would have been in a position to propose it. That Lopo was in fact in the southern Netherlands, and under the protection of the Spanish governor-general, by the summer of 1653, is proved by a letter sent by Leopold Wilhelm from Brussels, dated 17 July 1653, to the city authorities at Hamburg, lodging a protest on behalf of 'Lopo Ramirez'. The missive states that Lopo, having entered proceedings before the Hamburg magistracy against 'a certain merchant of that city called Duarte Nunes da Costa about a diamond of importance (*un diamante de importancia*), and obtained a favourable ruling, had still not succeeded in retrieving the diamond'.[68] The Spanish governor-general at Brussels demanded that the Hamburg Senate compel Duarte to return the diamond to Lopo. Not a word was said in the letter about Duarte being Lopo's brother.

The proposal to establish an organized Jewish community in Antwerp was taken seriously by both Brun and Leopold Wilhelm. The archduke decided to convene a high level committee, in Brussels, consisting of the archbishop of Mechelen, who at this time was the Jansenist Jacobus Boonen (d. 1655), the Chancellor of Brabant and four other members of the Council of State, Secret Council and Council of Brabant, to determine whether there was, in fact, any fundamental obstacle in the laws of Brabant to the Archduke's granting the requested permission.[69] These deliberations took place in December 1653. The commission compiled a lengthy report concluding that there was not any obstacle, either in Church law or the laws of Brabant, to the permitting of Jewish worship in Brabant but that it was necessary, should a Jewish community be established, that the Jews be made to live apart from Christians (for the protection of the latter) in segregated quarters, that is a ghetto, as was usual in Italy and Germany.[70] Finally, the commission recommended that the governor-general should allow the establishment of a Jewish congregation in the Antwerp suburb of Borgerhout in exchange for a substantial sum for the royal treasury.

[66] AGR SEG 257, fo. 133. Leopold Wilhelm to Philip IV, Brussels, 17 Apr. 1654.
[67] J. I. Israel, 'Menasseh ben Israel and the Dutch Sephardic Colonization Movement of the mid-Seventeenth Century (1645-1657)', in: Y. Kaplan, H. Méchoulan and R. H. Popkin, eds., *Menasseh ben Israel and his World* (Leiden 1989) p. 152.
[68] AGR Sécrétairerie d'état allemande 594, fo. 152. Leopold Wilhelm to the Hamburg Senate, Brussels, 17 July 1653.
[69] Ullmann, *Studien* (n. 65), p. 38-40; Hans Pohl, *Die Portugiesen in Antwerpen (1567-1648)* (Wiesbaden 1977) p. 342-343.
[70] Dequeker, 'Heropleving' (n. 65), p. 155.

However, formal negotiations for an organized Jewish community at Borgerhout were subsequently broken off after the Papal nuncio in Madrid was alerted by the internuncio at Brussels, Andrea Mangelli, a bitter foe of Archbishop Boonen, to what was afoot. The nuncio in Madrid, on orders from Rome, protested that His Holiness the Pope had been informed of the deliberations in Brussels 'que se havia comenzado a tratar en aquellos estados de abrir una sinagoga de hebreos en un lugar llamado Burgero [Borgerhout], pocas millas distante de Amberes'. The Pope wanted the king to cancel any resolution that might have been taken in the Spanish Netherlands in favour of allowing the readmittance of Jews and put a stop to all such discussions: 'supplica a Vra Magestad que se sirva de mandar se prohiba qualquiera resolucion sobre esto sino que se se arranque y quite de echo todo tratado en esta materia como lo espera de la rectitud y christiano çelo de Vuestra Magestad'.[71]

The nuncio's protest and the papal request were then sent to the full *Consejo de Estado* where the marqués de Leganes, the marqués de Valparaiso and other ministers considered the position on 7 February 1654. Twelve days later, a royal dispatch was sent off to Brussels in which the king referred to the Papal protest, averring that he could not believe that the Archduke could have given permission for a synagogue in Antwerp and that any such innovations would have the most damaging consequences. Replying on 17 April 1654, the governor-general explained that, through Ambassador Brun, some prominent Amsterdam Jews had proposed the establishment of a Jewish congregation in Antwerp and that, in view of the urgent need for cash for the army, he had supposed that the offer ought to be carefully considered.[72] In a subsequent letter, of 24 June 1654, the king ruled that in no circumstances, in exchange for money or on any other pretext, was formal toleration of Jewish worship to be granted in the Spanish Netherlands.[73]

Yet this was not quite the end of the matter. For if no organized community was permitted, it is clear that the Archduke Leopold Wilhelm had already, the previous year, taken Lopo Ramirez and his family, and a number of others, under his protection, granting them permission to live openly as Jews in Antwerp, exempt from the jurisdiction of the bishop. No doubt this was done in recognition of Lopo's services on behalf of the Spanish crown but probably money was also involved. What it amounted to was an informal, personal, privilege with the right to practice Judaism granted to Lopo Ramirez, in the first instance, but extending also to those living with him.

There is no doubt that Lopo enjoyed the governor-general's protection and, whilst residing in Antwerp, publicly avoided Christian worship, practicing Judaism without concealment. Not only does Isaac Aboab clearly assert this in the already

[71] Archivo General de Simancas, Estado 2185, consulta Consejo de Estado, 7 Feb. 1654; J. I. Israel, 'Spain and the Dutch Sephardim, 1609-1660', *Studia Rosenthaliana* 12 (1978) p. 1-61: 35.
[72] AGR SEG 257, fo. 133. Leopold Wilhelm to Philip IV, Brussels, 17 Apr. 1654.
[73] Israel, 'Spain and the Dutch Sephardim' (n. 71), p. 35.

cited notarial deed of 1673[74], but we have a number of other quite separate indications that this was the case. In the Aboab genealogy, for example, we are told that when Lopo's second son, Samuel, was born 'em Amberes', on 4 December 1655, 'foy aly serconsidado aos 8 dias', that is he was circumcized at Antwerp the customary eight days after birth.[75] The circumcizer might have been Isaac Aboab who tells us that late in the 1670s he personally circumcized his own sons[76], or else a *mohel* come specially from Holland or Middelburg. Lopo's third son, Isaac, according to the same source, was born in Antwerp on 30 November 1659, and he too 'foy aly sercuncidado aos 8 dias'. Still more remarkable is the fact that when he appeared in court in Antwerp, in 1657, Lopo insisted on swearing only 'more judaico' and that this was accepted by the court so that he was the first (and quite possibly the only) person ever to swear a Jewish oath in court in the Spanish Netherlands.[77]

One of the Portuguese New Christians with whom Lopo came in contact during the time he lived in Antwerp was a certain Gaspar de Victoria Pereira who was arrested for 'judaizing' a few years later by the Inquisition in the Canary Islands. Vitoria Pereira testified to the Canariote Inquisitors on 11 September 1662, recalling what he had seen in Antwerp some years before, that 'in the house of Lopo Ramirez, a Jew of the city of Antwerp against whom he had already given evidence, there lives a young man [Isaac Aboab], nephew and brother-in-law of Ramirez who is also a Jew'.[78] On 20 August 1663, the prisoner added that during the time he was in Antwerp he noted that 'neither Lopo Ramirez nor his brother-in-law, against both of whom he had borne witness, would go to the Exchange on Saturdays and that, in 1658, he had visited an inn in the street called La Mera which is frequented by Jewish travellers so that, if the Inquisitors thought fit, it would be easy to discover all who stay there'.[79] A fortnight later, he further testified that 'when in Antwerp he noticed a number of tents in a garden and was told by (he thinks) Don Geronimo Osorio de Silva, that the place belonged to Lopo Ramirez who lived in the tents with his family at a certain time of the year, to celebrate the feast of Tabernacles'.[80] The fact that Lopo, during his time at Antwerp, felt confident enough to dwell with his family in several *sukkot* during the festival of Tabernacles, shows how secure his position was.

Evidently, Lopo lived in Antwerp with his wife and children, observing Judaism more or less openly in the company of a number of other persons. In the first place there was Isaac Aboab (1631 – 1707), who was twenty-two when he accompa-

[74]   See again GAA NA 2242A, fo. 14.
[75]   Revah, 'Relation généalogique' (n. 5), p. 310.
[76]   *Ibid.*, p. 280; Crespo Fabião, 'O Cazo de David Curiel' (n. 17), p. 18-19.
[77]   Schmidt, *L'Histoire des juifs à Anvers*, p. 45.
[78]   L. Wolf, *Jews in the Canary Islands, being a Calendar of Jewish Cases extracted from the Records of the Canariote Inquisition in the Collection of the Marquess of Bute* (London 1926) p. 185.
[79]   *Ibid.*, p. 190.
[80]   *Ibid.*, p. 194.

nied Lopo to Antwerp and, by his own statement, dwelt in Lopo's house there, living as a Jew and observing the Jewish festivals, from 1653 to 1660. He subsequently married Sara Curiel, eldest daughter of Lopo and Rachel Aboab (his sister) who was therefore also his niece. He lived most of his later life in Amsterdam and it was there, in 1676, that he drew up the genealogy of the Aboab, Naar, Curiel and related families for which he is chiefly remembered. His father, Matatia Aboab, had been Lopo's ally in Amsterdam during the events of 1650-1653, but there is no sign that he joined Lopo and his son in Antwerp. He was to die in Amsterdam in October 1667. In his statement of July 1673, Isaac Aboab also attests that Judah (alias Luis) de Vega came a number of times, both during festivals and at other times, 'as a Jew among Jews' to Lopo Ramirez' house in Antwerp.[81] How far Lopo's house was also a centre for other Dutch Sephardi Jews staying for shorter or longer periods in Antwerp remains unclear. Victoria Pereira describes how he met a group of Jews from Amsterdam in Antwerp, in a house where they were staying, and had a meal with them of smoked meat and Passover bread, but made no mention of Lopo in this context.[82] He declared that one of the group was Isaac, son of Abraham Pereira.

Certainly, there were several other Amsterdam Jews who lived in Antwerp during the 1650s. The Spanish consul at Amsterdam, Jacques Richard, advised the new Spanish ambassador at The Hague, Don Esteban de Gamarra, in October 1655, that several Amsterdam Sephardi Jews were to be found in Antwerp, mentioning in particular two brothers, David and Jacob Mendez, who were tobacco dealers, a certain Romano Garcia and Miguel de los Ríos.[83] The latter is an especially interesting case, being the son of Joseph de los Ríos, one of the wealthiest and most prominent Amsterdam Sephardi merchants of the time. Joseph de los Ríos, who as a New Christian had been known as 'Martín Rodríguez', conducted an extensive trade with Spain, with business correspondents in Bilbao, San Sebastian and Madrid[84], and was a *parnas* of the Amsterdam Sephardi community in 1641, 1647, 1653 and 1658. Richard estimated his fortune at between two and three hundred thousand guilders. His son, Miguel, we are told, had been born and baptized in Rouen, and circumcized in Amsterdam around 1640. He had gone to Antwerp to marry the daughter of a rich Portuguese New Christian merchant of the city, Manuel Tavares, who had died some time before. Evidently Antwerp suited Miguel de los Ríos, for according to the official list of the 'Portuguese nation' living in the city in 1666, he was still a resident of Antwerp in that year.[85] There is no evidence, however, that

[81] GAA NA 2242A, fo. 14 (4 July 1673): *de welcke verscheijde maelen soo op hoochtijden als andersints als een Jood neffens andere Jooden ten huijse van de gemelte Lopo Ramires ... gecomen is.*

[82] Wolf, *Jews in the Canary Islands* (n. 78), p. 191-193.

[83] University College London, Mocatta Library, L. Wolf transcripts, 'Correspondance de Jacques Richard', p. 5-6.

[84] Israel, 'Spain and the Dutch Sephardim' (n. 71), p. 58.

[85] I. S. Revah, 'Pour l'histoire des Marranes à Anvers: recensements de la "nation portugaise" de 1571 à 1666', *Revue des Études Juives* 122 (1963) p. 123-147: 146.

any other household in Antwerp in the 1650s served as a focus for Jewish gatherings, observance and religious services in the way that Lopo's manifestly did.

Whilst Lopo dwelt in Antwerp, the provincial high court of Holland (*Hof van
Holland*) finally resolved the case of the inheritance of Rebecca Naar. On 30 September 1656, the Hof pronounced in her favour, ruling that the marriage of Francisco Ramires Pina and Sara Naar was in accordance with Jewish law and registered
by the 'Jewish nation', and that Rebecca was the legitimate daughter and heiress of
her father.[86] But his losing this case did not detract from the fact that Lopo's own
fortune remained one of the very largest among the Dutch Sephardi Jews of his
time. In the year 1660, Lopo left Antwerp and the Spanish Netherlands, moving to
Middelburg where there was a small Sephardi community, partly composed of refugees from what had formerly been Dutch Brazil. His seventh child, Abigail, was
born in Middelburg in March 1662. Subsequently, he moved to Rotterdam where
his eighth and last child, Abraham, was born on 2 November 1664.

Almost at the end of his life, in the summer of 1666, after thirteen years in
self-imposed exile – and during the very months when the messianic frenzy surrounding the figure of Shabbetai Zevi which was then sweeping the Jewish world
was at its height, not least amongst the Dutch Sephardim – Lopo, now elderly and
perhaps sick, decided to seek to be reconciled with the Amsterdam congregation and
Mahamad, offering to pay 1,000 guilders to the synagogue poor chest as a mark of
contrition. Lopo's offer was presented to the *Mahamad* by his nephew, Duarte's
son Jeronimo, 'Agent' of the Portuguese crown in the United Provinces. The *parnasim* resolved to accept Lopo's offering in view of the 'long time he has been away
and the present needs of the poor'.[87] Thus while Lopo is recorded as having died on
4 October 1666 at the age of seventy-two years and five months 'in the city of
Rotterdam', he was buried the next day in the cemetery of the Amsterdam community at Ouderkerk.[88] His family then migrated to Amsterdam, his widow Rachel
and his children being described in February 1667 as 'living in Amsterdam'.[89] Under
the Amsterdam tax register of 1674, the 'widow of David Curiel', as she is described,
was listed as possessing 117,000 guilders of taxable wealth, placing her fourth in
order of wealth among the Amsterdam Sephardi community after Antonio Lopes
Suasso, the widow of Gil Lopes Pinto (Abraham de Pinto) and Isaac de Pinto.[90]

His death and burial did not quite end Lopo's career as a source of contention
among Dutch Sephardi Jewry. Abraham, the illegitimate son of Sara Curiel, grew to
manhood and, on marrying at Amsterdam in May 1677, was authorized by the
parnasim – one of whom that year was his cousin Jeronimo Nunes da Costa – to

---

[86] Fuks, 'Een rechtsstrijd' (n. 56), p. 183-184.
[87] GAA Archives of the Portuguese Jewish Community 19, p. 562, Res. Mahamad, 15 Sivan 5426.
[88] Revah, 'Relation généalogique' (n. 5), p. 310.
[89] GA Rotterdam NA 110, deed of Rutger van den Burgh, 28 Feb. 1667.
[90] A. M. Vaz Dias, 'Over den vermogenstoestand der Amsterdamsche Joden in de 17e en de 18e
eeuw', *Tijdschrift voor Geschiedenis* 51 (1936), p. 165-176.

name Lopo as his father, in synagogue, during the wedding service. This procedure which contradicted what Lopo had always averred, and cleared the way for Abraham to proceed, with the support of the *Mahamad*, to claim a share of Lopo's fortune, was bitterly contested by Lopo's sons by Rachel, causing a whole new legal furore, interventions by the *Mahamad* and city magistrates and the obtaining of responsa from eminent Italian rabbis. Finally, in July 1682, the *Hof* of Holland ruled against Abraham, forbade him to name Lopo as his father in any Jewish prayer or ritual, and rejected his suit to be included among Lopo's heirs.[91]

Lopo Ramirez was, by any reckoning, a divisive and bizarre figure who left his mark on the history of Dutch Sephardi Jewry in numerous different contexts. But what above all was extraordinary was the unprecedented extent of his involvement, as a professing Jew, in the international statecraft and diplomacy over many years of both Spain and Portugal, during one of the most crucial phases in the history of the Iberian realms. But at no stage was he a more exceptional figure than during his seven years in the Spanish Netherlands as a resident of Antwerp, living openly as a Jew under the protection of the governor-general or, as Isaac Aboab expressed it, in his testimony of 1673, 'lived in Antwerp with the permission of his royal Majesty of Spain'.[92]

---

[91]   Fuks, 'Een rechtsstrijd' (n. 56), p. 185.

[92]   Aboab declared that he 'neffens Lopo Ramires sijn oom eenige jaren gewoont heeft tot Antwerpen met permissie van sijn conincklijcken Majesteyt van Spangien', see again GAA NA 2242A, fo. 14.

10

The Jews of Spanish Oran
and their Expulsion in 1669

In a letter of 5 May 1669 to the queen regent and her advisers in Madrid, the marqués de los Vélez, who was then governor of Spanish Oran, triumphantly reported his expulsion, the previous month, of all the Jews from the *plazas* of Oran and Mers-el-Kebir. But he also warned that those succeeding him as governor of Spain's principal enclave in North Africa, like his predecessors, were unlikely to share his view that expelling the Jews benefited the Spanish and Christian presence on the North African coast.[1] He suggested that the *Consejo de Estado* in Madrid, as the body which had pondered the Jewish presence in Oran and taken the decision to expel them, should reserve for itself the power to permit or refuse any element of Jewish presence in the *plazas* in the future. He urged that a royal order, or *cédula*, be issued to the effect that no future captain-general of Oran and Mers-el-Kebir should have the authority, on his own decision, to permit the return of any of those who had been expelled, or of other Jews. 'And I am not moved to propose this', he added, 'without good cause, for I know that when I leave this command there will be those who will introduce the proposal and that there have been many who have presumed to claim that the Jews were necessary to this republic' ('y no me muevo a pedir esto sin fundamento, porque sé, que en saliendo yo de este govierno ha

1. On the expulsion of the Jews from Oran, see J. Caro Baroja, *Los judíos en la España Moderna y Contemporánea*, 2nd edn. (Madrid, 1978), Vol. 1, pp. 231-3; J.I. Israel, 'The Jews of Spanish North Africa, 1600-1669', *Transactions of the Jewish Historical Society of England*, 26 (1979), 71-86; id., *European Jewry in the Age of Mercantilism* (Oxford, 1985), pp. 157-8; H. Kamen, *Spain in the Later Seventeenth Century, 1665-1700* (London, 1980), pp. 306-7, and H.Z. Hirschberg, *A History of the Jews in North Africa*, Vol. II, ed. E. Bashan and R. Attal (Leiden, 1981), pp. 62-7.

de haver quien introduzga la plática y muchos havía que presumían havían de hazer falta en esta republica los hebreos').[2]

The *Consejo de Estado* considered the point at its meeting of 27 May 1669, and recommended to the queen regent that a *cédula* should indeed be issued, in the name of the Council of War, the body which normally administered the North African strongholds, to the effect that in the future Jews should not be admitted to Oran by any governor.[3]

Los Vélez's claim, contrary to what his predecessors had maintained, that expelling the Jews actually strengthened the Spanish and Christian position on the Barbary Coast, is not easy to assess. But the Spanish grip apparently remained unimpaired after 1669, successfully resisting Muslim (both Moroccan and Turkish-Algerian) attacks and sieges in 1682, 1688, 1693, 1698, and 1700, before finally succumbing to the Turks in 1708 after a long and bitter siege.

My object in this present article is to extend, bring up to date, and present in a wider context the account of the sizeable Jewish community driven from Oran and Mers-el-Kebir in 1669, which I originally published in 1979 in the *Transactions of the Jewish Historical Society of England.* According to Los Vélez, the number of Jews — men, women, and children — ejected from Oran and Mers-el-Kebir in 1669 totalled 476.[4] They constituted a closely-knit, long-established Spanish-speaking Jewish community with deep roots in both Spanish and North African culture and one which in the past had played a crucial role in the life of the Spanish North African enclaves, as has also been stressed by H.Z. Hirschberg in his account of the episode in Volume II of his *A History of the Jews in North Africa.* In particular, I would like to draw attention to the heightened tension and complex conjuncture in Spain and the Mediterranean world more generally, which formed the context in which the expulsion of the Jews from Spanish Oran took place and which may conceivably also have

2. Archivo General de Simancas (hereafter AGS), Estado 4128, Los Vélez to queen regent, Oran, 5 May 1669, fol. 4.
3. Ibid., Consejo de Estado, consulta, Madrid, 27 May 1669.
4. Ibid., Los Vélez to queen regent, Oran, 5 May 1669, fol. 2v; I presume that the slightly lower figure of 466 given in the official printed account of the expulsion was an error for 476; see Luis Joseph to Sotomayor y Valenzuela, *Breve Relación y Compendioso Epitome de la general Expvlsion de los Hebreos de la Ivderia de la Ciudad de Oran* (n.p. and n.d. but the author dates his text Oran, 10 Jan. 1670), fol. 20. See also Hirschberg, *A History*, Vol. II, pp. 72, 74.

contributed to the decision to expel the Jews from Vienna, which was put into effect at the same time.

The original and, in the 1660s, still the essential reason for the Jewish presence in the Spanish North African *presidios* — there also were Jewish quarters (*juderías*) at Tangiers (Portuguese, but under the Spanish Crown from 1580 to 1643), Ceuta, Larache (Al-Araish), and Mazagan — was that Jews, who were fluent in Spanish as well as Arabic should form a connecting link between the Spanish garrisons and the Muslim hinterland. Their role was at once political, strategic, and financial. After the conquest of Oran early in the sixteenth century by King Ferdinand the Catholic, and at the prompting of Cardinal-Archbishop Ximenes de Cisneros, several former Spanish Jewish families, living in North Africa since 1492, were invited to settle in the town chiefly to facilitate contacts with the surrounding region.[5] According to Jewish, and to some extent general, tradition in Oran, there were seven original families, or *siete casas,* which had been individually authorized to reside in Oran at the time of King Ferdinand, and these were regarded as the seven pre-eminent families of the community.[6] Thus, in February 1657 a letter was sent from the Council of War in Madrid to the then governor of Oran, the marqués de San Román, asking for his view about a petition sent by the Jew Haim Albo in which he was styled 'citizen of the city of Oran, descended from one of the seven families that [King Ferdinand] ordered to settle in the said city'.[7] However, after instigating a search in the city's archives during the winter of 1668-69, prior to putting the expulsion into effect, Los Vélez claimed to have found only three *cédulas* authorizing the settlement of Jews in Oran, dating from the time of King Ferdinand, and that these three *casas de permisión* were those of the Cansino and Zemerro, who settled in the city in 1512, and of Rubi Satorra, who was then already in Oran serving the king as an Arabic interpreter.[8] The printed account of the expulsion published in 1670, denied that the Catholic kings who had 'at so much cost to themselves devoted themselves to purge the realms of Spain of insidious Jewish

5. Israel, 'Jews of Spanish North Africa', 72-6.
6. Ibid., 77.
7. British Library, London (hereafter BL), Add. MS. 28441, fols. 76-8. Queen regent to San Román, Madrid, 25 Feb. 1657: 'Ayen Albo hebreo vezino de la ciudad de Oran descendiente de una de las siete casas que su Magestad mando se abecindasen en la dicha ciudad'.
8. Sotomayor y Valenzuela, *Breve Relación*, fol. 8v.

remnants . . . creating the Holy Office of the Inquisition, wished to permit Satan to establish, in this new possession of the Church, a forbidden tree so hateful in the sight of the Almighty',[9] or, in other words, create a significant Jewish presence in Oran.

From an early date, it was the Cansino family (residents of Seville before the expulsion from Spain), who tended to monopolize the office of royal interpreter in Arabic at Oran. The holder of the post drew a regular monthly salary. The Jacob Cansino who headed the family in the mid-sixteenth century was sent to the Moroccan court on at least one occasion and played a notable part in the forging of closer Spanish-Moroccan relations in the 1550s, a time when both Spain and Morocco felt threatened by the spread of Ottoman influence westwards along the coast of North Africa.[10] In 1580 Jacob's son, Isaac Cansino, was summoned to Madrid where he spent several months assisting ministers at the time of Philip II's acquisition of the Portuguese crown and empire, which then included Tangiers and Ceuta. In 1608 Isaac's son, Haim Cansino, spent seven months at San Lúcar de Barrameda, on the Andalusian coast, at royal command, as interpreter and adviser to the duke of Medina Sidonia, who was then preparing ships and troops for the planned seizure and occupation of Larache and La Mámora, a pet scheme of the duke of Lerma.

But of all the members of the Cansino family of Oran who held the official post of royal interpreter in Arabic, the most outstanding figure was the Jacob Cansino, known as 'el sabio' (c.1600-1666), who held the interpretership from 1636 to his death in 1666. Given a royal pass for Madrid in 1625, this first visit to the court of Philip IV marked what has been described as the 'beginning of a friendship with Olivares'.[11] He obtained another permit in 1633 which enabled him to surmount his difficulties with the then governor of Oran, the marqués de Flores Dávila, who had imprisoned him briefly and, following the death of his brother, Aaron Cansino, in a cavalry fight with the Moors in 1633, refused to appoint him in his brother's place, as tradition required. Instead, he conferred the post on his rival, Yaho (Jacob) Saportas (or Caportas, or Sasportas) the Younger, who was *xeque* (sheikh), or secular head, of the Jewish Quarter, the figure who officially represented the community in its dealings with the governor, town

9. Ibid.
10. Israel, 'Jews of Spanish North Africa', 72.
11. J.H. Elliott, *The Count-Duke of Olivares: The Statesman in an Age of Decline* (New Haven, CT, 1986), p. 300.

council (*cabildo*), and ecclesiastical authorities.[12] The Council of War at Madrid eventually countermanded Flores Dávila's decision in this matter and, by *cédula* of November 1636, the royal interpretership, and accompanying salary, were transferred from Saportas to Cansino.

However, this suit was clearly not the reason Jacob Cansino resided in Madrid, from 1633 for some five years, living openly as a Jew and with the king's permission, residing for much of this time in the Calle de Olivo, opposite the home of the marqués de Valparaíso. Inevitably, his undisguised presence must have seemed a most bizarre phenomenon in the Spain of that time; it encouraged unfavourable comment and speculation that the Conde-Duque was preparing the ground for the readmission of the Jews to Spain.[13] And it is indeed probable that the question whether some form of readmission was feasible was one of the many topics discussed by Cansino and the Conde-Duque.[14] A clear indication that Olivares took a close interest in Cansino is that the latter was able to publish a book in Madrid, Moses Almosnino's *Grandezas de Constantinopla*, in 1638.[15] Since this publication was the only book published by a professing Jew in Spain before the abolition of the Inquisition it is, by any standard, a most extraordinary occurrence in both Spanish and Jewish history. Although Almosnino's work itself had no relevance to the relationship between Spain and the Jews, the edition was prefaced with a fulsome dedication to Olivares, complete with a full-page engraving, depicting the Conde-Duque sword in hand, slaying the dragon of the monarchy's enemies, followed by an account of the services of the Cansino family on behalf of successive Spanish kings.[16] While it is true that the Cansinos had been continuously in royal service, in Oran and elsewhere, since 1512, it was nevertheless sensational for this fact to be advertised with the support of the king's chief adviser — for without this, it could not have been publicized. Cansino's publication told all the world that the

---

12. Sotomayor y Valenzuela remarks that in 1668 Samuel Sasportas was given the 'xequia de los de su nacion (que es una tacita dignidad de gobernador della en quanto a sus constituciones', Sotomayor y Valenzuela, *Breve Relación*, fol. 11v.
13. Israel, *European Jewry*, pp. 110-12; Y.H. Yerushalmi, *From Spanish Court to Italian Ghetto*, 2nd edn. (Seattle, 1981), p. 167.
14. Israel, 'The Jews of Spanish North Africa', 74-5.
15. *Extremos y Grandezas de Constantinopla compuesto por Rabi Moysen Almosnino* (Madrid, 1638); the title page gives Jacob Cansino as the translator.
16. Yerushalmi, *From Spanish Court to Italian Ghetto*, p. 168; Elliott, *The Count-Duke of Olivares*, p. 301; the account of the Cansino family's services is entitled 'Relación de los servicios de Iacob Cansino y los de su padre'.

Spanish Crown employed Jews, that Philip IV and the Conde-Duque valued their services, and that Jews could expect to be rewarded for loyalty to Spain.[17] Even the required Inquisition license which accompanies the book seems to hint at a change in the relationship between Spain and the Jews, explaining to readers that the work has nothing wrong with it except that its authors belonged to a different faith than 'our holy Catholic religion', but that this was not an objection to reading it since Christians were permitted to read rabbinic authorities as well as pagan authors, including Tacitus 'who speaks so impiously of the Christians'.

It was the death of Jacob Cansino on 19 September 1666, we are told, which produced the situation in Oran which inspired the deliberations that eventually led to the expulsion of the Jews from the town.[18] The messianic frenzy surrounding the figure of Shabbatei Zevi was then at its height and seems not only to have exacerbated the usual tension between Christians and Jews in the *plazas*, but also to have caused serious dissension within the Jewish community itself.[19] One of the consequences of this was that there was stiff opposition to Jacob being succeeded by another Cansino. Unable to agree, the community asked the governor to present the names of three candidates to ministers in Madrid, so that the choice should be made there. It was at this point that the queen regent's advisers asked whether there was any reason that the principal interpretership in Oran should be held by a Jew rather than a Christian, to which Los Vélez had replied that while, originally, there had been a need for Jews as interpreters in the *plazas* this was no longer the case, since many of the Spaniards of Oran were entirely proficient in Arabic.

But the claim that there was no good reason why this enviable position, with a salary equivalent to that of a senior officer in the garrison, should be held by a Jew was not new and clearly contradicted the opinions on this point not only of Los Vélez's predecessors as governor, but also of other prominent Christians resident in Oran. Pedro Cantero Vaca, *vicario general* and head of the Catholic Church in Oran during the years 1631-36, for example, was no friend of the Jews, but was sufficiently objective to admit, in his description of Oran written around 1637, that, while there was also an official Christian interpreter, 'because [the Jews] go into the hinterland and have much more

17. Israel, 'Jews of Spanish North Africa', 75.
18. Sotomayor y Valenzuela, *Breve Relación*, fol 1.
19. Israel, 'Jews of Spanish North Africa', 81.

communication and correspondence with the Moors, they receive more information from them than does the Christian'.[20] Communication between the *plazas* and the countryside around was, indeed, at all times tightly regulated by the governor and garrison and, while the Jews, like the Christians, could only leave and re-enter the plazas with the governor's permission — and although Spaniards did also sometimes travel into the interior with such passes — it is evident that the Jews resident in Oran always had much more contact than the Spaniards with the interior.[21] Even the printed account of the expulsion, while insisting that the Jews were no longer needed, at the same time argued that they posed a danger to the security of the Spanish strongholds precisely because they had so much contact with the Moors and Turks ('por estar tan introducidos con los Moros y Turcos').[22] Moreover, though Muslim traders also entered and left the *plazas* with licenses now and again, they did not reside in them and the Crown made no use of their services, even for minor transactions, as it lacked any hold over them. Apart from slaves, the resident population of Oran consisted only of Christians and Jews. The group of friendly Muslim tribes living around Oran was known as the Banū 'Amir.

The tightly restricted and highly regulated nature of Spanish Oran's intercourse with the surrounding regions of the Barbary coast rendered the royal interpretership and *xequía* of the Jewish quarter positions of appreciable power and responsibility. There were numerous periods of insecurity and rising tension, owing to hostile movements and pressures, especially from the direction of Algiers. One such period of hostilities and tight controls was during the governorship of the marqués de San Román (1652-60), one of whose first steps on taking up his new command was to decree 'as necessary for the royal service and good government of those *plazas* that no Jew should dare leave for Barbary without first obtaining a license from me', stipulating that offenders would be treated as prisoners of war and enslaved ('pena de ser dado por de guerra y tomados por esclavos').[23] Soon after, in December 1652, he decreed that 'all the Jews who are in the *judería* of this city and who are not natives of it should leave for the hinterland within eight days of publication of the order'; non-compliance was to

20. Pedro Cantero Vaca, 'Relación de Oran (c. 1637)', ed. F. Jiménez de Gregorio, in *Hispania: Revista Española de Historia,* 22 (1962), 102.
21. Israel, 'Jews of Spanish North Africa', 73-4.
22. Sotomayor y Valenzuela, *Breve Relación*, fol. 2.
23. BL MS Add. 25682, fol. 10v.

be punished with enslavement, a punishment subsequently amended to six years in the galleys and a fine of 200 *reales*.[24] San Román likewise ordered that 'no Jew from outside and who is not one of the natives of the *judería* of this city shall dare to enter it without my license and permission'.[25]

Such tight regulation only enhanced the roles of the royal interpreter and *xeque*. In May 1654, San Román reviewed the royal license which had been assigned to Yaho (Jacob) Saportas, *xeque* of the *judería*, by the Council of War in Madrid on 24 January 1626, by which the captain-general of Oran at the time and his successors, were directed to 'permit him to correspond with the places of the Turk and Moors of those realms, both because of his services and loyalty and because it is useful to have in those *plazas* a person in whom we have full confidence, who obtains intelligence of what transpires in those parts'. San Román had no hesitation in confirming and reinforcing Saportas' powers in this respect. He determined that 'in consideration of how much, and well, Yaho Saportas has served in those *plazas* with his person and wealth for over 40 years . . . he can freely and securely correspond with the said districts in the same way that he has hitherto, without registering the letters which he sends out, and I hereby order the officers of the gates of this city that letters that arrive for the said Yaho Saportas be handed to him without being examined first by the interpreters, notwithstanding the decrees and instructions which I have issued to the contrary.'[26]

Outgoing and incoming letters were otherwise scrutinized, one of the chief tasks of the Jewish interpreter being to check such correspondence on the governor's behalf. The royal interpreter also had his own network of regular correspondents, 'Moorish confidants' as well as Jews, who sent in *avisos* from Algiers, Tlemcen, and elsewhere, supplying news of political and military developments and movements of Muslim rulers. Periodically San Román would ask Jacob Cansino for an account of recent intelligence which had come in from his confidential correspondents.[27]

A crucial aspect of the interaction between the *plazas* and the surrounding region was the buying of grain for the town's magazines and sometimes also, when grain prices in Barbary were much lower

24. Ibid., fols. 12v-13.
25. Ibid., fol. 13.
26. Ibid., fol. 57.
27. Ibid., fols. 59, 71, orders of 19 June and 18 Dec. 1654.

than in Spain, for the purpose of shipment to Spain. Usually grain was substantially cheaper in North Africa than in the Iberian Peninsula and the purchasing power of Spanish silver was greater, though there were also periods of dearth and severe shortages in Oran. Consequently ministers in Madrid preferred to provide Spanish Oran with ready cash rather than supplies. However, official remittances from Spain frequently arrived late, so that the governors were greatly hindered in arranging grain purchases at the most advantageous time — after the harvest and in the early spring. It was at such moments, and also when there were shortages but was insufficient money in the royal treasury of Oran to effect necessary purchases, that the *xeque*, royal interpreter, and other rich Jews of the town would advance cash, on loan, to the Crown.

The money made available to the captains-general in this way, however, was generally repaid very slowly and sometimes in the form of privileges and commercial concessions rather than cash. Thus, in June 1634, the Council of War in Madrid discussed a memorial from Yaho Saportas who, at that point was both *xeque* and royal interpreter in Oran, referring to sums advanced to the Crown in the early 1620s, during shortages and emergencies ('diferentes ocasiones de necessidades') which had not been reimbursed, asking that the money be repaid from tobacco and other duties on consumer goods collected in Oran.[28] In the following month, Isaac Saportas Cansino petitioned the council about 650 *escudos* he had lent the Crown for the purchase of wheat ten years before, likewise requesting that the money owed to him should be repaid by the usual method, out of returns from customs and duties on consumer goods collected in Oran.[29] Grain was always the most vital item but, at times, certain other products of the hinterland, especially horses for the garrison, were urgently needed. The governors and troops of Oran frequently sallied forth to show the flag and ensure that the name of the Spanish king was feared in the surrounding area, and also to raid and take slaves from hostile localities: for such activity a good supply of horses was essential. In September 1634 Jacob Cansino, described at that point simply as a 'Jew resident in Oran', reminded ministers in Madrid that 'by order of the captains-general of these *plazas,* he had advanced various sums of money at times of emergency to buy horses and other things for the garrison', requesting repayment.[30]

28. The total mentioned was 22,000 *reales;* AGS, Consejo de Guerra 1097, consulta de parte, 19 June 1634 and 28 Aug. 1634.
29. Ibid., consulta de parte, 14 July 1634.
30. Ibid., consulta de parte, 18 Sept. 1634.

But even when cash was available in the royal treasury at Oran, the governors of the *plazas* relied on the city's chief Jewish merchants, and especially the Cansino and Saportas, to make purchases for them from the Banū 'Amir, usually at Canastel or La Zafina de Jafa, for grain could be obtained with a considerable saving if buyers rode out from Oran to these fertile districts in the sierra, some distance away, to purchase at source. Early in 1657, for example, the marqués de San Román signed an order for 600 *reales* in silver to be given to Jacob Cansino 'so that he should use it to buy wheat in the Zafina de Jafa and Amayan at the most advantageous price he can, and as quickly as possible, which he must then bring back and store in the magazines'.[31] A week later, the treasurer was ordered to pay out another 800 *reales*, again to Jacob Cansino, to be used for purchasing grain in La Zafina.[32] Some months later, on 9 December 1657, the marquis ordered 1,800 *reales* in silver to be given to Jacob Cansino for use in buying 200 *fanegas* of barley and 50 of wheat, which, 'on my orders, he goes to purchase at La Zafina de Jafa at the price of twelve *reales* the wheat, and six for the barley, and which he must transport with the greatest possible speed to the royal magazines, with respect to the shortage of grain in which these *plazas* presently find themselves'.[33]

An active figure in these grain-purchasing expeditions was Aaron Cansino, son of Jacob, who petitioned the governor in July 1656 for a paid 'place' among the cavalry of the garrison in recognition of his numerous sorties into the countryside on the orders of the governor, 'to Canastel, the Zafina de Jafa and Hamayan to procure grain in times of urgent shortage', and his having, for this purpose, 'bought a horse at his own expense'.[34] He was duly assigned a 'place' by San Román.

When the governors sallied forth to show their banners, raid hostile localities, and seize Muslims as slaves, they did so accompanied by, and on the basis of information supplied by, a leading figure of the Cansino or Saportas family. Slavery was a central feature of life in the Maghreb and throughout the Islamic world, and it was the policy of the Spanish Crown, in reply to the enslavement of thousands of Christians taken by the Muslims at sea and on land, to enslave hostile Moors captured on sorties made from the *plazas*. Most of these slaves were then sold in Alicante, Cartagena, or Málaga and spent the rest of their

31. BL Add. MS 28440, fol. 132. order of San Román of 8 Feb. 1657.
32. Ibid., fol. 132v, order of San Román of 15 Feb. 1657.
33. Ibid., fol. 145, order of San Román of 9 Dec. 1657.
34. Ibid., fols. 124v-5, order of San Román, 27 July 1656.

days in south-eastern Spain.[35] They were a major source of the profits made by the captains-general of Oran in the performance of their duties. But to carry out slaving raids successfully required skilful preparation and guidance, and this was the task of the Jews. During the early and mid-seventeenth century, successive governors drew up slaving contracts with the head of the Cansinos, or else the Saportas, undertaking to pay a stipulated fee per slave captured, plus four slaves if a hundred or more were taken, in addition to a share in any horses or cattle seized.[36] During the sixteenth century, several members of the Cansino family were wounded or killed in clashes with hostile Moors while, in the seventeenth, Jacob's father, Haim, was shot in the arm, and, in a clash with the Beni-Raxas in 1633, his elder brother Aaron was killed. Isaac ben Haim Cansino, brother of Aaron and Jacob, and perhaps the most accomplished Hebrew poet of seventeenth-century Oran, wrote a funerary poem on his death.[37]

As the principal intermediaries between Spanish Oran and the interior, and a key factor in Oran's slave trade, the Jewish community played a large, and perhaps dominant, part in Oran's seaborne trade which was chiefly with Spain. The products exported from Oran, including the Moorish slaves, were obtained in the hinterland. To pay for their purchases of wax, lead, coloured plumes, and hides, Oran's Jews supplied various European and American products in demand in the Maghreb, and especially silver and tobacco.[38] Since silver was scarce and had a higher value in the Maghreb than in Spain, there was money to be made by exporting silver from the *plazas* to the interior in exchange for the North African commodities in demand in Spain. It was sometimes even claimed that the reason that the rulers of Algiers refrained from making an all-out effort to eliminate the Spanish presence from Oran was that the city was their principal source of silver.[39]

An unusual and exotic ingredient in this traffic were the fine, coloured plumes mainly utilized in Spain for the adorning of hats. 'It has come to my notice', proclaimed San Román, at the outset of his term as governor, 'that in the *judería* of this city are bought and sold

35. Kamen, *Spain in the Later Seventeenth Century*, p. 285.
36. Cantero Vaca, 'Relación de Oran', 107, 111; Israel, 'Jews of Spanish North Africa', 78.
37. *Encyclopaedia Judaica* (Berlin, 1928-34), Vol. V, p. 23.
38. Israel, 'Jews of Spanish North Africa', 76-7.
39. See the report written in 1661 by Diego Fernández de Humada, *vicario general* of Oran, in BL MS Add. 10262, fol. 201v.

many batches of plumes, both processed and unprocessed, which are shipped to Spain without paying the imposts which are due to the king'.[40] To put a stop to this evasion, the marquis ordered both 'Jacob Cansino, interpreter of the Arabic language' and 'Yaho Saportas *entretenido* (*xeque*) of the Jews' jointly to summon 'all those of your nation who are inhabitants of this city' and admonish them in the most rigorous terms that no one should dare buy or sell plumage treated or untreated, to anyone, inhabitant or outsider, without registering the sale with the chief customs officer, on pain of spending six years in the galleys.

Permission to trade with Spain without setting foot there in person required a special royal license which was a highly prized privilege, one of the chief rewards to be obtained by performing services for the Crown. Thus, in August 1656, Isaac Ballestero, 'Jew of Oran, son of Joseph Ballestero, and grandson of Jacob Ballestero', descendants of one of the *siete casas*, citing the many services he claimed he and his forebears had performed on behalf of the Spanish Crown, applied for permission 'to trade with Spain, with the inhabitants of Málaga and other ports, from the city of Oran without leaving it', importing wine, olive oil, brandy, and other permitted goods and exporting wax, hides, slaves and 'other products of the land'.[41] In February 1657 Haim Albo, likewise a descendant of one of the *siete casas,* requested permission to trade with Spain without leaving Oran, such as 'had been done with others of his nation'. It was estimated in 1652 that the plazas of Oran and Mers-el-Kebir annually consumed 4,000 *arrobas* of Spanish wine (1 arroba = 25 lb), 2,400 *arrobas* of olive oil, 1,800 *arrobas* of *aguardiente*, 1,600 *arrobas* of figs, 500 of dried cod, 1,200 *arrobas* of raisins, 400 *arrobas* of rice, and a quantity of sardines.[42]

Among the Spanish merchants with whom Oran's Jews traded in the last years before their expulsion was Don Felipe de Moscoso (1635-86), a son of Yaho Saportas, who converted to Catholicism in the mid-1650s and, after several years in Madrid, around 1660 settled as a merchant in Alicante. The conversion to Christianity of a son of Yaho Saportas seems to have lent added animosity to the traditionally strained relationship between the two principal families of Oran Jewry and would certainly have been a traumatic event in the life of the community, though, interestingly, there does not appear to have been a

---

40. BL MS Add. 28440, fols. 13v-14.
41. BL MS Add. 28442, fol. 41 'En nombre de Isaque Ballestero hebreo, vecino de esas placas', 8 Aug. 1656.
42. BL MS Add. 28440, fol. 27.

complete break between Moscoso and his family. At any rate, whilst in Madrid the convert vociferously sided with the Saportas in the aftermath of a violent affray in the main square of Oran in 1657, in which members of the rival families assailed each other with sticks, a scandal which moved the governor, who had a preference for the Cansinos, to banish several members of the Saportas family — Yaho Saportas the Younger, Muxi Saportas, and the latter's sons, Aaron and Arbi — to the *judería* of Ceuta.[43] For speaking disrespectfully about the governor, Moscoso was expelled from Madrid to Burgos. After establishing himself as a merchant in Alicante, he conducted a lively trade with Oran (where his main correspondent, in the 1660s, was Samuel Saportas), Livorno (where he traded among others with Duarte and Luis de Silva), Lisbon, Genoa, and, before long, London (where his correspondents were the Jewish firm of Jorge and Domingo Rodríguez Francia). At least in the 1660s Oran played an important part in his commercial world. In November 1663, after a visit to Oran, he wrote to a correspondent at Genoa: 'I purchased 26 slave girls and a quantity of wax, lead, and other commodities which have left me with a reasonable profit'.[44] Moorish slave girls, he informed a correspondent at Livorno the following year, were continually being sent to him from Oran.[45] Moscoso continued as an active merchant at Alicante down to his death in 1686, and became one of the principal merchants of the town. He has even been cited by a modern historian as evidence that seventeenth-century Spaniards did not lack zeal and aptitude for commerce, a curious conclusion given that he was raised among the Jews of Oran and never set foot in Spain until he was about twenty.[46]

Converts from Judaism to Christianity in Oran were relatively rare but Moscoso was by no means an isolated case. Indeed, a younger brother, Manuel, apparently also converted and later inherited his estate. On applying to the Council of War for a 'place' among the garrison of Oran in June 1634, Don Antonio Josepe, described as a 'Jew by nation, recently converted, a native of the *plazas* of Oran' ('de nacion hebreo, nuevamente conbertido, natural de las placas de Oran'), claimed that he had been cut off from his family, and reduced to poverty

43. BL MS Add. 28442, fols. 113, 123; on the latter page reference is made to 'D. Phelipe de Moscoso residente en esta corte, recien convertido, hijo de Jacob Caportas'; see also Israel, 'Jews of Spanish North Africa', 80, and Kamen, *Spain in the Later Seventeenth Century*, pp. 140-42, 267, 270-71, 285.
44. Kamen, *Spain in the Later Seventeenth Century*, p. 285.
45. Ibid.
46. Ibid., p. 144.

for the sake of the faith, pointing out that it was customary to concede such a 'place' to Jews who converted to Christianity in Oran.[47] The Council agreed that it behove the king to support 'those who convert to our holy faith', recommending that Josepe be assigned a 'place' in the garrison, paying two *escudos* monthly. During the expulsion of the Jews from Oran, in 1669, only one Jew preferred to convert rather than leave but this one exception, Isaac Cansino, was notable, as he was the older brother of the community's spiritual leader, Rabbi Abraham Cansino.[48] When the rest had departed, he stayed behind in one of the city's friaries to be instructed in the Christian faith.

The tension, social and religious, between Jews and Christians in Oran, as throughout the Mediterranean world, was ubiquitous and constant. The Cansinos and Saportas tried to minimize this tension in so far as they could, but it was always a threat to their community and themselves. There are various references in the sources to donations given by the Jews, and particularly the two leading families, to Oran's churches and friaries, contributions towards ransoming priests captured by the Muslims, and for the saying of prayers for departed Christian friends. Cantero Vaca who, in spite of himself, harboured a certain admiration for Jacob Cansino, tells us that he was assured by him 'many times' that the 'Cansinos had not participated in the crucifixion of Jesus since, at the time, they were living in Toledo',[49] which was also a discreet way of reminding him that there were Jews in Spain before there were Christians. But, in the nature of things, incidents apt to exacerbate sensibilities were continually occurring. Cantero Vaca relates how he himself clashed with Oran's Jews when he tried to convert an elderly Jew who was on his death-bed and from whom other Jews kept him away virtually by force. He alleges that the Jews went so far as to stifle the man before he could convert him, a serious offence which he afterwards brought to the attention of the Inquisition Tribunal of Murcia which had jurisdiction over the *plazas* of Oran.[50]

On the eve of Easter Friday 1663 an incident occurred which caused a riot in Oran. The author of the printed account of the expulsion, Sotomayor y Cuenca (who, in 1655, was described as a *capitan* and senior officer of the garrison),[51] a hostile witness, relates that while

47. AGS, Consejo de Guerra 1097, consulta de parte, Madrid, 18 June 1634.
48. Sotomayor y Valenzuela, *Breve Relación*, fol. 20v.
49. Cantero Vaca, 'Relación de Oran', 98.
50. Ibid.
51. BL MS Add. 28440, fol. 77.

church services were in progress the Jews inside the *judería* (which was then locked and where there were no Christians) put on a mock procession, carrying on their shoulders a Jewish girl called Miriam 'which in our language means Maria', and then threw her in a corner and spat on her, 'declaring that thus, if they could, would they treat the one the Christians call Mother of God' ('la escupieron y oprobieron todos, diziendo tratarían assi a la que los Christianos llamavan Madre de Dios a serles possible').[52] Some soldiers of the garrison, on duty on the walls, allegedly heard this and started the tumult which soon involved the whole body of the town's Christian population. The people wanted to kill the Jews there and then, but were calmed by being told that the Church authorities would investigate everything thoroughly and that those guilty would be exemplarily punished.[53] The subsequent Inquisition investigation accumulated a great mass of paper, but this mountain of 'evidence' led to no action. The Jews imprisoned after this incident were released.

Yet there are reasons for supposing that the normal friction between the three great faiths of the Mediterranean was abnormally acute precisely in the late 1660s, when the expulsion of the Jews from Spanish Oran was decided on and put into effect, and this for two reasons. Firstly, there was the Shabbatian frenzy of 1665-66 which suddenly, albeit briefly, especially infused the Sephardic Jewish communities with intoxicating messianic expectations and a new confidence and boldness which, we learn, frequently resulted in the making of provocative remarks in the presence of Christians, and, in a number of countries, led to something of a Christian backlash.[54] It is also evident that many Christians, although only for a short time, were somewhat taken aback by the transformation of the Jews' demeanour and, in some cases, impressed by their confident messianic predictions. We have no direct references to this in the case of Oran Jewry but we do know that the Jews of Oran, at this point, were fiercely divided,[55] presumably by dissension over Shabbetai Zevi. Also, it seems likely, as I have already suggested, that the rather cryptic passage in Los Vélez's report of May 1669 to the queen regent of Spain, where he writes 'and

52. Sotomayor y Valenzuela, *Breve Relación*, fol. 4.
53. Ibid.
54. Israel, *European Jewry*, pp. 211-12. Hirschberg describes how the Shabbatian frenzy caused a general heightening of tension amongst the Jews of North Africa and, in Morocco at least, also something of an Islamic backlash; see Hirschberg, *A History*, Vol. II, pp. 247-50.
55. Sotomayor y Valenzuela, *Breve Relación*, fol. 1.

it is miraculous that they have not caused the [Christians] to waver in
their faith, for their dominance reached such a point that they were
taken by everyone to be oracles' ('y milagrosamente no les han hecho
prevaricar en la fee, pues llego su dominio a tanto que de todos eran
tenidos por oraculos'),[56] refers to the exceptional atmosphere which
must have prevailed in Oran during the years 1665-66, just before Los
Vélez initiated the moves that eventually led to the expulsion. These
began following the death of Jacob Cansino, a few days after the public
apostasy of Shabbetai Zevi in Turkey, while Los Vélez's main appeal to
the inquisitor-general, and the queen regent's confessor and chief
minister, the Austrian Jesuit Juan Everado Nithard (as he was called in
Spain), to undertake the expulsion of the Jews from Oran, was dated
March 1667, exactly two years before the expulsion itself took place,
and only a few months after the Shabbatian frenzy.[57]

But besides the Shabbatian phenomenon there was also another
reason for the heightened religious tension gripping the Mediterranean
world in the late 1660s: the resumption of the Ottoman offensive to
conquer Crete and eliminate Venetian power (and papal authority) from
the Aegean. The Turks commenced their full-scale siege of the
principal Venetian bastion in Crete, Iráklion, in May 1667, long before
any decision had been taken in Madrid about the fate of the Jews of
Oran. The great siege of Iráklion was to last two and a half years, cost
countless lives, and generate a surprisingly strong and widespread
reaction throughout western and central Europe as well as the
Mediterranean. Throughout the winter of 1668-69, the Papacy launched
a vigorous publicity campaign to mobilize Christian help for Venetian
Crete, pressing Louis XIV, the Emperor Leopold, and the Spanish
Crown to act. Louis sent 6,120 troops under the dukes of Beaufort and
Navailles, many of whom perished and whose efforts accomplished
little. The Pope's call had a less tangible effect, however, in Vienna and
Madrid. It was reported in Rome just a few weeks before the expulsion
from Oran that the Pope, 'having complained', as the *London Gazette*
expressed it, to the French king

> that the Spaniards excused themselves from the assistance which
> the Venetians desired of them upon the pretence of their
> jealousies lest France might create them new troubles at home,

56. AGS Estado 4128, Los Vélez to queen regent, Oran, 5 May 1669, fol. 3; Israel,
    'Jews of Spanish North Africa', 81-2.
57. Sotomayor y Valenzuela, *Breve Relación*, fols. 1, 2v-3.

an express is here arrived in ten days, from Paris, to assure His Holiness that nothing shall be attempted against them for one year, in any part of their dominions, and that His Majesty hath ordered the Duke de Beaufort to embark with 18 men-of-war and 14 galleys [with the troops] who shall go under His Holiness' direction and banner for the relief of Candia (Iráklion).[58]

But Spain, recently humiliated by Louis XIV in the War of Devolution (1667-68), and in deep disarray internally — with Nithard's power collapsing in the face of strong opposition to his person at court and among sections of the Castilian nobility — was unable to undertake anything except send excuses to Rome and Venice. Meanwhile, in many parts of Italy, and on Malta, there was intense anxiety and fear for the future. The Pope publicly went down on his knees, in a succession of special services laid on for the preservation of Iráklion, beseeching the Almighty to intervene.[59] In the circumstances it was universally assumed that the Jews sympathized with the Turks. Indeed, just before the surrender of the Venetian forces in Crete, in September 1669, the Jews of Rome were punished, as was reported in the Dutch press, with a heavy fine for daring to 'laugh behind their hands that Candia is so weakened that it was unable to resist any more', and speaking 'very insolently' about Crete, if also partly for insulting the former Spanish inquisitor-general, the man chiefly responsible for the expulsion of the Jews from Oran, on his arrival, in exile, at Rome.[60]

The decision to expel the Jews from Oran was taken in Madrid more than a year after Los Vélez sent his long letter of March 1667 to Nithard, setting out the case for expulsion.[61] The governor of Oran first heard that at court there had finally been a positive response to his proposal, through a letter of 28 April 1668 from the queen regent, asking how the expulsion could best be put into effect and whether it would be necessary to supplement the garrison for the occasion.[62] By April 1668 Nithard's ascendancy at court was under challenge but was still largely intact, and above all in matters concerning the preservation of the faith he, as inquisitor-general, was the man who made the decisions. The underlying motive for deciding to expel the Jews from

58. *The London Gazette*, No. 347, report from Rome, 2 March 1688 (9).
59. *Hollandsche Mercurius,* 1669, p. 142.
60. Ibid.
61. Sotomayor y Valenzuela, *Breve Relación*, fol. 6v.
62. Ibid.

Oran at this juncture, I would suggest, was that it must have seemed a convenient, easy, and cheap way of bolstering the inquisitor-general's sagging prestige and image among the Spanish public and diverting attention (if only to a degree) from Spain's humiliation in the Low Countries and inability to help Venice against the Turks despite the repeated exhortations of the Pope.

During the following months, ministers in Madrid and the governor of Oran showed frequent signs of apprehension lest the Jews of Oran should discover what was afoot and collude with the Muslim powers of North Africa. In replying to the queen regent's letter of April 1668, Los Vélez stressed three points: the need to take every precaution to keep the Crown's deliberations and preparations secret lest the Jews should get wind of what was about to happen; the need to ship over an extra three to four hundred infantry to assist with the expulsion itself; and, finally, the necessity of ensuring that when they were finally ejected none of the expelled Jews should find their way to Algiers or anywhere else on the Barbary Coast.[63] Both the marquis and the Council of State, in Madrid, regarded it as essential that the entire Jewish community of Oran should be removed from the shores of North Africa, either to Italy or else to Salonica or another Jewish centre in the Levant.

In his account of the expulsion, Sotomayor y Valenzuela entered into a curious discussion about the additional troops sent over from Spain. This reinforcement from Cartagena arrived in Oran in March 1669; their coming was explained in terms of hostile movements among the Moors and Turks. He remarked that 'superficial observers' might suppose that the extra infantry were superfluous and that in dealing with 'people with so little valour and spirit as the Jews the ordinary garrison of the plazas would have sufficed'.[64] But such an assumption, he insisted, would be quite wrong. For had the Jews discovered what was to happen, they, a vengeful people, would have colluded with the Muslims, and had the Moors or Algerian Turks attacked before the expulsion could be put into effect, and the garrison been forced to go out to meet them, 'what defence would there be in the houses of the [Christian] inhabitants where there would be only women and children against enemies seditious, aroused and antagonized to the point of utter desperation?' He regarded it as almost miraculous that the expulsion of the Jews from Oran should have been under deliberation in Spain for more than two years before the event and yet that the Jews of Oran had no inkling of what was to occur.

63. Ibid., fols. 7v-9.
64. Ibid., fol. 14v.

The final decision to expel the Jews of Oran was taken by the Council of State in Madrid in October 1668, during the closing months of Father Nithard's ascendancy.[65] The subsequent delay was principally caused by the length of time it took to bring the extra troops across. Then, on 31 March 1669, to the amazement of Christian, Jew, and Muslim alike, the marquis called out the entire garrison, with the extra troops, in parade formation, drawing up 300 horsemen with numerous banners in the main square. Public buildings were decorated with banners and pennants. The marquis then took his seat at the centre of the square while the queen regent's hitherto secret decree of 31 October 1668, expelling the Jews from Oran, was read out to the assembled populace by the secretary to the municipality. The town's Christians were reportedly overjoyed; the Jews were plunged into utter confusion and despair. They were given eight days in which to sell their immovable assets and settle their affairs.

Various delays ensued, however, and it was not until 16 April that the exodus from the ghetto took place, a sad procession, flanked by soldiers, with the Cansinos at the head of the column. The garrison stood at the alert on the walls and at the shore, where the marquis himself remained virtually the entire day as the 476 Jews of Oran together with their belongings (and a few remaining slaves) were embarked on the large Genoese vessel which had brought the soldiers from Spain. The master was under the strictest instructions not to sail to any North African destination.[66] As the ship sailed away the people applauded and there were salvos of artillery from all the bastions and forts of the *plazas*, followed by a religious procession and *Te Deum* in the cathedral. Los Vélez's subsequent proposal to convert the synagogue into a church to be named after, and dedicated to, the 'Santo Christo de la Paciencia' (after the cult which originated in Madrid, in the 1630s, when a group of Portuguese *conversos* was alleged to have repeatedly whipped an image of Jesus) was approved by the *suprema* of the Inquisition in Madrid in June 1669.[67]

During the fortnight before their departure, there was continuous debate in the ghetto about where the community should go. They had to pay the cost of their own expulsion but could at least choose the

65. AGS Estado 4128, Los Vélez to queen regent, Oran, 5 May 1669, fol. 2; Sotomayor y Valenzuela, *Breve Relación*, fol. 17.
66. Ibid., fol. 2v; here the marquis says the Jews must not be allowed to go to Algiers 'por el daño que podia seguirse a estas plazas'.
67. AGS Estado 4128, queen regent to *Consejo de Estado*, Madrid, 10 June 1669.

destination, provided it was not in North Africa. Finally, they agreed, in the marquis's words, 'that they should be taken to Villa Franca de Niza [Nice], a port belonging to the duke of Savoy where he allows a ghetto for the sake of commerce'.[68] The Dutch newspaper *Hollandsche Mercurius* duly reported in July that a ship had arrived at Villa-Franca 'with 470 Jews who were expelled by the Spaniards from Oran due to suspicion of their conduct; these Jews brought great wealth with them and requested from the duke of Savoy freedom to establish their godless methods of trading at Villa-Franca'.[69]

Already before this event the English consul in Livorno had reported to London that '470 Jews are turned out of Oran on the Barbary Coast out of suspicion they corresponded with Taffilalte' (the region where the hostile Alawite sultan of Morocco was then massing his army).[70] Five weeks later the consul added:

> For of the 470 Jews banish'd from Oran in the African coast . . . all of which came to Villa-Franca, the Duke of Savoy has fix'd all the rich ones in that port and sent away 300 of the poor ones. Those Jews which are full of ready money there have wrote to the Jews in Leghorn [Livorno], telling them of the benigne reception they found from his Highnesse. This letter the Jewes in Leghorn sent to the Great Duke [Grand Duke of Tuscany] which made Count B. write another to them in Leghorn, assuring them that their poor should be received here, and that the said Duke would treat all their nation with more regard than they should meet with from any other prince.[71]

In conclusion, the expulsion of the Jews from Spanish Oran in 1669 took place amid a highly complex situation both in Spain itself and in the wider Mediterranean world. It was arguably both the result of, and

68. Ibid., Los Vélez to queen regent, Oran, 5 May 1669, fol. 2.
69. *Hollandsche Mercurius*, 1669, p. 122.
70. Public Record Office, London SP 98/10, fol. 176, Finch to Arlington, Florence, 7/17 May 1669.
71. Ibid., fol. 232, Finch to Arlington, Florence, 15/25 June 1669; clearly the statement in Toaff that 'quando nel 1669 la comunità di Orano fu finalmente espulsa dagli spagnoli, le 466 persone che la componevano vennero in parte a Livorno, ma non poterono trattenervisi se non in piccolo numero, e continuarono per Nizza e Villafranca, dove il Duca di Savoia fu pronto ad accoglierli' is incorrect; see R. Toaff, *La nazione ebrea a Livorno e a Pisa (1591-1700)* (Florence, 1990), p. 412.

was shaped by, a range of broader Mediterranean factors which, in themselves, had relatively little to do with the traditional role of the Jews in the Spanish North African strongholds or the long-standing friction between Spanish Christianity and the Jews. Especially important, I have suggested, were the Shabbatian frenzy in the Sephardi world of 1665-66, the temporarily heightened tension between the three great faiths of the Mediterranean following the resumption of the Ottoman offensive against Venetian Crete in 1667, and the precarious grip on power in Spain of the Austrian Jesuit, Father Nithard, who was then inquisitor-general and chief minister. It can not be said that the departure of the Jews decisively weakened the Spanish presence in North Africa;[72] for it was not until 1708 that the Turks succeeded in capturing Oran, during the War of the Spanish Succession, while the Spaniards subsequently regained control of the town in 1732 and held it for most of the rest of the eighteenth century, after again expelling its Jewish population. Finally, it is not true, as has been claimed, that 'this tragic little episode . . . rid all Spanish soil of Jews'.[73] After the expulsion from Oran, there were still Jewish communities at Ceuta and Larache. The latter was captured by the Muslims in 1689; the Jews were expelled from the former by the Spanish Crown in 1707.

72. J. de Bakker, *Slaves, Arms and Holy War. Moroccan Policy vis-à-vis the Dutch Republic during the Establishment of the 'Alawi Dynasty (1660-1727)* (Amsterdam, 1991), pp. 173-4, 177, 201.
73. Kamen, *Spain in the Later Seventeenth Century*, p. 307.

VetteKoe van Farao gy moet weeten, Dat gy van de magere künt werden gegeeten

FABEL
van de
Koeyen, de HERDER, en de WOLF.

De Wolf loerende op eenige vette Koeyen, vond sijn toeleg vergeefs, om dat haer Herder so wacker was; hun bloet-dorst en vraet-sucht, och ter, voorkomende een te verleyden, om dat lecker aes, so gebruyckte hy 't Voosjen, door welcke hy de vette en weeligste van allen alsoo sit aenspreecken. Wat baet het u Nichte, dat gy tot de buyck in 't klaver gaet dat uwe uyers gespannen staen, dat gy so veel melck leevert, U Herder sal u leeveren aen een vleeshouwer wanneer hy van u al de melck getrocken heeft, siet gy niet dat hy voor uwe melck, een nieuwe en suiverder staf gekreegen heeft. Wat macht heeft gy voor de byslcekenheyt, van de voordeelen die gy baeren andere opgeeft. Och dat gy wijs waert, gy siet nu uwe eygen sin vreyden en vry willen sijn, dit is immers dat Herders knoeyen, dat so draer, gy nier uwe hoorns toonde, door dick en dun uyt de weyde vloot. Moet hy niet u ontsien? Gy hem met...

Noch meer dan opgeblafen sijnde, en krachtig onder de hand, van de Wolf onderstcount, viel sy haer eygen Herder tegen, sy blies uyt haer neusgaten, sy schoymde in de mond, sy schopte de aarde op met haer klauweren, setter de kop met vlammende oogen tegen de grond en dreygde vervaerelijk met de hoornen, en liep recht tegen den Herder in...

Tot AMSTERDAM, Gedruckt voor Coppen Heertschops in de Spiegel voor de Raesbeeren.

The Fable of the Cows [the seven Dutch provinces], Cowherd [William III], and the Wolf [Louis XIV]. Political caricature by Romeyn de Hooghe (1684).

11

Toleration in Seventeenth-Century Dutch and English Thought

'Freedom', and particularly religious 'freedom', as Dutch writers of the seventeenth and eighteenth century frequently repeat, was at the centre of the aims and values of the Dutch Revolt against Spain. From the very commencement of the opposition to Philip II, in the 1560s, William the Silent and his adherents conceived of their struggle as a fight for the 'freedom' both of fatherland and of the individual, freedom here meaning both liberty of 'body and goods' and liberty of conscience.[1] It was no accident that the Inquisition became, in 1565, the principal target of opposition propaganda against the Habsburg regime. For in the popular mind the Inquisition had come to symbolize, neatly in one body, both Spanish tyranny over life and possessions and the regime's energetic persecution of heresy, whether in propagated form or buried in the private thoughts of the individual. The one and only general principal regarding religion enshrined in the articles of the Union of Utrecht of 1579 was the rule that every individual in the United Provinces should have the benefit of freedom of conscience, and that no-one was to be persecuted on account of his or her religious beliefs, or questioned about them.[2] This indeed was a notable landmark in the history of western civilization and was justly regarded, down to the fall of the Republic in 1795, as one of the pillars of 'Dutch Freedom'.

That a flexible, non-dogmatic and relatively tolerant attitude, infused with Erasmian influence, dominated the culture and attitudes of the civic elite (especially the regents), who led the Revolt and then governed the Republic, has often been emphasized by modern historians, and was clearly perceived by Dutch observers in the seventeenth century. Hugo Grotius, in one of his key political writings, his *Verantwoordingh* (or *Apology*) of 1622, insisted that, while William the Silent and the regents who supported him were no less convinced than the Reformed clergy of the need for a 'Reformation' to sweep away the 'superstition' and abuses fostered by the Catholic Church, the Reformation which the regents adopted contrasted sharply with that of the Reformed clergy, the former being as flexible, tolerant, and non-dogmatic as the latter's was rigid

---

[1] Martin van Gelderen, 'Machiavellian Moment and the Dutch Revolt: the Rise of Neostoicism and Dutch Republicanism', *Machiavelli and Republicanism* (ed. G. Bock, Q. Skinner, & M. Viroli, Cambirdge, 1990), p. 218.

[2] *Texts concerning the Revolt of the Netherlands* (ed. E.H. Kossmann & A.F. Mellink, Cambridge, 1974), pp. 169–70.

and unyielding. Grotius saw the 'Reformation' of the regents as rooted in the accommodating, irenic religious philosophy of Erasmus of Rotterdam, 'who was always very much inclined towards peace and accommodation'.[3]

No participant in Dutch intellectual debate during the Golden Age, not even the most hard-line Calvinists, ever disputed that liberty of conscience for the individual was an acknowledged and principal goal of the Revolt and pillar of the Dutch 'state' (as contemporaries called it) based on the Union of Utrecht. In view of this, it has often been supposed that the Dutch Republic in the seventeenth century represented an altogether exceptional phenomenon in Europe. It has been assumed that the success of the Revolt against Spain meant that the battle for toleration in the northern Netherlands was won, at least from the practical point of view, and that there was consequently neither a need for, nor any particular interest among the Dutch in analysing and debating the philosophical and theological principles and implications of toleration.[4] Dutch historians themselves have frequently assumed that the seventeenth-century debate about toleration in the United Provinces — insofar as it existed — was of little importance in the general European intellectual debate, and that developments in England before the Civil War, during the interregnum, and thereafter, were of far greater general historical significance in this connection.[5] But is it really true that a *de facto* toleration was already in place in the United Provinces by the end of the sixteenth century? Is it the case that, as a consequence, while the Dutch Republic might sometimes be held up as an example of the benefits of toleration, as English writers such as Henry Robinson were already doing by the early 1640s,[6] the English debate about toleration in the age before Locke and Bayle was the main one, and that the Dutch intellectual debate about toleration was largely or altogether marginal? I believe there are grounds for answering in the negative. Indeed, it will be argued here that both Dutch and English historians have greatly underestimated the significance of the Dutch debate before Locke for the intellectual development of both countries.

The concession of freedom of conscience to the individual is not the same thing as allowing freedom of public practice to faiths other than that of the state or public Church in an early modern state; indeed it may be far removed from it. Nor does freedom of conscience necessarily or even probably imply the freedom to discuss, let alone question, the doctrines of the established state, or public, Church. Dutch historians traditionally have great difficulty in conceding that the Dutch Reformed Church was a 'state Church', but, for the purposes of the present argument, the terminology is not critical. The point is that it

---

[3] H. Grotius, *Verantwoordingh van de wettelicke regieringh van Hollandt* ([Paris], 1622) pp. 29–32.

[4] See E.H. Kossmann, 'Freedom in Seventeenth-Century Dutch Thought and Practice', in *The Anglo-Dutch Moment. Essays on the Glorious Revolution and its World Impact* (ed. J.I. Israel, Cambridge, 1991), p. 282.

[5] *Ibid.*; and H.R. Guggisberg, 'Veranderingen in de argumenten voor religieuze tolerantie en godsdienstvrijheid in de zestiende en zeventiende eeuw', *Bijdragen en Mededelingen betreffende de Geschiedenis der Nederlanden*, XCI (1976), pp. 177–87.

[6] *Ibid.*, p. 190.

was the public Church in all seven provinces, and the public Church of the Union, its supremacy was acknowledged and total. It was the only Dutch church which was officially protected and financed by the provincial and civic governments as well as the federal government, and, by the 1590s, it was the only church which was officially and generally allowed to hold divine service in churches and for substantial gatherings of people. The Holland regents who stood at the helm of the new Dutch state may have been of Erasmian disposition, as Grotius claimed, and basically tolerant. Certainly they were committed to upholding the principle of liberty of conscience for the individual in the privacy of that individual's mind and home. But they were also determined to keep almost all places where religious services were held in the hands of the Reformed Church and, from 1573 onwards, to suppress the public practice of the Catholic religion. By the 1590s the Catholics in the United Provinces had been stripped by the provincial and civic governments of all the churches, chapels, cloisters and other formal places of worship which they had previously possessed, and they did not recover any of these until after the fall of the Republic. Neither Catholics, nor Lutherans, nor members of any other alternative church were allowed to challenge publicly, or even debate, the doctrines of the Dutch Reformed Church.

Whatever people thought of the public Church (and the authorities were well aware that only a minority of the population were well disposed towards it at the end of the sixteenth century), the non-Reformed majority were asked to keep their dissenting opinions to themselves, if not for the sake of their own salvation then for the good of the state and society. Outward religious conformity, or at least silence, was regarded by the political authorities as so necessary to the well-being of society and to the survival of the state in its struggle against Spain, that toleration in its seventeenth-century sense was generally rejected as a viable possibility. The conventional attitude of the Dutch political elite, however elastic and Erasmian their vision of the Reformation, was that open religious dissent was to be discouraged. It was a wordly attitude which was relatively tolerant by the standards of the time, but which was not conducive to the onset of full religious and intellectual toleration.

The conventional attitude of the Dutch political leadership at the close of the sixteenth century was summed up by the Flemish immigrant Simon Stevin in his book *Het Burgherlick Leven* (1590), where he urged those citizens of the United Provinces who privately did not accept the teachings of the Reformed Church to recognize it as their obligation, and as their own interest, to conform outwardly.[7] This was partly for moral and educational reasons, for if the authority of the public Church is undermined, or seen not to be respected, then children will not be in awe of the Church and will grow up without discipline, morality, and respect. But it was also for political reasons, to curb internal dissension. He argues that the pious individual who rejects the theology of the public Church and insists on the practice of another religion should move to another state

[7] Simon Stevin, *Het burgherlick leven* [1590] (Amsterdam, 1939), pp. 49–56.

where his own religion *is* that of the State Church. If the individual, for whatever reasons, does not move, then it his clear duty to conform outwardly and not to criticize the established Church.

The tolerationist philosophy of Justus Lipsius, the foremost political thinker of the Low Countries of the late sixteenth century, however erudite and intellectually sophisticated, was in essence rather conventional. The upholding of private religious freedom is one of the central motivations of Lipsius's thought.[8] But rather like Bodin, Lipsius saw in the strong absolutist prince the best chance of achieving social and political stability which to his mind was the *sine qua non* of the inner freedom of the individual. Lipsius's philosophy of spiritual and intellectual freedom clearly shows how distinct, even opposed in the late sixteenth-century Dutch context, were the ideals of liberty of conscience and full toleration. Lipsius rejected toleration, seeing it as incompatible with political stability and therefore destructive of liberty of conscience.

The great Dutch champion of full toleration during the period of the Revolt, Dirck Volkertsz. Coornhert, clashed bitterly with Lipsius, who regarded Coornhert's call for outward religious freedom as tantamount to calling for the destruction of both society and the state.[9] But if Lipsius abhorred Coornhert's philosophy of toleration, the Holland regents liked it scarcely any better. Coornhert argued, as seventeenth-century tolerationists were to do after him, that freedom of conscience both implies and necessarily involves freedom of practice as well. But it was precisely this point which made him such an isolated figure in the Dutch cultural milieu of his time despite his familiarity with regent circles and his great debt to Erasmus. Coornhert was a great man and, in many ways, representative of his time and place. Nevertheless, his thought, and especially his ideas on toleration, remained marginal in the sense that they were generally rejected by the Dutch political and intellectual elites of his time, and for decades remained discredited. In 1579 the States of Holland officially condemned him as a 'disturber of the public peace' or 'rustverstoorder'.

It is clear then that the intellectual battle for toleration had by no means been won in the United Provinces at the commencement of the seventeenth century. Indeed, Dutch society around 1600 cannot be said to have been particularly conducive to the spread of ideas of toleration. When in 1608 the Spanish negotiators at the truce talks in The Hague switched from seeking Dutch evacuation of the Indies to pressing for a limited but formal toleration of Roman Catholicism in the Republic as their main condition for a truce, in the form of one Catholic church in each main town, the response of Oldenbarnevelt and the Holland regents was sharply negative.[10] In 1612 the Jews of Amsterdam

---

[8] Gerhard Guldner, *Das Toleranz-Problem in den Niederlanden im Ausgang des 16. Jahr-hunderts* (Lübeck, 1968), pp. 96, 107–12; J. Kluyskens, 'De klassieke oudheid, propaedeuse van het Christendom: het streven van Justus Lipsius', in *Liber Amicorum Leon Voet* (ed. F. de Nave, Antwerp, 1985), pp. 434–7.

[9] H. Bonger, *De motivering van de godsdienstvrijheid bij Dirck Volkertszoon Coornhert* (Arnhem, 1954), pp. 13, 23–6, 81.

[10] J.I. Israel, *The Dutch Republic and the Hispanic World, 1606–1661* (Oxford, 1982), p. 11.

tried to build a public synagogue, but the Dutch Reformed Church in the city succeeded in persuading the city council to prevent them.[11] The public exercise of the Jewish religion, like the Catholic, was still forbidden throughout the Republic. Nor had the Lutherans yet convincingly crossed the threshold from private to public practice.[12] But there was little in the way of protest against, or discussion of, the situation. It was only with the onset of the great struggle between the Arminians and Counter-Remonstrants within the Reformed Church, and especially after the national Synod of Dordt (1618–19), that the real intellectual debate about toleration in the Dutch Republic commenced. Nor, once it began, was it a debate easily won. Even though a crucial shift towards toleration in the prevailing political and ecclesiastical situation was achieved in the 1630s, the debate nevertheless remained very much alive, just as it did in England, right down to the beginning of the eighteenth century.

I shall argue that there were two main intellectual impulses, or traditions of tolerationist thought in the seventeenth-century Dutch context. The first, preceding the other in time, and more theological in character, I shall call the Arminian tolerationist tradition, even though its real founder, and principal intellectual exponent, was not in fact Arminius but Simon Episcopius. Episcopius is a figure whose contribution to the debate about toleration has been consistently underrated since the eighteenth century, no doubt in part owing to the grudging manner in which (in common with so many other intellectual heroes of the seventeenth century) Bayle dismisses him in his great *Dictionnaire Historique*. Bayle conceded that Episcopius was 'un des plus habiles hommes du XVII siècle, et la principale colonne de la secte des Arminiens', but despite his own intense commitment to the cause of toleration, he has nothing more to say about Episcopius's contribution in this sphere other than that he 'ne guarda pas toujours la modération de style que ses principes de tolerance, joints aux devoirs évangéliques, exigeoient de lui d'une façon spéciale'.[13] Nonetheless, his importance in both the Dutch and the English contexts, as an intellectual proponent of toleration, was very substantial. The second intellectual tradition, more secular in character, I shall call the 'republican' tradition. It was to this stream of tolerationist thought that the De la Court brothers and Spinoza belonged. Both of the main impulses within the Dutch tolerationist tradition of thought have notable links and parallels with the seventeenth-century English context. For in England too there were several different tolerationist traditions of thought, two main streams of which can be termed the 'Arminian' and the 'republican'. The English 'Arminian' tolerationist tradition was, again, largely theological in inspiration and grew, at least in part, out of the Dutch Arminian tradition. The English 'republican' tradition, by contrast, owed less to Dutch

---

[11] J.I. Israel, *European Jewry in the Age of Mercantilism, 1550–1750* (Oxford, 1985), pp. 63–4.

[12] J. Loosjes, *Geschiedenis der Luthersche kerk in de Nederlanden* (The Hague, 1921), pp. 87–8, 100, 109.

[13] Pierre Bayle, *Dictionnaire historique et critique* (4 vols, Rotterdam, 1720) vol. II, pp. 1086–7.

intellectual influence, but was nevertheless remarkably similar to the Dutch 'republican' tradition in character and content.

Arminius himself, like Johannes Uyttenbogaert, the effective leader of the Arminian party within the Dutch Reformed Church during the crisis of the Twelve Years Truce period, was certainly of tolerant, indeed markedly irenic disposition, and believed firmly in dialogue between the churches. Like Episcopius later, Arminius distinguished between the relatively few fundamentals of Christian belief and the large number of subsidiary points over which, in his view, it was not necessary to insist on conformity. Arminius disliked the dogmatic rigidity of his hardline Calvinist opponents, urging flexibility and, within given limits, the accommodation of different views within the Dutch Reformed Church. It is by no means surprising, consequently, that the Arminians enjoyed from the beginning the tacit — and sometimes the not-so-tacit — support of many Mennonites, Lutherans and Catholics who resented the lack of freedom which they encountered in the early seventeenth-century Dutch Republic. The great poet Vondel, himself from a Mennonite background (though, later, he became a Catholic) mercilessly ridiculed Counter-Remonstrant intolerance and dogmatism in a series of anonymously circulated controversial poems.

Yet neither Arminius, nor Uyttenbogaert, nor any Arminian leader, during the period down to 1618, tried to construct a general theory of toleration or argued for a general toleration on principle. Oldenbarnevelt, Grotius, and the liberal Holland regents who were in power down to 1618, and who backed the Remonstrants, showed little inclination, however flexible their theological notions, to relax the general policy, in force since the 1570s, with regard to Catholics, Lutherans, Jews and others, more than marginally and on a *de facto* basis. Indeed, as Counter-Remonstrant critics of the Oldenbarnevelt regime pointed out, when it came to stifling separatist tendencies within the public Church, for example by refusing to allow the orthodox Calvinists to hold separate conventicles in towns where all the public churches and preachers belonged to the Arminian persuasion, they were actively intolerant. When a group of orthodox Calvinists at Gouda tried to establish their own services, and bring in a Counter-Remonstrant preacher to the town in 1614, the leaders of this initiative were punished by the pro-Remonstrant town council with fines and, in some cases, with banishment from the town.[14] When in the 1620s, under the leadership of Episcopius and Uyttenbogaert, the Dutch Arminians became advocates of toleration in the full sense, they were (not entirely without justification) accused by their opponents of inconsistency, opportunism, and hypocrisy.[15]

The Dutch Arminians shifted their position as a result of their defeat in 1618 and their subsequent bitter experiences. It was in the later 1620s that they made

---

[14] J.E.J. Geselschap, *Zeven eeuwen stad. Hoofdstukken uit de geschiedenis van Gouda* (Gouda, 1972), p. 306.

[15] Cornelius Dunganus, *Den vreedsamen christen, voorghestelt in een christelijke ende zedige aensprake aen den Remonstranten, over haren vryen godesdienst* (Utrecht, 1628), p. 9; Henricus Arnoldi, *Vande conscientie-dwangh* (Delft, 1629), pp. 8, 20.

their major contribution to the debate about toleration in an outburst of books and publications by Episcopius, Uyttenbogaert, Paschier de Fijne and also Grotius in his *De Veritate Religionis Christianae* of 1627. Grotius I shall interpret here as a giant bridging-figure linking the Arminian and republican traditions. Most of these works of the late 1620s were in fact published in Dutch rather than Latin, and clearly reveal their authors' purpose of seeking to sway the Dutch public. Yet, though closely linked to political circumstances, the shift represented by these publications cannot be described as mere intellectual opportunism. The traumatic confrontations, theological and political, of recent years, and their expulsion and exile were all bound to have a profound effect on the Remonstrant leadership. After the Synod of Dordt the bitter repression continued until the death of Prince Maurits in 1625. The hardships of these years were inevitably a decisive experience in the lives of all the Arminian intellectual luminaries. Thus the decisive shift in the Dutch debate about toleration took place within a short space of time, in very specific political circumstances. But it also achieved a profound, lasting change. As Grotius maintained, its origins reached back through the sixteenth century, ultimately to Erasmus.

Whilst Maurits lived, the Arminian leadership remained abroad. They could publish in the Republic only clandestinely, and at some risk to those involved, and Remonstrant religious conventicles in the Republic had to be furtive. Remonstrant preaching within the United Provinces was forbidden, and the Counter-Remonstrant civic regimes which Maurits had installed in 1618 throughout Holland, Utrecht, and in those Gelderland and Overijssel towns which had been pro-Remonstrant, were able to use the military, with the Stadtholder's permission, to suppress Remonstrant conventicles. Between 1618 and 1625 official religious and intellectual intolerance was extended also in other ways. This was especially the case with respect to Lutherans and Jews. Until the Synod of Dordt, there had always been a strong moderate block of the Dutch Reformed Church, as well as elements amongst the country's political leadership, eager to avoid a situation of out-and-out confrontation with the Lutheran Churches of Germany and Scandinavia, and which hoped that dialogue and ultimately even some form of reconciliation might be possible. Even at the commencement of the Synod of Dordt, before the formal expulsion of the Remonstrants, there was still talk of dialogue and exploring the possibilities for reconciliation, if not with the more orthodox Lutherans (the *rigidi*), then with the moderate party (*molliores*).[16] But by condemning and expelling the Arminians, the Counter-Remonstrants by the same token destroyed all chance of dialogue with the Lutherans, whose doctrine on will and salvation was much closer to that of Arminius than to that of orthodox Calvinism. Philippus van Limborch was later to refer to the breaking off of dialogue with the Lutherans as one of the most disastrous consequences of the Synod of Dordt both for the

---

[16] *Golden Remains, of the Ever Memorable Mr. John Hales, of Eaton-Colledge* (second edition, London, 1673), p. 66.

Dutch Reformed Church and for the Protestant world in general.[17] The German Lutheran Churches became more hostile to the Dutch Reformed Church
than hitherto, seeing it now as irredeemably hard-line Calvinist, while the Dutch
Reformed Church synods now sought to combat Lutheran activity more effectively within the United Provinces. The States of Holland were not prepared
to go as far in this direction as the Reformed Church urged but, in 1621, while
considering complaints about new Lutheran congregations being formed at
The Hague, Gouda, Bodegraven, Breda and elsewhere, the States did decree
that in all places where Lutheran worship had not previously been permitted it
would not henceforth be allowed, thereby effectively banning Lutheranism from
the countryside and most of the towns.[18] During these years successive Dutch
Reformed provincial synods also debated how to prevent the spread of Jewish
worship and enforce the ban on public synagogues.[19]

In the wake of Prince Maurits's death, however, the situation was rapidly
transformed. The new stadtholder, Frederick Henry (1625–47), a former pupil
and friend of Uyttenbogaert and a man of moderate disposition, had always
been neutral in theological matters and had distanced himself from the open
partisanship of his brother on behalf of the Counter-Remonstrant cause. While
reassuring the Counter-Remonstrants that he would adhere to the decisions of
the Synod of Dordt, he also, behind the scenes, took steps to end the persecution of the Remonstrants or at any rate mitigate it. Over the next two or three
years, most towns in Holland ceased their attempts to suppress Remonstrant
conventicles and clandestine preaching, especially after the disturbance at
Schoonhoven, in April 1627, following which the new Prince of Orange issued
orders that garrison commanders must not in future respond to requests from
burgomasters and town councils for troops to break up religious conventicles.[20]
The military were to support the town councils only in cases of serious disorder.
There was no general amnesty for those Remonstrants who were in exile, or in
prison, but gradually the pressure which kept them in exile, or behind bars,
eased. Although Grotius was an exception, and was not permitted to return,
the leading Arminian preachers were able to resume their public careers, albeit
along new lines, in the Republic. Episcopius returned to Holland from France,
in July 1626, as did Uyttenbogaert a few months later.[21]

With the civil authorities withdrawing from the fray, the Dutch Reformed
synods had now to come out into the open with theological and political arguments as to why the Remonstrants should not now be allowed to organize as a

[17] Philippus van Limborch, 'Voor-reden' to John Hales and Walter Balcanqual, *Korte Historie
van het Synode van Dordrecht* (The Hague, 1671), pp. 5–6.

[18] *Acta der Particuliere Synoden van Zuid-Holland, 1621–1700* vol. I (1621–33) (ed. W.P.C. Knuttel,
The Hague, 1908), pp. 6, 110.

[19] *Ibid.*, pp. 1, 75, 103–4.

[20] J.I. Israel, 'Frederick Henry and the Dutch Political Factions, 1625–1642', *The English Historical Review*, XCVIII (1983), pp. 7–8.

[21] Philippus van Limborch, *Leven van Simon Episcopius* [bound together with Simon Episcopius,
Predicatien] (3 vols, Amsterdam, 1693), vol. I, p. 133.-

separate church on the same basis as the Mennonites and (where permitted) the Lutherans. The Remonstrants petitioned the States of Holland for permission to gather and preach and launched a general intellectual and publicity campaign to persuade the public, and the regents, of the desirability of religious toleration on principle. A Counter-Remonstrant counter-campaign, arguing against toleration often in terms strikingly similar to those used by Roger L'Estrange, Thomas Tomkins, and Richard Perrinchief in attacking pro-toleration arguments in England during the Restoration period, was whipped up in the years 1627–30 by leading orthodox spokesmen such as Henricus Rosaeus at The Hague, Jacobus Trigland and Adriaen Smoutius at Amsterdam, and, most notable of all as far as the intellectual debate is concerned, Henricus Arnoldi of Delft.[22]

The South Holland synod submitted its remonstrance to the States of Holland, urging them to reject the Arminians' plea for freedom of practice, in July 1628. This text, drawn up by Arnoldi, denounces Remonstrant worship as both theologically and politically subversive since it encourages the spread of dangerously heretical, and especially Pelagian and Socinian, ideas.[23] The text cites a list of places where Remonstrant preaching had allegedly caused serious tension and turmoil, including not only major towns such as Rotterdam, Gouda and Delft, but also villages such as Hazerswoude, Oegstgeest and Warmond. The remonstrance also makes the general claim that toleration in the United Provinces had gone too far, giving dissenters too much freedom, and that it should be cut back.[24]

Arnoldi set out his arguments most systematically in his important tract *Vande conscientie-dwangh*, published at Delft in 1629. What is most remarkable here is that Arnoldi bases his doctrine of intolerance precisely on the principles of freedom enshrined in the Dutch Revolt and the articles of the Union of Utrecht. He insists, not unlike Rogert L'Estrange in 1663, that the suppression of freedom of practice, and with it freedom to publish, does not conflict with the upholding of freedom of conscience and, in a way, he was right. He pointed out that although Dutch Catholics had not been allowed freedom of practice since the commencement of the Revolt, they had not (and were not now) protesting that freedom of conscience and the articles of the Union of Utrecht were being infringed.[25] Another of Arnoldi's main points is that the States had never officially sanctioned the 'free exercise of their pretended religion to the Lutherans, or Mennonites, much less to the godless Jews, in these lands, but that their holding services in some places happens as a result of the civil authorities turning a blind eye'.[26] All church services taking place in the United Provinces,

[22] Philippus van Limborch, *Leven van Simon Episcopius* [bound together with Simon Episcopius, *Predicatien*] (3 vols, Amsterdam, 1693), vol. I, p. 133.

[23] *Acta* (ed. Knuttel), vol. I, pp. 239–45.

[24] *Ibid.*, pp. 1, 251.

[25] Arnoldi, *Vande conscientie-dwangh*, p. 20.

[26] *Ibid.*, p. 93.

in other words, other than those of the Dutch Reformed Church, were the result of connivance by the authorities and had no basis in the principles of the Revolt or in law. He adds that while toleration of Jews is damaging to a Christian society, 'since they insult the name of Christ', clearly implying that they should not be tolerated anywhere, Mennonites and Lutherans could be, and were, tolerated in some towns 'as long as they keep silent and do not concern themselves with politics or the public Church and avoid all conspiracy against the state of these [United] provinces'.[27]

Arnoldi deplored the doctrine of religious toleration expounded by Episcopius as something radically new on the Dutch scene, and something thoroughly subversive, insisting that the Arminians derived it not from 'God's Word, or out of Scripture . . . but from the books of Dierick Volckertsz. Corenhart [sic]',[28] in Arnoldi's day still a damning indictment. He also ridicules the Remonstrants' habit of citing Poland under King Stephen Bathory as a model of how beneficially and harmoniously a plurality of churches could co-exist, pointing out that Poland was a land of ceaseless religious strife and chaos.[29] Above all he derides Episcopius and Uyttenbogaert for having reversed their earlier, pre-1618 position on toleration.

It was especially Episcopius who spelt out the new doctrine. Uyttenbogaert and other Arminian writers in their publications of these years tended in the same direction but never quite reached as far as the Amsterdammer in setting out a clear, systematic and comprehensive theory of toleration. The dogged Remonstrant preacher, Paschier de Fijne, for example, who had continued preaching clandestinely in Holland throughout the years 1619–25, once escaping from Gouda, at the conclusion of a sermon, on a horse-drawn sledge along an iced-over canal, in several tracts vehemently denounced the intolerance and 'Calvinistic fury' of the Counter-Remonstrants, broadening this into a general attack on religious persecution of all kinds.[30] Religious persecution, he argues, is destructive of both human freedom and economic prosperity. He blamed the deep economic depression gripping Holland over the previous few years (in fact since 1621) on the intolerance of the Counter-Remonstrants, which had forced many Remonstrants, in all walks of life, to leave the country.[31] He also laments the loss of personal freedom: 'Since the Lord has released us from the Spanish yoke', he urges his countrymen, 'let us not burden each other with a Genevan yoke.'[32] Yet for all the fervour of Paschier's polemics against Calvinist intolerance, he does not set out systematically the arguments for a broad-based comprehensive religious toleration. He is pleading for freedom of practice:

---

[27] *Ibid.*, p. 94.

[28] *Ibid.*, p. 28.

[29] *Ibid.*, pp. 47–8.

[30] See, in particular, *Een broederlicke vermaninge* (1624), *Silvere naalde* (1624), and *Silvere vergulde naelde* (1625), in *Enige trataetjes van Paschier de Fyne, in syn leven predikant tot Haerlem* (2 vols, Amsterdam, 1735–6).

[31] De Fijne, *Broederlicke vermaninge in Eenige tractaetjes*, vol. II, pp. A2–5.

[32] *Ibid.*, vol. II, *Silvere naalde*, p. C2.

'what could be securer for the state and the prosperity of the land than that every inhabitant should be allowed the free exercise of his religion?'[33] But in arguing for toleration he tends to blur the distinction between freedom of conscience and freedom of practice and fails to discuss the position of the other dissenting churches.

The difference between Episcopius in writings such as his key tract *Vrye godesdienst* of 1627 (and subsequent writings), and Paschier de Fijne, or Uyttenbogaert, is that Episcopius derives his toleration plea clearly and systematically from his theology, above all from his doctrine that all Christians largely agree on the essentials and disagree in the main about inessentials. He therefore feels driven to be consistent in arguing for a comprehensive toleration, including freedom of expression as well as practice, for all churches.[34] The differences between various individuals' interpretations of Scripture he elevates into a good rather than dismissing it, like Arnoldi, as a plague, or ignoring the problem like most of the others.

Episcopius in his *Vrije godesdienst* strives to persuade his readers that public practice not only of the Remonstrant but of all faiths, far from being harmful to society, the state, or indeed religion itself, can only be beneficial. He couches his booklet in the form of a dialogue between a Remonstrant and Counter-Remonstrant, evoking echoes of the innumerable debates that had gone on in the Dutch universities, schools, taverns and town halls for two decades. The toleration he argues for is not only the freedom of practice for each church but also freedom from all doctrinal or intellectual coercion within each church. One of Episcopius's central propositions is that no human conscience is above another, or can be judge of another.[35] All have equal access to Scripture and to interpreting God's word. Like Paschier de Fijne, and Uyttenbogaert after 1619.[36] Episcopius argues that allowing a plurality of churches and upholding freedom of practice, far from destabilizing society, gives rise to a calmer and more stable society. But he also develops the point that any attempt to suppress dissent within churches and keep public expression of views (and the printing press), in the hands of those who merely reiterate official dogma, so as keep each church's teaching pure, is not a benefit but a disaster for religion.[37] Persecution and dogmatism are wrong not just because they cause resentment and tension, harm society and the economy, and destabilize the state, but even more because they stifle true debate about God's truth and reduce individuals to unthinking ciphers

---

[33] Paschier de Fijne, *Silvere vergulde naelde* (s.l., 1625), p. B.

[34] Philippus van Limborch, 'Voorreden' to Simon Episcopius, *Predicatien* (3 vols, Amsterdam, 1693) vol. I, pp. 2–4.

[35] [Simon Episcopius,] *Vrije godesdienst* (s.l., 1627) [Knuttel 3753], p. 43; [Simon Episcopius?,] *Verdediging van de confessie der Remonstraten* (s.l., 1627) [Knuttel 3770], p. 69.

[36] See for instance J. Uyttenbogaert, *Ondersoek der Amsterdamsche requesten tot verdedigingh der onschuldighe ende onder-rechtingh der misleyde* (s.l., 1628).

[37] Episcopius, *Vrye godesdienst*, pp. 36–7.

or, worse, to hypocrites who in their hearts accept nothing of what they profess to believe.[38]

Far from weakening the state as the Counter-Remonstrants claim, toleration (urged Episcopius) will also strengthen the state. Those states are securest and happiest where both individual conscience and religious practice are free. For in such a society no-one harbours deep-seated resentment against the state: the more churches and — within each church — the more points of view that are allowed, the less the fear, tension, and danger. Each faith holds the next in balance. Where religious freedom is suppressed, individuals lack patriotism and have no wish to support the state. It is only 'free minds and hearts that are willing to support the common interest'.[39] Seeing where this leads him, Episcopius takes the bull by the horns and makes his most controversial contention: he says that he sees no difficulty in allowing the free exercise of the Roman Catholic faith provided the 'Papists declare that they will conduct themselves as true and upright subjects according to the laws and decrees of the country', and also take an oath to this effect before a local magistrate 'with express renunciation of all those maxims which would dispense them from such an oath'.[40] Needless to say, no feature of Episcopius's toleration aroused the indignation of Arnoldi and his colleagues more than this.[41]

Episcopius's doctrine of toleration marks a step beyond that of the other Arminian writers in the period down to 1630. But subsequently his teaching took root and became integral in the outlook and published work of later Arminian leaders, especially Stephen Curcellaeus, who succeeded Episcopius in his chair at the Remonstrant Academy set up in 1634 at Amsterdam, and Philippus van Limborch, who was the son of Gertrude Episcopius, a niece of Episcopius, and who, through his parents, inherited a large part of Episcopius's papers.[42] Moreover, Episcopius's theologically based doctrine of toleration came to exert a measure of influence in academic circles in England, both in the Tew group in Oxford and, if Gilbert Burnet is to be believed, still more with the Cambridge Platonists.[43]

Of the writers who forged Dutch toleration doctrine in the 1620s, the one name which carried more weight in England than that of Episcopius was of course that of Grotius. There is indeed much in Grotius's *oeuvre* of the 1620s which parallels the writings of the Arminian religious leadership. There is in Grotius's *De Veritate Religionis Christianae* (1627) the same impulse towards a transcendent Christian truth over and above all denominational differences.

---

[38] *Ibid.*

[39] *Ibid.*, p. 37.

[40] *Ibid.*, p. 44.

[41] Arnoldi, *Vande conscientie-dwang*, p. 35; [Simon Episcopius?,] *Voorstant vande vryheyt der conscientie teghen den conscientie-dwang van Henricus Arnoldi van der Linden, predicant tot Delft* (s.1. 1630), p. 26.

[42] Jean Leclerc, *A Funeral Oration upon the Death of Mr Philip Limbroch, Professor of Divinity among the Remonstrants at Amsterdam* (London, 1713), pp. 8–10.-

[43] According to Burnet, 'they read Episcopius much'; quoted in A.A. Seaton, *The Theory of Toleration under the Later Stuarts* (Cambridge, 1911) p. 65.

There is also the same combination of high intellectual sophistication, the appeal to the most profound and learned, alongside the appeal to the common man who understands only Dutch. Indeed, *De Veritate* originally appeared in 1622 in a simpler, Dutch, rhymed version intended for the religious edification of mariners and other common folk. Grotius played a large part in generating the great cultural shift which took place in the United Provinces in the years around 1630. Grotius did not, however, join Episcopius in developing a comprehensive doctrine of toleration. While generally his writings stressed the vital importance of freedom of conscience, he is remarkably reticent on freedom of practice and expression. No doubt this was largely because of the great stress he had always placed on the importance of the national or state Church.[44] In his famous address to the Amsterdam city council of April 1617, Grotius defines toleration strictly in the narrow sense as meaning elasticity in doctrine within the public Church. He expressly states that the regime of which he was then a leading member 'connives' at Lutheran and Mennonite conventicles out of expediency rather than principle.[45] In his *Verantwoordingh*, written in 1622, he praises the 'wise and pious Camerarius for overturning the prevailing notion that diversity of views in religious matters disrupts the political sphere, since, on the contrary, the political sphere is disrupted when society refuses to accept freedom of conscience and oppresses men for their beliefs.[46] But here again there is no plea for freedom of practice, or of expression, on principle. Nevertheless, Grotius's *De Veritate* powerfully contributed to transmitting the new Arminian vision of an ideal, distilled Christianity which transcends all existing churches and which both churches and individuals must painstakingly work towards. By cutting back the dogmatic base of Christian belief to a minimum, Grotius, like Episcopius, laid himself open to the charge of being a sponsor of Socinianism.[47] The book was much detested by Voetius and other spokesmen of Calvinist orthodoxy in the Republic during the middle decades of the century.

In England, meanwhile, we find, in the period down to the 1630s, occasional pleas for 'toleration' such as that published in 1609 by Henry Jacob at Middelburg but addressed to James I, under the title, *An Humble Supplication for Toleration and Libertie.* This was a plea for freedom of practice in a particular case, but only out of political and social expediency, not principle. It does not, in fact, involve any genuine doctrine of toleration, rooted in a theological stance, and does not advocate toleration within the Church of England or any other

---

[44] 'In coningh-rijcken selve is de verscheydenheydt van publique religie ten hoochsten schadelijk: maer voor de republiquen t'eenenmael ruineux', Grotius, *Oratie vanden hooch-gheleerden voortreffelycken meester Hugo de Groot, Raed ende Pensionaris der Stadt Rotterdam ghedaen inde vergaderinghe der 36 raden der Stadt Amsterdam* (Enkhuizen, 1622), p. 52.

[45] *Ibid.*, p. 50.

[46] 'Den wijsen ende vromen Camerarius seyt dat het is ongefundeert te segghen dat diversiteyt van ghevoelen in saken van de religie de Politije verstroort: also ter contrarie de Politije werd verstroort so wanneer yemandt met de vryheydt sijns ghevoelens niet te vrede zijnde anderen daer over lastigh valt', Grotius, *Verantwoordingh*, p. 26.

[47] W.S.M. Knight, *The Life and Works of Hugo Grotius* (London, 1925), pp. 172–7.

church. Nor does it seek general freedom of practice. Jacob makes it clear that 'we doe humbly beseech you Ma. not to thinke that by our sute for the said Toleration we make an ouverture and way for Toleration unto Papistes, our sute being of a different nature from theirs, and the inducements thereof such, as cannot conclude ought in favour of them, whose head is Antichrist, whose worshippe is idolatrie, whose doctrine is heresie'.[48]

It is with the Tew group, during the 1630s, that we first encounter a power-ful tolerationist tendency based on an argued theological stance, strongly averse to the religious dogmatism and strife of past decades still so prevalent in England and in most of Europe. It has often been claimed that the group of Oxford dons which gathered at Tew around Lord Falkland were inspired by the Dutch Arminians, and in the case of John Hales it is clear that his spiritual develop-ment was moulded by his years in Holland and his role as observer at the Synod of Dordt.[49] It is also true that the most important writer of the group, William Chillingworth, in his main work, *The Religion of Protestants* (1638), develops a theological stance similar in spirit to that of Episcopius and Grotius. However, Chillingworth does not draw directly on either Dutch authors or Dutch situa-tions. The affinity with the Dutch Arminians lies above all in Chillingworth's insistence that

> by the religion of Protestants, I doe not understand the Doctrine of Luther, or Calvin, or Melanchton, nor the Confession of Augusta, or Geneva, nor the catechism of Heidelberg, nor the Articles of the Church of England, nor the Harmony of Protestant Confessions; but that wherein they all agree, and to which they all subscribe.[50]

But while they laid the theological base for toleration, neither Chillingworth nor his associates developed a comprehensive doctrine of toleration, includ-ing freedom of practice and expression as well as conscience, in the manner of Episcopius. Chillingworth, like Grotius, insisted on the freedom of the individual to interpret Scripture in his or her own way, without discussing toleration more generally.

In England it was only with the defeat of the King in the Civil War, and the temporary overthrow of episcopacy, with the onset of a period of *de facto* limited toleration, that freedom of practice became a pressing issue.[51] In his seminal essay, 'Toleration and the Cromwellian Protectorate', Blair Worden has shown that, in fact, Cromwellian toleration was rather more circumscribed phenomenon

---

[48] On Henry Jacob and the debate about toleration in early seventeenth century England, see Nicholas Tyacke, *Anti-Calvinists: the Rise of English Arminianism, c. 1590–1640* (second edition, Oxford, 1990); and *idem*, 'The "Rise of Puritanism" and the Legalizing of Dissent', in *From Persecution to Toleration: The Glorious Revolution and Religion in England* (ed. O.P. Grell, J.I. Israel & N. Tyacke, Oxford, 1991), pp. 23–9.

[49] Seaton, *Theory of Toleration*, pp. 51–4, 48; W.K. Jordan, *The Development of Religious Toleration in England* (4 vols, London, 1932–40) vol. II, pp. 205, 338–9, 372–9.

[50] William Chillingworth, *The Religion of Protestants. A Safe Way to Salvation* (London, 1638), p. 357.

[51] Guggisberg, 'Veranderingen', pp. 189–90.

than was formerly often supposed. In the new context, Arminian and Socinian influences, combined with rampant anticlericalism, could generate the sort of radical defence of freedom of expression and theological discussion advanced by Milton in his *Areopagitica* of 1644. Episcopius would have applauded warmly Milton's summons to Englishmen

> to be still searching what we know not, by what we know, still closing up truth to truth as we find it (for all her body is homogeneal and proportioned) this is the golden rule in theology as well as in arithmetic and makes up the best harmony in a church; not the forced and outward union of cold, and neutral and inwardly divided minds.[52]

Milton's toleration was based on his fervent conviction that the clergy of England had impeded, and held back, the spiritual development of the English people, his feeling that the real break-through in theology was yet to come, and would be born from free intellectual discourse, that 'God is decreeing to begin some new great period in his church'.[53] But the prevailing attitude in government and church circles during the later 1640s and the 1650s was by no means favourable to this sort of comprehensive toleration. Blair Worden has aptly styled the limited, *de facto* toleration which did prevail (using Cromwell's words) as a quest 'for the unity of the godly party in the several forms of it'.[54] Not only was there no freedom of practice for Episcopalians, Catholics, Quakers or Jews, but even freedom of conscience itself was curtailed. The Blasphemy Ordinances of 1648 proclaimed the death penalty for anti-trinitarian belief and harsh penalties for adherence to other condemned views.[55] Nor did the Presbyterian, Independent and Baptist blocks, which worked uneasily together to support the Cromwellian regime, evince much toleration either towards each other or amongst their own ranks. It was indeed with some justification that Anglican writers during the Restoration period, such as Thomas Tomkins in his *The Inconveniences of Toleration* (1667), described the so-called toleration prevailing under Cromwell as hypocrisy, indeed rabid intolerance masquerading as toleration.[56] Even Milton, in advocating that 'many be tolerated, rather than all compelled', added that 'I mean not tolerated popery, and open superstition, which as it extirpates all religious and civil supremacies, so itself should be extirpate'.[57]

---

[52] John Milton, *Areopagitica* [1644] (ed. K.M. Lea, London, 1973), p. 33.

[53] *Ibid.*, pp. 34–5.

[54] Blair Worden, 'Toleration and the Cromwellian Protectorate', in *Persecutin and Toleration* (ed. W.J. Shields, Oxford, 1984), pp. 206, 210, 216, 220.

[55] *Ibid.*, p. 220.

[56] [Thomas Tomkins,] *The Inconveniences of Toleration* (London, 1667) p. 17.

[57] Milton, *Areopagitica*, p. 40.

Milton's toleration, like his intellectual outlook generally, can best be described as a mélange of the two prime influences behind seventeenth-century toleration — the Arminian and the republican.[58] If the Dutch preceded the English in developing a theological base for toleration, the English preceded the Dutch in giving toleration its republican base, even though, in my view, the Dutch intellectual republican tradition reaches back earlier than the English, rooted as it was in Grotius. While Grotius did not himself develop a theory of toleration as broad and comprehensive as that of Episcopius, he not only made an important contribution to creating the theological base for toleration, but was arguably the originator of several major ingredients in the republican intellectual tradition. While J.G.A. Pocock is doubtless correct in asserting that the rise of English republican thought in the 1650s is characterized by the adoption of a political language and set of attitudes steeped in Machiavelli, the Dutch republican political thought tradition cannot be characterized in this way, even though Machiavelli and the Italian republican tradition was a powerful influence, at any rate on Pieter de la Court. To insist on the link with Machiavelli and Boccalini is to truncate Dutch republicanism which is an extensive and very important intellectual tradition beginning with Grotius and continuing down at least to Ericus Walten in the 1690s. Grotius is cited so frequently, by friend and foe alike during the second half of the seventeenth century, as the source of this tradition that I believe it makes little sense to define it in any other way than as a reworking and extension of his principles. Even the Orangist republicans, such as Walten, based their argument that tyrannical kings might legitimately be deposed by the people by force (and later their defence of the Glorious Revolution) on Grotius,[59] as indeed several English Williamite writers did.

It is often argued that Grotius was fundamentally ambiguous, that he changed his basic stance in politics, and was not truly a republican. But arguably Grotius was rather more consistent in his political thought than is usually supposed. The crucial political contention in the *De Jure Belli ac Pacis* is not the apparent defence of royal absolutism, a defence which he cleverly reserves for hardly any actual cases. Rather it is his powerful insistence that when a king possesses only part of sovereignty — which in his view is normally the case in France and England — and the rest is vested in the people or the 'Senate', and that ruler exceeds his rightful authority, then the Senate or people have the right not only to resist that king by force of arms and overthrow him, but also to dispossess him of that part of sovereignty that was previously his, and remodel sovereignty

---

[58] H.A. Enno van Gelder, *Getemperde vrijheid* (Groningen, 1972), pp. 259–63; see also Blair Worden, 'Milton's Republicanism and the Tyranny of Heaven', in *Machiavelli and Republicanism*, (ed. Bock, Skinner & Viroli), pp. 225–46.

[59] Ericus Walten, *De regtsinnige policey: of een nauwkeurig vertoog van de magt en pligt der koningen* (The Hague, 1689), pp. 136, 138.

within the state.[60] The *De Jure* embodies not only, as in Grotius's earlier writings, a full justification of the Dutch Revolt, but of all revolt, parliamentary or popular, against tyrannical monarchical power, and of the remodelling of constitutions within the state. But Grotius's doctrine that tyrannical kings might be overthrown and their dynasties removed from power, by parliaments and peoples, is only one of several strands which characterize the Dutch republican tradition as a whole. Equally fundamental is his doctrine that the public or state Church is a social and political necessity rather than a theological entity, and that while it need not have dogmatic cohesion its institutional cohesion is vital to both state and society. Directly flowing from this was his doctrine that Church and clergy must be subordinate to, and controlled by, the secular authorities, especially in republics. Finally, Grotius's Natural Law theories were important in strengthening the idea of the intrinsic dignity and freedom of the individual.

That the republican tradition was the second great impulse behind the rise of toleration theory in both Holland and England in the seventeenth century, and that in both countries it generated a separate tolerationist tendency, intellectually distinct (perhaps even in Milton) from the theologically based toleration of the Arminians, is readily shown. For the Arminians, and also for Milton whose doctrine of individual freedom (for all his republicanism) was ultimately rooted in the quest for a transcendent Christian truth,[61] the basis of toleration was the necessity to establish the spiritual independence of the individual and safeguard the expression and exchange of views. For republicans, by contrast, and here Grotius has a foot in both camps, the starting-point is the need to ensure the subordination of church and clergy to the political sphere if freedom in their sense, which Harrington calls 'intire civil liberty', their highest ideal, is to be realised. In other words, the one tolerationist tradition is chiefly concerned with spiritual and intellectual freedom, the other as much with political freedom.

Classical English republicanism, with a developed theory of toleration, was essentially the fruit of the 1650s, whereas for the Dutch the key decade was the 1660s. It was James Harrington who formulated the doctrine that liberty of conscience and freedom of religious practice are integral to civil liberty, and that neither can subsist without the other. A key feature of Harrington's toleration theory is his contention that freedom of conscience entails not only freedom of practice but also freedom from political and administrative disabilities for religious dissenters: 'Liberty of Conscience entire, or in whole, is where a man according to the dictates of his own Conscience may have the free exercise of his religion, without impediment to his preferment or imployment in the state',[62] a twist which it would not have occurred to the Arminians to introduce. If a man enjoys freedom of conscience and practice but, as a dissenter from the

---

[60] Hugo Grotius, *De Ivre Belli ac Pacis Libri Tres* (Paris, 1625), pp. 67–8, 113–14, 313.

[61] For an analysis of Milton's republicanism and doctrines of freedom, see Worden, 'Milton's Republicanism'.

[62] James Harrington, *A System of Politics in Short and Easy Aphorisms*, in *Oceana and His Other Works* (Dublin, 1758), pp. 505–6; and *The Art of Law-Giving*, in *Oceana*, p. 451.

state Church, 'is thereby incapable of preferment or imployment in the state', then, in Harrington's words, that particular society possesses only 'liberty of conscience in part'.[63] The other essential feature of Harringtonian toleration is that the state Church must not only lack coercive power over dissenters but must, if civil liberty is to be upheld, be stripped of coercive power with respect to belief and discipline over its own members. From this it followed that it is also essential to ensure civil control over the national Church, since, in his view, no national Church controlled by its clergy would long remain exempt from the corruption of power.[64] On this latter point, Harrington stands close to Grotius.

Classical Dutch republicanism, with its developed theory of toleration, was, by contrast, a product of the 1660s, being embodied principally in the writings of Pieter de la Court, Spinoza, and the Orangist Petrus Valkenier. The two works produced by Johan de la Court (d. 1660) and then reworked by his more famous brother Pieter, the *Consideratien van staat ofte politike weegschaal* (1660) and the *Politike discoursen* (1662), are markedly secular in character, steeped in Machiavelli, aggressively anticlerical, and insist that the outward forms of religion be regulated not by the Church but by the civil government. To ensure civil control of religious practice, and prevent ecclesiastical coercion of the individual, the De la Courts recommend the appointment of political commissioners to provide constant supervision of the clergy. In his *Interest van Holland* (1662), later reworked into what was virtually a new book, the *Aanwysing der heilsame politike gronden en maximen van de Republike van Holland en West-Vriesland* (1669), Pieter de la Court added a strong economic and social dimension to his doctrines.

By the 1650s much of what Episcopius and Uyttenbogaert had fought for in the sphere of toleration had been achieved. Nevertheless, freedom of practice was still denied to the Remonstrants in some places (including the town of Leiden), Catholics were denied the right of public exercise, Jews were excluded from most Dutch towns, and (from an intellectual point of view most sinister of all) the anti-Socinian campaign of the States of Holland was being used to curb the Collegiant movement in Amsterdam, Rotterdam and Rijnsburg. Anti-Socinianism was indeed as much as a preoccupation of the Dutch authorities in the 1650s as it was of the English. The threat to intellectual freedom increased further in 1656 with the partial success of the Dutch Reformed Church synods' campaign to persuade the States of Holland to legislate against the intrusion of philosophy into the domain of theology. Thus a great deal remained to be done before Dutch toleration could be considered complete, especially as regards widening the frame of intellectual freedom. Hence the central importance which toleration held and retained in the thought of Dutch republican writers. It is no accident that the neglected but rather important contribution of Adriaen Paets (1631–86), a Rotterdam Remonstrant regent much influenced by Grotius,

---

[63] Harrington, *A System*, pp. 500, 506.
[64] Harrington, *The Art of Law-Giving*, pp. 449–51, and Harrington, *Oceana*, pp. 181, 202.

arose specifically from his involvement in attempting to curtail the anti-Socinian campaign in Rotterdam in the wake of the anti-Socianian decree of the States of Holland of 1653.

It is typical of Pieter de la Court (and of all classical republicanism) that he sees the Inquisition in Catholic countries as evidence not just of the perversity of Catholicism but of the corrupt nature of ecclesiastical power in general.[65] He accuses the preachers of the Dutch Reformed Church of being inquisitors in spirit if not in fact. Toleration, in De la Court's eyes, is essential for the preservation of civil liberty in a republic, and integral to it. Toleration is also essential to the economic well-being not just of the Dutch Republic but of any republic. He explains the economic and general decline of the German city republics of Lübeck, Cologne and Aachen, since the Reformation, as a consequence of the city councils being persuaded — by bigoted clergy — to introduce policies which drive religious dissenters away.[66] Himself a textile manufacturer, he sees not only Leiden, his own town, but the whole economy of Holland as dependent on immigration if its vitality and prosperity are to be sustained, and he has no doubt that toleration, or 'vryheid van religie', is the most potent of all means to attract and retain foreign immigrants. In the period when De la Court was writing, a marked Catholic revival was taking place in Leiden as in other Holland towns. He had no doubt that this was a good thing and expressly insisted on the necessity to tolerate Catholic practice.[67] In this respect he goes much further than Harrington. De la Court admits that Dutch Catholics may well be enemies of the state, but says that they constitute only a fifth of the population and consequently cannot seriously threaten the state. Harrington, by contrast, advises that 'no religion, being contrary to or destructive of Christianity, nor the public exercise of any religion, being grounded upon or incorporated into a Foreign Interest, be protected by, or tolerated in, this state'.

Dutch republican toleration thought culminates, of course, in Spinoza. That Spinoza, in his political philosophy, was a republican (albeit less hostile to monarchs than Pieter de la Court), a great enemy of priests whether Christian, Jewish, or anything else, and a passionate champion of a general toleration based on untrammeled intellectual freedom, is altogether clear, and more evident than his debt to Machiavelli or Boccalini. Having himself been excommunicated from a religious community, the Portuguese synagogue of Amsterdam in 1656, and having frequently had cause to worry over the likely reaction of the Reformed clergy and the States to his ideas, even to the point of postponing indefinitely the publication of his principal work, the *Ethics*, Spinoza had a deep personal concern in the advancement of the cause of intellectual freedom and the means to preserve such freedom in the state.

---

[65] Pieter de la Court, *Aanwysing der heilsame politike gronden en maximen van de Republike van Holland en West-Vreisland* (Leiden-Rotterdam, 1669), p. 63.

[66] *Ibid.*, p. 65.

[67] *Ibid.*, pp. 66, 401.

How does Spinoza recommend organizing the religious life of society so as best to safeguard individual liberty and the stability of the state? A point worth stressing is that he regards it as essential that the patriciate should not be divided into theological sects and churches, and advocates a state Church, resembling that of Grotius, which is authoritative and cohesive but at the same time undogmatic and non-coercive. Spinoza believes that the state Church should have a clear primacy over the other churches in the state in the sense that it should loom larger and be more prestigious in the eyes of the populace. For, without this, it would not be a true public Church capable of impressing and guiding the public. He urges that the temples of the state religion in a well ordered commonwealth 'should be large and costly' while the tolerated churches, even though they might have as many temples as they please, 'yet these are to be small, and limited to a certain standard of size and on sites at some little distance from each other'. To achieve this combination of grandeur in the public Church combined with toleration it is essential in Spinoza's eyes that the state Church should be entirely under the control of the patriciate and that the main ceremonies of the Church should be conducted by the patriciate itself so as not to confer lustre and authority on a separate clergy. Preachers in the state Church must be appointed by, and completely subordinate to, the patricians.

Spinoza was, in most respects, anything but a typical representative of Dutch intellectual attitudes in the late seventeenth century. Yet his view of toleration can perhaps be said to be an uncontroversial, even somewhat typical contribution to the general Dutch debate about toleration in this period.[68] The question of whether or not to tolerate Catholic worship, still a problem in England, and still a difficulty for Locke, no longer had much relevance to the Dutch situation. Nor did the earlier problems of Remonstrant worship. Lutheranism, or the Jews. But this does not mean that all leading intellectual and church figures in the Dutch Republic now automatically accepted Bayle's

> droit inalienable que nous avons . . . de faire profession des doctrines que nous croions conformes à la pure vérité. Ce droit inalienable renferme tous les moiens honnêtes de répandre nos sentiments, d'avoir des docteurs et des ministres, de d'écrire contre ce que nous appellons des erreurs.[69]

On the contrary, the general feeling, even amongst those who were strong advocates of the toleration of dissenters, Catholics and Jews, was that toleration must not be allowed to go beyond certain bounds, or very serious consequences would follow. One major concern was to determine the nature of the relationship, in a tolerant society, between the public Church and the dissenting churches. That restrictions on the scope and character of Catholic, Lutheran, and Jewish worship should be continued was challenged by hardly anyone. As we have seen, even De la Court and Spinoza were anxious to maintain

---

[68] Enno van Gelder, *Getemperde vrijheid*, p. 270.
[69] Quoted *ibid.*, p. 288.

the visible and unquestioned supremacy of the public Church — this was indeed inherent in the Dutch 'republican' tradition, reaching back to Grotius. But a still greater problem for Dutch writers discussing toleration at the end of the seventeenth and beginning of the eighteenth century was that of the propagation of beliefs incompatible with the fundamentals of Christianity: anti-Trinitarianism, Spinozism, or anything that might plausibly be labelled as 'atheism'. Even Bayle had his fears on this score, and thought it better that Spinoza's work should circulate only in Latin, and Bayle's position was much more liberal than that of most Dutch contemporaries.

The Dutch Reformed Church had little choice, after the 1630s, but to give some ground to the tolerationists, and even to develop a toleration theory of its own. This was indeed inevitable if, during the second half of the century, the Dutch public Church was to acquiesce in the public toleration of Catholic, Lutheran, and Jewish worship, but still to combat vigorously the powerful Socinian and Spinozist tendencies in Dutch cultural life. Thus even the leading spokesman of the orthodox Calvinist wing of the Dutch Reformed Church during the third quarter of the century, Gisbertus Voetius, developed a coherent theory of toleration in his main work, the *Politica Ecclesiastica*, which on the one hand justified the acceptance by the public Church, and by the state, of Catholic, Lutheran, and Mennonite worship, arguing that their errors were not irredeemable and that their adherents might yet be claimed or won over to the 'true religion', while at the same time justifying the suppression and persecution of Socinians and 'atheists', those whose beliefs were so erroneous as to be beyond the pale, a dire threat to the well-being of society.[70] Voetius's theory of toleration was a theory of limited toleration which at the same time served as a potent instrument of intolerance. A work of which the Dutch Reformed Church wholeheartedly disapproved, such as Balthasar Bekker's *De Betoverde Wereld* (1691), could now be condemned on all sides, and vigorously acted against, on the grounds that it was conducive to the spread of the 'atheistic' ideas of Hobbes, Spinoza and Koerbagh.

The idea, then, that Locke, Bayle, Basnage and Leibniz, and indeed, all the participants in the European debate about toleration at the end of the seventeenth century, expressed ideas on the subject which had little relevance to the contemporary Dutch situation, and in which the Dutch themselves took little interest, may be rejected. On the contrary, there was a continuing Dutch intellectual debate about toleration in this period, to which Van Limborch, Bekker, Walten, and also Gerard Noodt (whose *De Religione ab Imperio Jure Gentium Libera* (1706) became well-known abroad in Jean Barbeyrac's French version of 1714) all made significant contributions.[71] These men were all intensely interested in the wider European toleration debate not least because of its pressing relevance

---

[70] G. Voetius, *Politica Ecclesiastica* (4 vols, Amsterdam, 1663–76), vol. I, pp. 924–5 and vol. II, pp. 538–44, 551, 380; O.J. de Jong, 'Voetius en de tolerantie', *De onbekende Voetius* (ed. J. van Oort, *et al.*, Kampen, 1989), pp. 109–16.

[71] G.J.J. van den Bergh, *The Life and Work of Gerard Noodt (1647–1725)* (Oxford, 1988), pp. 224–38.

to the Dutch domestic situation. Furthermore we can see, perhaps particularly clearly in the case of Van Limborch on the theological side, and in that of Walten and Noodt on the republican side, a constant referring back to Episcopius and Grotius which surely demonstrates the continuing vitality of the indigenous Dutch tolerationist intellectual tradition. It was that tradition which, in some respects, preceded the rise of the English toleration debate and which, to a not inconsiderable extent, influenced it.

12

William III and Toleration

POSSIBLY no other major statesman of early modern times came to be so closely associated with the cause of religious toleration in his own time and made so considerable a contribution to the advancement of religious and intellectual freedom in the Western world as the Stadholder-king, William III. His legacy in this sphere was of great importance, not only in Britain but also in the Dutch Republic and, more generally, in the European world of his day—including the North American colonies.[1] Even in Ireland, where his name, somewhat ironically, came to be identified with the rigidly Protestant settlement of 1697, his real role had been to try to mitigate, albeit not very effectively, the policies foisted on him by the English and Irish parliaments.

Even as a child William III was noted for his extreme reserve and taciturnity and was, as a man, frequently cold, aloof, and enigmatic.[2] His private correspondence with Hans Willem Bentinck and other close associates rarely affords any kind of glimpse into the inner world of his personal beliefs and convictions. Probably we must just accept from the outset that the historian has little prospect of ever penetrating William's own views on religion and freedom of conscience. Rather, 'King William's Toleration' to borrow a phrase

I would like to thank Graham Gibbs and Nicholas Tyacke for their advice on a number of points dealt with in this chapter.

[1] J. W. Schulte Nordholt, 'America and the House of Orange', in *William and Mary and their House* (New York and London, 1979), 22–5.

[2] N. Japikse, *Prins Willem III, de Stadhouder-koning* (Amsterdam, 1930–3), i. 75–6, 365–6, ii. 110, 115–18.

from the title of one of the Williamite pamphlets of 1689,[3] has to be treated as something basically political, moulded by the pressure of Dutch, British, and other European circumstances.

Admittedly historians have generally taken a somewhat different view. It is usual to point out that, as a child, William was for some years, from the ages of six to ten, in the energetic tutorial care of the Hague preacher Cornelius Trigland, son of Jacobus Trigland, one of the leading Dutch Counter-Remonstrant theologians of the era of the Synod of Dordrecht, and himself a pillar of Calvinist orthodoxy. It is customary to claim that the Prince, through his education, 'acquired a firm Calvinist faith', which then infused his thought and actions for the rest of his life.[4] Such leading authorities as N. Japikse and D. J. Roorda insisted that he was a man of deep Calvinist leanings and an authentic Protestant hero. But more recently there have been warning voices which have argued that William's outlook was perhaps really that of a thoroughgoing *politique*;[5] and it seems not only that this is a more convincing line of argument but that it should be urged more strongly than it has been hitherto. There is no evidence that Trigland's tuition had an enduring influence on the Prince's character and attitudes. It may be true that during his lifetime Protestant zealots, including many Huguenot *émigrés*, chose to regard him as a protestant champion, and that it sometimes suited William to play up to this image. But the modern scholar must take care not to swallow uncritically the wishful thinking of some contemporary orthodox Calvinists and be on his guard against the hagiographical tendencies which permeate some contemporary comment about him. After becoming king of England, William, like other Dutch politicians who came to London, occasionally let slip words of sarcastic contempt for the ritual and practice of the Church of England.[6] Daniel Defoe's comment that King William's scrupulous outward respect for the

---

[3] [J. Humfrey], *King William's Toleration: Being an Explanation of that Liberty of Religion, which may be Expected from His Majesty's Declaration* (London, 1689), dated 25 Mar. 1689.

[4] Japikse, *Prins Willem III*, i. 59–60, 111–12; H. H. Rowen, *The Princes of Orange. The Stadholders in the Dutch Republic* (Cambridge, 1988), 109.

[5] See, in particular, P. J. A. N. Rietbergen, 'William III of Orange (1650–1702) between European Politics and European Protestantism', in J. A. H. Bots and G. H. M. Postumus Meyjes (eds.), *La Révocation de l'Édit de Nantes et les Provinces-Unies 1685* (Amsterdam, 1986), 49–50.

[6] Japikse, *Prins Willem III*, ii. 277, 281.

Church of England was insincere is very likely justified.[7] But this need not mean that William was a man of strong Calvinist leanings. It is at least as plausible, and in my view more so, to cite Defoe further, that 'ambition or interest was ever at the bottom whatever face his outside politicks wore'.[8]

The only point that can be made with any certainty about William III's personal religiosity is that it was, by the standards of the time, decidedly tepid. One might agree or disagree with the proposition that the advancement of the cause of religious toleration in early modern Europe in general was a function of the steady waning of religious fervour in the post-Reformation context. But in William's own case his emphatic espousal of the cause of toleration does appear to have gone hand-in-hand with a marked lack of religious commitment. We see this from his life-style, from the company he kept, and also from the way he ran the Dutch army, though we must bear in mind that the army of the Dutch Republic included Catholic officers and men, and had never displayed a militantly Protestant character. The renowned liberal Calvinist theologian and savant Balthasar Bekker, who took service as an army chaplain with the Dutch forces in the Spanish Netherlands in 1678, left a vivid account of religious life, or rather the lack of it, to be found in William's camps. Although pastoral care for the German Lutheran, and also the Scottish regiments, was adequate, he was greatly troubled by the conspicuous lack of any concern to instil Calvinist motivation into the Dutch regiments. According to Bekker, the Dutch high command in William's day was so entirely indifferent to the need to see that the troops were preached to, or encouraged to participate in divine service, even on the eve of major battles against the forces of Louis XIV, that not the slightest attempt was made to organize marching, foraging, and other military duties in such a way as to avoid days and times when religious services were, or should have been, in progress.[9]

But a lack of strong personal religious commitment need not, as

---

[7] [Daniel Defoe], *King William's Affection to the Church of England Examin'd* (4th edn.; London, 1703), 18.

[8] Ibid.

[9] W. P. C. Knuttel, *Balthasar Bekker: De bestrijder van het bijgeloof* (1906; repr. Groningen, 1979), 123–4; Japikse, *Prins Willem III*, ii. 112; H. S. Haasse, 'Willem III gesloten en kwetsbaar? Een karakterschets', *Groniek: Gronings historisch tijdschrift*, 101 (1988), 25.

we see from the case of the Prince's father, Stadholder William II (1647–50), preclude the adoption, out of 'ambition or interest', of an uncompromising rigidity in matters of faith and conscience. Given the Prince's family and political background, and the tense, difficult circumstances in which he was elevated to the stadholderate in 1672, he had, after all, ample reason to contemplate throwing in his lot with the Calvinist orthodox.[10] For the previous 'stadholder-less' regime, under the leadership of Johan de Witt, had openly favoured the liberal Calvinist 'Cocceian' party during the early stages of the struggle between the rival factions of the Dutch Reformed Church which had been in progress in the Republic itself, and Calvinist districts of Germany, since the 1650s. Before 1672 Cocceian preachers had sided with the de Witt regime and, in accordance with the States of Holland ruling of 1663, omitted prayers for the 'Prince of Orange' from their services. It was the hard-line, orthodox 'Voetians', their opponents, who had opposed de Witt and the States party, preferring to retain the prayers for the Prince, and who had encouraged Orangist sentiment among the populace. It had been the Voetian clergy who in 1672 had helped mobilize the people and the civic militias against the regents.[11]

The bitter hostility of orthodox Calvinists towards the Cocceians and their 'Cartesian' allies within the Dutch Reformed Church stemmed from a deeply rooted conviction that Cocceius's theology and methods of biblical exegesis were subverting belief in the most fundamental Christian dogmas, including that of the Trinity, and eroding reverence for the literal meaning of Scripture, blurring the divide between theology and 'philosophy', which, for them, was a term of opprobrium. By diluting and de-emphasizing fundamental dogma and confessional dividing-lines, Cocceius and his adherents had allegedly also weakened the efforts of Church and state to combat Papist 'superstition' and Protestant dissent.[12] The Coccei-ans, in other words, like the Arminiàns with whom the Voetians continually compared them, stood for greater toleration. As long as

[10] D. J. Roorda, *Partij en factie* (Groningen, 1978), 248–9.

[11] A. Ypeij and I. J. Dermout, *Geschiedenis der Nederlandsche Hervormde Kerk* (Breda, 1818–27), ii. 503–6, iii. 174; G. Groenhuis, *De predikanten: De sociale positie van de gereformeerde predikanten in de Republik der Verenigde Nederlanden voor 1700* (Groningen, 1977), 96.

[12] A. Ypeij and Dermout, *Geschiedenis*, iii. 175–96; Knuttel, *Balthasar Bekker*, pp. 6–9.

de Witt remained at the helm, there was little the orthodox could do to arrest the progress of the Cocceians. But with William III's elevation to the stadholderate, it appeared that the boot was now on the other foot and that a new age of orthodoxy was at hand. The Voetians congratulated themselves that the leadership of the Dutch state was now in the hands of their assured and natural champion.

It was already the case, however, during the opening years of his stadholderate, that William's interventions in Dutch Church and academic politics in favour of his Voetian supporters were relatively infrequent. But, given the pressures of the Franco-Dutch War of 1672–8, orthodox Calvinists could appreciate that now was not the time to embark on a general purge of Cocceians, 'Cartesians', and other undesirable elements from the Dutch Reformed Church and universities. The United Provinces were caught up in a life-and-death struggle with France. Furthermore, the Republic's major allies at the time, Austria and Spain, were strongly Catholic powers hardly likely to look with equanimity on efforts to cut back the enhanced freedom which Dutch Catholics, as well as other non-Calvinists, had won during the de Witt era. And then the Prince did intervene on the Voetian side just often enough to keep alive the conviction that in the long run he would prove a true champion of the Calvinist orthodox. The best-known instance is his forceful intervention in 1676 at Middelburg.[13] Middelburg, the provincial capital of Zeeland, was a notorious hotbed of rivalry between the Dutch political and religious factions, both Voetians and Cocceians being strongly ensconced there. In 1676 Cocceian sympathizers, temporarily in the ascendant on both city council and consistory, appointed a well-known Cocceian, Wilhelmus Momma, to fill a preaching vacancy in the city. To block this, the Voetian faction in the consistory appealed to the classis of Walcheren, the body which exercised ecclesiastical jurisdiction over the whole island of that name, including Middelburg, and which had a Voetian majority. The ensuing furore in Zeeland was most unwelcome to the Prince, who was then encamped with his troops near Valenciennes and wanted no domestic distraction from his campaign. He wrote

[13] *Burger-kout wegens het Beroep van D. Momma tot Middelburgh* (Amsterdam, 1676), 5, 22–4; M. van der Bijl, *Idee en interest: Voorgeschiedenis: Verloop en achtergronden van de politieke twisten in Zeeland en vooral in Middelburg tussen 1702 en 1715* (Groningen, 1981), 25–6.

confirming the ruling of the classis cancelling the appointment of Momma. When the city council then disregarded this and insisted on retaining Momma, the Prince came in person to Middelburg some weeks later and not only removed the unwanted clergyman but also purged six of the most vocal Cocceian sympathizers from the city council.

It was only gradually during the 1680s and 1690s that the Prince, by his refusal to carry out more such interventions, and his general unresponsiveness to Voetian aspirations, profoundly disappointed the Dutch Calvinist orthodox, if not as some sort of Protestant hero in international politics then certainly as a champion of orthodoxy at home. Final disillusionment came in 1694 after the Voetians made a last attempt to enlist the aid of the Stadholder-king, as he now was, to convene a national synod, as Prince Maurice had done in 1618, to break the power of the Cocceians and expel them from the Church, as the Synod of Dordrecht had purged the Remonstrants. William, however, showed not the slightest inclination to perform the role of a Maurice, and co-operated closely with the States of Holland to impose a carefully devised *reglement*, or set of rules, on the Holland consistories, designed to damp down theological strife by (among other things) ensuring that henceforth preaching vacancies were filled exclusively with candidates willing solemnly to undertake not to engage in internecine controversy.[14] These States of Holland rulings of 1694 remained in force through the remaining decades of the Voetian-Cocceian controversy, through the first third of the eighteenth century, and prevented it from again seriously disturbing the stability of the Dutch Reformed Church and universities.

William's refusal to espouse the Voetian cause, his dislike of theological controversy, and his willingness to establish enduring working relationships with Catholic army officers and Jewish contractors and financiers, including his two principal military provisioners, Antonio Alvares Machado and Jacob Pereira, attests that he was a man of tolerant disposition and that this influenced his statecraft.[15] A further indication of his tolerant attitude was his allowing the Catholic majority in the county of Lingen—the

[14] Ypeij and Dermout, *Geschiedenis*, ii. 506, iii. 174–6.
[15] Jaap Meijer, *Zij lieten hun sporen achter: Joodse bijdragen tot de Nederlandse beschaving* (Utrecht, 1964), 83–4.

German territory lying to the east of Overijssel loosely attached to the Republic and administered almost as a personal fief of the Stadholder—a conspicuously enhanced degree of religious freedom despite the eagerness of the Dutch provincial synods for the imposition of a more emphatically Protestant policy there.[16] This was the more striking in that Lingen was a region where the Prince's father had sponsored a vigorously anti-Catholic policy in the late 1640s and where there had been initial indications, following the recovery of the county from the Catholic soldiery of the Bishop of Münster in 1674, that the Dutch would revert to a militantly Calvinist policy. But, whilst a general tendency towards a tolerant attitude, what Defoe later called his 'native aversion to all religious coercion'[17] is evident in William from the outset of his stadholderate, there nevertheless took place a crucial shift in the years 1688–9 which changed 'William's Toleration' from a personal inclination, albeit of considerable significance for Dutch domestic politics, into an international phenomenon of lasting importance for the entire Western world and which imparted to it a more systematically political character. For, while the Dutch intervention in Britain in 1688, and the ensuing English and Scottish Revolutions of 1688–90, contributed fundamentally to the rise of religious toleration and freedom of expression in Britain, it is also true that the massive Dutch intervention in Britain, accompanied as it was by a sustained propaganda effort throughout Europe, further strengthened and made more explicit the Republic's commitment to religious toleration both at home and in her foreign policy. During the short but crucial period of the British and Irish revolutions of 1688–91, for the only time in the history of the Dutch Republic the maintenance and extension of religious toleration became an expressed and fundamental objective of the Dutch state.

The principal reason why the Dutch regents decided in 1688 to co-operate with, and make possible, a large-scale invasion of

---

[16] Gregorio Leti, *La Monarchie universelle de Louys XIV* (Amsterdam, 1689), i. 455; it is noticeable that Rogier provides no evidence for his negative judgement of William's policy in Lingen; see L. G. Rogier, 'Het graafschap Lingen als deel van de Hollandse zending', *Archief voor de Geschiedenis van het Aartsbisdom Utrecht*, 64 (1940), 140–1.

[17] Daniel Defoe, *An Essay on the History of Parties, and Persecution in Britain* (London, 1711), 16.

Britain, using the Dutch army and navy, was their realization that the (since 1687) rapidly escalating economic conflict with France in which the United Provinces was then embroiled compelled the Republic either to go to war with France, to force Louis to cancel his new tariffs and restrictions on Dutch trade, or else to see the Dutch overseas trading system irreparably disrupted.[18] For, in the circumstances of 1688, the only way, in the view of the Holland regents, that the Dutch could fight France with any hope of winning was to invade the hostile but also weak, vacillating, and internally divided kingdom of England first and then turn England round against France.[19] It was this momentous decision of the Holland regents, and especially those of Amsterdam (who in 1683–4 had blocked William's efforts to mobilize the Republic in support of a European coalition ranged against France), which enabled the Stadholder to proceed with his plans for the invasion of Britain and amass 'una flotta non mai vista simile', as Gregorio Leti described it, a Dutch armada so huge that it dwarfed the Spanish armada of 1588.

But at the same time that the Amsterdam burgomasters concluded that they had to fight France (and that there was no other effective way of doing so in the circumstances of 1688 but to invade England first) they were still appalled by the immensity of the risks they were running.[20] Quite apart from the fact that an autumn seaborne invasion of a formidable island neighbour such as Britain was daunting and unprecedented—except, that is, for the unpromising example of 1588—the operation was attended by all sorts of other dangers. On 9 September 1688, nearly two months before the invasion took place, the French ambassador at The Hague had appeared before the States General and warned, in the name of his master, Louis XIV, that the moment the Dutch moved against his ally, the king of England, he would declare war on the Republic. The Holland regents were resigned to having to fight France in any case. But they felt deep anxiety that, with the pick of their forces

---

[18] J. I. Israel, *Dutch Primacy in World Trade, 1585–1740* (Oxford, 1989), 340–2; 'The Dutch Role in the English Revolution of 1688/9', in Israel (ed.), *The Anglo-Dutch Moment: Essays on the Background and World Impact of the British Revolutions of 1688/9* (Cambridge) (forthcoming).

[19] *Secreete Resolutien van de Ed. Groot. Mog. Heeren Staten van Hollandt en West-Vrieslandt* (Utrecht, 1710), iv. 230–4; res. 29 Sept. 1688.

[20] Jan Wagenaar, *Vaderlandsche Historie* (Amsterdam, 1749–59), xv. 426–7, 431, 435, 441.

campaigning in England, the Republic might well be exposed, unless the Austrians and Brandenburgers on the Rhine afforded sufficient cover, to another massive French invasion of its territory on the model of 1672. In addition, there was the evident danger that, if the Dutch intervened in Britain on the pretext that the Prince was coming to save the Protestant religion—and under what other pretext could the Republic invade England with any hope of enlisting sufficient local support to break James II quickly?—a damaging and possibly fatal wedge would be driven between the Dutch and their two foremost continental allies. For how could Catholic Austria and Spain, the powers on which the Republic's survival and prospects most immediately depended, be expected to tolerate, let alone support, a venture apparently intended to defeat the Catholic cause in Britain and Ireland?

Fear of appearing to Europe to be championing the Protestant cause, in collusion with Brandenburg, Hanover, and other German Protestant states which were supplying the troops to man the garrisons in the east of the Republic from which the invasion force for the armada was being drawn off, was actually a more persuasive factor in William's own mind, and that of his regent allies, during the summer and autumn of 1688 than any anxiety for the future of British Protestantism as such. It is no exaggeration to say that the Dutch leadership in 1688 felt little or no inclination to act out of Protestant motives, but a very powerful anxiety not to seem to be acting out of Protestant concerns—except in the specifically British context, where they had no choice but to play the Protestant card. Some of those Anglicans who either supported James II in the coming struggle or adopted a neutral stance, showing no enthusiasm for William (and there were a great many more of them than is often realized), understood this from the outset. One pro-James II, Anglican pamphleteer wrote in the autumn of 1688 that 'none that know the religion of the Hollander would judge the Prince or States would be at the charge of a dozen fly-boats or herring busses to propagate it, or especially the Church of England'.[21] He was pretty close to the mark. Nicholas Witsen, the leading Amsterdam burgomaster at the time, and his colleagues expressly rejected the argument that religion was a reason for the Dutch to invade

---

[21] *The Dutch Design Anatomized, or, a Discovery of the Wickednesse and Unjustice of the Intended Invasion* (London, 1688), 8.

England.[22] The Dutch intervened in Britain in 1688, not because Protestantism in England was in danger, but as a direct result of their confrontation with France.

The Dutch state had already commenced its propaganda campaign to project William III as a standard-bearer of the cause of religious toleration (in competition with James) but one who nevertheless was concerned to preserve the special position and privileges of the Anglican Church in England, Scotland, and Ireland with the famous *Lettre* written by the Pensionary of Holland, Gaspar Fagel, in consultation with William and his advisers, in the autumn of 1687.[23] This tract, in its various French, English, and Dutch versions (William expressed himself by preference in French), was crucially important in setting up a framework for the toleration debate which at this moment arose simultaneously in Holland, in England, and among the Huguenot refugee diaspora, and which generated a spate of pamphlets as well as John Locke's *Epistola de tolerantia*, albeit the latter was not printed and remained almost unknown before the Revolution.[24] Fagel's letter, rendered into English by Burnet, was printed in The Netherlands in unprecedented quantity and, with the help of opposition circles in both England and Scotland, distributed very widely, some 50,000 copies being shipped across the Channel.[25]

It was this *Lettre écrite par monsieur Fagel* which first assured Britain and Europe in the most emphatic terms that it was the view of William and Mary

que l'on ne doit faire violence à aucun Chrétien en sa conscience, et que l'on ne doit maltraiter personne, à cause qu'il diffère de la religion établie et dominante; c'est pourquoi ils peuvent bien consentir que les papistes en Angleterre, Ecosse, et Irlande soient soufferts avec la meme liberté de religion qui leur est accordée par les États dans ces provinces, dans lesquelles on ne peut pas nier qu'ils ne jouissent d'une pleine liberté de conscience.[26]

[22] J. F. Gebhard, *Het leven van Mr Nicolaas Cornelisz. Witsen (1641–1717)* (Utrecht, 1881), 321–2.

[23] Japikse, *Prins Willem III*, ii. 228–9.

[24] R. Ashcraft, *Revolutionary Politics and Locke's Two Treatises of Government* (Princeton, 1986), 486–7.

[25] J. Carswell, *The Descent on England* (London, 1969), 109.

[26] *Lettre écrite par Monsieur Fagel Pensionnaire de Hollande, à Monsieur Jacques Stewart, Advocat, pour l'informer des sentimens de leurs Altesses Royales, Monseigneur le Prince, et Madame la Princesse d'Orange sur l'abolition du Test et des Loix Penales* (The Hague, 1688), 2.

The other main point of the *Lettre* was that, despite this, their Highnesses took the view that Catholics should be excluded from office in England and that the Test Acts should be maintained. In subsequent Dutch amplifications of Fagel's letter, responding to attacks on it emanating from England, even more emphasis was placed on the Prince's commitment to moderation and toleration and his special qualities—as a Calvinist married to a princess who followed the rites of the Church of England, and being personally, and in his personal relations, exceptionally tolerant—as a champion of the cause of 'moderation'.[27]

But once the States of Holland and States General finally took their decision to invade Britain under the pretext that William was coming to save the Protestant religion and call a 'free parliament', a decision taken in September 1688, it became necessary, so intricate was the Republic's position in European politics at that point, to separate the two central strands in Dutch political propaganda. In order to enlist as much support for William as possible amongst Anglicans in England, it was seen to be necessary, for the moment, to concentrate on the Prince's commitment to defend the Anglican ascendancy in British life and to play down, as far as propaganda for distribution in Britain was concerned, his commitment to toleration. But at the same time it was seen as equally necessary, in the case of Dutch diplomacy and propaganda in continental Europe, to play down the commitment to Anglican supremacy as much as possible and place the whole emphasis on William's commitment to toleration, a toleration which expressly extended to Catholics.

From the end of October 1688 onwards the Dutch States General and the Stadholder, working hand-in-hand, sustained an intensive, formal, and informal diplomatic and propaganda campaign, using all the means at their disposal, to convince not just the rulers of Austria and Spain but all Europe that the United Provinces were not invading Britain out of Protestant motives and that the practice of Catholicism and Catholics in England, Scotland, and Ireland would be vigorously protected. Besides Vienna and Madrid, the Holland regents and the Prince were especially anxious to convince the papacy of this, as well as the German prince-bishops who had collaborate with Louis XIV against the Dutch in 1672 and who

[27] See, e.g., the *Aenmerkingen op een geschrift geintituleert Antwoort op den Brief gesupponeert te zyn geschreven door den Heer Fagel* (The Hague, 1688), 29–30.

now had to be kept neutral, and also their own Dutch Catholic subjects, who were widely reported to be reciting prayers in private for the success of Louis XIV in the great European conflict which was now beginning.[28] Dutch Catholics had to be persuaded not to withdraw their loyalty from the Republic, that there would be no repeat of the sort of anti-Catholic popular violence which had broken out at Leeuwarden in July 1687, and that Catholic worship in the Republic would not only be protected but extended. So the most energetic, intricate, and best orchestrated propaganda campaign ever launched by the Dutch Republic commenced on 28 October, just before the invasion armada set sail, when the States General instructed all the Dutch ambassadors in Europe to explain to rulers why the Republic was providing the army, navy, and resources with which William III was invading England, stressing that Protestant motives were entirely absent from its calculations.[29] The instructions insisted that the States General had no desire to try to dictate the future succession to the thrones of England, Scotland, and Ireland and 'moins encore pour exterminer la réligion catholique, ou pour la persécuter'.[30] The Dutch professed to be invading England purely out of reasons of state, to prevent James II from consolidating absolute power in England, and in order, by restoring England's Parliament and laws, to render Europe, as well as the Republic, more stable and secure. William participated fully in this effort, writing personally to the Emperor shortly before he set sail for England, reiterating his previous assurances that he would safeguard Catholic worship in Britain, including the recent advances Catholics had achieved under James II, and would generally ensure that British Catholics received very 'moderate', that is tolerant, treatment.[31] The Emperor replied to the Prince, now

---

[28] A month before the invasion they were also said to be praying 'ardently' for James II's 'preservation and for the success of his army against his enemies' (BL Add. MS 41816, fo. 231ᵛ, D'Albeville to Middleton, The Hague, 2/12 Oct. 1688).

[29] *Hollandsche Mercurius* (Haarlem, 1650–91), vol. for 1688, pp. 272–4; on the Dutch effort in Madrid, see BL Add. MS 41842, fos. 234ᵛ, 243, Stafford to Middleton, Madrid, 4 and 18 Nov. 1688.

[30] *Resolution contenant les raisons qui ont meües leurs Hauts Puissants Seigneurs d'assister son Altesse allant en personne en Angleterre avec des vaisseaux et de la milice* (The Hague, 1688); Abraham van Poot, *Engelands Gods-dienst en vryheid hersteldt door syn Hoogheyt den Heere Prince van Oranje* (Amsterdam, 1689), 103–4.

[31] N. J. den Tex, *Jacob Hop, gezant der Vereenigde Nederlanden* (Amsterdam, 1861), 138.

encamped in the west of England, that he placed great importance on the latter's guarantees, urging him to stick to his 'gute intentiones . . . das die catholische in ihrer gewissensfreyheit keine beschwarden zu befahren haben sollen'.[32]

As he had threatened, Louis XIV responded to the Dutch invasion of Britain with a prompt declaration of war on the Republic. Thus for France and the Dutch, and therefore also for the Dutch forces and Stadholder in England, the Nine Years War began in November 1688 and not, as was the case for England, in May 1689. Louis simultaneously unleashed a vigorous counter-propaganda campaign designed to convince Catholic Europe that the Dutch Republic and its Stadholder, together with their German Protestant allies and Sweden, *had* launched a *guerre de religion* and were intent on the destruction of the Catholic cause in Britain. This French propaganda effort, backed by James II's envoys in Europe, stirred up a good deal of European Catholic sentiment and, in particular, notably strengthened the hand of the pro-French *dévot* faction at Vienna.[33] In reply, the Dutch redoubled their own propaganda effort.[34] By the beginning of 1689 this vast Franco-Dutch diplomatic and publicity confrontation pervaded every niche of Europe's political life. To underline its commitment to a policy of religious toleration in Britain and elsewhere, the Dutch leadership, headed by the States of Holland, released a spate of key documents, including the resolution of the States General of 28 October and William III's First Declaration to the English People, also of October and originally published in English, in a series of Dutch, French, and German translations. These published documents were then supplemented with a variety of other writings, including several by the Italian Protestant city historiographer of Amsterdam, Gregorio Leti, whose works down to 1688 had been known for their generally anti-Spanish and pro-French bent. Leti enjoyed a European reputation for his uncompromising advocacy

[32] Ibid. 270–1.

[33] Ibid. 272–3; G. van Antal and J. C. H. de Pater (eds.), *Weensche Gezantschaps-berichten van 1670 tot 1720* (The Hague, 1929), i. 400–2; at Vienna, it was Cardinal Kollonitsch, the man behind the expulsion of the Jews from Vienna in 1669, who was regarded as the minister most 'ready to hold back the assistance those States might expect from hence' (BL Add. MS 41842, fo. 137, Carlingford to Middleton, Vienna, 19 Sept. 1688).

[34] P. J. W. van Malssen, *Louis XIV d'après les pamphlets répandus en Hollande* (Paris and Amsterdam, n.d.), 65–8.

of religious toleration and personal freedom—including that of women and Jews—and for his powerful sympathy for the Dutch Republic and its institutions.[35] From 1689 onwards he became equally well known for his defence of the Dutch in their defiance of Louis XIV, which he based on the propositions that it was not religiously motivated and that its success, in both Britain and continental Europe, would advance the cause of religious toleration and freedom in general. Over and over again Leti affirmed in his *Monarchie universelle de Louys XIV* (1689) and his *Teatro belgico* (1690) that the Dutch had launched a *guerre d'état* not a *guerre de religion*, that the principal Dutch objective was to prevent a joint Anglo-French attack on the Republic, and that the Dutch Stadholder could be relied on to protect English Catholics and Catholicism from the well-known anti-Catholic passions of the English.[36] One of his proofs was to cite the example of Lingen: 'les catholiques pourroient-ils souhaiter plus de douceur et d'humanité qu'ils en trouvent dans la comté de Linguen dont ce Prince est souverain?'[37]

To help convince Europe's rulers and Dutch Catholics, as well as the Catholics of England and Scotland, that the Prince's promises of protection for Catholic worship could be relied on, the preparations for the invasion of Britain were accompanied by a programme widening the frame of religious freedom in the Republic itself. This was judged necessary, not just to reassure Dutch Catholics but because, in the increasingly strained religious atmosphere which engulfed Europe following the Revocation of the Edict of Nantes in 1685, the United Provinces were swept by a formidable backlash of anti-Catholic sentiment often incited by Voetian preachers.[38]

[35] On Leti and his advocacy of Dutch toleration, see J. I. Israel, 'Gregorio Leti (1631–1701) and the Dutch Sephardi Élite at the Close of the Seventeenth Century', in A. Rapoport-Albert and S. J. Zipperstein (eds.), *Jewish History: Essays in Honour of Chimen Abramsky* (London, 1988), 267–84.

[36] Leti, *Monarchie universelle de Louys XIV*, i. 68–9, 243–5, 318, 418, 433, ii. 564; Gregorio Leti, *Teatro belgico o vero ritratti historici, chronologici, politici, e geografici delle sette Provincie Unite* (Amsterdam, 1690), i. 363, 394; see also Gregorio Letti, *Raguagli historici, e politici o vero compendio delle virtù heroiche sopra la fedeltà de suditti, e amore verso la patria* (Amsterdam, 1700), i. 257–65, 271, 291; Leti also composed a verse account of the 'miraculous enterprise of England': see Gregorio Leti, *Il prodigio della natura, e della gratia, poema heroestorico sopra la miracolosa intrapresa d'Inghilterra del real prencipe d'Orange* (Amsterdam, 1695).

[37] Leti, *Monarchie universelle de Louys XIV*, i. 455.

[38] L. Sýlvius, *Tweede vervolg van saken van staat en oorlog in, en omtrent de Vereenigde Nederlanden ... beginnende et het jaar 1687* (Amsterdam, 1698), 95; Rietbergen, 'William III of Orange', pp. 42–4.

The Holland burgomasters were determined to curb this backlash, but so equally was William III. Indeed, before he set sail for England, it was the Prince who took the lead in combating this potentially disastrous upsurge of popular feeling against the Catholic minority and in rejecting the proposals of the synods for reaffirming existing and introducing new anti-Catholic measures.[39] Prince and regents alike were adamant that this was a time for reinforcing, not watering down, the Republic's traditional adherence to policies of toleration.

Yet on the eve of his invasion of less tolerant Britain, William had simultaneously to step up his apparent espousal of the Protestant cause in order to work up the right image and publicity in England and Scotland. Briefly—but vigorously—he now adopted, purely for British consumption, what I would describe as an emphatic Protestant pose, which extended well beyond his printed invasion propaganda in English to his military arrangements and his own and Princess Mary's household organization. As James II's envoy at The Hague, the Marquis d'Albeville, reported to London on 9 October,

The Prince began to putt away ere yesterday all the Roman Catholicks about him, as his chief cook, and others who served him these many years very faithfully, as he acknowledges himself but the coniuncture of times requires to remove them. Her Royal Highness intends to make no more use even of popish tradesmen, which hitherto she ever made use of, but in England it must not be.[40]

The invasion armada itself was dressed up as a Protestant venture with more than merely banners and insignia. Hitherto, the Prince had pointedly always refrained from discriminating against Catholic officers in the Dutch forces. But he saw that in England 'it must not be'. He incorporated large numbers of Huguenot officers into his army of invasion, but deliberately left the Catholics behind to guard the homeland. As D'Albeville reported to London, 'the Prince brings with him none of the Roman Catholic coronels'.[41]

At the same time, William could not altogether avoid mentioning

---

[39] *Negociations de Monsieur le Comte d'Avaux en Hollande depuis 1679 jusqu'en 1688* (Paris, 1752–3), vi. 110; Rietbergen, 'William III of Orange', pp. 42–3.

[40] BL Add. MS 41816, fo. 227ᵛ, d'Albeville to Middleton, The Hague, 9 Oct. 1688.

[41] Ibid., fo. 239, d'Albeville to Middleton, The Hague, 15 Oct. 1688.

his projected toleration policy in his printed English propaganda. For, in addition to Anglican support, he also needed that of the English and Scots Dissenters and would subsequently need, should his invasion succeed, to square his promises to the English that he had come to safeguard their Established Church and laws (which was essentially untrue) with his assurances to Catholic Europe that Catholics and Catholicism in Britain would not only be protected but would actually benefit from his coming. Hence from the very outset, even in his First Declaration of October 1688, which was printed in exceptionally large numbers at Amsterdam, Rotterdam, and The Hague,[42] there is more than a hint that he intended to introduce significant changes in Britain. The Declaration appears to insist chiefly on his determination to safeguard England's Church and laws. But it also discloses what some Englishmen must have regarded as an amazing piece of presumption on the part of someone who was merely the Prince of Orange that he was coming also 'for making such other lawes . . . as may establish a good agreement between the Church of England and all Protestant dissenters, as also for the covering and securing of all such, who will live peaceably under the Government as becomes good subjects, from all persecution on account of their religion, even Papists themselves not excepted'.[43]

This text was drawn up by William and his Dutch, not his English, advisers and reflects serious intentions which were inherent in the Dutch intervention in Britain, the intention to introduce and maintain a framework of religious toleration which would cover Catholics as well as Dissenters. Indeed, William's First Declaration should also be read as a promise to the Jews. For, while the English Sephardi community was, and felt itself to be, insecure in the England of James II, the Dutch Sephardi leadership was extremely active in helping William finance and provision the invasion armada. Indeed the Jewish financier Baron Francisco Lopes Suasso was the

---

[42] BL Add. MS 41816, fo. 237.

[43] *The Declaration of His Highness William Henry by the Grace of God Prince of Orange, etc. of the Reasons Inducing him to Appear in Armes in the Kingdome of England, for the Preserving of the Protestant Religion, and for Restoring the Lawes and Liberties of England, Scotland and Ireland* (The Hague, Oct. 1688), 8; (Humfrey), *King William's Toleration*, p. 15; Leti, *Teatro belgico*, i. 363; see also the *Vertoog inhoudende dat d'expeditie van sijn hoogheyt den Heere Prince van Oranjen in Engelant, geensints op een oorlog van religie tegen de Rooms-Catholycken is aengesien* (Amsterdam, 1689), 5.

main figure involved in 'accepting' the secret and (as far as the English Crown was concerned) treasonable letters of exchange being remitted from London by English opposition circles to Amsterdam to help pay for the armada, and he took a considerable risk in paying them out in cash.[44] For he most certainly would have lost large sums had William's expedition failed. The Sephardi 'provisioners general' of the Dutch army, Machado and Pereira, and other leading Jews were also heavily committed to the success of the invasion.[45] Besides improving the position of the Jews in England, the Dutch Sephardi leadership most certainly also hoped to strengthen its commercial ties with the Sephardi communities (which were mostly of Dutch origin) of Barbados, Jamaica, and other English Caribbean colonies. At the time of his departure for England, prayers for the success of the invasion were recited not only in the Dutch Reformed churches of the Republic but in a variety of other churches as well. But probably few of the latter were as ardent for his success as the special service, held the day after William set sail, in the great 'Portuguese' synagogue of Amsterdam.[46]

During the first two weeks that the Dutch army of invasion operated in England, relatively few Englishmen rallied to the Prince's cause, especially in southern England where James's forces were concentrated and where the issue would be decided. It was only after James's fatal decision, of 23 November, to retreat from Salisbury Plain back to London that the initiative passed to William and sizeable support materialized. But the drama was not over yet. The royal army was still very much in evidence in and around London. The Prince, who was anxious as far as possible to avoid using Dutch troops against Englishmen, purposely opted to march on London in the slowest, most deliberate way possible to give James's collapsing authority every chance to crumble away of its own accord. This was an intelligent and effective strategy. But it

---

[44] *Negociations de Monsieur le Comte d'Avaux*, vi. 230; J. S. Silva Rosa, *Geschiedenis de portugeesche joden te Amsterdam, 1593–1925* (Amsterdam, 1925), p. 101.

[45] D. J. Roorda, 'De joods entourage van de Koning-stadhouder', *Spiegel historiael* (May 1979), 258–61; J. I. Israel, *European Jewry in the Age of Mercantilism, 1550–1750* (Oxford, 1985), 127–8, 130–1.

[46] D. F. Mendes, *Memorias do establecimento e progresso dos judeus portuguezes e espanhões nesta famosa citade de Amsterdam*, in *Studia Rosenthaliana*, ix (1975), 94–5, 98.

had a serious drawback in that it created something of a power vacuum in the south-east and much of the rest of England which lasted for several weeks. As a result the country was plunged into a nervous, chaotic, even panicky state, fuelled by pervasive fear of Catholic conspiracy and subversion, which led, in turn, to an alarming wave of anti-Catholic violence.[47] William, in response to the panic, issued his Third Declaration, which was published at Sherborne, presumably using the printing equipment which was brought with him on the armada, on 28 November. This was menacing in tone and only increased the panic, especially his warning that

we are certainly informed that great numbers of armed Papists of late resorted to London and Westminster, and parts adjacent, where they remain, as we have reason to suspect, not so much for their own security as out of a wicked and barbous design to make some desperate attempt upon the said cities, and their inhabitants by fire, or a sudden massacre.[48]

During the fortnight or so preceding the entry of the Dutch army into London, mobs of apprentices and other 'canaille', as the Dutch ambassador in London, Arnout van Citters, described them, roamed the streets of the capital searching for Catholic priests and terrorizing the Catholic population.[49] Anti-Catholic disturbances broke out also in Norwich, Lincoln, and Newcastle, and in January also at Edinburgh, conjuring up fears of a popular onslaught on Scottish as well as English Catholics. In London several people were killed on 11 December when the mob demolished the Catholic chapel at Lincoln's Inn Fields and a party of James's troops tried to intervene. Over the next few days the mob attacked the Catholic chapels at Clerkenwell, Lime Street, and Bucklersbury, wrecking and burning the images, paintings, and vestments.[50] They then sacked the chapel of the Spanish ambassador, Don Pedro de Ronquillo, envoy of one of the Dutch Republic's most important

---

[47] J. Miller, *Popery and Politics in England, 1660–1688* (Cambridge, 1973), 260–1.
[48] *The Prince of Orange His Third Declaration* (Sherborne, 26 Nov. 1688), 2–3; *Derde Declaratie van den Heere Prince van Oranje* (The Hague, 1688), 5–6.
[49] Van Poot, *Engelands Gods-dienst en vryheid hersteldt*, pp. 146–7.
[50] Ibid. 252; Lorenzo Magalotti, *Relazioni d'Inghilterra 1668 e 1688*, ed. A. M. Crino (Florence, 1972), 232; Otto Klopp, *Der Fall des Hauses Stuart und die Succession des Hauses Hannover in Gross-Britannien und Irland* (Vienna, 1875–87), iv. 265; R. Beddard, 'Anti-Popery and the London Mob, 1688', *History Today*, 37 (1988), 36–9.

allies against France, destroying his valuable collection of books, manuscripts, and art-works, turned on the embassy chapels of Venice, Tuscany, and Savoy, and pillaged a number of wealthy Catholic homes both in the City and in the outskirts, including two country houses outside Southwark.

The news of these anti-Catholic disturbances caused intense alarm amongst the Dutch political and military leadership, both at home and in William's camp. For English anti-Popery violence now threatened the most vital interests of the Dutch Republic. The general whom William had left in command of the Dutch forces at home, Georg Friedrich von Waldeck, wrote to the Prince of his fears that the anti-Catholic agitation in England might 'procure une paix entre le Pape et l'Empereur avec la France', pleading with William to write yet again to Vienna, Madrid, and Rome (and to Munich too for good measure) reiterating his guarantees that Catholics and Catholicism in Britain would be both tolerated and protected on the Dutch model.[51] 'J'ay bien de chagrin', the Prince answered Waldeck, 'que l'on est icy si violent contre les catholiques; je faits tout ce que je puis pour modérer les choses à leur eguardt.'[52]

The States of Holland responded to the anti-Popery outbreaks in Britain by assuring the diplomatic community at The Hague that 'dès qu'il sera possible d'appaiser la fureur du peuple, Monsieur le Prince d'Orange donnera de tels ordres que les catholiques se trouveront mieux dans leurs affaires qu'ils ne l'ont été par le passé'.[53] The Dutch leadership was telling Europe's leaders that it would see to it that Britain's Catholics were placed in better circumstances than they had ever been since the Reformation, and it meant it. Prince and States were fully at one on this. To calm the Dutch Catholic populace who were being accused by Voetian preachers (evidently with some justification) of being secret adherents of Louis XIV, the Holland town councils now gave guarantees to the Catholic clergy that they, their chapels, and their congregations would receive the full protection of the state.[54] Calvinist

[51] P. L. Muller, *Wilhelm III von Oranien und Georg Friedrich von Waldeck* (The Hague, 1873–80), ii. 121.

[52] William III to Waldeck, St James's Palace, London, 24 Dec. 1688, in Muller, *Wilhelm III von Oranien*, ii. 126.

[53] BL Add. MS 38495, fo. 73, Moreau to King of Poland, The Hague, 4 Jan. 1689.

[54] Ibid., fo. 74, Moreau to King of Poland, The Hague, 18 Jan. 1689.

preachers were summoned before the burgomasters and warned not to pronounce on the anti-Popery agitation in England in their sermons, being threatened with serious consequences if they disobeyed. Amsterdam and several other Holland towns went so far as to authorize the opening of several new Catholic chapels in order to underline their commitment to the toleration of Catholic worship.[55]

William meant what he said about suppressing the anti-Popery violence in England. His English advisers had urged him not to bring the main body of the Dutch army into London.[56] But the Prince did just the opposite. He brought the bulk of the Dutch troops into London, partly to ensure a smooth transfer of power, to secure the London area, and to maximize his own authority in England, but also in order to put a stop to the anti-Catholic disorder. All the English soldiery, including the palace guards, were ordered out of London and its immediate surroundings and relocated to billets in Kent, Essex, and elsewhere in the home counties, before the Dutch army marched in.[57] The Dutch troops occupied Westminster and Whitehall, including all the posts in and around St James's Palace, 'to the general disgust of the whole English army'; and also fanned out through the suburbs, occupying Chelsea, Kensington, and adjoining districts.[58] It was a high-profile occupation of London, and William paid a high price for it. Spectacles such as the parade on 19 February, when William lined up and reviewed nine thousand Dutch troops in Hyde Park (preparatory to a few of the regiments being sent home), offended local sentiment.[59] We know from the dispatches of the Amsterdam burgomaster Nicholas Witsen, who spent the first half of 1689 in London, that there was an alarming increase in anti-Dutch sentiment among Londoners during those months, in no small measure due to the

---

[55] BL Add. MS 38495, fo. 74.

[56] Gilbert Burnet, *History of my Own Time* (Oxford, 1833), iii. 357, 359; G. van Alphen, *De Stemming van de Engelschen tegen de Hollanders in Engeland tijdens de regeering van den koning-stadhouder Willem III (1688–1702)* (Assen, 1938), 8, 22.

[57] *The London Gazette*, no. 2411; Sir John Dalrymple, *Memoirs of Great Britain and Ireland* (London, 1790), ii. 221–2, 265.

[58] Dalrymple, *Memoirs*, pp. 221–2, 265; Burnet, *History of my Own Time*, iii. 357, 359.

[59] N. Luttrell, *A Brief Historical Relation of State Affairs from September 1678 to April 1714* (Oxford, 1857), i. 485–6, 503.

conspicuous presence of the Dutch army.[60] But for William the Dutch military occupation of London performed a vital service at the most crucial point of the Revolution. London was quiet and submissive. He, and he alone, was in charge of the English capital when the Convention Parliament met. Stability was restored, the Dutch regiments being highly disciplined. The anti-Popery agitation was stopped dead in its tracks. According to Burnet, never were the 'peace and order of the suburbs upheld better than over that winter'.[61]

Nevertheless, during the first month of the Dutch military occupation of the capital, London remained on edge, in the grip of fear of Catholic conspiracy and anti-Catholic passion. Initially, William continued with his apparently tough Protestant stance. On 14 January 1689 he issued a declaration from St James's Palace, upholding the 'order' of the Lords spiritual and temporal of 22 December requiring Catholics not normally resident in London to leave the city and 'places within ten miles adjacent'. Despite the latter order, decreed the Prince of Orange from Whitehall, 'great numbers' of Papists 'are still remaining in the said cities of London and Westminster, and places within ten miles adjacent, raising and fomenting jealousies and discontents, by false rumours and suggestions, deluding and seducing the unwary and conspiring civil dissentions and insurrections to destroy the peace and quiet of this kingdom'.[62]

Clearly this was language liable to inflame rather than dispel the menacing atmosphere which now hung over the Catholic cause in Britain. But behind the scenes William insisted that he disliked this proclamation and regretted the necessity for it. The Prince saw the Spanish ambassador on 13 January, and the Austrian envoy the following day, in order to reassure them that, whatever unfortunate impressions the decree might give rise to, it was, and would remain, his definite intention to establish in England and Scotland a broad and secure toleration for Catholics.[63] He urged them to have

---

[60] Amsterdam City Archives, archives of the burgomasters, oud nummer vii, Witsen to Amsterdam vroedschap, London, 31 May, 10 June, and 28 June 1689.

[61] Burnet, *History of my Own Time*, iii. 359.

[62] *The Declaration of His Highness the Prince of Orange concerning Papists not Departing from the Cities of London and Westminster* (St James's Palace, 14 Jan. 1689).

[63] Amsterdam City Archives, archives of the burgomasters, oud nummer vii, A. van Citters to Fagel?, London, 9/14 Jan. 1689.

confidence in his intentions and stiffen the resistance of the king and the emperor to the lying allegations of the French that his aim was to destroy Catholicism in Britain and Ireland. According to Van Citters, William told the ambassadors that 'although the humours of this nation are somewhat violent and impulsive so that at this early stage matters could not be so well regulated as he would wish, he was busy night and day to establish government more and more securely and wanted to ensure that in the future Catholics would be treated with the most complete moderation . . .'.[64]

In his subsequent letter to the Spanish king, William reiterated his promises to safeguard and improve the position of the Catholics in England, stressing, it is interesting to note, that the forcing of the individual conscience was something distasteful to himself. The Council of State at Madrid, at its meeting on 26 February, duly expressed satisfaction with William's guarantee 'que los católicos que se portaren con prudencia no sean molestados, y gocen libertad de consciencia, por ser contra su dictamen el forzar ni castigar por esta razón a nadie'.[65]

By the end of January southern England was calm except for the evident unease of the English soldiery and many Anglicans. But anti-Catholic disturbances continued in the north, and there was an increasingly chaotic and threatening situation in Scotland.[66] At the same time there was every indication that the Protestant–Catholic struggle in Ireland was intensifying. The Emperor continued to view the situation with great unease. Leopold was now at war with France and he was keen, William knew, to see England declare war on Louis. But there was no indication that he might be willing to recognize the deposition of James or was in any way sympathetic to the change of regimes in Britain. All that William knew for sure was that Leopold was becoming increasingly insistent on the need for Catholicism in Britain and Ireland to be tolerated. In late February Jacob Hop, the Dutch ambassador at Vienna, warned William that, while the Emperor was willing to trust the prince's assurances that he would secure the effective toleration of Catholicism in England, he would not be patient for long and was coming under growing pressure from *dévot* circles at his court, upon whom

---

[64] Ibid.; Van Poot, *Engelands Gods-dienst en vryheid hersteldt*, pp. 176–8.

[65] Quoted in T. B. Macaulay, *The History of England from the Accession of James the Second* (London, 1913–14), iii. 1247.

[66] Van Poot, *Engelands Gods-dienst en vryheid hersteldt*, p. 207.

Louis's propaganda, and the pleas of James II's envoy, were working with evident effect.[67] William, like Waldeck, was uneasily aware that it need not take much for Leopold to patch up his differences with Louis and leave both the United Provinces and the Prince stranded high and dry to face France on their own, with the situation in Scotland and Ireland still dangerously unstable.

William was in a tight corner. If he was to secure and retain Austro-Spanish (as well as Dutch) approval and support for his elevation as joint king of England, put together his projected European coalition, and shield the United Provinces from France, but, at the same time, was to retain the support of English Dissenters and stabilize his position in Britain, he had to goad Parliament with all possible speed into war with France and into toleration. Indeed, William's coronation (in April), which took place months before either Austria or Spain had indicated whether or not they would recognize him as king of England, England's declaration of war on France (in May), and the Toleration Act (also of May) were all intimately and indissolubly linked. For in the short and medium, and perhaps also the long term, the Prince's elevation to the throne of England, and those of Scotland and Ireland, would be backed by the United Provinces, his Catholic allies, and at least some Englishmen (he could dispense with the Scots and Irish possibly) only if his elevation was tied to war with France and the introduction of effective religious toleration in England, a toleration which extended also to the Catholics.

But how was the sort of toleration which William III needed to be achieved? Parliament was heavily dominated by Anglicans, most of whom were determined to minimize any concessions to the Dissenters and make no concessions at all to the Catholics.[68] We know that the unyielding attitude of the firm Anglicans in Parliament, grudging and basically intolerant towards Dissenters and Catholics alike, greatly exasperated William and his Dutch advisers in London.[69] Indeed, William's full programme of religious reform in England was unattainable. For he wanted, not only a broad toleration for Dissenters, Catholics, and Jews, but the abolition of

[67] Antal and de Pater, *Weensche Gezantschapsberichten*, i. 402.
[68] D. R. Lacey, *Dissent and Parliamentary Politics in England, 1661–1689* (New Brunswick, 1969), 237–8.
[69] Amsterdam City Archives, archives of the burgomasters, oud nummer vii, Witsen to Amsterdam, vroedschap, London, 12/22 Apr., 17/27 May 1689.

the Anglican sacramental test for office-holders so that all Protestants might hold office, and, as the inevitable result of all this, a weakening of the privileged position of the Church of England, his dislike of which he had scarcely troubled to conceal in the past and which he hid only with difficulty now. He knew that most Anglicans were ready at least to consider Comprehension, a 'widening of the entrance of the Church', by relaxing certain points of ritual and dogma sufficiently to create the possibility of bringing in some of the Dissenters, and that this could lead to a strengthening of the Church of England and of its grip on national life. But Comprehension was for William much less important than securing a statutory basis for toleration and improving the position of non-Anglicans in England. William's speech from the throne to the House of Lords of 16 March 1689, urging the 'admission to public office of all Protestants that are willing and able to serve', an initiative which he had discussed beforehand with his Dutch confidants in London but not with his English advisers, has been described as 'a monumental gaffe' because it strengthened the (correct) impression that he was no friend of the Church of England and wanted to weaken its position in English life.[70] It effectively destroyed the chances of securing a measure of Comprehension. But the Dissenters were in any case bitterly dissatisfied with the very grudging basis of Comprehension that was all that Parliament and the Church of England seemed willing to offer, and, by agreeing to hand the whole question of Comprehension over to Convocation—which effectively killed off any chance of a more generous form of Comprehension—the king's ministers engineered a deal whereby Parliament agreed to rush through a bill for toleration which the king desperately wanted.[71]

Historians nowadays show very little of the reverence for the Toleration Act of 1689 that they once did. Many prefer to call it the 'so-called Toleration Act'.[72] And, indeed, in some respects it was a grudging measure. Its stipulations were essentially an exempting of

---

[70] G. V. Bennett, 'King William III and the Episcopate', in G. V. Bennett and J. D. Walsh (eds.) *Essays in Modern English Church History* (London, 1966), 115; H. Horwitz, *Revolution Politicks: The Career of Daniel Finch, Second Earl of Nottingham, 1647–1730* (Cambridge, 1968), 88, 93.

[71] Horwitz, *Revolution Politicks*, p. 88.

[72] Ibid.; W. Troost, 'Willem III en de Engelse politici, 1688–1702', *Groniek: Gronings historisch tijdschrift*, 101 (1988), 83–4.

the Protestant Dissenters, including the Baptists and Quakers but excluding anti-Trinitarians, from the penalties of various laws.[73] It was intended by Parliament to grant effective toleration to most Nonconformists without expressly proclaiming unqualified toleration of their churches, so that, in the view of some scholars, it was not strictly a toleration act at all.[74] To Socinians (anti-Trinitarians), Deists, Catholics, and Jews, as well as other non-Christians, the measure offered nothing whatsoever—at least not explicitly. Yet, even with respect to its strict meaning, the Act was a much more fundamental landmark in English history than it is nowadays fashionable to suppose. Except during the Cromwellian Commonwealth, there had never, since the Reformation, been any statutory limitation on the exclusive control exercised by the Established Church over divine worship in England. As far as Parliament was concerned, prayer meetings of Nonconformists of whatever sort could not be legally held in England before 1689 and consequently lacked the protection of the law. During the Restoration period, the heyday of the Church of England's ascendancy over English life, mob-harassment of Dissenters' meeting-houses was far from uncommon. In contrast, during the reign of William III there was no legal, or popular, impediment to the undisguised, public practice of their forms of worship for Presbyterians, Independents, Baptists, and Quakers. These were now all free to take out licences, regularize their position in the eyes of the law, build their chapels, rebut the contentions of Anglican preachers from the pulpit, and, indeed, appeal publicly for more members. Dissenting clergy now went unhindered in the making of marriages and baptizing of infants.[75] Concomittantly, the power of the Church of England authorities to impede, investigate, and interfere with Nonconformist congregations and their activities was drastically curtailed. The practical impact of all this, as we see from the astounding proliferation of places of Dissenting worship which now ensued, was immense. In the first year of its operation, church licences for 796 temporary and 143 permanent prayer-houses were taken out under

[73] J. R. Jones, *The Revolution of 1688 in England* (London, 1972), 319; G. Holmes, *The Trial of Doctor Sacheverell* (London, 1973), 24.

[74] John Stoughton, *The Revolution of 1688 in its Bearing on Protestant Nonconformity* (London, 1888), 61.

[75] Ibid. 68, 92; A. T. Hart, *The Life and Times of John Sharp, Archbishop of York* (London, 1949), 258–9.

the terms of the Toleration Act, while the Quakers set up a further 239 meeting-houses without licences (or hindrance).[76] Between May 1689 and 1710 no less than 3,901 Dissenters' places of worship, temporary and permanent, were licensed.[77]

So even the Act itself was in reality a more fundamental change than some historians have recently been willing to allow. But to insist on the strict meaning of the statute is to fail, arguably, to grasp the true meaning of 'the Toleration' of 1689. It is usually assumed that 'the Toleration' of 1689 and the 'Toleration Act' are interchangeable terms. But careful examination of contemporary usage shows that this was by no means always the case. Furthermore, to insist that they were is to argue that the statute was the only significant engine of change on the toleration front, which, in the view of the present author, is to attribute far too much weight to Parliament and parliamentary politics in the making of the English Revolution of 1688–9 and not nearly enough to William, the Dutch Republic, and the Republic's Catholic allies on the Continent in the shaping of what actually happened in England, as well as in Scotland and Ireland. For the advancement of religious toleration and liberty of conscience, as well as the weakening of the grip of the church of England over English intellectual life generally, from 1688 cannot be understood simply in terms of what Parliament wanted, intended, or was prepared to accept. In no small measure it was also the outcome of what William, the Dutch regents, and their Catholic allies were determined to have. There is substantial evidence, as we have shown already, that William and his Dutch advisers always intended, whatever Parliament might want, that 'the Toleration' of 1689 should apply to Catholics as well as Dissenters and that William wanted to strengthen the position of the Dissenters and other groups, such as the Jews, in English life. His leverage arose first from the fact of military conquest and then from his new legal powers as king. Much as Louis XIV before 1685 had eroded the position of French Protestants despite the law by encouraging all manner of harassment of Protestant worship, so William, in mirror reverse of what his great antagonist had done, stabilized and consolidated Catholic, Jewish,

[76] G. V. Bennett, 'Conflict in the Church', in G. Holmes (ed.), *Britain after the Glorious Revolution, 1689–1714* (London, 1969), 163.
[77] Holmes, *The Trial of Doctor Sacheverell*, p. 36.

and other non-Anglican religious life in England, despite the law, by using his royal powers to direct the judges and curb popular and ecclesiastical interference and opposition. As Burnet aptly expressed it, 'the Papists have enjoyed the real effects of the Toleration though they were not comprehended within the statute that enacted it'.[78]

No doubt the improved position of Catholics in England after 1688 was partly the result of judicial and ecclesiastical inertia stemming from the vast proliferation of non-Anglican prayer-houses, by no means all of which were duly licensed, and the greatly increased difficulty of investigating Dissent and enforcing any kind of religious coercion in the new situation.[79] But it is clear that Catholic gains in England arising from the changes of 1688 were also the result of William's attitude and policy, and those of the Dutch regents and their Catholic allies. It may well be that in the spring of 1689 the new king was beset by a host of conflicting pressures. But there was little likelihood that toleration would slip from the forefront of his mind. Both the Emperor and Spain delayed their recognition of William's and Mary's joint elevation to the thrones of England, Scotland, and Ireland until as late as July.[80] When he did recognize William as king of England, Leopold deliberately coupled his offer of future political and military collaboration against France to the making good of William's assurances regarding English Catholics in his official letter of congratulation.[81] This was tantamount to publishing William's promise given 'both in the United Provinces and during his entry into England' that he would secure, and firmly establish, toleration for Britain's Catholics. Thus, from the summer of 1689 onwards, not only outright Jacobite opponents of the Revolution, but also 'High Flying' non-Jacobite Anglican critics of 'the Toleration' in its wider sense and a sprinkling of intolerant Dissenters, were able

---

[78] Burnet, *History of my Own Time*, iv. 21–2; see also John Bossy's comments, below, Ch. 14.

[79] J. C. H. Aveling, 'The Catholic Recusants of the West Riding of Yorkshire, 1558–1790', *Proceedings of the Leeds Philosophical and Literary Society*, x, part iv (Leeds, 1963), 256–80.

[80] Antal and de Pater, *Weensche Gezantschapsberichten*, i. 445, 447.

[81] Lambert van den Bos, *Het leven en Bedryf van Willem de derde, koning van Groot-Brittanie* (Amsterdam, 1694), i. 382; J. Tronchin du Breul, *Lettres sur les matières du temps* (Amsterdam, 1688–90), ii. 242–3; Sylvius, *Tweede vervolg*, iii. 153–4.

to make political capital out of William's no longer secret commitment to the Habsburg rulers.

The Stadholder-king, it emerged, had all along fully intended to extend, and (if necessary) impose, toleration for Catholics in Britain. This realization—that William was under obligation to his Catholic allies to introduce a firm toleration for Catholics in England— exposed him to some withering sarcasm from the anti-Revolution Press. Nathaniel Johnston actually states that, in order to obtain the support of the Emperor and king of Spain, as well as other Catholic princes, William 'gave them assurances that he would effectually accomplish that liberty for Roman Catholicks, which James, being a professed Papist, was not able to bring to pass: for the truth of this I need bring no other proof but the Emperor's expostulatory letter'.[82] He went on to ask, 'Where then was the crime of this most injured Prince [James II] in endeavouring to do that which the Usurper hath promised to do for him?'[83] 'I hope', commented Sir James Montgomery, a Dissenter and initially a Whig supporter of the Revolution who performed an ideological volte-face and turned Jacobite, 'those stretches in favour of Catholicks which were criminal in King James, are not become more legal and meritorious in King William; the exercise of the Dispensing Power in their favours, I hope, is as much a fault now as ever.'[84] But the disclosure of his commitment to the Catholic rulers also made it easier for William to explain the necessity of *de facto* toleration for Catholics and Catholic worship to his ministers, officials, and the circuit judges. Johnston noted that

Hence, when the judges, in the first circuit, desired to know his pleasure, how they should deal with Catholic priests, he told them, he was under an obligation to the Catholic Princes, not to molest them in the exercise of

---

[82] [Nathaniel Johnston], *The Dear Bargain, or, a True Representation of the State of the English Nation under the Dutch* (London, 1690), in the *Third Collection of Scarce and Valuable Tracts . . . Principally from the Library of Lord Somers* (London, 1751), iii. 249–50; on Johnson, see M. Goldie, 'The Revolution of 1689 and the Structure of Political Argument: An Essay and an Annotated Bibliography of Pamphlets on the Allegiance Controversy', *Bulletin of Research in the Humanities* (winter 1980), 497.

[83] [Johnston], *The Dear Bargain*, p. 250.

[84] [Sir James Montgomery], *Great Britain's Just Complaint for Her Late Measures, Present Sufferings and the Future Miseries She is Exposed to* (n.p. London?, 1692), 17; on Montgomery, see Goldie, 'The Revolution of 1689 and the Structure of Political Argument', pp. 498–500.

their religion; and that he was not so apprehensive of disturbance from them (because few and weak) as from the professed members of the Church of England.[85]

Another aspect of 'King William's Toleration', as distinct from the stipulations of the Toleration Act, which enfuriated many of his critics was the seemingly blatantly *politique* character—in reality, it was even more opportunistic and lacking in religious principle than the public realized—of his church policy in Scotland. It is doubly ironic that the Stadholder-king who was widely suspected of carrying barely concealed Calvinist leanings into the arena of English, Scots, and Irish ecclesiastical politics in fact made up his mind, on grounds of pure *raison d'état*, to try to retain episcopacy in Scotland against the wishes of most of the Scots Convention and public.[86] He was unable to do so in practice because the Scots bishops to a man, and the great mass of the episcopal clergy in Scotland, firmly rejected the Revolution and himself as king of Scotland. He had little choice but to concede the abolition of Scots episcopacy and the elevation of the Presbyterian church to the status of being the Established Church of Scotland. But in so doing he instantly came to be depicted in the minds of a great many English Anglicans and Scots episcopalians as the willing instrument of Presbyterianism north of the border.[87] It was generally assumed that it was William who encouraged, if he did not coax, the Scots Convention to 'establish that church-government which is most agreeable to the inclinations of the [Scots] people', in the eyes of Englishmen a rather shocking basis on which to base ecclesiastical principles.[88]

But while the Stadholder-king pursued a thoroughly *politique* Church policy in Scotland, and had no alternative but to ally with the Presbyterians, it is clear that he was appalled, as was Dutch opinion, by the violence against, and persecution of, episcopalians

---

[85] [Johnston], *The Dear Bargain*, p. 250.

[86] P. W. J. Riley, *King William and the Scottish Politicians* (Manchester, 1979), 4; B. Lenman, 'The Scottish Episcopal Clergy and the Ideology of Jacobitism', in E. Cruikshanks (ed.), *Ideology and Conspiracy: Aspects of Jacobitism, 1689–1759* (Edinburgh, 1982), 39; see also I. B. Cowan, 'Church and State Reformed? The Revolution in Scotland, 1689–90', in Israel (ed.), *The Anglo-Dutch Moment*, ch. 4.

[87] Daniel Defoe, *Presbyterian Persecution Examined. With an Essay on the Nature Necessity of Toleration in Scotland* (Edinburgh, 1707), 14, 23; G. Every, *The High Church Party, 1688–1718* (London, 1956), 37.

[88] [Johnston], *The Dear Bargain*, p. 251.

and Catholics which accompanied the Revolution in Scotland. From the outset he exerted himself to try to shield the episcopalians and Catholics from Calvinist repression and extend his *de facto* toleration policy to Scotland [89] though this only gave his Anglican and Jacobite opponents additional grounds to lambast him as a Machiavellian and hypocrite devoid of any principles. The usurper William, according to the Jacobite printer William Anderton,

> with his usual Arts of Dissimulation seemed to be very squeamish when he came to that clause of the Scots Coronation-oath 'We shall be carefull to root out hereticks', by declaring 'he did not mean by those words that he was under any obligation to become a persecutor', yet never made any scruple to set on foot and encourage one of the most violent persecutions we ever read of against the episcopal clergy there.[90]

Nathaniel Johnston was no less scathing: 'the inclination of the people it seems is the Word of God and the standard of church-government', adding that 'though [William] hath a double conscience, one for this and another for the north side of the Tweed, yet he hath but one Principle, that gain is great godliness and one Dutch soul, interest, to become all things to all men, to gain all to himself'.[91]

As for Ireland, historians have not yet sufficiently appreciated the extent to which it was William personally (albeit encouraged by his Catholic allies and the States General, who were anxious to get the Dutch forces out of Ireland as quickly as possible) who was behind the efforts to achieve a formal toleration of Catholic worship as well as retention of Catholic monasteries and schools in the country. Most accounts of the Limerick peace talks of 1691, which ended the Jacobite war in Ireland, assume that it was the Dutch commander of the allied army in Ireland, the Baron van Ginkel, who was responsible for the initially generous terms conceded to the disarming Jacobites and, in particular, the first clause which granted Irish Catholics 'such privileges in the exercise of their religion as are consistent with the laws of Ireland, or as they did

---

[89] W. L. Mathieson, *Scotland and the Union: A History of Scotland from 1695 to 1747* (Glasgow, 1905), 189–90.

[90] [William Anderton], *Remarks upon the Present Confederacy and Late Revolution in England* (London, 1693), 19.

[91] [Johnston], *The Dear Bargain*, pp. 251–2.

enjoy in the reign of Charles II', as well as 'protection' against Protestant persecution.[92] But there was nothing haphazard about the offer and it was not Van Ginkel who was behind it. For, even before this, the Stadholder-king (and Bentinck) had been trying to buy the Irish off with secret offers of the 'free exercise of their religion'.[93] It is in any case inherently improbable that van Ginkel was acting other than on the instructions of William. In any case, William afterwards did his best to push the draft terms through over the resolutely intolerant opposition of the English and (Protestant-dominated) Irish parliaments, his stance stiffened by the repeated interventions of the Emperor. In 1692 it was partly in response to the representations of Leopold's envoy in London, Count Auersperg, that William put his foot down on the issue of Irish monasteries and monastic schools, for the moment blocking the Irish Parliament's bill for their suppression.[94] It was only at the end of the Nine Years War that William's resolve (and the Emperor's leverage) weakened and the Parliaments had their way. In their final form, as adopted in 1697, the terms of the treaty of Limerick were shorn of their toleration content.[95]

During the 1690s the gap in practice between Parliament's Toleration Act and 'King William's Toleration' became painfully evident to those High-Church Anglicans who had abjured James II and, albeit often with some reluctance, accepted the Revolution settlement. For a majority of the Anglican clergy, and for many Anglican laymen, the 1690s were a time of growing anxiety and disillusionment with regard to the spiritual state of the nation. Indeed, by as early as the summer of 1689 a large part of the Church of England support which had initially welcomed the Revolution in 1688 had already reacted quite strongly against William.[96] The reaction was noticeable among both the lower and the higher clergy. Archbishop Sharp of York had never been keen on the

---

[92] J. G. Simms, 'The Treaty of Limerick', *Irish History Series*, 2 (Dundalk, 1961), 6–19; Wouter Troost, *William III and the Treaty of Limerick (1691–1697)* (Leiden, 1983), 33–5.

[93] Troost, *William III and the Treaty of Limerick*, pp. 30–1; [Johnston], *The Dear Bargain*, p. 250.

[94] Troost, *William III and the Treaty of Limerick*, pp. 42–3, 119, 164, 168.

[95] Ibid. 167–8.

[96] By August 1689 Nicholas Witsen considered 'de veranderlykheid der humeuren ongelofelyk'. See Amsterdam City Archives, archives of the burgomasters, oud nummer vii, Witsen to Amsterdam vroedschap, London, 6/16 Aug. 1689.

Revolution but had accepted it as a practical necessity and helped stop the hitherto routine attacks on the Dissenters from Church of England pulpits, abhorring that Anglican preaching should be 'prostituted to such purposes'.[97] But he soon became increasingly estranged as a result of the Anglican clergy's alarming loss of grip over ordinary parishioners. Even more striking is the case of Henry Compton, bishop of London, one of the leaders of the 1688 Revolution in England and one of the 'immortal seven' who had responded to William's urgent request to be sent an 'invitation' to intervene in England. Compton had participated in person in the insurrection against James in the Midlands and afterwards lent his support to the Toleration Bill as well as Comprehension.[98] But from 1689 onwards he became gradually more and more estranged from William and the Revolution and not just because of his jealousy of Tillotson, a liberal Low-Church prelate who became the Stadholder-king's most intimate English ecclesiastical adviser and who was preferred over Compton to the see of Canterbury. During the 1690s Compton, like so many of the Anglican clergy, came to believe that the Toleration Act was being vastly exceeded and abused with the collusion of the government, not just in the sense that the Dissenters were being permitted to interpret its provisions much too liberally, and to maintain Dissenting schools and academies (which were nowhere allowed in the statute) as well as prayer-houses, but also in that great numbers of parishioners were now absenting themselves from Anglican services on spurious claims that they were Dissenters. The latter was now a widely heard complaint.[99] The Toleration Act had in fact stipulated that the old laws concerning church attendance still applied to those who did not attend a licensed meeting-house—that is, that church-attendance was still compulsory for non-Dissenters.[100] But by releasing so many Dissenters from the grip of the ecclesiastical authorities, the Toleration Act in effect paralysed the pre-1688 mechanism for enforcing church attendance on ordinary parishioners, undermining

---

[97] Hart, *Life and Times of John Sharp*, pp. 258–60.

[98] E. Carpenter, *The Protestant Bishop, Being the Life of Henry Compton (1632–1713), Bishop of London* (London, 1956), 154, 161–2, 169, 174–5.

[99] E. Carpenter, 'Toleration and Establishment: Studies in a Relationship', in G. F. Nuttall and O. Chadwick (eds.), *From Uniformity to Unity, 1662–1962* (London, 1962), 294.

[100] Bennett, 'Conflict in the Church', pp. 162–3.

the clergy's control over church-going generally.[101] Apparently many of those who now assumed the liberty of not going to church on Sundays took to spending the Lord's Day relaxing in alehouses. The consequence of all this was a serious decline in the Church of England's prestige and authority and, especially in many growing towns in the Midlands and the North such as Birmingham, Manchester, Liverpool, and Leeds, a disastrous collapse in attendance.

Faced by so rapid and far-reaching an erosion of their pre-1688 ascendancy over English society and the English conscience, it is not surprising that a majority of the Anglican clergy quite quickly became seriously alarmed. They took fright at the unexpectedly dramatic proliferation of Dissenting congregations, at the scale of the popular defection from the Church of England, which was greater than anyone had feared, at the revival of English Catholicism, and not least at the impetus which 'the Toleration' lent to the spread of anti-Trinitarian and Deistic ideas. Indeed, for many the upsurge of such rampant heresy seemed considerably more shocking than the gains being made by the Dissenters and Catholics. 'Instead of Popery', wrote William Sherlock, an Anglican defender of the succession of William and Mary but a critic of 'the Toleration', 'men are now running into the other extremes of atheism, Deism, and a contempt for all reveal'd religion.'[102] If Socinian thinking had long had a precarious toehold in England, this had, until 1689, been all but imperceptible to the literate public. But since 1689, as the Principal of Jesus College, Oxford, expressed it in 1693, 'Socinian books ... swarm'd all upon a sudden, and have been industriously dispers'd through all parts of the kingdom, whereby many weak and unstable souls have been beguiled, and their minds corrupted from the simplicity which is in Christ'.[103] Historians have perhaps been insufficiently aware that the vigorous upsurge of anti-Trinitarian

[101] Ibid.; E. A. Payne, 'Toleration and Establishment; A Historical Outline', in Nuttall and Chadwick (eds.), *From Uniformity to Unity*, p. 262.

[102] William Sherlock, *A Vindication of Dr Sherlock's Sermon Concerning the Danger of Corrupting the Faith by Philosophy* (London, 1697), 12.

[103] Jonathan Edwards, *A Preservative against Socinianism* (Oxford, 1693), p. A1; according to Francis Atterbury, in 1697, the 'Trinity has been as openly denied by some as the Unity of the Godhead sophistically opposed by others; when all mysteries in religion have been decried as impositions on men's understandings, and nothing is admitted as an article of faith but what we can fully and perfectly comprehend' (G. Holmes and W. A. Speck (eds.), *The Divided Society: Party Conflict in England, 1694–1716* (London, 1967), 116).

thinking in England, which had so unsettling an effect on the Church of England in the 1690s, definitely preceded the expiry of the Licensing Act in 1695 and was in part a consequence of 'the Toleration' of 1689. And this, indeed, is how the phenomenon was seen at the time. Anglican clergymen knew where to lay the blame. It has been estimated that more than 80 per cent of the Anglican parish clergy came to reject 'the Toleration', not only in its wider sense, as distinct from the Toleration Act, but in the sense of anything but the very narrowest interpretation of the statute itself.[104] And following their lead, and that of the dons of Oxford and Cambridge, who, in general, despised 'the Toleration', many of the laity rejected it too. It was thus not the least of the many ironies of the English Revolution of 1688, as John Toland pointed out, that so many Anglican churchmen 'should so soon damn what they themselves and the whole nation had been acting at the Revolution'.[105] Their fear and anger led the majority to revert back to what their critics called 'persecuting principles'. It was not just the so-called 'High Flyers' but many so-called Anglican 'moderates' who 'turned tail', showed a growing susceptibility to the arguments of the Non-jurors and became filled, as Burnet expressed it, with the 'mad rage of zealots'.[106]

The Stadholder-king, whose aloof, misanthropic disposition caused him to derive a certain perverse pleasure from his own deepening unpopularity with the English, is unlikely to have been much troubled by the inflated anxieties of the mass of the Church of England clergy and laymen. But he was, of course, careful to secure the loyalty of the upper clergy, and so it was necessarily a key component of his English policy to ensure that Latitudinarian pro-Toleration sentiment predominated among the upper echelons of the Church hierarchy, where, in 1689, there were (conveniently) a considerable number of vacancies due to several deaths and the refusal of the Non-juring bishops to take the Oaths of Allegiance to himself and Mary.

It has been argued, it is true, that historians have been misled in thinking that William III 'favoured Latitudinarians'.[107] It has been

---

[104] Holmes, *The Trial of Doctor Sacheverell*, p. 35.

[105] John Toland, *The Jacobitism, Perjury and Popery of High Church-Priests* (London, 1710), 4.

[106] H. C. Foxcroft, *A Life of Gilbert Burnet, Bishop of Salisbury* (Cambridge, 1907), 314–15; M. Goldie, 'The Nonjurors, Episcopacy, and the Origins of the Convocation Controversy', in Cruikshanks (ed.), *Ideology and Conspiracy*, pp. 15–16.

[107] Bennett, 'King William III and the Episcopate', pp. 104–5.

claimed that 'after a disastrous initial intervention the king's personal policy or predelictions played little part', that William, hopelessly out of his depth amid the intricacies of English Church politics, was saved from continuing embarrassment by the experience and skill of key English ministers with close Church of England links, notably Daniel Finch, earl of Nottingham, and that most of the post-1689 preferments to English bishoprics were not in fact of 'Whig Latitudinarians' but of 'moderate' subscribers to a middle course between the Scylla of Non-juring rejection of the Revolution and the Charybdis of 'Church Whiggery'.[108] But this argument is by no means wholly convincing. In the first place, whilst William may have lacked sympathy for the Church of England, he was certainly not an ignoramus on the subject. On the contrary, William, Fagel, Bentinck, and other Dutch statesmen close to the Stadholder had been closely studying Anglican politics for years before 1688. The strategy of splitting the Tory Anglican camp was decided on by William and Fagel long before the Dutch invasion armada set out for English shores in November 1688. By the time Fagel drew up the Prince's Declaration to the English People of October 1688 the Whig leadership in Holland was already painfully aware that William was determined not to be tied to them and was making a strong bid to win over moderate Tory Anglicans.[109] Far from being initially bent on putting in Calvinists and known Whig Latitudinarians to key Church of England positions, William agonized for months during the summer of 1689 over whether to appoint the Latitudinarian John Tillotson or the more conservative Bishop Compton of London as Archbishop of Canterbury.[110] He chose Tillotson and Tillotson became from this point on much his closest English ecclesiastical adviser, which meant that he was frequently consulted on Church matters by Bentinck as well as by the King.[111] It may be true in the case of the see of Worcester that William was dissuaded from nominating the Calvinistic Dr Hall and instead chose Edward Stillingfleet. But it was precisely the likes of Tillotson and Stillingfleet who were the precursors of the future Low Church party, the men who had been willing to compromise

---

[108] Ibid. 105.
[109] Burnet, *History of my Own Time*, iii. 308–10.
[110] Bennett, 'King William III and the Episcopate', p. 117.
[111] Carpenter, *The Protestant Bishop*, p. 162; Stoughton, *The Revolution of 1688*, p. 55.

on Anglican ritual and make greater concessions to the Dissenters for the sake of a wider Comprehension.[112]

In any case it scarcely matters whether one calls William's bishops and deans 'moderates' or Latitudinarians, for the real point, as G. V. Bennett himself admits, is that the bulk of the Anglican lower clergy, in reacting against the tolerant tendencies of the 1690s, came to see Tillotson and his colleagues as the upholders and defenders of the spiritual state of affairs which they so abhorred and ultimately forced them into dependence 'on political Whiggery', thereby 'transforming them into the "Whig Latitudinarians" of continuing legend.'[113] It was Tillotson, Thomas Tenison (his successor as Archbishop of Canterbury on his death in 1695), Stillingfleet, Simon Patrick, Gilbert Burnet, William Lloyd, William Wake, and their associates who were the 'Dutch Churchmen', as Defoe dubbed them, the prelates criticized by most Anglicans for 'complying too far with the Dissenters and for giving up the decent ceremonyes and settled discipline, in exchange for a slovenly rude way of worship'.[114] It was these men, thoroughgoing compromisers, Liberals and Erastians, who had eventually to face a veritable revolt of the lower clergy against their direction of the Church and who were seen as responsible for the widening ideological split which by 1700 had divided the Church of England into warring High- and Low-Church parties.[115] Nor were the likes of Tillotson, Tenison, and Stillingfleet regarded as too compliant only with respect to the Dissenters. They were seen as being more generally in collusion with 'the Toleration' and even as being partly responsible for the sudden flood of Socinian tracts and influences, Deistic notions, talk of Spinoza, and other detested new tendencies.[116] Indeed, it was well known that the principal distributor of Socinian tracts in England during the 1690s, Thomas Firmin, was a personal friend of both Tillotson and Stillingfleet. Nor was there in High-Church minds the slightest doubt that it was ultimately William himself who was responsible for the changes. One Anglican Jacobite tract claims that William, finding the Church of England

[112] Stoughton, *The Revolution of 1688*, p. 55. Hart, *Life and Times of John Sharp*, pp. 117, 238.
[113] Bennett, 'King William III and the Episcopate', p. 130.
[114] [Defoe], *King William's Affection to the Church of England Examin'd*, p. 23.
[115] Holmes, *The Trial of Doctor Sacheverell*, pp. 30–1.
[116] Ibid. 26; Goldie, 'The Nonjurors, Episcopacy', pp. 15–16.

'opposite in the highest degree to his Designs . . . found it absolutely necessary to bring those principles into disreputation, and extirpate them . . . and to this purpose set up the noted Latitudinarian Gang'.[117] The same author denounced the 'new Latitudinarian religion' and contended that 'John Tillotson has contributed more to the spreading and rooting of atheism than fifty Spinosas, Hobbeses or Vaninis's'. To some High Flyers William seemed to be deliberately striving to render the Church of England 'odious and contemptible'.

Whilst the King lived, opposition to his Church policy and his politics of toleration, if intense, necessarily remained muted, at any rate outside Non-juring circles. It was not advisable to criticize the King directly. The result was a resort to coded talk about insidious 'Dutch' influences which gave a particular twist to the violent xenophobia purveyed by many opponents of 'King William's Toleration'. Firm Anglicans, Toland explained a few years after the Stadholder-king's death, 'used formerly to damn all the Dutch when they durst not expressly curse King William'.[118] Supporters of 'the Toleration' countered by taking up cudgels against this unedifying form of prejudice, a phenomenon which culminated in Defoe's celebrated poetic satire *The True-Born English-man* (1702), a merciless send-up of Anglican xenophobic reaction to the 1688 Revolution, which, among other things, ridiculed the Church of England parish clergy for their ingratitude to 'their deliverer'.[119]

For final proof that 'King William's Toleration'—defined as the situation created by William's own policies and Dutch and other European factors in addition to the parliamentary statute—marked a fundamental, indeed momentous, change in English life and one that remained profoundly controversial for decades after 1689, one need look no further than the reaction which set in following his death and the accession of Queen Anne. The new sovereign, who like so many of her countrymen detested her predecessor, evinced

[117] [Anderton], *Remarks upon the Present Confederacy*, pp. 19–21; according to one Jacobite observer, in May 1694, 'four parts out of five of the clergy are disposed to declare for the king (i.e. James)': see J. Macpherson, *Original Papers; Containing the Secret History of Great Britain, from the Restoration to the Accession of the House of Hannover* (London, 1776), i. 484.

[118] John Toland, *An Appeal to Honest People against Wicked Priests* (London, n.d. 1706?), 40.

[119] Daniel Defoe, *The True-Born English-man: A Satyr* (25th edn., Dublin, 1749), 29.

firm High-Church sympathies and, whilst she committed herself at the outset to the retention of the Toleration Act, to reassure the Dissenters, there was little doubt where her inclinations lay.[120] William's bishops promptly found themselves out in the cold. Sharp and Compton were back in favour; and both conspicuously intensified their hostility to the Dissenters.[121] Tory successes in the general election of the summer of 1702 reinforced the prevailing impression that 'the Church party' were now firmly in the ascendant.[122] Following William's death and the Tory election successes, a wave of dejection and anxiety swept Nonconformist circles in England, for which, it was soon seen, there was more than a little justification.[123] The demise of the Stadholder-king, the upholder and embodiment of 'the toleration' allegedly 'disappointed, mortified and humbl'd the Dissenters . . . so excessively, that they were ready to have thrown a blank to the Church'.[124] The High Flyers now had more scope to give vent to their frustrations, sense of betrayal, and resentment of William, creating an atmosphere fraught with tension and menace. The enemies of those who Toland dubbed the 'Protestant Jesuits' had to watch their step. Defoe was locked up for a lengthy spell in Newgate Prison for his *Shortest Way with the Dissenters* (1702), an anonymously published and ostensibly serious call to firm Anglicans to translate their resentment against the 'hodge-podge of a Dutch government' which had prevailed under William into drastic and bloody measures against the Dissenters and other undesirables, a summons greeted with rapture by several Oxford and Cambridge dons until they discovered that the tract was a hoax. Here and there the ecclesiastical authorities initiated prosecutions against Dissenters' schools and academies and, according to Defoe, 'began to threaten the Dissenters with shutting up their meeting-houses, and in many places rabbl'd,

---

[120] Daniel Defoe, *An Essay on the History of Parties, and Persecution in Britain* (London 1711), 17–20; Every, *The High Church Party*, pp. 108–9; Payne, 'Toleration and Establishment', p. 261.

[121] Every, *The High Church Party*, pp. 108–9; Carpenter, *The Protestant Bishop*, p. 186.

[122] Holmes and Speck (eds.), *The Divided Society*, p. 27.

[123] Defoe, *An Essay on the History of Parties, and Persecution in Britain*, pp. 18–20; Payne, 'Toleration and Establishment', p. 259.

[124] *The Memorial of the Church of England Humbly Offered to the Consideration of all True Lovers of our Church and Constitution* (London, 1705), 4.

pull'd down and burnt their meeting-houses.[125] This first appearance of High-Church mobs willing to resort to violence gave an ominous foretaste of the use of the Tory crowd to intimidate Low-Churchmen, Dissenters, and Whigs during the crisis of the Sacheverell trial in 1710.[126]

The High Flyers knew that they could not demolish all that William had done, and, indeed, their bark proved worse than their bite.[127] 'The heralds of war against the late reign', commented Defoe, 'will have the Toleration branded as a phanatick plot, and rail against it because they cannot have it repeal'd.'[128] But this was so in no small measure because 'King William's Toleration' had by 1702 achieved such an impact on national life that the Low Church, Dissenters, anti-Trinitarians, and free-thinkers had become altogether too numerous and well ensconced to be easily swept aside. 'The Church party' had little choice but to adopt a cautious, step-by-step policy, using as their main propaganda ploy the argument that the 1689 statute had never been intended to establish 'a Toleration' as such, seeking to whittle down 'the Toleration to such a pitch that they would no more have it allowed to be a Toleration but an exemption from the penalty of certain laws', precisely the (mistaken) interpretation which a number of modern historians have put on it.[129] But in the main the enemies of 'the Toleration' were thwarted. Those who had benefited from the effects of the Toleration Act knew that they had to stand together in league with the Whigs in Parliament to defend what Toland called 'all our present liberty'.[130] Moreover, in the furious national controversy which now ensued it was precisely the Low-Church element which William and his ecclesiastical allies had built up which took the lead and 'protected the Dissenters from the persecution of the High

[125] Daniel Defoe, *The Shortest Way with the Dissenters; or Proposals for the Establishment of the Church* (London, 1702), 3–4; J. R. Moore, *Daniel Defoe: Citizen of the Modern World* (Chicago, 1958), 109–10.

[126] Defoe, *An Essay on the History of Parties, and Persecution in Britain*, p. 20; see also Payne, 'Toleration and Establishment', p. 261.

[127] Bennett, 'Conflict in the Church', pp. 170–1.

[128] Daniel Defoe, *A New Test of the Church of England's Honesty* (London, 1704), 6.

[129] Defoe, *An Essay on the History of the Parties, and Persecution in Britain*, p. 20; Stoughton, *The Revolution of 1688*, p. 61.

[130] Toland, *The Jacobitism, Perjury and Popery of High Church-Priests*, p. 16.

Church, in order to maintain their own Liberty as well as that of the Dissenters'[131]

If William III's personality was deeply enigmatic, the same is true of his contemporary Dutch, British, and American reputation. In his own day, and after his death, there was remarkably little inclination to celebrate his major contribution to the advancement of toleration and freedom of conscience, even though western Europe was then on the threshold of the Enlightenment. Relatively few of the participants in the discussion of toleration in 1689, and over the next two decades, supported the concept on principle, as a definite social and intellectual ideal, and of those who did, such as Locke, Leti, Defoe, and the Dutch republican jurist Gerard Noodt, few if any were inclined to stress the personal contribution of the Stadholder-king. By the beginning of the eighteenth century more Englishmen were beginning to revise the traditionally negative English view of Dutch toleration. As one pamphleteer (probably Defoe) put it, 'Holland, a perfect Bog fit for nothing but what it was, the habitation of a few poor fishermen, is, by the great regard it has to the maintaining of Liberty and particularly Liberty of Conscience, become the very Garden of this part of the World'.[132] But it was still more usual, certainly among adherents of the Church of England, to deplore that 'in Holland there is a Toleration or free Liberty of Exercise and Profession to any and most blasphemous hereticks in the world, insomuch that it can not be properly said that there is any face of religion among them, the whole being but an oglio of opinions'.[133] Given this mentality, it is perhaps not surprising that the Stadholder-king made little effort to persist in print with the claims to be a champion of the cause of toleration which had been paraded before the world in the *Lettre écrite par Monsieur Fagel*. In general, it was probably more useful to him, at any rate in Britain and Ireland, to be celebrated as a Protestant hero.

Those contemporaries, and they were fairly numerous, that grasped the essentially *politique* character of the Stadholder-king's Church politics and religious principles were far more likely to

---

[131] [Daniel Defoe?], *The Case of Protestant Dissenters in Carolina* (London, 1706), 5.

[132] Ibid. 15.

[133] *The Ballance Adjusted; or, the Interest of Church and State Weighed and Considered upon this Revolution* (London, n.d. 1689?), 3.

condemn than to praise him for it. 'Are not the Catholics as much countenanced, and in the exercise of as much liberty for their religion, as ever?' exclaimed Sir James Montgomery with evident disgust.[134] 'What mortal wight can tell what religion he is of; or rather, is it not a contradiction to say he has any?' enquired William Anderton, adding, 'it's impossible he should be of the communion of the Church of England, which he found established by law, because he persecutes those with the utmost violence he can, whose defence he made one of the most specious pretences in his Declaration'.[135] 'They that bid most shall have it', commented Nathaniel Johnston acidly, 'for, as the Bishop of Worcester said of him, his religion is in his pocket.'[136] The injury to William's reputation was to prove an enduring one. Decades later, Dr Johnson accounted the Stadholder-king 'one of the most worthless scoundrels that ever existed'.[137]

But though the applause was scant, there is no denying that William III's contribution to the advancement of religious and intellectual freedom in both Britain and the Low Countries, as well as further afield, was immense. His *politique* stance played a crucial role in the consolidation of freedom of conscience in the United Provinces at a decisive turning-point in the history of the Republic, and in Britain at an even more decisive turning-point in the history of England and Scotland. His fight for toleration had a certain impact also in Ireland, albeit briefly, and, more lastingly, in the American colonies, where, for example, the new Massachusetts charter of 1691 substituted formal toleration for a long tradition of local intolerance.[138] Moreover, William's commitment to toleration in the Dutch context was intimately linked at all stages with his support for toleration in England and the territories England dominated. In the wake of the Revocation of the Edict of Nantes, he personally moved in the opposite direction to public opinion in both the Dutch Republic and Britain. He consciously strengthened Dutch toleration, in part to enhance his claims to be a champion of toleration in Britain, and strengthened toleration in Britain, in part

---

[134] [Montgomery], *Great Britain's Just Complaint*, p. 17.
[135] [Anderton], *Remarks upon the Present Confederacy*, p. 19.
[136] [Johnston], *The Dear Bargain*, p. 252.
[137] Quoted in Bennett, 'King William III and the Episcopate', p. 104.
[138] D. S. Lovejoy, *The Glorious Revolution in America* (Middletown, Conn., 1972), 348.

to reinforce his hand in Europe. It was his policy; but it was also a Dutch policy, one that he pursued hand-in-hand with the States of Holland. How apt was the remark of the seventeenth-century Dutch chronicler who recorded the failure of the North Holland Synod to enlist William's help in suppressing the Frisian Socinian Foecke Floris, who, on being expelled from his native province by the States of Friesland, took refuge in Holland, at Zaandam, in 1688: 'the Almighty did not wish either the States of Holland or the Stadholder to be seen to be countenancing this sort of evil in their own land just when His Majesty was striving to eradicate it from England'.[139]

[139] W. J. Kühler, *Het socinianisme in Nederland* (1912; repr. Leeuwarden, 1980), 179.

13

England's Mercantilist Response to Dutch World Trade Primacy, 1647–74

During the great period of the Dutch overseas trading system from 1590 down to about 1740, there were three major, sustained challenges to Dutch primacy in world trade.[1] First Spain with her embargoes and maritime raiding campaign down to 1647, then England from the Navigation Act (1651) until 1674, and finally France from Colbert's second tariff of 1667 down to the Peace of Utrecht (1713), all tried to mobilize every resource and expedient to break the Dutch system and siphon off the Republic's trade.

Of these three sustained challenges, that of England was the shortest in duration but was also the most dramatic and intensive. The Anglo-Dutch confrontation over commercial and colonial issues led to three bitter sea wars (1652–4; 1665–7; and 1672–4) which constitute the most direct and violent attack launched during the seventeenth century on Dutch trade and shipping. Yet it does not follow from this that England's challenge was actually the most serious or damaging of the three or, as we shall see, caused the kind of fundamental damage to the Dutch trading system that Spain and France were both able to inflict. For although England was a more successful trading and maritime power in her own right in this period than either Spain or France, and while the English navy posed a more formidable armed threat to the Dutch than the navies of either Spain or France, England nevertheless lacked the leverage over key markets which Spain and France both possessed and this, combined with the Dutch naval and privateering response, in the end largely frustrated England's efforts.

In this present study I shall endeavour to show why the English began to react so strongly to the Dutch overseas trading system in the years around 1650, and why they continued to do so for a quarter of a century; I shall then analyse English perceptions of Dutch commercial and maritime success, and finally set out the inherent limitations in England's position which effectively prevented her from seriously disrupting the Dutch overseas trading system.

To understand the background to the Anglo-Dutch Wars of the third quarter of the seventeenth century one must first of all grasp that this tremendous maritime conflict had relatively little, as Simon Groenveld has shown,[2] to do with the Anglo-Dutch quarrels about economic matters of the early part of the

---

[1] For a general analysis of the Dutch role in world trade during the seventeenth century, the reader is referred to my *Dutch Primacy in World Trade, 1585–1740* (Oxford, 1989).

[2] S. Groenveld, *Verlopend getij. De Nederlandse Republiek en de Engelse Burgeroorlog, 1640–1646*

century. The clashes in the East Indies of the 1613–23 period were still vividly remembered as was the wrangling of those years over the Cockayne Project and cloth dyeing and the Spitsbergen whale fishery.[3] But while, by the 1640s, Englishmen still spoke bitterly of real and alleged 'Amboina-like cruelties', all these encounters had long since faded into the background. By the time the new phase of Anglo-Dutch economic confrontation began in the late 1640s none of the specific quarrels of the 1613–23 period was any longer a live issue. It is true that English merchants had fresh cause for resentment after 1623 as they continued to lose ground to the Dutch in the furnishing of cloth to the Baltic and northern European commerce generally – except the traffic to Flanders.[4] But England's failure in the north was more than offset, especially since the Anglo-Spanish peace of 1630, by the triumphant success of her trade with Spain, Portugal, and the entire Mediterranean region.[5] Here the English had matters all their own way. By the early 1640s England was by far the leading northern trading power in the Iberian Peninsula, Italy and the Levant. When in 1644 Amsterdam merchants declared that the Dutch Levant trade, which had once, during the Twelve Years' Truce period, been in a flourishing condition, was now in a state of virtual collapse and that the valuable traffic had now fallen completely into English hands, they were not exaggerating.[6] England reigned not just supreme but unchallenged in Mediterranean commerce; and her ascendancy in this sector, one of the largest markets for pepper, spices and other East India commodities, enabled the English East India Company to recover from its serious reverses at Dutch hands of the 1620s.

England then was immensely successful in the 1630s and early 1640s in the maritime trade of southern Europe. But her supremacy in this sphere was based less on inherent strengths than on essentially external and basically precarious factors, as was realised by some perceptive onlookers at the time. Sir Thomas Roe, for example, commenting on England's trade in 1641 in the aftermath of the Portuguese secession from Spain, at a time when the Dutch were returning to the Portugal trade, thus giving English merchants a foretaste of what was later to happen on a larger scale, declared in Parliament that 'we enjoy almost the trade of Christendom, but if a peace happen betwixt France, Spain and the United Provinces, all these will share what we now possess alone, and

continued

(Dieren, 1984), pp.11–12; S. Groenveld, 'The English Civil Wars as a Cause of the First Anglo-Dutch War, 1640–1652', *Historical Journal,* " (1987), 545, 551.

[3] C. Wilson, *Profit and Power. A study of England and the Dutch Wars* (2nd printing, The Hague, 1978), pp.25–30; J. E. Elias, *Het voorspel van den eersten Engelschen Oorlog* (2 vol., The Hague, 1920), II, pp.92–6.

[4] J. K. Federowicz, *England's Baltic Trade in the Early Seventeenth Century* (Cambridge, 1980), pp.92–6.

[5] J. I. Israel, 'The Phases of the Dutch straatvaart. A Chapter in the Economic History of the Mediterranean', *Tijdschrift voor Geschiedenis*, XCIX (1986), 12–17.

[6] P. J. Blok, 'Koopmansadviezen aangaande het plan tot oprichting eener compagnie van assurantie (1629–1635)', *Bijdragen en Mededelingen van het Historisch Genootschap*, XXI (1900), 47f.

therefore we must provide for that day, for nothing stands secure but upon its own foundation.'[7]

The basic reason for England's supremacy in southern European trade between 1630 and 1647 was the prolonged impact of the Spanish embargo of 1621–47 against Dutch ships, goods, and Dutch-owned cargoes which was in force in all the territories of the Spanish crown, an embargo backed up buy a vigorous maritime raiding campaign waged from the Flemish sea-ports. The latter, which accounted for hundreds of Dutch merchant vessels during the 1630s and early 1640s, forced up Dutch freight and maritime insurance charges on all routes not only for Mediterranean destinations.[8] But except in the case of carrying Baltic stores and southern goods to the Flemish sea-ports (from which the Dutch were excluded by their own navy as well as the Spaniards), in northern European markets the English lacked the additional prop of the Spanish embargoes. It was the combination of embargo and crippling freight charges which had so devastating an effect on Dutch commerce with southern Europe between 1621 and 1647, and which gave England her southern ascendancy, so to speak, on a plate.

The moment the maritime raiding campaign ceased, however, with the French capture of Dunkirk in 1646, and when the Spanish embargoes against the Dutch were finally lifted in the summer of 1647,[9] the precariousness of England's trade hegemony in southern Europe and Flemish waters was suddenly revealed. And how very fragile it was soon shown to be! Within a year or two much of the edifice of English commercial supremacy in the Mediterranean world came crashing down with grim consequences for much of the rest of English economic life. With the Spanish embargoes and the Flemish privateering menace lifted, Dutch freight and marine insurance rates began to fall precipitately, wiping out the advantage previously enjoyed by English merchants shipping in Mediterranean waters.[10] England's recently flourishing transit traffic between Spain and Flanders evaporated almost overnight. Dutch ships and goods, and also Dutch factors, returned to the ports of Spain, Flanders and Spanish Italy on highly favourable terms, more favourable in some respects than those enjoyed by the English.[11] The Republic of Genoa which down to 1647 had, under Spanish pressure, purchased its grain and naval stores for the granaries and arsenals of the state from the English and Hanseatics lost no time in switching back to the Dutch whose costs were now appreciably lower.[12]

[7] H. Taylor, 'Trade, Neutrality and the "English Road", 1630–1648', *Economic History Review*, 2nd ser. XXV (1972), 239.

[8] J. Schreiner, *Nederland og Norge, 1625–1650. Trelastutforsel og handelspolitik* (Oslo, 1933), pp.48–50; J. Schreiner, 'Die Niederländer und die Norwegische Holzausfuhr im 17. Jahrhundert', *Tijdschrift voor Geschiedenis*, XLIX (1934), 323–6.

[9] J. I. Israel, *The Dutch Republic and the Hispanic World, 1606–1661* (Oxford, 1982), pp.354–6.

[10] M. P. Ashley, *Financial and Commercial Policy under the Cromwellian Protectorate* (Oxford, 1934), p.160; Israel, 'Phases of the Dutch straatvaart', p.17.

[11] Israel, *The Dutch Republic and the Hispanic World*, pp.346–7, 416–26.

[12] *Bronnen tot de geschiedenis van den Levantschen handel* (ed. K. Heeringa, 3 vol., The Hague, 1910–17), 1, p.112; John Thurloe, *A Collection of State Papers* (7 vol., London, 1742), II, pp.144–5.

The Dutch-Spanish peace and its many adverse effects on English overseas commerce was thus the main reason for the sudden sharp deterioration in English economic life at the end of the 1640s. To this we must add certain damaging consequences of the English Civil War, especially in the Caribbean area where the Royalists remained in control in Barbados, Surinam and elsewhere down to 1651, and where almost the whole trade of England's colonies in the region was re-channelled from around 1645 to 1651 into Dutch hands, with an appreciable slice of the Barbados sugar trade remaining in Dutch and Dutch-Jewish hands for long after that.[13] Taken together, the Dutch-Spanish peace and the English Civil War in the New World suddenly enabled the Dutch in the late 1640s to make very rapid progress at English expense in practically every important market – Spain, Italy, the Ottoman Levant, Flanders, the Baltic, Russia and the Caribbean. Of course, the English were not the only trading power adversely affected by the restructuring of the Dutch overseas trade system in the late 1640s. The Hanseatics, Danes and others lost ground also. But no other trading power lost ground so rapidly and in so many sectors at once as the English.

Clearly the restructuring of the Dutch trade system at the end of the 1640s was one of the most decisive factors in seventeenth-century English economic development. 'This sudden maritime crisis', as Ralph Davis expressed it, 'was the background to the first thoroughly worked out piece of English protective legislation – the Navigation Act of 1651 – and of the first Anglo-Dutch War'.[14] But it was also the background to what I shall term the classic phase of English mercantilist economic writing, by which I mean that batch of tracts and proposals which appeared between 1647 and 1672, which were concerned as a matter of great urgency with the problem of Dutch economic superiority, and which sought England's economic salvation in a wide-ranging protectionist system. Among the key examples of this mercantilist literature are Benjamin Worsley's *The Advocate* (1651), Thomas Violet's *The Advancement of Merchandise* (1651), Henry Robinson's *Certain Proposals* (1652) and Sir Josiah Child's *A New Discourse of Trade*, which was originally drafted in the mid-1660s. these writings were part of a spectrum of thought and action which consciously sought to erect a protective shield not only around England's overseas trade and shipping but also around her industries: for the Dutch restructuring severely damaged English shipbuilding and her cloth exports to Spain, [15]and caused serious damage to the English whaling and fishing industries. English fish exports to Flanders, for example, collapsed almost totally. 'In 1645', as Roland Baetens has shown, 'the vast majority of the fish [imported into the Spanish Netherlands] came from Britain . . .

---

[13] British Library (BL) MS Sloane 3662, fo. 58; V. Harlow, *A History of Barbados, 1625–1685* (Oxford, 1926), pp.65–70.

[14] R. Davis, 'English Merchant Shipping and Anglo-Dutch Rivalry in the Seventeenth Century', National Maritime Museum pamphlet (London, 1975), p.31.

[15] J. E. Farnell, 'The Navigation Act of 1651. The First Dutch War and the London Merchant Community', *Economic History Review*, 2nd ser. XVI (1963/4), 450.

whereas in 1648 virtually all of it came from the United Provinces'.[16] And like the other markets lost, this one was not subsequently regained.

English mercantilist deliberation, writing and action in the 1647–74 period sought to grapple with the specific problems posed by Dutch economic expansion during those years. Once the pre-1647 balance – almost a division of labour – between England and the Dutch in international commerce was overturned, a whole range of major economic challenges arose simultaneously. The most immediately pressing for English merchants trading with Spain and Italy, for the Levant company, and also for the Caribbean merchants, was the sudden post-1647 influx of commodities from these distant markets into England indirectly, carried by the Dutch, via the Dutch entrepot. Before 1647 there was no penetration of the English market by Italian silks, Canary wines or Zante currants shipped in via the Dutch entrepôt – at least not since 1621. Then all at once, from 1647, there was a massive and utterly disorientating influx. Benjamin Worsley was not exaggerating when he wrote in 1651 that 'at Spain, Canaries, Zante, with several other places in the Straits where they formerly rarely laded hither one ship of goods; they now lately laded hither more than we.'[17]

The obvious answer to this challenge was to seal off the English market, and also Scotland,[18] to merchandise shipped via the Dutch entrepôt. In 1645 the Greenland company, confronting the massive expansion of the Dutch whale fishery of the 1640s, had obtained from Parliament an Act forbidding the importing of whale products into England in any but their own ships.[19] What was now required was to generalize this principle. In January 1648 the Levant company in London petitioned Parliament 'against the importation of Turkey commodities from Holland and other places but directly from the places of their growth'.[20] Further pressure, including that of the Baltic merchants, built up rapidly from all sides. During 1650 the standing Council for Trade and the Council of State, assisted by Worsley who was the secretary of the former, and by Thomas Violet, laboured on a general measure designed to halt the flood of southern European and colonial commodities into England indirectly via Holland and Zeeland. After prolonged deliberation and several drafts all this endeavour finally gave birth to the Navigation Act of 1651, the most celebrated piece of English mercantilist legislation.

---

[16] R. Baetens, 'An Essay on Dunkirk Merchants and Capital Growth during the Spanish Period', in *From Dunkirk to Danzig. Shipping and Trade in the North Sea and the Baltic, 1350–1850* (ed. W. G. Heeres *et al.*, Hilversum, 1988), p.121.

[17] B. Worsley, *The Advocate or a Narrative of the State and Condition of Things between the English and Dutch Nation, in relation to Trade* (London, 1652), p.7.

[18] *Calendar of State papers. Domestic, 1651*, p.300.

[19] T. Violet, *The Advancement of Merchandize or Certain Propositions for the Improvement of the Trade of this Commonwealth* (London, 1651), p.7; Ashley, *Financial and Commercial Policy*, pp. 161–2.

[20] Public Record Office, London (PRO) SP 105/150, fo. 167, resolution of the Levant Company Court, 17 Jan. 1647 (1648); the Company renewed its complaint about importing 'indirectly . . . from the Netherlands' the following year, see *Calendar of State Papers. Domestic, 1649–50*, p.12.

But the Navigation Act dealt only with one particular aspect of the English 'maritime crisis' precipitated by the post-1647 restructuring of the Dutch trading system. What the Navigation Act did not, and could not, do was tackle the alarming deterioration in England's trading position in overseas markets, except where, as in the case of the Canaries wine trade and Puglian olive oil, England herself was the principal consumer. For the rest, other methods of intervention by the English state would have to be found. The Caribbean colonies required more than just the establishment of Parliament's authority, in 1651, and the Navigation Act for its solution, for most of the sugar output of Barbados and elsewhere brought up by the Dutch was destined not for England but for the sugar refineries of Amsterdam. In any case, the root of the problem was that the settlers in the Caribbean possessions preferred to buy the linen, tools, brandy and black slaves that they needed from the Dutch and from Dutch Jews because they knew that from them they would get a better deal than they would trading with London. 'The islanders here', it was reported from Barbados in 1655, 'much desire commerce with strangers [i.e. with the Dutch and Jews], our English merchants traffiquing in those parts generally being great extortioners'.[21] Despite the success of the authorities in seizing a considerable number of Dutch ships, often from Zeeland, attempting to trade with the colonies during the 1650s, an illegal contraband traffic using Dutch vessels continued to flourish at least into the late 1650s.[22] After that the direct Dutch traffic does seem to have tailed off. But this still left the problem of how to close the loopholes through which a largely Dutch-Jewish indirect traffic continued to flourish.[23] An important step here was the Act of March 1664 forbidding English vessels to sail to the colonies other than direct from an English port, thereby stopping English ships from sailing first to a Dutch port to load their goods and then from Holland or Zeeland on to the Caribbean. The English ambassador at The Hague, Sir George Downing, commented on this occasion that this Act

> doth very much trouble them here; for that it breakes all the Jewes correspondency att Barbados and elsewhere, and hinders them of their sale of vast quantities of the manufactures of the country; for that it will not quitt cost to send them first to England, and pay customes there, and then to ship them againe for his Majesty's plantations; but instead thereof, the English manufacturers are, and will be, new rented, which also will be felt in his Majesty's customes.[24]

But in the Caribbean and also North America, where the local Dutch loophole in the shape of New Netherland was suppressed by the simple expedient of

[21] Thurloe, *State Papers*, III, p.142.

[22] The parliamentary expedition sent to reduce Barbados to obedience in 1651 captured twenty-four Dutch vessels found trading there, five of them Zeelanders; eighteen more Dutch merchantmen trading with the island, or *Barbados-vaerders* as they were called in Dutch, were seized in 1655 and another six in 1658; Israel, *Dutch Primacy*, p.239.

[23] Harlow, *History of Barbados*, pp.93–4.

[24] 24. Sir George Downing to Lord Chancellor Clarendon, The Hague, 22 April 1664 in T. H. Lister, *Life and Administration of Clarendon* (3 vol., London, 1838), III, p.308.

sending out a military expedition in the autumn of 1664, England could rely on her superior political and military leverage to impose a framework advantageous to England no matter how disadvantageous to the local consumer. But the crux of England's difficulties was not the unco-operative attitude of her American colonists but her reduced competitiveness in European markets where she lacked the leverage to shut the Dutch out by political means or force. Until 1647 England had experienced no difficulty in selling great quantities of her manufactures, above all woollen products, in Spain, as there was no other way – with both Dutch and (since 1635) French goods excluded – that the merchants of Madrid and Seville could furnish Spain and Spanish America with an adequate range of textiles. In exchange for her cloth, fish and other products, England had bought up the bulk of Spain's wool and dyestuff exports and supplied much of the rest of Europe, including the Dutch entrepôt,[25] with these key commodities. But the trade revolution of the late 1640s had totally transformed the picture. 'That the commodities of Spaine are so inhanced', lamented one English onlooker,

> and bought up, and the cloathing of Holland within these few years so thriveth and increaseth that whereas we formerly brought home foure or five thousand baggs of cloth wooll and the Hollanders scarce a thousand, which they had then by re-shipping, theirs being prohibited, they now carry away five or six thousand and wee bring not past 12 or 1500 in the yeare at most.[26]

How was such a setback to be reversed? Some dreamed that England could somehow use her power and influence to pressure Spain into making special arrangements for English merchants, excluding the Dutch. One observer proposed that 'it can be done by the authority of the king of Spain' who should be persuaded 'by our state' to

> undertake for us the pre-emption of all the woolls of Segovia and Castile, which he will permit to be exported and that for a certain term of years, and at such a price as the owners of the wooll and the English contractor may both have reasonable content; and that the said king be obliged that no woolls shall be exported out of any of his ports but by the English contractor.[27]

But the only part of this reasoning which was at all realistic was that England did indeed need to prise the Spanish wool traffic out of Dutch hands if she was fully to restore her own previous position as an exporter of woollen textiles not only to Spain but also to other key markets such as the Baltic, Russia and Ottoman Turkey. This was not because England required Spanish wool as such; she

---

[25] *A Brief Narration of the Pesent Estate of the Bilbao Trade* (?London, ?1650), p.9; Taylor, 'Trade, Neutrality and the 'English Road', p.240; J. I. Israel, 'Spanish Wool Exports and the European Economy, 1610–1640', *Economic History Review*, 2nd ser. "III (1980), 205, 208.

[26] *A Brief Narration*, p.2.

[27] Thurloe, *State Papers*, I, pp.200–1; see also Wilson, *Profit and Power*, p.31. f

had her own plentiful supplies of wool albeit of a cheaper and less fine type than Castilian merino wool. The reason was that Spanish wool was the basic raw material of the Dutch fine cloth industry and it was with their high-quality cloth, *lakens* (made from Castilian wool) and camlets (made from Turkish mohair yarn) that the Dutch were making their most spectacular gains as suppliers of textiles to European markets. As one English commentator expressed it, 'our getting all the Spanish cloth woolls into our hands will totally dissolve the clothing of Holland, which, by means of the woolls, hath of late years mightily increased, to the destruction of the vent of all fine cloths of English making, both in Holland, France and the East lands [as well as Spain]'.[28]

The fall in English cloth exports to Spain since 1647 was rightly seen as inseparable from the post-1647 influx into Spain, and via Cadiz to Spanish America, of Dutch fine cloth and camlets. Clearly the most straightforward remedy for this state of affairs was to undermine the Dutch fine cloth industry by capturing the Spanish wool supply, through political influence or by force. But if such feverish plans were rife in the crisis atmosphere of the late 1640s and early 1650s, the frustrations of the indecisive Anglo-Spanish War of 1655–60 finally put paid to all such notions. This left no alternative but to concentrate on other, more practicable methods of restoring England's exports and competitiveness.

Dutch commercial superiority over England in the 1647–74 period had various aspects. There was the enviably low level of Dutch shipping costs, and their unrivalled shipping and shipbuilding capacity. There was the strength of Dutch financial institutions and their low interest rates. But no aspect of Dutch world primacy in these decades provoked greater anxiety in England than the universally admitted superior quality of Dutch manufactures: a most interesting strand of classic English mercantilist thought was concerned with improving the quality of English output by means of state intervention. Almost without exception English economic writers of the mid-seventeenth century were acutely conscious of, even obsessed with, the inferiority of English to Dutch processing and products.

In Worsley's view one of the principal strengths of the Dutch

> over us was the singular and prudent care they took in preserving the credit of those commodities which are their own proper manufactures, by which they keep up their repute and sale of them abroad, and by this means, likewise, very much damnifying and spoiling us.[29]

A Brief Narration drew attention to the somewhat tarnished reputation of English bays, serges, perpetuanes, says, fustians, and Norwich stuffs.[30] Henry Robinson pointed out how 'exceeding destructive' were the 'deceitfulnesse' and 'frauds'

---

[28] Thurloe, *loc. cit.;* see also *A Brief Narration*, pp.1–3, 9; and Henry Robinson, *Certain Proposals in Order to the Peoples Freedome and Accomodation in some Particulars, with the Advancement of Trade and Navigation of this Commonwealth in generall* (London,1652), p.11.

[29] Worsley, *The Advocate*, p.7.

[30] *A Brief Narration*, p.3.

prevalent in English cloth manufacture.[31] Sir Josiah Child, struck by the difference in repute between English and Dutch fish products, affirmed that English fish exports 'often prove false and deceitfully made and our pilchards from the West-Country false packed'.[32] All these writers saw the source of Dutch qualitative superiority, probably rightly, in the close – the Dutch economic writer Pieter de la Court thought stifling[33] – supervision exercised by the Dutch provincial, municipal and guild authorities over every aspect both of manufacture and of weighing, measuring and packaging. It was this meticulous, unceasing official scrutiny of the Dutch manufacturing process, according to Worsley, which was the 'cause of the so great thriving of our neighbour's cloathing, and of the so great ruine and decaie (on the contrarie) of our own'. He contrasts the scrupulous care of the Dutch authorities in this respect with the 'carelessness of this nation, in keeping our manufactures to their due contents, weight and goodness'.[34]

All these writers are much more concerned to stress the need to regulate the quality of English output, and improve it, than to specify by what official mechanisms this should be done. Henry Robinson merely states that fraud and 'deceitfulnesse' in cloth production should 'be enquired after and prevented in future'.[35] *A Brief Narration* advocates that English textiles 'be so regulated for goodnesse, so faithfully viewed, searched and sealed, for length, breadth and weight that men how unskilful soever, may buy them upon the credit of seals and contents upon them, without feare or hazzard of being abused or deceived by the makers of them.'[36] No doubt there was much entrenched resistance to the idea of closer regulation and relatively little was achieved. Nevertheless tighter public regulation of the processes of manufacture was certainly one of the central priorities of English mercantilist thought in its classic phase and there is some reflection of this in the legislative activity of the government. One of the early achievements of the Council for Trade, set up in August 1650 to deal with the economic crisis facing the country, was the steering through of an Act 'for regulating the making of stuffs in Norfolk and Norwich' which sought to set up new checking arrangements at Norwich to supervise their manufacture.[37]

Another central concern was that of wanting to provide England with the financial facilities and, above all, the very low interest rates which the Dutch entrepôt enjoyed and which were rightly identified as one of the major strengths

[31] Robinson, *Certain Proposals*, p.11.

[32] Child speaks also of the 'exact making of all their native commodities, and packing of their herring, codfish and all other commodities . . . ', Sir Josiah Child, *A New Discourse of Trade* (1672) (London, 1693), pp.2–3.

[33] T. van Tijn, 'Pieter de la Court, Zijn leven en zijn economische denkbeelden', *Tijdschrift voor Geschiedenis*, LXIX (1956), 316–25.

[34] Worsley, *The Advocate*, p.9.

[35] Robinson, *Certain proposals*, p.11.

[36] *A Brief Narration*, p.3.

[37] C. H. Firth and R. S. Rait, *Acts and Ordinances of the Interregnum. 1642–1660* (2 vol., London,1911), II, pp.451–5.

of the Dutch trading system. English mercantilist writers of the third quarter of the seventeenth century could not but be painfully aware of the gap between their country and the United Provinces in this respect. By 1670 Dutch interest rates stood as low as three per cent while English rates were at twice that level. Sir Josiah Child commented that 'Dutch low interest hath miserably lessened us in all trades of the world not secured us by laws, or by some natural advantage which over-ballanceth the disproportion of our interest of money'.[38] In the early 1650s Thomas Violet and Henry Robinson were both emphatic that the state must intervene to generate a better store of money and easier access to it, Robinson lamenting the ease with which in Holland money' was available to one and all at four or five per cent interest'.[39] He is also quite clear that the state should provide England with a public bank.

Seventeenth-century European mercantilism was not just the advocacy of increased, and more systematic, state intervention in order to promote the economic interest of the state, but also deregulation in the sense of removing all economic privileges, concessions and charters which restrict or obstruct the activity of the whole.[40]

English mercantilist thought, writing and action during the 1647–74 period were in this, as in other respects, fully typical of the wider phenomenon. It is well known that the old chartered companies were by no means looked on with favour by many of the new men in positions of influence under the Commonwealth regime. When the Council for Trade was set up in August 1650 it was set, as one of its specific tasks, to deliberate 'whether it be necessary to give way to a more open and free trade than that of Companies and Societies, and in what manner it is fittest to be done'.[41] No doubt in some sectors of European trade, privilege and charter were weakened during these decades. But there could be no generalized attack on the chartered company as such, for the Dutch themselves relied on such organizations, or other forms of cartel, for a great part of their traffic to the Americas and Africa, as well as to the East Indies and for regulating their fisheries. If England was going to compete successfully in regions such as Asia, Africa and the Levant then chartered companies not only had to stay; they had to be strengthened or in the case of the Royal Africa Company set up by Charles II, increased.

An element of deregulation and liberalization was also present regarding the issues of foreign immigration and religious toleration. Several English mercantilist writers lamented Dutch success in drawing off skilled workers to Leiden and urged the English state to endeavour to attract skilled operatives from the continent to England.[42] Thomas Violet, whose writings frequently

---

[38] Child, *A New Discourse of Trade*, preface; see also pp.8, 10.

[39] *Calendar of State Papers. Domestic, 1650*, pp.178, 183; Robinson, *Certain Proposals*, pp.10, 18–19.

[40] J. I. Israel, *European Jewry in the Age of Mercantilism, 1550–1750* (Oxford, 1985), pp.2–3.

[41] Firth and Rait, *Acts and Ordinances*, II, p.405.

[42] Thurloe, *State Papers*, 1, p.200: Violet, *The Advancement of Merchandize*, pp.10–11.

exemplify that mixture of advocacy of state intervention and deregulating tendencies so characteristic of English economic thought of the period, wanted Dover turned into a free port and England to be altogether more accommodating to 'merchants strangers', pointing out that Genoa, Livorno and Amsterdam had all achieved commercial greatness by granting foreigners 'equal privileges with their own natives'.[43] The pressure for the re-admission of the Jews into England, and subsequently the arguments for keeping them there, certainly emanated in part from mercantilist sources.[44] Sir Josiah Child judged that the commerce of the Jews, even if prejudicial to particular groups of established merchants in England, should be regarded as advantageous to England's trade as a whole.[45]

The central idea in the work of men such as Worsley, Violet, Robinson, Downing and Child, who shaped English mercantilist thought in its classic phase, was that

> for recovery of trade and commerce, the merchants need encouragement and protection from the state, at home and abroad, according to the practice of the lords of the United Provinces who are so vigilant over their traffic that, upon the least complaint of obstruction, they use all means, either by treaty or by force, to remove it.[46]

But how much of the state action inspired by this central idea proved effective? Certain strands of English mercantilist legislation, the Navigation Acts and the restrictions on shipping sailing to the colonies, undoubtedly had a considerable effect. Yet, all considered, the impact of England's mercantilist challenge to Dutch world trade primacy proved relatively weak. When it came to using the power of the state to manipulate markets and engineer shifts in international trade, it would seem that England could not really hope to match Spain or France. For there was nothing which the Dutch obtained from England which was essential for the functioning of their trade system, while England was never of the first importance as a market for Dutch products and re-exports.[47] Indeed, insofar as the Navigation Act reduced Dutch re-exports to England, and their carrying of goods from other markets to England, it served, paradoxically, to free the Dutch further from any reliance they may have had on England. How different was the position with regard to pre-1647 Spain or post-1667 France! Spanish and Spanish American commodities, in particular silver, dyestuffs and merino wool, were all vitally important to the functioning of Dutch overseas trade and Holland's industries, as were the commodities of France, especially wine, brandy, and salt. Similarly both Spain and France were many times more important than England as markets for Dutch products and re-exports.[48] In

[43] *Ibid.*, pp.2–3

[44] D. Katz, *Philosemites and the Readmission of the Jews into England, 1603–1655* (Oxford, 1982), pp.225–9; Israel, *European Jewry*, pp.158–60.

[45] *Ibid.*, p.160.

[46] *Calendar of State Papers. Domestic, 1650*, p.180.

[47] Israel, *Dutch Primacy*, p.285.

[48] *Ibid.*, pp. 285–6.

the case of Dutch exports of fine cloth and camlets and re-exports of spices, for example, France and Spain were the two largest markets whilst England was of almost negligible significance. Thus ultimately England had no other effective weapon against the Dutch trading system during the classic period of English mercantilism than her formidable naval power.

Potentially, England's naval might did represent an overwhelming threat to Dutch world trade primacy, and there were many foreign diplomatic observers who were of the opinion that England's navy and privateers would indeed soon overthrow Dutch hegemony over maritime trade.[49] In England, in the midst of the 'maritime crisis' which began in the late 1640's, the temptation to use the country's naval might to bludgeon the nation's way out of its difficulties was almost overwhelming. It was not mercantilist legislation such as the Navigation Act of 1651 which made the First Anglo-Dutch War inevitable but, as Simon Groenveld has shown,[50] the escalating English harassment of Dutch shipping in the Channel, North Sea, Irish Sea, and Caribbean. By 1651 English seizures of Dutch merchant vessels on the high seas on a variety of pretexts, such as that they were carrying arms to Ireland or Scotland, or trading with English colonies in the Caribbean – frequently well-grounded suspicions but not ones the Dutch authorities had any sympathy for – had reached intolerable levels. During 1651 no less than 140 Dutch merchant vessels were brought into English ports by the navy or privateers on one charge or another.[51] Another thirty Dutch ships were seized on the high seas in the month of January 1652 alone. For the Dutch, interference on such a scale was totally unacceptable. Either the Dutch state possessed the power to compel England to stop disrupting Dutch commerce, or it did not. If it did not then Dutch world trade primacy was at an end.

Nor is there any question that if it came to a fight, England's navy had the edge over that of the Dutch. Initially, the Dutch may have had more recent experience of naval warfare than the English, and it may be that their best commanders, Tromp and De Ruyter, had more flair than their counterparts. But England's navy had more and larger purpose-built warships and a decided superiority in terms of weight of guns.[52] By the time of the second war, the Dutch navy had been greatly strengthened, but so had England's, so that the gap in firepower was never closed. It was the potency of the English 'three-deckers' above all which persuaded Venetian, French and Swedish observers that it was English guns which would finally put an end to Dutch commercial greatness.

[49] Gugliemo Berchet, *Cromwell e la Repubblica di Venezia* (Venice, 1864), p.73; *Calendar of State Papers, Venetian, XXVIII* (1647–52), p.256; Wilson, *Profit and Power*, p.65.

[50] Groenveld, 'The English Civil Wars', pp.561–4.

[51] *Ibid.*, p.561.

[52] C. Boxer, 'The Anglo-Dutch Wars of the 17th Century, 1652–1674', National Maritime Museum pamphlet (London, 1974), pp.4–6, 15, 25.

Yet in this era of furious sea-wars with the Dutch, English sea-power in the end proved much less effective than expected. England was superior in naval power but failed to win the naval conflict. In the First War England won the big battles in the North Sea, but despite this failed to win any commercial or maritime concessions whatsoever from the Dutch. In the Second War the English were eventually beaten and induced to sign a peace by which Surinam, the English foothold in the Banda islands, Pulorun, and the former English West Africa base of Cormantine were handed over to the Dutch in exchange for New Netherland, which the Dutch considered indefensible in any case. England also conceded to the Dutch the much argued-over principle of 'free ship, free goods', which meant that England now abandoned all right to stop and search Dutch vessels suspected of trading with her enemies or breaking her laws.[53] Finally, in the Third War, in which the Dutch were all but overwhelmed by a joint Anglo-French attack, it seemed at first impossible that England should fail to make massive gains at Dutch expense. Yet not only, by 1674, was Charles II induced to make peace with the Dutch without having captured anything, but he failed even to recover Surinam, Pulorun or Cormantine, surely one of the most astounding results in the history of maritime conflict!

Why then in the end, despite all initial expectations, did England's naval might prove an ineffective instrument against Dutch world trade primacy? The answer is that the Dutch overseas trading system rested on a degree of leverage over markets and shipping resources, as well as financial power, which enabled the Dutch Republic to put such pressure on England that it proved impossible to sustain the naval offensive for long enough to do the Dutch real damage or to force them into maritime concessions. The First Anglo-Dutch War has traditionally been regarded as a victory for England. But this is only true with regard to the naval battles in home waters. Further afield the boot was very much on the other foot with extremely grim consequences for England's trade and shipping. The Dutch, in alliance with Denmark, closed the Sound to English shipping, shutting down the whole of the English Baltic trade for as long as the war lasted.[54] They had the upper hand in the Mediterranean also and, after their victory over the English at the battle of Livorno in March 1653, shut down the whole of the English trade with Italy and the Levant.[55] In the East Indies and the Persian Gulf the Dutch East India company swept the English off the sea.

---

[53] Ashley, *Financial and Commercial Policy*, p.172; this important concession was spelt out in detail under the Anglo-Dutch maritime agreement of February 1668; see H. C. Diferee, *De geschiedenis van den Nederlandschen handel tot den val der Republiek* (Amsterdam, 1908), p.325.

[54] Israel, *Dutch Primacy*, p.211.

[55] 'Our losses here have been so visible to all Europe, Asia, and Africa', reported the English consul at Livorno in January 1654, 'that they will not believe but our condition is as bad at home'; Thurloe, *State papers*, I, p.656.

In the Second War the Dutch again closed the Baltic to England and paralysed England's trade with the Mediterranean. Again the Dutch company had matters all its own way in the East Indies and on the coast of India. But this time there was also a new form of pressure: the Dutch mounted a highly effective privateering campaign of their own which, from the early stages of the war onwards, captured more, and more valuable ships, from the English than vice-versa.[56] In the Third War, attacked by both the French and the English, the Dutch States General kept all the merchant and fishing fleets in port making thousands of men redundant and forcing them, to feed their families, to sign on with the privateers. This time the Dutch privateers hunted the English in large packs off the east coast of Britain, in the Channel, around the coasts of Spain and Portugal, off Virginia and New England, almost everywhere. The result was the greatest disaster in England's maritime history. Daniel Defoe later stated that 'in the last war with the Dutch we lost 2,000 sail of ships great and small in the first year'.[57] This was an exaggeration. But the real total for the whole of the war was certainly well above 700;[58] and although the disaster was excised from the national record and is rarely if ever mentioned in modern history books, it had a tremendous, demoralizing impact at the time. In effect, England accepted in 1674 that she could not break the Dutch system by force.

To sum up, England's response to her post-1647 'maritime crisis', caused by the restructuring and strengthening of the Dutch overseas trade system in the wake of the Dutch-Spanish peace, was a sustained outburst of aggressive mercantilist deliberation, writing and legislation. Some of the legislation had far-reaching effects and did strengthen England's shipping and especially her colonial trade. Also the role of privilege in English trade was at least somewhat reduced and new elements, including the Jews, began for the first time to play a significant role. But it is also true that large parts of the English mercantilist programme, including the tightening of public regulation of manufacturing and packaging, and the establishment of Dutch –style financial institutions, failed to yield much result. Ultimately the English mercantilist challenge to the Dutch system, backed up though it was by superior naval force, proved to be largely ineffective.

---

[56] 56. J. R. Bruijn, 'Dutch Privateering during the Second and Third Anglo-Dutch Wars', *Acta Historiae Neerlandicae*, IX (1976), 89; Israel, *Dutch Primacy*, pp.278–9.

[57] 57. Daniel Defoe, *An Enquiry into the Danger and Consequences of a War with the Dutch* (London, 1712), p.4.

[58] 58. Bruijn, 'Dutch Privateering', p.89; J. R. Bruijn's research on this subject has totally transformed our perceptions of the role of Dutch privateering in the Anglo-Dutch Wars; nevertheless, as he himself admits, the figure he gives for Dutch prizes taken from the English are, certainly, considerably too low; see Israel, *Dutch Primacy*, pp.298–9.

14

The Amsterdam Stock Exchange
and the English Revolution of 1688

During the seventeenth century the Dutch maritime zone acted as the hub of world commerce and finance. The dimensions and apparatus of this, the first true world entrepot, were quite extensive. Harbours, warehouse complexes, shipyards, and processing plants of many kinds stretched over a relatively large area from the Scheldt estuary, at its southern end, to Friesland, in the north, linked by a continuous network of canals and waterways and dotted with commercial and industrial towns, fishing ports, and (especially along the Zaan) manufacturing villages. But the undeniable nerve-centre of this vast entrepot, and the world-wide overseas trading system which depended on it, was the Amsterdam Exchange. This famous bourse was the most important that existed anywhere in the seventeenth century and, perhaps, the most influential which has ever existed. 'La Bourse d'Amsterdam', as one foreign writer summed it up, 'est regardée par tous les négociants comme la plus considérable de toutes'.[1] A French official who in 1700 claimed that Amsterdam was 'le théâtre où tous les changes du monde se font' exaggerated but also testified to the unprecedented and unparalleled influence which the Amsterdam Exchange then exerted over the mechanisms of world trade and finance.[2]

The Amsterdam Exchange in its wider sense consisted of the 'Exchange' building itself (where most of the commodity dealing was concentrated, as well as much of the insurance and shipping brokerage), and a cluster of other institutions – the Wisselbank (Exchange Bank), the separate grain exchange, the Weigh-House, the civic Chamber of Insurance, and the brokers' informal meeting-places which, by the late seventeenth century, were often nearby coffee- and tea-shops. A major additional component, and the main theme of this present study, was the 'stock exchange' as historians generally call it, although in fact it was an unofficial, informal market, almost unsupervised, which met at certain times in the main Exchange building but also outside on the Dam[3], in front of the Town Hall, and, still more informally, in the city's nearby Jewish quarter.

Like any great business centre the Amsterdam bourse alternated between periods of relative stability and instability and occasionally was gripped by a serious

---

* I would like to thank Edgar Samuel, director of the Jewish Museum in London for his help with several aspects of this article.

[1] Jacques Savary des Bruslons, *Dictionnaire universel de commerce* I (3 vols., Paris 1723) 451.

[2] Cited in V.Barbour, *Capitalism in Amsterdam in the 17th Century* (3rd edn. Ann Arbour, Michigan 1976) 78.

[3] Joseph Penso de la Vega, *Confusión de confusiones* (1688) ed. M.F.J. Smith (The Hague 1939) 97.

panic or crisis. Much the best known of the major crises which hit the Amsterdam Exchange during the seventeenth century was the devastating crash of 1672, an experience which was to be long remembered. But another serious crisis, hitherto almost completely unknown to modern historians, occurred in 1688, the year of the Williamite political revolutions in England and Scotland. Moreover, it turns out that there are integral links between the Amsterdam stock market crisis of 1688 and the English Revolution of that year which are of considerable importance not only for gaining a fuller grasp of the workings of the Amsterdam stock market, and Exchange more generally, but also for understanding the role of the Dutch Republic in the making of the English Revolution. At the same time, this crucial episode, has, as we shall see, an important bearing on Jewish history.

As one would expect, Amsterdam merchants and financiers were accustomed to scrutinise business news from abroad of every sort. Like any bourse, the Amsterdam Exchange was always sensitive to news of developments and changes overseas of a kind liable to affect supply and demand and therefore commodity prices and freightage conditions. But in an age when statecraft and war impinged so powerfully on all market forces, an age of sweeping embargoes, tariff-wars, and trade restrictions, as well as naval blockades and privateering campaigns, Amsterdam was also highly sensitive to all kinds of European political and diplomatic news. Indeed, as I have argued elsewhere[4], the most dramatic and unsettling upheavals on the Amsterdam Exchange during the seventeenth century were caused not by shortages, subsistence crises, gluts, or any specifically economic factor, or factors, but by European political conjunctures of a sort liable to threaten the security of the Republic and its shipping.

Modern historical literature has had very little to say about the preoccupation of the Amsterdam Exchange as a whole, and the stock market in particular, with European statecraft and politics. But contemporaries often remarked on this sensitivity. In March 1664, for example, the English ambassador at The Hague commented that

'the very noise of the conference which I was to have this weeke, and had, concerning the East India Company and the rumours of a warre between England and the United Provinces like to be upon the matters now in difference, have already made the East Indie actions fall this weeke from 498 to 481'.[5]

Gregorio Leti, the Italian Protestant city historiographer of Amsterdam, pointed out in his book the *Teatro Belgico* (which he compiled during the dramatic events of 1688-1690) that there were two main regular influences on price movements in the Amsterdam share market.[6] Since the stock traded in consisted mainly of shares, or 'actions', lodged in the various chambers of the Dutch East and West India Companies, one of these main influences was business news from the Indies and, in particular, reports preceding and accompanying the arrival of a return fleet from the

---

[4] J.I. Israel, *Dutch primacy in world trade, 1585-1740* (Oxford 1989) 86, 255-256.

[5] Quoted in T.H. Lister, *Life and administration of Edward, first Earl of Clarendon* III (3 vols., London 1838) 300.

[6] Gregorio Leti, *Teatro Belgico, o vero ritratti historici, chronologici, politici e geografici delle sette Provincie Unite* II (2 vols., Amsterdam 1690) 243.

Indies when, if it proved richly laden, share prices would rise and, if disappointing, fall. The other main influence, according to Leti, was European political news, colonial stock tending to rise in value when prospects for peace were good and fall when there was talk of war. In his *Confusión de Confusiones,* the first ever extended account of the workings of a stock market (and a book likewise compiled in 1688) the Sephardi Jewish merchant-writer, Joseph Penso de la Vega, agrees that business news from the Indies, and prospects for peace or war in Europe, were two main influences affecting movements in the stock market but adds also a third main factor, namely the designs and machinations of the stock exchange dealers themselves.[7] There was, however, a great difference between the sort of impact which political news was liable to exert and that of business reports from the Indies and the doings of the brokers. For where the latter would affect only one, or both, sets of colonial share prices, encouraging, or disturbing, political news was apt to grip not just the stock market but all components of the Exchange, affecting other securities, notably States of Holland bonds or 'obligations', and insurance, interest, and exchange rates, as well as share prices. Political news, in other words, was more likely than business news, to transform the business scene as a whole. This was strikingly evident at times of major political alarm, such as in 1672 and 1688, when Dutch East and West India Company shares tended to fluctuate more or less together with 'obligations' and financial confidence generally. But it is noticeable also in more normal times that significant political events, and the interpretation put on them by the Amsterdam financial community, caused stock prices, 'obligations' and the money market to move together as aspects of a single bourse reaction. The sudden dissolution of Charles II of England's last Parliament, in April 1681, for example, which Amsterdam financial circles interpreted as meaning that for the moment the English crown was weak and short of money, and therefore unable to advance England's trade interests as vigorously as in the past, pushed up Dutch East India Company (VOC) shares from 408 to 422% and 'so proportionatly' as the English consul at Amsterdam described the movement 'other obligations on the land', that is the bonds issued by the Dutch provincial governments.[8]

Precisely because foreign news was so crucial to the functioning and fluctuations of the Amsterdam Exchange, the dealers in VOC and WIC (Dutch West India Company) actions were not content merely to remain passive recipients of news from neighbouring European countries and overseas. On the contrary, there are clear signs, certainly by the 1680s, that they had become highly skilled at exploiting the opportunities of leverage over share price movements arising from the fact that businessmen in that age frequently received information from abroad more quickly than diplomats and governments. Dealers in the seventeenth and eighteenth centuries had more scope for massaging news in order to precipitate trends in the stock exchange than was to be the case in more recent times.[9] And it was to this, above all, that the dealers in the late seventeenth century owed their somewhat unsavoury

[7] Penso de la Vega, *Confusión de confusiones*, 27: 'sabed que tienen las acciones tres estimulos para subir y otros tres para baxar: el estado de la India, la disposición de la Europa, y el juego de los accionistas'.

[8] British Library (BL) MS Add. 37981, fo.34v. Carr to Blathwayt, Amsterdam, 25 April 1681.

[9] See Jonathan I. Israel, 'Een merkwaardig literair werk en de Amsterdamse effectenmarkt in 1688: Joseph Penso de la Vega's *Confusión de confusiones*', *De zeventiende eeuw* 6 (1990) 159-161.

reputation. When, for example, Louis XIV met representatives of the Elector of Cologne in May 1687 and, over the next two months, negotiated a new military pact with the state which had been instrumental in the joint Anglo-French attack on the United Provinces in 1672, international tension inevitably rose and Amsterdam was awash with rumour-mongering. The Elector of Cologne ratified his offensive-defensive pact with Louis on 9 July. But it was during the preceding fortnight when everyone, diplomats and merchants alike, were striving to penetrate what was happening that the share dealers had their opportunity. News was 'given out by the actionists at Amsterdam', reported the English ambassador at The Hague, the marquis d'Albeville, that the

'French king...gave out letters of marque against [Dutch subjects] that Hanover was entered into alliance with the French as well as Colen. All these news being assured by the Jews and actionists at the same time my Memoriall [on behalf of James II] was given in, caused a consternation for a days tyme at Amsterdam; all was over the next day and the deceit of the Jews and actionists discovered.'[10]

The ambassador was particularly struck by the way his representation on behalf of James II was manipulated by the dealers. They were clearly reckoning on a fall in share prices; but some of the brokers were apparently spreading rumours designed to counter-act the drop, one actionist reporting that the 'marquis of Albeville sent 60,000 livers to Amsterdam to buy actions two days before he gave in his memorial, a Jew alledging that he had the money in h:s hands'. While expressing his annoyance, the marquis added that 'he wisheth that were true'.[11]

Not only did the brokers massage news to concert up and downward movements in share prices but according to Leti and the Amsterdam lawyer Nicolaas Muys van Holy who, in 1687, published a pamphlet highly critical of the doings of the actionists of the Amsterdam stock exchange, the dealers on occasion went so far as to fabricate completely bogus reports with the intention of stampeding the markets up or down.[12] In the circumstances, with methods of obtaining foreign news so rudimentary, there was simply no way, short of suppressing dealings in securities and shares altogether that such manipulation for profit could be prevented. The scope for exploiting restricted information was all the greater in that the buying and selling of state secrets was an integral part of the diplomatic scene at The Hague. An Englishman residing at Amsterdam in the 1680s vividly evoked the atmosphere of corrupt collusion between the Amsterdam dealers and the international diplomatic community at The Hague in a letter he wrote to the English resident there in February 1686:

'There are here some Actionists in the East India Company who, knowing of the honour I have to be known to your Excellency these many years, doe by me propose a handsome gratification if you think fitt to give them the first and best intelligence of things so farre as they may be usefull to give an influence to their way of trade : this I presume to propose daring to think that, as Your Honour would not expose the mysteries and main secrets of the state,   so,

[10] BL MS Add. 41814, fo. 267v. D'Albeville to Middleton, The Hague, 4 July 1687.

[11] Ibidem.

[12] Leti, *Teatro Belgico* II, 243; N. Muys van Holy, *Relaes en contradictie op de motiven om het kopen en verkopen van Oost- en West Indise actien, die niet getransporteert werden...te beswaeren met een impost* (Amsterdam 1687) (Knuttel, 12622) 1-2.

on the other side, I am bold to thinke that such a correspondency prudently and cunningly managed in this city would be able to doe the King [of England] a great deale of service by making these men to hazard their stocks and ruine themselves, or make it run into better hands, and so would procure the ruin in a great measure of their proud East India Company which is the only cause of all their insolencies against our traders in those eastern parts of the world: but, besides, I know that all ambassadors of foreign princes have pensions from these Actionists, and, as they have good intelligences, so they likewise communicate it to those ministers; and why may not such a thing be done with His Majesty's knowledge or connivance and he favour it for wise purposes and not repine at such small profits that may be made by his servants without prejudice to his service, for I would not dare to enter on it without his consent and connivance'.[13]

Sephardi Jews and the Amsterdam stock market

The 'Actionists' were thus a powerful force on the Amsterdam Exchange, and a factor in diplomacy, but also an element looked upon with some suspicion. It is also the case that by the 1670s, if not earlier, most of the regular *accionistas*, as Penso de la Vega calls them, those involved in the day-to-day fixing of trends in the market, were Sephardi (Spanish and Portuguese-speaking) Jews. After 1672 Sephardi Jews became much more prominent in the Amsterdam stock market than they had been before both as dealers and investors. Leading Sephardi merchants and financiers had begun to buy up large blocks of shares in both the VOC and WIC.[14] The most celebrated instance was that of the financier Antonio Lopes Suasso (1614-1685) and his son Francisco (both of whom were made barons by Charles II of Spain) who became internationally known (usually amalgamated into one personage) as the archetypal big Jewish investor in colonial stock. They were cited several times in English pamphlets of the 1690s concerned with East India affairs, usually in a misleading way to propagate the myth – which was then quite widely believed in outside the Republic – that the Jews owned most of the shares in the Dutch colonial companies.[15] 'It is well known and will not be denied', asserts one of the tracts, 'that the Jews have at all times the greatest share of actions in the Dutch East-India Company and that one Jew, Swasso by name, has had at one time more stock in that Company than ever an Englishman had or hath in this'.[16] Another pamphlet informs us that at one stage 'Swasso' owned £ 75,000 (or, some 750,000 guilders worth) of VOC shares.[17]

There is no doubt that in the years around 1688 there was a marked acceleration

[13] BL MS Add. 41818, fo. 235. Everard to Skelton, Amsterdam, 7 Feb. 1686.

[14] Before 1672 the only two really substantial Jewish investors in the WIC were Antonio Lopes Suasso and Jeronimo Nunes da Costa, see N.H. Schneeloch, *Aktionäre der westindischen Compagnie von 1674* (Stuttgart 1982) 33-34.

[15] One Italian observer wrote in 1678 that 'la compagnia delle Indie è formata dal numero di quei mercanti, che hanno parte in si gran traffico; i Giudei vi sono ammessi, e tre parti di tutti il capitale spetta a loro.', see G. Blom ed. 'Een Italiaansche reisbeschrijving der Nederlanden (1677-78)', *Bijdragen en Mededeelingen van het Historisch Genootschap* 36 (1915) 114; generally on Antonio (Isaac) and Francisco (Abraham) Lopes Suasso (c. 1657-1710), see M.H. Gans, *Memorboek. Platenatlas van het leven der joden in Nederland van de Middeleeuwen tot 1940* (Baarn 1940) 232, 236-237; L. Schönduve, 'Antonio en Francisco Lopes Suasso: joodse baronnen in Holland', *Holland. Regionaal-Historisch Tijdschrift* 20 (1988) 175-185.

[16] *Answer to all the material objections against the present East-India Company* (London 1695?) 2-3.

[17] *Third collection of scarce and valuable tracts* (from the library of Lord Somers) III (London 1751) 183.

in Sephardi acquisition of stock in the Dutch colonial companies and by no means solely in the Amsterdam chambers of the VOC and WIC. Where, for example, in 1680 only twelve Amsterdam Sephardi investors held stock in the Zeeland chamber of the VOC, based at Middelburg, stock amounting to 6.5% of the total, by 1690 thirty-four Sephardi investors held 15% of the shares while, by 1700, sixty Sephardi Jews owned no less than 34% of the total, a level at which the Sephardi role remained more or less fixed throughout the first half of the following century.[18] However, some of this stock certainly belonged to non-Jewish clients for whom these Sephardi businessmen acted as intermediaries and there is little doubt that actual Jewish ownership of shares in the great Dutch colonial companies amounted to much less than was often supposed. What is true is that by the 1670s and 1680s Sephardi Jewish brokers dominated the day-to-day dealings of the Amsterdam stock market. Whilst most of the officially licensed, or 'sworn', brokers in commodities, shipping, and insurance on the Exchange were Protestants, and usually Calvinist by background, the dealers in VOC and WIC shares were usually not licensed brokers of any sort and, in their great majority, were Sephardi Jews.[19]

There were a number of reasons for this state of affairs. In the first place, much of the commerce in which Dutch Sephardi Jewry had traditionally specialized, notably the traffic with Portugal and Brazil, was now in decline, and the community found itself under pressure to develop new business outlets. This was far from easy as most sectors of Dutch overseas commerce were already firmly dominated by well-established merchant élites and, even in relatively liberal Amsterdam, Jews were mostly excluded from shop-keeping and the crafts by guild and civic regulations.[20] Possessing capital, commercial expertise, and important trading links with the Iberian Peninsula and the Caribbean but few other openings, the Amsterdam Sephardi business community discovered in the stock market a focus for their energies quite uniquely suited to their needs. This was perhaps the one key area of business which was new, in a state of flux and not fenced around by restrictive and discriminatory regulations, which was, indeed, subject to hardly any supervision at all. Moreover, Dutch Sephardi Jewry, through its close links with Sephardi and Portuguese New Christian communities scattered all over western and southern Europe, the Levant, India, and Ibero-America, as well as the Dutch and English Caribbean colonies, disposed of a finely-tuned news gathering service which, in the world of that time, was of almost unparalleled scope and efficiency. It was perhaps also of some relevance that several leading members of the community, notably the Lopes Suasso, father and son, Baron Manuel de Belmonte, and Jeronimo Nunes da Costa (Moseh Curiel), acted as 'agents' in the United Provinces for the kings of Spain and Portugal, and the governor of the Spanish Netherlands, and for periods also as diplomatic 'chargés d'affaires' for those potentates, and consequently

---

[18] M. van der Bijl, *Idee en interest. Voorgeschiedenis, verloop en achtergrond van de politieke twisten in Zeeland en vooral in Middelburg tussen 1702 en 1715* (Groningen 1981) 206-207.

[19] Muys van Holy, *Relaes en contradictie*, 7; Leti, *Teatro Belgico* II, 243; J.G. van Dillen, 'Effectenkoersen aan de Amsterdamsche beurs, 1723-1794', *Economisch-Historisch Jaarboek* 7 (1931) 7; J.G. van Dillen, *Van rijkdom en regenten. Handboek tot de economische en sociale geschiedenis van Nederland tijdens de Republiek* (The Hague 1970) 455-456.

[20] J.I. Israel, *European Jewry in the age of mercantilism, 1550-1750* (2nd edn. Oxford 1989) 62, 177.

enjoyed access to a great deal of secret information relating to the Spanish and Portuguese Indies.[21]

By 1688 the role of the Sephardi Jews in the Amsterdam stock market was a conspicuous one. Even so, it was not until the stock market itself came under increased public scrutiny, and became more controversial, during 1687, the result of the mounting speculation and instability of share prices during the second half of that year, and the appearance of Muys van Holy's critical pamphlet, that the activities of the stock market dealers, and therefore of the Jews, became the object of a good deal of discussion and comment.[22] Indeed, it may well be that it was the speculative frenzy of late 1687 and early 1688, and the disastrous crash which followed, which originally gave birth to the modern myth of the malevolent 'stock exchange Jew', a new variant of the ancient antisemitic stereotype of the rich Jew who adeptly uses his financial power to strip honest Christians of their money. The modern notion of the 'stock exchange Jew' as a swindler and subverter of society which was to become such a potent theme in German-language antisemitic propaganda of the late nineteenth and early twentieth century is, it is true, no more than hinted at in Muys van Holy and the other pamphlets about the stock exchange printed at Amsterdam in 1687-1688. Nevertheless, it was suggested that the Jews who, as Muys van Holy says, enjoyed greater freedom at Amsterdam than almost anywhere else, were abusing their favourable position there to engage in financial activity – manipulation of the stock market – which had 'pernicious' effects on society.[23] Furthermore, as Penso de la Vega remarks, by early 1688 the practices of the stock market dealers was one of the principal topics of general conversation at Amsterdam and it is all too likely that much of the spoken comment linked the Jewishness of the brokers with what was alleged to be the 'pernicious' character of their dealings.[24] An anonymous English description of the Amsterdam stock market written shortly after 1688 and published in 1691 (not 1701 as Violet Barbour states) does clearly suggest that the modern antisemitic stereotype of the 'stock exchange Jew' was at this time in the making: the writer complains of the

'method used in the transactions of the Jews and others, who make a trade of buying and · selling the actions of the Company, the which is a great mystery of iniquity and where it enricheth one man, it ruins an hundred. The Jews are the chief in that trade and are said to negotiate seventeen parts in twenty in the East India Company; these actions are bought and sold four times a day at eight in the morning in the Jewes-street, at eleven on the Dam, at twelve and one o'clock upon the Exchange, and at six in the evening on the Dam, and in the colleges or clubs of the Jews until midnight, where many times the crafty Jews and others have contrived to coin bad news to make the actions fall, and good news to raise them, the which craft of doing at Amsterdam is not taken notice of, which is much to be wondered at, in such a wise government as Amsterdam is, for it is a certain truth they many times spread scandalous reports touching the affairs of state which pass amongst the ignorant for truth'.[25]

[21] Ibidem, 136-140.

[22] M.F.J. Smith, 'Inleiding' to Joseph Penso de la Vega, *Confusión de confusiones* (1688) ed. M.F.J. Smith (The Hague 1939) 23; H.I. Bloom, *The economic activities of the Jews of Amsterdam* (1937, 2nd edn.; Port Washington/New York 1969) 184.

[23] Muys van Holy, *Relaes en contradictie*, 7; Bloom, *Economic activities of the Jews of Amsterdam*, loc. cit.

[24] Penso de la Vega, *Confusión de confusiones*, 1,60.

[25] *A description of Holland, with some necessary directions for such as intend to travel through the Province of Holland* (London 1691) 40; Barbour, *Capitalism in Amsterdam*, 78.

The public controversy and exchange of pamphlets over the activities of the Amsterdam stock dealers confronted Dutch Sephardi Jewry with a situation fraught with social and moral dilemmas which ultimately reflected upon their position in Dutch society. Penso de la Vega's *Confusión de Confusiones* is not in any direct sense an exercise in Jewish self-defence. Written as it was in a highly literary Spanish, unsuited for translation into another language, it was clearly addressed not to the Dutch public but to the Sephardi community itself.[26] Nor is it a straightforwardly apologetic work which seeks to emphasize the good points of the trade in actions as against its negative aspects. On the contrary, the work is a deeply serious exploration of the issues which endeavours to show that the stock exchange, though fascinating and dangerous, is not intrinsically evil, that it has some good effects on society and that it is up to the individual to learn to understand what he insists is an extraordinarily complex phenomenon and minimize the potential risks to himself. He strives to distinguish between what he sees as the healthy trade in actions in a measured, responsible manner from the damaging and feverish 'gambling', and unhealthy speculation, which had got so out of hand during 1687-1688.[27]

What happened on the Amsterdam stock exchange, even when share price movements were unconnected with other financial developments, affected a great many people of various social backgrounds both inside and outside Dutch society. Penso de la Vega distinguishes three basic categories of investors in colonial company 'actions'.[28] The first group who he calls 'the princes' were those who inherited or purchased a share, or blocks of shares, which they retained on a long-term basis with an eye chiefly on the annual yield from dividends. This category viewed their shares as part of the family estate and, in the case of regent investors who held shares in the outlying chambers of the VOC, also as a political asset enabling them to become directors in the relevant chamber. Although the position doubtless varied from town to town, it is clear that VOC shares often made up a substantial part of the inherited wealth of Holland and Zeeland regent families.[29] This group were affected by long-term trends in share values but much less so by short-term fluctuations and, as a rule, had little need of the services of specialist brokers. Penso de la Vega's second category were 'the traders', those who bought in order to sell in the medium-term, content to make a profit from the underlying trend without paying much attention to the short-term fluctuations. This group were more likely to require the services of the specialist dealers, especially if they did not live in Amsterdam which was very often the case. These 'traders' might well be Dutch merchants or manufacturers but also included a significant sprinkling of foreign nobles and diplomats some of considerable social status. The most important client of the firm of Manuel Levy Duarte and Jacob Athias, diamond merchants who also acted off

---

[26] Smith, 'Inleiding', 26.

[27] Penso de la Vega, *Confusión de confusiones*, 289-292; Israel, 'Een merkwaardig literair werk', 163.

[28] 'Para mejor intelegencia deste assombro, deveis advertir que tratan en este negocio tres classes de personas, unos como príncipes, otros como mercaderes, y los últimos como jugadores', Penso de la Vega, *Confusión de confusiones*, 4; see also Ch. Wilson, *Anglo-Dutch commerce and finance in the eighteenth century* (1941, 2nd edn.; New York 1977) 82.

[29] Van der Bijl, *Idee en interest*, 209, 213; L. Kooijmans, *Onder regenten. De elite in een Hollandse stad. Hoorn, 1700-1780* (The Hague 1985) 104.

and on as share brokers during the 1680s, was Olympe Mancini, Countess of Soissons, a niece of Cardinal Mazarin and mother of Prince Eugene of Savoy who at the time was residing in Brussels. This famous lady purchased a consignment of VOC stock, through Levy Duarte and Athias, in 1680 which she later sold, through the same dealers, in 1685, achieving an overall profit of 7% on the transaction.[30] The third and last category were the 'gamblers', a class which included the actionists themselves and an array of other speculators, who were less near by, who closely followed and often became utterly obsessed with the intricacies of the market and the short-term movements in share prices. With one of his striking literary flourishes, Penso de la Vega tells us that the labyrinth of Crete was not more convoluted than the designs and obsessions of these stock market addicts.[31] They included some foreign speculators, often Sephardi or Portuguese New Christian relatives of Amsterdam dealers who, through their Amsterdam correspondents, were able to buy and sell actions on a short-term basis. Luis Alvares, for example, a wealthy jeweller who lived in Paris, gambled at times frenetically, in the Amsterdam share market through his distant relative Manuel Levy Duarte.[32]

After the 1672-crash

Until the autumn of 1687 the Amsterdam stock market, like the rest of the Exchange, had been relatively stable for a considerable period of years. Of course, the great crash of 1672 was still vividly remembered. But the staggering losses of that year were a wholly exceptional occurrence arising from exceptionally disastrous circumstances. The crash had ensued from the terrifying situation in which the Dutch had found themselves in June 1672 when the Republic was attacked by France and England jointly, in alliance with Cologne and Münster, and when the French overran three whole provinces of the Union – Gelderland, Overijssel and Utrecht – before being halted, by the flooding of a broad belt of land, just in time, a mere few miles from Amsterdam itself. Not surprisingly, this catastrophe had set off a financial panic such as had never been seen before.[33] There was a furious run on the Exchange Bank with millions of guilders and great quantities of bullion and jewellery, being transferred abroad. The quoted price of States of Holland 'obligations', a major element in many regent fortunes, slumped at one point to a ruinous 30% of their face value. The *agio*, or premium, on Amsterdam 'bank money' – normally the latter being safer, more readily changed, and paid out only in good coin – carried a 5% premium over cash-swung to a minus *agio* of 4 to 5% under. WIC shares became virtually worthless. Amsterdam's premier share, the actions of

---

[30] E.R. Samuel, 'Manuel Levy Duarte (1631-1714): an Amsterdam merchant jeweller and his trade with London', *Transactions of the Jewish Historical Society of England* 27 (1982) 19-20.
[31] 'No fué mas intricado el laberintho de Creta que el de sus designios, porque de aquel aun salió un Theseo con el hilo de Ariadne y deste hay muchos que no han podido salir sino con el hilo de la vida', Penso de la Vega, *Confusión de confusiones*, 5.
[32] Samuel, 'Manuel Levy Duarte', 19.
[33] Petrus Valkenier, *'t Verwerd Europa ofte politijke en historische beschryvinge der waare fundamenten en oorsaken van de oorlogen en revolutien in Europa* (2nd edn., Amsterdam 1742) 637; Savary des Bruslons, *Dictionnaire universel* I, 19-20; M.F.J. Smith, *Tijd-affaires in effecten aan de Amsterdamsche Beurs* (The Hague 1919) 64, 69, 71-72; L. Samuel, *Die Effektenspekulation im 17. und 18. Jahrhundert. Ein Beitrag zur Börsengeschichte* (Berlin 1924) 12, 15.

the Amsterdam chamber of the VOC, plummeted from a peak a short time before of 572% – a level which J.G. van Dillen took to be the high-point for the entire seventeenth century[34] – to 250% which was undoubtedly the low-point for the whole of the latter two-thirds of the century. The initial collapse was followed by a succession of wild swings. At one point, amid the despair, a few encouraging rumours, of little substance, sufficed to raise VOC actions to 340 and States of Holland bonds to 92% before both collapsed again.[35] Meanwhile, public building ceased, property rents slumped, and the art market suffered a paralysing dislocation from which it took decades to recover.

The great crash of 1672 administered a severe jolt. But the system took the strain. The markets bounced back after England, frustrated by Dutch maritime successes, withdrew from the war, in 1674, and the armies of Austria and Spain took the field, forcing Louis XIV to evacuate most of the Dutch territory which he had previously conquered. With the French evacuation the panic was over. Stability returned to the Amsterdam Exchange. By May 1675, the price of VOC shares at Amsterdam was fluctuating between 428 and 443 and, in July 1676, touched 450.[36]

Yet the recovery was incomplete and, for a variety of reasons, lost its initial momentum. For an entire decade from 1675 down to 1684 the Amsterdam Exchange, including the stock market, remained hesitant and, by pre-1672 standards depressed. Despite the end of the war with France and Louis XIV's conceding, under the terms of the treaty of Nijmegen (1678), the cancellation of his more aggressive anti-Dutch mercantilist measures, notably Colbert's draconian tariff-list of 1667, the feeling persisted in the early 1680s that the peace was fragile and that Amsterdam, as the English consul expressed it, 'decayes in its riches and trade'. In March 1681 the latter reported to London that the 'East India actions which in anno 1670 were 500 and once 550 are now but 406; and never as yet, since the war, could be brought up to 450 and so proportionally all other obligations on the land'.[37] On 25 March 1681, the consul reported that VOC actions at Amsterdam were at 408% and WIC actions at a dismal 54%.[38] Following Louis XIV's seizure of Strasbourg, in September 1681, and the consequent rise in international tension, VOC share price quotations at Amsterdam fell back further, sinking by November 1681 to 395½ before recovering by April 1682 to 447 and the following September to 462.[39]

Then, in September 1682, Louis XIV invaded the Spanish Netherlands, occupying Luxemburg and Dinant and, once again, the Amsterdam stock exchange went into a slide. The French invasion of the southern Netherlands was a slow, creeping affair, designed to hive off border areas rather than achieve large-scale gains, so there was no great panic. In mid-November the VOC share price at Amsterdam stood at 448%.[40] But the international political outlook continued to deteriorate

---

34 Van Dillen, 'Effectenkoersen', 12. 15.

35 Valkenier, *'t Verwerd Europa*, 637.

36 Gemeentearchief Amsterdam (hereafter GAA), PJG no. 858 (Archives of the Portuguese Jewish Community) 13; I am indebted to Edgar Samuel for bringing this valuable source, the business ledgers of Manuel Levy Duarte, to my attention.

37 BL MS Add. 37981, fo. 12v. Carr to Blathwayt, Amsterdam, 21 March 1681.

38 Ibidem, fo. 14, Carr to Blathwayt, Amsterdam, 25 March 1681.

39 GAA PJG 858, 471-472.

40 Ibidem, 340.

and a serious Dutch domestic quarrel broke out between the Stadholder, William III, and Amsterdam, over whether the Republic should expand her army and offer assistance to the Spanish Netherlands. Predictably, this had an adverse effect on the stock market. By August 1683 the VOC share price at Amsterdam was down to 397, one of the lowest levels reached between 1674 and 1688.[41] But the crisis passed and, by late 1684, the European situation was again calmer. The city of Amsterdam, by its stubborn opposition to William III's attempts to expand the Dutch army by 16,000 men, and build an armed European coalition against France, contributed significantly to the defusing of the crisis, even though this was, in effect, achieved by appeasing France with pieces of territory shorn from the Spanish Netherlands. The inevitable inference drawn from the Dutch domestic political imbroglio of 1682-1684 was that the Stadholder, whatever his intentions, could not mobilise the Dutch Republic and its resources against France without the agreement of Holland's greatest city and this Amsterdam simply would not concede as long as Louis refrained from directly bullying the Republic and kept to the accommodation of 1678 as regards commerce and tariffs.[42] Amsterdam's insistence that the Republic's true interest was to stick to her accommodation with France (however insatiable Louis' appetite for strips of German and Spanish Netherlands territory), that for the Dutch the safeguarding of their commerce and shipping should have priority over other considerations, was undoubtedly a major contributory factor in the increased confidence shown by the Amsterdam business community and Exchange over the next few years. The outcome of the Dutch internal political quarrel of 1682-1684 seemed, but as subsequent events were to prove, only seemed, to render the prospect of conflict between the Republic and its most dangerous potential adversary, France, much more remote.

The passing of the crisis of 1682-1684 set the scene for a more buoyant phase in the history of the Amsterdam Exchange and stock market. The 1680s were, indeed, on the whole, a fairly flourishing decade for Dutch commerce and shipping. It is true that the Baltic trade was now at low ebb by early seventeenth century standards and that, in the years 1683-1688, the United Provinces were locked in a damaging economic war with Denmark-Norway which further weakened Dutch trade with northern Europe. But Baltic commerce no longer had the same central importance in the Dutch overseas trading system that it had formerly had.[43] What mattered most now was the state of Dutch trade with France, Spain, the Levant, and the Indies east and west and it was precisely the 'rich trades' and long-distance traffic which were now flourishing. Both the Dutch East and West India companies appeared to be successfull, growing concerns and merchants could see that the relative importance of long-distance trade in the structure of Dutch commerce as a whole was increasing. In 1684 there began that long, steady climb in the value of all shares and securities on the Amsterdam Exchange which was to continue until the summer of 1688.[44] By late 1684 VOC actions were being quoted at Amsterdam at

[41] GAA PJG 334, fo. 688.

[42] G.H. Kurtz, *Willem III en Amsterdam, 1683-1685* (Utrecht 1928) 102-110, 125.

[43] Israel, *Dutch Primacy*, 299-358.

[44] *Relaes en contradictie op de motiven, om het kopen en verkoopen van Oost- en West-Indise actien* (Knuttel 12622a) (Amsterdam no date but 1687) 8; Gregorio Leti, *Il ceremoniale historico e politico* V (6 vols., Amsterdam 1685) 470.

470%.[45] The buoyancy of the Amsterdam financial markets was further heightened, as from 1685, with the large-scale exodus of Huguenots from France and the accompanying infusion of new cash at Amsterdam. Interest rates in the Amsterdam money market now sank to their lowest levels of the century and by early 1688 stood at a mere 2%.[46] Amsterdam was awash with spare cash some of which, no doubt, was used to fuel the rise in the values of shares and States of Holland 'obligations'. An additional factor in the rise of WIC share quotations was the decision of the Spanish crown, in February 1685, to transfer the monopoly, or *asiento*, for the supply of slaves to Spanish America to the Dutch house of Coymans whose factors obtained their slaves from the WIC slave depot at Curaçao.[47] This appeared to guarantee WIC dominance of the supply of slaves to Spanish America, and therefore also Curaçao's role as the principal Caribbean entrepot in the transit trade between north-west Europe and the Spanish colonies, at least in the medium term.

The rise in values on the Amsterdam Stock Exchange between 1684 and the summer of 1687 was slow, gradual and measured, though WIC share quotations seem to have risen more sharply than those of the VOC. By the autumn of 1687 when the speculative atmosphere surrounding the stock market became more intense, the VOC share price stood at, and around, 525%.[48] It was at this juncture when new and serious tensions entered into Dutch relations with France that, unaccountably in the eyes of some contemporary observers, the rise in share values began to accelerate.[49]

Prospects for Dutch European commerce sharply deteriorated as from August 1687 when a new round of economic warfare between France and the United Provinces began. Louis XIV had, in 1678, made major economic concessions to the Dutch, for the sake of political gains, but at the cost of mounting anger and resentment in France over the resumed success of the Dutch in the French market. It was perhaps only a matter of time before France's proud monarch lost patience with the growing stranglehold of the Dutch on large sections of France's overseas commerce. The new Franco-Dutch 'guerre de commerce' began with Louis' ban on the importing of Dutch herring into France, except where certified as having been salted with French salt.[50] Then, in September 1687, Louis tore up the tariff agreement of 1678 and re-imposed the 1667 tariff list on Dutch textiles entering France, at a stroke doubling the duty on imported Leiden 'lakens' and camlets and other Dutch textiles. The Leiden city council was outraged, protesting that 'soodanige zware belastinge in effect inhieldt een absolut verbod van inlandsche laeckenen in Vranckrijk te debiteren'.[51] By the end of 1687 imports of Dutch textiles and other manufactures such as Delftware, into France, had practically ceased.

[45] Leti, *Il ceremoniale* V, 470.

[46] BL MS Add. 41821, fo. 220, 'News from The Hague', 4 Aug. 1688.

[47] Penso de la Vega describes the Coymans *asiento* as the 'mas firme coluna desta fábrica', meaning that it was the main factor behind the sharp rise in WIC share quotations, Penso de la Vega, *Confusión de confusiones*, 94, 196; see also I.A. Wright, 'The Coymans Asiento (1685-1689)', *Bijdragen voor Vaderlandsche Geschiedenis en Oudheidkunde* 6th series, 1 (1924) 29-30.

[48] *Relaes en contradictie*, 8.

[49] Penso de la Vega, *Confusión de confusiones*, 1, 60.

[50] Ch.W. Cole, *French mercantilism, 1683-1700* (New York 1943) 12-13, 294-297, 307; Israel, *Dutch primacy*, 306.

[51] *Resolutien van de Staten van Hollandt en West-Vrieslandt*, res. 26 Nov. 1687.

All this was deeply disturbing. But the Amsterdam city council for the moment adhered to its policy of seeking to placate France and even suggested that there was some justification for French complaints about the poor quality of Dutch herring exports.[52] We know that many merchants and regents were appalled by the French measures; but it seems not yet to have occurred to the Amsterdam business community that this was a situation which could easily lead to war. It may even be that the deteriorating prospects for European trade for a time served to enhance further the attractiveness of the Dutch traffic with the East and West Indies. But whatever the reason the Amsterdam Exchange remained doggedly buoyant and the speculative fever intensified over the winter of 1687-1688. Not only was the puzzling behaviour of the stock market now one of the chief topics of conversation in the city but more and more investors were becoming obsessed with the short-term fluctuations of the market. Penso de la Vega tells of inexperienced, new 'gamblers, with little knowledge of the market, so obsessed with its intricacies that the latter filled their conscious thoughts and even their dreams'.[53]

The upward trend in share prices gathered momentum but was also punctuated by short, sharp, setbacks caused by political worries. In April 1688, for instance, James II's attempt to recall the English and Scots troops serving in the Dutch army briefly unsettled the market: 'the East India actions are considerably fallen this day', reported the English consul at Amsterdam, Daniel Petit, 'upon the news they had here of a memorial which the marquis d'Albeville, His Majesty's envoy at The Hague, had presented yesterday to the States'.[54] But the underlying trend soon resumed. 'The East India actions', wrote Petit on 23 April, 'are within these four days risen from 560 to 568', adding a few days later that the 'East India actions are still rising'.[55] In a letter to James II's secretary of state, the Earl of Middleton, written a few weeks later, Petit explained that the Dutch 'pretend to judge of peace and warre by the fall and rising of the actions', noting that the 'East India actions are risen within this week [17-24 May] from 566 to 576½'.[56] The Amsterdam Exchange evidently was still convinced that Europe and the Republic would remain at peace.

The inexorable rise in share values undoubtedly caused a certain amount of unease. One of the reasons for the public controversy about the Amsterdam stock market which broke out in 1687 was the feeling that the rise in stock quotations was unjustified and excessive.[57] On the other hand, the continuing rise also attracted new investors and strengthened confidence that prospects, both for peace and the two colonial companies, were bright. WIC shares which had languished at 54% in 1681 reached a peak in the spring of 1688 at 110% 'con la esperança', as Penso de la Vega explained, 'de que los retornos de Guiné y Curaçao serían floridos'.[58] When the VOC share price touched 580 many investors seem to have expected the rise to

---

[52] GAA vroedschapsresoluties no. 38 (Jan. 1688-June 1689) 17-18; res. 13 Jan. 1688.

[53] Penso de la Vega, *Confusión de confusiones*, 1, 60.

[54] BL MS Add. 41815, fo. 205. Petit to Middleton, Amsterdam, 6 April 1688.

[55] BL MS Add. 41815, fos. 237, 247. Petit to Middleton, Amsterdam, 23 and 27 April 1688.

[56] BL MS Add. 41815, fo. 258: Petit to Middleton, Amsterdam, 24 May 1688.

[57] Penso de la Vega, *Confusión de confusiones*, 74-75, 94.

[58] Ibidem, 94; R. Ehrenberg, 'Die Amsterdamer Aktienspekulation im 17. Jahrhundert', *Jahrbücher für Nationalökonomie und Statistik* 63 (1892) 817.

continue, assuming that that year's returning East India fleet would be richly laden, that a good dividend would be paid out, that the Company was continuing to expand and, as Penso de la Vega mentions, that they could rely on the 'paz de la Europa' (peace of Europe).[59] There was talk, amid the excitement, of the VOC share price possibly soon reaching 600%! Meanwhile the prices of shares in the out-lying chambers of the VOC and WIC were also rising, though less sharply than those for shares in the respective Amsterdam chambers. This meant that there was a widening gap in value between the Amsterdam and the outlying chambers for, as Penso de la Vega explains, the latter were ordinarily less susceptible to speculative pressures than the former and, consequently, tended to lag behind. At the time that Penso de la Vega was writing, shares lodged in the VOC chamber at Middelburg, were worth, according to him, 150 percentage points less than those of Amsterdam, those of Enkhuizen eighty points less, those of Hoorn seventy five points less, those of Delft seventy points less, and those of Rotterdam thirty points less.[60] The fact that shares in the Amsterdam chambers invariably stood higher than those in the other chambers, and were also speculated in more, was cited during the controversy of 1687-1688 in defence of the stock brokers: for if speculation pushed values higher was it not ultimately a benefit?[61]

During the early summer the situation continued much as during the spring. The underlying trend in the Amsterdam stock market remained bullish but there were still sudden sharp flurries of anxiety every time there was disturbing political news. Something of the dismay felt in England on the birth of a son and heir to James II, a birth which raised the prospect of the Stuart, and now Catholic, reign-- -dynasty establishing itself in the long term on the English throne, perculated through to Holland. 'The news of the birth of this prince', Petit reported to London, on 29 June, 'was no sooner known here but the East India actions fell from 572 to 567'.[62] The consul's own pleasure at the arrival of a male heir to the throne was somewhat marred as the banquet and fire-work display which he put on to celebrate the event were ruined by a hostile crowd which hurled insults against the King, and stones through his windows, loss and indignity for which James afterwards showed little inclination to compensate him.[63] Over the next fortnight VOC share prices first recovered and then eased back again owing to the onset of worries for the safety of the returning East India fleet. On 13 July VOC actions at Amsterdam stood at 569%. 'It is generally believed that they will fall more', commented Petit, 'because of the fear which the Dutch have that their Smyrna or East India fleet will be at-tacked by the English or French'.[64] Throughout July concern for the safe passage of the East India return fleet remained the main adverse pressure affecting the stock exchange. On 29 July VOC actions at Amsterdam stood at 566%.[65]

---

[59] Penso de la Vega, *Confusión de confusiones*, 17.

[60] Penso de la Vega, *Confusión de confusiones*, 109-110: 'valiendo ordinariamente las de Zelanda 150 por ciento menos que las nuestras, 80 las de Incusa, 75 la de Orne, 30 las de Roterdam y 70 las de Delef.'; in November 1681, shares in the Zeeland chamber of the VOC had been worth 95½ percentage points less than the Amsterdam chamber shares, GAA PJG 334, fo. 13.

[61] *Relaes en contradictie*, 8.

[62] BL MS Add. 41816, fo. 83. Petit to Middleton, Amsterdam, 29 June 1688.

[63] BL MS Add. 41821, fo. 213.

[64] BL MS Add. 41816, fo. 101. Petit to Middleton, Amsterdam, 13 July 1688.

[65] BL MS Add. 41821, fo. 210. 'News from The Hague; 29 July 1688.

Meanwhile, back in June, amid the utmost secrecy, the Stadholder, William III, had revealed to three of the four Amsterdam burgomasters his bold plan for armed Dutch intervention in England against James II.[66] The move was well timed. For already, in May, the States of Holland had concluded that Dutch diplomatic efforts to persuade Louis XIV to cancel his new 'guerre de commerce' against the Dutch had come to nothing and that there was now little alternative but to seek ways to exert more effective pressure on France.[67] At this point the discussion among the Holland regents was purely about economic retaliation, the Leiden city council, for instance, proposing the banning of French imports into the Republic. But it was already evident to many of the regents that the Republic might soon have no alternative but to go to war with France if Franco-Dutch commerce was to be restored to the basis on which it had been between 1678 and August 1687. The Prince of Orange who understood perfectly that 'le commerce est ce qui touche de plus près la nation hollandoise et que la France l'a entièrement rompue', as one of the diplomats at The Hague expressed it, now cleverly played on this perception. There is no doubt that Louis' well-aimed blows against Dutch trade since August 1687 had generated a tremendous amount of anger amongst the Dutch public and merchants, as well as the regents, and it is clear that it is this which made it possible for William to proceed with his plans for a Dutch invasion of England.[68] For if the Republic had to fight France in the circumstances of 1688 it was evident that the most effective way to do so would be to break Louis' tottering protegé, James II, and turn England round against France.

But none of this was yet disclosed to the States of Holland as a whole only to an inner circle of the most influential regents. Significantly, when, later, in September, the plans were formally revealed to the full States of Holland one of the reasons given as to why it had not been possible to do so earlier was that 'die interessen van die geene die sterk in Actien van de Oost- en West-Indische Compagnien waren handelende, de Geinteresseerdens obligeerden, om so veel doenlijk te penetreren in de secreten van den staat, ende so veel in haar was de deliberatien en resolutien na die haare interessen te doen formeren en uytvallen'.[69] Evidently there was a feeling that the influence of actions and 'actionists' reached so far that, through the interests in colonial stock of the regents, they could even sway on the resolutions of the state.

For the moment the secret was well kept. Those who knew of the plans at Amsterdam and elsewhere remained silent. Through July and the first three weeks of August there was no visible evidence that the Republic was planning to go to war with Louis XIV and James II. Although the naval and military preparations for the invasion of England were now underway, primarily at Amsterdam, though to a lesser extent also at Rotterdam, Middelburg, and in the West Frisian ports, these

[66] J.F. Gebhard, *Het leven van Mr Nicolaas Cornelisz. Witsen (1641-1717)* (Utrecht 1881) 316, 320.

[67] Gemeentearchief Leiden, Sec. Arch. 488, p.359. Vroedschapsresolutie 11 May 1688.

[68] BL MS Add. 38495, fo. 10, 28v: Moreau to king of Poland, The Hague, 31 Aug., 5 Oct. 1688; Jean Antoine de Mesmes, Comte d'Avaux, *Négociations de Monsieur le Comte d'Avaux en Hollande* VII (6 vols., Paris 1752-1753) 176, 208, 246, 288; see also my essay 'The Dutch role in the revolution of 1688' in: J.I. Israel ed., *The Anglo-Dutch moment. Essays on the background and world impact of the British revolutions of 1688/91* (Cambridge, 1991).

[69] *Secreete Resolutien van de Ed. Groot Mog. Heeren Staaten van Hollandt en West-Vrieslandt*, vol. 4 (1679-1696) 227. res. 18 Sept. 1688.

preparations were not yet on large enough a scale to attract much attention. At this stage, to all appearances, there was nothing at all unusual about the build-up in the ports, nothing of a sort liable to provoke unsettling speculation. Officially inspired reports at Amsterdam had it that the preparations were for an intended punitive expedition against the Algerian corsairs and, for the time being, this seemed perfectly believable. For those Amsterdam financiers who were not in the know all that showed on the surface was that the Amsterdam city council, still true to its former policy of seeking accommodation with France, was blocking the proposals put by Leiden, Haarlem and other towns for a ban on the importing of French products into the Republic – which were bound to antagonize Louis XIV further – in the hope that there might yet be a way out without war.[70] What D'Avaux's friends, the anti-Orangist element in the Amsterdam city council were hoping, was that the mounting evidence of Dutch anger, and the protracted discussion in the States of Holland about economic retaliation against France, would act as a sufficient lever to persuade Louis to pull back from the brink and cancel his unacceptable economic measures.

It is clear that for the first three weeks of August the Amsterdam stock exchange was entirely absorbed in the more immediate question of the returning East India fleet.[71] On 6 August Petit reported that the 'East India actions here are falling because of the uncertainty they are in here with what success their East India ships will come home'.[72] Then, on 7 August, the VOC directors at Amsterdam received firm news that their ships had in fact cleared the Cape of Good Hope two weeks before, that they were more numerous than had lately been expected, and that they would be arriving shortly.[73] A wave of jubilation swept the stock market. 'Auff diese gutte Zeitung', it was reported in the Hamburg press, 'sind die Actiones auff 575½ gestiegen'.[74] The VOC share price had jumped fifteen points on the news, and for a few days they kept on rising. 'The spirit of Ahab and the satans of Job', as Penso de la Vega expressed it, 'set to work with renewed vigour inspired by news so favourable for *la liefhebrería*'.[75] Van Dillen supposed that the high-point in the value of VOC shares at Amsterdam for the seventeenth century was reached late in 1671, or early 1672, when the share price had reached 572%.[76] But, as we now see, it was not in 1671-1672 but in 1688, and almost certainly in the ten days or so after 7 August, that the zenith for the century was attained. In late May, before the onset of anxiety over the safe home-coming of the East India fleet, the VOC share price at

[70] GAA vroedschapsresoluties no. 38, 139-142. res. 21 and 24 Sept. 1688; D'Avaux, *Negociations* VI, 190 200.
[71] BL MS Add. 41821, fo. 210; 'News from The Hague', 29 July 1688; see also the Hamburg newspaper *Relations-Coerier* 121 (1688) 7 (for this and the following references to German press reports of the summer of 1688, I am indebted to Dr. Johannes Weber of the Deutsche Presseforschung project of Bremen University Library).
[72] BL MS Add. 41816, fo. 138; Petit to Middleton, Amsterdam, 6 Aug. 1688.
[73] *Relations-Coerier* (Hamburg) no. 121 (1688) 7; *Sonntagischer Postilion* (Berlin) no. 32 (1688) 4; Penso de la Vega, *Confusión de confusiones*, 174.
[74] *Relations-Coerier*, no. 121 (1688) 7; *Sonntagischer Postilion*, no. 32 (1688) 4.
[75] Penso de la Vega, *Confusión de confusiones*, 174.
[76] Van Dillen, 'Effectenkoersen', 12, 15.

Amsterdam had already touched 576 before slipping back.[77] Now in mid-August the price regained that level and then rose higher. On 13 August VOC actions at Amsterdam climbed to 582 before easing back to 580.[78] These are the highest levels we know of, thus far, for the century, though it is likely that over the next few days, inspired by the news that Admiral Evertsen's warships had now joined the East India 'retourschepen',and were bringing them in, the price climbed even higher.

But no sooner was it learnt that the East India fleet was safe than letters arrived from the fleet providing information about their cargoes which caused a change of mood. On 17 August it was reported at the bourse that 'die Ladung ist so reich nicht als man sich eingebildet, sintemahl der Einkauff sich nur auff 34 Tonnen Goldes und 40,000 Gulden belaufft, welches ganz ausserhalb vermuthen ist, zumahl man die Retour viel grösser zu seyn gemeinet hat'.[79] Penso de la Vega describes the effect of this dispiriting news on the share market: investors were discouraged; share values began to slide.[80] But the fall that commenced on 17 August was merely a minor flurry, nothing out of the ordinary, a routine setback prompted by some disappointing business news. After a few days, the 'bulls', or 'liefhebbers' as they were then known in Amsterdam, were back on top and the market made up its mind that the actual value of the newly arrived cargoes was higher than initially estimated.[81] The downturn was reversed. It was not until a full eight days after the minor setback of 17 August that the real crash of 1688 began.[82]

The 1688-crash

While it has previously been noticed that in the fourth of the four dialogues of which the *Confusión de Confusiones* is composed, Penso de la Vega is concerned with a 'crisis which hit the market' at some point in 1688, this 'crisis' has hitherto remained completely buried in obscurity.[83] It is only in the light of new data from unpublished sources, revealing the circumstances and scope of the upheaval, that the significance of Penso de la Vega's highly literary and somewhat obscure discussion of the episode can be grasped. Just as the Amsterdam stock market recovered its poise after 17 August, he explains, the 'liefhebbers' were all at once overwhelmed by highly disturbing reports circulated by certain actionists who convinced the 'cabals', or dealers' gatherings, that they had 'penetrated' the deepest

[77] Several authors give 576 as the peak reached in 1688, see BL MS Add. 41815, fo. 258. Petit to Middleton, Amsterdam, 24 May 1688; Penso de la Vega, *Confusión de confusiones*, 138-139, 229; Leti, *Teatro Belgico* II, 243; Otto Pringsheim ed., *Don Joseph de la Vega. Die Verwirrung der Verwirrungen. Vier Dialoge über die Börse in Amsterdam* (Breslau 1919) xiv.

[78] BL MS Add.41821, fo. 236v., 'News from The Hague', 13 Aug. 1688.

[79] *Relations-Coerier* 127 (1688) 7.

[80] 'Divulgandose que la cargación no importava mas de 34 toneles, haviendo traido el año antecedente 50, començaron a desmayar los orgullos, a ofuscarse los corages, a rendirse los bríos', Penso de la Vega, *Confusión de confusiones*, 174.

[81] Ibidem, 173-175.

[82] Ibidem, 174.

[83] H. Kellenbenz, 'Introduction' to Joseph Penso de la Vega, *Confusión de confusiones* (1688) (abridged English edn., Harvard 1957) xiv, xvii, xx; Pringsheim, *Don Joseph de la Vega*, xiv.

secrets of the state.[84] What these 'accionistas' revealed was that they knew for certain that a major European war, in which the Republic was to participate, was about to break out. Penso de la Vega assures us that there had not hitherto been the least suspicion of this and we can be sure that he is right from the evidence of the dispatches of the diplomats at The Hague. It was not until 24 August that the French ambassador at The Hague, the efficient and extremely acute Comte d'Avaux, first grasped (or was alerted to) the fact that the preparations under way in Holland were intended for a full-scale invasion of England.[85] The Polish resident at The Hague wrote, on 24 August, that there were those at The Hague who were beginning to say 'que la flotte est destinée contre l'Angleterre' but was himself disinclined to believe this.[86] Clearly at this stage it was far from plainly evident what the preparations were for. 'They are at work night and day to get their ships ready', Petit reported to London, also on 24 August, 'but against whom is diversely spoken of, some guess it to be to oppose France in case that crown does by force undertake something in favour of the Cardinal Fürstenberg, others say that the equipping of this fleet is to prevent any design the two fleets of England and France may form to their prejudice'.[87]

Yet the revelations to the cabals of the stock exchange by certain actionists had such an impact that the share market all at once collapsed and in the most devastating manner. Clearly the cabals judged that the actionists who claimed to have 'penetrated' the deepest secrets of the state knew what they were talking about. On 25 August commenced what was almost certainly the second most disastrous crash to hit the Amsterdam Exchange of the entire seventeenth century. On the first day, according to one report, the VOC share price at Amsterdam dropped by eighty points from 580 to 500.[88] For four days the Amsterdam share market was in the grip of utter panic. It was all so sudden and catastrophic that the investing public was not just horrified but totally bewildered. What on earth could have caused this 'tan lamentable precipio', so ruinous a blow? Over the first four days of the crash the VOC share price slumped by 210 points to 370 while a full third was wiped off the value of WIC shares.[89]

The worst of the panic and the heaviest falls occurred during these opening few days. 'Good God, what a disaster!' exclaims the 'merchant' in Penso de la Vega's fourth dialogue. 'Almighty, what a catastrophe!' exclaims the 'philosopher' who has recently acquired shares in the VOC, 'what a collapse! What a thunderbolt!' Adding afterwards 'Blessed Heaven, what a gruesome day of judgement! Merciful Lord preserve my senses!'[90] The indescribable, initial panic was followed by a

---

[84] 'Esparcieron que havía guerra, que penetravan tales prevenciones, y tan secretas, que no podía dexar de haverla y que era precisa que, haviendola, deluviassen las imposiciones, se atropellasen los tributos y ardiesse la Europa con miserias, con horrores, con estragos', Penso da la Vega, *Confusión de confusiones*, 174-175.

[85] D'Avaux, *Négociations* VI, 203.

[86] BL MS Add. 38495, fo. 9. Moreau to king of Poland, The Hague, 24 Aug. 1688.

[87] BL MS Add. 41816, fos. 157-158. Petit to Middleton, Amsterdam, 24 Aug. 1688.

[88] J. Carswell, *The descent on England. A study of the English revolution of 1688 and its European background* (London 1969) 160; although the author does not state his source, this report seems to me more probable than Penso de la Vega's remark that on the first day of the crash the VOC price fell by thirty points, Penso de la Vega, *Confusión de confusiones*, 180.

[89] Penso de la Vega, *Confusión de confusiones*, 136, 173.

[90] Penso de la Vega, *Confusión de confusiones*, 227-229.

stunned silence: 'East India actions have been much at a stand these three days', noted Petit on August 31, 'the uncertain issue of the conjunctures are the occasion of it'.[91] At this point, Petit, D'Albeville, and most of the rest of the diplomatic community, except for D'Avaux, still had no clear notion of what the Dutch preparations were for or any firm suspicion that the Dutch were preparing to invade England. It was not until 7 September that Petit is convinced that the Dutch are preparing a major offensive expedition, though he says 'the discourses and reasons for this equipage are very various, one day they say they will demand reason of France [over commerce and Cologne], another that they will goe and cause a rebellion in England'.[92] It is only on 14 September that the Polish resident reported that 'le peuple ne fait plus de difficulté de dire que [la flotte] est pour l'Angleterre', though even then he is not entirely convinced, remarking a week later that 'si cela est le dessein c'est bien conduit et le secret bien gardé.[93]

Yet the stock market seemed to entertain no doubt. Nothing like the crash of late August and early September 1688 had ever been seen before. Frightening reports, rumours, revelations of secrets, had wiped over two hundred percentage points off the VOC share price in a few days! In June 1672 the Amsterdam stock market had fallen still more catastrophically but that was in the midst of an actual political and military disaster. Furthermore, in 1688 the slide went furthest in the days before the diplomatic community had made up its mind about the Dutch naval and military preparations. According to Penso de la Vega, the fall in the VOC share price bottomed out at 365%, a full 216 percentage points below the peak reached in mid-August.[94] Gregorio Leti speaks of a collapse from 550 to 300 but he was writing some time after the event and it is likely either that his recollection was at fault here or that his 300 is a slip for 360.[95] Daniel Petit confirms that on 5 September VOC actions were selling at Amsterdam at 366.[96]

Yet it was precisely when it became evident that the Republic was indeed intending to go to war with France or England, and probably both, that the stock market pulled out of its sensational collapse. What happened next was greeted by the participants in Penso de la Vega's dialogues, and no doubt by the investing public at large, with incredulity. In his book, Penso de la Vega explains that while rational considerations, namely commercial news from the Indies and news of the European political conjuncture, were the two prime determinants of movements in share prices, the responses of the actionists to these stimuli were far from being altogether rational. Emotional and psychological impulses – above all fear, hope, and patriotism – often decisively coloured the way incoming information was assessed.[97] Consequently, the stock market was capable of highly enigmatic, surprising and even irrational responses and at no time more so than when its nerves were tightly stretched. How right he was! For at precisely this moment the 'liefhebbers'

[91]   BL MS Add. 41816, fo. 16. Petit to Middleton, Amsterdam, 31 Aug. 1688.
[92]   BL MS Add. 41816, fo. 167. Petit to Middleton, Amsterdam, 7 Sept. 1688.
[93]   BL MS Add. 38495, fos. 14v, 19. Moreau to king of Poland, The Hague, 14 and 21 Sept. 1688.
[94]   Penso de la Vega, *Confusión de confusiones*, 138, 173; Pringsheim, *Don Joseph de la Vega*, xiv.
[95]   'Io ho veduto le attioni', wrote Leti, 'salire al valsente di 550 e diminuire sino a 300', Leti, *Teatro Belgico* II, 243.
[96]   BL MS Add. 41816, fo. 173v. Petit to Middleton, Amsterdam, 8 Sept. 1688.
[97]   Penso de la Vega, *Confusión de confusiones*, 2, 60.

took charge, halted the slide and engineered an amazing rally. Having suffered a ruinous collapse 'through fear of war', explains Penso de la Vega, VOC shares suddenly recovered a substantial part of what had been lost 'when it became known for certain that there would be war'.[98] 'The East India actions', wrote a staggered Daniel Petit, on 8 September 1688, 'are risen from 366 to 430 since Tuesday the fifth the last'.[99]

In fact Penso de la Vega's explanation is a slight oversimplification. Though it was now clear that the Dutch state was preparing a huge armada for use against France or England, the recovery began on the day the marquis d'Albeville submitted a highly conciliatory, not to say abject, memorial in the name of James II and the rise was obviously partly fuelled by hopes that there might not be war after all. Moreover, the recovery was abruptly reversed on 9 September with the appearance of the Comte d'Avaux before the States General in The Hague. The French ambassador announced that Louis XIV had taken note of the Dutch preparations, was convinced that 'cet armement reguarde l'Angleterre', and was resolved to stand by his friend and ally, His Brittanic Majesty. The moment that the Dutch moved their ships and troops against King James, Louis would declare war on the United Provinces.[100] This blunt but clear warning had an immediate effect and the slide in the stock market resumed. Yet Penso de la Vega's general point about the recovery of nerve on the Amsterdam Exchange is quite correct. D'Avaux's menacing speech had a sensational effect, as one can imagine, on the courts of Vienna, Madrid, Rome and Berlin, but a comparatively minor effect on the Amsterdam stock exchange and this, in turn, was soon reversed. After falling back fifteen or twenty points over the next few days, the VOC share price at Amsterdam recovered on 14 September from 414 to 424 and two days later was marked up to 433.[101] The actions then eased back again slightly but were now much more stable than previously and hovered at, and around, 420 throughout the next month.[102] This new-found stability arose from the feeling that the market now knew reasonably clearly what the facts of the situation were. An important factor mitigating investors' fears was the escalating quarrel between Louis and the Emperor Leopold and the entry of the French armies during September into the Palatinate. The stock exchange was particularly heartened by the news that the French had set siege to the great fortress city of Philippsburg, on the Middle Rhine, for this meant that there was unlikely to be a full-scale French assault on Dutch territory at least before the following spring. 'Le siège de Philippsburg', commented D'Avaux subsequently, 'fit augmenter les actions [à Amsterdam] de 10 pour cent et rendit les Etats Generaux fort insolens par la certitude que le Roi ne les attaqueroit pas ni les Pays-Bas espagnols'.[103]

The stock market was now out of the most catastrophic phase of the crash and had recovered some stability. But the intial shock and losses had been such that they were bound to have serious implications over the next months for the Amsterdam

[98] Ibidem, 184: 'las acciones…bolvieron a subir 100 despues de saberse ya con evidencia que hay la guerra'.

[99] BL MS Add. 41816, fo. 173v.; Petit to Middleton, Amsterdam, 8 Sept. 1688.

[100] See the resolutions of the States of Holland for 9 Sept. 1688.

[101] BL MS Add. 41821, fos. 254v and 257v. 'News from The Hague', 14 and 16 Sept. 1688.

[102] BL MS Add. 41816, fo. 236v. Petit to Middleton, Amsterdam, 15 Oct. 1688.

[103] D'Avaux, *Négociations* VI, 273.

Exchange and business community as a whole. The investors had lost staggering sums, each VOC share having a nominal value of 500 pounds Flemish, or 3,000 guilders.[104] During the initial *precipio*, Penso de la Vega's philosopher exclaims 'mas yo pierdo ya de 552⅔ a 370 que son 5,430 [guilders] en la partida'.[105] The losses on other shares and securities had also been enormous. In the opening days of the crash, WIC actions, according to Penso de la Vega, had plummeted from 110% to 75.[106] Since each WIC share had a face value of 1,000 pounds Flemish, or 6,000 guilders, the value of each individual share dropped in a few days from 6,600 guilders to 4,500 guilders. Furthermore, WIC actions are unlikely to have recovered during September and the next few months to the same extent as VOC shares as the news from Madrid was that the house of Coymans and the WIC were now to lose their monopoly of slave deliveries to the Spanish Indies.[107] 'West India actions', reported Petit on 5 October, 'are so inconsiderable that nobody will buy them'.[108] In the same letter he observes that the 'obligations upon the countrey [= States of Holland bonds] begin also to fall extreamly'. In fact they had already lost a great deal of ground since 25 August and it was noticeable during the further slide which followed D'Avaux's speech of 9 September that these securities had been slower to rally than had VOC actions.[109]

The most damaging aspect of the crash for the Amsterdam business community was not the nominal losses through the collapse of share values, though this wiped colossal sums off personal fortunes, but the financial dislocation which resulted from the panic selling at the end of August and in September. Investors and brokers simply sold faster than their correspondents and purchasers could settle their bills. A great deal of money owed was witheld. A disastrous confusion and loss of confidence ensued which led to a series of spectacular bankruptcies[110], especially in late September and early October. 'The East India actions', reported Petit on 28 September, 'which are of late so very much fallen and by which Monsieur van Beuningen loses already some tons of gold [= several hundred thousand guilders] have ruined a great many merchants; one worth above 150,000 pounds sterling is upon breaking'.[111] 'The great fall of the East India actions', he added a week later, 'has already ruined several of our greatest merchants here and many more must and will undoubtedly follow'.[112] The famous Amsterdam former burgomaster Van Beuningen had been showing signs of mental instability for some time; but it was now, under the impact of unwise speculation during the crash, and his immense losses, that his mind finally snapped. 'Monsieur Van Beuningen has lost his senses within these ten days past', reported Petit on 19 October, 'it proceeded from the very great losses which he and his relations suffer by the East India actions in which

---

[104] As Kellenbenz notes at the 1688 peak of 580% each VOC action was worth over 17,000 guilders, Kellenbenz, 'Introduction', xv.

[105] Penso de la Vega, *Confusión de confusiones*, 138.

[106] 'Sabed que las acciones del Oost se largan por 370 y las del West por 75', Ibidem, 136.

[107] Wright, 'The Coymans Asiento', 55-58.

[108] BL MS Add. 41816, fo. 214v. Petit to Middleton, Amsterdam, 28 Sept. 1688.

[109] 'Obligations sur la province d'hollande' did not begin to recover from D'Avaux's warning to the States General until 16 September when it was reported to London from The Hague that they 'valent maintenant 3 pour cent de plus', BL MS Add. 41821, fo. 257v. 'News from The Hague', 16 Sept. 1688.

[110] Penso de la Vega, *Confusión de confusiones*, 274-276.

[111] BL MS Add. 41816, fo. 199v. Petit to Middleton, Amsterdam, 5 Oct. 1688.

[112] Ibidem, fo. 214v. Petit to Middleton, Amsterdam, 5 Oct. 1688.

they were great traders'.[113] The English ambassador at The Hague also noted that 'Van Beuningen is turned mad for his losses by the actions...he might be rich and would not; this is the end of his philosophie and great witt'.[114] This great diplomat-politician was the most celebrated victim of the crash of 1688.

The initial panic selling, the unsettled accounts, and the general shaking of confidence which ensued from the stock market crash inevitably rebounded also on the Amsterdam money market. The effect in terms of interest rates may not strike us today as anything very dramatic but it has to be born in mind that abrupt movements in interest rates on loans were unusual in the seventeenth century and that in 1688 Amsterdam was awash with surplus cash, much of it emanating from Huguenot sources. The rise in interest rates seems to have begun before the stock market crash, influenced perhaps by the taking up of cash for the financing of William's armada. But the shift became more marked after 25 August and, apparently made quite an impression. D'Albeville noted with some surprise on 7 September that 'they say the refugiés have four per cent interests'.[115] The significance of this is confirmed by a report sent to London from The Hague a week later according to which money at Amsterdam had suddenly become so much tighter that 'on n'en peut avoir à moins de 4 pour cent d'interest en donnant de bonnes assurances, là où on pouvoit il n'y a que deux mois en trouver plus que suffisament à deux pour cent.'[116]

New confidence

Meanwhile the political and military dangers threatening the Dutch Republic continued to mount. Louis was in an implacable mood. Egged on by his contacts in the Amsterdam city council, D'Avaux warned his master repeatedly, from late August onwards, that the only way to mobilise the Holland regents against William III, and prevent the invasion of England and probable collapse of James II, was 'en rétablissant le commerce sur le pied du traité de Nimègue'.[117] If Louis did not agree to cancel the measures he had taken against Dutch commerce, then the invasion of England would certainly go ahead. Far from yielding to the pressure, Louis hardened his attitude and, at the end of September, came the sensational news of the arrest of the Dutch wine fleet which was then at anchor at Bordeaux, Nantes, and other French west coast ports. Reports circulating at The Hague and Amsterdam had it that some 300 Dutch vessels were seized – though the real figure seems to have been much lower. With this all remaining hesitation in the minds of the Amsterdam city council evaporated.[118] The work on the invasion armada accelerated and now without any idea of using the preparations merely as a psychological lever, to force Louis to make the desired economic concessions. The Holland regents, Amsterdam included, were now committed to the invasion of England.

During October, with an all but certain war with both France and England pend-

---

113 Ibidem, fos. 245-246. Petit to Middleton, Amsterdam, 19 Oct. 1688.
114 Ibidem, fo. 240. D'Albeville to Middleton, The Hague, 15 Oct. 1688.
115 Ibidem, fo. 170v. D'Albeville to Middleton, The Hague, 7 Sept. 1688.
116 BL MS Add. 41821, fo. 254v. 'News from The Hague', 14 Sept. 1688.
117 D'Avaux, *Négociations* VI, 208, 228, 245-246, 255.
118 GAA vroedschapsresoluties no. 38, 145-146, 153. res. 3 and 15 Oct. 1688.

ing, the trade recession which had begun on the Dutch entrepot the previous autumn began to deepen and the list of notable bankruptcies lengthened. 'Trade begins to be slender', reported Petit on 15 October, adding four days later that 'trade and navigation lye almost dead, bankrupts are dayly made among the great merchants here'.[119] Yet the stock exchange, as Petit also noted, remained remarkably calm. All trace of the unprecedented panic of late August, and the anxiety of early September seemed to have vanished: 'East India actions are at a stand viz about 420.'[120]

Penso de la Vega was much struck by the paradoxical character of the (partial) recovery of the Amsterdam stock market in the wake of D'Avaux's ominous intervention of 9 September, and the mounting evidence that the Republic was going to war, probably with both Louis XIV and James II.[121] And given the indescribable panic experienced at the end of August, the stability of the share market from mid September onwards is surely not the least enigmatic feature of these astounding months in Dutch history. To an extent which the diplomats at The Hague found difficult to account for, Dutch opinion at this juncture was remarkably confident that their armada against England would be as successful as Philip II's armada of a century before had been unsuccessful.[122] Despite the manifest risks inherent in the lateness of the season, and the possibility, even if William landed his army safely, that the pick of the Dutch forces would become bogged down in fighting in England leaving the homeland exposed to French attack, the Dutch seemed quite convinced that their Stadholder, and the States General, would smash James II quickly and turn the tables on France. The confidence displayed is perhaps still somewhat mystifying.

This confidence emanated from The Hague and above all from Amsterdam. The Dutch invasion of England in 1688 may have been planned mainly by William himself, together with Bentinck and Fagel, but, to a degree which historians have generally failed to appreciate, the financing and assembling of the armada of 1688 was essentially an Amsterdam affair. Only by means of the facilities which Amsterdam offered could so huge an operation have been prepared so quickly. Most of the raising of the necessary finance, hiring of the transports to carry the invasion army and their supplies, fitting out of the warships and transports and the provisioning of the armada went on at Amsterdam. Approximately 60% of the warfleet and naval manpower on the armada was provided by the Amsterdam admiralty college which, under the direction of its energetic secretary, Job de Wildt, was the nerve-centre of the preparations.[123] During late August, September and October, Amsterdam was a hive of frenetic activity. 'The people that are employed here by the Admiralty', reported Petit in the second week of October, 'are night and day att work, Sundays not excepted; they are about 1,800 in number'.[124] Apart from that

---

[119] BL MS Add. 41816, fos. 236v, 245. Petit to Middleton, Amsterdam, 15 and 19 Oct. 1688.

[120] Ibidem, fo. 236v.

[121] Penso de la Vega, *Confusión de confusiones*, 286-287.

[122] BL MS Add. 38495, fo. 28v. Moreau to king of Poland, the Hague, 12 Oct. 1688; D'Avaux, *Négociations* VI, 288.

[123] Algemeen Rijksarchief, The Hague (ARH), Archives of the States General 5625/ii. Gecommitteerden van de Collegien ter Admiraliteit to SG, The Hague, 4 Nov. 1688; J.C. de Jonge, *Geschiedenis van het Nederlandsche zeewesen* III (2nd edn. 5 vols., Haarlem 1858-1862) 44, 721-722.

[124] BL MS Add. 41816, fo. 234.

of the Rotterdam admiralty college which made a lesser but still substantial contribution, the contingents contributed to the armada by the other admiralty colleges were very small by comparison.[125]

The irony and paradoxical character of Amsterdam's special role in the preparing of the invasion of England was not lost on the diplomats. According to D'Albeville, the 'people generally are everywhere mad for warre both against England and France, those of Amsterdam more than any, and beyond all reason and imagination'.[126] The Polish resident, Moreau, wrote a remarkable passage on this theme, underlining the special significance of the Amsterdam business community's attitude to this, the Dutch Republic's most momentous gamble:

'La confiance paroît si grande dans les esprits, et l'espérance de réussir si certaine, que l'on peut dire avec vérité que les habitans de ces provinces semblent avoir changé d'humeur et de tempérament; car comme cet état est fondé sur le négoce et la navigation, chacun y souhaitte toujours ardemment la conservation de la paix parce que la moindre apparence de guerre fait baisser considérablement le capital de leurs biens qui consistent presque tout en obligations sur le pais, ou en ce que l'on appelle actions sur les Compagnies des Indes d'Orient et d'Occident; car pour les terres ils en ont si peu et elles payent d'ailleurs de si grosses sommes à l'état qu'elles sont à charge à ceux qui les possèdent. Cependent nous voyons aujourd'huy que ces mesmes gens qui ne peuvent faire valoir leur commerce et leur navigation que par la paix souhaitent la guerre avec fureur, et que sur la nouvelle du siège de Philippsbourg et l'entrée des troupes en Allemagne, le capital des biens a commencé à renchérir considérablement'.[127]

What all this shows is that the role of the Amsterdam business community, or elements of it, in the financing of the armada, in the advancement of the preparations, and in forming the psychological framework for the launching of the expedition was an extremely important one. In order to support their (totally unbelievable) pretension that the expedition was not their doing but solely the responsability of the Prince of Orange, the Holland regents made no official allocations for the armada. Some camouflaged Dutch government money was diverted to the costs of the invasion out of the four million guilders raised by the provinces back in July for the repair and strengthening of the Republic's border fortresses. But a good deal of money which was later paid back (in part from the £ 600,000 towards the costs allocated by the English Parliament in the spring of 1689) was raised through unofficial channels in Amsterdam. It is true that D'Avaux and D'Albeville were convinced that the bulk of this came from opposition circles in England itself.[128] But there are reasons for supposing that the various reports circulating in Holland and at Hamburg about massive remittances for the armada from England were part of an elaborate deception organized by William and Bentinck to reinforce the impression they were so anxious to foment (not least in England) that the whole business was basically an English affair. Certainly the report passed to London by the English resident at Hamburg strongly smacks of being part of a propaganda ploy:

---

125 De Jonge, *Geschiedenis* III, 44, 721-722.
126 BL MS Add. 41816, fo. 170v. D'Albeville to Middleton, The Hague, 7 Sept. 1688.
127 BL MS Add. 38495, fos. 28v-9. Moreau to king of Poland, The Hague, 12 Oct. 1688.
128 The Earl of Middleton was apparently sceptical but D'Albeville insisted that the quantities of weapons, stores and provisions being sent out to the waiting armada 'from Amsterdam, and other sea ports, is incredible, the like preparations was never done anywhere, and you may believe there what you will, the most part, if not all is done by money from England', BL MS Add. 41816, fo. 252; D'Albeville to Middleton, The Hague, 21 Oct. 1688.

'Tis advised hither they have very near fitted out their fleet with English money; and Baron Craeg, in his return through this place to Copenhagen told a publique minister here (from whom I had the story) that as he took his leave of Monsieur Petcomb (the Prince of Orange's Treasurer) he carryed him into a room where was on the floor such prodigious heaps of English gold as by his computation little must be left in the kingdome'.[129]

Even if these reports were true, elements of the Amsterdam financial elite must still have played a crucial role, for the secret letters of exchange in which form, reportedly, some of this alleged English cash was remitted had to be accepted and cashed at great financial risk to the Amsterdam bankers concerned and this the latter were hardly likely to undertake unless deeply committed to William and his cause. On 14 September D'Avaux reported to Paris that the 'Prince d'Orange avoit reçu plus de quatre millions [= of Dutch guilders roughly equivalent to £ 400,000] d'Angleterre, qu'on le savoit à n'en pouvoir douter; qu'une partie avoit été envoyée par lettres de change, dont Suasso en avoit payé quelques-unes, et le reste avoit ete porté en argent comptant dans un petit bâtiment anglois'.[130]

Sephardi financiers

D'Avaux is, of course, here referring to Baron Francisco Lopes Suasso who has long been known to have assisted with the financing of the armada, who regularly acted as an intermediary in the passing on of secret messages from Brussels and Madrid to the Dutch government and who, possessing one of the largest houses at The Hague, was a familiar figure there as well as at Amsterdam. It is fairly well known that William had established a personal relationship with several of the leading figures of the Amsterdam Sephardi financial circle as far back as 1673 and with Lopes Suasso at least since 1674.[131] What D.J. Roorda called the Stadholder's 'Jewish entourage' had personal links with him which reached back many years and which seem to have become even stronger, subsequently, in the 1690s. On the occasion of his first visit to Holland after becoming king of England, in 1691, William visited the Sephardi synagogue in Amsterdam, no doubt as a token of his appreciation for their support, talked with the community leadership and stayed three days in the house of Jeronimo Nunes da Costa, 'agent' at Amsterdam of the Crown of Portugal and, we may be sure, one of those who had performed services for the Stadholder.[132]

The services which William's Sephardi associates performed on his behalf in 1688, as throughout his stadholderate, were in the first place financial. But they were by no means only financial and were by no means simple business transactions. Even if we assume that there is no truth in the apocryphal story that in 1688, during the preparations of the armada, Lopes Suasso advanced two million guilders to the Stadholder without any security, merely commenting (he spoke

[129] BL MS Add. 41821, fo. 90; Wyche to Middleton, Hamburg, 18 Sept. 1688; Simon van Pettecum was one of William's closest aides.

[130] D'Avaux, *Négociations* VI, 230.

[131] D.J. Roorda, 'De joodse entourage van de koning-stadhouder', *Spiegel Historiael* May (1979) 258-261.

[132] David Franco Mendes, 'Memorias do estabelicimento e progresso dos judeus portuguezes e espanhoes nesta famosa citade de Amsterdam', *Studia Rosenthaliana* 9 (1975) 95.

fluent French) 'Si vous êtes heureux, je sais que vous me les rendrez; si vous êtes malheureux, je consens de les perdre'[133], it is a well-attested fact that both in 1688, and other years, Lopes Suasso did provide large sums for secret political and diplomatic uses of the Stadholder on no security, other than the Prince's friendship.[134] This was part of a pattern whereby Lopes Suasso and other Sephardi leaders, including Jeronimo Nunes da Costa, the father of the Duarte Nunes da Costa to whom Penso de la Vega dedicated his *Confusión de Confusiones*, on occasion risked and, in the short term, sacrificed, large sums for the sake of the prestige, influence and favours which accrued to them from their links with the Stadholder and the Dutch state. As we see from Leti's description of them, these men went out of their way to project an image of themselves as being willing and able to perform significant services for both the Prince and the States General.[135]

Two leading Sephardi financiers, both of whom were familiar figures in the Amsterdam stock market, Antonio (Moseh) Alvarez Machado and Jacob Pereira, had since 1673 served as official 'provditeurs generaal' (provisioners general) of the Dutch army on behalf of the States General, albeit at the particular wish of the Stadholder.[136] For many years they had been responsible for setting up stores for grain, procuring grain supplies, establishing bakeries near the field army, and supplying the troops with bread, fodder, and wagons. The Prince knew and trusted these men, retaining their services because they met his and the army's requirements efficiently and promptly. A few days before he set out on his expedition to England, the Prince drafted an agreement with Machado whereby the latter undertook to supply the Dutch army in the field on the Rhine, under Prince Waldeck, which had the vital task of shielding the Republic's eastern frontier from the French whilst the Stadholder and the pick of the Dutch forces were away in England.[137] At this point Machado and Pereira had already brilliantly carried out most of the task of provisioning the armada for the invasion of England. We know that the bulk of the provisioning of William's invasion fleet was organized at Amsterdam and, as all observers note, accomplished with astounding speed and efficiency, though it was not until early October that D'Albeville observed that at Amsterdam 'one Pereira, a Jew, is...[the fleet's] commissioner for victuals'.[139]

Care has to be taken not to exaggerate the significance of these facts. A group of Dutch Sephardi financiers played a not inconsiderable role in preparing the armada set to invade England. No doubt they did so out of self-interest but a self-interest which was not exclusively, or even mainly, financial in character. In effect, this group participated in a gigantic gamble which must have imparted a special

[133] Israel, *European Jewry*, 134.

[134] Ibidem; Roorda, 'De joodse entourage', 261.

[135] J.I. Israel, 'Gregorio Leti (1631-1701) and the Dutch Sephardi elite at the close of the seventeenth century' in: A. Rapoport-Albert and S.J. Zipperstein ed., *Jewish History. Essays in honour of Chimen Abramsky* (London 1988) 271-272. See below, chapter 17, pp. 375ff.

[136] F.J.G. ten Raa, *Het staatsche leger, 1568-1795* VI (11 vols., The Hague 1911) 28, 42, 53; J. Meijer, *Zij lieten hun sporen achter. Joodse bijdragen tot de Nederlandsche beschaving* (Utrecht 1964) 83-84.

[137] ARH Raad van State no. 109, fo. 520v. res. 25 Oct. 1688.

[138] Machado and Pereira 'also tendered for, and received,' states Childs, 'the contract to victual William's expedition to England in 1688', see J. Childs, *The British army of William III, 1689-1702* (Manchester 1987) 250.

[139] BL MS Add. 41816, fo. 229. D'Albeville to Middleton, The Hague, 9 Oct. 1688.

resonance to the service held at the great Portuguese synagogue in Amsterdam shortly before William's armada set sail for England 'to implore God to ensure the triumph of the Prince and his armada'.[140] To underline their commitment to the Dutch state in its hour of danger, the special prayer recited in the synagogue for the success of the 'States of Holland, States General and Prince of Orange' in their military undertakings (the allusion was to the invasion of England) was translated into Dutch and published.[141]

Against this background it is not difficult to see why there was a relatively strong impetus behind the 'patriotic' reaction in the stock market beginning on 5 September. One of the salient features of Penso de la Vega's discussion of the process of trend-fixing on the Amsterdam stock exchange is the way he presents the meetings of the accionists' cabals as encounters, even 'battles', between 'underminers' out to depress share price quotations for their own advantage, and the 'patriotic' element, concerned to support the colonial companies' shares and push up their value.[142] The emphasis which he lays on this is by no means surprising. For one of the central complaints of Muys van Holy and other critics of the stock exchange in 1687 was precisely that the (Jewish) accionists, out to profit at the expense of others, manipulated news and 'drove the price of actions down, belittling the Dutch state and the companies'.[143] The 'bears' of the market, or 'contraminores' as Penso de la Vega calls them clearly were seen as an anti-patriotic element, one particular Jew, called 'Mezquita' being singled out for having started a notorious run, or 'contramine', following an abrasive memorial from James II to the States General, very possibly the one submitted by D'Albeville which caused the fall in share prices in July 1687.[144]

But, if we accept that it was the Sephardi accionists in their cabals and smoke-filled coffee-shops by the Dam who fixed the trends in the stock market, we must by the same token attribute to them the 'patriotic' reaction from 5 September onwards which went some way to curtail the damaging consequences of the crash and restore confidence. That a sense of supporting the state and the companies was a major and conscious element in the psychological make-up of what Penso de la Vega calls 'la liefhebrería' is shown by the terms in which he discusses this phenomenon. Addressing a Sephardi audience, he urges his readers to avoid the practices of 'undermining' like the plague and to strive always to be responsible 'liefhebbers' who he repeatedly describes as 'patriotic', that is 'amantes de la patria, del estado y de la Compañía'.[145] At times, the 'liefhebbers' are forced to take great risks with their money but they are not afraid and by their boldness, accepting the risk, they assist the state.[146] Of course, we do not know which Sephardi financiers played the leading roles in checking the 'contraminores' of the stock market in September 1688,

[140] Franco Mendes, *Memorias,* 98.
[141] *Gebedt, gedaen op woensdag, sijnde den 27 oktober 1688, door de Portugeese Joden in hare kerck, ofte synagoge, binnen Amsterdam* (Amsterdam 1688) (Knuttel, 12784a).
[142] Penso de la Vega, *Confusión de confusiones,* 35-36.
[143] Muys van Holy, *Relaes en contradictie,* 1; Ibidem, 1-3.
[144] *Relaes en contradictie,* 9.
[145] Penso de la Vega, *Confusión de confusiones,* 36: 'continuamente dessean que las acciones suban y que vengan nuebas tan felices que en un punto caminen, corran, batan las plumas, y remontan las alas'.
[146] Ibidem, 'los liefhebberen son como la Zorafa que de nada se espanta'.

and in pushing share prices back up, but it would be surprising if Lopes Suasso, the largest Jewish investor, and Machado and Pereira, both of whom were experienced 'accionistas', had no hand in it.

With the success of William's invasion of England, and his subsequent elevation, along with Mary to the throne, VOC share prices at Amsterdam recovered further and the newly-regained stability of the market was placed on a securer foundation. Of course, the war situation and the various potentially dangerous developments of the next few years caused several further temporary surges of anxiety and, on at least one occasion, a fall of thirty percentage points in a single day.[147] But there was nothing at all comparable with the crash and panic of late August 1688 and the underlying trend was upwards back towards the 500% mark. The row between William and Amsterdam over the election of magistrates (schepenen) in the city, early in 1690, was thought highly disturbing by the Amsterdam business community and caused a notable setback in the stock market. The actionists continued to follow every political move with avid attention. On 10 March 1690, the English resident at The Hague reported that the 'actions at Amsterdam are risen prodigiously uppon hopes of an agreement'.[148] Yet there was no mistaking the new, underlying stability of the Amsterdam share market in the aftermath of the English Revolution of 1688 and England's subsequent entry into the Nine Years' War on the side of the coalition ranged against France. This is well illustrated by the reaction to the disastrous defeat of the Dutch army, under Waldeck, at Fleurus, in the Spanish Netherlands, in July 1690, a battle in which, according to Abel Boyer, the French killed 4,600 Dutch troops, wounded many more, and captured another 4,000 along with most of the Dutch field artillery.[149] William received the news of the disaster in Ireland three days after his victory over James II at the battle of the Boyne. Sorrowfully, he wrote to Waldeck ''t neemt mij 't eenemael weg de satisfactie over mijn eigen success'.[150] Yet, to the surprise of some of the diplomatic community, the actionists of the Amsterdam stock market seemed quite unperturbed by the defeat. 'There has been a big battle lost', remarked the English resident at The Hague, 'but there is not much consternation in Holland, the actions at Amsterdam are fallen onely from 496 to 487 and in another time they would have fallen fifty per cent.'[151]

In conclusion, we may say that the crash which began on the Amsterdam stock market on 25 August 1688, on the realisation that the Dutch state was preparing to invade England as part of a wider conflict with France, led to what was almost certainly the second most serious crisis on the Amsterdam Exchange of the entire seventeenth century. Many regents, merchants, and other members of Dutch society lost heavily as a result. The impact of the crash was reflected in a disastrous slump in the value of VOC shares, which lost 216 percentage points in a few days, WIC shares, and provincial 'obligations', and in an abrupt rise in interest rates, as

---

[147] Leti, *Teatro Belgico* II, 243.

[148] Public Record Office, London (PRO) SP 84/221, fo. 51; Aglionby to Warre, The Hague, 10 March 1690.

[149] A. Boyer, *The history of King William III* (3 vols., London 1702) II, 229.

[150] Quoted in N. Japikse, *Prins Willem III. De Stadhouder-koning* II (2 vols., Amsterdam 1933) 309.

[151] PRO SP 84/221, fo. 157v. Aglionby to Warre, The Hague, 7 July 1690.

well as a string of notable bankruptcies. It was in the midst of the crash that Coenraad van Beuningen became insane. But the financial dislocation might well have been much more severe than it was were it not for a strong counter-tendency, rebuilding confidence, which emerged at a time when the Republic was in a dangerous and extremely precarious situation in its relations with France and England. This reaction, which caused some surprise amongst diplomats and the investing public, was seemingly based in part on self-interest which was not strictly financial in character and which consciously projected itself as 'patriotic' and supportive of the Dutch state and Stadholder.

Appendix

Movements in the VOC share price (Amsterdam Chamber) at Amsterdam, 1671-90*

Date	Conjuncture	Share price levels and movements
(late 1671)		572
June 1672	French Invasion of the Republic	250/340
May 1675		428/443
13 July 1676		450
April 1681	Dissolution of English Parliament	408/422
Nov. 1681	French seizure of Strasbourg	395½
23 Jan. 1682		410
April 1682		441/447
Sept. 1682		461/462
Nov. 1682	French seizure of Luxemburg	448
May 1683	Quarrel between William III	427/402
June 1683	and Amsterdam; and confrontation	401/408
Aug. 1683	with France	395/403
(late 1684)		470
5 Feb. 1685		479
(late 1687)		525
April 1688		560/568
17/24 May 1688		566/576½
June 1688		572/567
13/29 July	Fears for returning VOC fleet	569/566
7 Aug. 1688	Safe return of VOC fleet	560/575½
13 Aug. 1688	Optimistic expectations of VOC cargoes	582/580
25 Aug. 1688	Onset of the great 'crash' of 1688	580/500
26/29 Aug. 1688	Panic on stock exchange	500/370
(Beginning of September 1688)	Nadir of the 'crash'	365
5/8 Sept. 1688	James II's weakness more evident	366/430
9/14 Sept. 1688	Louis XIV threatens war on the Republic	430/414
14/16 Sept. 1688	Fear of France and England subsides	414/433
15 Oct. 1688		420
July 1690	Battle of Fleurus	496/487

* The references for most of these share price quotations are given in the text, the remainder are from GAA PJG 334.

15

England, the Dutch and the Struggle for Mastery of World Trade in the Age of the Glorious Revolution, 1682–1702

During the third quarter of the seventeenth century, England, and the Dutch Republic went to war three times, in 1652–54, 1665–67, and 1672–74. These hard-fought maritime contests, all of which resulted in heavy losses of men, ships, and trade on both sides, were rooted in long-standing differences over commerce, colonies, and shipping. The wars were symptoms of a deep, underlying conflict of interest between the English and Dutch mercantile systems, which reached its most intense expression in the East Indies, West Africa, and the Caribbean region, but which also manifested itself in continual commercial and diplomatic rivalry in other key markets such as Spain, Italy, the Levant, and Russia, and in a ceaseless wrangle over the North Sea herring grounds. The latter were mainly exploited by the Dutch, but according to the English (and Scots) were a stolen resource, being located principally in the 'British seas'.

By 1688 Anglo-Dutch economic rivalry was thus a deeply entrenched, universally familiar feature of English and Dutch political life and attitudes. It is true that since the end, in 1674, of the Third Anglo-Dutch War, the rivalry had been somewhat less intense than previously, at any rate as reflected in the political and diplomatic spheres. But much of the old tension lingered on, above all (but by no means only) in the East Indies and Africa, and serious political clashes rooted in this continuing economic rivalry still occurred periodically. The gravest such incident in the period 1674–88 took place in 1682–83, when Dutch East India Company forces occupied the previously independent sultanate of Bantam at the western end of Java, an important center of the traffic in pepper and spices, and forced the sultan to concede exclusive control over Bantam's pepper output and exports to the Dutch. This was one of a series of actions taken by the Dutch during the early 1680s to shore up their hegemony over the commerce of southern Asia and curb the rapid growth of English competition. Their action at Bantam was, however, the most dramatic such intervention. The Dutch compelled the sultan to close the previously flourishing trade factories that the English, French, and Danes had all maintained there, and to expel Europeans who were not in Dutch service. By so doing, the Dutch company aroused the ire of three European rulers at once.

In response to Dutch pressure in the Indonesian archipelago, as well as in Bengal, where the English were now increasingly successful in challenging the Dutch for dominance of the region's commerce, Sir Josiah Child and other

English East India Company directors tried, unsuccessfully, to persuade the aging Charles II to authorize – and support – the dispatch of a major armed expedition to the East Indies to expel the Dutch from Bantam and generally tilt the balance. Child insisted that an uncompromising show of force was the right answer to Dutch 'insolence'. 'Besides their natural avarice,' he wrote to Charles's secretary of state,

> one thing that hath necessitated them to these dangerous and daring attempts to the provocation of three great kings of Europe at this time, I suppose, is the great increase of the English East India trade these few last years which did sensibly consume their stock; and my present thoughts are that they will endeavour to drive their designe of the sole trade of India through at any charge or hazard.[1]

Charles II was not interested in another armed confrontation with the Dutch. But the East India Company directors in London did not easily give up their plan. In a memorial to the king of July 1684 they again complained that the sultan of Bantam had been reduced to a 'mere slave to the Dutch . . . unable to stirr a step out of the castle without a guard of Dutch soldiers'.[2] Moreover, they still wanted the 'restitution of Bantam to the injured nations, viz. the English, French and Danes . . . and the Dutch forces entirely withdrawn'. In this they were to be thwarted. In the years after 1682 the Dutch were successful in drastically cutting back English trade with the Indonesian archipelago. But in Bengal, and in India generally, the English continued to make rapid progress at the expense of the Dutch.[3]

At the time of William III's intervention in Britain and the overthrow of James II, Anglo-Dutch commercial rivalry was still far from being a spent force. With William master of London, with Franco-Dutch relations at a nadir, and with the Dutch eager to enlist England against France, at least one foreign diplomat at The Hague remarked that it would be a more logical pursuit of Dutch interest to seek an accommodation with France, that in the long run there could be no Dutch alliance with England 'que leur commerce empeschera toujours qu'ils ne puissent être d'accord avec les anglois' (that their commerce will always prevent their coming to agreement with the English).[4] Following the 'Glorious Revolution' and William's elevation to the English throne jointly with Mary, England did become the ally of the United Provinces and in May 1689 entered the Nine Years' War on the side of the Dutch against France.

It also became an integral part of the Williamite propaganda of the day to insist that the French were England's real and natural foes, and that the Dutch

---

[1] Child to Middleton, Westminster, Sept. 6, 1683, BL, Add. MSS 41, 822, fol. 28.

[2] Directors of the English East India Company to Charles II, Westminster, July 9, 1684, ibid., fol. 48.

[3] K.N. Chaudhuri, *The Trading World of Asia and the English East India Company, 1600–1760* (Cambridge, Eng., 1978), p. 319; O. Prakash, *The Dutch East India Company and the Economy of Bengal, 1630–1720* (Princeton, 1985), p. 201.

[4] A. Moreau (the Polish resident) to the king of Poland, The Hague, March 1, 1689, BL, Add. MSS 38,495, fol. 168.

were England's natural allies in the fight to curb the overweening ambition of Louis XIV. One Williamite pamphlet, published the year after England's entry into the Nine Years' War, even went so far as to claim that the previous prolonged antagonism between England and the Dutch had been largely a result of cunning manipulation by the French, who had deliberately fomented 'several artificial insinuations of injuries received from the Dutch, as to Amboyna, and the Fishery' in England and gone to work 'with the same subtilty' on the Hollanders.[5] Englishmen were warned that all jealous thoughts of their Dutch neighbors were but aid and comfort to Louis XIV, who wanted nothing more than to split the new alliance of England and the Republic.

This was the line taken by the newly ensconced English regime, but such notions were far from prevalent in the minds of most Englishmen. One of the main arguments deployed by James II's regime in favor of its policy of religious toleration had been that toleration would greatly favor the advancement of English trade, industry, and shipping; furthermore it was clear from the outset that good, old-fashioned English antipathy to the Dutch would be one of the strongest assets of the emerging British anti-Williamite propaganda machine. From the moment that William landed in England, a not insignificant number of English Protestants, mostly conservative Anglicans, opted to back James rather than William. Once the initial flush of enthusiasm for the 'Glorious Revolution' had worn off, by the spring of 1689, more and more English and Scottish Protestants, especially traditionalist Anglicans and Scots Episcopalians, became, if not always exactly supportive of the exiled king, then certainly disillusioned with William and the Revolution and disinclined to sympathize with William's war against France.

During the first half of 1689 the Revolution became increasingly unpopular with significant sections of the populace. There were various reasons for this phenomenon, which was noticeable throughout Britain. According to Hugh Mackay, the commander of the Scottish brigades of the Dutch army whom William sent to Scotland early in 1689 to take command of his forces there, most of the population of Edinburgh 'appeared not well pleased with the late . . . so necessary . . . revolution'.[6] There is no doubt that one of the main features of this shift in public opinion was an alarming increase in anti-Dutch sentiment, caused partly by the continuing presence of the Dutch army in London and other parts of the country.[7] By July 1689, the Amsterdam burgomaster Nicholas Witsen, one of the three Dutch ambassadors extraordinary then in London, reported back to his colleagues on the Amsterdam city council that anti-Dutch feeling in England was now so prevalent as to be seriously hampering Anglo-Dutch

---

[5] *Nero Gallicanus: or, The True Pourtraicture of Lewis XIV* (1690), p. 11.

[6] Hugh Mackay, *Memoirs of the War Carried on in Scotland and Ireland, 1689–91* (Edinburgh, 1833), p. 7.

[7] G. van Alphen, *De stemming van de Engelschen tegen de Hollanders in Engeland tijdens de regeering van den koning-stadhouder Willem III*, 1688–1702 (Assen, 1938), pp. 37, 70–71.

naval and military cooperation against the French.[8] He also remarked on the brusque, paranoid reaction of the English to any suggestion that England's tough commercial regulations, and in particular the Navigation Act, might be amended in any way in favor of the Dutch.[9]

Clearly, at the time of the Glorious Revolution and the onset of the Nine Years' War, many Protestant Englishmen continued to view the Dutch, rather than the French, as England's real adversaries. Consequently, the stirring up of economic grievances and other resentment against the Dutch became a central theme of English Jacobite propaganda from 1688 onward and was arguably the most consistently effective expedient available to the Jacobites for working on those growing sections of British opinion inclined to be critical of William and his war against France.

Possibly the very first English pamphlet to attack William from a Protestant Jacobite standpoint (assuming the author's claim to be 'a true member of the Church of England' is genuine) was *The Dutch Design Anatomized, or, A Discovery of the Wickedness and Unjustice of the Intended Invasion,* a pamphlet which, from internal evidence, appears to have been written in October 1688, and in any case shortly before William's landing. William, his English allies, and the States General were claiming that what was about to take place was not an invasion and that the Dutch were playing what the propaganda of the States General called only an 'auxiliary' role. *The Dutch Design Anatomized* set the tone for subsequent Jacobite propaganda by roundly labeling William's enterprise an 'invasion' by 'the Dutch', accompanied by a few English auxiliaries.[10]

Why were the Dutch 'invading England'? The anonymous author scoffs at William's pretensions that he was intervening for the sake of English liberty and religion. With some justification, the author notes that the Dutch Republic had never acted in the international arena out of religious motives, or anything remotely resembling them: 'I think that none that know the religion of an Hollander would judge the Prince or States would be at the charge of a dozen flyboats, or herring busses to propagate it or especially the Church of England as by law established'.[11] The true authors of the invasion, the pamphlet insists, are not William and his English supporters, but the States of Holland and the States General, whose fleet and army the prince was using, the goal being to exploit the opportunity to overthrow James II to clinch and consolidate Dutch economic supremacy over England.[12] The writer bases this contention on the argument that James II's policy of religious toleration had secured great gains for England by making the country safe for merchants and artisans of various

[8] Amsterdam City Archives, archives of the burgomasters, vol. 7: Witsen to Amsterdam *vroedschap,* Westminster, April 16–26, May 21–31, June 18–28, June 25, July 5, 1689.

[9] Ibid., May 31, June 10, 1689.

[10] *The Dutch Design Anatomized, or, A Discovery of the Wickedness and Unjustice of the Intended Invasion, and a Clear Proof, That It Is the Interest of All the King's Subjects to Defend His Majesty and Their Country Against it* (1688).

[11] Ibid., p. 8.

[12] Ibid., pp. 6–8.

creeds, and that the Dutch were 'very sensible that this liberty [of conscience] would be more prejudicial to them in their traffick than anything that had been done by England against them in many years'.[13] After reminding his readers 'by what perfidiousness, over-reaching and barbarity the Dutch have wormed us out of the trade of the East Indies', he goes on to urge his countrymen to consider the Dutch as would-be 'conquerors that come for no other end but to seize on all your effects in trade and put them into Dutch bottoms and Dutch hands'.[14]

The tract entitled *Some Reflections on the Prince of Orange's Declaration*, which was written shortly after William's landing, is another early example of Jacobite mocking at William's pretensions that cites economic motives for the Dutch invasion. Its author urges his countrymen not to believe the assurances of the prince and the States General. 'Dutch good-nature we very well know', he remarks, 'at all the markets in the world: liberty of conscience gave them their trade, and that mighty wealth they have; and they fear the consequence of it here, lest what we should get, they might in a great degree lose.'[15] The author roundly denounces this 'present invasion that cannot be thought to end without making many fatherless and widows, and spoiling, wasting and impoverishing the country'.

Up to a point there is an important element of truth in these anti-Williamite propaganda tracts. It is certain (though modern historians have been curiously reluctant to make the point) that the role of the States of Holland and the States General was crucial, William being merely stadholder, with no independent power to dispose of the Dutch army and navy.[16] It is also abundantly clear that the Dutch regents' reasons for embarking on so risky and momentous an enterprise as invading England had little to do with religion, and nothing at all to do with English liberty, except insofar as the States of Holland (as we know from their secret resolutions on the invasion) calculated that an English regime dominated by Parliament would be more likely than a Stuart absolutist monarch to join an anti-French coalition and less likely to make secret deals with Louis XIV. The States further reckoned that the strengthening of England's Parliament would make England a safer and more useful neighbor for the Dutch.[17] Jacobite propagandists were also correct in their claim that economic considerations were uppermost when the States decided to launch the Dutch forces in a full-scale invasion of England.

[13] Ibid., pp. 4–5.

[14] Ibid., pp. 7, 30.

[15] *Some Reflections upon the Prince of Orange's Declaration* (1688), in *A Collection of Scarce and Valuable Tracts . . . from the Collection of Lord Somers* (11748), vol. 1, p. 295.

[16] See J.I. Israel, 'The Dutch Role in the Glorious Revolution', in J.I. Israel (ed.), *The Anglo-Dutch Moment: Essays on the Glorious Revolution and its World Impact* (Cambridge, Eng., 1991), pp. 105–62.

[17] *Secreete Resolutien van de Ed. Groot. Mog. Heeren Staaten van Hollandt en West-Vriesland* (The Hague, n.d. [1679–96], vol. 4, pp. 224–33, resolutions of Sept. 18 and 29, 1688.

Where the Jacobite pamphleteers were wide of the mark was in their assumption that the politico-economic worries that shaped Dutch policy at this decisive juncture centered chiefly on England. In fact, England was only an incidental factor in Dutch calculations at this time. The Dutch saw England as their most dangerous rival for the trade of the world, but not as a political and military threat to the Dutch trading system as such. On the contrary, England's political and military weakness during the last years of Charles II and under James II was regarded, not least by the Amsterdam stock exchange, as rather reassuring.

France, however, was another matter entirely. As long as Louis XIV had been willing to abide by the tariff and other commercial clauses of the Treaty of Nijmegen (1678), as he had done through most of the 1680's, the Dutch had been able to sell their goods in France, a market many times more important to Dutch business than England which, since 1651, had largely been closed to Dutch products. France was indeed a crucially important market for the Dutch, both for the sale of Holland's main export products – herring, textiles, dairy produce, spices, whale products, and Baltic naval stores – and as a source of the wine, brandy, and salt that figured so largely in Dutch traffic with northern Europe. Louis's reversion in the autumn of 1687 to outright economic warfare against the Dutch, first shutting out their herring, then their textiles, and finally, in September 1688, seizing the Dutch wine fleet in French ports, not only infuriated the regents and merchants of Holland and silenced the previously influential pro-French (anti-Orangist) faction on the Amsterdam city council, but convinced the Dutch that it was only by going to war with France that they could protect their trading system from irreparable damage.[18] It was because the Dutch had made up their minds that they had to fight France that they invaded England. For the States of Holland saw the opportunity of overthrowing James II (Louis's protégé, as they regarded him) and allying England with Holland as offering the best means of defeating Louis. It was Louis's attack on Dutch trade with France that sealed James's fate.

During the months of the Revolution in England, from November 1688 to the spring of 1689, and during the opening months of the war with France, Jacobite pamphleteers continued to denounce the Dutch as conquerors by subterfuge, seeking to gain economically at England's expense by means of a Machiavellian religious policy built on a mixture of hypocrisy and a total lack of religious scruple. The author of *Whether the Preserving the Protestant Religion was the Motive* asserted,

> It is no slander to say that the Deputies of the Seven Provinces, who sit governing at The Hague, never enter into war or peace upon any other instigation, or views and ends, save those of a secular concernment. Nor would it move or impress them to

---

[18] Polish resident at The Hague to king of Poland, The Hague, Oct. 5 and 12, 1688, BL, Add. MSS 38,495, fols. 28, 29v; *Négociations de Monsieur le Comte d'Avaux en Hollande* (Paris, 1752–53), vol. 6, pp. 190, 208, 228, 246, 288, Israel, 'Dutch Role', pp. 111–19.

see all the inhabitants of these three kingdoms turn Pagans or Mahometans farther than it may affect their trade, and disturb their civil tranquility.[19]

He then went on to remind his readers of how, in 1628, the Dutch had supplied warships to enable Louis XIII to besiege La Rochelle, the maritime stronghold of their Huguenot co-religionists, and to accuse the Dutch of a shameful betrayal of Christianity in Japan, where, for the sake of economic advantage, Dutch factors carried instructions not to try to propagate Christianity among the Japanese. The author of this tract, too, sees the main motive of the Dutch intervention in Britain as being the Hollanders' desire to stifle James II's policy of religious toleration, a motive based on the fear of the commercial implications of that policy.

But the most dramatic expression of this theme is the piece entitled *Min Heer T. van C's Answer to Min Heer H. van L's Letter of the 15th of March 1689*, apparently written in the spring of 1689. In this purported letter from one Dutch regent to another we are told that 'if the Liberty of Conscience which [James II] was going to establish had not been prevented, the most considerable of our merchants (who lives amongst us because they are not molested in the free exercise of their religion) would have been removed, and drawn their effects to England, where the ports being more secure, they would, without hazarding their religion, have run less danger of their goods'.[20] The purported regents go on to congratulate themselves that Prince William will prevent freedom of conscience and will ally with the Church of England, 'by which means all conscientious Dissenters will with the Jews, be again forced to take their retreat amongst us'.[21] With the Revolution's apparent stifling of freedom of conscience on behalf of the Church of England, the supposed Dutch leaders boast that 'we have . . . established our Interest upon a firm and lasting foundation, by their utter ruin, being now masters of the whole Trade of the inhabitable world'.[22] For the first time we also encounter the idea that the Dutch attempt to drag England into war with France was essentially a stratagem to serve Dutch economic interest: 'tis manifest also and foreseen, by our wisest men, that whilst it was impossible for us to stave off a war with France, King James, whose industry and application to the advancement of trade, made him embrace all occasions to incourage it, would have preserved a neutrality to our utter ruin'.[23]

By the summer of 1689, with the Toleration Act on the statute books and William himself obviously strongly committed to a de facto toleration that

---

[19] *Whether the Preserving the Protestant Religion Was the Motive unto, or the End, That Was Designed in the Late Revolution* (n.p., n.d. [1689]), p. 33.

[20] *Min Heer T. van C's Answer to Min Heer H. van L's Letter of the 15th of March 1689, Representing the True Interests of Holland, and What They Have Already Gained by Our Losses* (1689), in *A Collection* (1748), vol. 4, p. 126.

[21] Ibid., p. 128.

[22] Ibid., p. 127.

[23] Ibid., p. 126.

encompassed Catholics and went far beyond the actual terms of the act,[24] the argument that the Dutch had invaded England to prevent the establishment of religious toleration there had become entirely unpersuasive. Manifestly, it was not Dutch policy to destroy liberty of conscience in England. But the idea that England had, as a result of the Revolution, come under the thumb of the Dutch had by no means lost its grip on the English imagination. According to *The Dear Bargain,* one of the hardest-hitting of the anti-Williamite tracts of the 1690's, the Dutch 'have been always our rivals, and are now our masters'. The author claimed, 'We give them up our trade, and pay them too,' referring to the 600,000 that Parliament paid to the States General in 1689 to reimburse the expenses of William's expedition 'for their enslaving us.'[25] 'For now we are under Dutch comptrollers,' lamented Samuel Grascombe, 'and as nothing must be done, so nothing must be said, that may be offensive to the Hogen Mogens.' This enduringly potent propaganda myth that the Dutch 'hector and domineer in our country' was partly built on the political realities of the situation and the conspicuousness of the Dutch troops and courtiers in the country.[26] There was certainly a strong aversion to William III's reliance on Hans Willem Bentinck and a small group of other Dutch advisers, what *The Dear Bargain* calls 'a secret cabal of Dutchmen', in the shaping of England's foreign policy. There was resentment too that 'they buy the estates of our impoverished gentry, and Dutch pages are made English nobles'. Since it was inadvisable to criticize the new king openly, there was a marked tendency for any political resentment of William to manifest itself, in conversation and print, as anti-Dutch sentiment in general. As John Toland put it, High Church Anglicans became accustomed to 'damn all the Dutch when they durst not expressly curse King William'.[27]

The idea that what Grascombe called 'Dutch practices' in England were intended to undermine England economically and consolidate Dutch trade hegemony remained a central component of Jacobite and antiwar propaganda, albeit now necessarily based on arguments rather different from those concerning religious toleration that had figured so prominently at first. During the 1690's it increasingly emerged as the centerpiece of this type of anti-Williamite agitation that the mounting fiscal burdens and the disruptive effects at sea of the war against France were all part of a deep stratagem to exhaust England and divert her vitality to the republic. In some instances William himself was depicted as a 'humble, obedient and active' instrument 'for emptying the English Treasures into Dutch Exchequers'.[28]

---

[24] See J.I. Israel, 'William III and Toleration', above, pp. 263–304.

[25] Nathaniel Johnson, *The Dear Bargain, or, A True Representation of the State of the English Nation Under the Dutch* (1692), in *A Collection of Scarce and Valuable Tracts . . . of the Late Lord Somers,* ed. Sir Walter Scott (13 vols., 1809–15), vol. 10, pp. 353, 354.

[26] Samuel Grascombe, *An Appeal to All True English-men (If There Be Any Such Left)* (n.p. [London], n.d. [1696]), pp. 3–5.

[27] *Dear Bargain,* p. 374; John Toland, *An Appeal to Honest People Against Wicked Priests* (n.d. [1708]), p. 40.

[28] *Great Britain's Just Complaint for Her Late Measure, Present Sufferings, and the Future Miseries She Is Exposed to* (1695?), in *A Collection* (1748), vol. 1, p. 498.

One of the most systematic expositions of the economic case against 'Dutch William' and his henchmen was the tract *The People of England's Grievance*, by James Montgomery. This tract, resonant with anti-Dutch feeling, roundly blames the 'great decay' of England's trade on the Revolution and the Dutch. The author argues that under pretense of being her allies, the Dutch have ensnared England in a trap: 'For England and the United provinces are rivals for the trade of the world, and as such, have mighty crossing and interfering interests, and will be always jealous of one another.'[29] In support of this general contention, the author depicts the joint Anglo-Dutch trade embargo of France as nothing other than a device to divert English business to Holland, where, he alleges, the blockade was only ostensibly enforced. 'It is notoriously known', he remarks, by way of illustration, 'that we have had champaigne wine (the undeniable product of France) by way of Flanders and Holland, and at so great a rate, that it could not be sold in taverns here for less than 10 shillings a flask.' *The Dear Bargain* also cites the joint embargo of France as one of the devices by which the Dutch were 'mastering' the English.[30]

The huge outpouring of cash from England to the Continent in the early and mid-1690s, money used to support the English forces in Flanders and to subsidize the German allies of England and the Republic, led to a serious shortage of coin in England and an unprecedented epidemic of coin clipping in both England and Holland. That epidemic for a time became a major, controversial issue in English public life. Not surprisingly, Montgomery and other exponents of the economic case against the Dutch chose to see the fact that 'our best coin is exported to Holland and Flanders, and a great part of it there clipt and demolish'd' as yet one more example of Dutch malevolence and scheming to ruin England.[31] Remarkably, Montgomery also depicts the establishment of the Bank of England as an example of Dutch artifice and cunning, though the logic of his argument, that the creation of the bank would set off a massive drain of funds from England to the Republic, is hardly convincing. Dutch bankers, he insists, had advanced millions of guilders to the newly set up Bank, 'by which they will in a short time devour the whole treasure of the nation: for in Holland money is put out but at 3 per cent and for money put into the Exchequer here 8 per cent is allow'd: so that the Dutch will thereby be clear gainers 5 per cent and 6 per cent, for remitting our money into Holland'.[32]

He was correct, insofar as the gap in interest rates between Amsterdam and London at this juncture was extraordinarily wide. In the first part of 1688, until

---

[29] James Montgomery, *The People of England's Grievances Offered to Be Enquired into, and Redress'd by Their Representatives in Parliament* (1695), in *A Collection* (1748), vol. 1, p. 521, 523.

[30] *Dear Bargain*, pp. 251–52.

[31] Montgomery, *Grievances*, p. 520. See also the discussion of the English cash outflow in D.W. Jones, *War and Economy in the Age of William III and Marlborough* (Oxford, 1988).

[32] Montgomery, *Grievances*, p. 522.

the great crash on the Amsterdam Exchange that resulted from the business community's fears of war with France and England, Dutch interest rates, depressed by the heavy influx of Huguenot cash since 1685, had probably been at their lowest point for the whole of the seventeenth century – 2 per cent.[33] As a consequence of the panic, which had begun on August 25 and had precipitated massive falls in the value of Dutch East and West India Company shares, interest rates in Amsterdam had doubled to 4 per cent and lending had greatly slowed.[34] But with the success of William's expedition, Dutch interest rates (despite the outbreak of war with France) had then eased again, as Montgomery states, to 3 per cent. Never had the gap between Dutch and English rates been more conspicuous. But it should have been obvious that this huge gap would serve to suck massive Dutch funds into England rather than vice versa.

One tract – *Remarks upon the Present Confederacy and Late Revolution in England* – makes liberal use of the economic case against the Revolution but has a rather different emphasis than do the tracts discussed above. It heaps the blame on William personally (and to a lesser extent on his Continental allies) rather than on the Dutch and the States of Holland. This tract was written by a fervent sympathizer of the nonjurors and the pre-1688 Church of England. His primary purpose is to lambaste William as 'a true Machiavelist' who, finding Anglican attitudes and principles 'opposite in the highest degree to his Designs', set about undermining and debasing the Church of England by subverting it with the 'new Latitudinarian religion' in alliance with 'one John Tillotson [William's archbishop of Canterbury, who] has contributed more to the spreading and rooting of Atheism than 50 Spinozas, Hobbeses, or Vaninas's'.[35] The author is so enraged against William that he reserves all his anger for 'the usurper', almost ignoring the rest of the Dutch. Nevertheless, aware of the appeal of economic grievances, he makes full use of them, blaming William for policies that he says serve Dutch economic interests. He, too, refers to the flow of English coinage into Holland, where it is 'irrecoverably lost, to our vast impoverishment and the enriching of our sworn enemies'.[36] He cites the damage done by the joint Anglo-Dutch embargo of France. He stresses the disruption that the war has caused to English trade with the West and East Indies and the Levant. He puts particular emphasis on the mistakes in English naval strategy and especially the inefficiency and delays in convoying English merchant fleets and the failure to contain the depredations caused by the French privateers. William's maritime convoy policy he describes as a 'design to ruin our commerce and gratifie the

---

[33] 'News from The Hague', Aug. 4, 1688, BL, Add. MSS 41,821, fol. 220.

[34] On the financial crash of 1688, see J.I. Israel, 'The Amsterdam Exchange and the English Revolution of 1688', above, pp. 318–47.

[35] *Remarks upon the Present Confederacy, and Late Revolution in England* (1693), in *A Collection* (1748), vol. 3, p. 567. Tillotson was regarded by the nonjurors as the 'head' of the schism in the English Church; see G. Every, *The High Church Party, 1688–1718* (1956), p. 67.

[36] *Remarks*, p. 557.

Dutch'.[37] 'Are not we forced by this means', he asks, 'to trade with them for ready cash, or bullion, for those commodities which we used to fetch in our own bottoms from abroad?' His conclusion is that William (whom he styles 'the Prince of Orange') is guilty of a 'design to betray our trade to the Dutch, for it is impossible to avoid such a reflection'.[38] England's interests, he urges, have been lamentably neglected, 'trade in general decreasing, basely and designedly betrayed and rendered almost impracticable'.[39] But unlike Montgomery – who insists that 'English hatred of the French is turning apace in all sorts of men, into an hatred of the Dutch: our very soldiers by sea and land, as well as their commanders, wish for a war against the Dutch' – this author is less concerned that the Dutch are incorrigible enemies of the English than that 'it's impossible for us to retrieve our commerce so long as the Prince of Orange continues here; because we can never hope to be at peace; or masters of the seas so as to secure it'.[40]

The end of the Nine Years' War, in 1697, lifted the heavy pressure of war and, for the moment, some of the burden of William's and Parliament's relentless taxation. Yet there was little sign of any falling off in the intensity of anti-Dutch feeling in England during the last years of the reign of William III. On the contrary, English xenophobia in general and anti-Dutch sentiment in particular seem to have risen to a new peak in the aftermath of William's death, which rendered the expression of anti-Dutch feeling even more uninhibited than before.[41] Daniel Defoe, in his satirical poem *The True-Born Englishman*, a send-up of the xenophobic tendency of the time, derided this upsurge of hatred of foreigners and popular aversion to William as something both contemptible and ludicrous. And so, in many ways, it was. But the phenomenon was nevertheless an extremely important aspect of English reaction to the Revolution of 1688 and its outcome which Defoe, in mockery of the xenophobes, styled 'your new hodge-podge of a Dutch government'.[42] It reflected deep-seated economic anxieties, a way of viewing England's economic problems as basically symptoms of confrontation with the Dutch, symptoms that by the 1690s had been prevalent for a century. It reflected also a deep sense of the unnaturalness of being shackled to an alliance with a people with whom many, or most, Englishmen felt themselves to be fundamentally at odds, the Dutch being 'our enemies in trade'.

The bitter complaints about the Dutch who were 'planted amoung us; some in the King's Council, some in the army and the common traders [who] have possessed themselves of the outskirts of the city, often contriving to have

---

[37] Ibid., p. 569.

[38] Ibid.

[39] Ibid., p. 557.

[40] Ibid., p. 568.

[41] Albeit as part of a wider reaction against religious and intellectual toleration; see Daniel Defoe, *An Essay on the History of Parties, and Persecution in Britain* (1711), pp. 16–20.

[42] Daniel Defoe, *The Shortest Way with the Dissenters* (1702), p. 3.

themselves naturalized or made denizens',[43] may today seem rather absurd. But they reflect the real and widespread fear that took hold in England during and after the Revolution, the fear that in the Revolution the Dutch had found an effective means finally to settle, in their favour, the age-old conflict between themselves and the English for mastery of the world's trade. To many, the consequences appeared dreadful in the extreme. In his tract *Gloria Cambriae* (1702), Robert Price joined the chorus of those denouncing the alliance with the Dutch as unnatural on account of the rivalry of the two countries in trade; Price voiced the fear that the alliance would ultimately reduce England to 'extreme poverty', that 'we shall be supplanted by our neighbours and become a colony to the Dutch'.[44] Price was far from being alone in concluding that the events of 1688–89 had produced a revolution in England that far from being 'glorious', was humiliating, disruptive, and economically ruinous.

[43] Robert Price, *Gloria Cambriae: The Speech of a Bold Britain in Parliament, Against a Dutch Prince of Wales* (1702), in *A Collection* (1748), vol. 1, p. 102.

[44] Ibid.

16

Propaganda in the Making of the Glorious Revolution

One of the most sensational publications in 17th-century Dutch and English history, and indeed one of the greatest propaganda coups of early modern times, was William III's *Declaration* to the English people issued simultaneously in Britain and on the continent in November 1688.[1] The text is dated The Hague '10 October 1688' but its release was delayed by over a month so as to coincide with the landing of William III and his army of invasion at Torbay on 15 November (new style). In an age in which normally even the most noticed controversial tracts were rarely printed in more than two or three editions, or more than 2000 or 3000 copies,[2] William III's *Declaration* stands out as altogether exceptional given the very large quantity of copies printed, the large number of editions, and the variety of languages into which it was translated. In an era when propaganda tracts generally circulated only in a fairly restricted geographical area, William III's *Declaration* became well-known all over Europe and on both sides of the Atlantic. Finally, in an era in which it was unusual to report the impact of a piece of printed propaganda, in this case there is a range of contemporary evidence testifying to the crucial impact of this text on the course of the Glorious Revolution, one of the great events of world history.

Indeed, it is remarkable that William III's 'manifesto', as it was frequently referred to in England at the time, was recognised as a publication of exceptional importance even before its contents were known to more than a small circle of the Prince's confidants. As soon as he heard of its existence, the English ambassador at The Hague at the time, the Marquis d'Albeville, made energetic efforts to obtain a copy, but without success. 'It would be of the greatest importance imaginable to His Majestie', wrote James II's secretary of state, the Earl of Middleton to D'Albeville, from London, on 28 September, 'to see the *Declaration* they intend to sett out, as soon as it is possible, and this I am well assur'd, that you have us'd your best endeavours to gett it, yet the better to enable you,

---

[1] The historian who has hitherto most emphasised the importance of the *Declaration* of William III is L.G. Schwoerer: see Lois G. Schwoerer, 'Propaganda in the Revolution of 1688–89', *The American Historical Review 82* (1977), 852–5; Lois G. Schwoerer, 'The Bill of Rights: Epitome of the Revolution of 1688–89' in J. G. A. Pocock (ed.), *Three British Revolutions, 1641, 1688, 1776* (Princeton, 1980), pp.235–6; L.G. Schwoerer, *The Declaration of Rights, 1689* (Baltimore, 1981), pp.17–18, 115–16.

[2] Mark Goldie, 'The Revolution of 1689 and the Structure of Political Argument', *Bulletin of Research in the Humanities*, vol.83 (1980), 479–80.

you are to spare for no money, nor stick at any summe, that may procure it'.[3] Normally, not sticking 'at any summe' was more than enough to procure vital documents from the secret corridors of The Hague. But not on this occasion. 'You may imagine I have taken all possible care to come by the *Declaration* which I hear is on the press', D'Albeville replied, but 'the States printer is not to be corrupted; I have employ'd some to see if any of his servants can be; they are all sworn, and their places so lucrative they will not endanger them; I will leave no stone unmoved.'[4]

Three days later, on 15 October, D'Albeville further reported that the

> manifesto or *Declaration* can not be yett had at any rate for I have offer'd consider-
> ably for it, and you will, I believe, see it there sooner than we here. They give out
> they will insert in it a copy of a capitulation between both kings [i.e. James II and
> Louis XIV] notwithstanding all assurances given to the contrary, engaging to sup-
> press the Protestant religion and destroy these states for that end.[5]

On the same day, the English consul at Amsterdam, Daniel Petit, reported to Middleton that 'order is come hither from The Hague for the printing of 20,000 copies of the Prince's manifest', adding that 'a proportionable number is print-ing at Rotterdam and att The Hague, and are to be distributed at the same time that the Fleet putts to sea'.[6]

Security at the printers employed by the Prince and the States at Amsterdam and Rotterdam was evidently as tight as at The Hague, for on 21 October, D'Albeville wrote to Middleton that the 'manifest can not be had for any money that I offer'd', giving as a main reason that several of William's English ac-complices 'are so describ'd, tho not nam'd, that they may be easily discover'd'. He then added the following information: 'all the manifests printed were brought to the Prince himselfe, and seal'd up by him, except two that were given to the author, before they were brought to Benting's quarters'.[7] This reveals not only the scrupulous care which William took to guard the secrecy of his *Declaration* until what he judged was the right moment but also that Bentinck, the Stadtholder's closest associate in the work of planning the invasion of Britain, and who we know from other evidence masterminded the distribution of the *Declaration* in England, was from the outset put in charge of the entire stock of copies and made responsible for ensuring that there were no leaks.

Actually D'Albeville had finally obtained several copies 'with the arms of England upon it' by 20 October (new style) which, given the long delay in the sailing of the fleet, due to the contrary winds and stormy weather, should have given James much more time to react to William's propaganda coup than he

[3] BL MS Add.41823, f.76v. Middleton to D'Albeville, London 28 September 1688 (old style).
[4] BL MS Add.41816, f.232v. D'Albeville to Middleton, The Hague, 2/12 October 1688.
[5] Ibid, f.238v. D'Albeville to Middleton, The Hague, 5/15 October 1688.
[6] Ibid, f.237. Petit to Middleton, Amsterdam, 15 October 1688.
[7] Ibid, f.251. D'Albeville to Middleton, The Hague, 21 October 1688.

HIS HIGHNESSES

DECLARATION.

IT is both certain and evident to all men, that the publike Peace and Happines of any State or Kingdome can not be preſerved, where the Lawes, Liberties and Cuſtomes eſtablished, by the Lawfull authority in it, are openly Tranſgreſſed and Annulled: More eſpecially where the alteration of *Religion* is endeavoured, and that a *Religion* which is contrary to Law is endeavoured to be introduced: Upon which thoſe who are moſt Immediatly concerned in it, are Indiſpenſably bound to endeavour to Preſerve and maintain the eſtablished Lawes Liberties and Cuſtomes: and above all the *Religion* and worship of God, that is Eſtablished among them: And to take ſuch an effectuall care, that the Inhabitants of the ſaid State or Kingdome, may neither be deprived of their *Religion*, nor of their Civill Rights. Which is ſo much the more Neceſſary becauſe the Greatnes and Security both of Kings, Royall families, and of all ſuch as are in Authority, as well as the Happines of their Subjects and People, depend, in a moſt eſpeciall manner, upon the exact obſervation, and maintenance of theſe their Lawes Liberties, and Cuſtomes.

Upon theſe grounds it is, that we cannot any longer forbear, to Declare that to our great regret, wee ſee that thoſe Councellours, who have now the chieffe credit with the King, have overturned the *Religion*, Lawes, and Liberties of thoſe Realmes: and ſubjected them in all things relating to their Conſciences, Liberties, and Properties, to Arbitrary Government: and that not only by ſecret and Indirect waies, but in an open and undiſguiſed manner.

Thoſe Evill Councellours for the advancing and colouring this with ſome plauſible pretexts, did Invent and ſet on foot, the Kings *Diſpencing power*, by vertue of which, they pretend that according to *Law*, he can *Suſpend* and *Diſpence* with the Execution of the *Lawes*, that have been enacted by the Authority, of the King and Parliament, for the ſecurity and happines of the Subject and ſo have rendered thoſe Lawes of no effect: Tho there is nothing more certain, then that as no Lawes can be made, but by the joint concurrence of King and Parliament, ſo likewiſe lawes ſo enacted, which ſecure the Publike peace, and ſafety of the Nation, and the lives and liberties of every ſubject in it, can not be repealed or ſuſpended, but by the ſame authority.

For tho the King may pardon the puniſhment, that a Tranſgreſſour has incurred, and to which he is condemned, as in the caſes of *Treaſon* or *Felony*; yet it can not be with any colour of reaſon, Inferred from thence, that the King can entirely ſuſpend the execution of thoſe Lawes, relating to *Treaſon* or *Felony*: Unleſſe it is pretended, that he is clothed with a Deſpotick and Arbitrary power, and that the Lives Liberties Honours and Eſtates of the Subjects, depend wholly on his good will and Pleaſure, and are entirely ſubject to him; which muſt infallibly follow, on the Kings having a power to *ſuſpend* the execution of *Lawes*, and to *diſpence* with them.

Thoſe Evill Councellours, in order to the giving ſome credit to this ſtrange and execrable Maxime, have ſo conducted the matter, that they have obtained a Sentence from the Judges, declaring that this *Diſpencing power*, is a right belonging to the *Crown*; as if it were in the power of the twelve Judges, to offer up the Lawes, Rights, and Likerties, of the whole Nation, to the King, to be diſpoſed of by him Arbitrarily and at his Pleaſure, and expreſſly contrary to Lawes enacted, for the ſecurity of the Subjects. In order to the obtaining this Judgment, theſe Evill Councellours did before hand, examine ſecretly, the Opinion of the Judges, and procured ſuch of them, as could not in Conſcience concurre in ſo pernicious a Sentence, to be turned out, and others to be ſubſtituted in their Rooms, till by the changes which were made, in the Courts of Judicature, they at laſt obtained that Judgment. And they have raiſed ſome to thoſe Truſts, who make open Profeſſion of the Popiſh Religion, tho thoſe are by Law Rendred Incapable of all ſuch Employments.

It is alſo Manifeſt and Notorious, that as his Majeſtie was, upon his coming to the Crown, received and acknowledged by all the ſubjects of *England*, *Scotland*, and *Ireland*, as their *King* without the leaſt oppoſition, tho he made then open profeſſion, of the *Popiſh Religion*, ſo he did then Promiſe, and Solemnly Swear, at his Coronation, that he would maintain his ſubjects, in the free enjoyment of their Lawes, Rights, and Liberties, and in particular, that he would maintain the *Church of England as it was eſtabliſhed by Law*: It is likewiſe certain, that there have been at diverſe and ſundry times, ſeverall Lawes enacted for the preſervation of thoſe Rights, and Liberties, and of the Proteſtant Religion: and among other Securities, it has been enacted that all Perſons whatſoever, that are advanced to any Eccleſiaſticall Dignity, or to bear Office in either Univerſity, as likewiſe all others, that ſhould be put in any Imployment, Civill or Military, ſhould declare that they were not Papiſts, but were of the Proteſtant Religion, and that, by their taking of the Oaths of *Allegeance*, and *Supreamacy* and the *Teſt*, yet theſe Evill Councellours have in effect annulled and aboliſhed all thoſe Lawes, both with relation to Eccleſiaſticall and Civill Employments.

A 2   In

was actually to have.[8] D'Albeville sent a copy 'by an express' and then another copy to Lord Middleton in London but his messengers were 'detained as well as the couriers of Spayne and France at Maerdyk, nobody being suffer'd to pass that way or by any other till the Prince set sayle'.[9] On 28 October (new style), two and a half weeks before the landings at Torbay, and several days after sending off the couriers with the copies of the manifesto, D'Albeville wrote: 'I doubt not but this memorial has allready come into your Lordship's hands, some thousands having been sent into England to be dispers'd at the prince his landing; they are not to be had here as yett'.[10] But in fact the security measures taken in the Republic, and Bentinck's careful undercover methods in Britain, worked so well that, despite the long delay in the sailing of the fleet, the Prince's *Declaration*, though now present on a massive scale in both Britain and the Netherlands, remained concealed from the eyes of the government in London almost to the last moment. Bentinck had instructed his agents to begin distribution only after hearing of the landing, but, in fact, the first copies seem to have started circulating in London after the fleet made its first attempt to set out, at the end of October.

According to the contemporary Hugenot historian Abel Boyer, 'just as the Prince was about to leave, Captain Langham who belonged to one of the English regiments in Holland was seized [in London] upon suspicion, and in his portmantle were found a parcel of the Prince of Orange's *Declaration* which were the first that were brought over'.[11] However, according to what James II himself told the Archbishop of Canterbury and other bishops whom he summoned to the palace on 2 November (old style) 'he had seized a person who had brought into the city a great number of the Prince of Orange's declarations, and had begun to disperse them; for His Majesty had received five or six copies from several persons, to whom they have been sent in penny-post letters, which he had thrown into the fire; but that he had still one copy'.[12] James's purpose in discussing the Prince's *Declaration* with the bishops, on 2 November, was to challenge them, as he had the Bishop of London, Henry Compton, the day before, on the passage in the text where the Prince claimed that he had been 'invited' to appear in arms in England by numerous 'lords temporal and spiritual'. James assured the bishops that he did not believe a word of what was in the *Declaration* concerning them – Compton brazenly lied to the King in denying any involvement – but asked them to issue a public statement denying that they had 'invited' William to invade. The bishops agreed to discuss the matter among themselves; but, subsequently, on various pretexts, refused to issue any statement. In the interview of 2 November the King did not actually

[8] BL MS Add.41816, f.249. D'Albeville to Middleton, The Hague, 20 October 1688.

[9] Ibid, f.263. D'Albeville to Middleton, The Hague, 28 October 1688.

[10] Ibid

[11] Abel Boyer, *The History of King William the Third* 3 vols (London, 1702), 1, 229.

[12] *The Correspondence of Henry Hyde, Earl of Clarendon . . . with the Diary*, edited by S.W. Singer, 2 vols, (London, 1828), II, 494.

The entry of
William III and
the Dutch army
into Salisbury,
December 1688.

permit the bishops to see the copy which he held up as he spoke and had already refused the previous day to put it into Compton's hands. James had a secretary read the relevant passage concerning the bishops 'pointing to the place where he would have him begin and end'.[13] The bishops were thus sent off without having actually perused a copy and without having a copy to discuss amongst themselves. On 3 November, Lord Clarendon 'being at the King's levee, His Majesty took me into his closet, and showed me the Prince's *Declaration*, as he had done yesterday to the bishops', but again James avoided parting with the copy he showed Clarendon. Later that day – two days before William III landed at Torbay – Clarendon waited on Princess Anne: 'she lent me the Prince of Orange's Declaration', saying 'the King had lent it her, and she must restore it to him tomorrow'.[14] No doubt James expected that she would be as shocked as he was by the contents of the *Declaration* and not least the doubt it cast on the legitimacy of her five-month old brother, the heir to the throne, James, Prince of Wales.

James's initial response, then, was to endeavour to suppress the text at court and 'keep the Prince's *Declaration* from the knowledge of the people'.[15] He issued a royal proclamation from Whitehall, on 2 November, denouncing the treasonable declaration designed to 'seduce our people and (if it were possible) to corrupt our army, a very great number whereof being printed, several persons are sent and employed to disperse the same throughout our kingdoms'. The proclamation warned

> all our subjects, of what degree or quality soever, that they do not publish, disperse, repeat or hand about the said treasonable papers of declarations, or any of them, or any other paper or papers of such like nature, nor presume to read, receive, conceal or keep the said treasonable papers or declarations . . . without discovering and revealing the same as speedily as may be . . . to the justices of the peace or other magistrates, upon peril of being prosecuted according to the utmost severity of the law.'[16]

With the landing of the Prince's invading army, at Torbay, on 5 November, however, Bentinck's distribution machine suddenly sprang into action and his agents began distributing copies everywhere. In London, evidently, one of the main suppliers of the *Declaration* was the Spanish embassy.[17] Simultaneously, the *Declaration*, which the States General's printers had prepared in Dutch, French and German, as well as English, editions, was released in the Republic, D'Albeville

---

[13] *Correspondence of Henry Hyde II*, 494.

[14] Ibid, II, 199–200.

[15] Boyer, *History of King William the Third* 1, 231; [Edmund Bohun], *History of the Desertion*, (London, 1689), 34; Schwoerer, 'Propaganda in the Revolution of 1688–89', 870.

[16] BL G5302. Proclamation of James II, Whitehall, 2 November 1688.

[17] [Bohun], *History of the Desertion*, 35–6.

writing to Sunderland on 6 November from The Hague that the 'manifesto is now sold publickly, and in all languages'.[18]

So great was the impact of the *Declaration* in the days immediately following the landing that James's ministers were quickly brought to the realisation that the King's initial policy of suppression was not just ineffectual but positively dangerous. The manifesto had to be resolutely and effectively confronted. Not only was London inundated with copies but the *Declaration* was now circulating in abundance all over England. Also both the main *Declaration*, and the separate Declaration of the Prince for Scotland, were circulating north of the border.

James thus switched to a very different tack. Using the *London Gazette*, then the only licensed, regular newspaper in England, the King now deliberately drew attention to the 'late [*Declaration*] published by him', announcing to the public that its seemingly high-sounding principles and phrases were, in reality, just 'specious and plausible pretences', the Prince of Orange's real aim being

> an absolute usurping of our crown and royal authority, as may fully appear by his assuming to himselfe in the said *Declaration* the regal style, requiring the peers of the realm, both spiritual and temporal and all other persons of all degrees, to obey and assist him in the execution of his designs, a prerogative inseparable from the imperial crown of this realm.[19]

During the next month, as the struggle unfolded and William's army advanced slowly towards London, the government tried to press home its counter-attack by having the *Declaration* reprinted in London – and also Edinburgh – along with, as Boyer expressed it, 'a preface and some frivolous animadversions upon it'.[20]

These government-inspired versions of the *Declaration*, complete with hostile commentary, concentrated on denouncing the tone of the *Declaration*, with its obvious resonances of regal authority, the lack of any attempt in it to demonstrate a conspiracy between James II and Louis XIV against the United Provinces, and the slur contained in the *Declaration* regarding the legitimacy of James II's five-month old son, the heir to the throne, James, Prince of Wales.

The style of the *Declaration*, attacked by James already in the *London Gazette*, was made much of. 'To use in England the style of We and Us, commanding, having of Parliaments and settling the nations, and last of all that he will then send back his Army which sheweth he intends to stay behind himself, can declare nothing else to us but that his design is to be King.'[21] As for the alleged Anglo-French conspiracy, D'Albeville had already pointed out that William, in his propaganda in the Netherlands, had made much of the alleged plot of the two

[18] J. Macpherson, *Original Papers; containing the Secret History of Great Britain*, 2 vols (London, 1776) 1, 286.

[19] *The London Gazette*, no.2397 (5–8 November 1688), p.1.

[20] Boyer, *History*, 1, 231.

[21] *Some reflections upon the Prince of Orange's Declaration* in *A Collection of Scarce and Valuable Tracts . . . from the Collection of Lord Somers*, 4 vols (London, 1748), 1, 292.

kings, James and Louis, against the Protestant religion and, as part of this, against the United Provinces, in order to sway Dutch opinion in favour of intervention in Britain at a time when James was experiencing difficulties with his domestic opposition. The absence of any reference to this alleged conspiracy in the *Declaration* was pounced upon by James's propagandists as clear evidence of William's cynical manipulation of public opinion in both the Republic and Britain: 'the first thing I looked for', wrote one of James's commentators on the *Declaration*,' was the exposing of our clandestine League with France, so much talk'd of, to excuse the Dutch preparations and invasion; but I find after all, not one word said of France, or any such secret league, the main thing pretended and expected'.[22] Another of James's commentators told how the rumours of a 'secret league between His Majesty of Great Britain and the French king to extirpate all Protestants' had been 'with so much art and cunning spread, as to startle the most considering Protestants of all persuasions, whence nothing could be more eagerly desired, than a sight of the Prince of Orange's *Declaration*'; however, 'there not being one word of any such treaty, we cannot see why it is that the Prince comes over'.[23] In addition to his 'usurping a regal style, and commanding obedience from the King's subjects', misleading the public about James's relations with the French king, and outrageously insulting the birth of the Prince of Wales whom William, allegedly, well knew to be the legitimate heir to the throne, there was some sarcastic comment about the methods William customarily used to get his way with the Dutch provincial assemblies and States General, one of the Jacobite commentators on the *Declaration* calling him a 'Prince who having well nigh enslaved his own States, is come to fight us into Liberty'.[24]

The points made by James II's publicists were both pertinent and hard-hitting. Yet the enormous impact which the *Declaration* made in Britain was wholly advantageous to William. The government's 'animadversions on it' appear to have had little effect. Later Jacobite and French propaganda unswervingly pointed to the Prince's *Declaration* as having played a key role in 'debauching' the English public, making them forget their true allegiance and turn against their legitimate monarch.[25] But discerning pro-Revolution writers, especially those who had no reason to stress the contribution of William's Whig allies to the actual invasion, were just as emphatic in seeing the *Declaration* as crucial. 'Though there was not all that men had fondly expected in this *Declaration*', recalled Edmund Bohun, a moderate Tory pro-Revolution writer,

[22] Ibid

[23] *The Prince of Orange His Declaration : shewing the Reasons why he Invades England, With a short Preface and some modest remarks on it* (Edinburgh, 1688), p.2.

[24] *Seasonable and Honest Advice to the Nobility, Clergy, Gentry, Souldiery, and other the King's Subjects, upon the Invasion of His Highness the Prince of Orange* (London, 1688), p.2.

[25] See, for instance, Antoine Arnauld, *Le véritable portrait de Guillaume-Henri de Nassau. Nouvel Absalom, Nouvel Herode, Nouveau Cromwell, Nouveau Néron* (gives Brussels [but Paris?], 1689,), pp. 34–5, 40, 50, and the *Esprit politique ou l'histoire en abregé de la vie et des actions de Guillaume III de Nassau, Roi de la Grande Bretagne* (gives Amsterdam [but Paris?]), 1695), p.137.

yet there was enough to satisfie any rational man that the expelling this Prince and his Army before our Religion, Liberties, Properties and Government were effectually settled in Parliament, and those who had so outrageously attempted the ruine of them were call'd to account, would certainly end in the ruine of them, and was a kind of cutting up our Laws and Religion with our swords. This and nothing else was the cause that wherever the Prince's *Declaration* was read, it conquered all that saw or heard it, and it was to no purpose to excite men to fight against their own Interest, and to destroy what was more dear to them than their lives.[26]

During the early weeks of the Glorious Revolution, both William himself in southern England, and his Whig and Tory accomplices in other regions of the country, used the *Declaration* as the main justification for the Prince's 'appearing in arms' in England, as the invasion was euphemistically termed, and for Englishmen supporting the invasion.[27] On entering Exeter, the first important town occupied by the Dutch army, William summoned those of the Anglican clergy who remained – the bishop and dean had fled – to the cathedral where Gilbert Burnet 'read aloud the Prince's *Declaration* and reasons for this his expedition'.[28] In the first fortnight, hardly anyone among the English dared come out in support of William. When the nobility did begin to desert James, they used the *Declaration* to justify their doing so. In early December, on seizing Durham, Lord Lumley read out the *Declaration* to the gentry of the county at Durham Castle.[29] In the north-west, the Williamite rebels, having disarmed James's troops at Chester, 'read the Prince's *Declaration* and declared for him'.[30] Lord Delamere, who seized Manchester the next day, also had the manifest publicly read there.[31] At Oxford the Glorious Revolution culminated in the blowing of a trumpet at Carfax and the Prince's *Declaration* 'being read openly to the multitude by Lord Lovelace'.[32] Much the same scene was re-enacted all over England, from Leeds to Portsmouth and from Bristol to King's Lynn.

In her discussion of the significance of William III's *Declaration*, Lois Schwoerer has assumed that it was essentially a Whig document and that, by making use of it, William provided the basis for the limiting of his own power, in the shape of the Declaration of Rights, when he replaced James as king: 'in a certain sense

---

[26] [Bohun], *History of the Desertion*, 72.

[27] *Engeland Beroerd onder de Regering van Iacobus de II en hersteldt door Willem en Maria, Prins en Princesse van Orangie* (Amsterdam, 1689), pp.246–55; Abraham van Poot, *Engelands Gods-dienst en vryheid hersteld door sijn Hoogheid den Heere Prince van Oranjen* 2 vols (Amsterdam, 1689), II 167, 205, 213, 231; see also J. I. Israel, 'Introduction' to *The Anglo-Dutch Moment: Essays on the Glorious Revolution and its World Impact*, edited by J. I. Israel (Cambridge, 1991), pp.15–16.

[28] Schwoerer, *Declaration of Rights*, 116.

[29] W.A. Speck, 'The Revolution of 1688 in the North of England', *Northern History*, XXV (1989), p.194.

[30] *The London Courant*, no.4 (18/22 December 1688) p.1.

[31] G. G. Arconati Lamberti, *Mémoires de la dernière révolution d'Angleterre*, 2 vols (The Hague, 1702), I, 596.

[32] *The Life and Times of Anthony Wood, Antiquary of Oxford, 1632–1695*, edited by A.Clark, 5 vols (Oxford, 1891–1900), III, 286–7.

William really was hoisted on the petard of his own propaganda'.[33] The fact that the *Declaration*, which was designed to 'persuade the public of his selfless purposes' was published in his name was, she has argued, 'a central consideration in persuading the Prince to agree to a statement which he otherwise might well have refused'.[34] But the view that the *Declaration* was basically a Whig initiative which had the effect of boxing the Prince in is, arguably, greatly to exaggerate the role of Parliament and parliamentarians in the making of the Revolution. It is also to misrepresent what was in fact the basic purpose of the *Declaration.*

An exact assessment of the political significance of the *Declaration* has to begin with the undoubted fact that it was not a Whig, or in any sense an English parliamentary, document. It was actually written, under William's close supervision, by his righthand-man in the States of Holland, the Pensionary Gaspar Fagel, and then translated into English by Gilbert Burnet. [35] Its basic purpose was two-fold: firstly, it was intended to justify William's armed intervention in Britain as self-proclaimed guardian of the English and Scots constitutions; secondly, it was designed as a legitimation of the Prince's seizure and exercise of *de facto* power in the interim period that would necessarily intervene before the Prince, as he promised to do in his *Declaration*, could convene a Convention Parliament. Although the drafting of the *Declaration* by Fagel was preceded by the submission of various proposed drafts for the Declaration by William's Whig accomplices, the actual text concocted by William and Fagel was concealed from the Whig leadership in Holland, as it was from everyone else, because William's aims were not the same as theirs. When the Whig leadership with the invasion armada, at Hellevoetsluis, did eventually see the text, many of them were angered by its moderate tone and obvious intention of appealing to Tory, as well as Whig, sentiment.[36]

During the first crucial three months of the Glorious Revolution, down to the beginning of February 1689, William was not yet concerned with how he might evade, or water down, the parliamentary Declaration of Rights which, in the appendix to his *Declaration*, he had promised. During the decisive phase of the Revolution, that is in the period preceding Parliament's intervention, the Prince's main concerns were still to undermine James by winning extensive English support for the invasion; secondly, to justify his own seizure of power in England as regent with the acquiescence of the peerage – or a selection of it – and the city of London, and lastly, to persuade Parliament to make him king. Hence, even when William and his army were approaching London, and James was clearly beaten, William and Bentinck, far from distancing themselves from

---

[33] Schwoerer, 'Propaganda in the Revolution of 1688–9', 872.

[34] Schwoerer, 'The Bill of Rights', 235.

[35] G.Burnet, *History of His Own Time*, 6 vols (Oxford,1833), III, 300; N. Japikse, *Prins Willem III, de stadhouder-koning*, 2 vols (Amsterdam, 1933), II, 251.

[36] Burnet, *History*, III, 308–10.

the *Declaration*, went out of their way to remind everyone of it at every opportunity.[37] When, on his approach, the officers of the London militia sent an address to his camp, assuring him that they would not only support him but that 'it was their firm resolution to venture all that was dear to them to attain the glorious ends of His *Declaration*',[38] they were not trying to box him in but conveying their submission to his constantly reiterated assurances.

Once he had London effectively in his grasp, the Prince continued to deploy his *Declaration* systematically as his chief means of explaining and legitimating every step in his political programme. At the meeting of former members of Parliament which the Prince convened in London a week after his arrival, he asked them to 'advise the best manner how to pursue the ends of my *Declaration*'.[39] In the letters which William, as regent, sent out to the constituencies directing that members of Parliament be elected to attend the Convention which he was summoning, he explained that 'we' were doing so, 'heartily desiring the performance of what we have in our *Declaration* expressed'.[40] On opening the Convention Parliament, on 22 January, the Prince urged members to act with all haste so that the 'ends of my *Declaration* will be attained'.[41]

As Parliament deliberated what to do about the throne and the succession, William was not yet concerned to preserve his future monarchical power as far as possible from constitutional limits because it was very much an open matter whether Parliament would make him king at all. We know that initially there was a great deal of reluctance in both houses to contemplate William as sole, or joint, monarch and that in the Lords there was large majority against elevating him to the throne.[42] We also know that through his Dutch favourites, Bentinck and Dijkveld, the Prince brought every kind of pressure to bear, threats as well as carrots, to sway members to vote as he wanted. But the most important instrument of pressure was the *Declaration* which was continually kept ringing in members' ears. In other words, in so far as the *Declaration* set limits on royal authority, the manifesto was an asset rather than a handicap to William at the most vital moment of the Revolution and of his political career.[43] The Prince's supporters bombarded wavering MPs with the proposition that 'his unchangeable adherence to what he promised in his *Declaration* shews with what sacredness he will observe his oath as king'.[44]

---

[37] *Correspondence of Henry Hyde II*, 215.

[38] *A Collection of State Tracts Publish'd on Occasion of the Late Revolution in 1688*, 3 vols (London, 1705), III, 71.

[39] Israel, 'Introduction' p.16

[40] *The Journals of the House of Commons*, x (1688–93) pp.5, 8.

[41] 41. Israel, 'Introduction' p.16.

[42] 42. E. Cruickshanks, D. Hayton, and C. Jones, 'Divisions in the House of Lords on the Transfer of the Crown and other Issues, 1689–94: Ten New Lists', *Bulletin of the Institute of Historical Research* LIII (1980), 61–5.

[43] 43. Arnauld, *Le véritable portrait de Guillaume-Henri*, 71.

[44] 44. [R. Ferguson], *A Brief Justification of the Prince of Orange's Descent into England and of the Kingdoms Late Recourse to Arms* (London, 1689), p.36.

The paradox of the Convention debate on the future of the throne, however, is that William's *Declaration* also emerged, at this point, as the chief weapon of the Tory loyalist opposition to the dethroning of James.[45] So successful had William's propaganda coup been that his *Declaration* was now conceded by everyone, on all sides of the political equation, as the only basis on which possible courses of action could be taken. For the Whigs it opened up the prospect of setting limits on the crown. For loyalists it was an instrument by which they could hope to exploit the ceaseless assurances of William and Bentinck that the Prince sought only the aims set out in the *Declaration* and was not after the throne for himself. Clarendon saw at once that the Prince's *Declaration* offered the Tories the best hope of saving James, by following a policy of urging Parliament to concede only what was in the *Declaration*.[46] This then became the strategy of the loyalist grouping as a whole, the bishop of Ely recalling afterwards that 'we saw no other hopeful way to save [the King] and serve him but by treating with the Prince on the foot of his *Declaration*'.[47]

Consequently, when the Convention met everyone was willing to adopt the *Declaration* as a basis of action. Tory MPs such as Sir Robert Seymour, representing the University of Cambridge, and Sir Thomas Clarges, MP for Oxford University, being at the forefront of the clamour. It was Clarges who pronounced: 'I think wee sit here to pursue the ends of the Prince of Orange's *Declaration* and therefore I move that the *Declaration* may be read'.[48] The entire text of the *Declaration* was later reprinted in the opening pages of the Commons journal recording the Convention debate complete with William's promise that 'it is plain that there can be no redres nor remedy offered but in Parliament by a Declaration of the Rights of the Subjects that have been invaded'.[49] Parliament on drawing up the Declaration of Rights duly concluded with the words 'to which demand of [the King's subjects] rights, they are particularly invited by the *Declaration* of His Highness the Prince of Orange'.[50]

Modern historians, Whig and Non-Whig in tendency, have alike been intent on focusing attention on the role of the Convention in the making of the Glorious Revolution and have virtually all tended to de-emphasise the role of William III and the Dutch intervention. Along with the Prince and the Dutch state, historians have down-played the Prince's *Declaration*. Whole books of documents on British constitutional history in the late 17th century have been

[45] 45. Lois G. Schwoerer, ' A Jornall of the convention at Westminster begun the 22 of January 1688/9', *Bulletin of the Institute of Historical Research* XLIX (1976), 253, 256.

[46] 46. *Correspondence of Henry Hyde II*, 244,246; Nicholas Witsen, 'Uitreksels' in J. Scheltema, *Geschied- en Letterkundig Mengelwerk*, 6 vols. (Amsterdam, Utrecht, 1817–36), III, 150–1.

[47] 47. Robert Beddard, 'The Loyalist Opposition in the Interregnum: a Letter of Dr Francis Turner, Bishop of Ely, in the Revolution of 1688', *Bulletin of the Institute of Historical Research*, XL (1967), p.106.

[48] 48. Schwoerer, 'A Jornall of the Convention', 256.

[49] 49. *The Journals of the House of Commons*, X (1688–93), p.5.

[50] 50. Ibid, p.23.

published without including so much as an extract from the Prince's *Declaration*. Yet, it is arguable that this manifesto was by far the most important single document of the Glorious Revolution not excepting even the Declaration of Rights which, to a considerable extent, repeated its stipulations and assertions. Certainly, contemporaries regarded it as *the* document of the Revolution, a text of overriding significance. Furthermore, its contents were much more widely and vigorously debated than those on the Declaration of Rights and this continued to be the case through the 1690s. William III's *Declaration* to the English people, of 10 October 1688, is without doubt an exceptional, even perhaps extreme, instance of the power of the press. With its vast impact, it proved one of the most decisive publications of modern history.

The house of the Baron Belmonte at Amsterdam *c.*1700. Engraving by Romeyn de Hooghe

17

Gregorio Leti (1631–1701) and the Dutch Sephardi Élite at the Close of the Seventeenth Century

It is remarkable that Gregorio Leti's pages on the Amsterdam Sephardi élite of the 1680s and 1690s are never mentioned, much less analysed, by scholars of Dutch Jewish history. Leti's extensive discussion of this select group undoubtedly constitutes a major source of information on the subject, providing detail and opening up perspectives which, in some cases, are wholly new. The reason for the undeserved neglect of Leti as an observer of the Dutch Jewish scene, one can only presume, is that the relevant sections of text have simply escaped attention, buried as they are in unlikely places in his prolific output, none of his many volumes bearing titles which suggest that they are likely to yield material of Jewish interest.

Leti, the illegitimate son of a Milanese nobleman, was a literary adventurer who led a colourful and most unconventional life. After leaving his native Italy filled with fury against petty despots and the Catholic clergy, he settled and married at Geneva and became a Calvinist. However, in 1679, after a public investigation of his writings, and in particular his historical commentary on the role of the 'true Reformed faith' and alleged adoption of the maxims of Machiavelli, he was expelled from Geneva as an undesirable influence on public morality.[1] After this, the pivotal experience of his life, he migrated to Paris and then London. But despite his growing reputation as a writer of fashionable works on the political history of Italy, Spain, France and other countries, he failed to find much favour in either capital, largely on account of his anti-Catholicism. In 1683, on leaving England, he decided to try his fortune in Amsterdam and, finding it much to his taste, there he stayed for the remaining eighteen years of his life. He was an early example of a professional writer who lived by his pen and it is this which explains the profuseness as well as the often hack nature of his writings. Although on arriving in Holland he knew no Dutch, such were his international reputation and his connections that he rapidly moved to the forefront of the Dutch literary *monde* of the day.[2] The Amsterdam city council appointed him city historiographer, in October 1685, at a yearly salary of four hundred guilders. His duties included the giving of regular seminars on historical topics in

---

[1] L. Fassò, *Avventurier della penna del seicento. Gregorio Leti, Gerolamo Arconati Lamberti, Tomaso Tomasi, Bernado Guasconi* (Florence, 1923), pp.71, 88,100.

[2] Ibid., pp. 219–20.

French to the sons of Amsterdam's regent oligarchy. His appointment was confirmed in 1689 and his salary increased to first five then six hundred guilders. Among the more obviously political literary ventures of these years was the monumental heroic poem that he wrote and published on the subject of William III's passage into England and successful bid for the English throne.

The works which Leti wrote during his Dutch period, though often facile, repetitious and filled with tiresome flattery, do also have a serious side which, still today, deserves a measure of attention. He was always a forthright, eloquent champion of religious and intellectual freedom and a frequently scathing critic of Lutheran and (Swiss) Calvinist as well as Catholic bigotry.[3] Moreover, he went further than probably any other seventeenth-century writer in elevating the Dutch Republic to the status of a political ideal, comparing the United Provinces favourably not only with Europe's monarchies and petty principalities but also with the (in his view) despotic republics of Venice, Genoa and Geneva.[4] What he cherished most about the Dutch Republic was the unique combination to be found there of a high, indeed unparalleled, level of political, religious and intellectual freedom – and not least the great freedom enjoyed by foreigners such as himself[5] – with order, security and good government.[6] What Leti says about the Jews has to be placed in this wider context and linked perhaps especially with his defence of the unprecedented freedom enjoyed by Dutch women.[7] It is difficult for us today, in our more liberal age, to grasp fully that the prevailing image of the Dutch Republic among Europe's educated classes in the late seventeenth century was not always a flattering one and that there was frequently an undercurrent of contempt fed especially by feelings of distaste for the exceptional position of women and Jews in that country.[8] It took a somewhat unconventional intellect, such as that of this flamboyant Milanese token Calvinist, expressly to champion freedom of women and Jews in print.

The substance of Leti's defence of freedom of women in Holland was his contention that its effects were largely beneficial and did not lead to unrestrained licentiousness in society. Again and again Leti returns to the theme that Dutch

---

[3] A. Cameroni, *Uno scrittore avventuriero del secolo XVII. Gregorio Leti. Appunti critici* (Milan, 1893), pp.162–4.

[4] See G. Leti, *Raguagli historici e politici o vero compendio delle virtù heroiche sopra la fedeltà de'suditi, e amore verso la patria*, 2 vols (Amsterdam, 1700), vol. 1, raguaglio iii, pp.262–5 *et seq.*

[5] 'Ma a proposito di forastieri', averred Leti, 'diro che questi hanno grandissima libertà, poiche entrano e escono a loro piacere, senza esser tropo ricercati ne esaminati come se fa in Italia, o in Francia, o . . . in Germania': G. Leti, *Teatro Belgico, o vero ritratti historici, chronologici, politici, e geografici, della sette Provincie Unite*, 2 vols (Amsterdam, 1690), vol. 2, . 406.

[6] See, e.g., Leti (note 4 above), vol. 1 raguaglio iii, pp.408–10.

[7] See, e.g., G. Leti, *Il ceremoniale historico e politico, opera utilissima a tutti gli Ambasciatori, e Ministri publici*, 6 vols (Amsterdam, 1685), vol. 5, p.734.

[8] *ibid.* This is perhaps especially so of German opinion: see Julia Bientjes, *Holland und die Holländer im Urteil deutscher Reisender, 1400–1800* (Groningen, 1967), pp.91–4, 223–4; the writer Heinrich Benthem contemptuously noted of Holland, in 1698, 'Denn hier krehet die Henne und der Hahn muss nur keckeln', *ibid.*, p.223.

women enjoyed an altogether exceptional degree of freedom, and in every respect, but that despite this they were not in any way more forward sexually than French or Italian women. In fact, quite the contrary. In a number of passages Leti lavishly praises the modesty of Dutch women, remarking for instance on the fact that in contrast to France, Dutch women of all classes scrupulously kept neck, shoulders and bosom covered up, however taken they might be with French fashions in other respects.[9] Leti is also at pains to defend Amsterdam against the widely-held notion that harlotry and prostitution were allowed to flourish there to excess. [10]Leti compares what he considers the relatively small number of thirty *bordelli* found in Amsterdam with the much larger concentrations of houses of ill-repute encountered in Rome and Venice. 'For every one of these bordelli to be seen in Amsterdam,' he insists, 'there are for sure ten in so-called "holy" Rome and more than twenty in Venice.' He went so far as to assert that the Venetian regime deliberately encouraged sexual licentiousness as an instrument of state, to deflect the attention of the populace from political matters. Nor did he consider the number of brothels the only relevant factor. In Italy, asserts Leti, one is far more likely to meet seductive, brazen and promiscuous behaviour in public places than in Holland.

Leti's principal reason for broaching the subject of Dutch Jewry is that he (once again) wishes to show that one of Europe's chief prejudices against the Dutch Republic – that it allows Jews too much freedom – is unwarranted. But Leti was certainly no defender of Judaism as such. Like so many figures of the early Enlightenment, he boldly asserts the right of Jews to a place in society, and their potential worth to the state and general culture, while totally dismissing the rites and culture of the Jews themselves. We meet this attitude in his book on England, where he describes the Bevis Marks Synagogue in London. Services in Bevis Marks, claims Leti, are unsightly, unpleasant to the ear, and characterized by '*gesti ridicolosissimi*'.[11] And later, in his *Teatro Belgico,* he is scarcely any more flattering about the proceedings in the great Portuguese Synagogue at Amsterdam:

> concorrono giornalmente, e sopra tutto il sabbato, la matina, e il dopo pranso nell'hora degli esecizii Giudaici, numero grande di Christiani, che vengono per vedere, e la sinagoga, e le ceremonie de' Giudei, che per dire il vere son di poca edificatione, gridano, cantano salmi con voci senza tuono, e senza concerto, con i soliti veli sul cappello, ma no veggo gran differenza della maniera con la quale negotiano nella

[9] Leti (note 5 above), vol. 2, pp.28–9

[10] Leti (note 4 above), vol. 1, raguaglio iii, p.269; in another passage, written a few years after the notorious booklet *Le Putanisme d'Amsterdam* (1681) lent further currency to Amsterdam's reputation as a den of sexual promiscuity, Leti noted that the combination of unparalleled religious toleration and alleged licentiousness generated '*un certo horrore*'abroad, Leti (note 7 above), vol. 5, p.734: Bientjes (note 8 above), pp.175–6.

[11] G. Leti, *Del teatro Brittanico o vero historia dello stato, antico e presente, ... della Grande Brettagna,* 2 vols (London, 1683), vol. I, pp.251–2, 549–50.

Borsa, e quella con la quale si tengono nella sinagoga; ma piacesse a Iddio che i Christiani potessero in cio rimproverarli, senza esser rimproverati.[12]

Nor, in contrast to so many seventeenth-century writers, does Leti place much emphasis on the economic activities of the Jews. He does believe that tolerating at least some categories of Jews brings economic benefits and has no doubt that where Spain, for instance, ruined herself by expelling her 'Jews, Marranos and Moors' such states as Venice, Tuscany and Hamburg, as well as the Dutch Republic, had enriched themselves by encouraging Jewish immigration.[13] But he also recognizes the prevalence of poverty among the German Jews and tends to dismiss them as being of little value to society. One point he does stress is that allowing the Jews more freedom, and better terms of residence, does not, as many people fear, lead to a huge, uncontrollable influx of impoverished Ashkenazi Jews.[14] To illustrate this point he provides some most interesting statistics which, though accurate enough as far as the Sephardi community is concerned, wildly underestimate the size of the German-Jewish community in the Dutch state. He tells us that in Amsterdam there are 450 Portuguese Jewish families without counting a number of destitute families.[15] Since in all his works Leti habitually multiplies numbers of families by six to reach his estimates of total numbers of souls, this implies a total of just over three thousand, which is precisely the figure modern historians generally postulate for Amsterdam Sephardi Jewry at this time. Leti's estimate for Rotterdam Jewry, which he puts at eighty families,[16] can probably also be accepted as reasonably accurate though there is little other evidence with which to compare it. But then in a wild underestimate of the number of Ashkenazim in Amsterdam, he tells us '*in quanto al numero de Guidei tedeschi non arrivano a cento famiglie che vuol dire, sei cento persone in circa*'.[17] Elsewhere in the *Teatro Belgico,* Leti states that the total number of

---

[12] Leti (note 5 above), vol. 2, p.337.

[13] Leti (note 7 above), vol. 5, pp.731–2.

[14] *ibid.*, p.724; Leti (note 5 above), vol. 2, p.132; in his account of the court of Brandenburg, of 1687, Leti describes Berlin Jewry as being small in number: 'e di poca figura, se non fosse il signor Joost Libman d'ottimi portamenti, che gode il privileggio d'esser Gioielliere de queste serenissimi Altezze, e che in fatti serve con puntualità, e confedeltà, virtù che l'hanno accreditato appresso la persona di S.A.E. che con somma humanità lo vede di buon' occhio, e come spesso si fa veder nella corte, viene da tutti i corteggiani ben visto, più di quello che permette quell'uso ordinario de'Christiani verso i Giudei; perche in fatti dico e buona persona e honorevole,' G. Leti, *Rittrati historici, politici, chronologici e genealogici della Casa Serenissima, e elettorale di Brandenburgo,* 2 vols (Amsterdam, 1687), vol. 1, p.334.

[15] Leti (note 5 above), vol. 2, p.336.

[16] *ibid.*, p.132; the provision of seating in Rotterdam's new synagogue, built in 1725, suggests that the Ashkenazi community then numbered around 100 families; see C. Reijnders, *Van 'Joodsche Natiën' tot joodse Nederlanders* (Amsterdam, 1970), p.154.

[17] Leti (note 5 above), vol. 2, p.336; earlier Leti had estimated the total number of Sephardi and Ashkenazi families in Amsterdam at 570, or around 3420 souls in all, adding that in any case 'certo e che non arrivano a quatro mila'; Leti (note 7 above), vol. 5, p.725.

Jews in the United Provinces amounted to no more than 1400 families, yield-ing a grand total of 8400 Jews, which, as far as we can tell, was only about half the real figure.[18]

But Leti's central point in his discussion of Dutch Jewry is that the Republic, by granting Jews citizenship and public honours, if not access to public office or economic equality with non-Jews, thereby assigning the Jews a higher status than they enjoyed anywhere else in Europe, derived only benefit. They demonstrated a loyalty and political good faith which reinforced the Dutch state, and were an asset culturally also. His discussion of Dutch Jewry thus focuses mainly on the life-style and attitudes of a group almost without parallel in Europe – Amsterdam's Jewish quasi-aristocratic élite, cultivated and wealthy, who live in what Leti styles *palazzi e case nobilissime* who have performed political and financial services for the state and in other ways contributed to the prosperity and well-being of Amsterdam. Leti is aware, as everyone living in Amsterdam was, of the great contrast in life-style and attitudes as between the Sephardi and Ashkenazi communities and shows no interest at all in the latter. It is the Portuguese Jews that interest him and then only their élite. He agrees that the Sephardi community as a whole is impressive. '*La sinagoga de' Portoghesi*,' he wrote, '*sembra un seggio di Nobili, gente ben fatta, quasi tutta civile, ben vestita, ricca e che fa gran figura.*'[19] But when he goes into detail he confines his attention to a handful of leading figures, those who had indisputably performed services for the state, for literature and for general culture.[20]

Essentially, then, Leti concentrates on the Sephardi elite because they fitted his arguments better than any other Jewish group, and best lived up to the political and cultural criteria of his distinctive brand of early Enlightenment republican idealism. But there is also the issue of his personal relations with the group in question. Leti, as a recent southern European immigrant with (at least at the outset) an inadequate knowledge of Dutch, spent much of his time with other members of Amsterdam's flourishing immigrant communities, especially Italians and French Hugenots but on occasion, it would seem, also

[18] Leti (note 5 above), vol. 2, p.132; with regard to Anglo-Jewry, Leti gives two different statistics, asserting in one place that there were 300 Jewish families in England in the early 1680s and in another 200; see Leti (note 11 above), vol. 1, pp. 251, 549.

[19] Leti (note 7 above), vol. 5, p.728.

[20] Besides those whom he discusses in detail, Leti lists the Amsterdam Jewish élite, or at least their menfolk, as follows: il Barone Antonio Lopez Suasso, David Emmanuel de Pinto, Giacob Perera, Giacomo del Prado, Giacomo de Pinto, Giacomo Aboaf Ozorio, Francisco Emanuel Dias Jorge, Moise Pereira, Henrique Mendes de Silva, Abramo del Soto, Emanuele de Pinto, Giosepe e Abramo Felix, Giacomo e David Bueno de Meschita, Abramo Telles, Antonio Alvare (Machado), Simone e Luigi Rodrigues de Soze, Emanuel de Vega, il proveditore di Mascado, Emanuel Goma de Silva, e altrui; Leti (note 7 above), vol. 5, p.725. The Giacomo del Prado mentioned here is the same as the Isaac de Prado who was a *parnas* that year as was Isaac (Manuel?) de Pinto and Isaac (Henrique) Mendes da Silva; Abraham Telles was *parnas* in 1681 as was Jacob de Pinto in 1682 and Jacob Bueno de Mesquita in 1683; regard-ing the wealth of the community, Leti says 'molte sono quelle Famiglie che godono gran richezze, e ne sono due, o tre che non hanno meno d'un milione di facoltà ciascuna; più di sei di mezo milione al meno, in somma tra queste 450 famiglie si fa il conto che vi siano più di venti milioni di facoltà, la maggior parte in gemme in contanti, in buone lettere'; Leti, (note 5 above), vol. 2, p.336.

Portuguese Jews. Clearly he visited and enjoyed hospitality at several of their houses and cultivated the acquaintance of at least several of those whom he describes. He may have obtained some financial benefit from his relations with them. Certainly he shows that the Sephardi élite now formed an integral part of the patronage network which supported Amsterdam's increasingly cosmopolitan community of men of letters at the close of the century. With one of the leading figures whom he describes, Baron Manuel de Belmonte, Resident, or as Leti calls him 'Agent-General', of the Spanish crown in the United Provinces, we know that he came in contact at the very outset of his sojourn in Amsterdam. This was whilst he was finalizing his manuscript of *Il ceremoniale historico* for publication when word got out that there was a great deal in it about the European powers, especially France and Spain, and that the first volume was dedicated to Louis XIV.[21] At the instigation of the Spanish ambassador in The Hague, Belmonte was sent to see Leti and offered him a large sum of money for the deletion of passages derogatory of Spain. Leti afterwards proudly claimed to have refused both the money and any deletions, asserting that his unwavering goal was historical truth.

The Amsterdam Jewish personality to whom Leti devotes most space is Jeronimo Nunes da Costa (Moses Curiel) (1620–97) who had had the title of 'Agent of the Crown of Portugal in the United Provinces' since May 1645.[22] Jeronimo Nunes da Costa, Leti explains, had performed many important services on behalf of Portugal, and during the long periods in which there had been no resident Portuguese ambassador at The Hague had in effect functioned as Portugal's minister in the Dutch Republic. Leti recalls in the *Raguagli historici*, first published in 1698, a year after Jeronimo's death, and then reissued in 1700, that the Portuguese Council of State, in Lisbon, was so satisfied with his services that no sooner did word reach Portugal of his death than patents were dispatched appointing his eldest surviving son, Alexandre Nunes da Costa[23], to the same

---

[21] Fassò, (note 1 above), p.230.

[22] Quite a lot has now been written about this personality, see D. Swetschinski, 'An Amsterdam Jewish Merchant-Diplomat: Jeronimo Nunes da Costa alsia Moseh Curiel (1620–1697), Agent of the King of Portugal', in L. Dasberg and J. N. Cohen (eds),. *Neveh Ya'akov. Jubilee volume presented to Dr Jaap Meijer on the occasion of his seventieth birthday* (Assen, 1982) pp.3–30; and J. I. Israel, 'The Diplomatic Career of Jeronimo Nunes da Costa: an Episode in Dutch-Portuguese Relations of the Seventeenth Century', above, chapter 8, pp. 171ff; *id.*, 'An Amsterdam Jewish Merchant of the Golden Age: Jeronimo Nunes da Costa (1620–1697), Agent of Portugal in the Dutch Republic', *Studia Rosenthaliana*, vol. 18 (1984), pp.21–40. Jeronimo was ennobled as a 'cavalheiro fidalgo da casa real' by John IV of Portugal in 1646.

[23] Alexandre Nunes da Costa (Selomoh Curiel) (1655–1712) was much less active in his capacity as 'Agent of Portugal' (1697–1712) than his father had been, being mainly employed to send miscellaneous items of various kinds needed by the king and his ministers in Portugal: however, the Portuguese ambassador, Sousa Pacheco, during his temporary absence from the United Provinces in 1698 did name Alexandre as his chargé d'affaires, asking the States General to 'respondere, pendante ejus absentia memorialibus ab Alexandro Nunio a Costa, Regis Domini sui Amstelodami Agent praesentandis'; see Algemeen Rijksarchief, The Hague (ARH), Archive of the States General 7104. Francisco de Sousa Pacheco to SG, The Hague, 11 February 1698; Alexandre was elected

post and with the same honours and privileges as his father had enjoyed 'e con lettere obligantissime'.[24] But having acknowledged Jeronimo's services on behalf of Portugal, Leti at once goes on to say that this pre-eminent Sephardi personage had also performed many notable services for the Dutch state. He was regarded as a citizen of such merit, Leti tells us, that in recognition '*del suo instancabile zelo verso la republica*' he had been presented with '*una bellissima catena d'oro, e misteriosissima medaglia*' and with the much-prized privilege of exemption from taxation such as was enjoyed by scarcely ten other men in the whole of the Dutch Republic, apart from fully accredited ambassadors.[25] Among other details he gives, and which indicate some familiarity with the Da Costa household, Leti reports the exact date of Jeronimo's death, 16 January 1697, and says that Alexandre continued to preside over the family firm, together with his youngest brother Alvaro, but that out of veneration for their departed father, the brothers continued to trade under the name 'Geronimo Nunes da Costa e figli'.[26]

Another Sephardi personage to whom Leti devotes detailed attention is Baron Manuel de Belmonte, who had been first Agent, then Agent-General, and finally Resident of Spain in the United Provinces.[27] Once again, Leti points out that during the sometimes politically crucial periods when there had been no Spanish ambassador in The Hague, Belmonte had in practice served as Spain's representative to the States General. Belmonte had indeed done much on behalf of Spain, but what Leti is even more anxious to point out is that he had also

---

continued

parnas of the Amsterdam Sephardi community in 1700 but refused the honour and was not subsequently elected, see Gemeente Archief, Amsterdam, Archive of the Portuguese Jewish Community no. 1323. 'Registro dos parnasim'.

[24] This detail suggests that Leti had actually been shown the patents; Leti (note 4 above), vol. 2, raguaglio i, p.123; Alexandre seems also to have inherited his father's position as one of the two permanent deputies of the Amsterdam Sephardi community to the non-Jewish authorities – together with Baron Belmonte; it was in this capacity – and not as I. S. Emmanuel states as a *parnas* – that he went to see the West India Company directors in January 1702, together with Belmonte, to convey Curaçao Jewry's protest at the attempts of the governor of Curaçao to make them send their slaves to work on the island's fortifications on the Sabbath; Belmonte was then a *parnas* of the community but Alexandre was not, see ARH Archive of the West India Company 357 fo.15.res. 17 January 1702 and I. S. and S. A. Emmanuel, *History of the Jews of the Netherlands Antilles*, 2 vols (Cincinatti, 1970), vol. 1, p.100.

[25] On the presentation of the gold chain and Jeronimo's tax exemption, see Israel, 'Diplomatic Career' (note 7 above), vol. 5, pp.182–3, 186–7; Leti (note 7 above), vol. 5, p. 728; id. (note 4 above), vol. 2, raguaglio i, p.128.

[26] Jeronimo Nunes da Costa had four married sons, the eldest of whom, Duarte Nunes da Costa (Aaron Curiel) (1650–95) – to whom Joseph Penso de la Vega dedicated his *Confusion de Confusiones*, in 1688 – died two years before his father; a third son, Francisco Nunes da Costa (Jacob Curiel) (1660–1703), died only five years after his father, so that of the four only the youngest, Alvaro Nunes da Costa (Nathan Curiel) (1666–1737) lived beyond 1712. Given that Alvaro was born in 1666 and that his father was an enthusiastic supporter of Sabbatai Sevi in 1665–6, it may be that Alvaro was given his Jewish name, Nathan, in honour of Nathan of Gaza. (I am indebted to Edgar Samuel, Director of the Jewish Museum, for the dates of birth and death of Jeronimo's sons.)

[27] Leti (note 7 above), vol. 5, p.728.

actively assisted and served the interests of the Dutch state. So highly had his activity been appreciated by the States General that he too had been granted tax exemption. Leti adds that Belmonte was always full of the latest European news, which we can well believe; we know that he regularly corresponded with Spanish diplomats in other European countries as well as with ministers at The Hague, Brussels and Madrid. A third figure whom Leti mentions as having played a significant political role was Baron Francisco Lopes Suasso. He tells us that this personality was held in high esteem by the States General and all Dutch ministers as well as by the diplomatic confraternity at The Hague, where he normally lived, and by the Dutch Stadholder, William III, king of England. In particular, Leti alludes to Lopes Suasso's major role in buttressing the finances of the Spanish régime in Brussels and the payments to the Spanish army of Flanders during the 1690s, remarking that during the 'last war' (i.e. the Nine Years War 1689–97) Lopes Suasso had performed '*rilevanti serviggi alla causa commune de' collegati*', that is on behalf of the coalition of European powers allied against Louis XIV's France.[28]

Awareness of their merits and public services, Leti maintains, was the reason that Amsterdam's Jewish élite had come to be not just accepted, but sought after, in the most select circles. Jeronimo Nunes da Costa, he assures us, was esteemed and visited by everyone. Besides a host of lesser dignitaries and noblemen who had visited his famous town house in Amsterdam, and supped at his table, Leti records that the Electress Sophia of Hanover (the mother of the future George I of England) had lodged for some time in his house, as, on one occasion, had the French ambassador, the marquis de Croissy, the 'other Colbert'.[29] And Jeronimo's deceased wife, Ribca Abaz, whose family, as Leti remarks, had been ennobled by the Holy Roman Emperor in the early seventeenth century, had reputedly been just as accomplished and assured in entertaining noble ladies, and welcoming them to her home, as had Jeronimo in receiving noblemen and diplomats.[30] Leti also says that after Jeronimo's death, his sons Alexandre and Alvaro succeeded in maintaining the high social standing which their parents had achieved, and in this he was certainly right. Both Alexandre and, after his death, Alvaro, who was Agent of the crown of Portugal in the United Provinces from 1712 until his death in 1737, are known to have had frequent dealings with an assortment of aristocratic diplomats, most notably

---

[28] On Lopes Suasso's role in the financing of the Spanish army of Flanders during the 1690s, see J. I. Israel, *European Jewry in the Age of Mercantilism, 1550–1750* (Oxford, 1985), p.134.

[29] Actually both the elector, Ernest Augustus, and the Electress lodged at Jeronimo's house when they visited Amsterdam in 1679. Whilst there, the Elector fell ill and had to be attended by Jeronimo's physician who was none other than the famous Isaac Orobio de Castro; see E. Bodemann (ed.), *Briefwechseln der Herzogin Sophie von Hannover mit ihrem Bruder dem Kurfürsten Karl Ludwig von der Pfalz* (Leipzig, 1885), p.369.

[30] 30 Leti (note 7 above), vol. 5, p.728; Rivbca Abaz (1634–86) was a daughter of the Dias Jorge family which (whilst still ostensibly Catholic New Christians) had been ennobled by the Emperor Rudolph II under patents of 1610 and 1614; see Heinrich Schnee, *Die Hoffinanz und der moderne Staat*, 6 vols (Berlin, 1953–4), vol. 4, p.315.

Luis da Cunha and the conde de Tarouca who were among the most outstanding Portuguese statesmen of the eighteenth century. These personages spent a good deal of time in the United Provinces especially during the 1712–13 European peace congress at Utrecht. Alexandre and Alvaro were, of course, assisting their diplomatic work and, among other things, arranged their accommodation at Utrecht.[31] But it does seem that they also formed a genuine friendship with these men. The Portuguese Protestant writer Francisco Xavier de Oliveira, who knew Alvaro Nunes da Costa in Amsterdam in the 1730s records that Alvaro

> étoit sans cesse visité de toute la noblesse du pais, et de presque tous les ministres étrangers qui passoient à Amsterdam pour se rendre à la Haye. Deux grands ministres du Portugal, le Comte de Tarouca, et Dom Luis da Cunha, avoient pour lui la plus parfaite considération.[32]

Moreover, it is likely that Luis da Cunha's well-attested philo-Semitic attitude, and hostility to the Portuguese Inquisition, began with, or was at least fomented by, his encounter with the Nunes da Costa at Amsterdam.[33] If so, this would figure as a key instance of the Amsterdam Sephardi élite's success in elevating the standing and improving the image of western Jewry in the eyes of educated non-Jews through their assiduous cultivating of the travelling aristocratic and diplomatic *monde* of their time.

But as Leti emphasizes, the Nunes da Costa, if among the most successful, were by no means alone in finding acceptance in the most select circles. Several other figures were no less notable in this respect. Don Isaac Senior Teixeira, for example, who arrived in Amsterdam from Hamburg in 1698, at the age of fifty, is described by Leti as an immensely cultivated gentleman who had not only performed numerous public services on behalf of the republic of Hamburg but also whilst living there had been constantly visited by distinguished personages. He tells that Queen Christina had lodged in his house on many occasions after her abdication of the Swedish throne and that the Elector and Electress of Brandenburg had lodged with him in 1682.[34] According to Leti, Baron Lopes Suasso was likewise greatly esteemed by '*rappresentanti publici e nobiltà straniera*' and since it is well known that he had many dealings with the Stadholder-king

---

[31] 31 Gemeente Archief, Amsterdam, Notarial Archive 7958 ii, p.88, a deed of 25 April 1712 by which Alexandre pledged 13,000 guilders as surety for payment for the hire, for Dom Luis da Cunha, of a large house in Utrecht belonging to the Utrecht nobleman, the heer van Deijl.

[32] 32 F. Xavier de Oliveira, *Discours Pathétique au sujet des calamités présentes arrivées en Portugal* (London, 1756), p.41.

[33] 33 See the *Instrucões inéditas de D. Luis da Cunha a Marco António de Azevedo Coutinho* (Coimbra, 1929), pp.75–6, 87, 95–7.

[34] 34 Leti (note 7 above), vol. 5, pp. 557–8; id. (note 4 above) , vol. 2, raguaglio i, pp.126–7; H. Kellenbenz, 'Königin Christine und ihre Beziehungen zu Hamburg', in *Queen Christina of Sweden. Documents and Studies* (Stockholm, 1966), pp.188–9.

William III, there is no reason to question this.[35] And as for Baron Belmonte, Leti reveals the highly significant, though by no means surprising, fact that Spain's ambassadors to the Dutch Republic, when on visits to Amsterdam from The Hague, where the embassy was, were accustomed to lodge at his house.[36] Possibly part of the explanation as to why Baron Belmonte chose to reside at some distance from the Jewish quarter of Amsterdam, while Jeronimo Nunes da Costa and other Sephardi leaders resided within it or at its edge, was his need to prevent embarrassment to his aristocratic Spanish guests, envoys of the crown which in 1492 had expelled the ancestors of Holland's Sephardi community from Spain.

Besides their activity in support of the Dutch state and its allies, and their success in finding acceptance in high society, what most impressed Leti about Amsterdam's Sephardi élite was its seigneurial life-style and its zeal for literature – especially for men of letters such as himself. This is a theme which recurs in several of his descriptions of leading Amsterdam Sephardi personages and opens up a new dimension to our perceptions of this group whom historians are accustomed to think of as patrons of Jewish, or at any rate of Sephardi literature, but not as patrons of non-Jewish literatures. Jeronimo Nunes da Costa, according to Leti, not only won the affection and esteem of all who knew him but was always zealous to *'proteggere, accarezzare e beneficiare letterati'*. [37]Likewise, Leti assures us, that highly cultivated gentleman Don Diogo Teixeira de Mattos, eldest son of Isaac Teixeira, enthusiastically emulated his father *'nel favorire e accarezzare i letterati'*. [38]Oddly enough, Leti does not mention Baron Belmonte in this connection, though other evidence suggests that Don Manuel was the most serious of all the Amsterdam Sephardi patricians in the sphere of literary patronage. It was Baron Belmonte who set up late seventeenth-century Amsterdam Sephardi Jewry's two literary salons, the Academia de los Sitibundos (1676) and the Academia de los Floridos (1685), modelled on the Spanish literary fraternities of the day, and it was to Baron Belmonte that Isabel Correa dedicated her monumental Spanish rendering of Guarini's *Il Pastor Fido*.[39]

But when Leti asserts that the Amsterdam Sephardi elite zealously associated with, and cultivated, men of letters what exactly is he telling us? In the case of Sephardi writers, on both religious and secular topics, it is clear enough that the Dutch Sephardi patriciate assisted financially, especially towards the costs of publication; and that they, in turn, were rewarded for their outlay by being festooned with flowery dedications. But in the case of non-Jewish writers there are no known instances of this type. What Leti seems principally to have

[35] 35 Leti (note 4 above), vol. 2, raguaglio i, pp. 127–8.

[36] 36 Leti (note 5 above), vol. 2, p.406.

[37] 37 Leti (note 4 above), vol. 2, raguaglio i, p.124.

[38] 38 *ibid.*, i, p.127

[39] 39 Isabel Correa dedicated her poem on 15 November 1693, in Antwerp, to 'Don Manuel de Belmonte, Baron de Belmonte, Conde Palatino y Regente de su Magestad Catholica', see I. Correa, *El Pasto Fido, Poëma de Baptista Guarino* (Antwerp, 1694); see also D. M. Swetchinski, 'The Portuguese Jews of seventeenth-century Amsterdam: Cultural continuity and Adaptation', in F. Malino and P. C. Albert (eds), *Essays in Modern Jewish History: A Tribute to Ben Halpern* (New York, 1982), p.71–3.

in mind is the liberal hospitality regularly showered on Amsterdam's resident colony of foreign writers by the Sephardi patricians. It seems clear enough that Leti himself was a frequent guest. Jeronimo Nunes da Costa, he tells us, was fond of nothing more than of extending hospitality to foreign visitors and was used to *'ricevere con nobilissimo accoglio gli stranieri in sua casa'*. Similarly, Baron Lopes Suasso, though he normally resided near the government buildings at the centre of The Hague, was accustomed to offer *'speso tavola ad amici e stranieri'*.[40] In his account of the German Empire, published a decade before Isaac Teixeira's move from Hamburg to Amsterdam,[41] Leti remarks that Hamburg was known everywhere as being one of the chief centres of hospitality and culture in Central Europe, but that no one in Hamburg had a greater reputation for hospitality among travellers of quality than Don Isaac:

> Et in questo genere il signor Resident Teixeira fa grande honore alla città, poiche so sforza più d'ogni altro ad honorare e accarezzare gli stranieri, e a trattar con molta prudenza e amorevolezza con cittadini, di modo che la sua casa splendidissima in ogni cosa, sembra un Teatro, e un Albergo della gentilezza.[42]

But if we now go on to ask why foreign literati were regularly included among the dinner guests of the Sephardi patriciate, we see at once that the function of the non-Jewish men of letters in the life-style of the Sephardi élite must have been very different from that of the Sephardi authors whom they patronized. By assisting the publication of works, religious and secular, by Portuguese Jewish writers, the Amsterdam Sephardi patriciate were consciously striving to enhance their standing and prestige within their own community and the Jewish world at large.[43] For the same reasons, there were sometimes sermons and

[40] 40 'D'ordinario stantia con la sua famiglia nell'Haga, con carozza a sei, servitù, e livrea decente . . .'; Leti (note 4 above), vol. 2, raguagli i, p.127. The Lopes Suasso residence on the Nieuwe Voorhout was regarded in the early eighteenth century as one of the finest houses in The Hague; see M. Henriquez Pimentel, *Geschiedkundige aanteekeningen betreffende de Portugeesche Israelieten in Den Haag en hunne synagogen* (The Hague, 1876), p.35.

[41] 41 Another detail for which we must thank Leti is that he tells us, in the *Raguagli historici*, that Teixeira's move from Hamburg to Amsterdam took place in September 1698; in his notes on Teixeira, Henriques de Castro observes that the move must have taken place only shortly before Teixeira's election as *parnas* of the Amsterdam community in 1699. Such a speedy elevation to the highest communal honour so soon after arrival in Holland would seem to have been unprecedented; Leti (note 4 above), vol. 2, raguaglio i, p.126; D. Henriques de Castro, *Keur van grafsteenen op de Nederl. Portug. Israel. begraafplaats te Oudekerk aan den Amstel*, 2 vols (Leiden, 1883) vol. 1, p.106.

[42] 42 G. Leti, *Ritratti historici* (note 14 above), vol. 2, p.378; in this connection, Teixeira's role as host, as well as manager of the income and business agent of Queen Christina of Sweden takes on an added dimension. For Christina regarded herself as the standard-bearer of culture, and especially of French and Italian refinement, amid what she considered to be the cultural wastes of Germany and Scandinavia, so that both her initial choice of and subsequent unbroken adherence to Teixeira, indicate that she must have regarded him as not just a reliable business manager but as in some sense an embodiment of refined culture in the Hamburg context.

[43] 43 The most important such secular work was, of course, Joseph de la Vega's treatise *Confusion de Confusiones*, on the workings of the Amsterdam stock exchange which was published in 1688 and dedicated to Jeronimo's then eldest son, Duarte Nunes da Costa.

prayer-gatherings in their homes. Thus, during passover 1690, Jeronimo Nunes da Costa invited the pick of the Amsterdam Sephardi community, together with three or four rabbis, to his home for a study session. One of those present, Rabbi Samuel da Silva de Miranda, delivered a sermon which was subsequently published, no doubt at Jeronimo's expense, and dedicated to him.[44] In 1683, Joseph Penso de La Vega, one of the most active members of the Amsterdam Sephardi literary coterie, published a flowery panegyric on the 'Divine law of Moses' which he dedicated to the 'merit and zeal' of Jeronimo Nunes da Costa under his synagogue name, Moseh Curiel.[45] In some cases, the works patronized by the Dutch Sephardi élite, though written by Sephardi authors, were essentially intended to boost their standing in the non-Jewish Spanish- and Portuguese-speaking world. This was the case, for example, with Manoel de Leon's *Triumpho Lusitano* (1688), a eulogy of King Pedro II of Portugal on the occasion of his second marriage, paid for by and dedicated to Jeronimo Nunes da Costa, which Jeronimo specially had published in Catholic Brussels so as to facilitate its sale in Portugal and the Portuguese colonies.[46] This publication, essentially a piece of political propaganda, bore an engraved title-page, representing the arms and insignia of Portugal, of remarkable beauty. Another such general work was Abraham da Fonseca's *Orthographia Castellana* (1663), a treatise on Spanish orthography published at Amsterdam and again dedicated to Jeronimo Nunes da Costa.[47] In the same way, the Amsterdam Sephardi élite gained added lustre from the inflated baroque poetic eulogies which flowed from the ready pen of Daniel Levi de Barrios.

But the reasons for cultivating non-Sephardi writers were different. A man such as Leti could be of no service to building up the image of the Amsterdam Sephardi élite either in the Hispanic world or the European Jewish Diaspora. But where such non-Jewish literati who, being resident in Holland, were generally either Protestant or nominally so, could be of great service was in acting as a cultural bridge between the Sephardi patriciate, on the one hand, and the aristocratic milieu of courtiers and diplomats with which they aspired to rub shoulders, on the other. For Amsterdam's Portuguese Jewish patricians needed more than mere titles, splendid houses, liveried servants and richly laden tables to attract princes, ambassadors and noblemen, and their wives, to their doors. Also indispensable was the capacity to provide the right sort of conversation. Thus culture, and especially the refined talk of fashionable literati, became a zealously sought-after commodity among Amsterdam's quasi-aristocratic Sephardi patricians.

[44] 44 A. Neves, *Bibliografia Luso-judaica* (Coimbra, 1913), p.22.

[45] 45 J. Penso de la Vega, *La rosa panegirico sacro en encomio de la Divina Ley de Mosseh* (Amsterdam, 1683).

[46] 46 M. de Leon, *Triumpho Lusitano. Applausos festivos* (Brussels, 1688); see also M. Kayserling, *Biblioteca Española-Portugueza-Judaica* (Strasbourg, 1890), p.57.

[47] 47 Kayserling (note 46 above), p.46.

Leti abundantly attests to the Sephardi patricians' interest in cultivating elegant conversation. He tells us that Don Isaac Senior Teixeira *'parla molte lingue con gran franchezza e tra le altre cose ama molto la compagnia de' letterati che accoglie in sua casa con grand' affetto'*.[48] His son, Don Diogo (Abraham Senior) Teixeira de Mattos, according to Leti, was an even more polished conversationalist:

> Don Diogo può veramente dirsi huomo ad ultrumque paratus, perche parla di tutto, discorre di tutto, e intende a perfettione quel tanto che conviene nella società civile ad un galanthuomo, essendosi spesso esercitato nella lettura di differenti opere de' più celebrati scrittori, essendo in oltre la gentilezza istessa.[49]

Similarly Baron Lopes Suasso, asserts Leti, whatever his riches in money, was even richer *'in suoi tesori dell'animo, con li quali rende sempre più accreditata la sua nattione'*.[50] And as for Jeronimo Nunes da Costa, none could match him *'nella destra condotta, e accorta prudenze di sapersi maneggiare con tutti'*.

The houses of the Sephardi patriciate of Amsterdam and The Hague, then, were more than just luxurious residences; they also served as the forum for a highly intricate and richly cosmopolitan cultural ritual. The magnificence of at any rate the three-best known Amsterdam Jewish patrician houses – those of the Nunes da Costa, Belmonte and De Pinto – has often been remarked upon. But it is questionable whether the extent to which they functioned as show-cases for both Sephardi and general culture has been fully grasped. It is evident that they were among the major tourist attractions of Amsterdam. Together with their accessories – coaches, barges and liveried servants – they were intended to impress noblemen as well as Jewry and the public at large. Leti describes Baron Belmonte's residence as a *'casa nobilissima'*, equipped with a *'carrozza bellissima con le armi di Spagna'*. On the famous Romeyn de Hooghe engraving of the house, we see these arms also over the front entrance and carved on the back of Belmonte's imposing barge. Still more impressive, according to Leti, was the home of Jeronimo Nunes da Costa

> la più commoda, esplendida casa della città almeno tiene un giardino che non ve n'e alcuno altro che l'ugagli; e foura la gran porta della sua casa si vede l'arma di Portogallo; in oltre un carrozzino per suo uso, e una bellissima barca, con l'arma ancora di Portogallo, e è certo che fa nobil figura, e nella sua casa sembra esservi una corte, per il gran concorse de' stranieri . . . [51]

---

[48] 48 Leti (note 7 above), vol. 5, p.558; in his book on Germany, Leti describes Don Isaac as a 'signore cortese, e civile, e inclinato con molta generosa gentilezza a far servitio ad ogni uno, onde comunemente viene amato da tutti'; id., *Ritratti historici* (note 14 above), p.375.

[49] 49 Leti (note 4 above), vol. 2, raguaglio i, p.127.

[50] 50 *ibid*

[51] 51 Leti (note 11 above), vol. 2, p.406; the arms of Portugal were still in place above the front entrance several decades later, for Oliveira records that on arriving in Amsterdam from Lisbon in 1734 'à la vue de l'Ecu des Armes de Portugal arboré sur le grand porteil de la maison de cet Agent, j'en fus d'abord un peu desconcerté'; Oliveira (note 32 above), p.40.

Thus, according to Leti, Jeronimo's garden, of which we snatch just a glimpse on Romeyn de Hooghe's famous engraving, through the open front entrance, and which we know from other sources was exceptionally large for an Amsterdam town house,[52] was arguably the most outstanding in the city. At any rate, it was a particularly fine garden. From this and other evidence, we see that the Nunes da Costa were among the chief propagators of an enthusiasm for fine gardens which arose among the Dutch Sephardi élite at this time.[53] From a letter of Alvaro Nunes da Costa to a Portuguese minister, written in 1712, we learn that a specialist gardener was employed at the house and that the family had a decided interest in new and rare varieties of plants, examples of at least some of which they shipped to Lisbon, intent on delighting the Portuguese court with the spectacle of varieties previously unknown in Portugal.[54] The effort which went in to cultivating fine gardens, we may conclude, was yet another means of seizing the attention of visiting envoys and aristocrats.

But the principal attraction contained in the houses of the Amsterdam Portuguese Jewish patriciate were the precious objects, rarities and exotic items stored in cabinets and display cases within. If the cultivation of elegant conversation about literary topics was one method of forging a path into fashionable society, another (and among the merchant élites of Venice, Antwerp and Amsterdam the traditional) method, was to amass noted collections of antiquities and remarkable objects of fineness, rarity and beauty guaranteed to arrest the eye of eminent visitors. These collections did not necessarily exclude Judaica. In this period, the Dutch Sephardi élite were striving to raise the standing of Jewish culture in the eyes of non-Jewish society, as well as to convert themselves into the embodiment of all that was finest in general culture. Among the items on display in the Nunes da Costa household, for example, was a mediaeval illuminated Hebrew Bible of exeptional beauty which Jeronimo's father, Duarte Nunes da Costa, had purchased from a Spanish Jew from North Africa whilst in Pisa in 1618, and which was regarded as the oldest and most venerable possessed by Dutch Jewry.[55] Nor were the Sephardi patricians in the least inhibited about displaying the various patents of nobility they had received from the kings of Spain and Portugal and letters of appointment from various other princes. But the chief categories of objects on display were the exotica and rarities, especially fine jewels. Paintings and other works of art were included also, but appear to have received less emphasis in these Sephardi homes. When the De

---

[52] 52 J. S. da Silva Rosa, 'Een drietal prenten van joodsche patriciërshuizen te Amsterdam uit het einde der 17e eeuw'. *De Vrijdagavond*, vol.5, no. 3 (20 April 1928), pp.42–3.

[53] 53 The garden of David de Pinto at his country residence, Tulpenburg, was described by a visitor in 1736 as 'le plus beau jardin de toute la Hollande', M. H. Gans, *Memorboek* (Baarn, 1971), p.114.

[54] 54 Biblioteca Pública de Evora, Cod. cxx/2–4, p.10. Alvaro Nunes da Costa to conde Unhão, Amsterdam, 18 October 1712.

[55] 55 Duarte himself noted on the inside of the cover that he had bought it for its beauty and rarity with a view to passing it on to his heirs. *Catalogue de vente de la succession de feu N. D. Henriques de Castro* (Amsterdam, 1899), pp.44–5.

Pinto house was pillaged during the riots in Amsterdam in 1696 one of the display cases dragged out into the street contained medallions and old coins.[56]

Jewish wealth in Amsterdam was thus on display, presented to the public, in ways that were to be met with nowhere else in Europe. But much care was taken by the Sephardi patricians to project only what was deemed the right image. No Jewish beggars were allowed to congregate around their doors. Indeed, both the Sephardi and Ashenkazi leadership in Amsterdam were greatly concerned to keep the Jewish destitute as far as possible off the streets. Both communities operated a comprehensive system of community welfare, the net effect of which, as far as an outsider such as Leti was concerned, was to keep the Jewish poor virtually out of sight. But what one did see congregating around the doors of the Sephardi patricians were crowds of Christian beggars whom the former took good care to ply with coins. The Sephardi Jewish community, explains Leti, '*si sogliono raccogliere e spendere dieci mila scudi per anno d'elemosine, e pero tra di loro non vi vedono poveri andar per le porte se non fossero Christiani a quali sogliono dare alcuni bene spesso*'. [57]But while all the Sephardi patricians acted thus, Baron Belmonte stood out in this respect. Belmonte, says Leti,

> si fa conoscere grande amico de' poveri onde hà ristretto di molto gli atti di cortesia, di gratitudine, e di civilità, per esser più generoso verso gli stessi mendici, de' quali se ne vedono spesso in gran copia innanzi la porta della sua casa. Alcuni l'accusano di fare egli questo per ostenttatione, per vanità, ma comunque sia i poveri ne profittano.[58]

Exactly how this strategy influenced popular perceptions of the Amsterdam Sephardi élite is hard to say. Certainly there was in Amsterdam relatively little of the overt popular hostility to the Sephardi patricians which surged up so strongly in the late 1690s at Hamburg, precipitating the flight of the Teixeira to Holland. The leading Sephardi figures felt sufficiently secure to parade their wealth and pretensions in an unprecedentedly public manner, and it is clear that theirs were household names known to practically everyone who lived in the city. Still, there is no reason to suppose that they were looked on with affection by the masses and it is noteworthy that their houses were among the relatively small number of Amsterdam patrician residences – the Christian houses in the group belonging to persons who were particularly unpopular with the mob – which were attacked during the so-called *Aansprekersoproer* (undertakers' riot) of 1696. The De Pinto house, whose owners were then away at The

---

[56] 56 See J. Craffurd 'Een generaal en kort verhaal vande schrickelycke beroerte binnen Amsterdam voorgevallen en begonnen op den 30 Januarij des s'avonds, ende volcomen t'ondergebragt ende gestilt op den 6de Februarij 1696', in R. M. Dekker, *Oproeren in Holland gezien door tijdgenoten* (Assen, 1979), p.74.

[57] 57 Leti (note 7 above), vol. 5, p.726.

[58] 58 Leti (note 4 above), vol. 2, raguaglio i, p.128; this imparts a new relevance to Levi de Barrios' descriptive couplet about Belmonte: 'Residente leal del Rey hispano/piadoso al pobre, atento al cortesano': D. Levi de Barrios, *Estrella de Jacob* (Amsterdam, 1686), p.65.

Hague, was the only Jewish residence actually plundered. The mob invaded the house, smashing the porcelein *'dat daer in grote menigte was en zeer costelijck, in stucken'* and carried off jewels, coins and other 'rarities'. But before this the crowd had 'seriously threatened' the residence of the 'Palsgraaf Belmonte' as he was generally known in the city, withdrawing leaving the building intact only because the baron had barricaded himself in so strongly.[59] The same happened at the house of Jeronimo Nunes da Costa, who

> hadde zijn huijs van binnen meede wel bezorgt, de deuren met dwarsboomen 's cruisweegs toegemaakt en verscheijde gewapende in elcke kamer die aan de straat en op de tuijn uijtzien.[60]

The crowd withdrew after being warned from one of the windows that they would be fired on if they came closer.

But whatever the undercurrents of popular resentment against the Jews, Leti was confident that the new finesse, discretion and exemplary conduct of Amsterdam's Sephardi élite were the right tools by which the Jews could win the esteem and affection of all. It was the ancient pride and arrogance of the Jewish people which in the past had brought down so many calamities on their heads.

Leti's central conclusion, then, from his observations on Dutch Jewry, was that the Republic which had taken them in and given them unprecedented freedom was now reaping its just reward. The Jews in Holland had been transformed into valuable citizens capable of rendering significant services both to the state and to culture. As for Jewish religion and tradition, these had no value whatever in Leti's eyes. This was the characteristic stance of the European Enlightenment towards the Jews. Leti's vision extended to the possibility that one day society might accept the Jews as equals and that then, finally, the Jews would show themselves, in their capacity for political service and general culture, to be fully the equals of others:

> nella società civile gli Huomini son tutti uguali, di modo che basta una buona condotta per acquistar gran merito. E *come apud Deum non est ecceptio personarum*, lo stesso deve seguire della società civile, ond'e che in Holanda si da indifferentemente la cittadinanza.[61]

---

[59] 59 Craffurd (note 56 above), p.73.
[60] 60 *ibid.*
[61] 61 Leti (note 4 above), vol. 2, raguaglio i, p.128.

18

The Dutch Republic and its Jews during the Conflict over the Spanish Succession, 1699–1715

During the first half of the seventeenth century, the commercial system of Dutch Sephardi Jewry was based on Portugal and the Portuguese colonial empire.[1] The Portuguese Jews of Holland engaged in a narrow range of economic activity, based largely on the traffic, via Portugal, in Brazilian sugar. But within this limited context, their activity was an important factor in the functioning of the entire Dutch trading and colonial system.[2] As the Portuguese ambassador at The Hague noted in 1648, when Portugal and the Dutch Republic were on the verge of war over Brazil, the Sephardi Jews had come to play a "considerable" role in the Dutch body politic.[3] It was during the great struggle between the two countries for control of northern Brazil (1641–1661) that Dutch Jewry first emerged as an active and influential force in the policies of the Dutch state.

During the second half of the seventeenth century, the trading system of Dutch Sephardi Jewry was radically restructured, due to a number of developments — the collapse of Dutch Brazil in 1645–54, the decline of trade with Portugal, the Republic's new relationship with Spain after 1648, when the Treaty of Munster was signed, and the rise of the Sephardi communities in the Dutch and English Caribbean.[4] After 1648, and especially in the period 1672–99 when the United Provinces and Spain

---

1 Jonathan I. Israel, "The Economic Contribution of Dutch Sephardi Jewry to Holland's Golden Age, 1595–1713," *TvG* 96 (1983), p. 507.
2 See Jonathan I. Israel, "Dutch Sephardi Jewry, Millenarian Politics, and the Struggle for Brazil (1640–1654)," and above, chapter 7, pp. 145–70.
3 *Correspondência diplomática de Francisco de Sousa Coutinho durante a sua embaixada em Holanda* (3 vols., Coimbra, 1920–55), vol. 2, pp. 313–14: "E como os judeus fazem hum membro consideravel destas Provincias como o mais rico. . . ."
4 Israel, "Economic Contribution," pp. 521–27.

were allied against France, political and economic relations between the two powers became as close as the Catholic-Protestant divide would allow. This was mainly due to the military supremacy of France and the policy of territorial expansion pursued by Louis XIV. Both powers felt the need to collaborate against France; but their common fear of English expansion in the Caribbean also played a part. This growing Dutch-Spanish political and economic collaboration was exceptionally favorable for Dutch Sephardi Jewry. Their trade with Spain and Spanish America (via Cadiz) was accepted and legalized by the Spanish crown.[5]

When, starting in the early 1660s, the Spanish contractors (*asentistas*) in Spain charged with supplying black slaves to the American colonies began obtaining most of their slaves from the Dutch entrepôt at Curaçao, Dutch Sephardi Jewry was in a favorable position to take advantage of the unofficial transit trade from Holland — via Curaçao — to the Spanish colonies, which developed in the wake of the legal slave trade. At the same time, Dutch-Spanish military collaboration in the South Netherlands was conducive to the activities of the Dutch Sephardi army contractors, Antonio Alvares Machado and Jacob Pereira, and their associates, financiers like Baron Lopes Suasso,[6] and Spain's Jewish "resident" at Amsterdam, Manuel (later Baron) de Belmonte. By the 1670s, the role of the Amsterdam-Lisbon-Recife circuit had largely been displaced as the foundation of Dutch Sephardi enterprise by Amsterdam-Antwerp-Cadiz-Curaçao. It was against this background that Holland's Sephardi Jews came to play a central role in the policy and actions of the United Provinces during the crisis over the succession to the Spanish throne, which began in 1699.

From the beginning of the crisis to the outbreak of the War of the Spanish Succession (1702–13), acute anxiety over future prospects for Dutch commerce, shipping, and finance was general among the Dutch mercantile and governing elite. No one in a position of influence or involved in commerce had any doubts about the profound importance of the Spanish succession for the United Provinces. But whereas for non-Jewish Dutch merchants, or rather non-Sephardi Dutch merchants, the

---

5 Ibid., p. 521; Silva Rosa, pp. 84–85.

6 In the early 1690s, Lopes Suasso, as the Amsterdam correspondent of the Madrid banker the baron de Tamari, handled the official *mesadas*, or supposedly monthly payments, of the royal subsidy from Madrid to Antwerp: Frans van Kalken, *La fin du régime espagnol aux Pays-Bas* (Brussels, 1907), pp. 104–105.

trade with Spain and Spanish America were only two strands of the Dutch commercial system, which included the Baltic, Muscovy, Levant, and East India trades, the trade with Spain and the Spanish Caribbean were the only major branches in which the Sephardim were heavily involved. This special intensity of the Dutch Sephardi preoccupation — political and commercial — with Spanish trade and Spanish American bullion was conspicuous enough to catch the attention of more than one French envoy sent to The Hague during the closing stages of the war. The Sieur de Saint Maurice reported back to Paris that the Jews of Amsterdam were the most implacable and vociferous opponents of any peace with France and Spain that would leave the Bourbon claimant, Louis's grandson Felipe V, on the Spanish throne.[7]

The Spanish succession crisis began during the final months of life of Spain's last Habsburg king, Carlos II (1665–1700). Madrid, during these months of acute tension, was a hive of diplomatic intrigue, in which Francisco Schonenberg (alias Jacob Abraham Belmonte), the special envoy at the Spanish court of William III, stadholder of the Dutch Republic and king of England, Scotland and Ireland, played a prominent role. In accordance with William's instructions, Schonenberg worked closely with the court faction headed by the marqués de Leganés, which was endeavoring to secure the entire Spanish inheritance for the Austrian Habsburg claimant, the Emperor's son the Archduke Charles.[8] Had these efforts succeeded and the dying Spanish monarch bequeathed his global legacy to his Austrian relative, Spain would have been secured for the Anglo-Austro-Dutch coalition against France and the Dutch primacy in both the official Cadiz trade and the Caribbean transit trade with the Spanish Indies would have been confirmed. During Carlos the Second's last months, however, at the end of 1699, opinion among the childless king's ministers in Madrid gradually shifted in favor of France. No doubt there were various reasons for this, but one of them was the feeling among Charles's ministers that if the Austrian archduke did gain possession of

---

7 Bernhard Blumenkranz, *Documents modernes sur les juifs (XVI–XX siècles): 1. Depôts parisiens* (Toulouse, 1979), p. 390.

8 *Documentos inéditos referentes a las postrimerias de la Casa de Austria*, ed. Gabriel Maura Gamazo and Prince Adalberto of Bavaria (5 vols., Madrid, 1927–31) vol. 5, pp. 118, 166, 16, 247; R. J. H. Gottheil, *The Belmont-Belmonte Family: A Record of Four Hundred Years* (New York, 1917) pp. 68–70; Julio Caro Baroja, *Los Judíos en la España moderna y contemporánea* (3 vols., Madrid, 1978²), vol. 2, p. 169.

Spain and its empire, with the help of England and the United Provinces, it would inevitably lead to further concessions to the Dutch and English in the Indies and a growing risk that heresy might gain a foothold in the Spanish American dependencies.[9]

Francisco Schonenberg, though viewed with distrust and enmity by most of the court at Madrid, was an able man with an exceptional knowledge of Iberian and Spanish American affairs. Moreover, he was not only the personal envoy of William III, the head of the allied coalition against France, but also the official envoy of the Dutch States-General, though he lacked the title of ambassador. May we also see Schonenberg as in some sense an unofficial envoy of the Dutch Sephardi elite? I believe that we can. He was the representative of Dutch Sephardi interests in the Peninsula not only in the sense that the Dutch Sephardim as a group opposed the Bourbon succession in Spain and favored the Austrian claimant, nor that he was expert in dealing with the *Casa de Contratación* in Seville, the administrative body that regulated the Indies trade and was a vigilant defender of Dutch mercantile and shipping interests in the Peninsula.[10] There are also indications that Schonenberg collaborated closely with his uncle, the Baron de Belmonte, and other Jews, in arranging their affairs in the Peninsula, that his services were highly esteemed by the Dutch Sephardi elite, and that this continued to be the case after the outbreak of the War of the Spanish Succession, in May of 1702, when Schonenberg transferred his activities from Madrid, now an enemy capital, to Lisbon. It is revealing that in 1707, when Schonenberg was pressing the States-General to award him at long last the prestigious title of "ambassador" which had so far been denied him, the English minister at The Hague reported to London that the "Jews here sollicite hotly to obtain that honour for him but there is not yet great disposition to gratify *them* in that."[11]

In Portugal after 1702, as previously in Spain, Schonenberg was a great believer in mixing commerce with diplomacy; he thus displeased the Portuguese ministers as much as he had previously displeased those of Carlos II. In 1709 the Portuguese court tried to have Schonenberg recalled, the Portuguese envoy in Holland alleging that he had "defrauded the king

---

9 *Documentos inéditos*, vol. 5, p. 247.
10 *Documentos inéditos*, vol. 3, p. 392.
11 Public Record Office [hereinafter PRO], London, SP 84/229. Dayrolle to Harley, The Hague, 4 Feb. 1707.

of his custome in a considerable quantity of Ingots of silver brought on shore and to his house by his servants and coaches." "What success the envoy will have," commented the English resident at The Hague, "one can not very well judge, for Schonenberg has here a great many protectors, among them some perhaps who are concerned in the ingots."[12] In fact, this was probably part of the silver originating in Spanish Peru which was shipped to Europe via Rio de Janeiro, avoiding Spain, as payment for Dutch goods shipped out to the Spanish Indies before 1702.[13] The States-General had entrusted Schonenberg with retrieving bullion belonging to Dutch merchants from the Portuguese; we can be sure that some of it belonged to Amsterdam Jews.

After Carlos II died in Madrid in November 1700, Schonenberg continued to work with Leganés and to intrigue against the French and the Bourbon succession. Louis XIV's ministers were well aware of this and soon noticed also his connection with Baron Belmonte. In December 1700, Louis instructed his minister at Madrid, the Marquis d'Harcourt, that

> Il est nécessaire aussi de veiller à la conduite de Schonenberg, agent des Etats Généraux. Vous savez qu'il est très mal intentioné. Il ne faut pas cependant le faire sortir tant que l'ambassadeur d'Espagne demeurera en Hollande; mais il est bon que la Junte lui fasse parler fortement sur le retardement que les Etats-Généraux apportent à reconnaître le roi d'Espagne [i.e., Felipe V] et à le féliciter son avènement à la couronne.[14]

A few weeks later, Harcourt warned Paris in reference to Schonenberg that

> son oncle [i.e. Baron de Belmonte] sert le roi d'Espagne en qualité de son resident à Amsterdam. Comme on ne peut plus prendre aucune confiance en lui pour cet emploi, il serait nécessaire de le donner à quelqu' autre plus fidèle et attaché aux seuls intérets du Roi Catholique.[15]

---

12 Ibid. SP 84/232, fol. 47. Dayrolle to Boyle, The Hague, 27 Feb. 1709.
13 ARA, The Hague, SG 7018/i. Draft letter from States-General [hereinafter SG] to king of Portugal, The Hague, 12 July 1706.
14 Cited in Gottheil, *Belmont-Belmonte Family*, pp. 70–71.
15 Ibid., p. 71.

It is likely that one of Felipe the Fifth's first actions as king of Spain was to strip Belmonte of his agency for Spain in Amsterdam, though as yet no evidence of this has come to light.

Carlos II died on 1 November 1700, bequeathing the whole of the Spanish Empire in the Indies and Europe to the Bourbon candidate, Philip of Anjou. The maritime powers, England and the United Provinces, had suffered a disastrous diplomatic defeat; but, after considering their position, decided for the moment not to embark on war against France and Spain. After some hesitation the English and Dutch therefore recognized Felipe V as king of Spain, only to withdraw that recognition later, after the outbreak of war. The prospect of war against the combination of France and Spain was daunting. In the previous war, when Spain had been on their side, Louis XIV had fought the allies to a stalemate. But developments during 1701 seemed so threatening to the interests of both the English and the Dutch that in the end they decided that they had no choice but to form an alliance with Austria and declare war. The main factors in their decision were the advance of the French army into the Spanish Netherlands, forcing out the Dutch garrisons stationed there under the terms of the Peace of 1698, and the loss to Dutch and English commerce of the Spanish and Spanish American markets. From the Dutch point of view both developments, strategic and commercial, were disastrous. As early as March 1701, Amsterdam firms engaged in the Spanish America trade via Cadiz, were instructing their factors in Cadiz, Malaga, and Alicante to empty their warehouses and transfer their stock to neutral Genoese and Hanseatic firms.[16] Schonenberg sent details to The Hague of every step taken by Felipe the Fifth's ministers against Dutch trade, of the increasingly tense atmosphere at Cadiz, of the orders sent from Madrid to Spanish governors in the Caribbean banning Dutch slave ships from Spanish American ports, and of the seizure of several vessels belonging to the Dutch West India Company off the coasts of Spanish America. The grave view he took of the situation was confirmed by dispatches from the Dutch consul at Cadiz and from the governor of the Dutch island of Curaçao.[17] Then, in September 1701, as Schonenberg immediately informed The

16 ARA SH 2548, fols. 138v, 155, 173.
17 Ibid., fols. 115, 138v, 155, 161, 173, 192v; for instance, on 19 May 1701 Schonenberg reported to The Hague that "dit hof heeft door het geheele rijk circulaire ordres gezonden om generalijk alle de vreemde tabacquen geen gewasch wezende vande Spaensche dominien in America, strengelyk te prohiberen."

Hague, Felipe V transferred the *asiento*, the royal contract for the supply of slaves to the Spanish Indies, from the Portuguese Guinea Company (which, in the late 1690s, had been servicing the *asiento* in collaboration with the Dutch West India Company, obtaining most of the slaves from Curaçao) to the French Guinea Company based at St. Malo, which was proposing to obtain its slaves in West Africa, bypassing the Dutch as much as possible.[18] By the beginning of 1702 feeling against the kings of France and Spain in the United Provinces was running so high among all sections of society that there was practically no opposition to the Republic's joining with England and Austria and declaring war.

Whether or not he was actually stripped of his title as Agent of the Spanish crown in the United Provinces, Belmonte was certainly working against Felipe V as early as 1701, and probably earlier. The transfer of the *asiento* was a direct blow to his own personal interests, since he, together with the Amsterdam Sephardi firm of Luis and Simão Rodrigues da Sousa, had been acting as the Amsterdam factors of the Portuguese Guinea Company and as its delegates to the Dutch West India Company.[19] They also had direct financial involvement in the slave shipments from Dutch West Africa to the factors of the Portuguese company at Cartagena, Porto Bello, Havana and the other distribution centers in the Spanish Caribbean.[20] Thus it is hardly surprising to find Belmonte, then still nominally Spanish agent at Amsterdam, writing to William the Third's London secretary, Blathwaite, shortly after the transfer of the *asiento* to the French, and expressing his hope that the French slave company would soon collapse through lack of funds and slaves and his opposition to French endeavors to obtain financial assistance in Amsterdam and London.[21]

18 Georges Scelle, *La traité negrière aux Indes de Castille et traités d'Assiento* (2 vols., Paris, 1906) vol. 2, pp. 35, 48, 67, 134; Jorge Palacios Preciado, *La trata de negros por Cartagena de Indias* (Tunja, 1973), pp. 62, 70, 86.
19 ARA WIC [= West Indies Company] 356, fols. 287, 290, 310v. res. 8 Nov. and 6 Dec. 1701, and 357, fols. 41, 238. res. 14 Feb. and 21 Nov. 1702; the firm of Luis and Simão Rodrigues da Sousa was one of the largest Sephardi investors in the Dutch West India Company in the late seventeenth century and after the Nunes da Costa probably the most active Sephardi firm in Amsterdam trading with Portugal, Brazil, and the Azores; the firm was clearly well known to the authorities in Lisbon: see Bloom, pp. 37 and 126.
20 ARA WIC 356, fols. 287, 290, 310v.
21 British Library MS 34340, fols. 115–16. Belmonte to Blathwaite, Amsterdam, 1 Nov. 1701 (I am indebted to Daniel Swetschinski for drawing my attention to this letter).

In the first year of the war, the Archduke Charles's claim to the Spanish throne had a hollow ring. But when early results suggested that the allies might gain the upper hand in Flanders and Germany, the English and Dutch, in May of 1703, managed to persuade Portugal to join the coalition against France and Spain. The allies now had a firm base in the Iberian Peninsula and could plan their assault on Spain. The archduke and his shadow court took up residence in Lisbon. From the first, Jews were prominent among his contacts, agents, financial backers, and suppliers, including Don Joseph Cortizos, who was soon to become principal army contractor for the allied forces based in Spain.[22] As the preparations for the invasion of Spain progressed, the Dutch Sephardi elite became increasingly involved in the Archduke's cause, especially following the decision of the English, Dutch and Portuguese to follow Austria in recognizing him as "Carlos III of Spain." In May 1704, the archduke, in contact with Holland through Schonenberg, wrote to the States-General from Lisbon asking that Baron Belmonte be recognized as his "minister resident" in the United Provinces and that the States "aurez aussi pour lui [Belmonte] tous les égards favorables que nous devons nous promettre de votre amitié et la bonne correspondance que vous maintenez avec nous."[23] The States-General had already accorded provisional recognition to Belmonte as "resident" of "Carlos III of Spain," at Belmonte's prompting, by a resolution of 4 May 1704.[24] The States-General also recognized as "consul of Spain" to work with Belmonte a certain Judah Senior Henriquez, presumably a relative of the brothers David Senior and Captain Felipe Henriquez who had been factors for the slave *asiento* on Curaçao in the 1690s and had for many years been among Belmonte's Curaçao correspondents.[25] Senior Henriquez, who acted as agent in The Hague of Joseph Cortizos and served as his link with the States-General,

door syne Majesteyt den koningh van Spaengen Carel den derden

---

22 See Charles Rubens, "Joseph Cortissos and the War of the Spanish Succession," *Transactions of the Jewish Historical Society of England* 24 (1975), pp. 114–43.
23 ARA SG 7100/i. The Archduke Charles to the States-General, Lisbon, 30 May 1704.
24 Ibid., extract res. SG 4 May 1704.
25 Ibid., "Memorie van J. Senior Henriquez, 16 July 1704'; the captain's Jewish name was Jacob Senior; significantly the brothers' mother, Sara Lopes, was a sister of Baron Lopes Suasso. see I. S. Emmanuel, *Precious Stones of the Jews of Curaçao* (New York, 1957) pp. 302–304; see also Edgar Samuel, "Manuel Levy Duarte (1631–1714): An Amsterdam Merchant Jeweller and his Trade with London," *Transactions of the Jewish Historical Society of England* 27 (1982), p. 24.

aengestelt zijnde als desselfs consul in deese Vereenighde Nederlanden, met maght om in de plaatsen daer hij in persoon selfs niet en kan resideren, een ander in desselfs plaetse te substitueeren...,

was installed as consul-general in The Hague, with supervisory powers over the Spanish consulships in Rotterdam and Middelburg — though how, in practice, this affected Daniel de la Penha and Isaac Semach Ferro, who had been installed in the 1690s by Carlos II as Spanish consuls in Rotterdam and Middelburg, respectively, remains unclear.[26]

Baron Belmonte died in 1705, just as the allied invasion of Spain was getting under way. The archduke at once nominated Don Manuel's nephew, Baron Francisco (Isaac) Ximenes Belmonte — who was also a nephew of Jeronimo Nunes da Costa — his successor "als sijn rezident" in the United Provinces. Ximenes Belmonte presented his credentials to the States-General in January of 1706, signing himself "Don Francisco Ximenes Belmonte."[27]

The allies' good fortune reached its zenith in 1706. Following the duke of Marlborough's crushing victory over the French at Ramillies, in May, Anglo-Dutch forces overran the whole of Flanders and Brabant and imposed an Anglo-Dutch political-economic condominium on the southern Netherlands. Dutch Jews were now free to enter the South Netherlands. Indeed, the economic arrangements forced upon Brussels were much more in the Dutch than in the English interest.[28] The commercial regulations and tariffs of the Spanish Netherlands were reorganized to suit the Dutch, Dutch garrisons reappeared in numerous South Netherlands towns, and the Dutch, including the Sephardi contractors, resumed their control over provisioning and military finance. At the same time, the allies' two-pronged invasion of Spain, from Portugal and through Catalonia (which rose in support of the Austrian claimant) for the moment seemed likely to succeed. The forces of Felipe V were driven back, most of eastern Spain declared for "Carlos III," who transferred his headquarters to Valencia, Anglo-Dutch

---

26 Daniel de la Penha, who lived until 1718, had been installed as consul at Rotterdam in 1693: see D. Hausdorff, *Jizkor: Platenatlas van drie en een halve eeuw geschiedenis van de joodse gemeente in Rotterdam* (Baarn, 1978), pp. 17–19.

27 Don Francisco's mother, Gracia, was a sister of Jeronimo; his own daughter, Esther, had married Jeronimo's grandson, also called Jeronimo Nunes da Costa (Moseh Curiel) at Amsterdam in 1699 (I am indebted to Edgar Samuel for this information).

28 Israel, *Dutch Primacy*, 372.

and Catalan forces penetrated into Castile, and allied troops even briefly occupied Madrid. When the news of the fall of Madrid reached Holland, congratulations were at once dispatched to "Carlos III"; there was intense excitement among the regents, merchants, and the Jewish community. Holland's regents assumed that the struggle was as good as won and that it was time to extend the offensive to the Caribbean, which had all along been a major objective of the Republic's ruling circles, as it was also of the Dutch Sephardi elite.[29]

The conquests in the South Netherlands and Spain seemed to open up major new possibilities for the Jews. It appeared likely that the Dutch Sephardim would become a major factor in the economic life of the South Netherlands, despite the resistance of local merchants. Antonio Alvares Machado died in 1706, but another Dutch Jew, Sir Solomon de Medina, took over the "contracts for supplying bread and bread-wagons to the forces in the Low Countries in the Queen of Great Britain's pay," which he serviced in the years 1707–11, working together with his brother Joseph de Medina in Amsterdam and his son, Moseh, in London, and with various other Jewish financiers.[30] Quite a number of Dutch Jews were involved in the complex business of supplying the various Dutch garrisons in the South Netherlands, procuring horses and fodder, and many other aspects of military provisioning. Among the more prominent of these were Don Manuel Cardoso, based for some years in Brussels, and Joshua Castanho, who, towards the end of the war, built himself an imposing residence in Antwerp.[31] Besides provisioning and the munitions trade, there was also the matter of financing the war. The Dutch Republic possessed the most advanced fiscal machinery of any European state of the day and serviced a huge public debt. But raising cash and credit through the provincial states and municipalities was slow; there were numerous occasions, as William III had found in 1688, when the swift procurement of funds from the Sephardi financial elite offered distinct advantages. This was again the case during the War of the Spanish Succession; there was even an element of competition between public and Jewish finance in the Republic. In

29 See, for instance, Gemeente Archief Haarlem, vroedschapsresoluties 33, fols. 84–5, res. 7 June 1706.
30 O. K. Rabinowicz, *Sir Solomon de Medina* (London, 1974) pp. 38–42.
31 M. de Lamberti Arconati, *Mémoires pour servir à l'histoire du XVIIIe siècle* (14 vols., Amsterdam, 1735–40), vol. 7, p. 366; E. Schmidt, *L'Histoire des juifs à Anvers* (Antwerp, 1969²), p. 55.

February of 1709, for instance, it was reported to London from The Hague that:

> Four Hundred Thousand Florins will be borrowed here very soon for the service of the Low Countreys at 5 per cent, upon the security of the customs and tolls of Fort Maria. A Jew whose name is Baron Swazzo [i.e., Lopes Suasso] has offered to lend that money himselfe alone but was refused.[32]

Though thwarted on this occasion, the second Baron Lopes Suasso was certainly closely involved in a good deal of Sephardi activity in the Spanish Netherlands during these years.

Still more exciting possibilities appeared to be opening up in Spain itself and in the Caribbean. The war had caused the Inquisition to cease its activity against *conversos* in Spain so that, for the moment, the descendants of Portuguese New Christians in Spain enjoyed more security and freedom than at any time since they had first begun to settle in the country in the late sixteenth century. Nor were some of them inhibited about making or resuming contact with Dutch Sephardi Jewry and with Carlos the Third's various Sephardi and New Christian agents. One result of this was that Dutch Jewry had by far the best intelligence service inside and outside Spain of any group involved in the War of the Spanish Succession, of which they made extensive use. War news from Spain often reached the governments of England and the Republic via the Sephardi community in Amsterdam. In February 1708, for example, it was reported from The Hague to London that:

> Here are some advices among the Jews from Madrid of the 23rd of January which mention the Earl of Galloway was dead at Tarragona the 11th and that the French men-of-war were sailed from Cadiz for the Canaries in order to secure the Gallions which were expected very soon with Du Casse's squadron.[33]

A few months later the English minister at The Hague reported to London that:

> By letters from Madrid of the 5th in the hands of the Jews here we hear that the Marquis de Bay having passed the sierra with his army,

32 PRO SP 84/232, fol. 40v. Dayrolle to Boyle, The Hague, 15 Feb. 1709.
33 PRO SP 84/231, fol. 51v. Dayrolle to Harley, The Hague, 14 Feb. 1708.

the Portuguese were advanced and were then in sight of the enemy so that a battle was expected in those parts.[34]

As Cadiz and Seville remained in Bourbon hands, there was no question of the Dutch Sephardim restoring their lost trade links with those ports. But now that Barcelona, Valencia, and Alicante were in the hands of the forces of "Carlos III" and the allies, and the allies were dependent on supplies and munitions brought by sea through the straights of Gibraltar, often via the newly conquered port of Gibraltar, there were clearly openings along the Spanish east coast. There is evidence that some Dutch Sephardi firms took steps to establish or restore contact with this region. The Amsterdam Sephardi firm of João and Luis Mendes da Costa, for example, one of the most prominent Jewish firms forced out of the Spanish trade in 1701, petitioned the States-General in 1706 to intercede with the archduke to secure the latter's protection for their former factor in Valencia, a gentleman by the name of Gombeau, who was now proposing to return and resume business in Valencia.[35]

But the most dramatic breakthrough in Spain, from the Sephardi point of view, was of course Gibraltar. Between its conquest in July 1704 and the Peace of Utrecht in 1713, Gibraltar was not a British colony, but part of "Carlos the Third's Spain," a free port ruled in his name by a German governor and garrisoned jointly by the British and Dutch. In 1705 there were two Dutch regiments stationed at Gibraltar, and Dutch subjects had considerable standing there.[36]. There was even an Amsterdam-style "music-house," a tavern *cum* brothel for the Dutch soldiers and seamen. Sephardi Jews, encouraged by the departure of most of the pre-1704 Spanish population,[37] began to settle there almost from the moment of its conquest. Most of the several dozen Sephardi families who settled in Gibraltar before 1713 came either from Morocco or Livorno, though in most cases they were Spanish- or Portuguese-speaking. But there were also a number of Marranos from Portugal, and probably also from Spain itself, as well as a handful of Dutch Sephardim.[38] There is no doubt, moreover,

---

34 Ibid., fol. 259. Dayrolle to Boyle, The Hague, 22 June 1708.
35 ARA SG 7100/ii. SG to Carlos III, The Hague, 2 August 1706.
36 British Library MS Add. 10034, fols. 89v–90.
37 Some 1,200 Spanish Catholic families left Gibraltar following the capture of the town by the Anglo-Dutch expeditionary force.
38 British Library 38329 fol. 161v. Jos. Bennett, "Some Remarks concerning Gibraltar" (1712); ibid., MS Add. 38853, fols. 85–7.

that developments at Gibraltar aroused keen interest among the Jews in Holland. Because most of the town's houses had been abandoned by their original Spanish inhabitants, Gibraltar attracted many other foreigners besides Jews, especially Greeks and Genoese. But it was the Jews who captured the largest share of trade.

Gibraltar never had greater strategic importance than in the years 1704–13, when it was the lifeline of the allied forces operating in eastern Spain. The grain, fodder, and munitions supplied by Don Joseph Cortizos to the allied armies in Catalonia and Valencia, though procured from Holland, Portugal and Morocco, were stored and shipped in from Gibraltar.

Amsterdam Sephardi firms trading with eastern Spain also needed factors in Gibraltar; to this end they sent out a number of young Jews from Holland. Among them were Alvaro de Silveira (alias Aron Sasportas) and Michael de Ribera (Isaac de Mattos), described as "marchans de la ville d'Amsterdam," who in June 1707 obtained a letter of recommendation from the States-General asking the governor of Gibraltar to take them under his protection as "Dutch subjects."[39] These two settled in Gibraltar and briefly acted for a number of Amsterdam Sephardi firms, but apparently not very satisfactorily; in 1708 the merchants concerned, sent out Manoel Rodrigues Henriques, another Dutch Sephardi Jew, to reorganize matters and close accounts with Silveira and de Mattos.[40]

Besides provisioning, financial involvement, and their news service, Dutch Sephardi Jewry also participated in the war against the Bourbons through privateering. Amsterdam Jews had first participated in a privateering campaign on a significant scale more than fifty years earlier, when they played a prominent role in backing the massive onslaught mounted by the Zeeland privateers on Portuguese shipping in the Atlantic in 1647–48.[41] During the War of the Spanish Succession the Zeelanders again mounted a large-scale privateering campaign, especially against French shipping; there were also privateers based in Rotterdam, Amsterdam, and the West Frisian ports. In this period, Sephardi participation in Zeeland privateering was marginal, involving only two or

39 ARA SG 7102, minute of SG to governor of Gibraltar, The Hague, 2 June 1707.
40 ARA SG 7103. SG to governor of Gibraltar, The Hague, 19 Jan. 1708.
41 *Correspondência diplomática de Francisco de Sousa Coutinho,* vol. 2, pp. 53 and 314.

three ships out of a large number.[42] At Amsterdam, however, several prominent Sephardi firms were involved, notably that of Simão and Luis Rodrigues da Sousa, while at least nine out of 30 Dutch privateers operating out of Rotterdam were financed, equipped, and managed by Joseph and Daniel de la Penha.[43] Joseph, David, and Daniel de la Penha, among the most active of the Dutch Sephardi supporters of the Habsburg cause, were by far the most prominent Jewish privateering entrepreneurs of early modern times. One of Daniel's privateers operating out of Rotterdam, the *Grote Eendracht*, captured a French ship off Havre de Grace during the great allied breakthrough in the South Netherlands in the summer of 1706.[44]

But nowhere was Sephardi involvement in Dutch shipping activity, including privateering, more important than at Curaçao.[45] In peacetime there were as many as 70 or 80 barques trading out of Curaçao to the coasts of Venezuela and New Granada, to Puerto Rico, Cuba, and Santo Domingo, and to the Danish island of St. Thomas. During the war this number was reduced to 20 or 30. But these were the larger vessels, armed and equipped for wartime conditions. Most of the munitions and naval stores for these craft were shipped out on West India Company vessels from Amsterdam consigned by Sephardi merchants, notably Gabriel Alvares Corres, Aaron Henriques Morão, Luis and João Mendes da Costa, and Simão and Luis Rodrigues da Sousa.[46] It was this fleet of Curaçao trading barques, manned by Dutch seamen and flying the Dutch flag, that fulfilled the vital function of maintaining Dutch commerce in the Caribbean during the War of the Spanish Succession; a high proportion, possible more than half, were owned and managed by Jews. In general, the Caribbean was not favorable terrain for Dutch privateering, as relatively few French and Spanish ships were inclined to risk the Caribbean sea lanes during a war with both England and the Dutch Republic; and the English,

---

42 Two Zeeland privateers were managed by Daniel de la Penha: J. Th. H. Verhees-van Meer, *De Zeeuwse kaapvaart tijdens de Spaanse Successieoorlog, 1702–1713* (Middelburg, 1986), p. 186.

43 Ibid., pp. 197–98.

44 ARA SG 5644. David de la Penha to SG, 11 Sept. 1706.

45 Although I. S. Emmanuel makes this point, it seems to me that he fails to bring it out strongly enough: I. S. and S. A. Emmanuel, *History of the Jews of the Netherlands Antilles* (2 vols., Cincinnati, 1970) vol. 1, p. 83.

46 ARA WIC 357, fol. 178v; 359, fol. 353; vol. 364, fols. 187v and 300; and vol. 365, fols. 99v, 255v, 260.

based at Jamaica, had the lion's share of such privateering activity as there was.[47] Nevertheless, a few of the more heavily armed barques were used as privateers, and Curaçao Jewry did have some prizes to its credit. In 1702, for example, a privateer fitted out at Curaçao by Abraham Henriques Morão, Mordechai de Crasto, Mordechai Henriques, and Moseh Lopes Henriques — the last a close business associate of the Baron Belmonte — captured two Spanish vessels loaded with half a million pounds of cacao off the coast of Venezuela.[48]

The prime object of the War of the Spanish Succession, as far as the Dutch Sephardi elite was concerned, was to secure Dutch trade with Spanish America; consequently it was in the efforts to expand the Dutch role in the Caribbean that Jews exerted their greatest influence on Dutch policy and activity. This was the case at all levels, from secret parleys over grand strategy at The Hague to attempts to retain and extend Dutch control over specific markets in Spanish America. Apart from an abortive, small-scale Dutch attempt — with five ships — to seize La Guaira, the port of Caracas, in 1702, the Dutch scarcely deployed force in the Caribbean during this war. But this was because the Republic, fielding an unprecedentedly large army in Flanders and with expeditionary forces fighting alongside the English and their Iberian allies in Portugal, Catalonia, and Gibraltar, could not launch a major expedition to the Caribbean until some of these forces were released — it was hoped through a speedy collapse of the Bourbon cause in Spain. But there was a good deal of feverish discussion among the ruling class in the United Provinces, especially in the years 1706–10, as to how best to mount an Anglo-Dutch expedition, with the blessing of "Carlos III," which would seize and hold in his name sizeable portions of Spanish America — some slices of which (it was expected) would be permanently annexed to the Dutch and English colonial empires as a reward for their help in gaining for the Habsburg claimant what was allegedly his by right.[49] From their secret resolution we know that the directors of the Dutch West India Company, for example, had specific designs on Puerto Rico as a future Dutch colony.[50]

---

47 ARA WIC 200, fol. 392. Governor Beck to WIC directors, Curaçao, 6 March 1703.
48 ARA WIC 358, fol. 148. res. Amsterdam directors, 15 June 1703.
49 In June 1706, for example, the Haarlem burgomasters declared that they regarded it
      as a matter of the highest priority that Dutch trade with Spanish America be secured
      by the dispatch of a powerful expedition, GA Haarlem vroedschapresoluties 33, fols.
      84–5. res. 7 June 1706.
50 ARA WIC 447, secret resolutions of 12 Jan. and 12 April 1712.

Apart from the Amsterdam burgomasters and directors of the West India Company, key figures in the secret Dutch deliberations over Spanish America were the Pensionary of the States of Holland, Heinsius, and the Habsburg claimant's "minister" at Brussels, Don Francisco Bernardo de Quiros. Baron Belmonte, of course, was the key participant from the Jewish side until his death in 1705. Subsequently this role seems to have been played less by his successor as Spanish Resident at Amsterdam, Baron Isaac Ximenez Belmonte, than by Don Joseph de la Penha and, to a lesser extent, Daniel de la Penha, the Spanish consul at Rotterdam. Certainly in 1708, when the Dutch were planning a major expedition to the Caribbean (which, owing to the deterioration of the allies' position in Europe, never actually materialized) Joseph de la Penha was the Sephardi leader who was brought in — clearly as a main participant — to Heinsius' secret deliberations, in conjunction with the Amsterdam city council and with Quiros, about grand strategy in the Americas.[51] It is clear that at this crucial juncture the leaders of the Dutch state considered de la Penha's advice to be extremely important.

For Dutch Jewry, as for the Dutch state, one of the most vital aspects of the War of the Spanish Succession was the scramble by the European powers after the commerce of Spanish America. After the Anglo-Dutch attack on the Spanish treasure fleet at Vigo, in October 1702, the official Spanish trans-Atlantic trade was effectively suspended for the duration of the war. The whole of Europe's trade with the Spanish Indies was thrown into confusion and disarray. The colonists in Spanish America, unable to obtain the textiles, spices, and other wares that they were accustomed to receive from Europe, via Spain, turned to contraband and direct trading with other Europeans. During the early years of the war the Dutch, with their excellent harbor, large stocks of goods, and fleet of barques at Curaçao, were well placed to exploit the opportunity and assume effective control of the Spanish American market. The English at that stage were forbidding their Caribbean colonists to trade with the Spanish colonies. This, of course, worked to the advantage of the Dutch, though the English privateers, in their efforts to keep the Dutch from trading with the Spanish colonies, captured and brought in to Jamaica no fewer than 20 Curaço barques and sloops between the start of the war and March 1704.[52] Thanks

---

51 *De Briefwisseling van Anthonie Heinsius, 1702–1720*, ed. A. J. Veenendaal, volume for 1708–10 (The Hague, 1985) pp. 361, 499, 514
52 ARA WIC 447, fols. 246–47. N. van Beck to WIC directors, Curaao, 1 March 1704.

to this fairly flourishing traffic in the opening years of the war, there was a substantial flow of silver as well as of Venezuelan cacao, tobacco and other Spanish Caribbean products from Curaçao back to Amsterdam, though the quantities of silver were small compared with the amounts sent in peacetime via the official route to Cadiz. Although a clear majority of the participants in this traffic were Jews, the handful of Christian merchants involved in the transit traffic from Holland to Spanish America via Curaçao in fact handled most of it. The handful of Sephardi firms that regularly handled a large slice are shown in Table 1.

Table 1

The major Amsterdam Sephardi Firms involved in the transit trade with Spanish America via Curaçao during the War of the Spanish Succession (1702–13) and their Curaçao correspondents[53]

Amsterdam	Curaçao
Abraham Fundão	Felipe Henriques and David Senior
Gabriel Alvares Correa Simão and Luis Rodrigues da Sousa	Manuel Alvares Correa[54]
Aaron Henriques Morão	Abraham Henriques Morão[55]
Manuel and Elias de Crasto	Mordechai de Crasto[56]
Luis and João Mendes da Costa Selomoh and Jacob Lopes Henriques Baron Manuel de Belmonte Baron Francisco Ximenes de Belmonte	(Jacob Semah?) Ferro and Neira Moseh Lopes Henriques[57]

53 This table is based on data from the West India Company's "Curaçao books": see ARA WIC 566, 567, 568, 569.
54 Manuel Alvares Correa was presiding *parnas* of the Curaçao Sephardi community in 1705 and 1715; he was born in Livorno (1650); his family emigrated to Amsterdam in 1652; his son Gabriel was born in Curaçao: see Emmanuel, *Precious Stones*, pp. 231–32.
55 Part of this family had been settled in Curaçao since 1674; Abraham was *gabbay* of the Curaçao community in 1698 and second parnas in 1705: ibid., pp. 145–46.
56 Mordechai was second *parnas* of the Curaçao community in 1702 and 1705: ibid., pp. 229–30.
57 The Lopes Henriques had close connections with the Semah Ferro family: see ibid., p. 45.

Through Curaçao the Dutch dominated the Venezuela trade during these years, accounting for the great bulk of the cacao then reaching Europe, and also extended a more general trade dominion over New Granada and, via the Andean corridors running inland from Coro, Maracaibo, and Rio de la Hacha, over commerce with Quito and more loosely with Peru itself.[58] But the English eventually reversed their policy on trade with the Caribbean colonies; by 1706 their factors based at Jamaica, controlled most of the Caribbean market from Cartagena westwards and were rivalling the Dutch in the Maracaibo area. Meanwhile the French enjoyed an increasing success with their traffic through the Straits of Magellan and up the Pacific coast of South America to Peru.[59] In the later years of the war the Curaçao trade fell off markedly as the main European rivals informally split up the traffic to the Spanish Indies. The English were pre-eminent in the western Caribbean and the French in the Peru trade; the Dutch were left with Venezuela, Puerto Rico, and some of the trade with Quito. During the final years of the war the merchants of Curaçao considered their commerce to be in a chronic state of decline.[60]

Dutch Sephardi Jewry, then, was intimately involved in almost every aspect of the Dutch and allied war-effort between 1702 and 1713. Perhaps no other comparable group had as great a preoccupation with the course of the war or interest in its outcome. French reports that Dutch Jews were acting as a pressure group against Felipe V of Spain and exerting a conspicuous influence on Dutch policy are confirmed by the clear evidence that key Sephardi figures such as Baron Belmonte, Joseph de la Penha, and Francisco Schonenberg were formally giving advice at the highest levels, and being listened to up to a point. Here and there we also have tantalizing glimpses of informal contacts at high levels. In July 1704, for example, Joseph Cortizos, the *proveedor general* of "Carlos III," who was then at Lisbon with Schonenberg, at the archduke's side, sent Heinsius two reports on the situation in Spain, written in Spanish. An associate at Lisbon, presumably Schonenberg, appended a note to Heinsius on the first

58 Scelle, *La traité negrière*, vol.2, pp. 309–10.
59 F. W. Dahlgren, *Le Commerce de la Mer du Sud jusqu'à la Paix d'Utrecht* (Paris, 1909), pp. 102 and 439.
60 ARA WIC 203 fols. 69-70, petition of merchants to the governor of Curaao, 17 March 1711; ibid., vol. 205, fol. 414.

report, in Dutch, explaining that as "Monsieur Corticos" knew "weinig Duyts" he had composed his piece in Spanish; should Heinsius require a translation of this secret report he could ask Manuel Levy, "who lives next door to the treasurer-general [Jacob] Hop," in The Hague.[61] At the time Hop was one of the most powerful and wealthiest men in the Republic; it is intriguing to find that his next-door neighbor was the eminent Sephardi merchant jeweller, Manuel Levy Duarte, who is known to have been a close associate of Baron Lopes Suasso and Judah Senior Henriques, among others.[62]

The allied successes in 1704–6 had aroused great excitement among Dutch Sephardi Jewry. Blenheim, Ramillies, and the invasion of Spain had seemed to open up the prospect of a new era, but were followed in fact by stalemate, failure, and disillusionment. No doubt there were recriminations and a deep sense of missed opportunity. The feeling among the Dutch Sephardi elite was that the Republic had failed to do enough to secure its vital interests, and in particular to wrest control of the Spanish America trade from the French. There was much criticism of the strategies adopted and, understandably enough, bitter complaint over the role of Britain, which brought the war to an end by making a deal with France behind the backs of the Dutch and Austrians. By the Peace of Utrecht (1713), the Dutch-Spanish peace treaty (1714), and the so-called Barrier Treaty between the United Provinces and Austria (1715), the Dutch did wind up with some gains — specific guarantees for their trade in Spanish America on an equal basis with the British and French (except that the British were to have the official slave trade), important commercial privileges in the (henceforth) Austrian Netherlands, and the right to garrison specified towns there. But these seemed paltry gains in return for the vast effort and treasure expended. As a result of the British deal with France, Felipe V remained on the Spanish throne, the cause of "Carlos III" outside the South Netherlands was abandoned, and the slave *asiento* for the Spanish Indies was transferred to Britain, along with Gibraltar and Minorca. Britain's successes were certainly perceived as a setback to Dutch and Curaçao Sephardi Jewry as well as to the Dutch state itself. By 1707, in the wake of the Methuen treaty, Britain practically monopolized the trade

---

61 *Briefwisseling van Anthonie Heinsius*, vol. 3 (1704), p. 215.
62 Edgar Samuel explains that the "final phase of Manuel Levy Duarte's life was spent at The Hague, where he lived from 1696 to 1713" (Samuel, "Manuel Levy Duarte," p. 24).

of Portugal, a development that Schonenberg regarded with utter dismay.[63] He was also deeply suspicious of British designs on Gibraltar, warning Heinsius as early as 1704 that if Britain managed to appropriate Gibraltar for herself this would be highly "prejudicial" to the Dutch Mediterranean trade.[64]

In his repeated criticisms of allied strategy in Spain, Schonenberg lamented the decision to base the main allied expeditionary force in Catalonia, so far from the Atlantic sea lanes and so difficult to provision. The correct strategy, he urged Heinsius all along, would be to invade Andalusia while simultaneously blockading the province from the sea. According to Schonenberg, Andalusia, a region close to Portugal and facing the Atlantic, rich in provisions and abundant in horses suitable for cavalry, was the key to victory. An invasion of Andalusia, culminating in the capture of Cadiz, would have enabled the allies to wrest control of the Spanish America trade and paralyze France by cutting her out of it entirely.[65] In a key passage he wrote to Heinsius:

> . . . ik altoos, nevens diegheenen die het werk best verstaan, van sentiment ben geweest dat men sigh van Andalusiën ende specialijk van Cadiz behoorde meester te maaken, als kunnende den oorlogh aldaar door de opulentie van die provintie, de quantiteyt van goede paarden voor de cavallerie, de nabuyrschap van Portugael, de bequaemheyt der havenen en zeeplaatsen om de nodige descentes en secoursen te effectueeren ende door meer andere commoditeyten met veel meer convenientie voortgeset worden, waarbij komt de inponderable importantie om van de geheele West-Indische navigatie en commertie meester te worden ende door 't afsnijden van den Fransen handel Vrankrijk tot reden te dwingen, gelijk meermalen omstandiger-en overtuygenderwijse aan den staat en waar het verders te passe quam, geremonstreert hebbe.[66]

This plan for an Anglo-Dutch invasion of Andalusia to seize Cadiz, together with an expedition to the Caribbean, can be regarded, I believe, as the characteristic and typical approach of the Dutch Sephardi leadership to how the war should have been fought.

---

63 *Briefwisseling van Anthonie Heinsius*, vol. 6 (1707), p. 278.
64 Ibid., vol. 3(1704), p. 455.
65 Ibid., vol. 6 (1707) pp. 278 and 592.
66 Ibid., p. 278.

Index

(Illustrations are shown in bold)